A. Gasper

S0-ARK-331

West Bar Review
A West Publishing Affiliated Company
901 Fifteenth Street, N.W., 10th Floor
Washington, D.C. 20005
1–800–6–WESTBAR

Steven H. Levine
President

Stanley D. Chess
Chairman and CEO

Dear Law Student:

Welcome to law school—and congratulations. But be wary. The law school experience that you're about to undertake is unlike any educational experience you've ever had.

Law school requires you to learn new concepts, new terms, and, most importantly, a new way of thinking. Over and over, you'll be told to "think like a lawyer."

And over and over, you'll be told something by second and third year students that you might think is strange. They'll tell you that the sooner you enroll in your bar review course the better off you are.

Now this does sound strange. After all, you'll be sitting for the bar exam *after* you graduate from law school. The last thing you want now is to plan how you'll spend the summer of '98. And most first-year students have no idea in which state they'll be accepting their first job.

So why enroll in the West Bar Review during your first year? Because enrolling early in the West Bar Review can save you a good deal of money and help you greatly during your three years of law school.

WestBar will provide you with first-year study aids, so that you can save money on Sum and Substance and other materials used in preparing for finals. WestBar will provide you with first-year lectures, so that you can hear Harvard Prof. Arthur Miller on Civil Procedure, University of Virginia Dean Robert Scott on Property, other top WestBar lecturers on all the important subjects. In fact, more law students have learned civil procedure from Prof. Miller than from anyone else!

During your second or third year we'll prepare you for your Multistate Professional Responsibility Exam (the "MPRE"). And we'll give you an early start on your bar exam.

Along with WestLaw and the West Publishing Company, West Bar Review is dedicated to your legal experience. We'll help you through law school, we'll help you through your bar exam, and then we'll be with you for the rest of your legal career.

If you have any questions, or if you would like to become a WestBar student representative, please call us at 1–800–6–WESTBAR. Your future is our future. We intend for it to be successful.

Sincerely,

Stanley D. Chess

West
Bar Review™
1-800-6-WestBar

West Bar Review™

LAST NAME	FIRST	INITIAL	PERMANENT ADDRESS (if different)

CURRENT STREET ADDRESS (Do not use P.O. Box — This address used for course materials.)

CITY	STATE	ZIP	CITY, STATE, ZIP

(_____) _____   (_____) _____
AREA CODE   HOME PHONE   AREA CODE   ALTERNATE PHONE   TELEPHONE

LAW SCHOOL   GRADUATING (MONTH) (YEAR)   E-MAIL ADDRESS

I am enrolling in West Bar Review with a deposit of $ _____

Date: _____

Referred by ❏ Student Rep/Name & School _____

        ❏ Ad   ❏ Other

I am interested in bar exam information for the following states:

_____

I plan to take the MPRE in
❏ November   19 _____
❏ March   19 _____
❏ August   19 _____

(to receive MPRE materials a total non-refundable payment of $75 is required)

METHOD OF PAYMENT

❏ CASH   ❏ CASHIER'S CHECK   ❏ PERSONAL/BUSINESS CHECK   AMOUNT

TO CHARGE PLEASE COMPLETE: ❏ VISA   ❏ MASTERCARD

CARD # _____ EXP. DATE _____

AMOUNT CHARGED TO CREDIT CARD $ _____ CARDHOLDER'S NAME _____

SIGNATURE _____ DATE _____

❏ Bill my law firm

Name _____
Address _____
City _____
State/Zip _____
Attn. _____

FOR OFFICE USE ONLY	Total Tuition Due _____	EED _____	Other _____
Date ____ Amount Paid _____	Balance _____	Materials _____	Date Issued _____ Shipped Via _____
Date ____ Amount Paid _____	Balance _____	Materials _____	Date Issued _____ Shipped Via _____
Date ____ Amount Paid _____	Balance _____	Materials _____	Date Issued _____ Shipped Via _____

- -

Thank you for your enrollment in West Bar Review.

West Bar Review™

STUDENT NAME: _____

COURSE: _____   TOTAL TUITION: _____

AMOUNT PAID: _____   ❏ CASH ❏ CHECK ❏ CC RECEIVED BY: _____

West Bar Review schedules and information will be mailed to you at the above address. If there are changes in your enrollment information, please contact your West Bar Review representative or call 800/693-7822.

Sum & Substance

QUICK REVIEW

™

CONTRACTS

**Professor
Robert D. Brain**

Casebook Table
◆
Case Squibs
◆
Summary of the Law
◆
Essay & Multiple
Choice Q & A
◆
10 - 5 - 2 Hour Study Guide
◆
Capsule Outline

WEST Professional Training Programs, Inc.
Sum & Substance • West Bar Review

SECOND EDITION

Editor: Roberta Simon, Esq.

Production Coordinator: Seth Barondess

Cover Design: William Johnson

WEST'S COMMITMENT TO THE ENVIRONMENT

In 1906, West Publishing Company began recycling materials left over from the production of books. This began a tradition of efficient and responsible use of resources. Today, up to 95% of our legal books and 70% of our college texts and school texts are printed on recycled, acid-free stock. West also recycles nearly 22 million pounds of scrap paper annually—the equivalent of 181,717 trees. Since the 1960s, West has devised ways to capture and recycle waste inks, solvents, oils, and vapors created in the printing process. We also recycle plastics of all kinds, wood, glass, corrugated cardboard, and batteries, and have eliminated the use of Styrofoam book packaging. We at West are proud of the longevity and the scope of our commitment to the environment.

Production, Prepress, Printing and Binding by West Publishing Company.

 TEXT IS PRINTED ON 10% POST CONSUMER RECYCLED PAPER    PRINTED WITH SOY INK

COPYRIGHT © 1996 by   WEST PROFESSIONAL TRAINING PROGRAMS, INC.
1231 Third Street Promenade
Santa Monica, CA 90401
1-800-876-4457

ISBN 0–940366–56–8 Sum and Substance *(1-800-876-4457)*
ISBN 0–314–07621–2 West Professional Training Programs, Inc.

Sum & Substance Quick Review of Contracts is a publication of
Sum & Substance, a division of West Professional Training Programs, Inc.

This product was printed and published in the United States of America.

SUM & SUBSTANCE
LEGAL & PROFESSIONAL PUBLICATIONS

The "Outstanding Professor" Series Audiotapes

America's #1 Selling Law School Audiotape Series

Administrative Law *Prof. Steven Finz*	$ 49.95
Agency *Prof. Chris Munch*	39.95
Antitrust *Prof. James McCall*	49.95
Bankruptcy *Prof. Douglass Boshkoff*	49.95
Civil Procedure *Prof. Arthur R. Miller*	64.95
Civil Procedure *Prof. Doug Blaze*	49.95
Commercial Paper *Prof. Douglas Whaley*	49.95
Community Property *Prof. Max Goodman*	39.95
Conflict of Laws *Prof. Tom Fischer*	49.95
Constitutional Law *Prof. Mary Cheh*	49.95
Consumer Law *Prof. Douglas Whaley*	39.95
Contracts *Prof. Douglas Whaley*	49.95
Copyright Law *Prof. Robert Gorman*	39.95
Corporations *Prof. James Cox*	49.95
Criminal Law *Prof. Joshua Dressler*	49.95
Criminal Procedure *Prof. Joshua Dressler*	49.95
Environmental Law *Prof. William Rodgers Jr.*	39.95
Equitable Remedies *Prof. Arthur Miller*	39.95
Estate & Gift Tax *Prof. John McNulty*	49.95
Evidence *Prof. Steven Goode*	49.95
Family Law *Prof. Marc Perlin*	39.95
Federal Income Tax *Prof. Frank Doti*	49.95
Future Interests *Prof. Julian Juergensmeyer*	15.95
Insurance Law *Prof. John Dobbyn*	39.95
Jurisprudence *Prof. Jeremy Miller*	49.95
Labor Law *Prof. Robert Gorman*	49.95
Land Use *Prof. Julian Juergensmeyer*	39.95
Partnership *Prof. Chris Munch*	39.95
Product Liability *Prof. Steven Finz*	24.95
Prof Responsibility *Prof. Michael Josephson*	49.95
Real Property *Prof. Julian Juergensmeyer*	49.95
Sale & Lease of Goods *Prof. Douglas Whaley*	39.95
Secured Transactions *Prof. Douglass Boshkoff*	39.95
Sports Law *Prof. Ray Yasser*	39.95
Torts *Prof. Steven Finz*	49.95
Trusts *Prof. Gerry Beyer*	39.95
Wills & Succession *Prof. Ira Shafiroff*	39.95

The "Essential Skills" Series Audiotapes

Intensive Exam Writing (Essay) Seminar	
See description below	$ 95.00
Exam Writing: Essay *Prof. Steve Bracci*	24.95
Mastering Multiple Choice (MBE) *Prof. Steven Finz*	24.95
How to Win at Law School *Scott Pearce, Esq.*	15.95
Law Firm Interviewing *Kirk Pasich, Esq.*	19.95
Winning at Moot Court *Adj. Prof. Matthew Moffett*	39.95

Quick Review Outline Series

Contains all of the features necessary to succeed and excel in law school.

Civil Procedure *Prof. Doug Blaze*	$ 18.95
Conflict of Laws *Prof. Tom Fischer*	18.95
Constitutional Law *Prof. Phil Prygoski*	18.95
Contracts *Prof. Robert Brain*	19.95
Corporations *Prof. James Cox*	17.95
Criminal Law *Prof. Steve Friedland*	18.95
Evidence *Prof. Steven Goode*	18.95
Family Law *Prof. Marc Perlin*	17.95
Professional Responsibility *Prof. Percy Luney*	18.95
Real Property *Prof. Julian Juergensmeyer*	18.95
Torts *Prof. Larry Levine*	18.95

"Intensive Exam Writing (Essay) Seminar"

The most effective 6 hours you will spend in law school:

- Dramatically increase available time through effective studying;
- Learn how to write the A+ essay and excel in law school;
- Covers case briefing, outlining, memorization, exam analysis, issue spotting, IRAC, assumptions, time allocation and much more!
- Authored by the nation's leading expert on exam writing and excelling in law school, Professor Ira Shafiroff, Southwestern University, School of Law;
- Rated A+ by seminar attendees!!
- Program cost: $95 — Includes 4 audio cassettes (6 hours) and a 200 page comprehensive workbook.

SEE YOUR BOOK STORE OR CALL TOLL-FREE: 1-800- 876-4457

TABLE OF CONTENTS

CASEBOOK
TABLE

QUICK REVIEW CHAPTERS AND SECTIONS	Burton Principles of Contract Law 1995	Calamari, Perillo & Bender Cases and Problems on Contracts 1989 (2d ed)	Crandall & Whaley Cases, Problems and Materials on Contracts 1993 (2d ed)	Dawson, Harvey & Henderson Cases and Comment on Contracts 1992 (6th ed.)	Farnsworth & Young Cases and Materials on Contracts 1988 (4th ed.)	Fuller & Eisenberg Basic Contract Law 1990 (5th ed.)	Kessler, Gilmore & Kronman Contracts Cases and Materials 1986 (3d ed.)	Murphy & Speidel Studies in Contract Law 1991 (4th ed.)	Murray Contracts Cases and Materials 1991 (4th ed.)	Summers & Hillman Contract and Related Obligation: Theory, Doctrine, and Practice 1992 (2d ed.)
CHAPTER TWO Mutual Assent	145-149	28-30; 84-85, 92; 113, 375	1-20; 196; 742-750	203-216; 306-307; 328-334; 336-337; 339-340	56-60; 89-94	80-99	141-179; 238-257	173-178; 265-275	41-50; 250	68-76; 360-385
CHAPTER THREE Offers, gen	27-35	16-33, 80-84	1-36	216-217; 349-374; 396-414; 450-451; 612-614	137-159	328-330; 359-367	183-186; 315-348; 357-364; 689-700	276-306; 312-319	41-90	385-395; 464-471
Definitions §3 0-3 2					137	359	180-181	276-279; 294-303	74	385
Advertisements §3 214	28-34	22-25, 27, 89-90	26-31	349-352; 357-360	145-149	365-368	183-186	276-294; 321-334; 352-357	75-82	385-387
Auctions §3 5	34-35	25-27	85					303-306	174	
CHAPTER FOUR Acceptance, gen.	27, 35-71; 185-191	84-110, 122-142	37-155	370-435; 447-451	149-218	368-526	238-257; 315-381; 689-694	306-373	91-174	395-464
General Offers §4 333	40	83-86, 140	56-57, 85-90	216-217; 370-374; 612-614	71-72	387-391	377-381	327-330	93; 140-141	
Silence §4 57	63-68	93-95, 100-102	51-56	447-451	174-75	461-469	238-247	344-348	96	406-407
Mailbox Rule §4 6	68	110-117; 140	103-112	441-444	191-193	414-421	348-350	337-340	103-109; 121	458-464
CHAPTER FIVE "Battle of the Forms"	80-82; 373	134-140	112-130	425-435	193-213	377-378; 596-627	181; 257-272	361-369	175-206	497-514
CHAPTER SIX Indefiniteness	31-35; 82-102	33-84	130-155	349-360	245-252; 596-647	491-526	121-123; 129-131; 179-201	411-460	66-71	464-485; 712-722

QUICK REVIEW CHAPTERS AND SECTIONS	Burton Principles of Contract Law 1995	Calimari, Perillo & Bender Cases and Problems on Contracts 1989 (2d ed.)	Crandall & Whaley Cases, Problems and Materials on Contracts 1993 (2d ed.)	Dawson, Harvey & Henderson Cases and Comment on Contracts 1992 (6th ed.)	Farnsworth & Young Cases and Materials on Contracts 1988 (4th ed.)	Fuller & Eisenberg Basic Contract Law 1990 (5th ed.)	Kessler, Gilmore & Kronman Contracts Cases and Materials 1986 (3d ed.)	Murphy & Spidel Studies in Contract Law 1991 (4th ed.)	Murray Contracts Cases and Materials 1991 (4th ed.)	Summers & Hillman Contract and Related Obligation: Theory, Doctrine, and Practice 1992 (2d ed.)
CHAPTER SEVEN Consideration, gen.	124-166	146-240	157-301	196-248	1-125; 302-312	1-189	37-38; 55-66; 279-314; 348-363	97-188	212-283	26; 46-78; 353
Definitions §7.0-7.1	130-132; 138	146-149	157-168	205-217, 233-234, 291-294	40-45; 54-56; 71-72	41-53	279	26-30	228-233; 245-257	47-50
Types §7.2-7.3	134, 139-151	104-106, 152-156; 168-170, 206-214, 216		208-212, 224-228, 293-294, 306-307	48-60; 73-77; 99-103	2-4; 8-9, 43-45; 72-74		105-132; 352-357	228-233; 245-257	47-68
Gift promises §7.51	125-127, 134			196-197, 203-205, 217-218	46-48	7-10, 106-107	284, 472-480	213-216	287-288	48-49; 51; 53-54
Moral or Past Consideration §7.52	191-202	230-239	198-240	217-218, 233-248	56-60; 116-124	167-189	510-551	30-33; 203-216	312-326	134-136
Adequacy §7.61	135-138	675-676	170-177	213-219	302-312	10-15	84-87	132-150; 352-357	219-228	77-78; 552-583
Illusory Promises §7.62	149-155	209-213	185-198	295-296, 304-307, 781-785	86-93				249-250	68-76
Output, Requirement, & Exclusive Dealing Contracts §7.623-7.6241	149-151	206-211	146-155, 196-197	308-312	24-29; 82-89; 599-601	92-97	418-453	171-179; 910-922	256-260	68-71
Pre-Existing Duty §7.63	151-154; 164; 590; 596-611	158-162; 166-174	216-240	224-228, 289-293	317-330; 562-563	99-147	76-79	158-172	262-267	76-77; 606-625
Settlements (Accords) §7.634, 24.33	151-154, 158	171-174	231-240	577-589; 596-607	363	136-151	688-674	999-1003	274-280	628-629

QUICK REVIEW CHAPTERS AND SECTIONS	Burton Principles of Contract Law 1995	Callmari, Perillo & Bender Cases and Problems on Contracts 1989 (2d ed.)	Crandall & Whaley Cases, Problems and Materials on Contracts 1993 (2d ed.)	Dawson, Harvey & Henderson Cases and Comment on Contracts 1992 (6th ed.)	Farnsworth & Young Cases and Materials on Contracts 1988 (4th ed.)	Fuller & Eisenberg Basic Contract Law 1990 (5th ed.)	Kessler, Gilmore & Kronman Contracts Cases and Materials 1986 (3d ed.)	Murphy & Spidel Studies in Contract Law 1991 (4th ed.)	Murray Contracts Cases and Materials 1991 (4th ed.)	Summers & Hillman Contract and Related Obligation: Theory, Doctrine, and Practice 1992 (2d ed.)
CHAPTER EIGHT Promissory Estoppel	125-126, 131-132, 164-191	241-277	240-301	264-293; 402-414	94-107, 218-237	22-40; 98, 514-516	282; 308-314; 320	33-36; 111-114; 216-271; 399-410	283-312	2; 33; 44; 79-107
CHAPTER NINE Statute of Frauds	102-123	757-801	503-599	95-98, 269-275; 278-281; 957-974	253-289	B1-B39	753-819	36-40; 682-745	329-369	66; 78; 82; 94; 115-117; 139; 182-198; 396; 473; 683-684
CHAPTER TEN Incapacity	206-209	313-324	771-780	235-240; 297; 546-569, 964-965	290-301			512-527	261; 325; 341	
CHAPTER ELEVEN Mistake & Misunderstanding	12-26, 220-244	353-367	20, 633-675	364-373, 402-409; 615-641	356-364	334-342; 653-695	862-891	480-508; 949-957	431-453	873-904
CHAPTER TWELVE-CHAPTER FOURTEEN Duress, Undue Influence, & Misrepresentation	138-139, 153-158, 209-220	186-196, 326-351	29-30, 584-675, 700-738	283-284, 296-298; 488-495; 563-574; 596-603; 647-658; 700-726	289, 314-318; 330-336, 342-351	47-53; 549-553; 684-691	84-104; 196-201; 657-663; 674-678	528-582; 637	456-466	520-537, 556-559; 678-679
CHAPTER FIFTEEN Unconscionability	266-280	370-378, 490-501	780-827	513-515, 526-542; 710-725	364, 379, 389, 403-427	53-67	275; 284; 561-649; 1097-1101	62-67; 582-623	466-481	565-583
CHAPTER SIXTEEN Illegality	209-220	817-846	738-771	145-150, 431; 453-457, 489-495, 516-531; 770-773	440-470		60-61; 97-98	624-682	509-523	539-545
CHAPTER SEVENTEEN & CHAPTER NINETEEN Parol Evidence Rule	372-389, 399-405	278-288, 301-311	561-631	457-508	544-558; 588-591; 301-602, 663-666	527-578	821-859	753-776	369-372	641-684

QUICK REVIEW CHAPTERS AND SECTIONS	Burton Principles of Contract Law 1995	Calamari, Perillo & Bender Cases and Problems on Contracts 1989 (2d ed)	Crandall & Whaley Cases, Problems and Materials on Contracts 1993 (2d ed)	Dawson, Harvey & Henderson Cases and Comment on Contracts 1992 (6th ed.)	Farnsworth & Young Cases and Materials on Contracts 1988 (4th ed.)	Fuller & Eisenberg Basic Contract Law 1990 (5th ed)	Kessler, Gilmore & Kronman Contracts Cases and Materials 1986 (3d ed.)	Murphy & Speidel Studies in Contract Law 1991 (4th ed.)	Murray Contracts Cases and Materials 1991 (4th ed.)	Summers & Hillman Contract and Related Obligation: Theory, Doctrine, and Practice 1992 (2d ed.)
CHAPTER EIGHTEEN Interpretation	397-398, 406-419, 426-430	289-301	548-631	330-340; 356-57; 366-367, 375-377, 432-435, 471; 498-508, 741-745	569-615	328-358, 584-594		804-827	402-430	684-712
CHAPTER TWENTY Conditions, gen	458-487, 512-542, 548-564	379-438	865-906	727-826	74-75; 649-693	899-982	973-1059	804-888	525-561	742-868
Express Conditions §20.0-20.1121	459-474	379-408, 480-483	867-899	727-773	74-75; 649-670	899-952	985-987	804-848	539-545; 549-550	742-760; 763-764; 775; 804-805
Constructive Conditions §20.123-20.125	480-483, 484-487	410-446	899-906	786-826	670-693	953-982	985-987	846-888	549-561	743-745; 805-847
Distinguishing Promises from Conditions §20.3	458-464	389-396, 516-518		727-734	688-70	900-921	979-981		531-539	745-747; 760-775
Divisibility, Breach, Waiver & Forfeiture as Excuse §20.4	464-474; 542-543	447-501	944-976	591-596; 744-746; 750; 755-769; 778-779; 822-825; 857-859	559-586, 635-640; 677-678, 725-735; 782-794	937-952	1021-1059	828-846; 873-888; 1034-1036	603-612	776-804, 827-832
CHAPTER TWENTY-ONE & CHAPTER TWENTY-TWO										
Order of Performance §21.0-21.1; 22.1	544-548	418-419; 433	905-907	798-809; 802-805; 818-823	692-693	958-961	983		553-558	804-815

QUICK REVIEW CHAPTERS AND SECTIONS	Burton Principles of Contract Law 1995	Calamari, Perillo & Bender Cases and Problems on Contracts 1989 (2d ed.)	Crandall & Whaley Cases, Problems and Materials on Contracts 1993 (2d ed.)	Dawson, Harvey & Henderson Cases and Comment on Contracts 1992 (6th ed.)	Farnsworth & Young Cases and Materials on Contracts 1988 (4th ed.)	Fuller & Eisenberg Basic Contract Law 1990 (5th ed.)	Kessler, Gilmore & Kronman Contracts Cases and Materials 1986 (3d ed.)	Murphy & Speidel Studies in Contract Law 1991 (4th ed.)	Murray Contracts Cases and Materials 1991 (4th ed.)	Summers & Hillman Contract and Related Obligation: Theory, Doctrine, and Practice 1992 (2d ed.)
Material v. Immaterial Breach §21.2-21.251; 22.1	512-541; 549-550	419-423, 427-433	899-905; 925-926	822-859	679-697	877-900, 974-981	106-110; 1021-1058	44-49; 859-873; 1010-1111	574-588	756-759, 815-842
Substantial Performance §21.26	512-541	427-433	907-926	779-781; 829-830, 837-844	501-506, 694-701	877-900	1050-1058	44-49; 859-873	574-588	756-759, 815-837
Perfect Tender Rule §22.1	544-548	430-439	927-940	826-836	715-717	888-890	1002-1007	1028-1034	586-588	842
CHAPTER TWENTY-THREE Anticipatory Repudiation	487-507	518-537, 580-583	979-1001	38-44, 53-60; 802-804, 852-871	735-761	983-1027	1061-1328	41-44, 1011-1026	591-599	847-868
CHAPTER TWENTY-FOUR										
Substituted Agreements (including Novations) §24.1-24.2		806-812, 816	1008-1010	607-611; 965-966	943-944			997-999	279-280	1035-1037
Accord & Satisfaction §24.3	151-154, 158	171-180, 809-811	231-240	289-293; 577-607; 607-611	363-364	136-151	668-674	999-1003	279-280	634-637
Mutual Rescission §24.4		802-807	633-634	526-531; 583	319-328					612

QUICK REVIEW CHAPTERS AND SECTIONS	Burton Principles of Contract Law 1995	Calamari, Perillo & Bender Cases and Problems on Contracts 1989 (2d ed.)	Crandall & Whaley Cases, Problems and Materials on Contracts 1993 (2d ed.)	Dawson, Harvey & Henderson Cases and Comment on Contracts 1992 (6th ed.)	Farnsworth & Young Cases and Materials on Contracts 1988 (4th ed.)	Fuller & Eisenberg Basic Contract Law 1990 (5th ed.)	Kessler, Gilmore & Kronman Contracts Cases and Materials 1986 (3d ed.)	Murphy & Spidel Studies in Contract Law 1991 (4th ed.)	Murray Contracts Cases and Materials 1991 (4th ed.)	Summers & Hillman Contract and Related Obligation: Theory, Doctrine, and Practice 1992 (2d ed.)
CHAPTER TWENTY-FIVE Impossibility, Impracticability & Frustration	566-590	538-587	827-864	658-700	809-873	696-742	911-973	924-987	615-656	904-954
CHAPTER TWENTY-SIX Modification	151-154, 590-611	183-205, 228-229; 423-427	231-240; 301; 523-524	286-289, 583-603	318-319, 558-559	19, 118-128; 952	79-84	171-172; 571-582; 828-833; 987-997	274; 392-402	606-637
CHAPTER TWENTY-SEVEN Third Party Beneficiaries	628-667	688-721	1003-1046	877-917	874-923	744-794	1329-1439	1335-1390	753-802	984-1006
CHAPTER TWENTY-EIGHT & CHAPTER TWENTY-NINE Assignments & Delegations	667-693	722-756	1047-1111	917-956	924-996	795-838	1441-558	1281-1334	806-849	1007-1037
CHAPTER THIRTY & CHAPTER THIRTY-TWO Equitable Remedies	220-231; 291-299	657-687	452-472	93-95; 156-184; 700-707	6; 19-35; 88; 302-309; 404; 446; 499; 744-745; 807	288-299	9-10; 1068-1108; 1257	426-433; 1180-1190; 1195-1213	744-752	214-215; 321-336; 551-552; 559-565
CHAPTER THIRTY-ONE & CHAPTER THIRTY TWO Damages, gen.	3-9, 279-364, 501-507	588-650	303-452	1-150; 832-876	1-12	192-287; 300-305	1061-1069; 1108-1201	49-62; 1036-1152	25-36; 657-745	35-41; 204-281
Interest Analysis & Basic Damage Formulations §31.0-31.3; 31.5	3-9; 166, 279-280; 289-364	588-606	303-325	1-8; 29-32; 35-44; 82-93; 525-526	16-18; 94-106; 108-116; 413-416; 471-532	33; 192-287; 300-305	1061-1069; 1132-1134	49-62; 1036-1058; 1064-1065; 1085-1086; 1090-1099; 1101-1107; 1117-1129; 1139-1152	25-36; 657-732	35-41; 208-209; 204-236; 268-281

QUICK REVIEW CHAPTERS AND SECTIONS	Burton Principles of Contract Law 1995	Calamari, Perillo & Bender Cases and Problems on Contracts 1989 (2d ed.)	Crandall & Whaley Cases, Problems and Materials on Contracts 1993 (2d ed.)	Dawson, Harvey & Henderson Cases and Comment on Contracts 1992 (6th ed.)	Farnsworth & Young Cases and Materials on Contracts 1988 (4th ed.)	Fuller & Eisenberg Basic Contract Law 1990 (5th ed.)	Kessler, Gilmore & Kronman Contracts Cases and Materials 1986 (3d ed.)	Murphy & Speidel Studies in Contract Law 1991 (4th ed.)	Murray Contracts Cases and Materials 1991 (4th ed.)	Summers & Hillman Contract and Related Obligation: Theory, Doctrine, and Practice 1992 (2d ed.)
Damages in Employment Contracts §31.32-31.33		606-611		44-53, 109-113	478-479, 492-498, 527	209-226		1099-1101		222-226
Damages in Construction Contract Cases §31.34-31.35		621-624	388-389		472, 490-92, 501-506, 520-524			44-49, 1070-1074; 1107-1112	704-710	
Damages in Sales of Goods Cases §31.38, 31.32-33.5	300-313, 501-507	611-619	406-416	22-25, 35-38, 53-65, 810-818, 832-862	479-485, 490-524, 717-725; 806	227-236	1129-1138; 1165-1171	59-60, 1064-1065; 1085-1099; 1101-1107; 1117-1128; 1139-1148	29-32; 710-725	35, 227-234; 818-819
Limitations on Expectation Damage Recovery §33.4	334-346	588-613, 620-624; 644	336-354, 365-380	38-51, 65-80,	490-524	236-238	1138-1165; 1269-1328	56-59, 1065-1069; 1128-1152	32-36; 674-693; 716-725	236-242; 256-273; 278-281
Emotional Distress Damages §31.6, 33.7			364-365	73-76	524-526	192-201; 268-273		49-56, 1038-1044	682-686	38-41; 262-265
Liquidated Damages §31.7, 33.6	286-289	639-651	380-400	119-126, 133-151	532-543	271-287	1223-1243	1214-1235	693-704	281-294
Punitive Damages §31.8, 33.7	279-286	629-635	400-406	22, 26-29, 75-76, 192	5; 36	273-274	1212-1221	73-77; 1045-1058	497	18, 21; 24-26; 265-266
CHAPTER THIRTY-THREE Restitutionary Recovery	195-202; 364-371; 507-512	439-440, 651-657	304; 416-452	60-64, 98-132; 228-247, 665-692	107-116, 486-489	305-325	33-34; 1186-1188	17-21; 193-203; 460-468, 629; 668-669, 878-888; 983-987; 1074-1085; 1127-1128	36-40; 366; 655-666, 733-744	131-132; 304-321; 960-961

Sum & Substance QUICK REVIEW of Contracts

SUMMARY OF CONTENTS

TABLE OF CASES CITED IN TEXT

I. INTRODUCTION

About the Author —

 Professor Robert D. Brain has taught Contracts, Sales, and other courses at Pepperdine University School of Law in Malibu, California and at McGeorge School of Law, in Sacramento, California. Since his graduation from University of California, Boalt Hall School of Law in 1980, Professor Brain has practiced law with Gibson, Dunn & Crutcher, tried cases for the Los Angeles District Attorney's Office, and authored a number of publications in several areas. He is a past Executive Board Member of the American Association of Law Schools Teaching Methods Section. In addition to his teaching and publishing responsibilities, he volunteers his time as an arbitrator for commercial disputes in the Los Angeles area, and serves on several ABA and other Bar Association Committees. Professor Brain is a graduate With Honors and With Distinction in Biology from Stanford University in 1976, and received his M.S. in Biochemistry from Stanford in 1977.

From the Author —

Two of the most difficult tasks for a first year law student to master are the abilities to ascertain "the big picture" and "the little picture" about certain topics. That is, you will probably find it relatively easy to get a general idea of what is going on after reading your assignment for a particular topic and to get the gist of what is important about that topic after listening to and participating in class discussion. However, two weeks later, when you start preparing your outline of the material, you may have trouble explaining exactly where that topic fits into the overall picture of the course; or deciding which particular exception is applicable to what particular rule or rules; or determining what issue is addressed by the three-part test you spent so long formulating in class.

Therein lie the purposes of this outline. It is organized in a structured framework so that you can easily tell where a doctrine or rule fits into the big picture of contracts. It tells you what the issues are and what legal tests and principles apply to which issues. Moreover, most of the rules that initially seem hard to grasp are illustrated with a number of examples, so that the details, or the little picture, of various doctrines can be quickly ascertained. In addition, to help you initially develop the right approach, a discussion of the important issues found in the major contracts cases is included. Finally, to check your understanding, both essay and multiple choice questions are provided, along with answers that explain the correct analysis of the particular issues tested.

Acknowledgement —

I would very much like to thank and acknowledge my former colleague Professor Mark Scarberry at Pepperdine for his helpful comments, the countless hours he spent with me discussing contracts issues, and for his permission to use certain essay and multiple choice questions and answers, which I have edited for the purposes of this outline.

I would also like to thank Ellyn Garofalo, Esq. and Richard Turner, Esq. for their tireless research and proofing efforts. In addition, I am grateful to Selina Lozier, Esq. for her editorial assistance.

This outline could not have been completed without the secretarial assistance of Dorothy Aiken, Dorothy Olbricht, and Leslie Darough; their dedication was much appreciated.

II. 10-5-2 HOUR STUDY GUIDE FOR CONTRACTS

This study guide is designed to help you maximize your performance on Contracts examinations. These materials, of course, **do not** and **cannot** replace the notes and insights gleaned from the cases you have read and from your classroom experiences. This **Quick Review** is intended to complement your notes, briefs, and other class materials. With this in mind, the **10-5-2 Hour Study Guide** does not suggest that you begin your preparation for a final examination with only ten hours of study time before it is to be given. Contracts, like all first year classes, is simply too vast and complex for cramming.

Accordingly, this **Study Guide** assumes that you will complete the following, in advance:

___ Thoroughly review your class notes and case briefs, always making sure you not only understand the holding of a particular case, but also why that case was included in the case book and where its holding fits into the structure of the course as presented by your professor.

___ Use **Quick Review** to resolve any confusion or incomplete understanding in your review of the cases and topics covered in class.

___ Review previous examinations given by your professor. Professors generally test on the same issues time and again, so it is worth your while to spend a few hours looking at old exams and model answers. If answers have not been released, take an exam yourself under the stated time limits and ask your professor to review what you have written. If your professor does not have old exams on file, take an exam from **Quick Review** under examination conditions, and ask if your professor would review it.

___ Prepare your own outline of the course. Students differ on whether making an outline is worth the time and trouble, but most feel that the experience of synthesizing the course in their own words is invaluable. If you decide to make your own outline, use **Quick Review** as a guide to its structure.

With that in mind, the following will be helpful as the exam approaches.

10 Hours of Study Time Before the Final Examination

___ Review the **Capsule Outline**. If you understand all the concepts outlined in the **Capsule**, you are well on your way. Examine the **Summary of the Law** for any areas you do not understand.

___ Answer the objective questions in **Quick Review** as a means of checking your understanding of how to apply rules.

___ Review "major" cases covered in class. As a general rule, there is a rough proportionality between how much time you spent in class covering a topic and the amount that topic will be tested on the exam. Hence, if you spent one class (or most of a class) covering one particular case, it will probably be worth your while to **make sure** you understand that case well.

___ Begin to formulate an idea of how you will address certain issues. You should have in mind a way to approach a question that presents an issue as to whether something was an offer, how you will discuss an illusory promise issue, your approach to a UCC §2-207 problem, etc.

5 Hours of Study Time Before the Final Examination

___ Quickly scan through your class notes (or your own outline), taking the time to re-learn any issues which still present difficulty.

___ Review the main **Capsule Outline**. At this point you may wish to annotate the **Capsule Outline** with your own notes or with points from your own outline.

___ Take one last look at the **Case Squibs** to review any "major" cases covered in your class.

2 Hours of Study Time Before the Final Examination

___ Review the Table of Contents to make sure everything makes sense.

___ Take one last look at your notes covering those areas you feel will most likely be tested.

___ Mentally review those issues for which you have developed an approach.

___ Relax! Take a break a few minutes before exam time.

III. INTRODUCTION TO CONTRACTS

CHAPTER ONE: A CONTRACTS OVERVIEW

A. SOURCES OF CONTRACT LAW. [§1.0] Contract law is derived from several different sources. Despite this fact, contract law is fairly uniform throughout the United States. Mostly this is because lawyers, judges and legislatures generally agree on what the basic principles of contract law should be, but it is also because contracts are so frequently made and so heavily relied upon that a common nationwide set of rules governing the formation and operation of contracts is almost an economic imperative. The main sources for contract law are: (1) common law judicial decision-making; (2) treatises; (3) the Restatement of Contracts; and (4) the Uniform Commercial Code.

1. COMMON LAW. [§1.01] Most of our contract law is common law based, meaning (although this puts it a bit too simply) that it has been shaped through judge-created doctrines, rather than through legislative statutes. However, when commentators or professors speak of "the common law rule," they are likely referring to a long-standing rule that was probably developed by the pre-Revolutionary War English courts or, perhaps, by 18th or 19th century American courts.

2. TREATISES. [§1.02] Every contracts student comes across references early on in the course to Professor Williston's and Professor Corbin's treatises. Professor Williston's treatise was published in 1920, and Professor Corbin's between 1950-1960 in several volumes. Each was massively influential and largely shaped common law decisions after their publication. To write these works, each of the authors studied virtually all of the cases and writings on contracts existing at the time they were published; both extracted the rules governing contractual agreements and structured those rules into an organized set of legal principles with citations to support them. Modern day authors of contracts law treatises include Professors Farnsworth, Murray, and Calamari and Perillo.

3. RESTATEMENT OF CONTRACTS. [§1.03] The American Law Institute, a prestigious group of law professors, judges, and practitioners, published the Restatement (First) of Contracts in 1932. The Restatement set forth a series of black letter rules governing contract formation, operation, breach, etc., by restating in a unified way the **majority rules** governing those principles adopted by courts throughout the country. Some thirty years later, the First Restatement was revised to take into account newer thinking about contract law, and the Restatement (Second) of Contracts was published in 1962. The Restatement is not "the law" anywhere, but it does set forth the rules regulating contract law adopted by the courts of most states. Moreover, due to the prestige of its drafters, the "Restatement 2d" is frequently cited in modern case law as articulating the correct rule of law. Unless indicated otherwise, all citations to the Restatement in this book are to the Restatement 2d.

4. THE UNIFORM COMMERCIAL CODE. [§1.04] The Uniform Commercial Code ("UCC") is a set of statutes that govern commercial transactions throughout the United States. It is divided into nine substantive sections, called Articles, only three of which are cited with much frequency in a typical first year contracts course. These are: Article 1, dealing with general rules and general definitions used under all Articles of the Code; Article 2, entitled "Uniform Commercial Code—Sales"; and Article 9, entitled "Uniform Commercial Code—Secured Transactions." Of these, Article 2 has the most influence on contract law, and its rules are discussed in some detail in this outline. The first edition of the UCC was published in 1953 and it has been revised several times since then. The UCC was drafted as a joint project by the American Law Institute and the National Conference of Commissioners on Uniform State Laws, a group similar to, but having a different membership from, the American Law Institute. Unlike the Restatement, the UCC is "the law" throughout the United States, with the exception of Louisiana, and even Louisiana has adopted many of its provisions. That is, 49 state legislatures (and the governing bodies for various territories, including Puerto Rico, etc.) have adopted the UCC as the Commercial Code for their state or territory, although it should be noted that each state has amended the uniform act slightly when enacting it into law.

While the provisions of the UCC apply with the force of law to contractual relations within its scope, it is important to understand that **the UCC does not apply to all contracts**. By its terms, Article 2 applies only to "transactions in goods," and thus does not apply to contracts for the sale of land, to contracts for services, or to leases of goods [UCC §2-102] (see also the further discussion of the applicability provisions of Article 2 in Chapter Thirty-Four). Thus, the first step in analyzing any problem potentially governed by the Code is to determine whether the UCC and its rules apply, or whether more general common law contract rules apply.

> **a. The Uniform Sales Act. [§1.041]** Many early American contracts cases refer to the Uniform Sales Act ("USA"), and so that you won't be confused, a brief mention of the Act is included here. In some ways, the USA was a precursor to and set up roughly like the UCC. The USA was drafted by Professor Williston and eventually adopted by more than 30 states after its release in 1906. However, unlike the UCC, its scope was quite limited. For example, it did not deal with issues such as what remedies were appropriate upon a contractual breach. Indeed, it was a dissatisfaction with the limited scope of the USA that caused the UCC to be drafted.
>
> Note also that there was a British Sales of Goods Act published in 1893. In very old contracts cases there are sometimes references to both Uniform Sales Acts and while they are similar, you should realize they are two separate statutes.

B. DEFINITION OF CONTRACT. [§1.1] Perhaps surprisingly, there is no one agreed upon definition of a contract. What follows are the two most frequently cited definitions.

> **1. RESTATEMENT DEFINITION. [§1.11]** Under §1 of the Restatement 2d, "A contract is a promise or set of promises for the breach of which the law gives a remedy, or the performance of which the law in some way recognizes as a duty." In essence, under the Restatement, a contract is a promise or set of promises that are enforceable in our courts.

> **2. UCC DEFINITION. [§1.12]** §1-201(11) of the UCC defines a contract as "the total legal obligation which results from the parties' agreement . . ."

> **3. SIGNIFICANCE OF DISTINCTION BETWEEN RESTATEMENT AND UCC DEFINITIONS. [§1.13]** In most cases, a contract under the Restatement will also be one under the UCC. The one place where there will be a contract under the UCC, but not one under the Restatement, is when *both* parties complete all of their performance at or about the time their agreement is made. For example, if June offers Bill $100 for his watch, Bill accepts, and they exchange the money for the watch on the spot, there is likely no "contract" under the Restatement 2d because there are no "promises" of either party left to be enforced. There would be a UCC contract, however, for their agreement does give rise to legal obligations, e.g., if the cash were counterfeit, Bill would have a right to sue her as a result of their agreement.
>
> Note that if they agreed to the deal, but chose to make the exchange of the watch for the cash next Thursday, there *would* be a contract under the Restatement 2d for each party would have promised something — Bill to show up and bring his watch next Thursday;

and June to bring $100 at the same time. Similarly, if Bill had given up his watch on the spot in return for Jill's promise to pay him next Thursday, there would also be a Restatement 2d contract for there would be at least one unperformed (or, in contract terms, "unexecuted") promise remaining after the agreement had been made. Thus, if Jill failed to make good on her promise without a legally sufficient excuse, Bill would have a remedy for the breaking of her enforceable promise in a breach of contract action.

Most Contracts cases deal with contracts having at least some executory performance, i.e., with at least some promised acts that remain unperformed at the time the contract is formed, and so when this book refers to a "contract," it will usually be in the Restatement sense.

C. **ELEMENTS OF A CONTRACT.** [§1.2] A contract typically consists of:

1) an **offer** by one party;

2) an **acceptance** by the other;

3) and **consideration**.

An **offer** is a manifestation by a party reasonably indicating a willingness to be legally bound to a particular transaction on certain terms (Restatement 2d §24; Chapter Three).

An **acceptance** is a manifestation by the other party of a similar willingness to be legally bound to that same transaction (Restatement 2d §50; Chapters Four and Five).

Consideration is the main doctrine governing which promises made by the parties will be enforceable through our legal system. It may seem surprising, but courts will not enforce all promises exchanged between two parties. In general, courts will only enforce those with "consideration." As a general rule, for consideration to be present, the promises of one party must induce (or at least appear to induce) the promises or actions of the other, i.e. the parties' promises must be the result of a "bargained for exchange." (Restatement 2d §71; Chapter Seven). If consideration is not present, a party's promises may still be enforced to some extent if **promissory estoppel** (loosely defined as "a moral obligation") is present. For the doctrine of promissory estoppel to apply, the party seeking to enforce a promise must both reasonably and actually rely on that promise, and it must be demonstrated that it would be unjust if the promise were not enforced. (Restatement 2d §90; Chapter Eight.)

D. **TYPES OF CONTRACTS.** [§1.3]

1. **UNILATERAL CONTRACTS.** [§1.31] Unilateral contracts are those in which only **one party makes a promise, in the form of an offer, which calls for the other to render some sort of performance as acceptance.** For example, Jill and Ed agree that Jill will pay Ed $1,000 if Ed completes painting Jill's house. If Ed finishes the painting, they have entered into a unilateral contract because only one party, Jill, has made a promise, i.e., to pay; and that promise is conditioned on Ed's rendering performance, i.e., the painting, in order to accept. In other words, Ed's performance in painting the house (and not any promise to paint) acted as the acceptance of Jill's offer. (See §3.31)

2. **BILATERAL CONTRACTS.** [§1.32] Bilateral contracts are those in which **both parties make mutual promises to each other.** For example, suppose Jill promises to pay Ed $1,000 if he will agree to paint her house next Thursday. At this point, Jill has made an

offer to enter into a bilateral contract for she seeks a promise in return from Ed. If, in response to Jill's offer, Ed promises to do the painting next Thursday, then Ed has accepted Jill's offer and a bilateral contract has been formed. (See §3.32)

3. **EXPRESS CONTRACTS. [§1.33]** An express contract is one in which **the parties' contract results from words**, whether oral or written.

4. **IMPLIED-IN-FACT-CONTRACTS. [§1.34]** An implied-in-fact contract is one that is **reasonably implied by the parties' conduct**, rather than by express words. For example, a sign in Sally's Barber shop states, "We only give hair cuts and we only charge $12.00." Bruce walks in, sits in the barber chair and allows Sally to cut his hair, all without saying a word. An implied-in-fact contract has been formed, for it is reasonable to imply that he is agreeing to the $12 contract price when he sits in the chair. **The legal effect of an implied-in-fact contract in exactly the same as that of an express contract.**

5. **IMPLIED-IN-LAW CONTRACTS OR "QUASI-CONTRACTS." [§1.35]** Implied-in-law contracts or "quasi-contracts" (the terms are synonymous) **are not really contracts at all,** for there is no offer and acceptance agreed to by the parties. Rather, the terms refer to a limited group of situations where, to avoid inequity and unjust enrichment, a court will hold that one party must pay the other when he or she has benefitted from services provided by the other, even though the benefitted party neither explicitly nor implicitly agreed to pay for such services. In these situations courts **imply** that the benefitted party has agreed to pay for the benefits received, and require the party to pay the fair market value for those services. Note that because there is no "contract" in these cases, many modern commentators do not use the terms implied in law contract, or "quasi-contract" at all. Instead they describe such situations as giving rise to quasi-contractual "claims" or quasi-contractual "recovery" (see §32.4 for a further discussion of quasi-contractual recovery).

    a. **Example. [§1.351]** Georgia, a doctor, sees Fred lying unconscious in the street and renders emergency medical treatment. Fred is liable for the fair market value of Georgia's services under an implied-in-law, contract, or quasi-contract theory. Even though Fred never agreed to pay for those services, and thus never formally "accepted" Georgia's offer (which would be necessary for formation of a "contract"), the court will nevertheless impose that obligation on Fred as a matter of law. The idea is that Fred probably would want such aid, and it would thus be inequitable and unjust under the circumstances for Fred to be benefitted by Georgia's treatment and not pay the fair market value or "going rate" for it.

IV. OFFER AND ACCEPTANCE

CHAPTER TWO: MUTUAL ASSENT

A. MUTUAL ASSENT: DEFINED AND DISCUSSED. [§2.0] For a contract to be valid, the parties must manifest a **mutual assent to be bound** [Restatement 2d §18]. In other words, it is necessary to show that one party wished to exchange a particular item or service for specified terms, and that the other party agreed to that exchange. The rationale for this requirement, also known as **mutuality of obligation**, is that contract making is a form of risk allocation and it is important that the commercial risks associated with a contract be shared symmetrically. This concept is discussed immediately below.

1. **EXAMPLE OF MUTUALITY OF OBLIGATION. [§2.01]** Joe contracts to sell his car to Sally for $5,000. By offering his car at that price, Joe is taking a risk that he is making a "bad" (for him) deal in that other buyers might offer him $6,000 for the car. However, Joe is also taking the chance he has made a "good" (for him) deal in that no other buyer would offer him more than $4,000 for the car. By accepting the offer, Sally is taking reciprocal risks. That is, she is taking a risk that she has entered into a "bad" (for her) deal, whereby she has purchased a $4,000 car for $5,000. But she also may have made a "good" (for her) deal in that she bought a $6,000 car for $5,000. Because Joe and Sally share equal, but opposite, risks, their transaction is said to evidence **mutuality of obligation** and thus be enforceable.

   If there were a point at which only one party, say Joe, was bound, but Sally was not, then Sally could engage in speculation at Joe's expense. That is, she could explore the market, find out if anyone was interested in buying the car from her for $6,000, and if not, simply walk away from the deal. Obviously Sally is free to make such inquiries **before** she enters the contract. Also, she is free to engage in such speculation if she paid Joe for that right, i.e., if she entered into an option contract (see §4.421). However, absent an option contract situation, contract law views as unfair a situation where one party is bound and the other is free to speculate. Indeed, this idea of symmetrical risk allocation is at the heart of modern contract doctrine. It is often said that contract making is a form of mutual risk allocation, and so if parties do not share mutual, but opposite, risks, then they do not have mutuality of obligation, and there is no enforceable contract.

B. MUTUAL ASSENT JUDGED BY OBJECTIVE, NOT SUBJECTIVE TEST. [§2.1] Whether mutual assent has been achieved is judged by the **objective theory of contracts**, i.e., whether a reasonable person would conclude that a contract had been formed. Under this test, it is thus irrelevant what either party subjectively meant by what he or she said or did during contract negotiation. That is, it may be possible that one party to an enforceable contract does not believe that he or she has entered into such an agreement. However, if a reasonable person in the position of the **other** party would believe a contract has been formed, both parties will be bound.

1. **ELIMINATION OF "MEETING OF THE MINDS." [§2.11]** While the phrase "there was no contract because there was no **meeting of the minds**" is still bantered about, it is now meaningless. At common law, contract law used a subjective test to determine mutuality and so it was important that the parties' minds in fact "met" and that they both agreed to the same deal. Today, however, it is only important that a reasonable person in the position of one party would conclude that the other party intended to be bound **even if at the time that party did not intend to be contractually bound.**

2. **EXAMPLE OF *HAWKINS V. MCGEE*.** [§2.12] A surgeon told the parents of a boy ready for hand surgery that he would "guarantee" to make the hand "100% perfect," if the parents agreed to contract for his services. At trial, the doctor claimed he did not intend for his statements to act as a contractual commitment, especially in light of all his warnings that it was experimental surgery. **Held:** The question of whether the doctor had made an enforceable promise is one for the jury to determine under an objective test. As the jury concluded that a reasonable person in the position of the parents would believe that the doctor made an offer to be legally bound to produce a 100% perfect hand, and that the parents accepted that offer, a contract was formed, regardless of whether the doctor subjectively believed he had made a "contractual" promise to cure the hand. (See §3.2153 and Case Squibs Section, *Hawkins v. McGee*.)

3. **PRESUMPTION AGAINST MUTUAL ASSENT TO CONTRACT IN DOMESTIC OR SOCIAL SITUATIONS.** [§2.13] Under modern contract law, there is a presumption against finding a mutual assent to contract if the parties are social friends making promises to each other (e.g., if you'll give me a ride to the football game, I'll buy you a hot dog), or if the parties are living in an amicable domestic situation (e.g., where a brother promises to iron his sister's clothes in return for her promise to wash his car). The presumption against contractual intent can be overcome by admissible evidence that a binding legal commitment was intended, but the general rule is that the legal system will not enforce such promises or award damages for their breach. The rationale for this rule is that it is unlikely a reasonable person would believe that friends or family intended to be legally bound when making such casual promises. However, when parties are not in an amicable living situation, e.g., where a husband and wife are living together in the same house while waiting for a divorce, a modern court will usually find promises made between such partners to be enforceable.

C. **PRECISE TIME OF MAKING OF CONTRACT IRRELEVANT FOR DETERMINING MUTUAL ASSENT.** [§2.2] Occasionally, it is difficult to tell exactly when the parties entered into a contract. For example, sometimes two companies will negotiate a contract by phone and, instead of signing a single document as a contract they will sign identical duplicates of the same agreement so that both duplicates will be their contract. However, it is unlikely they will sign those separate documents at the same time. Rather than say they had no contract (the argument being that one party was bound for a time while the other was not, and they therefore lacked mutuality (see §2.01), both the Restatement and the UCC take the position that so long as mutual intent to be bound can be found at *any* point in time, valid contract is formed. Thus, under modern contract law, **mutuality of obligation can still be satisfied even if the precise moment of contract formation cannot be determined** [Restatement 2d §22(2); UCC §2-204(2)].

D. **MUTUAL ASSENT AS TO ALL TERMS NOT REQUIRED.** [§2.3] To have a binding contract, it is not necessary that the parties manifest mutual agreement to all possible terms. Rather, it is only necessary that there be agreement as to the **essential terms**. For example, if Sue manifests an intention to sell her car to Fred for $2,000, and Fred manifests an intention to buy the car for $2,000, the contract will still be upheld even if they do not agree, e.g., on where delivery is to take place, for there has been mutual assent to the essential terms (see Chapter Six: Indefiniteness).

CHAPTER THREE: OFFERS

A. OFFER: DEFINED AND DISCUSSED. [§3.0] An "offer" is the manifestation by one party (the offeror) of a willingness to enter into a bargain with another (the offeree) on certain terms. To be a valid offer, the manifestation must raise a reasonable expectation in the offeree that nothing more than acceptance is needed by the offeree to create a contract [Restatement 2d §24]. Offers can be written, oral, or expressed by conduct. In a simple negotiation, offers are typically the next-to-last communication before contract formation (acceptances being the last), but in complicated, long-distance negotiations, it may be difficult to pinpoint exactly which document or draft was an offer (see §2.2).

B. EFFECT OF AN OFFER. [§3.1] A valid offer creates in the offeree the **power of acceptance.** In other words, an offeree with the power of acceptance has the power to conclude a contract merely by accepting a valid, outstanding offer (see §4.3 et seq.).

C. HOW TO DETERMINE WHETHER AN OFFER WAS MADE: THE OBJECTIVE THEORY OF CONTRACTS. [§3.2] Whether an "offer" has been made is judged by **whether a reasonable person, in the position of the offeree,** would believe that only his or her expression of assent is necessary to form an enforceable contract. In other words, offers are judged under the **objective theory of contracts.** That is, a court may determine that someone has made an offer, even when the person himself or herself had no intention of making a legal commitment. So long as a reasonable person in the offeree's position would believe an offer was made, that offer is enforceable. The test is **not** whether this particular offeree believes an offer was made. Rather it is whether a **hypothetical reasonable person,** standing in the position of the offeree, **would have believed** an offer to have been extended.

In making the determination as to whether an offer was made, it is important to consider both the specific words and conduct of the offeror, and the context in which such words or actions were made. For example, a reasonable person would take the statement "Right, I'm going to offer to sell you this new $1,000 compact disc player I have for $500 because you're such a swell guy" very differently depending on whether it was said sarcastically to a friend while sharing beer and pizza than if it was said earnestly by a sales representative in an electronics store.

1. **DISTINGUISHING OFFERS FROM OTHER TYPES OF COMMUNICATIONS.** [§3.21] Over time, problems with common fact patterns have surfaced in analyzing whether an offer has been extended. Each of these is discussed below, but it is important to remember that the key question is **whether, to a reasonable person in the offeree's position, the offeror's statement creates an immediate power of acceptance in the offeree.** If it does, an enforceable offer has been made.

   a. **Offer Distinguished From Statement of Future Intention. [§3.211]** A statement that a party is thinking about making an offer or may be willing to be bound in the future is not an offer. Instead, such statements are deemed only **statements of future intention or invitations to make an offer** [Restatement 2d §26, Com. d]. Typically, phrases such as "I'm thinking about . . .," or "I may be interested in . . ." are only statements of intention and thus not offers. On the other hand, phrases like "You can have it for . . ." or "I'll sell you . . ." will be deemed offers.

      (1) **Example. [§3.2111]** Ted tells Barbara, "I decided last night to sell my sailboat for $5,000.!" Barbara immediately tenders Ted a check for $5,000 and says, "I'll take it." No contract is formed. This is because it has been determined, as a matter of contract law, that a reasonable person in Barbara's position would conclude that

Ted was merely stating his future intention to make an offer and is not presently offering Barbara a chance to bind him to those terms. In other words, there is no manifestation of Ted's commitment to sell the boat to Barbara. However, **Barbara** would be found to have made an offer, for a reasonable person in Ted's position would conclude that she is manifesting a commitment to be bound to the deal if Ted accepts.

b. **Offer Distinguished From Request for Price Quotation. [§3.212]** When someone merely asks for a **price quotation**, no offer is made, for there is no manifestation of intention to be bound and such a statement does not create a power of acceptance in the other party.

   (1) **Example. [§3.2121]** Sam calls up the hardware store and says, "Could you please give me a price quote for three boxes of 2 1/2-inch finishing nails?" Sam is clearly not making an offer to purchase the nails for he is not manifesting an intention to be bound no matter what the price turns out to be.

c. **Offer Distinguished from a Preliminary Negotiation/Invitation to Make an Offer. [§3.213]** A statement that solicits the other party to make an offer is not an offer itself, but rather a **preliminary negotiation** or **invitation to make an offer** [Restatement 2d §26]. Phrases such as "Are you interested in . . . " or "Would you give . . . " are typically deemed invitations to make an offer, for a reasonable person would not find a power of acceptance created in the presumptive offeree by such statements. Once again, there is simply no commitment to be bound in a transaction expressed by these kinds of statements.

   (1) **Example. [§3.2131]** Bruce tells Gloria, "Would you consider selling your car for $1,000?" and Gloria, responds, "It's yours." It is Gloria, not Bruce, who has made the offer. This is because to a reasonable person in Gloria's position, Bruce has merely entered into a preliminary negotiation with Gloria and is really trying to solicit an offer from her rather than make one himself. That is, he has not agreed to pay Gloria $1,000 for her car, but instead has merely invited Gloria to begin to negotiate with him. Gloria's response shows that it is she who is making the offer. Obviously if Bruce had said, e.g., "If you will agree right now to sell your car to me, I'll give you $1,000 for it," he will be deemed to have made an enforceable offer.

d. **Offer Distinguished from Advertisements/Catalogue Descriptions. [§3.214]** A staple of first year contracts classes is analyzing the effect of an advertisement in the newspaper or a description of an item in a mail-order catalogue. The question is whether the advertisement or description is itself an offer, or is a preliminary negotiation/invitation to make an offer as discussed in §3.213. **The general rule is that an advertisement or a description in a catalogue is not an offer, but rather a solicitation to make an offer.** Thus, it is the reader of the advertisement who is deemed to make the offer when he or she tries to purchase the item.

However, if the advertisement or catalogue description both:

(1) specifies a particular quantity of goods to be offered at the invited price; and

(2) indicates to an offeree what specific steps need to be followed in order to accept that offer without further communication from the seller, such as the goods are being sold on first come, first-served basis, such advertisement or catalogue description will be considered an offer [Restatement 2d §26, Com. b].

(1) Rationale for Rule. [§3.2141] The rationale for the general rule is, in part, based on the consequence of deciding whether or not a contract is formed. If the advertisement or catalogue were an offer, and the customer accepted that offer by attempting to purchase the item, the seller would be in breach of contract every time the seller ran out of the item and couldn't produce it when an "offer" was made.

However, if the seller specifically offers buyers a particular quantity of goods, and explains to buyers how they may accept the offer, then the store has taken sufficient steps to protect itself from the breach problem described above and has manifested an intention to be bound on the described terms. That is, to a reasonable person in the position of a buyer, there is no expectation that the store is offering an unlimited supply of goods; rather, the reasonable expectation is that once the specified quantity of goods has been sold to others, the offer expires by its own terms. There thus cannot be an over-acceptance of the offered goods.

(2) Example. [§3.2142] A clothing store advertised a famous line of suits in these terms, "Nationally advertised suits. Normally at $220, today only at $150." Alvin came to the store in response to the advertisement, selected a suit, and tendered $150. Is there a contract? No; the advertisement stated no quantity and the cases hold such advertisements to be mere statements of intention to sell or solicitations to a buyer that the buyer make an offer.

(3) Example of *Lefkowitz v. Great Minneapolis Surplus Stores*. [§3.2143] The following advertisement appeared in a store window: "3 Black Lapin Stoles, Beautiful, Worth Up to $139, $1 First-Come First-Served. . . ." Customer was the first to the store and tendered the $1. **Held:** Because a quantity was given and because the advertisement stated what steps needed to be taken to accept without further communication from the store, the advertisement constituted an offer. Thus, upon customer's tender of the $1, an enforceable contract was formed. *Lefkowitz v. Great Minneapolis Surplus Stores*, 251 Minn. 188, 86 N.W.2d 689 (1957).

e. Offer Distinguished from Statements Made in Jest, in Anger, in a Grumbling Manner, or While Intoxicated. [§3.215] Under the objective theory of contracts, it is irrelevant whether a party intended his or her statements or conduct to create an offer. Thus, **so long as an offeree reasonably believes that the offeror was manifesting an intention to be bound upon acceptance by the offeree, the fact that the offeror was only kidding, or was intoxicated, was grumbling, etc., does not prevent a valid offer from being made** (see §2.1 et seq.).

(1) Example. [§3.2151] Joe has just purchased a $30,000 car which he loves. He tells Larry, "I'll sell my new car to you for $1,000." With only this much of the story, it is impossible to tell whether Joe has made an enforceable offer or not. To determine whether a valid offer was made, it is important to know the circumstances surrounding the communication, e.g., were Joe and Larry joking, were they old friends, did they make "offers" like this often between themselves, did Joe really need $1,000 at that point in his life, etc. Obviously the price disparity makes it unlikely that it will be deemed an enforceable offer, but that alone is not enough to conclude that the offer was not a serious one. The question is whether a reasonable person in Larry's position would conclude that Joe had manifested a commitment to be bound to a deal on the proffered terms.

(2) **Example of** *Lucy v. Zemer.* **[§3.2152]** After a night of some drinking and "needling" conversation, Zemer offered in writing to sell Lucy his farm for $50,000, a fair price. Lucy accepted and Zemer later contended that no contract had been formed because he was "higher than a Georgia Pine" when he made the offer and because he believed the offer to be a joke. **Held:** Zemer made a valid offer to sell the farm because, to a reasonable person in the position of the offeree, it appeared that Zemer made a sincere offer. It is thus irrelevant what Zemer subjectively believed. (See Case Squibs section, *Lucy v. Zemer.*)

(3) **Example of** *Hawkins v. McGee.* **[§3.2153]** (See §2.12 and Case Squibs section, *Hawkins v. McGee.*)

D. **TYPES OF OFFERS. [§3.3]** Generally contracts scholars identify three types of offers, each of which is discussed below.

1. **OFFER TO ENTER INTO A UNILATERAL CONTRACT. [§3.31]** A unilateral contract offer is one in which the offeror is seeking *performance* of an act by the offeree. For example, "I promise to pay you $1,000 if you actually paint my house." The offeror is not seeking the painter's promise to paint the house, but instead is saying that he or she is offering to pay on completion of a specified act. [See §1.31 for a discussion of unilateral contracts].

2. **OFFER TO ENTER INTO A BILATERAL CONTRACT. [§3.32]** An offer to enter into a bilateral contract is one in which the offeror seeks a *promise of performance* by the offeree. For example, "I promise to pay you $1,000 if you agree to paint my house by the end of the month." Obviously the offeror expects that the offeree will eventually follow through and paint the house if the offeree accepts, but at the present time, the offeror is only bargaining for the promise of performance, not for the performance itself. [See §1.32 for a discussion of bilateral contracts].

   a. **Significance of the distinction between unilateral and bilateral contract offers. [§3.321]** Many first year students wonder why anyone would ever make a bilateral contract offer, and are surprised to learn that most offers are bilateral in nature. That is, why would someone only want a promised performance when you could bargain for performance itself? The answer is lies in the concept of breach and settled expectations. If an offeree says, "I will only pay you if you complete painting my house," he or she cannot reasonably rely on the house being painted. Because, after all, the offeree has not promised to start; or once started, the offeree has not promised to finish. (See §4.134 for a more thorough discussion of this issue).

   On the other hand, if the offeree promises to paint the house by a certain date, the offeree has a right to expect that the work will be done, and if it is not, he or she will have a right to sue for breach of contract if there is no justifiable excuse for the offeree's non-performance.

3. **GENERAL CONTRACT OFFERS. [§3.33]** A "general" offer is an offer phrased in such a way that a large, and in some cases, potentially unlimited, number of people can accept it. For example, a Bank that offers a reward for information leading to the arrest and conviction of someone who robbed one of its branches. Almost always, general contract offers are unilateral in nature, i.e., the offeror is only offering to pay upon the completion of some act. However, general offers carry with them peculiar problems regarding acceptance and revocation, which is why they are typically discussed separately. (See §4.33 for a discussion of the acceptance and revocation problems associated with general offers).

E. THE OFFEROR IS "MASTER OF THE OFFER." [§3.4] It is often said that the offeror is "master of the offer." This means that the offeror is free to dictate all the terms of the offer. However, when the cases speak of the offeror as being the "master of the offer," they generally are referring to two specific things:

(1) **the offeror's power to specify how the offer is to be accepted**, e.g., the offer may only be accepted by telegram received before 10:00 a.m. tomorrow; and

(2) **the offeror's power to dictate who may validly accept the offer**, e.g., the offer may only be accepted by members of your club.

Once an offeror has limited either how the offer can be accepted or who may accept it, an offeree is required to abide by such limitations in accepting the offer (see §§4.5, 4.3).

F. SPECIAL RULES REGARDING OFFERS MADE AT AUCTIONS. [§3.5] There are special rules for dealing with offers made at auctions. The key to analyzing an auction transaction is to determine, as between the auctioneer and the bidder, which party is the offeror and which is the offeree. The answer depends on whether the auction is **with reserve** or **without reserve** [Restatement 2d §28; UCC §2-328]. Each type of auction is discussed below.

1. **AUCTIONS WITH RESERVE. [§3.51]** Auctions are assumed to be "with reserve" unless otherwise indicated [Restatement 2d §28(1)(a); UCC §2-328(2)]. "Reserve," this context, means that the auctioneer reserves the right to remove the goods from the auction at any time before the hammer falls. **Thus, in an auction with reserve, the auctioneer is deemed merely to solicit offers from bidders and it is the bidders themselves who are the offerors.** The auctioneer, as offeree, has the power to accept or decline the bids, and signifies acceptance of the last offer by letting the hammer fall. Thus, even if there are bids outstanding, the auctioneer can choose to reject them and withdraw the goods from the auction simply by never letting the hammer fall and thus never "accepting" any offer.

2. **AUCTIONS WITHOUT RESERVE. [§3.52]** If the auction is specifically stated to be **without reserve, the auctioneer is the offeror and each successive bidder is an offeree** [Restatement 2d §28(1)(b); UCC §2-328(3)]. By placing the goods on sale, the auctioneer is deemed to have made an irrevocable offer to sell, which cannot be withdrawn after the first bid is made. Each bid acts as a conditional acceptance, subject to the conditions that: (a) it is not withdrawn before the hammer falls; and (b) no higher bid is made. Once the hammer falls without a retraction of the final bid and without a higher bid being made, the conditional acceptance becomes an enforceable acceptance, and a contract is formed with the last bidder.

3. **WITHDRAWAL OF BID. [§3.53]** Whether or not an auction is with reserve, the bidder is free to withdraw his or her bid at any time prior to the auctioneer's announced completion of the sale. In such an event, earlier bids are **not** automatically restored [Restatement 2d §28(1)(c); UCC §2-328(3)].

CHAPTER FOUR: ACCEPTANCE

A. ACCEPTANCE: DEFINED AND DISCUSSED. [§4.0] An "acceptance" is a manifestation by the offeree that he or she is willing to be bound by the terms of the offer. Acceptance can be written, oral, or expressed by conduct. In a simple negotiation, acceptance is the last communication which results in contract formation. To be valid under §50 of the Restatement 2d, an acceptance must be made:

    (1) by someone entitled to accept the offer (see §4.3);

    (2) by an offeree whose power of acceptance has not been terminated (see §4.4); and

    (3) in a manner permitted under the contract (see §4.5).

B. EFFECT OF ACCEPTANCE. [§4.1] Assuming the existence of valid consideration, timely acceptance of a valid offer in a permissible way by an authorized person creates an enforceable contract. A valid acceptance cuts off the offeror's right to terminate the offer, and, of course, also cuts off the offeree's right to reject the offer.

C. WHETHER ACCEPTANCE HAS TAKEN PLACE IS JUDGED UNDER THE OBJECTIVE THEORY OF CONTRACTS. [§4.2] Whether or not an offeree has accepted an offer will be judged under the **objective theory of contracts. The test is whether, to a reasonable person in the position of the offeror, the offeree has manifested a willingness to be bound by the terms of the offer**. If so, an acceptance has been made. The test is not whether the actual offeror believed an acceptance had been made, but whether a hypothetical person, standing in the shoes of the offeror, would believe that the offeree has manifested a willingness to be bound.

A somewhat strange, and relatively uncommon (except in law school hypotheticals), effect of the objective theory of contracts is that sometimes an offeree may accept an offer without even knowing its contents. That is, so long as the offeree at least knew that some sort of offer had been tendered (even if its exact terms are unknown), and as long as a reasonable person in the offeror's position would have believed an acceptance had been tendered, the acceptance will be valid.

    1. EXAMPLE. [§4.21] Frank, a law student, sends a letter to his college roommate, Jim, offering Jim one-half of his upcoming summer's earnings if Jim will pay one-half of Frank's spring semester tuition. Frank truthfully and seriously explains that he is experiencing cash flow problems and figures Jim, who now has a high paying corporate job, may want to make such an investment and help Frank out. Jim receives the letter, but loses it before he gets a chance to read it. When Frank calls and asks, "Do we have a deal as outlined in the letter?" and Jim replies (because he's embarrassed about losing the letter), "You bet we do, good buddy," a contract is formed because a reasonable person in Frank's shoes would believe Jim had manifested an intention to be bound. Jim's ignorance of the exact terms of the offer are irrelevant, for he knew from Frank's question that an offer had been made.

    2. CROSS-OFFERS. [§4.22] Occasionally parties will exchange identical offers to each other in the mail. That is, the buyer will send an offer to the seller stating that he or she is willing to buy particular goods on certain terms, and the seller will also send an offer to the buyer indicating a willingness to sell those same goods on those same terms. **The exchange of cross-offers does not form a contract,** for while both parties have manifested a willingness to be bound on his or her own suggested terms, **neither has**

manifested a willingness to accept the offer of the other party. Recall that the definition of acceptance requires a "manifestation of assent" by the offeree, and there is no such manifestation in a cross-offer.

D. WHO IS ENTITLED TO ACCEPT THE OFFER. [§4.3] When an offer is made to someone, the offeree is said to have a **power of acceptance**. The general rule is that **an offer may only be accepted by the person or persons in whom it is reasonably apparent that the offeror intended to create the power of acceptance when the offer was made** [Restatement 2d §§29, 52]. When an offeror specifically limits who may accept the offer, such a limitation will be effective, for the offeror is the "master of the offer." However, when no specific person is mentioned, an offer may be accepted by anyone to whom it reasonably appears the buyer was intending to give the power of acceptance. In cases of doubt, it is for the court to decide who is in the class of authorized, but unnamed, offerees. A court makes such a determination through an examination of the circumstances under which the offer was made, e.g., was it made in a face-to-face meeting, in front of a large group, in a newspaper, etc.

1. **WHO IS AN ELIGIBLE OFFEREE IS JUDGED BY THE OBJECTIVE THEORY OF CONTRACTS. [§4.31]** Whether an individual is an authorized offeree, and thereby eligible to accept an offer, is determined under **the objective theory of contracts**. Thus, if a reasonable person in the purported offeree's shoes would believe the offer was being made to him or her, that person has the power to accept it. Hence, once again, the subjective intention of the offeror as to whom the offer was intended is irrelevant.

2. **POWER TO ACCEPT IS NOT GENERALLY TRANSFERABLE. [§4.32]** On occasion, an eligible offeree will try to transfer his or her power of acceptance to another. In the absence of an option contract (see §4.42), such a transfer has no legal effect [Restatement 2d §52]. That is, the power to **accept an offer**, as opposed to the right to delegate duties after the contract has been formed, is not legally transferable.

   a. **Example. [§4.321]** In a face-to-face conversation, Barbara offers to sell her stereo to Elaine for $500. Elaine decides she does not want the stereo, but mentions the offer to Mary and tells Mary she can go ahead and buy Barbara's stereo if Mary wants, for Elaine will give Mary her power of acceptance. Mary thereafter walks up to Barbara and says, "I'll take the stereo you offered Elaine for $500 — Elaine said I could have her power of acceptance." No contract is formed, for Elaine cannot assign her power to accept. Barbara is still the master of the offer and need not sell her stereo to Mary if she does not wish to do so. However, Mary will be judged as having made an offer to purchase the stereo, and thus, Barbara can decide to accept or decline Mary's offer.

   b. **Review Problem. [§4.322] Dennis places an order for $1,000 worth of shelving from Bill's Lumber Yard. Before Bill's has accepted, Bill's premises and inventory are bought by Lumber Co. Question: Can Lumber Co. accept Dennis' offer?**

      Answer: Even though Dennis will be getting the same goods at the same price from Lumber Co., Lumber Co. cannot validly accept Dennis's offer. This is because the power of acceptance in Dennis's offer was in Bill's and it cannot be transferred. Dennis is free to choose either to make a new offer to Lumber Co. for the goods, or to take his business elsewhere. If Lumber Co. sends him the shelving as a purported acceptance, it would in fact be an **offer** by Lumber Co., which Dennis could accept or not as he wished.

c. **Exception: Right to Accept Under an Option Contract is Generally Transferrable.** [§4.323] Absent an express agreement to the contrary, if the offeree has entered into a valid option contract, the offeree gains a **right** to accept the offer rather than merely a **power** to do so. As such, the right of acceptance is transferable under the general rules governing the assignability of all other contract rights (see §4.42 and Chapter Twenty-Eight).

3. **SPECIAL PROBLEMS CONCERNING WHO CAN ACCEPT "GENERAL" OFFERS.** [§4.33] A "general" offer is an offer that creates powers of acceptance in a large, and in some cases an unlimited, number of people. For example, an offer by a bank of $5,000 for information leading to the arrest and conviction of the party who robbed the Main Branch. (See §3.33)

A general offer presents four problems regarding acceptance:

(1) whether acceptance by one person extinguishes the power of all others to accept the general offer;

(2) whether the offeree must know of the general offer in order to accept it;

(3) how a general offer can be retracted by the offeror so as to terminate the power of acceptance; and

(4) whether an offeree must give notice to the offeror of his or her intention to accept before beginning performance.

These issues are discussed below in the context of rewards, which are the most common form of general offers.

a. **General Reward Offers Can Usually be Accepted By Only First Person. [§4.331]** Contract law has determined that a general reward offer, e.g., the bank will offer $5,000 "for information leading to the arrest and conviction of (an offender)," can only be accepted by the **first** person supplying such information. Obviously the terms and circumstances of the offer itself may amend the rule, but if nothing is said one way or the other as to who may accept, only the first supplier of information may accept the offer [Restatement 2d §29, Com. b, Ill. 1].

(1) **Example.** [§4.3311] Bank posts a reward for information leading to the conviction of the individual who robbed it's Main branch. On Monday, Julie calls the police and gives some information about the robbery. On Tuesday, Bruce provides different information. Even if Bruce's information was essential to the conviction, and even if Bruce did not know about Julie's previous conversation, Bruce is not entitled to the reward because he was not the first person to comply with the terms of the offer.

(2) **Example.** [§4.3312] The owner of a large company promises a $500 reward to "any employee" who never takes a sick day for two years. While probably a general offer if the size of the company is large enough, the words and circumstances of the offer itself make it clear that the offer may be accepted by any and all employees who meet the requisite conditions.

(3) Exception: General Offer Whose Conditions Make it Unlikely that an Unlimited Number of People Can Accept is Effective as to All Who Meet Those Conditions. [§4.3313] Contract law holds that a general offer that imposes conditions which make it likely that only a small number of people can accept, because only a small number of people are likely to meet all the conditions, is effective as to any and all persons who do, in fact, meet the conditions.

    (a) Example of *Carlill v. Carbolic Smoke Ball Co.* [§4.3313-1] Manufacturer of a carbolic smoke ball (a kind of incense, shaped into a ball, with medicinal qualities claimed by the manufacturer) placed advertisements in several publications offering a £100 reward to anyone who caught the flu after purchasing the product and using it as directed. This was held to be a valid offer to anyone who met the conditions. The case stands, in part, for the rule given in §4.3313. That is, if the nature of the conditions given in a general offer make it likely that only a limited number of people can meet those conditions, the offer is valid as to all who actually meet those conditions and otherwise do the acts necessary to accept the offer. *Carlill v. Carbolic Smoke Ball Co.*, 1 Q.B. 256 (1893). (See also §§4.3341;4.562.)

b. Offeree Must know of Reward Offer in Order to Accept it. [§4.332] In order to accept a general offer, an offeree must know of the existence of the offer. Note that the offeree need not know of the offer before starting the actions necessary to collect it, but must know of the offer before finishing those acts [Restatement 2d §§51, 23 (see esp. Com. c, Ill. 2)]; (see also §7.53). Note, also, that the offeree need not know exactly what the terms of the reward offer are in order to accept it (see §4.2). The requirement is only that he or she must at least know generally that some sort of a reward is being offered for the kinds of actions being undertaken by the offeree before the reward can be validly accepted.

    (1) Example. [§4.3321] On Monday, a public spirited citizen reports that she saw a certain individual climbing out of the bank window at 2:00 a.m. The following Wednesday, citizen hears about the bank's reward for information leading to the conviction of the robber. Regardless whether the individual she named is convicted of the crime, she is not entitled to the reward because she did not know of its existence before she gave the information.

    (2) Example. [§4.3322] On Monday, public spirited citizen sees something suspicious at 2:00 a.m. in the bank. She begins an investigation. On Wednesday, she learns that the bank is offering a reward of some sort for information leading to the conviction of the robber. On Thursday, she tells what she knows to the police, and ultimately the information she provided is instrumental in securing the conviction of the robber. She is entitled to the reward, even if she didn't know about it when she started investigating, or even if she did not know of the amount of the reward when she turned over the information.

    (3) Rationale for Rule that Offeree Must Know of Reward Offer to Accept it. [§4.3323] The rationale for the rule that an offeree must at least know of the existence of a reward offer before it can be validly accepted is twofold. The first is that the offer of a reward is designed to motivate people into taking actions that they would not otherwise take. Thus, if a person was going to come forward with incriminating information about a criminal anyway, when he or she does so there is no manifestation that such actions are intended as an acceptance of the reward offer (see also §7.55). The second reason revolves around the nature of a reward contract. If an offeree who knows of the reward discovers the required information and is the first to report it, he or she has a legitimate expectation of payment. However, if the "offeree" did not know of the offer, he or she has no expectation regarding payment when doing the acts called for in the offer. Accordingly, it is thought that there is no reason for the legal system to reward actions which carry with them no promissory expectations.

(4) Police Officers. [§4.3324] In most jurisdictions, a police officer who arrests a criminal may collect a reward offered for the apprehension of that criminal only if the officer performs acts which are outside of his or her official duties. If the required acts are within the officer's official duties, the promise to pay the reward is unenforceable due to lack of consideration under the pre-existing duty rule (see §7.63) or, perhaps more realistically, because it would be against public policy to have citizens offering extra compensation to police officers to do the jobs they are already paid to do.

c. **Revocation of general offers: The "Equal Publicity Rule". [4.333]** The general rule is that until an offer is accepted, it can be revoked at will by the offeree. However, typically the offeree must be specifically told about the revocation before it can be effective. (See §4.413 et seq.) The problem with a general offer is that the offeror, such as a bank which makes a reward offer, will usually not know who has seen the original published offer and may be working to try and collect the reward. Accordingly, if the bank wishes to revoke the offer before it's been accepted, it will not know who to contact. Contract law has solved this problem by means of the "**equal publicity rule.**" That says that if a general offeror gives equal publicity to its retraction as it did in making the offer, i.e., publishes it in the same places, with the same prominence and frequency, etc., the offer will be retracted as to all offerees, regardless whether they ever had actual notice of the retraction. [See §4.4132-1]

d. **Notice of Intent to Accept General Offer Not Required. [§4.334]** Unless specifically and unambiguously required by the offer itself, an offeree need not give notice to the general offeror of his or her intent to accept the offer.

(1) Example of *Carlill v. Carbolic Smoke Ball*. [4.3341] Manufacturer placed an advertisement in several publications promising to pay £100 to any one who caught the flu after purchasing and using the smoke ball as directed. Carlill purchased and correctly used it, but nevertheless caught the flu. Manufacturer asserted that it should not have to pay because Carlill gave it no notice that he was intending to accept the general unilateral offer before he began performance. **Held:** Carlill (offeree) was under no duty to inform the manufacturer (offerror) of his intention to accept the general offer before beginning performance. *Carlill v. Carbolic Smoke Ball*, 1 Q.B. 256 (1893). (See also §§4.3313-1; 4.562)

E. WHEN MAY AN OFFER BE ACCEPTED: DURATION OF THE POWER OF ACCEPTANCE. [§4.4]
A purported acceptance of an offer after the power of acceptance under that offer has been terminated is an invalid acceptance. There are different rules regarding when and how the power of acceptance under an offer terminates, depending on whether the offer is revocable or irrevocable, and these rules are discussed extensively below in §§4.41 et seq. and 4.42 et seq. However, it is important to understand that regardless of whether the offer was revocable or irrevocable when made, once it has been effectively terminated, the offeree has thereafter neither the power nor right to accept the offer, and any purported acceptance by the offeree is really a counter-offer.

Note that you will often see in cases and other sources a reference to "termination of an offer." While this is descriptive, it is not technically accurate. **What terminates is not the offer, but rather the offeree's power to accept the offer.** Nonetheless, on occasion this book uses the terms "termination (or expiration) of an offer" to be consistent with the cases and other sources that use these words to mean termination of the power of acceptance.

1. **GENERAL RULES GOVERNING TERMINATION OF THE POWER OF ACCEPTANCE UNDER REVOCABLE OFFERS. [§4.41]** A revocable offer may be accepted so long as the power of acceptance under it has not been terminated [Restatement 2d §35]. There are eight ways such termination may occur:

    (1) upon **rejection or counter-offer** by the offeree (discussed in §4.411 et seq.);

    (2) by **lapse of time** (discussed in §4.412);

    (3) upon **revocation** by an offeror (discussed in §4.413);

    (4) upon **death or incapacity of the offeror** (discussed in §4.414);

    (5) upon **death or incapacity of the offeree** (discussed in §4.415);

    (6) upon **death or destruction of a person or thing essential for the contract's performance** (other than the offeror or offeree) (discussed in §4.416);

    (7) **by supervening illegality** (discussed in §4.417); and

    (8) by the **non-occurrence of any condition of acceptance** under the terms of the offer (discussed in §4.418).

    a. **Termination of Offers Through Rejection and Counter-offer by the Offeree. [§4.411]** A **rejection** occurs upon any manifestation by the offeree that he or she does not accept the offer and is unwilling to be bound under its terms [Restatement 2d §38].

    A **counter-offer** is an offer made by the offeree, to the original offeror, relating to the same matter as the original proposal, but on different terms than those proposed in the original offer. It has the effect of rejecting the original offer (thereby terminating the power of the offeree to thereafter accept the original offer) and proposing a new one in its place [Restatement 2d §39].

    Both rejections and counter-offers may be communicated by words or by actions, and their effect is to terminate the power of acceptance by the offeree.

    (1) **Counter-offer Need Not Explicitly Reject Offer. [§4.4111]** All counter-offers are effective as rejections of the original offer, regardless of whether they specifically mention the original offer. In effect, **when the offeree makes a counter-offer, he or she is implicitly rejecting the original offer and telling the offeror, "I do not want to proceed on the terms you proposed, and am willing to be bound only on the different terms I am now proposing."** [Restatement 2d §39, Com. a]. For example, Sam offers to sell his car to Bob for $5,000. Bob replies, "I am only willing to buy it for $4,000, and I will never go higher." At this point, even without mentioning the offer specifically, Bob has rejected it. Thus, Bob has terminated his power to accept Sam's $5,000 offer. Thus, if Sam declines Bob's $4,000 counter-offer, Bob cannot validly accept the original $5,000 offer for Bob's

power to do so has terminated. If he tries to accept for $5,000, it is Bob who will be deemed to have made a new offer to purchase the car at that price, which Sam may accept or reject.

(2) Rejections and Counter-offers are Judged Under the Objective Theory of Contracts. [§4.4112] Whether or not an offeree has rejected an offer, whether by counter-offer or otherwise, is determined under the **objective theory of contracts**. Thus, the test is whether a hypothetical reasonable person, in the position of the offeror, would believe that the offeree was rejecting the offer or making a counter-offer. Once again, even if the offeree did not subjectively intend to reject an offer, or to make a counter-offer, such intention is irrelevant. In making the determination of whether a rejection has taken place, the context of the situation, as well as the words and actions of the offeree, are to be taken into account.

(3) Common Law Rule: Counter-offer Found if Purported Acceptance Differed from the Offer in the Slightest Respect. [§4.4113] At common law, if the terms of a purported acceptance deviated from the terms of an offer in the *slightest respect,* it was deemed to be a counter-offer and not an acceptance. Modern contract law, most notably under the UCC, has changed this rule substantially (see Chapter Five).

(4) Rejections and Counter-offers Distinguished from Other Types of Communications. [§4.4114] As with any legal classification, in close cases it is difficult to say whether an offeree's statement falls on the rejection/counter-offer side of the line, or sould be interpreted as something else. Of course the answer to such an inquiry is often of crucial importance, for it will often decide whether or not a contract was formed and if so, what its terms are. Over time, contract law has been able to classify various situations and develop rules for determining when statements are rejections, counter-offers, or something else. Each of these situations is described below. However, once again the guiding principles in determining whether a statement is a rejection, counter-offer, or something else are:

    (1) **To be an effective rejection, the offeree must manifest an intention not to accept the offer; and**

    (2) **To be an effective counter-offer, the offeree must manifest an intention to be bound only on different terms from those made in the offer.**

(a) Example: A Neutral Comment is Neither a Rejection nor a Counter-offer. [§4.4114-1] Dave offers to sell a ring to Sally for $10,000. Sally says, "Gee that's expensive. I don't know if I can afford it." Sally has made only a **neutral comment**, and has not rejected the offer, for a reasonable person would not believe her to have manifested an intention not to be bound. Thus, Sally still retains the power to, and may validly, accept Dave's offer.

(b) Example: A Mere Inquiry/Preliminary Negotiation is Neither a Rejection nor a Counter-offer. [§4.4114-2] Bernice offers to sell her watch to Jane for $500. Jane replies, "Would you consider $450?" Jane has not rejected the offer under the objective theory and has made a **mere inquiry** or a **preliminary negotiation** as to whether Bernice might be willing to negotiate the price. Jane's statement does not rise to the level of a counter-offer because Jane has neither expressed a commitment to be bound to a $450 price, nor manifested an intention to proceed only on different terms from those made in the offer. In the contracts meaning of the term, Jane has made only a preliminary negotiation on the road to a possible offer (see §3.213). Therefore, Jane still retains the power to accept Bernice's $500 offer [Restatement 2d §39, Com. b, Ill. 2].

(c) **Example: Rejection or Counter-offer Immediately Cuts Off Power of Acceptance, Even if Offer was to be Open for Longer Period. [§4.4114-3]** An antique store owner offers to sell Jack a grandfather clock for $7,500 and tells him to "take a week to think it over." Jack immediately responds, "I will offer to buy it for $6,000 and that is all I'll pay you for that thing." Jack has manifested an unwillingness to go forward on the terms contained in the offer (i.e., the $7,500 price) and has indicated a willingness to be bound only on different terms (i.e., a $6,000 price). Thus, Jack has made a counter-offer and has thereby immediately lost his power to accept. Thus, even if Jack comes back to the store the next day and says, "O.K. I'll pay the $7,500," such statement is only a new offer to buy, not an acceptance of the store's offer to sell, for Jack's power to accept the original offer has terminated [Restatement 2d §38, Com. a, Ill. 1].

(d) **Example: Request for Modifications do not Terminate the Offeree's Power of Acceptance. [§4.4114-4]** In response to an offer to sell him a $2,000 stereo on no-interest 90-day credit, Moe says, "O.K. I'll take it, but will you give me a 5% discount for cash?" Moe has accepted the stereo at $2,000 and has made a **request for modification** of the contract regarding the cash discount, which may be accepted or rejected by the store (see Chapter Twenty-Six for a further discussion of modification). Note that if Moe had said, "I'll accept only if you give me a 2% discount for cash," then it would be a counter-offer, as a reasonable person would believe Moe was rejecting the offered price and willing to be bound only at the lower one.

(e) **Example: A Grumbling Acceptance does not Terminate the Offeree's Power of Acceptance. [§4.4114-5]** In response to an offer to sell him a used refrigerator for $1,500, Bernie says, "O.K. I'll take it, but the price is way too high. I should only have to pay you $800 for it." Bernie has accepted, even if he is not happy about it. Such a situation is known as a "grumbling acceptance".

(f) **Example: Rejections and Counter-offers Where the Offeree Manifests an Intention to Take the Offer under Further Advisement. [§4.4114-6]** Laura offers to sell her watch to Jean for $600 and tells Jean to "take a week to think about it. I won't sell to anyone else before then." The next day Jean says, "I am unwilling pay $600 today, and if you would like to close the deal right now, I'll give you $525 for the watch. However, I am keeping your $600 offer under advisement for the rest of the week." Jean's power of acceptance has **not** been terminated, for she has manifested an intention to keep the offer open. Thus, to a reasonable person in the position of the offeror, Jean would not be seen as manifesting an unwillingness to be bound by the original offer, but rather making a preliminary inquiry as to whether the price was negotiable. As such, Laura is not entitled to rely on Jean's statements as terminating the offer, and, if nothing more is said, Jean may validly accept the $600 offer later in the week [Restatement 2d §38(2), Com. b; §39(2), Com. b, Ill. 3].

(g) **Example: When Offeror Manifests Intention to Continue Offer even in Light of Counter-offers. [§4.4114-7]** Very occasionally, an offeror may say something like, "I'm willing to sell my car to you for $25,000, and I'll hold the offer open for 30 days. However, I will be willing to receive a counter-offer from you in the meantime." Fred makes a counter-offer of $21,000, which is turned down by the offeror. Fred still has the power to accept the $25,000 offer until the 30 days runs out, despite his counter-offer. This is, of course, because of the offeror's manifestation to keep the offer alive even in light of the counter-offer [Restatement 2d §39(2), Com. c].

(5) When a Rejection is Effective. [§4.4115] The general rule is that a **rejection is effective when it is received by the offeror**. In the vast majority of cases, the determination of exactly when a rejection is received is undisputed or unimportant, e.g., the rejection comes during a face-to-face conversation, or during a phone conversation, or for other reasons the parties do not contest the time of rejection. However, occasionally a party will mail an acceptance and then change his or her mind and want to signify rejection (e.g., by a phone call) before the offeror has received the mailed acceptance. Similarly, an offeree may originally mail a rejection and then want to accept by phone before the offeror receives the mailed rejection. These situations, and others, are covered by the **mail box rule** (see §4.6).

b. **Termination of the Power of Acceptance through Lapse of Time. [§4.412]** Sometimes an offer specifies when it will terminate, e.g., "This offer is valid until 5:00 p.m. on October 1." The offeror, as "master of the offer," is entitled to make such a specification and if the offeree has not accepted it within the specified time, the offeree's power of accece terminates. If there is no mention of an expiration time in the offer, the power to accept terminates after a "reasonable time." [Restatement 2d §41(1)].

(1) Determination of "Reasonable Time." [§4.4121] A reasonable time regarding the termination of an offer with no specified time limit will vary depending on the circumstances existing when the offer was extended and when the acceptance was made [Restatement 2d §41(2)]. The question of whether the acceptance was made within a reasonable time is one of fact, not law, (meaning that it's for the jury's determination not the judge's, in a jury trial), and the circumstances which can be used to answer the question include the subject matter of the contract, the manner in which the offer was made, any previous dealings between parties, etc. **The test of what constitutes a reasonable time for acceptance is how long would a reasonable person in the position of the offeree believe he or she had to accept** [Restatement 2d §41, Com. b]. If the acceptance comes before that time elapses, it is effective.

(2) Common Presumptions about what Constitutes "Reasonable Time." [§4.4122] There are some general rules regarding certain types of transactions that have developed over the years. While the precise rule for a particular case may change depending on exactly what is communicated between the parties, the general presumptions are as follows:

(a) Offers Made in Direct Negotiations: Reasonable Time Terminates at End of Negotiation. [§4.4122-1] When parties deal directly over the phone, face-to-face, or via interactive computer, **the offeree's power to accept the offer generally terminates when the negotiation has concluded.** For example, if Ann offers Bill her record collection for $300 in a telephone conversation and Bill declines, unless Ann specifically extends the offer, Bill could not accept it during a face-to-face meeting a few hours later, for it terminated when the phone conversation ended.

(b) Offers in Letters: Acceptance Timely if Made on the Day of Receipt. [§4.4122-2] Generally, an acceptance by letter of an offer made by letter is timely if the acceptance is mailed on the date the offer is received, or early the next day if it was received towards the close of business. However, more (or less) time may be allowed before the power of acceptance terminates depending on the circumstances surrounding the particular offer. However, the general presumption is that when the parties are at some distance from each other, the time for acceptance extends at least to the normal time for transmission of the offer and for the sending of the offeree's reply by the same medium [Restatement 2d §41(3), Com. e].

(c) Offers in Telegram, Overnight Delivery, or Facsimile: Indications that Acceptance Must be Expedited to be Timely. [§4.4122-3] Anytime an offer is made via an expedited mode of communication, such as facsimile machine, telegram, or overnight mail, it is evidence that acceptance also must be expedited to be effective. In any situation, all the circumstances will have to be weighed, but the fact that an offeror chose a quick means of communication is an important factor in assessing how long the offeree's "reasonable time" period will extend before the offer lapses.

(d) Offers Dealing with Price-Volatile Subject Matter: Acceptances Usually Need be Expedited to be Effective. [§4.4122-4] As a general rule, the more the subject matter of a contract is subject to rapid price fluctuations, e.g., commodities, the shorter the period of time the offeree has to accept.

(3) Interpretation of Ambiguous Time Provisions in an Offer. [§4.4123] Even if an offer specifically limits the time period for an effective acceptance, such limitation may nevertheless be ambiguous. For example, if a letter ends with, "This offer is effective for 10 days," it is not clear on its face whether the offer can be accepted 10 days from the date of the letter, from the date of the postmark, from the date of receipt, whether this means 10 calendar days, 10 working days, etc. In such cases, it is up to the court to interpret what the offer meant in light of all relevant circumstances, such any previous dealings between the parties, the business practices of the industry, etc. (see §6.4). The general principle is that a court will try to ascertain what it was reasonable for a person in the position of the offeree to believe as to how long the offer was open. If after applying such interpretation rules a court still cannot come up with a definitive answer, generally any ambiguity is resolved *against* the offeror since, after all, the offeror could have made the provisions clearer.

(4) Effect of Delay in Communication of Offer. [§4.4124] While it doesn't happen often, occasionally offers sent, for example, by U.S. mail, are delayed through no fault of either the offeror or offeree. The rule in this situation is that **if the offeree knows or has reason to know of the delay in communication at the time he or she receives the offer, the delay does not extend the time during which the offeree can accept**. Thus, if on November 15, an offeree first receives a letter dated and post-marked October 1, notifying her that the offer described in the letter may be accepted during the next 10 days, the offeree cannot accept it because she has reason to know of the delay in transmittal. That is, the offeree's power to accept terminated sometime in mid-October. However, if the offeree does not know or have reason to know of the delay, e.g., where a letter is undated and the postmark is hard to read, then the offer may be accepted within the period it could have been accepted had it arrived in a timely manner [Restatement 2d §49]. Thus, in the case described above, the offeree would have ten days from the date of receipt to accept.

c. **Termination of Offers by Revocation. [§4.413]** In the absence of an option contract (see §4.421), or a UCC Merchant's Firm Offer (see §4.422), **offers are freely revocable by the offeror up until the moment of acceptance.** That is, so long as they have not been accepted, the offeror can "take back" an offer, even if he or she promised to keep it open. Thus, if an offeror says, "I'll sell you my watch for $500. You don't have to decide now — I'll give you a week to think about it," and five minutes later says, "I've changed by mind, I don't want to sell it to you," the offer is validly revoked and with it the offeree's power to accept. Similarly, if an offeree is on his or her way to accept an offer, but the offeror sees the offeree first and says "I revoke, the deal is off!" the revocation is immediately effective.

(1) **Revocations are Judged Under the Objective Theory of Contracts. [§4.4131]** Whether a revocation has occurred is judged under the objective theory of contracts. Thus, **the test is whether by words or actions, and in light of all other relevant circumstances, does it appear to a reasonable person in the position of the offeree that the offeror has manifested an unwillingness to continue to be bound by the terms of the offer.** If so, the offer is revoked and with it, the offeree's power of acceptance. Once again, whether the offeror subjectively believes he or she has revoked an offer is irrelevant.

(2) **Revocations Generally Effective only on Receipt by the Offeree. [§4.4132]** The general rule is that **a revocation is ineffective until it has been "received" by the offeree.** A written revocation is deemed received when the writing comes into the possession of either the person (including a corporation) to whom it is addressed, the person's authorized agent, or a person's designated place for receipt of such communications [Restatement 2d §68; UCC §1-201(26)]. Thus, a revocation lost in the mail is ineffective. This makes sense, the offeree should not lose his or her power to accept an offer when the offeror has subjectively decided to revoke unless the offeror tells the offeree that the offer is no longer outstanding. The rule that revocations are only effective upon receipt also has implications under **the mail box rule** (see §4.6).

(a) **Exception for Revocation of a General Offer: The Equal Publicity Rule. [§4.4132-1]** A general offer is one that can potentially be accepted by an unlimited number of people (see §4.33, supra). There is a problem when the maker of a general offer, e.g., a reward for information that was made in a newspaper advertisement, on a sign posted on a bulletin board, etc., wants to revoke that offer. The problem is that there is no way to ensure that everyone who saw the offer will also see the revocation. If a person does not see the revocation, then under normal rules he or she may later accept it (if the power to do so has not otherwise terminated), because the revocation would not be effective against someone who has not received it under the rule stated in §4.4132. Contract law solved this problem by adopting the **equal publicity rule**, which states that **so long as the revocation of a general offer is given equal publicity as the offer itself, the offer will be deemed revoked** [Restatement 2d §46]. Thus, if the revocation is posted in the same place, for the same number of days, in the same sized print, etc. as the offer, it will be effective even against someone who honestly did not see it.

(3) Indirect Revocation. [§4.4133] An indirect revocation occurs when the offeree hears from a third party, rather than from the offeror directly, that the offeror has revoked the offer. There are two requirements for an **effective** indirect revocation:

(1) the offeror must have taken a definite act inconsistent with an intention to enter into the proposed contract; and

(2) the offeree must have heard about the offeror's conduct from a reliable source. [Restatement 2d in Section 43].

According to the Restatement, the "definite act" requirement is to be construed narrowly, and essentially means that the offeror must have unequivocally disposed of the property that was the subject of the offer to another party e.g., by selling it, giving it away, or perhaps by leasing it on a long-term basis. Similarly, the source from which the offeree hears of such disposition of the property sale must appear to be reliable to a reasonable person acting in good faith [Restatement 2d §43, Com. d].

(a) Example of *Dickenson v. Dodds*. [§4.4133-1] Dodds offered to sell a piece of land to Dickenson for a given price, and promised Dickenson two days to think it over. The next day, before Dickenson had either accepted or rejected the offer, Dodds sold the property to Allan. From a reliable source, Dickenson heard that Dodds was selling (or perhaps had sold) the property to Allan, but nevertheless sent what would otherwise have been an effective acceptance. **Held**: There was no valid acceptance by Dickenson because the offer was indirectly revoked, and with it Dickenson's power of acceptance. *Dickenson v. Dodds*, (See Case Squibs).

(b) Rationale for the Indirect Revocation Doctrine. [§4.4133-2] The rationale behind the indirect revocation doctrine is straightforward. If the original offeree really knew that the offeror had already sold the goods, property, etc. in question, then there is only one reason the offeree would still try to "accept" the offer — namely to make the offeror a breaching party liable to the offeree for damages. That is, by "accepting" the offeror's promise to deliver what the offeree knows the offeror can't produce, the offeree is setting the offeror up for a breach of contract action. Contract law will not allow the offeree to set up the offeror in this manner.

(4) Special Problems Surrounding the Revocation of Unilateral Offers. [§4.4134] A unilateral offer seeks actual performance, not the promise of performance, in return for a promise (see §§1.31; 3.31). Thus, an offer under a unilateral contract cannot be "accepted" until the requested performance is completed. If the performance takes some time to complete, as is usually the case, this presents a potential problem for the offeree. That is, if an offeror can revoke the promise to pay any time before acceptance, it might be that an offeree will have spent a good deal of time, effort and money to get to a point where the performance is almost completed, and then have the offeror revoke the offer so that all the offeree's efforts are for naught. There are different approaches to solving this problem.

(a) The "Brooklyn Bridge" Hypothetical. [§4.4134-1] Probably the most famous hypothetical illustrating this issue is where Bill offers John $100 upon John's completion of a walk across the Brooklyn Bridge. John starts, but just before he takes the last step, Bill yells, "I revoke" and claims no contract was ever formed because there was no acceptance (no **completion** of the walk across the bridge) before the revocation. Your professor may, of course, substitute a more modern fact pattern to illustrate this point, e.g., Bill offers John $800 when John finishes painting Bill's house and Bill revokes just before the last little bit is painted, etc.

The three theories as to how to treat this situation are:

(i) **There is No Contract until the Offeree Accepts. [§4.4134-1A]** One theory holds that no contract is ever formed. This view provides no exception to general common law rules when dealing with unilateral contracts. That is, general contract law holds that an offeror such as Bill is entitled to revoke his offer at any time before acceptance without contractual liability, and since there was never acceptance as per terms of the offer, there was no contract. Under this view, there should be no special rules governing this practice just because the offer is for a unilateral contract and not a bilateral one. Obviously this is unfair to the offeree and if it ever was the prevailing view, it is no longer so today.

[handwritten margin notes: TRADITIONAL; Look at it like • I unilateral ①– option k ②– §45, reliance ③– Traditional. • II bilateral; Preparation Counts; Preparation doesn't count]

(ii) **There is a Unilateral Option Contract upon the Offeree's Beginning Performance: Restatement 2d §45. [§4.4134-1B]** Under §45, the Restatement 2d takes the position that as soon as the offeree begins performance, the agreement between the parties has been transformed into a unilateral option contract, binding the offeror but granting the offeree the right to complete performance or not at the offeree's option. That is, upon the beginning of performance, an implied irrevocable option contract springs into existence whereby the **offeror is required both to hold open the offer and give the offeree a chance to complete performance within a reasonable time**. Upon completion of performance, the offeree has then accepted, and the offeror is bound under the terms of the offer. However, this option contract is unilateral only, in that **the offeree is not bound to complete performance and may walk away at any time after performance is begun without breaching the contract.**

Under this view when John "began performance," i.e. started over the bridge, an **irrevocable** (for a reasonable time) unilateral contract offer arose. At that point, John has a reasonable time to "accept," i.e. to complete the walk called for in the offer, and if he does, Bill must pay him. However, John was never contractually obligated to finish his walk and if he chooses to walk away at any time before completion, he may do so without incurring contractual liability. **This view is the majority one today.**

(iii) **There is a Bilateral Contract upon the Oferee's Beginning Performance. [§4.4134-1C]** The third view as to how to treat this issue is to say that the beginning of performance by the offeree acts to form an implied, but enforceable, bilateral contract. That is, as soon as the offeree starts to perform, the offeror is deemed to make an offer for a bilateral contract (i.e., a promise that he or she will pay in return for a return promise from the offeree that the offeree will complete performance); and by beginning performance, the offeree is deemed to make a promissory acceptance in return (i.e., a promise that he or she will complete the task he or she has started in return for the promise to pay).

In the Brooklyn Bridge hypothetical, under this view once John started across the bridge, Bill and John were both contractually bound to an implied bilateral contract, and neither could revoke or fail to complete performance without incurring liability for breach of contract.

Note that this approach has drawn criticism, for it seems contrary to the idea that the offeror is the master of the offer. In these situations, the offeror has indicated that he or she is bargaining for performance, not a promise of performance. Thus, to say that a unilateral contract offer can be satisfied by an implied promissory acceptance seems contrary to usual formation rules, especially when the offeree has, in fact, expressly promised nothing.

(5) Special Problems Surrounding Revocation of Offers Foreseeably Inducing Pre-Acceptance Preparation by the Offeree. [§4.4135] There are some occasions in which an offeree may undertake substantial expense, or forego lucrative alternatives, in response to an offer but before acceptance actually occurs. Sometimes these actions can be deemed "beginning performance" in response to a unilateral contract offer and thus either bind the offeror to a unilateral option contract under §45 of the Restatement 2d (see §4.1341-B) or bind both parties under a bilateral contract (see §4.1341-C). However, sometimes the circumstances surrounding these actions are such that it is impossible to treat them under the "beginning of performance" rules, either because the offer was originally for a **bilateral** contract (which has not yet been accepted by a promise of the offeree), or because the actions taken by the offeree were not **specifically** called for by the offer. Under certain circumstances, contract law will provide relief for the offeree and find an enforceable agreement in these kinds of situations. Under Restatement 2d §87(2):

> **An offeror's power to revoke is terminated, and an option contract is completed whereby an offer is deemed irrevocable to the extent necessary to avoid injustice, when:**
>
> (a) an offeree takes action (or forebears to take action) of a substantial nature in response to an offer; and
>
> (b) **such action is reasonably foreseeable given the nature of the offer.**

In other words, when an offeree relies on the offer to a substantial degree in making pre-acceptance preparations, and when those acts are reasonably foreseeable, the offer becomes irrevocable for a reasonable period. Thus, upon the initiation of these pre-acceptance actions, the offeror is bound to hold the offer open for a reasonable time and must allow the offeree to accept the offer during that period.

(a) Example of *Drennan v. Star Paving Co.* [§4.4135-1] Star Paving, a subcontractor, submitted a bid to Drennan, a general contractor, for paving work to be done on a large project. Drennan used Star Paving's bid in preparing its quote for the overall project. Drennan was awarded the contract to build the overall project. However, before Drennan could inform Star Paving that Star Paving's offer to do the paving was accepted, Star Paving tried to revoke its bid. Star Paving's argument was that normal contract rules provide that it had an absolute right to revoke an offer to enter into a bilateral contract before that offer was accepted, and that Drennan had never accepted. Drennan stated that it could not accept before it was awarded the contract to build the project by the developer, for unless it had such a contract, it had no use for Star Paving's services. **Held:** Drennan prevailed under the rules set forth in §87(2). That is: (a) Drennan took action of a substantial nature in response to Star Paving's offer; (b) the reliance on Star Paving's offer was reasonably foreseeable given the nature of the contracting business; and (c) it would be unjust not to enforce the offer given the foreseeable reliance by Drennan in using Star Paving's offer in preparing its own bid. Thus, an option contract was implied whereby Star Paving's offer was deemed irrevocable for a reasonable time as soon as Drennan relied upon it. In this case, a reasonable time was defined as a few days after Drennan learned it was awarded the development contract for the entire project; and since Drennan accepted within this period, the acceptance formed a valid contract (see §8.342, for a more detailed discussion of the general contractor/subcontractor relationship). *Drennan v. Star Paving Co.*, 51 Cal. 2d 409, 333 P.2d 757 (1958).

Note that the rule of §45 of the Restatement 2d (see §4.4134-1B) would not apply to this situation for Star Paving's offer was for a bilateral contract and §45's implied unilateral option doctrine applies only to offerees who begin performance in response to offers to enter into a **unilateral** contract. That is, Star Paving sought Drennan's **promise** to pay it for the paving work rather than for the work itself. Thus, absent a rule such as that fashioned in §87(2), Star Paving would have been entitled to revoke its offer before it was accepted.

(b) Example of *Kucera v. Kavan*. [§4.4135-2] Owner of farm entered into a long-term lease with tenants and later gave the tenants an option to purchase the farm at any time within five years at a fixed price. Tenants, with owner's approval and at considerable expense, substantially improved the farm buildings and the farm land within the next three years. Upon completion of these improvements, but before exercise of the option by the tenants, owner tried to revoke his offer to sell the land and made a new offer to sell the farm to the tenants at a substantially higher price. **Held:** The substantial and foreseeable reliance on the part of tenants, coupled with the justice of the situation, made owner's offer to sell at fixed price irrevocable throughout remainder of five-year period. [Restatement 2d §87(2), Com. e, Ill. 4].

d. Termination of Offeree's Power to Accept upon Death or Incapacity of Offeror. [§4.414] Upon the death of the offeror, the offeree's power of acceptance of an outstanding revocable offer is immediately terminated, even if the offeree has no notice of the death and accepts the offer in good faith. Similarly, incapacity of the offeror occurring after an offer is made, but before it is accepted, also immediately terminates the offeree's power to accept, even if the offeree has no notice of such incapacity and accepts the offer in good faith [Restatement 2d §48].

(1) Criticism of Traditional Rule. [§4.4141] The rule that death or incapacity of the offeror immediately terminates the offeree's power of acceptance, even without notice, has been criticized as being incompatible with the objective theory of contracts. That is, if a reasonable person in the position of the offeree would believe that an offer could still be accepted, the objective theory of contracts would seem to indicate that such acceptance should be validated. [Restatement 2d §48, Com. a.] Nevertheless, the general rule stated in §4.414 seems firmly entrenched.

e. **Termination of Offeree's Power to Accept upon Death or Incapacity of the Offeree.** [§4.415] In general, only a designated "offeree" has the power to accept an offer (see §4.3). Thus, if the offeree dies or becomes incapacitated before acceptance, the offer cannot be accepted. Of course, if an offer is made to more than one offeree, the death or incapacity of one offeree will not affect the rights of the others to accept.

f. **Termination of Offeree's Power to Accept by Death or Destruction of a Person or Thing Essential for Performance (Other than the Offeror or Offeree).** [§4.416] If a thing or person necessary for the contract's performance either is destroyed or dies after the offer is made, but before its acceptance, the offeree's power to accept thereby terminates, even without notice to the offeree of such death or destruction [Restatement 2d §36, Com. c]. For example, if Charles offers to sell Bluebelle, a prize-winning racehorse, to Tony for $100,000, and if before Tony accepts the offer Bluebelle dies, Tony cannot thereafter validly accept (and thereby put Charles in breach since Charles will not be able to deliver) because the "thing essential for performance" is "destroyed" prior to acceptance.

Note that if the horse died after acceptance, it would be an impossibility/impracticability issue, not a formation issue (see Chapter Twenty-Five for these and related issues).

g. **Termination of Offeree's Power of Acceptance by Supervening Illegality.** [§4.417] A contract calling for an illegal act is "void" and therefore unenforceable (see Chapter Sixteen). Sometimes, however, when an offer is made the act called for by the offer is legal, but before it is accepted that act is rendered illegal through supervening legislation, court decision, etc. As soon as the act called for in the offer becomes illegal, the offer is thereby terminated and cannot be validly accepted.

h. **Termination of Offeree's Power of Acceptance by the Non-Occurrence of any Condition of Acceptance Specified in the Offer.** [§4.418] Just as the offeror may specify a time limit for an offeree's acceptance, the offeror may also make the offeree's right to accept conditional upon the occurrence (or non-occurrence) of an event. Thus, if the specified event does not occur (or does occur), the power to accept is terminated. For example, assume Mike says to Al, "I'll sell you my car for $10,000 and hold it open for a week, but if the prime interest falls below 7% before then, the deal's off." Mike has made a valid offer but has also made Al's acceptance conditional on an event. If the prime rate falls below 7% during the next week, the occurrence of that condition terminates Al's power to accept.

2. **GENERAL RULES GOVERNING TERMINATION OF IRREVOCABLE OFFERS.** [§4.42] Most contracts are freely revocable by the offeror. This is true even when the offeror has promised to hold an offer open (see §4.413). However, there are two ways the parties can ensure that the offeror's promise to hold the offer open for a period of time is enforceable, and that the offer thereby becomes **irrevocable** during that period. The first of these is when the offeror and offeree enter into an "**option contract**" (see § 4.421 et seq.), and the second is when the offeror makes a "**Merchant's Firm Offer**" under UCC §2-205 (see §4.422).

a. **Option Contracts: Defined and Discussed** [§4.421] An option contract is a special kind of contract where the purpose of the agreement is the limitation of the offeror's power to revoke an offer [Restatement 2d §25]. Thus, because an option contract is a separate contract in and of itself, in order for it to be enforceable there must be a separate offer regarding the offeror's promise not to revoke, a separate acceptance of that offer, and separate consideration (or, in some cases, promissory estoppel) supporting the promise.

Probably the most familiar use of option contracts is in real estate transactions, e.g., where, for $1,000 now, someone purchases an "option" to buy a piece of land at a specified price sometime within the next three years.

(1) Effect of Option Contract on Termination of Offers: The Difference Between a Power of Acceptance and the Right to Accept. [§4.4211] Once the offeror has bound himself or herself in an option contract not to revoke an offer, the offeree's **power of acceptance** transforms into a **contractual right of acceptance.** The transformation from a power to a right to accept is significant, for under an option contract, the offeree's right to accept the underlying offer is **not** terminated by:

    (1) rejection (see §4.411 et seq.);
    (2) counter-offer (see §4.411 et seq.);
    (3) revocation (see §4.413 et seq.);
    (4) death or incapacity of the offeror (see §4.414 et seq.); or
    (5) death or incapacity of the offeree (see §4.415 et seq.).

However, stating that offers under an option contract are "irrevocable" may be using too broad a word, **for the offeree's right of acceptance under an option contract can be terminated:**

(1) if the time period in which the option can be exercised, as specified in the option contract, has expired (see §4.412 et seq.); or

(2) by destruction or death of a thing essential for performance under the contract (see §4.416); or

(3) by supervening illegality (see §4.417); or

(4) by the non-occurrence of a condition, the occurrence of which is necessary to accept the offer as specified in the option contract (see §4.418) [Restatement 2d §37].

Probably the important thing to note about "irrevocable offers," i.e., offers governed by an option contract, is that, unlike revocable offers, they **may not be terminated by the offeror.**

(a) Example. [§4.4211-1] Sara offers to sell Lance her stereo for $500 on Monday. Lance asks for a few days to think about it, to which Sara replies, "Sure, I'll hold my offer open for a week." On Wednesday, Sara tells Lance she's changed her mind and won't sell him the stereo. Sara has effectively revoked, as there was no separate enforceable option contract as to her promise to keep the offer open for a week.

(b) Example. [§4.4211-2] Sara offers to sell Lance her stereo for $500 on Monday. Lance asks for a few days to think about it, to which Sara replies, "For $5 now, I will keep my offer open for a week." Upon payment of the $5, Lance has a right to accept at any time within a week. Thus, if Sara tells Lance on Wednesday that she's changed her mind, that attempted revocation is ineffective and Lance may still accept any time within the week. Similarly, if Lance tells Sara on Wednesday, "$500 is too much. I'm only willing to buy it from you for a $400 price," Lance still retains the right to purchase it for $500, as a counter-offer does not terminate a right of acceptance granted under an option contract. If at the end of the week Lance decides not to purchase the stereo,

Sara is entitled to keep the $5, for it served as the consideration for the option contract, i.e., as consideration for Lance's right to decide whether he wanted to exercise the option. Note, that if on Wednesday the stereo was destroyed, Lance could not thereafter accept the offer, since destruction of a thing essential for performance under a contract *will* terminate even an "irrevocable" offer under an option contract.

(2) **"Purported Consideration" and Option Contracts. [§4.4212]** Ordinarily, an option contract is not contractually enforceable unless the offeror's promise not to revoke is supported by valid consideration. However, the Restatement takes the view that so long as: **(a) the underlying deal is fair; (b) the offer to enter into the option contract is in writing; and (c) the offer is signed by the offeror, then the contract need only recite "purported consideration" to make the offeror's promise not to revoke enforceable.** That is, if the conditions are met, the parties need only *state* that something of value was exchanged for the option, regardless of whether or not it actually was exchanged, to make an option contract enforceable (see also §§7.661;17.241) [Restatement 2d §87(1), Com. c].

For example, if a written contract states that for $5 received today, I hereby grant Lance the right to buy my stereo for $500 until March 31, Lance has an option to purchase the stereo until March 31, Lance has an option to purchase the stereo until March 31 even if he never pays the $5.

(3) **Implied Option Contracts. [§4.4213]** As seen previously (see §§4.41341 et seq. and 4.4135 et seq.), there are two situations in which contract law imposes an **implied-in-law** option contract as a means of avoiding both injustice and unfair enrichment.

(a) **Implied Option Contract Recognized upon Offeree's Beginning of Performance in Response to a Unilateral Offer. [§4.4213-1]** Under §45 of the Restatement 2d, the offeree's beginning performance in response to an offer seeking a unilateral contract impliedly forms a valid unilateral option contract between the parties. Under this implied option contract the offeror may not revoke until the offeree is given a reasonable time to complete performance (see §4.4134-1B).

(b) **Implied Option Contract Recognized upon Offeree's Foreseeable and Substantial Pre-Acceptance Preparations. [§4.4213-2]** Under §87(2) of the Restatement 2d, a unilateral option contract is also formed when an offeror makes an offer which he or she should reasonably expect to induce substantial reliance by the offeree before acceptance and which does, in fact, induce such reliance. As soon as the offeree undertakes acts in reliance on the offer, i.e., by taking (or refraining from taking) some action of a substantial nature, the offeror may not revoke the offer for a reasonable time and the offer is enforceable to the extent necessary to avoid injustice (see §4.4135).

b. **Merchant's Firm Offers. [§4.422]** Under §2-205 of the UCC, an offeror may be bound by his or her promise not to revoke an offer even in the absence of any consideration supporting that promise. That is, under §2-205, a promise to keep an offer irrevocable can be enforceable, even in the absence of an option contract. For this to occur, the following must be true:

(1) the offeror must be a **merchant**, within the definition of UCC §2-104(1);

(2) the offer must be **in writing**;

(3) the writing must be **signed by the merchant offeror**; and

(4) the writing must **expressly state that the offer is intended to be irrevocable, will be held open,** or the like.

If these criteria are met, the offer will be irrevocable during the time period stated in the writing, or if no time period is stated, for a reasonable time. However, in neither case can the period of irrevocability exceed three months. If the parties wish to extend the period for greater than three months, they may do so either by having the merchant send another letter at or near the end of the first three-month period, or by entering into a standard option contract supported by consideration.

F. HOW AN OFFER MAY BE ACCEPTED: PERMISSIBLE METHODS OR MODES OF ACCEPTANCE. [§4.5] As master of the offer, the offeror can set forth which of the only four possible ways an offer may be accepted:

(1)   by requiring the offeree to **promise to perform** the action requested in the offer;

(2)   by requiring the offeree **actually perform** the action requested in the offer;

(3)   by requiring the offeree to **begin to perform** the action requested in the offer; or

(4)   in certain cases, by **silence and/or inaction** of the offeree.

When an offeror is clear as to how an offer can be accepted, determining the permissible mode of acceptance for the offeree is, of course, no problem. However, when an offer is unclear as to how it should be accepted, there can be a problem in determining which of these methods is "permissible" in response to a particular offer. The rules governing this problem are discussed below.

1. GENERAL RULE REGARDING ACCEPTANCE OF AN OFFER WHICH SPECIFIES METHOD OF ACCEPTANCE. [§4.51] When the offer specifically states how it is to be accepted, the offeree must comply with such statement in order to have a valid acceptance. [Restatement 2d §58]. This means that an unambiguous offer to enter into a unilateral contract can only be accepted by promising the performance called for in the offer. In addition, it also means that an offeror is entitled to limit acceptance to particular words or conduct. Thus, if an offer says that no other acceptance will be honored but the delivery of a telegram containing the words, "I accept wholeheartedly," then transmitting a facsimile print-out with that message, or sending a telegram with just the words, "I accept" does not act as a valid acceptance. Rather, those communications would themselves be counter-offers.

2. GENERAL RULES REGARDING ACCEPTANCE OF AN OFFER WHICH DOES NOT SPECIFY EXPLICITLY METHOD OF ACCEPTANCE. [§4.52] If an offer does not specify how it is to be accepted, it may be accepted in any manner and by any medium reasonable under the circumstances. [Restatement 2d §29(2); UCC §2-206(1)(a).] Thus, if the offer, and the circumstances under which it was made, do not explicitly specify a method of acceptance, the offeree may accept either by performing, by promising to perform, or by beginning performance, so long as such action is reasonable [Restatement 2d §32]. However, in making the determination whether a particular form of acceptance is reasonable, it is important to examine the surrounding circumstances. It may

well be that even though the offer is silent as to whether a promissory acceptance or acceptance by performance is permitted, the circumstances clearly point to one of these options being the only "reasonable" method of acceptance.

    a. **Example of *Hamer v. Sidway*.** [§4.521] Uncle writes to his nephew, who is then 16, offering to pay nephew $5,000 if nephew will refrain from drinking or using tobacco until age 21. Under the circumstances, an immediate promise by the nephew to refrain from drinking and using tobacco would be ineffective to bind Uncle, for Uncle clearly is bargaining for performance, not a promise of performance. (See §7.22; Case Squibs, *Hamer v. Sidway*.)

    b. **REVIEW PROBLEM.** [§4.522] Jeff says to Grace "I'll pay you $1,000 to paint my house next Monday." Question: How can Grace accept?

        Answer: It is unclear whether Jeff is asking for a promise to paint his house or for actual performance. As such, Grace may accept by using either method.

3. **SPECIAL RULES FOR OFFER TO PURCHASE GOODS FOR PROMPT SHIPMENT UNDER UCC.** [§4.53] Unless there is an unambiguous indication to the contrary by the offeror, **an order to buy goods for prompt shipment invites acceptance either by prompt shipment of, or by a prompt promise to ship, the goods.** Thus, if Jack places an order to a lighting store for "3 halogen lamps, Model No. XB-15, A.S.A.P.," the store may accept either by promising to ship the lamps or by actually shipping the lamps. If the store accepts by actually shipping, however, it must notify Jack of its acceptance within a reasonable time or the contract becomes unenforceable [UCC §2-206]; (see §4.5423, for a further discussion of the subsequent notice requirement).

4. **SPECIAL PROBLEMS WHEN BEGINNING PERFORMANCE IS INTENDED TO ACT AS AN ACCEPTANCE.** [§4.54] When an offeree begins performance in response to an offer, the question as to whether such activity serves as a valid acceptance is a complicated one, depending on the type of offer it is, and on the circumstances surrounding its making.

    a. **Beginning Performance in Response to an Unambiguous Offer for Unilateral Contract.** [§4.541] As noted earlier, there are different theories as to the effect of beginning performance in response to a clear offer for a **unilateral** contract. One theory says that the offer is not accepted by such conduct and full performance must occur before there is acceptance; the Restatement 2d §45 says that a unilateral option contract is formed upon the beginning of performance, whereby the offer becomes irrevocable for a reasonable period of time, thereby ensuring that the offeree will have a reasonable attempt to complete performance and thus accept the offer; and a third view holds that the beginning of performance acts to transform the agreement into an enforceable bilateral contract (see §4.4134, et seq.).

    b. **Beginning Performance in Response to an Unambiguous Offer for Bilateral Contract.** [§4.542] If an offer is one to enter into a bilateral contract, and thus unambiguously calls for a promissory acceptance, and only a promissory acceptance, then beginning performance will not be an effective acceptance for it was not what the offeror requested.

    c. **Beginning Performance in Response to an Offer that is Ambiguous as to what Mode of Acceptance is Called for.** [§4.543] As noted in §4.52, an offer that is unclear as to the mode of acceptance called for can be accepted by beginning performance, so long as such action is "reasonable under the circumstances" [Restatement 2d §29(2); UCC §2-206(1)(a)]. However, there are some special considerations when the offeree attempts to accept in this manner, which are discussed below.

(1) **Treatment of Beginning Performance in Response to an Ambiguous Offer.** [§4.5431] If the commencement of performance is a reasonable means of acceptance in response to an offer that is unclear as to how it should be accepted, the **beginning of performance will simultaneously also imply a promise by the offeree to complete performance** and thus, result in an enforceable bilateral contract between the parties. That is, if the offeror does not make it clear whether he or she is seeking actual performance, or promised performance as acceptance, (i.e. if it is unclear whether the offer is for a unilateral or a bilateral contract) then either mode of acceptance is permitted.

But once the offeree starts performance, he or she is bound and has thus deemed to have made and implied promise to complete the performance. In other words, once an offeree begins performance in response to an offer whose mode of acceptance is ambiguous, a bilateral contract is formed and if the offeree unjustifiably does not complete performance, a breach has occurred.

(a) **Example.** [§4.5431-1] John offers Nina $1,000 to paint his house next Wednesday. The mode of acceptance called for under that offer is ambiguous, so Nina may accept either by painting the house next Wednesday or by promising to do so. However, suppose Nina starts painting and John orders her off his property. At that point she has neither performed nor made an express promise to perform, and thus John would like to argue that since his offer has not been accepted, he may revoke it. However, as soon as Nina began working, she is deemed to have accepted John's offer by promising to finish, thereby completing the formation of a bilateral contract. As there has been a valid acceptance to an outstanding offer, John would be in breach if he does not allow Nina to finish. Similarly, if Nina walked off the job after starting to paint (without a justifiable reason), she would be in breach for by beginning performance, she has made an implied promise to finish.

(2) **Necessity of Giving Notice to Offeror when Beginning Performance Validly Acts as Acceptance.** [§4.5432] In those cases where beginning of performance acts as an effective acceptance, a problem sometimes arises because the offeror does not know that the offeree has accepted. This will almost always be true when the offeror and offeree are in different cities. Under Restatement 2d §54(2), if the offeree has reason to know that the offeror has **no adequate means of learning about the beginning of performance**, the offeree must notify the offeror of his or her actions within a reasonable time. The UCC, in §2-206(2), makes the requirement even plainer — an offeree who accepts by beginning performance must *always* give the offeror notice as to the acceptance within a reasonable time.

(a) **Exceptions: When an Offeree Need Not Give Notice.** [§4.5432-1] An offeree who reasonably accepts an offer by beginning performance need not give notice that he or she has started to perform in three cases: (1) if the nature of the performance is such that the offeror would know of the acceptance, e.g. an offer to paint a house that the offeror lives in so that when the offeree starts, such performance would come to the offeror's attention; (2) when the offeror states in the offer that such notice is unnecessary; and (3) if past dealings between the parties indicate that such notice is not required.

(3) Effect of Failing to Give Notice. [§4.5433] Under both the Restatement and the UCC, if an offeree who has validly accepted by beginning performance fails to give the required notice after a reasonable time, the contractual duties of the offeror are discharged [Restatement 2d §54; UCC §2-206(2)]. Thus, sending the notice in such situations is treated as a condition subsequent to the offeror's duties under the contract. That is, a valid contract is formed upon the beginning of performance, but if the condition is not fulfilled (i.e., if the notice is never sent), the duties of the offeror become unenforceable (see §20.112 for a more thorough discussion of conditions subsequent).

However, note that under §54 of the Restatement, once an offeree begins performance, he or she is promising to finish regardless whether the offeree gives notice. That is, while the offeror is not bound to accept the offeree's completed performance in such a case (for there was no effective acceptance upon the failure to send notice), the offeror can **sue** the offeree for any damages suffered if the offeree does not complete performance on time. So when the offeree begins performance without giving notice when notice is required, the offeror is in a very strong position — he or she need not accept performance, but is entitled to sue if the failure to complete the performance causes the offeror damage.

5. **THE "UNILATERAL CONTRACT TRICK" UNDER THE UCC. [§4.55]** Under common law rules, a breach did not always occur when an offeror sent non-conforming goods; sometimes there was a counter-offer. For example, assume a retailer (offeror) orders 100 21-inch television sets from a manufacturer (offeree) and does so on a unilateral contract basis, i.e., the retailer makes clear that payment will be forthcoming only when the 21-inch sets arrive. If the manufacturer shipped 19-inch sets, at common law there was no breach because there was never an acceptance. That is, the only way the offer could be accepted was to ship 21-inch sets. As such, shipment of the 19-inch sets acted as a counter-offer. This rule was unfair to the offerors, for such party was relying on receiving conforming goods in response to the offer. Therefore, while the offerors could reject the non-conforming 19-inch sets when the sets arrived, at that point the offeror had to start over, at some inconvenience (if not at some financial sacrifice), and place another order for 21-inch sets with someone else. Further, the offeror could not bring a breach of contract suit against the seller, for there was never an enforceable contract on which to sue.

UCC §2-206(1)(b) has changed the common law rules. Now, when sending goods is a reasonable means of acceptance, the offeree (in the case above, the manufacturer) who sends the 19-inch sets is deemed to have both simultaneously accepted the offer to send 21-inch sets and to have breached that contract by sending non-conforming goods. Thus, under the "unilateral contract trick" of simultaneous formation and breach, when non-conforming goods are sent, the buyer is entitled either to accept them and **sue for breach of warranty**, or to reject them and **sue for breach of the promise to deliver conforming goods.**

Note that the UCC §2-206 applies whenever it is "reasonable" to accept by shipment. Thus, despite its name, the "unilateral contract trick" does not apply only to situations where the offeror has made a unilateral contract offer; **rather, it applies whenever an offer is ambiguous as to the requested mode of acceptance.** That is, when an offer is ambiguous as to calling for shipment or a promise of shipment, the sending non-conforming goods by the offeree acts as a simultaneous promissory acceptance of the offer and a breach of the resulting contract.

a. Accommodation Shipments. [§4.551] If the offeree wishes to send non-conforming goods, but also to keep such action as a counter-offer and not have it be treated as a simultaneous acceptance and breach under §2-206(1), the offeree may send an "accommodation" shipment. Under an accommodation shipment the seller notifies the buyer (typically in a cover letter) that the goods the seller has shipped are not what was requested in the offer, but also expresses a good-faith belief or hope that the buyer can use them anyway [UCC §2-206(1)(b)]. With such notice there is no unilateral contract trick, and the seller's actions can only be deemed a counter-offer, to be accepted or not as the buyer wishes.

6. **NOTICE PROBLEMS IN ACCEPTANCE UNDER UNILATERAL CONTRACTS.**
   [§4.56] When an offeror makes an offer for a unilateral contract, an issue sometimes arises as to whether the offeree need give the offeror notice of his or her intention to accept. The answer is no. That is, if an offer can be accepted by performance, then the acceptance is effective regardless of whether the offeree has previously given notice of his or her intention to accept. However, upon acceptance, the offeree may have to give reasonably prompt notice that he or she has performed the acts specified in the offer. Under Restatement 2d §54, the offeree must give notice of acceptance if the offeror has no adequate means of learning the performance with reasonable promptness or certainty. If such notice is not given, then the offeror's duties are discharged and he or she will not be in breach for failing to perform.

   a. Example. [§4.561] Laura has a vacation cabin 200 miles from her principal residence. She has made a unilateral offer to a painter that she will pay him $500 to paint her cabin by June 1. The painter need not give Laura notice that he intends to accept her offer, and may validly accept it by painting the cabin in accordance with the terms of the offer. However, as Laura will not have an adequate means of learning of the acceptance within a reasonable time after the painter's performance, he is under an obligation to give her reasonably prompt notice. If he does not, her duties under the contract will be discharged. Of course, even if her duties **under the contract** are discharged, Laura's promise to pay may be enforced by promissory estoppel (see Chapter Eight), or she may be liable in restitution (see Chapter Thirty-Four).

   b. Example of *Carlill v. Carbolic Smoke Ball*. [§4.562] Manufacturer placed an advertisement in several publications promising to pay £100 to any one who caught the flu after purchasing and using a carbolic smoke ball as directed. Carlill purchased and correctly used the smoke ball, but nevertheless caught the flu. **Held:** Carlill was under no duty to inform the manufacturer of his intention to accept the unilateral offer (i.e. purchasing the ball, using it correctly, and catching the flu). Thus, by doing the acts called for in the offer, his acceptance was effective, despite the lack of prior notice. However, he was obligated to let the company know of his acceptance within a reasonable time, as it would have no adequate means of learning of Carlill's performance with reasonable promptness and certainty (see also §4.3313-1 and Case Squibs section for a further discussion of the case). *Carlill v. Carbolic Smoke Ball Co.*, 1 Q.B. 256 (1893).

7. **ACCEPTANCE BY SILENCE OR INACTION. [§4.57]** The general rule is that an offeree's silence cannot act as a valid acceptance. However, there are a few particular situations where the offeree's silence may act to bind him or her to the terms of an offer.

   a. Silent Acceptance of Services. [§4.571] Where an offeree silently takes the benefit of offered services, having reason to know the offeror expected to be paid for them, and having an opportunity to reject them, the offeree's silence operates as an acceptance.

This rule is a specialized application of the general rule regarding implied-in-fact contracts, i.e., a situation where an acceptance is deemed effective because, to a reasonable person in the position of the offeror, the conduct (rather than the words) of the offeree indicates the offeree's intention to be bound by the terms of the offer (see §1.44); [Restatement 2d §69(1)]. For example, a medical clinic has a sign outside that says, "Today only. Physicals $5.00." If Ann enters the clinic, waits in line for the physical, and receives the physical, all without saying anything, Ann is liable for the $5.00.

b. **Silent Acceptance at Direction of Offeror. [§4.572]** Sometimes an offeror will try to structure an offer so that the offeree's silence or inaction will be deemed an effective acceptance, e.g., an offer may state, "There is no reason for you to inform me of your acceptance. I am so sure you will want our product, your silence or inaction will be deemed acceptance by me and we will bill you in 30 days." Perhaps surprisingly, such an offer **may** be effective and silence **can** serve to bind the recipient. The key factor is whether the offeree intends to accept the offeror or not. That is, if the offeree remains silent but intends to accept the offer, the silent acceptance is valid. However, if the offeree remains silent and intends to reject the offer, then the silence is not a valid acceptance [Restatement 2d §69(1)(b)]. While this puts the offeror in a position of uncertainty as to whether or not the offer is accepted, it is the offeror's fault for phrasing the offer as he or she did in the first place.

c. **Silence can Act as a Valid Acceptance because of Previous Conduct. [§4.573]** So long as the parties' previous dealings make it reasonable, silence and inaction by the offeree may act as effective acceptance [Restatement 2d §69(1)(c)]. The most familiar example of when the parties' prior conduct is sufficient to create acceptance by silence is, e.g., a Compact-Disc-of-the-Month club. When the offeree joins, he or she promises that inaction will constitute acceptance of the monthly shipment, and in such cases that arrangement will be enforced.

d. **Silent Acceptance of Property by Acting Inconsistently with Owner's Interest. [§4.574]** If an offeree acquires property (personal or real) as part of an offer, and acts inconsistently with the offeror's ownership interest in that property, then there has been an acceptance by conduct, even if no express acceptance was ever made [Restatement 2d §69(2); UCC §2-606(1)(c)]. For example, through the mail Bud is sent a cassette tape along with a letter saying, "If you wish to purchase this exciting tape, do nothing and it's yours. We will bill you $11.00 later. However, if you don't want it, just put it in the prepaid envelope and return it to us." If Bill gift wraps it and gives it to his daughter for her birthday, he has accepted the offer to purchase the cassette by silence, for he has acted inconsistently with the offeror's ownership interest. Once again, this rule is a particularized example of an implied-in-fact contract.

G. **POSTING PROBLEMS: THE MAILBOX RULE. [§4.6]** On a cost-benefit analysis most students put learning the mail-box rule far on the debit side. However, it is not as confusing as it first appears, and when you understand the problems the mail box rule seeks to resolve, rather than just trying to learn some disjointed rules, the doctrine makes a good deal of sense and solves some recurring problems.

There are two types of posting problems inherent in transmitted offers and acceptances. The first concerns **when** a communication is effective, e.g., if an offer says it's open for ten days, and on the tenth day the offeree mails an acceptance that doesn't reach the offeror until the twelfth day, has the offer been timely accepted? The second issue revolves around when a party **changes his or her mind**, e.g., if an offeree accepts by mail, but two hours later, before the offeror gets the letter, the offeree telephones the offeror and rejects, which is the effective communication — the first sent written acceptance or later made the oral rejection? Although it will be necessary to learn the rules for each situation, the general rule set down in the 1818 English case *Adams v. Lindsell* (see Case Squibs), is:

(1) **offers, revocations, and rejections are effective on *receipt* by the offeror;** but

(2) **acceptances are effective on *dispatch* by the offeree.**

1. ACCEPTANCES EFFECTIVE ON DISPATCH. [§4.61] If an offeree accepts an offer by mail, the timeliness of the acceptance is measured by the time of its dispatch. This means that a properly dispatched acceptance will be effective, **even if it never gets to the offeror.** However, it is important to note the "time of dispatch" means more than just, e.g., giving a letter to a secretary to mail — it means putting the letter out of the offeree's ability to recall it. Usually, this is the time of actually delivering the letter to a mailbox [Restatement 2d §63]. Note that for the acceptance on dispatch rule to apply, two criteria must be met:

(1) **the letter must be properly addressed and stamped;** and

(2) **acceptance by mail must be a permissible mode of acceptance.**

Each of these requirements is discussed below.

a. **Letter Must be Properly Addressed. [§4.611] The acceptance must be properly addressed for it to be effective upon dispatch.** If the letter is not properly addressed, it is usually effective only upon *receipt*. Note however, under §67 of the Restatement 2d, even if an acceptance is misaddressed it will nonetheless be treated as effective on dispatch **if** it arrived within the time a properly addressed letter would normally have arrived. Thus, if the offeree transposed two numbers of the zip code, but the post office was able to timely deliver the letter anyway, the acceptance will be effective upon dispatch.

b. **Acceptance by Dispatched Letter must be an Authorized Mode of Acceptance. [§4.612]** An offer may specify that acceptance can only be effective upon receipt by the offeror. If it does, then the dispatch rule is not followed. Similarly, the offer may indicate that acceptance by another medium, such as a telegram, or by performance, is the only way to accept the offer. Once again, if the offer specifically limits the mode of acceptance so that acceptance by dispatch of a letter is not an authorized mode of acceptance, then the dispatch rule will not control. Lastly, even if the offer is silent as to how and when it is to be accepted, any purported method of acceptance must be "reasonable under the circumstances" (see §4.4122 et seq.). Thus, if the circumstances, such as where the offeree knows that the offeror has competing bids, indicate a quicker form of acceptance to be used, such as a telephone, telegram, or facsimile machine, then a mailed acceptance will only be effective upon receipt. Note however, that under §67 of the Restatement 2d, even if the offeree uses an unauthorized means of communication to transmit an acceptance, it will nonetheless be treated as effective on dispatch **if** that communication arrives within the time in which a properly dispatched acceptance would normally have arrived.

c. **Offeror Loses Power to Revoke after a Dispatched Acceptance. [§4.613]** One consequence of acceptance is that the offeree thereafter loses the power to revoke. Hence, even if the offeror has not yet received the properly dispatched acceptance, and thus reasonably believes he or she has the power to revoke, he or she may not do so because acceptances are effective on dispatch. (See Case Squib section, *Adams v. Lindsell*.)

d. Special Rules Regarding Option Contracts. [§4.614] Unless explicitly provided to the contrary, **acceptance under an option contract is not effective until it is received by the offeror** [Restatement 2d §63]. This is clearly an exception to the normal rule. Note, this is not acceptance of an offer to enter into an option contract. Rather, it is acceptance of the offer that is **the subject of** an option contract. In other words, this rule assumes an option contract has previously been entered into and the offeree is now exercising his option granted under the option contract.

2. REJECTION NOT EFFECTIVE UNTIL RECEIPT. [§4.62] Rejection of an offer is not effective until it is received by the offeror. A communication need not be read to be "received." Rather, it is received when delivered into the control of the addressee. Thus, a rejection typically becomes effective when it arrives at the offeree's address [UCC §1-201(26)].

3. EFFECT OF AN OFFEREE FIRST SENDING A REJECTION, FOLLOWED BY AN ACCEPTANCE. [§4.63] If an offeror first mails a rejection, and then changes his or her mind and communicates an acceptance, the rule is **the acceptance is effective if it arrives first; and the rejection is effective if it arrives first.** In some respects, this rule for this situation is a rejection of *Adams v. Lindsell*, i.e., the acceptance is **not** effective on dispatch, it is only effective if it gets there first. However, given that the offeree has first rejected the offer, the rule makes sense. Note, that if in this situation the rejection arrives first, the later-sent and later-received acceptance can act as a counter-offer.

4. EFFECT OF AN OFFEREE FIRST SENDING AN ACCEPTANCE, FOLLOWED BY A REJECTION. [§4.64] If an offeree first mails an acceptance, and then changes his or her mind and communicates a rejection, the rule is **the acceptance is effective on dispatch unless: (1) the rejection arrives first; and (2) the offeror changes his or her position in reliance on the rejection.** For example, if the rejection overtook the acceptance, and upon receiving it the offeror entered into a contract for the same goods with someone else, the offeror changed position in reliance on the rejection and it is thus effective. Otherwise the acceptance of the offer will be binding on the offeree.

CHAPTER FIVE: WHEN THE "ACCEPTANCE" VARIES FROM THE OFFER: THE MIRROR IMAGE RULE AND UCC §2-207

A. COMMON LAW VIEW: THE MIRROR IMAGE RULE. [§5.0] Under the common law, an effective acceptance had to accept the offer unconditionally and entirely. That is, the acceptance had to be the "mirror image" of the offer. If the purported acceptance added an additional term, had one fewer term, or even slightly changed a term, it was considered a counter-offer, not an acceptance.

B. UNFAIRNESS OF MIRROR IMAGE RULE. [§5.1] The mirror image rule makes sense in face-to-face transactions, for it seems only fair to say in those situations that unless the parties agree as to all the terms they have not manifested the mutual assent necessary for a valid contract. However, in modern commercial transactions, where the parties often do not deal face to face, and where offer and acceptance are often made via pre-printed forms, the mirror image rule often leads to unfairness. This unfairness comes about in two ways, each of which is described by example below.

1. EXAMPLE OF UNFAIRNESS WHERE ONE PARTY DOESN'T PERFORM. [§5.11] On September 1, a farmer in Kansas sends a "Purchase Order" form to a grain supplier in Illinois. On the Purchase Order are blanks which the farmer fills in by hand to indicate she wants 1,000 pounds of corn to be delivered on or before next February 15, at quoted prices. Clause 36 of her Purchase Order is preprinted and states that delivery shall be made by U.P.S. Upon receiving the Purchase Order, the grain supplier sends out a preprinted form entitled "Acceptance of Purchase Order." The owner fills in the blanks to indicate the grain company is promising to supply 1,000 pounds of corn to be delivered on or before February 15, and promises to sell the corn at the same price quoted in the Purchase Order. However, clause 31 of the Acceptance is also pre-printed and says that delivery is to be made by "any common carrier." When the Acceptance form arrives, Farmer checks only to ensure that the quantity, price, and delivery dates are correct, and puts the document in her files. If grain company never delivers the corn, under the mirror-image rule there is no breach of contract because no contract was ever formed. Because of the discrepancies in the delivery term, ("U.P.S." versus "any common carrier") the Acceptance was only a counter-offer which was never itself accepted. Obviously, this is unfair to Farmer.

2. EXAMPLE OF UNFAIRNESS WHERE THE PARTIES PERFORM: THE "LAST SHOT" DOCTRINE. [§5.12] Builder places an order for 100 front doors from lumber company. On the Purchase Order builder uses to order the doors is the clause, "Supplier warrants that all doors supplied under this contract shall be of stainable quality." Lumber company sends back an acknowledgment form that is identical to the Purchase Order in every respect, except that its form states "Supplier represents its products are only of paintable, not stainable, quality." Neither party looks at the other's form and the doors are delivered and paid for. Later, when the doors turn out to be unstainable, builder sues lumber company. Under the mirror image rule, the parties never had a contract based on the exchange of forms. Further, the lumber company's form was the pending offer at the time the parties performed for it was a counter-offer due to the different warranty clauses. As such, common law held that when the builder paid for the doors, he or she implicitly accepted lumber company's counter-offer, and thus became bound to a contract whose terms included the paintable only quality warranty. This rule is sometimes called the "last shot" doctrine and resulted in a contract by performance being made on the terms of the last party to submit a form. While perhaps not quite as unfair as the situation described in §5.11, the last shot doctrine did deprive offerors of some of the benefits they thought they were getting under these types of contracts. Recall, the scenario is that neither party reads the fine print and boiler plate language contained in the other party's form, and thus neither party really knows what terms are truly in the deal. The drafters of the UCC attempted to deal with these issues and cure these types of unfairness in §2-207 which is discussed below.

C. **UCC §2-207: AN OVERVIEW.** [§5.2] §2-207 of the U.C.C. is intended to lessen, if not eliminate, the unfairness of the common law view. It does so by eliminating the strict mirror-image rule and allowing for a valid acceptance to contain terms different from or additional to an offer. However, it is important to note that not only does §2-207 govern whether the parties have a contract (i.e., whether there was an offer and an acceptance) but it also determines what the terms of that resulting contract are. It is only in this latter capacity that §2-207 becomes complicated.

D. **EXAM APPROACH TO ANALYSIS OF §2-207 PROBLEMS.** [§5.3.] After ascertaining that the rules of Article 2 of the UCC govern the transaction (see Chapter Thirty-Seven), nearly all §2-207 problems can be analyzed in only three steps:

> (1) **Do the parties have a contract based on the exchange of their writings under §2-207(1)?** (i.e., is the purported acceptance actually an effective acceptance or is it a counter-offer as would be true under common law?);

> (2) **If the offeree's form is an effective acceptance, then the terms of the contract are dictated by §2-207(2)**;

> (3) **If the offeree's form is not an effective acceptance, then the parties do not have a contract based on their writings under §2-207(1). In that case it is necessary to examine whether they have a contract by conduct under §2-207(3), and if they do, to use §2-207(3) to determine the terms of that contract.**

Example. Assume a typical §2-207 problem: the offeror is a buyer who orders a product on a Purchase Order form, and the offeree is a seller who purports to accept that order by an Acknowledgment form which differs from the Purchase Order in some respect.

1. **FIRST STEP: DO THE PARTIES HAVE A CONTRACT BASED ON THEIR WRITINGS UNDER §2-207(1).** [§5.31] The first issue is whether the parties have a contract based on their exchanged writings. This is determined by judging their writings under the provisions of §2-207(1). The only function of §2-207(1) is to determine if the Purchase Order and Acknowledgment together constitute a binding offer and acceptance. This is done in two sub-steps:

> (1) **determining whether the seller/offeree's Acknowledgment is a "seasonable expression of acceptance;"** and

> (2) **ascertaining whether the seller's acceptance is "expressly made conditional" on the buyer/offeror's "assent to [any] different or additional terms."**

The analysis for each of these sub-steps is described below.

a. **First Sub-Step: Does the Offeree's Document Act as a "Definite and Seasonable Expression of Acceptance?"** [§5.311.] The first question is whether the purported acceptance is really intended to act as an acceptance. Usually this is not a problem, as most seller's forms evidence a desire to sell the same goods the buyer wishes to purchase, at the same price the buyer wanted to pay. However, if the purported acceptance is too different from the offer, or contains a different quantity (or perhaps even too different a price) term from that found in the Purchase Order, it is **not** an acceptance, but will be deemed a counter-offer, and the determination of whether the parties have a contract is judged under §2-207(3) not §2-207(1). In other words, §2-207(1) will allow a purported acceptance to be an effective acceptance even if it contains different or additional terms from the offer, but when either the number of the differences between the seller's and buyer's forms gets too great, or when the seller's form differs sufficiently in an essential term from that found in the Purchase Order, the Acknowledgment will be deemed a counter-offer, not an acceptance.

b. Second Sub-Step: Does the Offeree's Document "Expressly Make [Acceptance] Conditional on [the Offeror's] Assent to the Additional or Different Terms." [§5.312.] While §2-207(1) holds that most purported acceptances with different or additional terms are, in fact, acceptances and not counter-offers, a question remains as to how an offeree can make a valid counter-offer if he or she does not want to accept one or more of the offeror's terms. To solve this problem, §2-207(1) provides that if the seller's form makes acceptance "expressly . . . conditional on assent to the additional or different terms," found in seller's form, then the Acknowledgment will be treated as a counter-offer and not an acceptance. Once again this makes sense, for if the seller indicates: (a) that the seller is proposing a deal on different terms; and (b) that the seller is only willing to go forward if the buyer agrees to the seller's terms, then the seller should be treated as having made a counter-offer and not an acceptance.

(1) To be Effective, an "Expressly Made Conditional On Assent" Clause must Require Express, Not Implied, Consent from Offeree. [§5.3121.] Occasionally a seller will try to include a clause on its form that makes inaction or silence on the part of the buyer an implied acceptance of the additional or different terms contained in the seller's form. For example, an offeree-seller's form may have language like, "Buyer must notify seller of any objection to any term contained in this document within ten days of receipt; otherwise Buyer agrees that the terms of this Acknowledgment are binding." In including this type of clause, the offeree-seller is intending to do two things: (1) make its form a counter-offer rather than an acceptance under §2-207(1); and (2) devise a way that the buyer will be deemed to have accepted the counter-offer by silence or inaction, so that the seller's terms will control the deal. However, under the UCC this type of clause is **not** effective. It is not a counter-offer, because **to be a counter-offer under §2-207(1), the offeree-seller's form must clearly communicate both:**

(1) **that the seller is unwilling to go forward on the terms of the offer; and**

(2) **that its own terms will not control unless the buyer-offeror EXPRESSLY, not implicitly, assents to the seller's different or additional terms.**

Further, a seller cannot sneak terms into the deal which result in an unbargained for advantage by setting up an acceptance by silence situation for the offeror, i.e., a situation where the offeror implicitly "accepts" the terms put forth by the seller if he or she does nothing. Indeed, such a result would resurrect the last shot doctrine (see §5.12), something §2-207 was designed to prevent, and would make acceptance by silence binding, something traditional common law contract formation will not usually permit (see §4.57 et seq.).

(2) Example of Incorrect Approach under §2-207(1): *Roto-Lith v. F.P. Bartlett & Co.* **[§5.3122]** Perhaps the most criticized §2-207 case ever is the one virtually every first-year student is initially assigned, *Roto-Lith, Ltd. v. F.P. Bartlett & Co.* 297 F.2d. 497 (1st Cir. 1962). The reason the case is so widely criticized is that it fails to recognize that point made in the immediately previous section. In *Roto-Lith*, the seller-offeree's acknowledgement form both disclaimed all warranties and contained the following clause, " . . . if these terms are not acceptable, buyer must notify seller at once." Buyer did not notify the seller of any objection and eventually purchased the goods. When the goods turned out to be sub-standard, the buyer tried to sue for breach of warranty. The court held that the quoted language made the offeree's acknowledgement a counter-offer, which was implicitly accepted by the buyer when it accepted the goods. However, this analysis is incorrect, **for a clause that does not call for an express manifestation of the buyer's assent to the different terms found in the offeree's document is insufficient to render that document a counter-offer under §2-207(1).** Rather, the seller's document should have been classified as an *acceptance*, and because the warranty disclaimer materially altered the offer (see §5.322 for a discussion of the material alteration issue), the disclaimer should not have been deemed to be part of the contract.

(3) Examples of Correct Approach under §2-207(1): *Dorton v. Collins & Aikman Corp* and *C. Itoh & Co. v. Jordon International.* **[§5.3123]** The two cases cited in the heading, taken together, establish the correct analysis under §2-207(1). In both cases the seller was the offeree, and its form contained an additional term calling for arbitration of certain disputes under the contract, rather than litigation of those claims. In *Dorton*, the seller's form also stated " . . . [our] acceptance of your order is subject to all the terms and conditions [in this document], including arbitration." The court correctly held that the "is subject to" language was insufficient to transform the purported acceptance into a counter-offer because the language did not require the buyer's specific affirmitive **assent** to those terms before they became part of the contract. Hence, the seller's form became a valid acceptance, and the question of whether the arbitration term became part of the contract was decided by reference to §2-207(2) (see §5.322). In *Itoh*, the seller's form stated that its acceptance was "expressly conditional on Buyer's assent to the additional . . . terms and conditions set forth below." The court correctly held that the "expressly made conditional on Buyer's assent" language was sufficient to turn the purported acceptance into a counter-offer, and thus the parties had no contract based on the exchange of their writings. Whether they had a contract at all was determined by reference to §2-207(3). (See Case Squibs Section, *Dorton* and *Itoh*.)

2. **SECOND STEP: IF THE PARTIES HAVE A CONTRACT BASED ON THEIR EXCHANGED WRITINGS UNDER §2-207(1), THEN §2-207(2) GOVERNS WHAT TERMS MAKE UP THE CONTRACT. [§5.32]** Once it is determined that a contract is formed by the exchanged writings under §2-207(1), i.e., it is determined that the offeree sent a definite and seasonable expression of acceptance and that it was not a counter-offer, the provisions of §2-207(2) provide the rules to determine what the terms of that contract are. The proper analysis under §2-207(2) depends on whether the parties are merchants.

a. **If Either Party is a Non-Merchant, Additional Terms are only Proposals to Contract. [§5.321]** If either party to the contract is a non-merchant, then any additional terms contained in the acceptance are merely proposals for addition to the contract, which may be accepted or not by the offeror. That is, such terms do not automatically become part of the contract, and are treated as nothing more than suggestions of possible additions to the deal presented to the offeror.

b. **If both Parties are Merchants, Additional Terms are Still Probably Not Part of the Contract. [§5.322].** Even if both parties to the contract are merchants, it is still likely that the additional terms in the acceptance will not become part of the contract. However, §2-207(2) phrases this concept awkwardly. It says when both parties are merchants, any additional terms **are** part of the contract **unless**:

  (1) the offer expressly limits acceptance to the terms of the offer [§2-207(2)(a)];

  (2) the additional terms in the acceptance materially alter the offer [§2-207(2)(b)]; or

  (3) notification of objection to the additional terms has already been given, or is given within a reasonable time after notice of them has been received [§2-207(2)(c)].

Thus, only if **none** of these three conditions apply will the additional terms become part of the contract. It is very rare that such will be the case.

In the four examples given below, assume both parties are merchants.

(1) **Example. [§5.3221]** Offeror/Buyer's Purchase Order says, "Acceptance of this offer is limited to the terms of this offer." Offeree/Seller's Acknowledgement is the same as the offer, except it does not contain the quoted language above, and contains a "no modification except in writing" clause. The "no modification except in writing" provision does not become part of the contract, because the offer expressly limited acceptance to only those terms found in the offer [UCC §2-207(2)(a)].

(2) **Example. [§5.3222]** Offeree/Seller's Acknowledgement is the same as the offeror/buyer's Purchase Order, except that it says, "No goods sold under this contract shall be sold with any warranty, express or implied, including the warranty of merchantability." If seller's form is judged an acceptance under §2-207(1), the warranty disclaimer does **not** become part of the contract because it materially alters the contract [UCC §2-207(2)(b)]. (For examples of those terms which do and do not materially alter a contract, see UCC §2-207, Com. 4 and 5.)

(3) **Example. [§5.3223]** Seller's Acknowledgement is the same as the offeror's Purchase Order, except it says, "Any dispute arising under this agreement shall be resolved by arbitration, not litigation." A day or two after receiving seller's form, buyer notices the arbitration provision and notifies buyer that he or she objects to that provision. Because the objection is made within a reasonable time after buyer has notice of it, the arbitration provision does not become part of the contract [UCC §2-207(2)(c)].

(4) **Example. [§5.3224]** Seller's Acknowledgement is the same as the offeror's Purchase Order, except it says, "Any Delivery of Goods made by Seller is to be made after 8:30 a.m. on the date of delivery." If this term is not objected to by the buyer, and if the offer does not limit acceptance to only the terms found in the offer, the "after 8:30 a.m." provision becomes part of the contract, assuming it does not materially alter the offer.

c. **The Curious Treatment of "Different" Terms under 2-207(2). [§5.323]** Section 2-207(1) states that an expression of acceptance can act as an effective acceptance, "even though it states terms additional to or **different from** those offered or agreed upon . . . ." However, in §2-207(2), there is no mention of "different" terms. The provision states only, "[T]he **additional** terms are to be construed as proposals for addition to the contract . . . . " Thus, often the parties will end up in a situation where an acceptance is found under §2-207(1) despite the presence of a different term or two in the acceptance; however, there is no guidance as to whether that different term is or is not part of the resulting contract.

Several theories have arisen to explain how different terms should be handled under §2-207(2), only two of which have much support. The first and most widely held is that different terms should be treated the same as additional terms, for it was just an oversight that the word "different" was left out of §2-207(2). There is support for this theory in Comment 3 to §2-207, which states "Whether or not additional **or different** terms will become part of the agreement depends upon the provisions of subsection (2)." The second theory is that additional terms simply drop out altogether and can never become part of the agreement. That is, the presence of a different term in a seller's acknowledgement will not prevent a contract from being formed based on the writings under §2-207(1), but once it is determined that a contract has been made, the different terms have no legal significance and can never, under any circumstances, be part of the contract. The support for this theory comes from the plain language of the statute, i.e., the phrase "different terms" is included in 2-207(1) and not in 2-207(2).

3. **THIRD STEP: IF NO CONTRACT IS FORMED UNDER 2-207(1) BASED ON THE EXCHANGED WRITINGS, AN IMPLIED-IN-FACT CONTRACT MAY BE FORMED ON THE PARTIES' CONDUCT UNDER §2-207(3). IF SO, §2-207(3) WILL ALSO GOVERN WHICH TERMS BECOME PART OF THE CONTRACT.** [§5.33] If the offeree's form is found not to constitute an effective acceptance, either because it was not a "seasonable expression of acceptance," or because it was expressly made conditional on assent to additional or different terms, then the analysis of a §2-207 problem must proceed to §2-207(3). That is, §2-207(2) has absolutely no significance in such a case, and is by-passed completely in analyzing such a problem, for §2-207(2)'s only function is to provide the rules for determining what terms are part of the contract **if** a contract is made by exchange of the writings under §2-207(1). Under §2-207(3), "conduct by both parties which recognizes the existence of a contract is sufficient to establish a contract although the writings of the parties do not establish a contract." Thus, even if the offeree is deemed to have sent a counter-offer that is never formally accepted, the parties can establish an implied-in-fact contract by their conduct. Thus, if the seller sends the goods called for in the offer, and the buyer accepts them, they have made a contract by conduct under §2-207(3).

(Note that if the parties do have a contract based on the exchange of their writings, its terms **must** be governed by §2-207(2). In other words, resort to §2-207(3) can only be made when **no** contract is formed based on the parties' exchanged writings as judged by application of the rules in §2-207(1)).

a. **The Terms of an Implied-In-Fact Contract by Conduct under §2-207(3) Are Determined under the "Knock-Out" Rule. [§5.331]** Under the common law's last shot doctrine, the terms of an implied-in-fact contract made under §2-207(3) would be the terms stated in the last form exchanged between the parties, i.e., the other party would be deemed to have impliedly accepted whatever offer (or counter-offer) was last exchanged between them (see §5.12). Section 2-207(3) changes the rule. Once a contract by conduct has been found under the first sentence of 2-207(3), the second sentence of that provision states that the **terms** of such a contract "consist of those terms on which the writings of the parties agree, together with any supplementary terms incorporated under any other provision of this Act." Thus, all the terms which are in both parties writings become part of the contract, but any term that is not found in **both** documents is "knocked out," and does not become part of the contract. In other words, the contract consists of all the terms both parties agreed on, but no term on which only one party put forward. If at the end of the "knock-out" process the contract is left with no term regarding price, time of delivery, place of delivery, time of payment, or place of payment, such terms can be supplied by the UCC's "gap fillers" which are some of the "supplementary terms" referred to in §2-207(3) (see §6.21 for a discussion of gap fillers). In addition, other such supplementary terms include, e.g., the implied warranty of merchantability [UCC §2-314], and the implied warranty of fitness for a particular purpose [UCC §2-315].

4. **WHEN THE ADDITIONAL OR DIFFERENT TERMS ARE FOUND IN A CONFIRMATION INSTEAD OF AN ACCEPTANCE. [§5.34]** Until now, the analysis under §2-207 has assumed that the parties have exchanged a written offer and a written "acceptance" that differs from the offer. However, a close reading of §2-207(1) reveals that it also applies where one party sends the other "a written confirmation . . . within a reasonable time which states terms additional to and different from those . . . agreed upon." In other words, if the parties have made, e.g., an oral contract over the telephone, and one party thereafter sends the other a written confirmation of the oral contract, but the confirmation contains different or additional terms than those agreed to on the phone, §2-207 is implicated.

   a. **Effect of Confirmation Containing Additional Different Terms. [§5.341]** The §2-207 analysis of a problem where the confirmation, rather than the acceptance, in the operative document varies only slightly from the normal §2-207 analysis. The principal difference is that there is no need to inquire whether the parties have entered into a contract based on their exchanged writings under §2-207(1). By definition, a "confirmation" confirms that a contract exists, and merely serves to restate the terms of that contract. Thus, if the confirmation recites that it is intended to confirm a contract previously made by the parties, analysis proceeds directly to §2-207(2) to determine the terms of the contract. Under §2-207(2), the terms of the confirmation are compared against the terms of the previously made contract. To analogize a "confirmation" situation to a more typical §2-207 analysis with exchanged writings by both parties, think of the oral contract as the "offer" and the written confirmation as the "acceptance" under §2-207(2). As a result, it is unlikely that the party sending the confirmation will be able to slip in a term not present in the original oral contract. It is only in the unlikely event that: (A) both parties are merchants; (B) the party to whom the confirmation is sent does not notify the other of his or her objection to the additional terms of the confirmation (§2-207(2)(c)); and (C) those additional terms do not materially alter the contract (§2-207(2)(b)), that the terms of the confirmation become part of the contract. Otherwise, the additional terms are only proposals that may be accepted or not by the recipient of the confirmation. (If the terms of the confirmation are "different" rather than "additional," the analysis would proceed as described in §5.323.) This rule makes sense, for it would be manifestly unfair for a party sending a written confirmation to be able to slip in a material term not agreed to by the other party.

(1) REVIEW PROBLEM. [§5.3411] Charles, the owner of a retail health and fitness store, telephones Terri, the owner of a company that manufactures exercise equipment. Charles places an order for fifteen $1,000 HEM-100 home exercise machines. They agree that the machines will be delivered to Charles's store on Monday, April 10, and that Charles will pay for them within 30 days after their receipt. Nothing is said as to whether Charles is liable for interest if he is late in paying. Later that day, Terri sends Charles a "confirmation," stating accurately the terms of the deal, except she has added a term stating "Buyer will owe interest to seller at a rate of 0.75% per month if seller does not pay within 30 days of delivery. Charles receives the confirmation and does not object. Question: Does their contract now contain the 8% interest clause?

Answer: Yes. The analysis is as follows: First, since the writing at issue is a confirmation, §2-207(1) is bypassed and the situation is analyzed under §2-207(2). For a §2-207(2) analysis, the oral contract (without the interest term) is to be compared with the confirmation containing the interest term. Under §2-207(2), because both parties are merchants, the interest provision becomes part of the contract unless §2-207(2)(a), (b), or (c) applies. Section §2-207(2)(a) does not apply, for the contract says nothing explicitly about being limited only to its terms. Section §2-207(2)(b) does not keep out the provision, because according to Com. 5 to §2-207, an interest on overdue balance clause does not materially alter the transaction. Section 2-207(2)(c) does not apply because Charles did not object. Thus, the additional term of the confirmation "become[s] part of the contract" under §2-207(2).

E. SUMMARY. [§5.4] The steps involved in analyzing a §2-207 problem have been discussed in this chapter in some detail. As a result, it is often easy to get lost in the detail and forget what is truly at issue. Recall, there are only three steps to applying §2-207 in a typical case:

(1) Is the purported acceptance truly an acceptance under §2-207(1) despite the presence of additional or different terms, or is it a counter-offer (usually because it contains a clause, e.g., "this Acceptance expressly conditioned on Buyer's assent to any additional or different terms");

(2) If the purported acceptance is deemed a valid acceptance, then the terms of the contract are determined under §2-207(2) (and §2-207(3) is never used); and

(3) If the purported acceptance is found not to be a valid acceptance, the parties have no contract based on their exchanged writings (and §2-207(2) is never used). However, they may have a contract by conduct under §2-207(3), and if they do, the rules of §2-207(3) also determine that contract's terms.

For those who prefer a diagram, a flow chart of the steps involved in analyzing a §2-207 problem is as follows:

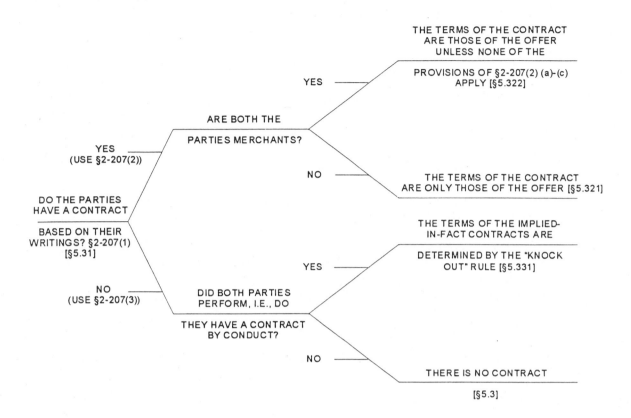

1. **Example. [§5.41]** Construct Co. sends a Purchase Order form to Door Co., seeking to purchase 100 oak doors. Door Co. sends an Acknowledgment of Order form back to Construct Co., acknowledging the order. The pertinent portions of these forms are as follows:

Purchase Order	**Acknowledgment of Order**
100 oak entry doors, 6 ft. x 3 ft.	100 oak entry doors, 6 ft. x 3 ft.
$300/door, payment due on delivery	$300/door, payment due on delivery
Delivery on 4/1/92	Delivery on 4/1/92
Doors of Stainable Quality	No Warranty, Either Express or Implied, Including the Implied Warranty of Merchantability Regarding the Stainable Quality of the Doors

Question: Do they have a contract and if so, what are its terms?

Analysis: (1) **Is there a contract based on these writings under §2-207(1)? YES. First**, the Acknowledgment is clearly a definite and reasonable expression of acceptance under the UCC, as the presence of the different warranty terms is insufficient, in and of itself, to make the Acknowledgment a counter-offer. **Second**, there is no "expressly made conditional on [buyer's] assent to different or additional terms" clause, thus the Acknowledgment is a valid acceptance under § 2-207(1), despite the fact it contains different warrant provisions. Thus the analysis must proceed under §2-207(2) to determine the terms of the contract.

(2) **Does the different term found in the Acknowledgment become part of the contract under §2-207(2)? NO. First**, are the parties merchants? Yes. Then there is a small chance that the "no stainable quality" term might become part of the contract. (If either party were not a merchant, there is no chance the term would become part of the contract). **Second**, are any of the provisions of §2-207(2)(a)-(c) implicated. **NO**. There is no objection by the buyer to any different terms, either in the Purchase Order itself, or afterwards. Hence neither §2- 207(2)(a) or (c) are satisfied. The "no stainable quality" terms certainly materially alters the deal, and thus, it could not become a term of the contract under §2-207(2)(b). (Recall there are two theories as to how to deal with "different" as opposed to "additional" terms under §2-207(2) [see §5.323]. One theory says that "different" terms drop out all together, and thus under this approach, the no stainable warranty provision would never have legal significance).

2. Example. [§5.42] Same parties as above, except this time the relevant forms are as follows:

Purchase Order	**Acknowledgment of Order**
100 oak entry doors, 6 ft. x 3 ft.	100 oak entry doors, 6 ft. x 3 ft.
$300/door, payment due on delivery	$300/door, payment due on delivery
Delivery by 4/1/92	Delivery by 4/1/92
Doors of Stainable Quality	No Warranty, Either Express or Implied Including the Implied Warranty of Merchantability.
	Regarding the Stainable Quality of the Doors, Seller, Door Co., is unwilling to accept Buyer's offer and enter into a contract with Buyer unless Buyer expressly assents to the additional and/or different terms found in this Acknowledgment.

Neither party looks at the form of the other, except to ensure the quantity, price, and delivery terms are correct. Non-stainable quality doors are shipped and accepted, and three months later Construct Co. sues for breach of warranty, claiming the doors are not of stainable quality as called for in the contract.

Question: Is there a contract and, if so, what are its terms?

Analysis: (1) Is there a contract based on the writings under §2-207(1)? NO. While the Acknowledgement is a definite and seasonable expression of acceptance, its final clause turns the document into a counter-offer. It clearly states Door Co. is unwilling to go forward on anything other than its own terms and states that no contract based on the writings can be formed without the *express* assent of Construct Co. Therefore, analysis must proceed to §2-207(3).

(2) **Is there a contract by conduct under §2-207(3)? YES.** Door Co. shipped doors to Construct Co., who accepted and paid for them. Thus, a contract by conduct was formed.

(3) **Does the different warranty term in the Acknowledgment become part of the contract under §2-207(3)? NO.** Under §2-207(3), the terms of an implied-in-fact contract by conduct consist of only the terms *both* parties agreed upon, plus the supplemental terms of the UCC. Thus the contract was for 100 doors, at $300/door, with payment and delivery due on April 1. However, under the knock-out rule [see §5.331] the quality terms of each party are knocked out (for they only appear in their own forms) and do not become part of the contract. Instead, the Code's implied warranty of merchantability under §2-314 will supply the quality term. (See §36.2 for a discussion of the warranty of merchantability)

F. **THE RESTATEMENT VIEW. [§5.5]** Sections 59 and 61 of the Restatement 2d appear to adopt many of the rules embodied in UCC §2-207. Thus, in non-UCC transactions, e.g., service contracts, real estate contracts, etc., there is support for abolition of the mirror-image rule. However, these Restatement provisions have not proven quite as persuasive as other Restatement sections, and it is fair to say that some courts might still hold that to be valid, an acceptance must match exactly and reciprocally the terms of the offer in non-UCC transactions.

CHAPTER SIX: THE INDEFINITENESS DOCTRINE

A. **THE INDEFINITENESS DOCTRINE: DEFINED AND DISCUSSED.** [§6.0] The indefiniteness doctrine states that an agreement will be unenforceable if a court cannot determine its essential or material terms with reasonable certainty, or fashion an appropriate remedy for its breach. Indefiniteness is an issue with respect to the entire agreement, so the fact that a particular offer may not contain many essential terms is not necessarily fatal to the **offer**. The test is whether the **entire contract** is sufficiently definite to be enforced.

1. **RATIONALES FOR THE INDEFINITENESS DOCTRINE.** [§6.01] Three reasons are generally given as to why a court will not enforce a contract where it cannot ascertain essential terms with sufficient certainty:

   (1) if a court does not know what a term is, the court cannot tell whether the term was breached;

   (2) if a court does not know what a term is, it cannot fashion an appropriate remedy for the breach; and

   (3) courts have traditionally expressed a reluctance to rewrite a contract for the parties, which they would have to do in order to enforce an indefinite agreement. Sometimes this is put "courts interpret contracts, but do not write them."

   a. **Example.** [§6.011] Max enters into a contract with Kathleen whereby Kathleen is to build a custom made grandfather clock for Max. They agreed as to the price and the design of the clock, but they did not agree as to when delivery was due. Eight months later, the clock has still not been delivered and Max sues for breach of contract. Under a strict application of the indefiniteness doctrine, Kathleen would prevail because the agreement would be unenforceable. This is so because:

   (1) the court cannot tell when delivery is due, so it cannot tell whether the contract has been breached;

   (2) even if the court could tell that the contract has been breached, it cannot fashion an appropriate remedy, for it is impossible to tell on what date damages began to run; and

   (3) to make the contract definite, the court would have to rewrite it and insert a delivery term, something courts are generally unwilling to do.

2. **TYPES OF INDEFINITENESS CASES.** [§6.02] There are three types of fact situations where the indefiniteness doctrine comes into play:

   (1) **where the parties to a contract have not agreed to a term;**

   (2) **where the parties have agreed to a term, but the term itself is so ambiguous that it is impossible to ascertain its meaning;** and

   (3) **where the parties have "agreed to agree" to a term sometime after contract formation, but then never reach an agreement on that point.**

   a. **Example Where Parties Have Not Agreed to a Term.** [§6.021] The hypothetical between Kathleen and Max described in §6.011, is an example of a case where the parties **have not agreed to a term**.

b. **Example Where an Agreed Upon Term is Too Ambiguous to be Enforced:** *Varney v. Ditmars*. **[§6.022]** Employer promises employee his salary "plus a fair share of the profits" if employee does good work. This is an example of a situation where the parties have reached an agreement as to a term, but the **term is so ambiguous** that a court has no basis on which to determine whether it is breached, or no basis to fashion a remedy even if it could be determined that a breach occurred. (See Case Squibs section, *Varney v. Ditmars*.)

c. **Example When There is an "Agreement to Agree." [§6.023]** Elliot tells June, "We've got a deal. I'll get back with you later on and we'll work out the payment terms." June agrees with this statement. However, if the parties do not ever reach an agreement as to the payment terms, either because they never discuss it, or because they do discuss it but cannot reach a subsequent agreement, it is an example of the **"agreement to agree"** type of indefiniteness problem.

3. **INDEFINITENESS DISTINGUISHED FROM FAILURE TO MAKE A CONTRACT. [§6.03]** The more essential terms the parties leave out of a deal, the greater the likelihood that they never had a contract in the first place. However, whether they exhibited sufficient mutual assent to establish a contract is an issue of formation, not indefiniteness. The indefiniteness doctrine pre-supposes the parties had a contract, but states that one or more terms may be so indefinite that a court may choose not to enforce the contract.

4. **INDEFINITENESS DOCTRINE ONLY APPLIES TO ESSENTIAL TERMS. [§6.04]** While it is sometimes difficult to establish what is an "essential" or "material" term and what is not, it is clear that a failure to agree on an immaterial term will not prevent enforcement of the contract under the indefiniteness doctrine. Typical "essential" terms are treated in the next section.

B. **COMMON LAW RULE ON INDEFINITENESS. [§6.1]** While scholars disagree as to exactly what terms were so essential to a contract before a common law court would find the agreement sufficiently definite and thus enforceable, the general thinking is that the parties had to manifest agreement about:

(1) the **subject matter** of the contract;

(2) the **quantity** to be purchased;

(3) the **price**;

(4) the **time performance was due;**

(5) the **place** performance was due; and

(6) the **payment** terms.

The common law courts were relatively strict in applying the rule, and failure to include any of these terms in a particular deal probably was enough to run afoul of the indefiniteness doctrine and render a contract unenforceable.

C. **MODERN RULE ON INDEFINITENESS. [§6.2]** Modern contract law has relaxed, but not eliminated, the indefiniteness rule. It has **not** done so by changing the wording of the rule itself, for under both the Restatement and the UCC a contract will fail for indefiniteness if the court cannot find a reasonably certain basis to determine the existence of a breach or to fashion an appropriate remedy [Restatement 2d §33; UCC §2-204]. Rather, modern contract law has relaxed the indefiniteness rule by applying it differently. It has done so in two ways.

First, regarding cases in which the parties have agreed to a term, but the term seems ambiguous on its face, courts are now more willing to examine the circumstances surrounding a transaction so as to **interpret** the language in a way to give definite effect to an ambiguous term (see Chapter Eighteen).

Second, as to those cases in which the parties have not reached an agreement as to a particular term, modern courts are far more willing to examine the circumstances surrounding a transaction so as to **imply** a reasonable term that is to fill in the gaps left by the parties. However, there are limitations to each of these doctrines and thus the real question in modern cases is under what circumstances will a court act, and under what circumstances will it refuse to act, to cure any indefiniteness problem. As shown below, in cases arising under Article 2 of the UCC, a court has a much easier time implying operative terms than in a non-UCC context.

1. **THE UCC APPROACH TO INDEFINITENESS: THE GAP FILLERS. [§6.21]** The approach taken to indefiniteness by the drafters of the UCC has been to include provisions that become operative if the parties have not reached final agreement on these issues under their contract. That is, when the parties have left "gaps" in their contract on these issues, the UCC provides "gap fillers" that spring into existence so that a court has a basis to decide whether a party is in breach and how to fashion a remedy to deal with that breach. The UCC-gap fillers govern:

> (1) the **price of the goods** the buyer must pay and the price the seller must accept [UCC §2-305];
>
> (2) the **mode of delivery** [UCC §2-307];
>
> (3) the **place of delivery** [UCC §2-308];
>
> (4) the **time of delivery** [UCC §2-309]; and
>
> (5) the **time and place for payment** [UCC §2-310].

Before discussing each gap filler individually, three points need be made.

> a. **Gap Fillers Are NOT Effective Unless an Otherwise Enforceable Contract has been Formed. [§6.211]** While gap fillers play an important role in the operation of a contract, they play no role in its formation. Thus, if the parties agree on all terms except time of delivery, and leave a negotiation saying, "We've almost got a deal; if we can just work out the time of delivery, we will have a contract," the fact that there is a gap filler for time of delivery is irrelevant and the parties do not have an enforceable contract. In other words, the parties still must evidence a mutual intention to be bound before a gap filler can operate [UCC §2-305(4)].
>
> b. **Gap Fillers ARE Effective when the Parties Make Agreements to Agree. [§6.212]** Under the UCC, a gap filler is effective when the parties evidence a mutual intent to be bound, but agree to agree later on about a term covered by a gap filler. If, after contract formation, they do not reach an agreement as to that term, either because they forget to talk about it or because they do talk about it and cannot later agree, an applicable gap filler will be operative [UCC §2-305, Com. 1].

c. **Gap Fillers Are NOT Effective if the Parties Make a Specific Agreement to the Contrary. [§6.213]** Gap fillers only spring into existence if the parties to an enforceable contract have not agreed about a term covered by a gap filler. If the parties otherwise reach an agreement on that issue, it is their agreement, not the gap filler, which controls.

2. **SPECIFIC GAP FILLERS UNDER THE UCC. [§6.22]** The gap fillers are located in Part 3 of Article 2 of the UCC. Each is discussed below.

   a. **Gap Filler as to Price: Reasonable Price. [§6.221]** One of the more remarkable aspects of the UCC is that it allows the parties to an enforceable contract even though they do not agree on the price to be paid for the good. **If nothing is said as to price, or if the price is left to be agreed upon by the parties and they later fail to agree, the price for the goods will be "a reasonable price at time of delivery"** [UCC §2-305]. Thus, when a builder calls a hardware store and orders 100 feet of PVC pipe to be delivered to a job site, the contractor has implicitly made an enforceable promise to pay a reasonable price pending at time of delivery for the pipe. Generally, the reasonable price under the UCC is the market price for the goods.

   b. **Gap Filler Regarding Mode of Delivery: Delivery in Single Lot. [§6.222]** The general rule is that a **buyer is entitled to demand delivery of all goods called for in a single contract in one lot; similarly the seller is entitled to deliver them in one lot** [UCC §2-307]. However, where circumstances make it **reasonable** either to make or accept delivery in several lots and, in **good faith**, the other party would **not be harmed** by such action, several lot delivery or acceptance is required [UCC §2-307, Com. 3]. For example, if the buyer does not have the storage space to accept all the order at once, and if delivering the shipment in lots would not unduly inconvenience the seller, buyer can demand delivery in lots.

   c. **Gap Filler Regarding Place of Delivery: The Seller's Place of Business. [§6.223]** The general rule is that **if nothing is agreed regarding where delivery is to take place, delivery is to occur at the seller's place of business or residence, or for a specific good which the parties know at the time of contracting is somewhere else (e.g., a racehorse in a particular paddock), then the place of delivery is that other place** [UCC §2-308]. In other words, in the absence of a contrary agreement, the cost of delivery is always on the buyer and not assumed to be included in the sales price.

   d. **Gap Filler Regarding Time of Delivery: Reasonable Time. [§6.224]** If no time for shipment or delivery is agreed upon, **the seller must tender the goods within "a reasonable time."** What is reasonable depends on all the circumstances, e.g., how complicated the good is to make, past dealings of the parties, the practice within the industry, etc. [UCC §2-309].

   e. **Gap Filler Regarding Time of Payment: Payment Due at Time and Place of Delivery. [§6.225]** In the absence of an agreement as to payment terms, **payment is due at the time and place at which the buyer is to receive the goods** [UCC §2-310(a)].

   f. **No Gap Filler Regarding Subject Matter of the Contract or Regarding Quantity. [§6.226]** In deciding what the gap fillers would be, the drafters of the UCC tried to decide what the parties probably would have chosen had they reached an agreement on the matter. However, there are two things about which it is impossible to say what the parties "probably" would have done had they reached an agreement: (1) **what the** parties bargained for, i.e., the subject matter of the contract; and (2) the **quantity** of goods the parties would want to exchange. Thus, there is no gap filler for these terms, and a failure to agree on them will result in the contract being deemed unenforceable due to indefiniteness even under the UCC, for there is no way to determine the existence of a breach of these terms, or should a breach occur, to fashion an appropriate remedy [UCC §2-204].

3. **THE RESTATEMENT APPROACH TO THE INDEFINITENESS DOCTRINE. [§6.23]** Like the UCC, the Restatement also directs that the common law indefiniteness rule should be loosened. However, unlike the UCC, the Restatement does not explicitly provide gap fillers that the courts can automatically turn to when the parties do not reach an agreement about a particular material term. Nonetheless, the comments to Restatement 2d §33 suggest that there are appropriate circumstances for a court to imply UCC gap fillers by analogy (or even to apply other court-fashioned "gap fillers") in non-UCC transactions. These comments state that it is proper for a court to review the circumstances surrounding a transaction and to imply a sufficiently definite term in order to enforce the contract under §33. However, under the Restatement 2d, a court cannot simply decree what a term should be without a basis for doing so. Rather, it may imply a term **only if it believes that term is what the parties implicitly agreed to** even if it was not expressly stated in their agreement. For example, in a contract for the sale of a residence, where no date for transfer of the deed is mentioned, if the buyer can show that the seller has hired a moving van to move out of the house on July 1, a court is entitled to imply July 1 as the closing date for the transaction.

   a. **Agreements to Agree in Non-UCC Transactions. [§6.231]** Traditionally, courts have been reluctant to enforce non-UCC contracts where the parties have agreed to agree, but subsequently failed to do so. However, the Restatement suggests that at least for some terms, courts should take the UCC approach and imply a reasonable term to fill in when the parties fail to reach a post-contractual agreement. Thus, there is reason to think the modern trend will be a greater enforcement of contracts in which a particular promise is left for future negotiation and agreement on that issue is never reached.

D. **PAST PERFORMANCE AS A CURE FOR INDEFINITENESS. [§6.3]** Under both the UCC and the Restatement, past performance of a contract may act to cure an indefinite contract and make it enforceable. For example, a grocery store makes a contract with a fruit wholesaler for the delivery of "10 bushels of apples per week for the next year." The contract, as written, may fail for indefiniteness, for it is not possible to tell on its face what kinds of apples are contemplated. However, if the wholesaler delivers Granny Smith apples each week for three months, and the store accepts them, this past performance has likely cured any future indefiniteness problem.

E. **USAGE OF TRADE, COURSE OF DEALING, AND COURSE OF PERFORMANCE AS CURES FOR INDEFINITENESS. [§6.4]** When appropriate, a properly proven usage of trade, course of dealing, or course of performance can be used to cure an indefinite contract (See §19.1121 for a definition of these terms). For example, a contract calls for Contractor to deliver "a load" of gravel to a building. If within the trade "a load" has a more specific meaning, e.g. 100 pounds, then usage of the understood trade will make the contract enforceable.

V. CONSIDERATION AND ITS "SUBSTITUTES"

CHAPTER SEVEN: CONSIDERATION

A. THE CONSIDERATION DOCTRINE. [§7.0] Not all promises made in offers and acceptances are enforceable. The doctrine of consideration is the theory that separates those promises in offers and acceptances that will be enforced by the courts from those that will not. If an agreement is not supported by valid consideration, that agreement is not an enforceable contract. However, certain promises in an otherwise unenforceable agreement may be enforced under a promissory estoppel theory (see Chapter Eight).

B. DEFINITIONS OF CONSIDERATION. [§7.1] Over time, the generally accepted definition of consideration has changed. However, as noted in §7.15, while it is important to study these definitions, none of them completely explain all the situations in which consideration will be found by modern courts. Thus, while the concepts contained in the various definitions are important and need to be learned, you should keep in mind that no one theory completely describes all the contours of the consideration doctrine.

1. THE "WILL" THEORY. [§7.11] This theory was most prevalant in *early* common law. Under it, a promise was supported by consideration (and thus enforceable) so long as the promisor "willed" to be legally bound at the time the promise was made. Given the highly subjective nature of this test, and given both the trend and need for an objective test of consideration, the "will theory" is no longer used.

2. THE "BENEFIT/DETRIMENT" THEORY. [§7.12] Under this theory, a promise is deemed supported by consideration (and thus enforceable), whenever:

(1) The promisee either acts, or promises to act, **in exchange for the promisor's promise;** and

(2) The promisee's act or promised act is either **a legal detriment to the promisee** or a **legal benefit to the promisor.**

While the definition sounds a bit complicated and technical, in practice it is fairly straightforward as illustrated immediately below.

a. Example: Unilateral Contract. [§7.121] Eric makes an offer to enter into a unilateral contract with Holly, promising to pay her $1,000 for her watch. If Holly gives Eric her watch in exchange for his promise to pay the $1,000 (thereby accepting the offer), Eric's promise to pay the $1,000 is enforceable under the benefit/detriment theory. That is Holly, the promisee, suffered a **legal detriment** (i.e., she gave up possession of her watch), and Eric, the promisor, received a **legal benefit** (i.e., he obtained possession of the watch). Further, the detriment and benefit were given **in exchange for Eric's promise** to pay the $1,000. Thus, the parties have entered into a valid, enforceable unilateral contract with a promissory offer, an acceptance by conduct, and consideration to enforce Eric's promise to pay.

b. Example: Bilateral Contract. [§7.122] Assume that instead of immediately handing the watch to Eric in response to his offer to pay $1,000 for her watch, this time Holly promises to give Eric her watch at a later point. Eric's promise to pay is enforceable, for Holly suffered a **legal detriment** (she promised to give up possession of the watch), and Eric received a **legal benefit** (he was promised possession of the watch) **in exchange for his promise** of the $1,000 payment. Note also that **Holly's** promise to give up the watch (i.e., her promissory acceptance) is also enforceable. Eric suffered a legal detriment (promised payment of $1,000), Holly obtained a legal benefit (the receipt of Eric's promise to pay), **in exchange** for Holly's promise to tender the watch. As such, the parties have entered into a valid, enforceable bilateral contract, with a promissory offer, a promissory acceptance, and consideration to support the executory promises.

3. **THE RESTATEMENT'S "BARGAIN" THEORY. [§7.13]** The Restatement (both First and Second) rejected the benefit/detriment theory in favor of "the bargain theory." Under this approach, "[t]o constitute consideration, a performance or return promise must be bargained for" [Restatement 2d §71(1)]. Thus, under the Restatement, it is irrelevant that a party either suffers a detriment or reaps a benefit, so long as the return promise or requested performance sought by the promisor is bargained for [Restatement 2d §79(a)].

Of course, this definition raises the question of when is a promise "bargained for." Under §71(2) of the Restatement 2d, a performance is bargained for if:

(1) it is **sought by** the promisor in exchange for his or her promise; and

(2) it is **given by the promisee in exchange for that promise.**

Once again, while the definition may seem formidable, its application is also relatively straightforward as seen below.

a. **Example: Unilateral Contracts. [§7.131]** (Assume the same facts in the Holly/Eric transaction as set forth in §7.121.) Eric's promise to pay the $1,000 is enforceable under the bargain theory. That is, Holly's act in giving up the watch was "bargained for" because it was both **sought by** Eric (the promisor), and given by Holly (the promisee), **in exchange** for Eric's promise to pay. Thus, the parties entered into a valid enforceable unilateral contract, with a promissory offer, an acceptance by conduct, and consideration sufficient to enforce Eric's executory promise.

b. **Example: Bilateral Contracts. [§7.132.]** (Assume the same facts in the Holly/Eric transaction as analyzed in §7.122.) Eric's promise to pay the $1,000 is enforceable, for Holly's promised performance (her promise to tender the watch at a later time), was "bargained for"; i.e., it was **sought by** Eric, and **given in exchange** for Holly's promise to pay. Similarly, Holly's promise to tender the watch is enforceable, for Eric's performance (his promise to pay $1,000), was **sought by Holly,** and **given in exchange** for her promise to deliver the watch. Thus, the parties entered into a valid, enforceable bilateral contract, with a promissory offer, a promissory acceptance, and consideration sufficient to enforce the executory promises.

4. **MODERN CONTRACT LAW'S ACCEPTANCE OF THE BENEFIT/DETRIMENT AND BARGAIN THEORIES OF CONSIDERATION. [§7.14]** The Restatement 2d's bargain theory of consideration is the preeminent view of consideration used in modern contract law. However, the idea that the promisee must suffer a legal detriment or the promisor must obtain a legal benefit is still recited to a great extent by modern courts when discussing consideration principles. (Indeed, on occasion some courts have even combined the two tests, stating that consideration is present only when there has been a benefit and/or detriment that was **bargained for,** rather than merely given "in exchange"as required by the earlier test.) The reason benefits and detriments are still recited so frequently by courts is probably that, as a practical matter, there are few occasions in which a promise will be enforceable under one theory and not the other, and also probably because the benefit/detriment theory is studied so much in law school. However, it is clear that there are some cases in which a promise would be enforceable under the benefit/detriment theory but not under the bargain theory.

Probably the most significant type of transaction in which the two theories would yield different results occurs when a return promise or performance is given by a promisee **in exchange** for a promise, but not as part of a **bargain for** that promise. For example, suppose Dan, who is a fast typist, promised to type Mary's moot court brief simply because they were friends. In response, Mary was so pleased that she promised to wash Dan's car. Mary's promise was not **bargained for**, in that it was not **sought by** Dan when he promised to type Mary's paper. Thus, it would not be enforceable under the Restatement's bargain theory of consideration. However, Mary's promise was given in exchange for Dan's promise, and resulted in both a **detriment** by Mary, (i.e., she promised to do something she otherwise did not have to do) and a **benefit** to Dan (i.e., the promise of a clean car). Thus, under the benefit/detriment theory, Mary's promise would be enforced.

5. **CRITICISM OF CONSIDERATION DEFINITIONS. [§7.15]** Many prominent contracts scholars have criticized both the benefit/detriment and bargain theories of consideration as insufficient to explain all cases. There are times when a promisee suffers a legal detriment or a promisor reaps a legal benefit in exchange for a promise, and there still will be no consideration present (see e.g., §7.5 et seq.). Similarly, there are cases in which a party's promises or performances are clearly bargained for, yet they still will not be enforced (see e.g., §7.63). As a result, it is probably easier to think of consideration as the general doctrine that governs which promises will be enforced, and to concentrate on learning the rules governing the different types of transactions described in this chapter, rather than trying to "fit" the definitions of consideration into each of these types of transactions.

C. **TYPES OF CONSIDERATION IN UNILATERAL CONTRACTS. [§7.2]** In a unilateral contract, the consideration supporting the offeror's promise consists of one of the following bargained for elements:

   (1) an **act**;

   (2) a **forbearance**; or

   (3) the **creation, modification, or destruction of a legal relationship** [Restatement 2d §71(2), (3)].

To be considered valid consideration to support the enforceability of the promises made in a unilateral contract, one of these three elements must be sought by the promisor and undertaken by the promisee in exchange for the promise made in the offer.

1. **EXAMPLE. [§7.21]** Frank offers to pay Larry $800 for Larry's couch if Larry will deliver it to Frank's house by 5:00. Larry's delivery of the couch is sufficient consideration to make Frank's promise to pay enforceable, for it is an **act** taken by the promisee (Larry), which was both **sought by the promisor (Frank)**, and **given in exchange for the promise to pay**.

2. **EXAMPLE of *Hamer v. Sidway*. [§7.22]** Uncle offers to pay 16 year-old nephew $1,000 if nephew refrains from smoking or drinking until age 21. If nephew does not drink or smoke until age 21, the uncle's promise to pay is supported by consideration (and thus enforceable), for nephew undertook a **forbearance in exchange** for uncle's promise, and that forebearance was **sought by** Uncle when he made his offer. (See Case Squibs section, *Hamer v. Sidway*.)

3. **EXAMPLE. [§7.23]** Greg has a 30-year $100,000 mortgage at 4% interest. He offers to pay $90,000 in cash today if the bank will cancel the 30-year loan. If the Bank agrees and cancels the loan, that act is sufficient consideration to enforce Greg's promise to pay, for it is a **destruction of a legal relationship**, undertaken **in exchange** for Greg's promise, and was a type of action **sought by** Greg in making his offer.

4. **EXAMPLE. [§7.24]** Helen gratuitously offers to give her friend Ilene a ride to the airport next month, which Ilene gratefully accepts. Ilene is so pleased, that she rushes out and sends Helen flowers with a note saying, "Thanks for agreeing to give me a ride." Ilene's acts are insufficient consideration to enforce Helen's promise to provide a ride under the bargain theory, for Ilene's act in buying the flowers was not made as part of a bargained for exchange. That is, Ilene may have purchased the flowers **because** of Helen's promise, but that act was not **sought by** Helen when she made the promise to drive Ilene to the airport. In other words, Ilene's purchase of the roses was a gift, and hence not part of the **bargain** struck for the promise of a ride to the airport. Note, however that Helen's promise may be enforceable by promissory estoppel (see Chapter Eight).

D. **TYPES OF CONSIDERATION IN BILATERAL CONTRACTS. [§7.3]** In a bilateral contract, **each party's promise serves as consideration for the return promise of the other** if, but only if:

    (1) each promise was **sought by,** and was given in exchange for the other; and

    (2) the performance promised by each party would be valid consideration if it were carried out [Restatement 2d §75].

In other words, any promise made in a valid offer to enter into a bilateral contract serves as consideration for any promise made in the acceptance, and **vice versa**, so long as the offer and acceptance were bargained in exchange for each other, and so long as the promised performance, if completed, would be valid consideration.

1. **EXAMPLE. [§7.31]** Ken offers to pay a furniture store $1,200 in three equal monthly payments for a living room set. Furniture store accepts that offer, promising to deliver the furniture next week. The contract is supported by consideration because:

    (1) the promise to pay and the promise to deliver the furniture were sought by each other, and were given in exchange for each other; and

    (2) if completed, the acts called for by each party's promise would be valid consideration, i.e., delivery of the furniture and payment would not be considered "invalid" as "past" consideration (see §7.53); "moral" consideration (see §7.53); as "gift" promises (see §7.51); as "illusory" promises (see §7.62); or as violative of the pre-existing duty rule (see §7.63).

2. **REVIEW PROBLEM. [§7.32]** Sally, a police officer, is under a public duty to apprehend criminals. However, Hal offers Sally $1,000 if she will promise to work hard to catch the robber who stole Hal's record collection. Sally promises to work hard on Hal's case while on the job and ends up arresting the robber the next week as part of her official duties. Question: Do they have an enforceable contract?

Answer: Sally and Hal have no enforceable contract, for although their promises were bargained for and given in exchange for each other, the acts called for by Sally's promise would not be sufficient consideration even if performed, for Sally was under a pre-existing duty to arrest the robber (see §7.63 for a discussion of the pre-existing duty rule).

E. **THE RETURN PROMISES OR PERFORMANCES BY THE PROMISEE CAN BE VALID CONSIDERATION EVEN IF GIVEN TO A THIRD PARTY. [§7.4]** Consideration can still be valid even if it is a third party that either gives a return promise or undertakes an action in a transaction. So long as the promisee's performance or promised performance was bargained for and given in exchange for the promisor's promise, the consideration is valid even if it goes to or comes from a third party [Restatement 2d §71(4)].

1. **EXAMPLE. [§7.41]** Claire owes Barbara $10. Additionally, Claire owns a cassette tape that Ann wants. If Ann agrees to pay Barbara $10 to settle Claire's debt, in return for Claire's promise to give Ann the tape, the promise to pay the $10 and the promise to deliver the cassette are enforceable, even though a third party was involved. That is, because each promise was sought, bargained for, and given in exchange for the other, consideration is present to enforce the contract.

F. **TRANSACTIONS WITHOUT CONSIDERATION BECAUSE THEY LACK A BARGAINED FOR EXCHANGE. [§7.5]** As mentioned above, to be enforceable under the bargain theory, the performance or promised performance of the promisee must be "bargained for," i.e. sought by and given in exchange for the other party's promise [Restatement 2d §§53, 71]. There are two types of promises or actions which historically have been deemed insufficient to provide consideration for a contract, for they lack this "bargained for exchange" element: (i) gifts or gift promises; and (ii) "unsolicited actions." These types of return promises or actions may, in fact, be given **because of** a promise, but they do not serve as consideration to support a contract for they are not **sought by** and given **in exchange** for the promise. Each is discussed below.

1. **GRATUITOUS OR GIFT PROMISES. [§7.51]**

   a. **Traditional Rule: Gift Promises Are Unenforceable because They Are Not Supported by Consideration. [§7.511]** The traditional common law rule was that a promise cannot act as consideration if it is made as a gift, rather than as part of a bargained for exchange.

   (1) **Example. [§7.5111]** Aunt says to nephew, "Because today is your birthday, I promise to give you $1,000." Nephew says, "I accept your gracious gift." If the aunt does not pay, her promise cannot be enforced as part of a contract for she only made a gift promise. That is, she did not seek any return promise or action by the nephew when she made her promise. In other words, there was no "bargain" struck between them. As such, the aunt's promise is deemed only a gift or gratuitous promise, and therefore unenforceable.

   (2) **Completed Gift Not Affected By Lack of Consideration. [§7.5112]** Note that the consideration doctrine only makes a gift **promise** unenforceable. If the promisor has already made the gift to the promisee, the rights of the promisor potentially to reclaim it are governed by the law of property, not of contract.

(3) Acts Incidental to a True Gift Promise Are Insufficient Consideration To Enforce The Promise. [§7.5113] Occasionally, a promisor will require the promisee to take some sort of action in order to obtain the benefits of a gift promise. **If such action is deemed only incidental to the true gratuitous nature of the promise, the taking of such action is insufficient to act as consideration.** In order to determine whether the act is incidental or not, the key inquiry is whether the promisor made the promise in order to "get something" from the exchange, i.e. did the promisor seek, or bargain for, some sort of benefit resulting from the promise, or does the act called for merely make more convenient the giving of a gift.

(a) Example. [§7.5113-1] Jay tells his friend Ted, "Drop by tonight on your way home from school because I have a present for you — the mystery novel you've been talking about." Even if Ted drives to Jay's house, such action is likely not sufficient consideration to make Jay's gift promise enforceable. Jay was not benefitted from making the promise and his request for action was incidental to the true nature of the agreement, i.e. the making of a gift. It only made the giving of the gift more convenient. As such, because Jay did not seek or **bargain for** anything as a result of his promise to transfer possession of the book, the promise to give it to Ted is unenforceable. Hence, if Ted fails to deliver the book, Jay cannot successfully sue him for breach of contract since the "duty" to deliver the book is not supported by consideration.

Note that if Ted can establish that Jay was lonely, and thus actually bargaining for Ted's company, then consideration may be present because Jay then would have "gotten something" from the transaction. That is, by promising to deliver the book, he would have sought or bargained for a return action by Ted (Ted's company), and Ted's company would have been given in exchange for the promised delivery of the book. (Even if Ted's actions were judged merely incidental to a gift promise, however, he may be able to recover at least the expenses of his drive to Jay's house under a theory of promissory estoppel [see Chapter Eight, infra]).

(b) Example of *Kirksey v. Kirksey*. [§7.5113-2] Relative wrote to recently widowed sister-in-law, "If you come down and see me, I will let you have a place to raise your family." Sister-in-law moved to Alabama with her family, but father-in-law would not provide her a place to live. **Held:** The offer of a place to live was only a gift promise and thus the actions requested of sister-in-law were merely incidental to the true nature of the offer. In other words, the father-in-law's offer was a gift, and while it is true that to take advantage of the gift she had to come to Alabama, that trip does not change the fundamental nature of father-in-law's gift promise. As such, her travel to the father's-in-law's farm was deemed only incidental to the gift, and thus insufficient to make the promise of a place to live enforceable. Note that the sister-in-law could recover at least the expenses for her trip to Alabama, and perhaps more, under a theory of promissory estoppel [see Chapter Eight, infra].

b. Modern Rule: Some Gift Promises To Repay Otherwise Uncollectible Pre-Existing Indebtedness Can Be Enforced. [§7.512] Assume Joe has borrowed $10,000 from Bridget and has failed to re-pay it when due. After awhile, if Bridget does nothing, the debt becomes unenforceable because the statute of limitations runs, or possibly because it becomes discharged if Joe files for bankruptcy. At common law, if Joe promised to pay the debt after it became unenforceable, Joe's promise would be classified as a gift promise arising out of a perceived moral obligation, i.e. a promise of a gift of money to someone who is not legally entitled to it because it is the "right" thing to do. As such, it would have been unenforceable.

However, under the Restatement 2d, Joe's new promise is likely enforceable as part of the Restatement's relaxation of the rules regarding gift promises in "moral" consideration settings. These rules are explained in §7.64, infra.

2. PAST CONSIDERATION (OR "MORAL" OBLIGATION). [§7.52]

a. **Traditional Rule: Past Consideration and Moral Obligation are Insufficient to Make Promises Enforceable. [§7.521]** Traditionally, where a promise was made in response to some act or forbearance **previously undertaken**, or to some promise **previously made**, the promise was held insufficient to act as consideration. This is because, by definition, the promise could not have been made as part of a bargained for exchange. The promise could only have been made after the event occurred and while it may have been made *because of* the event, it could not have been *sought by* the person precipitating the previous event.

(1) **Example of *Mills v. Wyman*. [§7.5211]** Mills cared for Wyman's adult son who fell ill during a sea voyage. Upon reaching port and finding out what had occurred, Wyman wrote Mills expressing his thanks and promising to reimburse Mills for all the expenses incurred in the care of his son. When Wyman ultimately did not pay, Mills sued. **Held:** Wyman's promise was not supported by sufficient consideration. While Wyman may have felt a moral obligation, the only consideration to support the promise was past consideration. In other words Mills was not *seeking a promise of payment* from Wyman when he cared for Wyman's son. As such, there was no bargained for exchange necessary to make Wyman's promise enforceable.

b. **Modern Rule: Past Consideration and Moral Obligation Can Make *Some* Promises Enforceable. [§7.522]** The Restatement 2d, reflecting a general dissatisfaction with the common law rule as to past consideration, takes a more flexible approach to this issue. Under §86:

A promise made in recognition of a benefit previously received by the promisor is enforceable to the extent necessary to prevent injustice, *unless*:

(1) the promisee intended the benefit received by the promisor as a gift; or

(2) the value of the promisor's promise is disproportionate to the benefit he or she received.

Note that this is not a full abandonment of the past consideration rule, and so each provision if §86 must be read and applied carefully.

(1) **Example of *Webb v. McGowin*. [§7.5221]** Webb saved McGowin's life and was rendered handicapped in the rescue. To show his gratitude, McGowin promised to make biweekly payments to Webb of $15 until Webb's death. Under the Restatement 2d approach, McGowin's promise would be enforceable because:

(1) McGowin's saving of Webb's life was not intended as a gift (even though it was not induced by a promise of payment); and

(2) its value ($30 per month) was not disproportionate to the benefit received by McGowin.

(2) Example of *Mills v. Wyman*. [§7.5222] [The facts of *Mills v. Wyman* are given in §7.5311]. Even under the Restatement 2d, Mills still could not enforce Wyman's promise for the benefit conferred by Mills was received not by the promisor (Wyman), as required by §86, but rather to the promisor's son [Restatement 2d §86, Ill. 1].

(3) REVIEW PROBLEM. [§7.5223] Sue saw Elena, a friend of hers, at another table in a fancy restaurant and asked the waiter to send a bottle of champagne to Elena "with her compliments." Elena was thrilled by the gesture but came over to Sue and said, "That was lovely of you, but I insist on paying you for the champagne."

Question: Is Elena's promise enforceable?

Answer: Even under the Restatement 2d approach, Elena's promise is not enforceable. While the promise was made in recognition of a benefit previously received by the promisor (the sending of the wine to Elena), and while the value of the promise is proportionate to the benefit received (Elena promised to pay the price of the wine), the promise still cannot be enforced because Sue originally intended the benefit received by Elena (the champagne) as a gift.

3. UNSOLICITED ACTIONS ARE INSUFFICIENT TO ACT AS CONSIDERATION. [§7.53] For a promisee's *actions* to be sufficient consideration so to make the other party's promise enforceable, those *actions* must be sought by, and taken because of, an existing promise. Actions taken without regard to the promise are not sufficient to serve as consideration. This issue most often arises when a party fortuitously accomplishes the acts called for by an offer, but is unaware of the offer while he or she is doing them.

a. Example. [§7.531] In the local newspaper, Harry places an advertisement promising a $100 reward for the return of his lost wallet. Tara, who is unaware of the ad, finds the wallet and independently returns it to Harry. Even though Tara did the acts called for in Harry's offer, her actions were not made as part of a bargain with Harry. That is, she did not return the wallet in exchange for Harry's for the promise to pay the reward. Thus, her acts cannot serve as consideration under the bargain theory [see also §4.332].

G. SPECIFIC TYPES OF TRANSACTIONS RAISING CONSIDERATION ISSUES. [§7.6] There are certain types of transactions whose very natures raise consideration issues. Each is discussed separately below but once again, the overriding principle is that as long as the promises or performances of one party are both sought by the other in making a promise, and are given in exchange for that promise, consideration is probably present.

1. TRANSACTIONS IN WHICH THE CONSIDERATION OF ONE PARTY IS WORTH SUBSTANTIALLY LESS THAN THE OTHER: THE "PEPPERCORN" THEORY OF CONSIDERATION. [§7.61] Typically, courts will not inquire into the adequacy of one party's consideration, even if its economic value seems disproportionate to the economic value of the other party's [Restatement 2d §79]. The reason is that the courts will let parties make their own judgments as to how much a return promise or return performance is worth and will not try to impose some objective economic proportionality standard regarding the validity of consideration. Thus (at common law), a peppercorn, or (today) a dollar, etc., can generally serve as valid consideration for any promise, no matter how extravagant, so long as the promise was freely bargained for and freely given in exchange for the peppercorn, dollar, etc.

a. **Inadequate Consideration may be Evidence of Fraud, Duress, or Undue Influence.** [§7.611] Although no inquiry will normally be made into the adequacy of a party's consideration, the presence of an unusually great economic disproportionality in the parties' benefits and detriments under the contract may occasion a court to look closely for evidence of fraud, duress, or undue influence in the transaction. For example, if Bill "contracts" to sell his $25,000 painting to Mary for $100, the disparity in the value of the consideration coming to Bill entitles a court to examine the transaction for duress, fraud, undue influence, etc. on Mary's part. (See Part VI of this outline for a discussion of these doctrines.) Thus, while a court will not refuse to enforce a contract based solely on the adequacy of consideration, a disproportionate economic benefit realized by one party may serve as circumstantial evidence of the existence of a doctrine that would allow one party to avoid the contract, and entitles the court to examine the transaction carefully to ensure that the promises of the parties were freely and voluntarily bargained for.

b. **Inadequate Consideration May Be Evidence of Sham Consideration.** [§7.612] Uncle wants to give his 16-year old niece his $5,000 antique desk on her 18th birthday. Knowing gift promises to be unenforceable, uncle agrees to "sell" the desk to niece now for $1, with delivery to be in two years. If the "bargain" is only a pretense to disguise a gift promise, niece's payment of $1 is not consideration for uncle's promise to deliver the desk. Hence, if uncle never delivers the desk, or if he becomes incapacitated before the desk is delivered, the contract cannot be enforced by niece. Hence, inadequate consideration may also serve as evidence of a sham transaction which is unenforceable under contract law [see §7.65].

2. **ILLUSORY PROMISES.** [§7.62] An illusory promise is one in which the promisor gives the illusion of making a valid promise to act or forebear, but in reality does not bind himself or herself to do anything. For example, if in response to an offer to purchase a couch for $500, Bill responds, "I promise to pay you $500 for the couch if I decide I want to, otherwise I will not take the couch and will pay you nothing," Bill has made no real commitment, and thus no enforceable contract is formed. The rule governing illusory promises is that **a true illusory promise cannot serve as consideration.** While the general rule is of long standing, the question of what is and what is not a true illusory promise has changed over time.

a. **Traditional Rule: Unless a Definite Commitment was Evident, a Promise Lacked Consideration.** [§7.621] The common law rule was clear: **unless the promisor made a definite commitment to be bound, the promise was illusory** and thus insufficient to act as consideration. For example, if Joe promised to accept and pay $500 for a portrait "if I like it when it's done, otherwise I'll reject it and pay nothing," no enforceable agreement was ever formed between Joe and the artist because Joe's promise was illusory. He had made no definite commitment.

b. **Modern Rule:** *Any* **Restriction, Either Express or Implied, on a Promisor's Actions Makes a Promise Enforceable — The Duty of Good Faith and Fair Dealing.** [§7.622] Modern contract law has changed the rules in two ways regarding when a promise is illusory. First, contract doctrine now holds that *any* **restriction on a promisor's freedom of action, whether express or implied, will prevent a promise from being classified as illusory.** Second, it provides that one of the implied restrictions on a promisor's freedom of action is **an implied duty of good faith performance**. That is, in **every contract**, the parties will be deemed to have agreed to perform under the contract in good faith [Restatement 2d §205; UCC §1-203]. (The definition of good faith under both the Restatement 2d and the UCC is "honesty".) This construction thus permits the courts to hold that the promisor has implicitly restricted his or her actions, i.e., the promisor is obligated to perform in good faith, and such restriction on the promisor's freedom has been deemed sufficient to keep the promise from being truly illusory.

(1) **Example. [§7.6221]** Joe engages an artist to paint his portrait, promising to pay $500 if he likes it when it is completed. Under modern contract law, this is an enforceable contract, as the court will imply that Joe must exercise his judgement as to whether he likes the painting in good faith, i.e., honestly. With this construction, Joe suffers a detriment, i.e., he has obligated himself to do something he did not have to do — pay $500 if he honestly likes the picture. As such, the contract is supported by consideration.

(2) **Example of *Wood v. Lucy, Lady Duff Gordon*. [§7.6222]** Lady Duff Gordon promised to grant Wood an exclusive right to sell her clothing line for a year in return for his promise to pay her half of any profits he might make from selling them. Under their agreement she provided him with the exclusive rights to sell her clothing line, but he was not specifically obligated to sell (or even to try to sell) any. He only promised to split any profits he **might** make with her. When she sold the rights to sell her clothing to someone else during the year, Wood brought suit to enforce the exclusivity provision. Her defense was that the contract was unenforceable because Wood's promise was illusory in that he promised to do nothing under the contract. **Held:** Wood's promises under the agreement were sufficient consideration to make enforceable Lady Duff Gordon's promise of an exclusive right to sell, for the court implied a duty of good faith, i.e., a duty of "reasonable efforts," on Wood's part. Thus, the court found that Wood impliedly bound himself at least to try and market the clothes (meaning that Lady Duff Gordon could sue him for breach of his duty of good faith performance if he did not use reasonable efforts to sell the clothes), and therefore his promise was a sufficient detriment to Wood to constitute consideration. Note that the rule of this case has now been codified in §2-306(2) of the UCC regarding exclusive dealing contracts (see also §7.624). *Wood v. Lucy, Lady Duff Gordon*, 222 N.Y. 88, 118 N.E. 214 (1917).

 c. **Treatment of Illusory Promises in "Requirements" and "Output" Contracts. [§7.623]** A requirements contract is one in which a buyer agrees to purchase all of a particular good or service it needs from one seller. An output contract is one in which a seller agrees to sell all its output of a particular good or service to one buyer. Such contracts are arguably illusory because, in a requirements contract, the buyer may say it requires none of the goods or services that are the subject of the contract, and thus not be obligated to buy anything. Similarly, in an output contract, the seller may say it will not provide any of the services, or produce any of the goods, that are the subject of the contract, again arguably not obligating itself at all under the contract. Nonetheless, such contracts are common in industry. Accordingly, contract law has determined such agreements to be enforceable by imposing a good faith requirement on the parties to them. That is, UCC §2-306(1) states that under output and requirements contracts, the parties have bargained for "such actual output or requirements **as may occur in good faith**." The rule for non-UCC requirements and output contracts, such as those concerning services, is similar.

(1) Example. [§7.6231] Gas Co. signs contract agreeing to provide any and all pure oxygen needed by Metal Co. in manufacturing steel over the next two years. A year and a half into the contract, Metal Co. decides it is paying too much for the oxygen, and tells Gas Co. if it does not reduce its price, Metal Co. will simply stop producing steel for the next six months, and Gas Co. will have no sales. (At the end of the six months, Metal Co. plans to work its plant overtime to make up for the steel it did not make during this six months period.) Gas Co. refuses to lower its price, Metal Co. stops manufacturing steel, and Gas Co. sues for breach of contract.

Metal Co. may try to defend such a suit by asserting that the parties never had a contract because Metal Co.'s promise was illusory as it never bound itself to do anything. It would argue that it agreed to buy oxygen from Gas Co. only if it needed any, and that it could decide it did not need the gas at any time. However, that defense would fail, for the contract is enforceable because of the implied obligations of good faith. That is, under modern contract law, Metal Co. will be deemed to have bound itself to purchase in good faith all the oxygen it needed. In a case like this, where Metal Co.'s asserted lack of need for oxygen was made for a bad faith reason, the contract will be enforced. Thus, in the subsequent lawsuit, Metal Co. will be deemed to have breached its implied duty of good faith, and Gas Co. can recover damages resulting from Metal Co.'s failure to purchase a good faith amount of oxygen.

(2) Requirements and Output Contracts Generally Have No Implied Floor, but Do Have an Implied Ceiling. [§7.6232] Occasionally, a buyer will enter into a requirements contract and then, due to some event or another, end up not needing to purchase any of the goods or services that are the subject matter of the contract. For example, assume a tire company who supplied tires to Ford enters into a requirements contract with a rubber producer. Just before the requirements contract is supposed to start, the tire company loses its contract with Ford and can find no one else to purchase its products. At that point, it may legitimately have no rubber requirements. Courts and commentators have interpreted UCC §2-306(1) as providing that so long as the buyer acts in good faith in such a circumstance, and really does not need any of the product that was the subject matter of the agreement, he or she is not obligated to purchase any. In other words, there is no implied floor of a minimal order present in requirements contracts.

On the other hand, courts and commentators have interpreted §2-306(1) as containing an implied ceiling on the amount that can be required under a requirements contracts. For example, suppose the tire company mentioned in the previous paragraph all of a sudden got contracts to supply tires not just for Ford, but also for Toyota, General Motors, and Chrysler. As a result, instead of the amount of rubber it might have needed under the contract when signed, it now needs 25 times more. Under §2-306(1), it cannot require the rubber supplier to supply a "disproportionately" large amount of rubber under the contract, even if in good faith it needs more rubber. The rationale for that rule is that it would be unfair to hold the supplier in breach for failure to deliver an unreasonably large amount of product in those circumstances.

The rules are similar for output contracts. That is, if a supplier in good faith produces none of the goods that are the subject matter of the agreement, it may do so without fear of breach, for there is no implied floor as to the amount of goods it must produce. However, it is not entitled to suddenly start producing a "disproportionately" large amount of product and require that the buyer accept it.

d. **Treatment of Illusory Promises in Exclusive Dealing Contracts. [§7.624]** An exclusive dealing contract is one in which one party is given an exclusive right to sell or otherwise deal in goods or services owned or controlled by the other party [UCC §2-306(2)]. Typically, the party given the right to sell or otherwise deal in goods under an exclusive dealing contract agrees to pay the supplier a percentage of what is sold. However, because the seller does not promise to sell anything, but only promises to turn over a fee or a percentage of what **may be** sold, there is at least an argument that such contracts are illusory, for the recipient of the exclusive right to deal has not promised to do anything. As with requirements and output contracts, exclusive dealing contracts are made enforceable by implying a duty of good faith. Under UCC §2-306(2), the recipient of an exclusive right to sell impliedly promises to use his or her "best efforts" to supply or promote the sale of the goods or service. As such, the seller is deemed to make an enforceable promise, and thus exclusive dealing contracts do not fail for lack of consideration.

(1) **Example of *Wood v. Lucy, Lady Duff Gordon*. [§7.6241]** The arrangement between Wood and Lady Duff Gordon was an exclusive dealing agreement and the case is discussed and analyzed in §7.6222.

e. **Treatment of Illusory Promises in Contracts with Expressly Conditional Promises: Such Contracts are Enforceable Unless the Condition is Within the Unfettered Discretion of the Promisor. [§7.625]** When a party's promise under a contract is expressly conditioned upon the occurrence or non-occurrence of a particular event, there is an issue as to whether such a promise may be sufficient consideration under the illusory promise rule. To determine whether a conditional promise is illusory, it is necessary to examine who controls the occurrence of the condition. **If the occurrence of the condition is in the unfettered discretion of the promisor, then the promise is illusory.** However, if the occurrence of the condition is **at all** outside the **unfettered** control of the promisor, the promise is enforceable.

(1) **Example. [§7.6251]** Rich makes an offer to purchase Ed's air conditioner next Friday for $500 "on the condition that the temperature doesn't fall below 70 degrees by then." Ed accepts that offer. They have made an enforceable contract, for Rich's promise is not illusory, since the occurrence of the condition (the temperature falling), is outside of Rich's control.

(2) **Example. [§7.6252]** Bill says to Mary, "I'll pay you $1,000 for your couch on the condition I feel like doing so next week." Even if Mary accepts the offer they will have no enforceable contract. Bill's promise is unenforceable under the illusory promise doctrine, as the occurrence of the condition is within his unfettered discretion.

(3) **Even if the Occurrence of a Condition is to *Some* Extent Within the Discretion of the Promisor, the Promise is Nonetheless Enforceable if any Restriction on the Promisor's Discretion can be Implied. [§7.6253]** If a bargained for contractual promise is expressly made conditional on the occurrence (or non-occurrence) of an event which is dependent only to *some* extent upon the discretion of the promisor, such promise is sufficient consideration to make the

contract enforceable if any limitation on the promisor's exercise of discretion can be found. As with the case of promises which are not expressly conditional, modern contract law has found such limitations on the exercise of a promisor's discretion by implying a duty of good faith on the promisor's performance.

(a) **Example. [§7.6253-1]** Rob agrees to purchase Holly's house for $150,000, "on the condition a loan for purchase of the house can be obtained from Central Bank." It is arguable that Rob has explicitly promised nothing, for while he has agreed to buy the house *if* he gets the loan, he has not promised to apply for the loan. Nevertheless, because the duty of good faith will be implied to him, a court will find that he implicitly promised to try in good faith to obtain a loan. Such restriction on Rob's actions therefore prevents his promise from being deemed illusory, and the contract is valid. Note that implying the duty of good faith to Rob means that if he does not apply for the loan, he could be liable in a contract action for a breach of his implied duty.

(b) **Example: Aleatory Promises. [§7.6253-2]** An aleatory promise is one conditional upon the happening of a reasonably chance event. An aleatory promise is not illusory because, by definition, the occurrence of the event is not within the complete unfettered discretion of the promisor. For example, if Sid promises Sally that he will share half of any future lottery winnings with her if she will pay him $1,000 today, such promise will be enforceable, assuming Sally agrees to it, so long as the promise was bargained for and not made under duress, influence, or the like [Restatement 2d §76, Com. c].

f. **Special Illusory Promise Problems Regarding Termination-At-Will Clauses. [§7.626]** A contract that is terminable at will presents illusory promise issues. For example, assume that Rex's Pizza House places an order with Sandy's Cheese Company for 100 pounds of cheese per week for the next year, but Rex reserves the right "to terminate at any time." It is arguable that Rex has made an illusory promise, i.e., he has merely said, "I promise to order from you unless I change my mind." The treatment of such situations has changed over time.

(1) **Traditional Rule: Contracts with Termination-at-Will Clauses Illusory and hence Unenforceable. [§7.6261]** At common law, a termination-at-will clause rendered a contract unenforceable under the illusory promise doctrine.

(2) **Modern Rule: Contracts with Termination-At-Will Clauses Probably Enforceable. [§7.6262]** Today most courts hold that even under a termination-at-will clause, the party terminating the contract must give notice to the other. Under this theory, the fact that the terminating party must give notice is itself a sufficient detriment, i.e., a sufficient restriction on the promisor's actions, so as to render the promise enforceable. In other words, the requirement that the promisee give notice is a sufficient bargained for restriction on the promisee's actions to constitute consideration. Note that if there had been a specified notice period, e.g., "I will hire you for a one year period, but either of us can terminate this contract upon 30 days notice," there is no consideration problem because the promisor has at least bound himself or herself to pay the employee for at least 30 days.

(3) **The UCC Approach to Terminable-At-Will Contracts: The Reasonable Notification Requirement Avoids Illusory Promise Issues. [§7.6263]** Under UCC §2-309(3), in order to terminate a contract validly, termination must take place either upon the happening of an agreed event or after reasonable notification is

received. Thus, because reasonable notice must be given before termination is effective is an *explicit* requirement under the UCC, termination-at-will clauses in contracts governed by the Code do not present illusory promise issues.

3. **THE PRE-EXISTING DUTY RULE. [§7.63]** If a promisor is already under a duty to take some sort of action, a reaffirmance of his or her intention to take that same action is generally not consideration, even if the reaffirmance is bargained for and given in response to a new promise. That is, if the promisee is under a pre-existing duty to do something, a subsequent promise to do that same thing cannot be part of a valid bargained for exchange [Restatement 2d §73].

   a. **Example. [§7.631]** Police officer investigates a residential burglary. Homeowner promises to pay officer $1,000 if officer gets the homeowner's stereo back to him in a week. Even if officer performs such action, there is no consideration for the promise to pay, because the officer was under a pre-existing duty as a public official to recover stolen property and return it to its true owner. This is true even if the parties can establish that the promise of the $1,000 payment was bargained for, and even if the officer can establish she took action because of the promise and worked especially hard to try to find homeowner's stereo. Some commentators have suggested that this doctrine is not really a consideration rule, but rather is an expression of a public policy against the wealthy being able to offer additional compensation to public servants to get better service when public servants should seek to solve all citizens' problems with equal diligence regardless of a particular citizen's wealth.

   b. **REVIEW PROBLEM. [§7.632] Sam agreed to type Laura's Ph.D. thesis for $500. A week before it is due, when it would be virtually impossible to find someone else to type it, Sam demands another $300 to finish, which Laura reluctantly agrees to pay. Question: Is Laura's promise enforceable?**

      Answer: No. Laura's promise to pay the extra $300 is unenforceable by Sam, for Sam was under a pre-existing duty to type the thesis for $500. That is, if Laura does not pay it, and Sam tries to sue her for breach if she only pays him $500, Sam will lose, for there is no consideration to support Laura's promise to pay the extra $300. She does have to pay him the originally agreed to $500, however.

   c. **Special Rules Regarding Consideration Necessary for Contract Modification. [§7.633]** Both the Restatement and the UCC have adopted special rules regarding whether extra consideration is necessary for contract modification. Under UCC §2-209(1), no consideration is needed in order for the parties to make a valid modification of their contract (although other requirements, such as the Statute of Frauds, must be met). Similarly, under §89 of the Restatement 2d, the parties can make an enforceable modification to any executory, i.e., unperformed, portion of a contract without consideration as long as the modification is fair, equitable, and either: (a) is made because of circumstances unanticipated at the time the contract was made; or (b) has induced reliance by a party to the agreement (see §§26.1; 26.2).

   d. **Special Rules Regarding Consideration in Accords and Substituted Contracts. [§7.634]** Often parties to a contract get into a dispute as to what, if anything, is owed under it. In the great majority of such cases, they reach a settlement whereby the creditor agrees not to sue (or continue a suit) to collect the full debt in return for an immediate payment by the debtor of a percentage of what is claimed. This kind of agreement, i.e., where the parties attempt to discharge their obligations under one contract by entering into a new one, is a form of accord or substituted contract (see Chapter Twenty-Four). To be enforceable, this new contract must be formed by a valid offer, a valid acceptance, and supported by valid consideration. This last element sometimes poses problems because it is arguable that the debtor's promise of part payment of the lesser sum is insufficient consideration to support the creditor's promise to surrender the lawsuit. That is, if the debtor was already under a pre-existing duty to pay the entire debt, he or she did not promise anything new by agreeing to settle the case and pay only a percentage of the debt. However, if parties in a dispute under a contract could not enter into enforceable settlement agreements, no debtor would ever settle a claim, for there would be no enforceable benefit in doing so. Accordingly, traditional contract law adopted the following rule:

An agreement to surrender a claim under a contract in return for part payment of that claim is almost always supported by valid consideration.

It is only **not** supported by valid consideration when all three of the following are present:

(1) the claim is for a liquidated (i.e., certain) amount;

(2) there is no *bona fide* dispute over whether the debtor owes it; **and**

(3) the creditor does not receive any benefit in addition to those he or she is due under the contract as a result of the agreement to compromise the claim.

However, as explained in §7.635, it appears that under both the Restatement and the UCC, even these elements need not be proven, and any valid settlement of a claim arising from a breach of contract is enforceable despite the absence of consideration. Nevertheless, the traditional contract rules are discussed here and in the following sections since they are usually covered in some detail in first year contracts courses.

(1) **Example of *Foakes v. Beer*.** [§7.6341] On a certain date, Dr. Foakes was obligated to repay Ms. Beer £2,090. If he did not pay on the date their contract provided, he would owe her interest on the principal until the entire debt was repaid. Dr. Foakes claimed he could not pay on the due date, and the parties entered into a settlement whereby Dr. Foakes would pay £500 on the due date, with the remainder of the principal to be paid on an agreed schedule. In return, Ms. Beer agreed to waive the interest. Dr. Foakes paid according to the schedule, and after the last payment was made, Ms. Beer nevertheless sued him for the interest owing under the original debt. **Held:** Dr. Foakes was still obligated to pay the interest, for his promise to pay a portion of what he already owed was insufficient consideration to make the settlement enforceable. *Foakes v. Beer*, L.R. 9 App. Cas. 605 (H.L. 1884).

Note that although a few states have rejected *Foakes*, the case would come out the same way under the more modern rule given above in §7.634. That is: (a) the settlement was for a **liquidated amount** (£2,090); (b) there was **no bona fide dispute** about whether Dr. Foakes owed the money (both Dr. Foakes and Ms. Beer agreed he did); and (c) Ms. Beer received **no additional benefit** from the settlement that she was not already entitled to under the original contract (payment of the debt). Dr. Foakes would, of course, argue that Ms. Beer did receive an additional benefit, i.e., she would have gotten nothing on the due date in the absence of the settlement agreement, and would have had to sue for the principal, incurring delay, attorneys' fees, etc. However, these "benefits" to Ms. Beer are insufficient under contract law to constitute consideration, for the contract law looks at the issue more simply, i.e., before the due date Dr. Foakes promised to pay £2,090 plus interest; after the new agreement Dr. Foakes, promised only to pay

£2,090. As nothing new was added in the settlement that benefitted Ms. Beer, no consideration was present for Dr. Foakes only reaffirmed what he had a pre-existing duty to do.

(2) **Example. [§7.6342]** Creditor claims she is owed $6,000 for interior decorating work done on debtor's home. Debtor, in good faith, questions the quality of the work and believes it only to be worth $5,000. The parties enter into a settlement agreement whereby debtor promises to pay $5,500 in return for creditor's promise to surrender the claim. As this is a good faith settlement of: (a) **a bona fide dispute** of (b) an **unliquidated debt**, where (c) **both parties receive additional benefits** they might not otherwise have received under the original contract, the mutual promises are sufficient consideration for each other to make the settlement agreement enforceable.

e. **Modern View: Accords and Substituted Contracts Likely Valid Even Without Consideration. [§7.635]** Under §277(1) of the Restatement 2d, and under UCC §1-107, a written settlement of a claim arising out of a breach of contract is enforceable even without consideration. Thus, if the parties to an agreement enter into a written accord or substituted contract to settle a claim **arising from a breach**, then the subsequent contract need not be supported by consideration to be enforceable (see also §24.4). Note that the UCC provision cited above, §1-107, is an Article 1, not Article 2, provision. Thus, it applies to more than just contracts for the sale of goods (see §34.1).

4. **PROMISES TO PAY DEBTS MADE UNENFORCEABLE UNDER THE STATUTE OF LIMITATIONS OR BY BANKRUPTCY. [§7.64]** A valid obligation owing under a contract can become unenforceable either because the statute of limitations governing the claim has run, or because the debtor has discharged the obligation in bankruptcy. Despite the unenforceability of the debt, debtors will sometimes promise to "make good" the debt out of a moral obligation. Ordinarily, such promises would be deemed unenforceable under the moral consideration or gift promise rules (see §7.531 et seq. and §7.512 et seq.).

However, the Restatement 2d has drafted special rules governing these situations:

If the debtor acknowledges that he or she still owes a debt, despite the running of the statute of limitations, or if the debtor promises not to assert the statute of limitations as a defense in a subsequent collection suit, such promises are enforceable against the debtor [Restatement 2d §82].

In addition, if a debtor expressly promises to pay all or part of a contractual debt that is discharged in bankruptcy, or is dischargeable in bankruptcy proceedings begun before the promise was made, that promise is binding against the debtor [Restatement 2d §83].

Most states have adopted the rule of §82, but require that such promises be **in writing** to be effective. Note that under this provision, it is only the *new* promise to pay that is enforceable, not the original debt.

a. **Example. [§7.641]** Jack borrows $10,000 from Joy, but fails to pay it back. The statute of limitations expires, and Jack tells Joy he's sorry, and promises that he will pay her at least $7,500 by the next January 31. If Jack doesn't pay anything by the following January 31, Joy may only sue him for $7,500 — the value of the newer promise — and not $10,000 — the value of the original debt.

5. **SHAM CONSIDERATION IS NOT EFFECTIVE CONSIDERATION. [§7.65]** Sham consideration is a return promise or performance which is not bargained for and is, in truth, given in an attempt to make a gift promise enforceable (see §7.612). While courts are reluctant to look into the purpose for which consideration was given and generally will uphold a bargain if there is any reasonable way to do so, **when it is apparent that the nature of the transaction is a gift, and that the consideration is a pretense to disguise the gift, the resulting contract will not be enforceable due to a lack of consideration.**

6. **PURPORTED, BUT UNPERFORMED, CONSIDERATION IS NOT EFFECTIVE CONSIDERATION. [§7.66]** Purported consideration is consideration that is intended to have taken place in exchange for a promise, but which in fact never occurred. For example, a signed document may say "For $500 received from buyer, I hereby sell to him my antique desk." If the $500 is never actually paid, the seller can sue the buyer for breach, regardless of the fact that the "contract" says the $500 was paid. Similarly, if the $500 is never paid, the buyer cannot seek to enforce the seller to deliver the desk because purported consideration is not sufficient to make a promise enforceable.

   a. **Exception: Purported Consideration Sufficient for Option Contracts. [§7.661]** Under §87 of the Restatement 2d, purported consideration is sufficient to make effective the promises made in an option contract, as long as the offer for the option contract is in writing, is signed by the offeror, and proposes a fair exchange [Restatement 2d §87, Com. c], (see §4.4212).

   Hence, if a written option contract recites that for $20 received, seller gives buyer an option to purchase her car for $5,000 within 30 days, the buyer is obligated to sell the car to the buyer if he tenders the $5,000 within 30 days, even if the buyer never paid the original $20.

7. **VOIDABLE PROMISES CAN SERVE AS VALID CONSIDERATION. [§7.67]** If a party makes a promise that is voidable, e.g., because the promisor is a minor and lacks capacity, because the promise violates the Statue of Frauds, etc., the promise may still act as valid consideration for the contract [Restatement 2d §78; See Part VI of this Outline for a listing of those things that make a contract voidable.].

   a. **Example. [§7.671]** Kevin, a 15 year old, promises to pay $300 for Rebecca's stereo. The contract may be voidable by Kevin because of his age, but if he wishes to enforce it, his voidable promise nevertheless serves as valid consideration for Rebecca's promise to tender the stereo.

CHAPTER EIGHT: PROMISSORY ESTOPPEL AND THE SEAL

A. THE PROMISSORY ESTOPPEL DOCTRINE. [§8.0] The doctrine of promissory estoppel is based on the premise that where the promises of one party have led the other to justifiably and reasonably rely on those promises being carried out, the promises should be enforced even if they were only gratuitous or not otherwise supported by consideration. In essence, the doctrine estops (prevents) a party from denying reasonable obligations foreseeably resulting from reliance on his or her promise, and estops a party from being able to deny liability on the technical ground that no "bargained for exchange" resulted upon the acceptance of an offer. At its heart, promissory estoppel is a moral doctrine that makes enforceable promises our sense of justice suggests should be enforced, even though they are not supported by consideration.

B. PROMISSORY ESTOPPEL IS NOT A "SUBSTITUTE" FOR CONSIDERATION. [§8.1] It is often said that promissory estoppel is a "complete substitute" for consideration, i.e., that it will "step in" when a deserving contract is held unenforceable due to a lack of consideration and render that contract enforceable. This is not technically true. First, recovery under a promissory estoppel theory is not a recovery based on "contract." Rather, it is a recovery based on a mixture of equitable and tort law principles. Second, even when promissory estoppel applies to a promise, it does not automatically make that promise fully enforceable. Rather, promises governed by promissory estoppel are only enforceable to the extent that "justice requires," which may fall short of full enforceability (see §8.4). Third, promissory estoppel does more than make enforceable gratuitous promises exchanged as "offers" and "acceptances." For example, it also serves to make some offers irrevocable (see §§8.34 and 8.35), and to enforce some promises made during preliminary negotiations which do not rise to the level of offers (see §8.342). Note, however, that some cases have held promissory estoppel to be a species of consideration (see e.g., *Feinberg v. Pfeifer*, 322 S.W. 2d 163 (Mo. App. 1959), Case Squibs Section, but this idea has not been generally adopted).

C. ELEMENTS OF PROMISSORY ESTOPPEL UNDER THE SECOND RESTATEMENT. [§8.2] Section 90 of the Restatement 2d states that a promise is binding if:

> (a) **in making the promise the promisor should reasonably expect to induce action or forbearance on the part of the promisee;**
>
> (b) **the promise does in fact induce foreseeable action or forbearance by the promisee; and**
>
> (c) **injustice can be avoided only by enforcement of the promise.**

If these criteria are met, the promise may be enforced, but only to the extent "justice requires."

1. EXAMPLE OF *RICKETTS V. SCOTHORN*. [§8.21] Grandfather is upset to find granddaughter working and gives her a $2,000 promissory note, redeemable on demand, telling her the note will to see to it that she will never have to work to survive. Granddaughter quits work immediately, but did not attempt to redeem promissory note until several years later, after grandfather had died. His executors refused to pay. **Held:** The promise to pay the $2,000 is enforceable under a promissory estoppel theory. The promise could not be upheld under a consideration theory, for the grandfather's promise to pay was clearly a gift promise. However, because it was a promise that: (a) reasonably could be expected to induce action on the part of the granddaughter in reliance on it (quitting her job); (b) actually did induce such action (she did quit); and (c) would be unjust not to enforce under the circumstances, the promise was enforceable under promissory estoppel to the extent justice requires. In this case, justice required full enforcement of the promise. (See Case Squibs section, *Ricketts v. Scothorn.*)

2. **DIFFERENCE BETWEEN PROMISSORY ESTOPPEL UNDER THE FIRST AND SECOND RESTATEMENT OF CONTRACTS. [§8.22]** Most contracts professors ask their students to compare the differences between §90 the Restatement (First), and §90 of the Restatement (Second). The differences are these:

(1) The Restatement (First) required that the reliance by the promisee be actual, reasonable, and "of a definite and substantial character." The Restatement (Second) only requires the reliance to be actual and reasonable for promissory estoppel to apply;

(2) As written, the First Restatement states that if promissory estoppel applies to a promise, it will be enforced *in its entirety,* **regardless of whether the promisee relied completely on the promise or not.** For example, if Grandfather tells adult Granddaughter to go out and buy a $1,000 stereo and he will pay for it, and Granddaughter buys only a $750 stereo, by a strict reading of its terms the Restatement (First) would enforce the promise entirely and Grandfather would have to pay $1,000 to Granddaughter. While some commentators have questioned whether that is what §90 of the First Restatement truly meant, it is what Professor Williston, the reporter for the First Restatement says he intended such and it is what the section, on its face, says. Section 90 of the Restatement (Second) only enforces such promises to the extent justice requires, and so in the Grandfather/ Granddaughter example, the Grandfather's promise would only be enforceable to $750 (see §8.4 for a further discussion of this issue); and

(3) The First Restatement did not make any special provision for promises to make donations to charities (or to marriage settlements), whereas the Restatement (Second) has §90(2), which states that such promises are binding even without any reliance by the promisee.

D. **TYPES OF PROMISES ENFORCEABLE UNDER PROMISSORY ESTOPPEL. [§8.3]**

1. **GIFT PROMISES. [§8.31]** By far, the most common types of promises supported by promissory estoppel are gratuitous or gift promises (see §7.51). Hence, if a gift promise meets the requirements of §90, it will be enforceable to the extent justice allows.

2. **ORAL PROMISES TO CONVEY LAND. [§8.32]** If Paul makes an un-bargained for, oral promise to convey Blackacre to Dan, Dan relies on the promise by moving onto the land, making improvements, etc., and Dan is reasonable in believing he is entitled to make these improvements, most courts will hold that the promise to convey is binding against Paul under a promissory estoppel theory [Restatement 2d §§90, 139]. Whether Dan will get specific performance of the promise or simply be recompensed for his work on the land will depend on what "justice requires" given all the circumstances (see §4.4135-2 and §8.4). Note that in this type of case the promissory estoppel doctrine not only overcomes a "no consideration" defense, but also overcomes a Statute of Frauds defense as well (see §9.2), thereby making enforceable an oral promise to convey an interest in land.

3. **CHARITABLE SUBSCRIPTIONS. [§8.33]** The rule regarding the enforceability of promises to donate to a charity is different from the rules governing most promissory estoppel situations. Under §90(2) of the Restatement 2d, **a pledge to a charity is enforceable even without proof that the promise induced any reliance whatsoever by the organization.**

   a. **Example. [§8.331]** Ellen calls a March of Dimes telethon and pledges $100. The promise is enforceable by the March of Dimes under §90(2) of the Restatement 2d, even though it was gratuitous (and thus without consideration) and even if the March of Dimes did not take any action in reliance on Ellen's promise.

4. **OFFERS THAT INDUCE FORESEEABLE RELIANCE OF A SUBSTANTIAL NATURE BECOME IRREVOCABLE. [§8.34]** Under §87(2) of the Restatement 2d, promissory estoppel will also serve to make any other type of offer irrevocable (at least to the extent necessary to avoid injustice) if:

   (a) **the offeror should reasonably and foreseeably expect the offeree to undertake substantial action in reliance on the offer;** and

   (b) **the offer actually does induce that reliance.**

   a. **Example. [§8.341]** Food Co. makes an offer to Farmer promising her that it is willing to buy all the carrots Farmer grows this season at a fixed price. Food Co. tells Farmer she may think about the offer for a month and need not accept before then. Farmer immediately purchases carrot seed and within two weeks has dedicated a substantial portion of her farm to growing carrots. At this point, Food Co.'s offer is irrevocable until the end of the month, since Food Co. should reasonably have expected Farmer to rely on the offer to a substantial degree, and because Farmer has, in fact, relied on Food Company's promise.

   b. **Offers by Sub-Contractors. [§8.342]** The most common application of the rule in §87(2) of the Restatement 2d is in dealings between general contractors and subcontractors. To fully appreciate the applicability of §87(2) to this kind of situation, some understanding of the general contractor/subcontractor relationship is necessary.

   In the construction industry, general contractors are awarded contracts by developers for constructing large projects. General contractors almost never do all the work on a large project by themselves. Thus, in preparing their bids to submit to the developer, general contractors ("general") solicit offers for various parts of the projects from subcontractors, e.g., the same or different subcontractors ("subs") may bid (i.e., make offers) to do the paving work, the electrical work, etc. The general will then use the subs' bids in determining its own price for the entire project. Occasionally a sub will change its mind about its bid after the general has already relied on it by using it as part of the general's bid to the developer, but before the general has formally "accepted" the sub's bid. (That is, although a general will use the sub's bid in making its bid to the developer, it will not accept the sub's offer until the developer has accepted the general's bid to develop the entire project. The reason is that a general will not want to commit to paying the sub unless the general is awarded the development contract). Under normal formation rules, an offer such as the one made by the sub is freely revocable until the time of acceptance (see §4.41 et seq.). However, under §87(2), **promissory estoppel makes the promisor's (i.e., the subcontractor's) offer irrevocable until the general contractor has a reasonable chance to accept.** Typically, that "reasonable time" extends to a day or two after the developer has awarded the bid to the general. That is, within the construction industry, a general using a sub's bid to develop its own bid is considered reasonable, foreseeable, and an act of substantial reliance. As such, it is deemed unjust to allow the subcontractor to revoke the offer once it has been communicated to the general (see the discussion of *Drennan v. Star Paving*, §4.4135-1).

5. **ACTIONS TAKEN IN RELIANCE ON PROMISES MADE IN PRELIMINARY NEGOTIATIONS. [§8.35]** Some courts (although certainly not all) have held that a rather vague promise, of the type typically found in preliminary negotiations, may be enforceable to some extent if reliance on that promise was both foreseeable and reasonable.

 a. **Example of *Hoffman v. Red Owl Stores*. [§8.351]** Red Owl franchises supermarkets. Its representative promised Hoffman that he would be awarded a franchise if he gained the necessary experience and invested $18,000. Hoffman started a two year quest to gain the necessary experience by quitting his then-present job, moving to another city to go to work in another grocery store, borrowing $18,000 from a relative, etc. At the end of the two years, Red Owl stated the $18,000 franchise could not be paid with borrowed money and refused to award Hoffman a franchise. **Held:** No contract existed because there was no offer from Red Owl. While Hoffman may have been promised a franchise, there were simply too many details left open as to the terms of that franchise to call it an offer, e.g. where the store was to be located, how soon he could operate it, etc. At most, the promise was part of a preliminary negotiation. Nevertheless, because Red Owl should have foreseen Hoffman would have relied on the promise to his detriment, and because Hoffman did in fact rely on the promise, it would now be unjust not to enforce the promise to some degree. Thus, under a promissory estoppel theory, Hoffman could recover the out of pocket costs he spent in reliance on the promise. *Hoffman v. Red Owl Stores*, 26 Wis.2d 683, 133 N.W.2d 267 (1965).

 Note that this case also sets forth the rather controversial doctrine that the parties owe a duty of good faith to each other not only in the performance and enforcement of the contract, but also during its **negotiation**. As such, it extends dramatically and (almost) uniquely the obligation of good faith set forth in the Restatement 2d §205 and UCC §1-203.

E. **REMEDIES WHEN A PROMISE IS ENFORCED UNDER PROMISSORY ESTOPPEL. [§8.4]** When a promise is made enforceable under promissory estoppel, it is not necessarily enforceable to its full extent. Rather, when a party breaches a promise that is made enforceable under promissory estoppel, "the remedy granted for breach may be limited as justice allows." Usually, the promisee is entitled to recover his or her full expectation interest, i.e., the full amount to which he or she would have been entitled had the contract gone forward, but where the expectation interest is greatly disproportionate to the promisee's actual reliance, or where the circumstances make it unjust (or impossible) to award the complete expectation interest, a promisee is only entitled to his or her reliance damages (see §§31.3 and 31.5).

1. **EXAMPLE. [§8.41]** A famous hypothetical illustrating this principle assumes that a well dressed, obviously wealthy woman becomes concerned about a man who is not warmly dressed and is standing outside during a snow flurry. The woman tells the man to go into the clothing store down the street and to buy a $300 coat to keep him warm and that she will pay for it. The man goes into the store and buys a coat for $200. The question is, should he be entitled to $200 from the woman (the value of his out-of-pocket reliance), or $300 (the value of the full expectation interest). Although Professor Williston disagreed, most commentators hold that in these circumstances justice requires that enforcement of the promise should be limited so that only the man's actual reliance is compensable.

2. **EXAMPLE OF** *HOFFMAN V. RED OWL STORES.* [§8.42] (The facts of *Hoffman* are given in §8.351.) It was impossible to award Hoffman any expectation damages because it was impossible to ascertain what profits, if any, he would have made running the grocery store. Given the uncertainty of the expectation interest, it was proper to award him his reliance damages.

F. **EXAM APPROACH TO PROMISSORY ESTOPPEL PROBLEMS.** [§8.5] Contracts professors are usually wary of students relying too heavily on promissory estoppel to enforce promises, and thereby relying too little on the intricacies of consideration when writing exam answers. In theory, many (if not most) of the promises supported by consideration could just as easily be supported by promissory estoppel, i.e., most of the time, it is reasonable to foresee that a bargained for promise will be relied upon by the other party, and usually it is actually relied upon as well. Given such action, it typically would be unjust not to enforce the promise. However, as Justice Holmes once said, "[a] pervasive use of promissory estoppel would cut up the doctrine of consideration by the roots." Accordingly, in your analysis of formation issues for your essay tests, you should **first** determine whether a promise can be supported by consideration. If it can, your analysis should proceed from there. It is only when the promise is gratuitous, or for some other reason cannot meet the requirements of consideration, that you should examine whether the promise can be enforced by promissory estoppel.

G. **THE COMMON LAW SEAL.** [§8.6] At common law, any promise contained in a document delivered with the promisor's seal (i.e., a wax impression, usually formed by pressing a signet ring or the like into molten wax dripped onto the document) was binding even in the absence of consideration. However, the UCC in §2-203, has formally declared seals to be inoperative, and most states have followed suit in non-UCC transactions as well. However, §95 of the Restatement 2d still permits a sealed document to be enforced without consideration so long as the document is "delivered," and so long as the promisor and promisee are either named or identifiably described in the document. Despite this provision, the seal as a substitute for consideration is, for the most part, a dead issue.

VI. VOIDABLE AND VOID AGREEMENTS

INTRODUCTORY NOTE ON THE CONCEPTS OF VOID AND VOIDABLE AGREE-MENTS: An agreement may be formed by a valid offer with a matching acceptance and be supported by valid consideration, yet nonetheless still be unenforceable. This can happen if the agreement is "voidable" by a party, or is "void" from the beginning (void *ab initio*).

If a contract is voidable by a party, that party holds the option either to enforce it, or to disaffirm (avoid) it, i.e., terminate the contract without contractual liability. Another way to look at it is that the party who has the option to disaffirm the contract has a defense to his or her non-performance. That is, the party with the disaffirmance option can fail to perform what he or she promised in the contract, and assert the reason allowing the voidability as a defense in a subsequent breach action brought by the other party.

If a contract is "void," a party cannot enforce it even if he or she wishes, for a "void" contract has no legal effect.

A contract is **VOIDABLE** if:

(a) it does not satisfy the requirements of the **Statute of Frauds** (discussed in Chapter Nine);

(b) one of the parties to the agreement is **without the capacity to contract** (discussed in Chapter Ten);

(c) it is entered into under **mistake** (discussed in Chapter Eleven);

(d) one of the parties entered the contract under **duress by improper threat** (discussed in Chapter Twelve);

(e) one party **unduly influenced the other** into entering into the contract (discussed in Chapter Thirteen);

(f) it was entered into by means of **fraud as to the inducement** (discussed in Chapter Fourteen); or

(g) one or more of its terms is **unconscionable** (discussed in Chapter Fifteen).

A contract is "**VOID**" if:

(a) it is entered into **under duress by physical force** (discussed in §12.1);

(b) one party enters into it under a **fraudulent misrepresentation as to the very nature of the document itself (fraud in the *factum*)** (discussed in §14.3); or

(c) it calls for a performance that is **illegal, or otherwise violates public policy** (discussed in Chapter Sixteen).

CHAPTER NINE: THE STATUTE OF FRAUDS

A. THE STATUTE OF FRAUDS DOCTRINE. [§9.0] The Statute of Frauds does nothing more than evidence a choice to enforce written, rather than oral, agreements in certain situations. It states that in some cases, and under some circumstances, the legal system will enforce promises made in a contract *only* if they are in writing. Sometimes this serves a good purpose as the Statute of Frauds can prevent fraudulent practices. For example, suppose Phil and Georgia never entered into contract. Nevertheless, assume Phil tries to sue her for "breach" of contract anyway, hoping to win a nuisance settlement. The Statute of Frauds, if applicable and not satisfied, will provide Georgia with a complete defense to the suit for the "contract" was not in writing.

However, sometimes the operation of the Statute serves an unjust purpose as it can serve to protect fraudulent practices. For example, suppose Phil and Georgia actually did enter into an oral contract, that Georgia does not perform, and that Phil sues her for breach. The Statute of Frauds, if applicable and not satisfied, would still provide Georgia with a complete defense to the action. It is partly for this latter reason that Parliament (which passed the original Statute in 1677) repealed most parts of the Statute in 1954, so that it does not apply to most kinds of contracts in England any longer.

1. **PURPOSES OF THE STATUTE. [§9.01]** By requiring a signed writing in order to make a contract enforceable, the Statute of Frauds is said to serve several purposes:

   (1) to provide evidence that the parties truly entered into a contract;

   (2) to provide a written record of what they agreed to, rather than having to trust the memories of the parties as to what the terms of the contract were; and

   (3) to make unsophisticated parties aware that they are entering into an agreement with legal ramifications, i.e., when a party has to "sign" something it appears more formal, and thus more significant, than just making an oral promise.

2. **EFFECT OF STATUTE APPLYING. [§9.02]** Students spend a lot of time learning what contracts are covered by the Statute (see §9.1) and what it takes to satisfy a contract that is covered by the Statute (see, e.g., §9.23). Sometimes, however, the exact effect of the Statute gets overlooked.

Probably the best way to think of the Statute is that, when it applies and is not satisfied, it gives a party a defense to a breach of contract lawsuit. For example, assume that Janet orally contracts with Bob to sell him her stereo for $2,000. Their contract is never reduced to writing. This kind of contract is subject to the Statute (see §9.6 et seq.), and thus must be in writing to be enforceable. Now assume that Janet never delivers the stereo. Bob sues her for breach. The Statute, because it applies and is not satisfied, provides Janet with a defense to the breach action. She did not perform what she promised, but her non-performance is excused, because she has a legally recognized *defense* — namely the applicability of the Statute.

Note that the Statute has *nothing whatsoever* to do with contract formation. For example, let's assume that Bob owes Janet $2,000, and gives her a check for that amount to pay off the loan. However, Bob later claims the check was for Janet's stereo, and sues her for breach for failing to deliver the stereo. Although the Statute applies to this transaction, it has been satisfied by Bob's payment of the check to Janet, even though it was for another purpose (see §9.643). However, the fact that the Statute is satisfied does not mean that

Janet will lose the breach of contract suit. All it means is that she has lost one defense to that suit. She still has others, e.g., that she never entered into the agreement to sell her stereo in the first place. So the fact that the Statute is satisfied does not mean that, somehow, a contract is formed where one never existed. Once again, all it means is that a single defense — the defense of the Statute — is unavailable in that action. [See §§9.632; 9.644]

B. **MAJOR TYPES OF CASES COVERED BY THE STATUTE. [§9.1]** While contract law refers to a "Statute of Frauds," in fact there is not a single clause or provision that governs all the issues dealt with in this chapter. (Nevertheless, for convenience's sake, this outline will go along with the majority and discuss the doctrine as "the Statute.") However, it is more accurate to think of the Statute as a general doctrine that affects five major types of contracts:

(1) **Contracts for the transfer of an interest in land** (see §9.2);

(2) **Contracts which, by their terms, cannot be performed within a year** (see §9.3);

(3) **Contracts made in consideration of marriage** (see §9.4);

(4) **Contracts where one party agrees to act as a surety for another** (see §9.5); and

(5) **Contracts for the sale of goods for $500 or more** (see §9.6).

(See §9.10 for a mnemonic to summarize these principles.)

1. **NOMENCLATURE UNDER THE STATUTE OF FRAUDS DOCTRINE. [§9.11]** Often the hardest part of mastering the Statute of Frauds is learning the terminology. The following paragraph explains most of the seemingly tricky word choices.

If a contract must be in writing to be enforceable, the contract is said to be "within the Statute." If it can be enforced even though oral, it is said to be "without the Statute" or, more often, "outside the Statute." A contract can be outside the Statute either because no part of the Statute applies to it, or because a particular exception to a rule takes the contract outside the Statute. If a contract is within the Statute, then it will only be enforced if the Statute is "satisfied," usually by some sort of signed writing. When the contract is within the Statute and a party fails to satisfy the Statute (e.g., because that party has not signed a writing), then any oral promises made by that party are unenforceable by the other.

C. **TYPE ONE: CONTRACTS FOR THE TRANSFER OF AN INTEREST IN LAND. [§9.2]** In general, **any contract for the transfer of an interest in land, other than a license, must be in writing to be enforceable** [Restatement 2d §125].

1. **THE TRANSFER OF VIRTUALLY ALL INTERESTS IN LAND, EXCEPT LICENSES, ARE COVERED BY THE STATUTE. [§9.21]** The scope of the term "interests in land," the transfer of which must be in writing to be enforceable, is quite broad. Essentially, it includes any interest in real property other than licenses, which are only permissive uses of property. Thus agreements to transfer mortgages, leases, easements, future interests, rights under restrictive covenants, or any other legal or equitable interest in land, except licenses, are within the Statute [Restatement 2d §127]. Note however, that some states provide that short-term leases, generally those for less than a year, do not need to be in writing to be enforceable, and also that if a transfer of a mortgage is really the transfer of a debt secured by a mortgage, such transfer is outside the Statute.

Sum & Substance QUICK REVIEW of Contracts

a. **"Transfer of Interest in Land" Includes Option Contracts. [§9.211]** An option contract regarding the sale of land must be in writing in order to be enforceable. Note that offers alone, whether offers for option contracts or offers for some other transfer of land, need not be in writing to be effective **offers**. It is only the resulting **contract** that must be in writing to be enforceable.

b. **Contracts for the Transfer of Things Attached to Realty Like Crops, Minerals, Timber, Structures and the Like. [§9.212]** A question has arisen as to whether the term "interest in land" as used in the Statute includes items which may be attached to land when they are sold, but are capable of being severed and sold by themselves. Under UCC §2-107(2), the sale of **growing crops, timber to be cut, or any other object capable of being severed without material harm to the land should be treated as a sale of goods and not a transfer of interest in land, but only if the crops, timber, etc. are in fact sold separately, apart from the land.** In other words, if a buyer contracts for the wheat presently growing on a farm, the contract is to be treated as a sale of goods. If the contract is for the sale of land with wheat on it, it should be treated as a transfer of an interest in land.

Under UCC §2-107(1), a "sale of **minerals or the like (including oil and gas) or of a structure . . . to be removed from realty is a contract sale of goods . . . if they are to be severed by the seller,**" but should be considered as a transfer of an interest in land if they are to be removed by the buyer. In other words, a contract for coal located on someone's property should be treated as a contract for the sale of goods if the seller is to remove the coal, but as a sale of land if the buyer is to remove it. (See also §34.4.)

Note that labelling a transaction as a sale of "goods," as opposed to "land," does not automatically mean it does not have to satisfy the Statute of Frauds. Section 9.6 et seq. sets forth the requirements for the Statute of Frauds as applied to the sale of goods. Classifying a transaction as one of goods and not of land means only that the transaction need not satisfy the "transfer of interests in land" portion of the Statute, but it still may have to satisfy other parts of the Statute to be enforceable.

c. **Promises to Pay in Return for a Present Conveyance Are Outside the Statute. [9.213]** If a purchaser makes a promise to pay in the future in exchange for the present transfer of an interest in land, **the executory promise to pay may be enforced even if it is oral.** This is because all that is unperformed under the contract is the buyer's obligation to pay money, and not the seller's obligation to transfer a land interest. As such, the agreement at this point is outside the Statute. However, the opposite is not true. A contract whereby the purchaser pays presently in return for the seller's promise to transfer land in the future is within the Statute, for there remains an obligation to transfer land, and not just an obligation to pay money. Thus, in such a case the unperformed promise to transfer land must be in writing to be enforceable [Restatement 2d §125, Com. e].

2. **REASONABLE RELIANCE BY THE PURCHASER MAKES A PROMISE TO TRANSFER AN INTEREST IN LAND ENFORCEABLE. [§9.22]** An oral contract to transfer an interest in land is enforceable if the purchaser can establish that:

   (a) he or she has relied on the promise of the seller to sell the property, and on the continuing assent of the seller to sell the property;

   (b) such reliance was foreseeable and reasonable; and

(c) injustice can only be avoided by enforcing the promised transfer [Restatement 2d §§90, 129].

Whether the buyer will be able to obtain specific performance or is limited to reliance damages depends on the circumstances surrounding the transaction and what justice requires.

    a. Example. [§9.221] Manny orally sells Whiteacre to Jack. With Manny's knowledge, Jack moves onto the property and begins to make substantial improvements to it. Manny now tries to evict Jack, stating that their agreement for the sale of the property is unenforceable because it was oral. Jack may equitably enforce Manny's promise to sell him the land, even though oral, for the elements listed in the previous section have been met. Whether Jack will only be permitted to recover his out-of-pocket expenses (i.e., his reliance interest), or will be permitted to take title to the property (i.e., to get specific performance), depends on what "justice requires" after evaluating all the circumstances.

3. SATISFYING THE STATUTE. [§9.23] If a contract for the transfer of an interest in land is within the Statute, the party seeking to enforce the contract must show:

    (a) the existence of a writing reasonably identifying the interest in land that is being transferred;

    (b) that the writing is signed by the other party, i.e., the party against whom the contract is being enforced; and

    (c) that the writing sufficiently evidences that the parties have intended to transfer that interest [Restatement 2d §131].

    a. The "Merger" Doctrine. [§9.231] Sometimes, all the essential terms, the signature of the party to be charged, and the intent to enter into the transaction cannot be found on only one writing, but can be found if two or more writings are taken together. All modern courts allow a party to "merge" the terms of two or more writings to satisfy the statute of fraud.

D. TYPE TWO: CONTRACTS WHICH, BY THEIR TERMS, CANNOT BE PERFORMED WITHIN A YEAR OF THEIR MAKING. [§9.3] The general rule is that if even a single promise made in a contract cannot be fully performed in a year from when the contract is made, all the promises in the contract are within the Statute of Frauds and thus must be in writing to be enforceable. This rule is not quite as broad as it sounds, for the requirement that a promise "cannot" be performed within a year is construed quite strictly.

1. IT IS ONLY WHEN, BY ITS OWN TERMS, COMPLETED PERFORMANCE OF A PROMISE IS *IMPOSSIBLE* WITHIN A YEAR OF ITS MAKING THAT THE STATUTE APPLIES. [§9.31] If completed performance of a promise is theoretically possible, even if factually unlikely, within one year from the date it was made, the contract is outside the Statute and can be enforced even if oral.

    a. Example. [§9.311] Phil's Construction Company is awarded a contract for $2 billion to build an office tower twice as high and twice as large as the Sears Tower in Chicago. While it is factually unlikely that such a project could be completed in less than a year, there is nothing inherent in the contract itself that makes the completion of performance impossible within a year, and therefore the Statute does not apply. Thus, the contract can be enforced, even if oral.

b. **Example.** [§9.312] Brian agrees to serve as Rose's butler for a two year period. Since by its very terms Brian's promise cannot be completed within a year, the contract is within the Statute and must be in writing to be enforceable.

c. **Example.** [§9.313] On September 1, Sam agrees to work as a research assistant to Professor Smith for a three month period beginning next July 15. The contract is within the Statute, for **by its terms** it cannot be completed within one year **of its making**. Thus, it must be in writing to be enforceable.

2. **SPLIT OF OPINION AS TO WHETHER CONTRACTS WITH TERMINATION OPTIONS WITHIN A YEAR ARE WITHIN THE STATUTE.** [§9.32] There is a difference of opinion whether contracts that are for fixed terms greater than a year, but which also give one or both parties the power to terminate them within a year, are within the Statute. An example of such a contract is where Steel Company contracts with Gas Company to purchase a supply of pure hydrogen for three years, but the contract allows either party to terminate the contract on 30 days notice. The **majority view** holds that the Statute applies, for under this view "termination" is not "completed performance," and thus by its terms the promise to deliver gas cannot be completely performed within a year. The holders of this view would therefore require the contract to be in writing to be enforceable.

However, a **minority**, including **the Restatement**, states that exercising the right to terminate is simply an alternative means of performance under the contract. That is, Steel Company can perform by either accepting the hydrogen every month for three years and paying for it, or by terminating the contract with 30 days notice. Either action is a completed performance under the contract. Since exercising the termination provision can be done within a year, this minority view holds the contract to be outside the Statute, and thus enforceable even if oral.

3. **FULL PERFORMANCE BY ONE PARTY TAKES THE CONTRACT OUTSIDE THE STATUTE.** [§9.33] Most (but not all) courts hold that where one party has **completely** performed his or her obligations under a contract where the other party's performance cannot be completed within a year, the contract is thereafter taken outside the Statute and can be enforced by the party who has performed. For example, Lou and Gina orally contract whereby Lou promises to deliver a load of firewood to Gina next week, in return for Gina's promise to make 18 monthly payments of $30 to Lou. At the time of its making, the contract would not be enforceable because Gina's promise cannot be completed within a year from the making of the contract. However, once Lou delivered the wood, Lou's performance is completed and at that point most courts would find the contract is taken outside the Statute, and Gina's oral promise to make monthly payments is enforceable by Lou. This rule makes sense for there is obviously evidence that the parties made a contract, i.e., it is unlikely Lou would deliver the wood otherwise, and to leave him no contractual recovery in such a case would be unfair. Those states that do not provide recovery for Lou on the contract would allow him to recover in restitution (see Chapter Thirty-Two for an explination of restitution).

a. **Part Performance Does Not Take the Contract Outside the Statute.** [§9.331] Where one party has only partially performed his or her obligations under a contract where one party's performance cannot be completed within a year, most courts hold that the contract is still within the Statute, even if theoretically divisible. For example, in the Lou and Gina hypothetical stated above, if Lou promised to make two deliveries of firewood, one next week and one three months later, no part of the contract would be enforceable by Lou after delivery of only the first load. Of course, after the second load is delivered, Lou's performance is then complete and the courts would find the contract outside the statute (see §9.33).

4. **SATISFYING THE STATUTE IN A CONTRACT WHICH, BY ITS TERMS, CANNOT BE PERFORMED WITHIN A YEAR. [§9.34]** A party seeking to enforce a contract which, by its very terms, cannot be performed within a year of its making must establish:

> (a) the existence of a writing reasonably identifying the subject matter and essential terms of the contract;

> (b) that the writing is signed by the other party, i.e. the party against whom the contract is being enforced; and

> (c) that the writing sufficiently evidences that the parties have intended to make a binding agreement [Restatement 2d §131].

> Note that the merger doctrine (§9.231) applies to satisfy the Statute in these types of contracts.

E. **TYPE THREE: CONTRACTS MADE IN CONSIDERATION OF MARRIAGE. [§9.4]** A contract for which all or part of the consideration is marriage, or the promise to marry, is within the Statute, and thus must be in writing to be enforceable [Restatement 2d §124]. For example, assume Julia proposes to Richard, and to induce Richard to agree she also promises to give him a new car if he accepts her offer. If Richard accepts, both the promise to marry and the promise to give Richard a car are within the Statute and thus, must be in writing to be enforceable. This is because the promise to give Richard the car was, in part, bargained for and given in exchange for Richard's promise to marry.

1. **PRE-NUPTIAL AGREEMENTS. [§9.41]** The key in determining whether a pre-nuptial agreement is within or without the Statute is to determine whether it was made in **consideration of marriage**, i.e., as part of a bargain in which one party wanted to induce the other to marry (or to promise to marry), **or whether it was made only in contemplation of marriage**. In the former case, it is within the Statute. In the latter, it is outside the Statute and thus, enforceable even if oral. For example, if Lisa and Rod agree to be married and a few weeks later begin discussions and eventually agree on a pre-nuptial agreement, the agreement is outside the Statute, for it was only made in contemplation of marriage, and not in return for one party's promise to marry. That is, it was not entered into with one party's agreement of marriage being part of the bargained for exchange.

F. **TYPE FOUR: CONTRACTS WHERE ONE PARTY ACTS AS SURETY FOR ANOTHER. [§9.5]** In general, **a promise to pay the debt or default of another is within the Statute, and thus must be in writing to be enforceable** [Restatement 2d §112]. This part of the Statute is known as the "suretyship" provision.

1. **DEFINITION OF SURETY. [§9.51]** A surety is a person who is secondarily liable for the duty of another, called the principal (or the debtor). As a result of a suretyship agreement, both the surety and the principal are liable to a third party, called the obligee (or creditor). However, it is important to note that the surety is only liable if the principal

does not discharge his or her duty. In other words, in a suretyship the creditor must seek performance by the principal first, for the principal is primarily liable, before he or she can look to the surety, who is only secondarily liable.

a. **Example. [§9.511]** The most common example of a surety is where the surety agrees to pay a debt if the principal defaults on some credit obligation. Assume Paul wants to buy a car but his credit rating is not the best and the bank won't lend him any money unless he gets a co-signer. If Sally co-signs the loan, typically she will promise to pay any of Paul's remaining obligations under the car loan should Paul default. Sally is a surety; Paul is a principal (or debtor); and the bank is the obligee (or creditor). Should Paul default, the bank must first look to Paul to pay the remaining balance, and only if he is unable to do so may the bank seek to enforce Sally's promise.

2. **WHERE THE SUPPOSED SURETY IS PRIMARILY, NOT SECONDARILY, LIABLE, NO SURETYSHIP EXISTS AND THE CONTRACT IS OUTSIDE THE STATUTE. [§9.52]** If the obligee extends credit or other services based solely on the credit or representations of the putative **surety**, rather than of the principal, no suretyship exists because the liability of the purported surety is primary rather than secondary. Accordingly, any oral promises made in such a contract are enforceable, as the transaction is not within the Statute [Restatement 2d §112, Com d].

a. **Example. [§9.521]** Shirley telephones flower shop and instructs the shop to deliver a dozen roses to Peter, telling the florist that "if Peter doesn't pay for them, I will." In this case, Shirley is primarily, not secondarily, liable because the flower shop extended credit based on her representations, not Peter's. Accordingly, she is not a "surety." Thus the contract is outside the Statute, and her promise to pay the flower shop is enforceable by the shop even though it is oral.

3. **THE "MAIN PURPOSE" OR "LEADING OBJECT" EXCEPTION. [§9.53]** If the main purpose for which the surety makes the promise to answer for the duty of the principal is to secure an economic advantage for the **surety**, rather than to provide a benefit for the **principal**, the transaction is outside the Statute under the **main purpose (or leading object) rule**. [Restatement 2d §116.] This rule is illustrated below.

a. **Example. [§9.531]** Jim owes Claude $1,000. To collect, Claude is about to levy an attachment on Jim's house. Ron, who is also a creditor of Jim's, is afraid that if Claude levies on Jim's house, Jim will declare bankruptcy and the chance of Jim paying Ron the full amount of the debt would be reduced. Thus, Ron orally promises Claude that if Claude will hold off any attachment proceedings for six weeks, Ron will pay Claude the $1,000 if Jim doesn't pay it during this period. Even though Ron's promise was an oral surety, it is nonetheless enforceable under the **main purpose, or leading object exception**. That is because the main purpose of Ron's promise was to benefit himself, not Jim [Restatement 2d §116, Ill. 2].

b. **Example. [§9.532]** Jim owes Claude $1,000. To collect, Claude is about to levy an attachment on Jim's house. Ron, a friend of Jim's, wants to avoid his friend's embarrassment, and so orally promises Claude he will pay the $1,000 if Jim does not, so long as Claude promises to hold off any attachment for six weeks. The main purpose of Ron's promise was to benefit Jim, the principal, and not Ron, the surety. As such, the main purpose rule does not apply, and Ron's oral promise is within the Statute and thus unenforceable [Restatement 2d §116, Ill. 1]. (Of course, if Claude relied on Ron's promise, it may be enforceable under a promissory estoppel theory.)

4. SATISFYING THE STATUTE IN SURETYSHIP CONTRACTS. [§9.54] A party seeking to enforce a contract for suretyship against the surety must establish:

(a) the existence of a writing reasonably identifying the debtor, surety, obligor, and the essential terms of the suretyship agreement;

(b) that the writing is signed by the surety; and

(c) that the writing sufficiently evidences an intent by the parties to enter into a suretyship agreement [Restatement 2d §131].

Note that the merger doctrine (§9.231) applies to satisfy the statute in suretyship contracts.

G. TYPE FIVE: CONTRACTS FOR THE SALE OF GOODS FOR $500 OR MORE UNDER UCC §2-201. [§9.6] The general rule provided by UCC §2-201 is that to enforce a **contract for the sale of goods for $500 or more against a party, that party must have signed a written contract.** However, that general rule is subject to several exceptions and alternate means of satisfaction other than by a signed writing, and thus, each of the three sections of §2-201 needs to be studied carefully and independently.

1. STRUCTURE OF UCC §2-201. [§9.61] Section 2-201 is divided into three sections:

§2-201(1) sets forth the general rule given in §9.6 and describes what sort of writing is usually necessary to meet the requirements of that rule (see §9.62).

§2-201(2) sets forth an alternative way to satisfy the Statute when the contract is made between merchants (see §9.63).

§2-201(3) sets forth exceptions to the general rule of §2-201(1), describing three situations is which contracts for the sale of goods in excess of $500 can be enforced even though there is no writing signed by the party against whom the contract is sought to be enforced (see §9.64).

A party need not satisfy or meet the requirements of all three sections to have satisfied the statute. If an agreement satisfies only one section of §2-201, it is enforceable.

Note that the UCC has three other Statutes of Frauds dealing with transactions other than the sale of goods, i.e., contracts for the sale of certain securities [UCC §8-319]; for the creation of a security interest [UCC §9-203(1)(a)]; and for the sale of personal property in excess of $5,000 [UCC §1-206 (a)]. As these provisions are tangential at best to most contracts courses, they are not dealt with in this book.

Note also that the merger doctrine (§9.231) can be used to help satisfy the Statute for sales of goods contracts for $500 or more.

2. SATISFYING THE STATUTE UNDER §2-201(1). [§9.62] Under §2-201(1), a contract for the sale of goods for $500 or more is not enforceable unless:

(1) it is **in writing**;

(2) it is **signed** by (or on behalf of) the party against whom enforcement of the contract is sought;

(3) the writing **evidences that a contract for sale** (as opposed to merely an offer, preliminary negotiation, etc.) has been made between the parties; and

(4) the writing contains a **quantity term**.

a. **Example. [§9.621]** Fred orally agrees to sell his car to Bill for $2,000. Fred sends Bill a letter saying, "I'm glad you agreed to buy my car. I think $2,000 is a fair price. As we discussed, I'll deliver it to you next Friday. /s/ Fred." Bill later changes his mind and refuses to accept delivery of the car or to pay for it. If Fred sues Bill, **Bill will prevail**, for the contract is not enforceable against him. While the contract is for the sale of goods for $500 or more, and while there is a writing which specifies a quantity and evidences that a sale was made, **the writing was not signed by the party against whom it is being enforced, i.e., Bill**. Instead, it was only signed by the party seeking to enforce it, Fred. Thus, as to Bill, it is unenforceable.

Note that if Fred decided to breach by failing to tender the car, the contract **would** be enforceable against him, and Bill could sue him successfully. This is because there is a writing, signed by the party against whom the contract is being enforced, i.e., Fred, that evidences a contract for the sale of a specified quantity of goods.

b. **Typical Problems under §2-201(1). [§9.622]** The following sections discuss and explain how to resolve the typical issues arising under §2-201(1).

(1) **Divisible Contracts. [§9.6221]** Suppose the parties agree on the sale of three identical vases for a total of $600. There is an issue as to whether such agreement is one contract, and thus within the Statute, or whether it is really three contracts for $200 each, each of which is outside the Statute. The rule is that if the parties intended to make one contract, it is within the Statute. If they intended to make three contracts, all are without the Statute. Ascertaining the parties' intent is an issue of interpretation for the court (see Chapter Eighteen).

(2) **Decision to Limit Enforcement of Agreement to Less Than $500. [§9.6222]** Suppose Wanda and Susan had an oral contract for the sale of a good costing $550. If Wanda decided not to go through with the deal, could Susan sue for breach and only seek to enforce the contract for $499? The answer is no. Either the contract as a whole is within, or is outside, the Statute. If it is within, as this one is, it cannot be enforced *at all* if it is oral.

(3) **A Contract Cannot be Enforced beyond the Quantity Shown in the Writing. [§9.6223]** The Statute is fulfilled if there is a quantity term in the signed writing, even if the quantity term is in fact "wrong" because it misstates the true agreement of the parties. However, the contract cannot be enforced beyond the quantity set forth in the writing [UCC §2-201(1)].

(4) **A Contract Containing No Formal "Signature" Can Nonetheless Fulfill the "Signed by" Requirement. [§9.6224]** Occasionally a case will arise where, e.g., a company issues an unsigned written purchase offer on its letterhead, which the other party accepts by signing at the bottom. At that point, there is no formal signature by the company-offeror and thus, there is an issue as to whether the contract can be enforced against the company. The answer is that such a document

is deemed "signed" by the offeror, even if it does not contain a formal signature. This is because under UCC §1-201(39), a writing is considered "signed" if it includes "any symbol . . . adopted by a party with present intention to authenticate a writing." As a party's letterhead is a symbol that is conventionally adopted so as to authenticate that the written offer was made by that company, it is a "signed" writing for purposes of §2-201(1).

3. **SATISFYING THE STATUTE UNDER §2-201(2): THE MERCHANT'S CONFIRMATORY MEMORANDUM. [§9.63]** Under §2-201(2), the sending of a "confirmatory memorandum," i.e., a document that, by its terms confirms the making of an oral contract, can satisfy the Statute **against the one who receives it** if:

(1) the transaction is **between merchants;**

(2) the **memorandum is sent within a reasonable time** after the contract was made;

(3) it is actually **received by the other party** and that party **has reason to know of its contents;**

(4) the confirmatory **memorandum satisfies the requirements of 2-201(1) against the sender;** and

(5) it is **not objected to in writing within ten days** after its receipt.

The effect of such a confirmatory memorandum is that, if all these elements are met, a party who has not signed anything will still lose its defense under the Statute, and his or her oral promise will become enforceable.

a. **Example. [§9.631]** Acme Company telephones an order for a new $10,000 transducer to Nadir Company, which is accepted on the phone by Nadir. (At this point, the contract is not enforceable against either party as it is not in writing). The next day, Nadir sends a "Confirmation of Order" to Acme in which it confirms Acme's promise to pay for, and Nadir's promise to ship, a new transducer for $10,000. The confirmation is signed by a Nadir Vice-President. (At this point, Nadir has lost its Statute of Frauds defense and the contract can be enforced against it. That is, Nadir has signed a writing evidencing a sale of one transducer, and thus the contract can be enforced against it under §2-201(1)). However, Acme is **not** bound at this point for it has not signed anything and has only made an oral promise to pay.

Thereafter, Acme receives the confirmation, and does not respond to it for ten days. (At this point, **both** parties have lost their Statute of Frauds defense and either can enforce the contract against the other. Nadir lost its defense under §2-201(1) when it sent the signed memorandum; Acme lost its defense under §2-201(2) because it failed to object to the merchant's confirmatory memorandum within ten days.) Hence, even though Acme failed to sign anything, it has no statute of frauds defense if it fails to tender payment to Nadir.

b. **Effect of Failure to Object Within Ten Days. [§9.632]** The only effect of a party's failure to object within ten days is that it loses its Statute of Frauds defense. The failure to object has **nothing to do with contract formation.** This is a **common** mistake and thus, is both frequently tested on and important to learn.

(1) Example. [§9.6321] Ralph's Tire Company ("Ralph's") has never had anything to do with Joe's Rubber Supply Co. Nevertheless, one day Ralph's gets a confirmatory memorandum from Joe's "confirming" an order of $5,000 worth of rubber to be delivered next month. Thinking it is a joke, Ralph's throws the confirmation away and does not object. Joe's tenders delivery of the rubber a month later and when Ralph's does not accept and pay for it, Joe's sues. The fact that Ralph's didn't object to the memo means **only** that Ralph's has lost its Statute of Frauds defense in the suit by Joe's. It does **not** mean that Ralph's has somehow implicitly consented to the existence of the contract, or implicitly waived its right to try to prove that the alleged contract never existed. Ralph's still will have the chance to prove at trial it never ordered from, or had any dealings with, Joe's. True, Ralph's will have to explain why it did not object to the confirmatory memorandum, but it is entitled to make such an explanation. The key, however, is to realize that the only effect of its failure to object is that Ralph's will not be entitled to have the action dismissed before trial on Statute of Frauds grounds. Assuming truth will prevail at trial, Ralph's will win and is not obligated to pay for the rubber. [see §§9.02; 9.644]

c. Effect of Objecting Within Ten Days. [§9.633] If the party receiving the confirmatory memorandum objects within ten days, whether it keeps its Statute of Frauds defense or not depends on what it says in its objection. If it disclaims knowledge of the contract, i.e., if it says something like, "Our company has never dealt with you, we do not know what you are talking about, and we certainly have no contract with you," the objecting party has preserved its Statute of Frauds defense. But if the receiving party says something like, "You have misstated our deal. Our contract was for one transducer at $9,500, not $10,000," **it loses its Statute of Frauds defense**. It does not lose the defense under §2-201(2), for it has timely objected. However, it loses it under §2-201(1), for in its objection it has sent a **signed writing**, evidencing a **sales transaction**, with a given **quantity** term in sending the objection. Thus, it has satisfied the Statute against itself under §2-201(1).

d. Effect of Either Party Not Being a Merchant. [§9.634] Section 2-201(2) applies **only** where both parties are merchants. Thus, if Willie (an individual) receives a "Confirmation of Order" from a Bicycle Shop, confirming an oral order for a new 10-speed bicycle, the stated agreement cannot be enforced against Willie based only on the confirmation regardless of whether Willie objects to the writing within 10 days. That is, because Willie is not a merchant, and because there is nothing he has signed, the contract cannot be enforced against him under either §2-201(1) or §2-202(2).

e. Effect of the Confirming Memorandum Not Satisfying §2-201(1) Against the Sender. [§9.635] Assume manufacturer sends a written confirmation to retailer stating, "This will confirm our telephone conversation today whereby you ordered the transducers for shipment on April 10. As we agreed, we will expect payment 30 days after you receive the transducers. /s/ V.P. Manufacturer." This letter will not satisfy the requirements of §2-201(2), and thus, the contract is still unenforceable against the retailer, and will continue to be so even if there is no objection by the retailer. The reason is that while both parties are merchants; while the confirmatory memorandum is signed by the manufacturer; and while it was received by the retailer, **the letter was not sufficient to bind the sender under §2-201(1)**. That is, one of the requirements for an effective merchant's confirmatory memorandum is that the writing be sufficient under §2-201(1) as against the sender. In the above confirmation, there is no mention of a particular quantity. Thus, because the letter does not satisfy the requirements of §2-201(1) so that it could be used to enforce the agreement against the manufacturer, it is not an effective confirmatory memorandum. As a result, the agreement is voidable at the option of the retailer under the Statute, despite the merchant-retailer's failure to object.

4. **SATISFYING THE STATUTE UNDER §2-201(3). [§9.64]** Section 2-201(3) provides three exceptions to the writing requirement set forth in §2-201(1). None of these exceptions is limited to merchants.

   a. **Specially Manufactured Goods. [§9.641]** Under §2-201(3)(a), an oral contract for the sale of goods for $500 or more is enforceable if the contract is for specially manufactured goods and the seller has at least begun manufacture or made commitments in reliance on the buyer's order. Perhaps surprisingly, there is no definition of "specially manufactured goods" in the UCC. However, under the most widely agreed definition, a specially manufactured good is one the manufacturer could not readily sell in the ordinary course of its business to anyone other than the original buyer. That is, it is in some sense a "custom made" product.

   b. **Admission. [§9.642]** Under §2-201(3)(b), if the party against whom enforcement of the contract is sought admits either in a pleading, a deposition, at trial, or otherwise in a court-related proceeding while under oath, that an oral contract was made for the sale of goods for $500 or more, the oral contract becomes enforceable. According to most modern commentators, this provision means that no motion to dismiss on statute of limitations grounds is possible until the plaintiff at least has had the opportunity to ask the defendant under oath whether a contract was formed, i.e. until the plaintiff has taken the defendant's deposition.

   c. **Performance. [§9.643]** Under §2-201(3)(c), if the buyer has completely paid for the goods ordered under an oral contract for the sale of goods for $500 or more, or if the seller has completely delivered all goods called for under such a contract, the remaining promises under the contract are enforceable.

      (1) **Part Performance. [§9.6431]** Section 2-201(3)(c) speaks only in terms of full performance, i.e., full payment or full delivery. Often, however, a buyer will leave only a partial payment as a deposit on ordered goods. Today the rule followed by a vast majority of courts is that such part performance will also take the contract out of the Statute, and will render an oral contract enforceable. Note that this is different from the rule on part performance of contracts that cannot be performed within a one year period (see §9.331).

   d. **REVIEW PROBLEM. [§9.644]** Printing House has a slow month and decides, on its own, to print 100,000 calendars with the "Acme Department Stores" logo on the bottom. It sends the calendars, with a bill for $50,000, to Acme, which Acme refuses. Printing House sues Acme for breach of contract Question: Analyze the contractual liability of the parties and the effect of the Statute of Frauds.

      Answer: The Statute of Frauds applies because it is a sale of goods for $500 or more (see §9.62), and the Statute is satisfied under the "specially manufactured goods" exception of §2-201(3)(a) (see §9.641). Hence, Acme cannot use the Statute of Frauds as a defense to the lawsuit. However, because it never entered into a contract in the first place, it has no contractual liability to Printing House. [See §§9.02; 9.6321]

H. ENFORCEMENT OF PROMISES IN CONTRACTS WITHIN THE STATUTE OTHER THAN TRANSFER OF LAND INTERESTS BY RELIANCE.

[§9.7] Reliance by a party as to an oral agreement to transfer an interest in land is a universally recognized way to satisfy the Statute. (see §9.22) However, there is a difference of opinion as to whether reasonable reliance on an oral promise by one party will make other agreements subject to the Statute enforceable. The Restatement, and a majority of states, provide that a reliance exception to the Statute exists. Thus, upon reasonable and foreseeable reliance on an oral promise, the promise is enforceable by the relying party to the extent justice requires [Restatement 2d §139]. In many ways, this is a specialized application of the promissory estoppel doctrine. Further, while "reasonable reliance" is not a statutory exception under UCC §2-201, many jurisdictions have nevertheless recognized the doctrine even in sales of goods transactions, and thus will enforce oral sales of goods contracts for $500 or more where one party reasonably relied on the promises made in the agreement.

I. THE STATUTE AS APPLIED TO MODIFICATIONS OF EXISTING CONTRACTS.

[§9.8] If the parties to a written contract within the Statute wish to modify it orally, there is a question as to whether such oral modification is enforceable. The Restatement provides that if the contract, as modified, is within the Statute, then all its terms must be in writing for the newly modified contract to be enforceable. If they are not in writing, then the originally agreed upon terms are effective [Restatement 2d §149]. The UCC seems to take a similar position (see §26.3).

J. CONSEQUENCE OF NOT SATISFYING THE STATUTE OF FRAUDS.

[§9.9] While the test for whether a particular type of contract is within the Statute varies depending on the nature of the transaction, **the effect of the Statute on all transactions to which it applies is identical**:

> **If the Statute applies and is not satisfied, the contract is voidable by the party who has the Statute of Frauds defense. Thus:**
>
> (a) the party with the defense can enforce the contract against the other, so long as the other party has satisfied the Statute; and
>
> (b) if the party with the defense does not wish to go through with the contract, he or she does not have to. Thus, that party can simply cease performance without contractual liability. If the other party brings a breach of contract action for such nonperformance, the action will fail for the Statute provides a complete defense. (See §§9.02;9.6321;9.644)

Some have characterized the Statute as an "evidentiary gate" which controls whether the jury will hear **any** evidence about the contract. If the Statute applies and its requirements are met, (or if the Statute does not apply), the evidentiary gate is lifted and all evidence that either party wants to introduce about the contract is admissible. Of course the rules of evidence and the parol evidence rule may limit such evidence, but the point is that once the Statute has been satisfied, the Statute of Frauds doctrine will not limit evidence surrounding the making of the contract or its terms. On the other hand, if the Statute applies and is not satisfied, the evidentiary gate remains closed and the party seeking to allege a breach of contract against the party who never signed a contract will **never** get to put on any evidence of the contract or its terms. Once again, the non-signing party has a complete defense to the action.

1. **EXAMPLE. [§9.91]** Paul agrees to sell his car to Mary for $1,000 and both parties sign a written contract to that effect. The Statute has been satisfied and thus, there is nothing in the Statute to prevent Paul from suing Mary claiming that the deal really was for $1,250. Note of course that there are other doctrines that might limit such evidence, but once the Statute is satisfied, there will be no prohibition under the Statute of Frauds limiting any evidence either party wishes to introduce about the contract or its terms.

2. **EXAMPLE. [§9.92]** Mark orally agrees to sell his leasehold interest in a mobile home park to Terry. A few weeks later, Mark decides not to go through with the deal and Terry sues him. Since the Statute applies and is not fulfilled, Mark has a complete defense to the breach action, and Terry will not be permitted to introduce evidence that he and Mark ever entered into a contract.

3. **RESTITUTION REQUIRED UPON DISAFFIRMANCE. [§9.93]** The party who avoids a contract under the Statute is entitled to restitutionary recovery from the other. However, that party must also make restitution, if appropriate. That is, each party to such a contract will have to pay the other the fair value for any benefits received under the agreement before it was avoided (see Chapter Thirty-Two for a discussion of restitution).

K. **MNEMMONIC SUMMARY. [§9.10]** For those who use mnemonics to help summarize legal principles, a well-used one in the Statute of Frauds area is "**MY LEGS**," which is explained below:

M arriage Contracts — **Only** contracts where consideration is marriage or the promise of marriage.

Y ear Contracts — Contracts that **by their very terms** cannot be performed in a year.

L and Contracts — Contracts for the transfer of an interest in property of anything other than a license.

E stoppel (reliance) exception — A party that reasonably relies on an oral promise otherwise subject to the SOF may enforce the promise to the extent justice allows. Always applies to land contracts; majority rule applies to other contracts as well.

G uaranty (Surety) Contracts — Contracts where one party guarantees the debt of another.

S ales of Goods — A UCC contact for $500 or more.

CHAPTER TEN: INCAPACITY

A. THE INCAPACITY DOCTRINE. [§10.0] In order to enter into a valid contract, t[...]
mandates that a party have sufficient judgment to decide to bind himself or herself to an
enforceable promise. There are two classes of persons that the law presumes not to have such
judgment — minors and the mentally infirm.

B. INCAPACITY DUE TO INFANCY/MINORITY. [§10.1] The general rule is that until a
person reaches the age of majority (almost universally 18), any contract entered into by that
person is **voidable** at the option of the minor [Restatement 2d §§12, 14]. Note that the test is
not whether the **particular** minor who entered into a contract is sufficiently mature to
understand the nature of entering into a legal bargain. Rather, the test turns solely on the age
of the individual. Note also that the minor is entitled to void the contract at any time while a
minor, even if he or she has enjoyed the benefits under the contract.

1. **EXAMPLE. [§10.11]** Fred just turned 17 and signs a contract to purchase a used car on
   credit for $6,000. If Fred wants to go through with the deal, he is entitled to do so, for he
   is not required to terminate (or avoid) the transaction. However, if he does not wish to go
   through with the deal, he does not have to. As the contract is voidable at his option, he
   can terminate it anytime up to the age of majority, and even a reasonable time after that
   (see §10.123). If he takes possession of the car for six months and makes six months
   worth of payments, and then decides he does not want to go through with the deal, he is
   entitled to avoid the contract at that point. He simply has to return the car, and he will be
   entitled to the return of all the payments he has made.

2. **RATIFICATION OF A CONTRACT ENTERED INTO BY A MINOR. [§10.12]** Upon
   reaching majority, a minor can **ratify** a contract, thereby turning it from a voidable one
   into a binding one. Note that **ratification cannot validly take place until the minor
   reaches majority,** for it is only then that contract law assumes the party has attained the
   capacity necessary to enter into a binding contract. **Generally, ratification needs no new
   consideration to be valid**, and can occur in three ways:

   (a) express ratification;

   (b) implied-in-fact ratification; or

   (c) ratification by silence.

   a. **Express Ratification. [§10.121]** If a former minor expressly indicates by words,
      whether written or oral, that he or she wishes to be bound by the promises made in a
      contract entered into during minority, such ratification is valid and will serve to
      deprive the former minor of the further power to avoid the contract.

   b. **Implied-in-Fact Ratification. [§10.122]** If the former minor manifests by action that he
      or she is apparently willing to be bound to the promises made in a contract entered into
      during minority, such ratification is valid and will take away the former minor's further
      power to avoid the contract. For example, in the hypthetical with Fred in §10.11, if
      Fred continues making payments after he turns 18, he will be deemed to have made an
      implied in-fact ratification of the contract. Thus, he may no longer avoid it, and if he
      stops making payments and tries to return the car, he will be deemed in breach.

c. **Ratification by Silence: Implied-in-Law Ratification. [§10.123]** Ratification by silence, or implied-in-law ratification, is the most common form of ratification. This occurs where a former minor says and does nothing one way or the other about a contract entered into during minority. The rule is that **a minor is given a reasonable time to disaffirm the contract after reaching majority. If it is not disaffirmed within such reasonable time, ratification will be implied.** While the facts of each contract need to be examined to determine what is a reasonable time, one factor is that the more benefits the minor has received under the contract, the less the amount of time he or she will have to disaffirm upon attaining majority. Conversely, the more the benefits under the contract are still executory, i.e. unperformed, as to the former minor, the greater the amount of time the former minor will have to disaffirm.

3. **DISAFFIRMANCE OF CONTRACTS ENTERED INTO BY MINORS. [§10.13] A party may disaffirm (i.e., declare void) a contract at any point during his or her minority, and may continue to do so after reaching majority up until the time the contract is ratified.** Such disaffirmance may be by words (written or oral), or by conduct.

a. **Treatment of the Economic Benefit Received by the Minor While in Possession of the Goods: No Restitutionary Recovery Permitted in Credit Sales. [§10.131]** The disaffirmance doctrine can act unfairly to sellers. For example, suppose Ace Car Company sells a new car to Larry, a mature looking 17 year old, for 24 monthly payments of $600. Larry keeps the car for ten months (until just before he turns 18) and then tells Ace he is disaffirming the contract. Because the contract is voidable, Larry is entitled to disaffirm it and is entitled to all his money back. However, the car Ace gets back is not the car it sold, i.e., the car is now a used one and is worth considerably less. In all states except those following the "New Hampshire" rule (see §10.1311), **the non-minor (here Ace) has no right to recover, even in restitution, for this lost value.** That is, Ace would not be entitled to recover any fair rental value, depreciation, mileage etc. for the car. This inability to seek an offset would be true even if Larry smashed the car and totally wrecked it. All Larry would have to do is disaffirm the contract (assuming it had not yet been ratified), and he would then be entitled to all his payments back, while Ace would only be entitled to the return of the wrecked automobile. If the car is stolen, the same result would follow except that Ace would not be entitled to anything back except the transfer of Larry's right to get the car back if it is ever found.

(1) **The "New Hampshire" Rule. [§10.1311]** A few states have agreed with the New Hampshire Supreme Court that where a minor has contracted with someone who is not a minor, the non-minor is entitled to restitutionary (fair value) recovery upon the disaffirmance of a credit sale by a minor, so long as the minor would be unjustly enriched from the use of the goods without having to pay for such use. (See Chapter Thirty-Two for a further discussion of Restitution).

b. **Treatment of the Economic Benefit Received by the Minor While in Possession of the Goods or Services: Restitutionary Recovery Permitted in Cash Sales. [§10.132]** A different situation occurs when the minor pays cash for goods or services and later seeks disaffirmance. For example, assume Joyce gives guitar lessons for $30 per hour. If Paula, a 17-year old, pays the $30 and gets the lesson, it would be unfair to allow Paula to turn around at the end of the lesson and say she was disaffirming the contract and demand her money back. However, the minor is still deemed to be without the judgment necessary to contract. Contract law solves this dilemma as follows: **where the minor receives goods or services in return for a cash payment,the minor is still** entitled to avoid the contract. However, upon disaffirmance by the minor, the non-infant is entitled to full restitutionary recovery. Thus, in the Paula/Joyce example, Paula is entitled to avoid the contract and demand her $30 back (because she is a minor) at the end of the lesson. However, when that occurs, Joyce is entitled to seek the reasonable (restitutionary) value of her services from Paula, which is most likely $30 (see Chapter Thirty-Two for a discussion of restitution).

    c. Restitutionary Recovery Permitted upon Disaffirmance of a Contract for "Necessities." [§10.133] If a minor contracts for "necessities," generally including at least food, clothing, and shelter (and perhaps other things if, e.g., the minor is emancipated and/or married), he or she will be liable in restitution for such necessities upon disaffirmance of the contract. This is true in all jurisdictions, regardless of whether the contract is a cash sale or a credit agreement. For example, assume Lloyd and Nan are both 17 years old and married to each other. They enter into a month-to-month lease for an apartment for $600 per month. At the end of the month they are entitled to disaffirm the lease contract based on their minority, but if they do so they will be liable in restitution for the fair rental value of the apartment for the month (see Chapter Thirty-Two for an explanation of restitution).

    d. Misrepresentation of Age by Minor. [§10.134] If a minor affirmatively misrepresents his or her age to the other contracting party as being over 18, the non-infant party generally can get full restitutionary recovery for any benefits conferred on the minor should the minor later disaffirm, even in a credit sale. Some states go even further and hold that upon an affirmative misrepresentation of majority, a minor is **bound under the contract** and may no longer disaffirm it.

C. INCAPACITY DUE TO MENTAL INFIRMITY: THE "COGNITION" THEORY. [§10.2] The general rule is that **if, at the time of the making of a contract, a party lacked the ability to understand the nature and consequences of the agreement, i.e., could not appreciate what he or she was doing, then the contract is voidable at the option of the mentally infirm party, or by his or her guardian** [Restatement 2d §15]. This is called the "cognition" test. Note that the test is **not** whether the person is "insane" or "senile," etc. A person can be judged "insane" for some purposes and still have the capacity to contract if he or she can appreciate the legal consequence of the agreement at the time it was made. In other words, if the party knows what he or she is doing when entering into a contract, and knows that such actions carry with them legal consequences, then the party has the capacity to contract, and the resulting agreement or contract entered into by the mentally infirm person is not voidable. However, if the party lacks such cognition, any contract entered into by the party is voidable under the rules set forth in §10.22.

    1. **RATIFICATION. [§10.21]** Ratification of a contract entered into by someone with mental incapacity is treated just like ratification of a contract entered into by a minor (see §10.12). That is, ratification cannot take place while the party continues under the infirmity (although it can be ratified by the person's guardian), and when the party no longer suffers from the infirmity, he or she has a reasonable time to void the contract or it will be deemed ratified by silence. In addition, upon gaining sufficient cognition, ratification can be by words (either oral or written), or by action (implied-in-fact ratification).

    2. **DISAFFIRMANCE OF CONTRACTS ENTERED INTO BY THE MENTALLY INFIRM. [§10.22]** A party suffering from a mental infirmity cannot validly disaffirm a contract (although his or her guardian can). If the person recovers from the mental infirmity, he or she may disaffirm the contract until it is ratified. Disaffirmance can be by words, oral or written, or by action.

a. **Restitutionary Recovery Often Permitted upon Disaffirmance of Contract. [§10.221]** The majority rule is that if a mentally infirm party (or his or her guardian) disaffirms a contract, the non-infirm party is entitled to restitutionary recovery for any benefits conferred on the infirm party, unless the incompetency would have been obvious to a reasonable person at the time the contract was made. The minority view believes that restitution should be allowed even if the incompetency was obvious.

b. **Restitutionary Recovery Permitted upon Disaffirmance of Contract for Necessities. [§10.222]** All jurisdictions permit the non-infirm party to recover in restitution for the supply of necessities to a mental incompetent, even if the incompetency was obvious to the other party (see §10.133 for a discussion of necessities).

3. **THE EFFECT OF TEMPORARY MENTAL INCAPACITY: INTOXICATION AND OTHER DRUG USE. [§10.23]** Most states provide that **a party who, at the time of making a contract, is rendered incompetent under the cognitive test due to intoxication by alcohol or other drug use, is entitled to disaffirm the contract to the same extent as all other classes of mental incompetents. This is true regardless of whether the intoxication is voluntary or involuntary.** That is, it would apply equally to someone who became drunk at a bar, or to someone who had taken prescription medication that had a mind-altering effect, and who was unaware of such effects. However, the Restatement 2d takes the view that a contract entered into by an intoxicated person is voidable only if the intoxicated party fails the cognition test **and** the other party has reason to know of the intoxication [Restatement 2d §16]. Some states, although probably not a majority, follow this view. In the others, the contract is voidable regardless of the non-intoxicated party's knowledge, so long as the intoxicated party fails the cognition test. As such, this view seems to run afoul of the "objective" theory of contracts by allowing a contract to be avoided, even though the intoxicated person objectively appeared to have capacity.

CHAPTER ELEVEN: MISTAKE AND MISUNDERSTANDING

A. THE MISTAKE DOCTRINE. [§11.0] The mistake doctrine is a difficult one to study for a couple of reasons. The first is that when applying it, courts do not always use the same terms to mean the same thing. The second is that the doctrine is intended to be flexible, so that it can be applied by different courts to different fact situations. The most important thing in studying the mistake doctrine is to learn a structure for analyzing mistake problems. Such a structure is provided below.

B. DEFINITION OF "MISTAKE." [§11.1] For purposes of contract law, **a mistake is a belief that is not in accord with the true facts** [Restatement 2d §151]. Note that a mistake does **not** mean an improvident act, e.g., the making of a contract in which a party lost money. Thus, a person who enters into a "bad" deal, without more, cannot use the mistake doctrine to avoid the contract.

1. ERRONEOUS BELIEF AS TO THE FUTURE IS NOT A "MISTAKE." [§11.11] **Mistake is measured by the facts as they exist at the time the contract is made.** Thus, a poor prediction or erroneous belief as to what will occur in the future is not a "mistake" entitling the poor predictor to relief under the mistake doctrine (although erroneous beliefs as to future events may give rise to the doctrine of impracticability (see Chapter Twenty-Five)).

2. MISTAKE OF LAW CAN BE A MISTAKE OF FACT. [§11.12] A contracting party may have an erroneous belief as to the legal consequence of its promise in a contract. The existing law at the time the contract is made is generally considered a "fact," and thus, relief can be granted for a mistaken belief as to the operation of the law, assuming all the other elements for applying the mistake doctrine are present [Restatement 2d §151, Com. b].

3. "MISTAKE" DISTINGUISHED FROM "MISUNDERSTANDING." [§11.13] A misunderstanding occurs when two parties attach different meanings to their communications. As such, it is not an erroneous belief as to a fact, and it is analytically distinct from (although often confused with) the mistake doctrine. Misunderstanding is discussed in detail in §11.5.

C. UNILATERAL AND MUTUAL MISTAKE. [§11.2] The Restatement 2d and the courts treat differently the situations where only *one* party to a contract is under a mistaken belief as to the true facts, from those in which *both* parties are under such a mistake. In general, **it is easier for the party adversely affected by the mistake to get relief when the mistake is mutual rather than when it is unilateral.** The rules regarding mutual mistakes are treated immediately below, and those regarding unilateral mistakes are explained in §11.4.

D. MUTUAL MISTAKE DEFINED. [§11.3] Mutual mistake occurs when both parties to a contract are under substantially the same erroneous belief as to the true facts present in an exchange [Restatement 2d §152]. If a party is adversely affected by a contract entered into under mutual mistake, the contract is **voidable** at the option of that party.

1. ELEMENTS NECESSARY TO ESTABLISH MUTUAL MISTAKE. [§11.31] If a party to a contract formed under a mutual mistake is adversely affected by the mistake, Restatement 2d §152 sets forth three criteria that must be met in order for that party validly to avoid the contract:

(1) The mistake of both parties must be as to a **basic assumption** on which the contract was made (see §11.311);

(2) the mistake must have **a material effect** on the agreed exchange of performances (see §11.312); and

(3) the party seeking to avoid the contract **must not bear the risk** of that mistake (see §11.313).

Each of these elements is discussed below.

a. **The Mistake Must be as to a "Basic Assumption" on Which the Contract Was Made. [§11.311]** There is no agreed upon definition for "basic assumption," but the idea is that the shared mistake must change the **essential nature** of the contract. That is, whatever the parties thought they were agreeing to must be vastly different, i.e., different not just in kind, but in essential nature, from what they actually agreed to.

b. **The Mistake Must Have a "Material Effect" on the Agreed Transaction. [§11.312]** To meet this requirement, it must be demonstrated that it would simply be **too unfair to enforce the bargain as called for in the contract**, for one party would get far more than both parties thought he or she was bargaining for, or alternatively, one party would get far less than both parties thought he or she was bargaining for. In other words, if it appears one party is getting too large an unbargained for windfall, or the other is suffering too large an unknowingly-risked detriment, the mistake has a material effect on the transaction. The availability of other remedies is taken into account in determining whether a party will reap a sufficiently large windfall or suffer a sufficiently large detriment.

c. **The Party Seeking to Avoid the Contract Must Not Bear the Risk of Making the Mistake. [§11.313]** Under the Restatement 2d §152, if the party seeking relief under the mistake doctrine "bears the risk of the mistake," that party cannot avoid the contract under the mistake doctrine. Under Restatement 2d §154, there are three alternative grounds for finding that a particular party bore the risk of the mistake:

(1) **the risk was allocated to that party by express agreement of the parties;**

(2) **the party is aware, at the time the contract is made, that he or she has only a limited knowledge of the true facts, but decides to treat that limited knowledge as sufficient;** or

(3) **as a matter of law the court finds it reasonable to place the risk of the mistake on that party.**

The first of these alternatives is almost never an issue, for if the risk was expressly allocated in the contract, usually the parties do not dispute it. The second and third alternatives are frequently litigated in mistake cases.

2. EXAMPLES APPLYING MUTUAL MISTAKE PRINCIPLES. [§11.32]

a. **Example of *Sherwood v. Walker*. [§11.321]** Buyer and seller contract for the sale of a cow, the now infamous (to contracts students) Rose 2d of Aberlone. According to the seller, both parties were experienced farmers and reasonably believed the cow to be unable to breed, and thus worth the $80 contract price. If the cow could breed, the cow would have been worth around $800. After delivery to the buyer, it was discovered that Rose was pregnant and seller sought to avoid the contract based on mutual mistake. **Held:** Mutual mistake is available. First, the difference between a breeding cow and a non-breeding one is a change in the **essential nature** of the contract — i.e., what the buyer thought he was buying and what the seller thought he was selling turned out to be a completely different thing than what was actually exchanged between them. **Second**, the buyer would receive such a **great unbargained for windfall** in the transaction that it would be unfair to enforce the contract. Note that this was not a case where the buyer thought there was a chance the cow was breedable and thus entered the contract hoping it would end up a good deal for him, i.e., a case where he bargained for the *risk* of a favorable result. This was a case where any benefit he received from the breeding capabilities of the cow was a surprise, and thus an unbargained for windfall. **Third**, the **risk of this mistake was not on the seller**, for none of the provisions of Restatement 2d §154 apply, i.e., the seller did not expressly assume the risk, it was not a case where he entered into the contract aware that he did not know very much about the breeding properties of cattle, and there is nothing in the contract that would make it reasonable for the seller, as opposed to the buyer, to bear the risk of the mistake. *Sherwood v. Walker*, 66 Mich. 568, 33 N.W. 919 (1887).

b. **Example of *Wood v. Boynton*.** [§11.322] The owner of a small unpolished stone did not know either what it was, or its value. She took it to a jeweler who, in good faith, also professed an uncertainty as to what it was. The jeweler suggested that it might be a topaz. The owner sold it to the jeweler for $1, a fair price for a topaz. In fact, it turned out to be a diamond worth $700. Thereafter, the seller sought to avoid the transaction based on mutual mistake. **Held:** The seller was not entitled to relief based on mutual mistake. It is arguable that the mistake changed the essential nature of the deal, i.e., a contract for the sale of a supposed topaz is essentially different from a contract for the sale of a diamond. Similarly, it is arguable that the jeweler would reap a huge unbargained for windfall, as the thing he thought was a $1 topaz turned out to be worth 700 times what he paid. However, under Restatement 2d §154, the owner bore the risk of the mistake, for **she knew she did not know exactly what the stone was, but instead of investigating further, she went ahead with the deal**. As some have put it, this was not a case of "mistake," but rather of **conscious ignorance** on the part of the seller. In other words, if contract making is risk allocation, she consciously took the risk that the stone might turn out to be more valuable than she thought. *Wood v. Boynton*, 64 Wisc. 265, 25 N.W. 42 (1885).

c. **Example of Land Sales.** [§11.323] Occasionally, a party will sell land at a price which would be fair if the land is used for farming or for residential purposes, but later turns out to be much more valuable because, unbeknownst to both parties at the time of contracting, there are e.g., mineral deposits hidden underneath the land. The seller, of course, wants to avoid the contract. In this type of case, the courts will generally not permit the seller to disaffirm based on mutual mistake, on the ground that the nature of land sales transactions makes it reasonable to impose the risk of making such a mistake on the seller.

3. **LIMITATION ON WHEN A PARTY MAY VOID A CONTRACT BASED ON MUTUAL MISTAKE: REASONABLE TIME AFTER DISCOVERY.** [§11.33] The adversely affected party in a contract entered into under mutual mistake must seek to disaffirm or avoid it within a reasonable time after discovery of the mistake. What constitutes a reasonable time will vary depending on the circumstances, but if **disaffirmance is not sought within such time, the contract will be deemed ratified by the adversely affected party**.

4. **EFFECT OF MUTUAL MISTAKE. [§11.34]** If the contracting party adversely affected by a mutual mistake can establish the elements of mutual mistake, **the contract is voidable by that party** [Restatement 2d §154]. In other words, because such a contract is voidable, and not "void," a party harmed by the mutually shared mistake has the option to either avoid the contract, or to waive the mistake and treat it as if it never occurred, at that party's option. In addition, certain types of mutual mistake may justify reformation of the contract.

   a. **Restitution Required if Contract Avoided on the Basis of Mutual Mistake. [§11.341]** If the party whose expectations under the contract were adversely affected because of a mutual mistake chooses to avoid the contract, full restitution is required for any benefits conferred under the contract up until the time it was avoided. Of course, that party must also make restitution (i.e., pay the reasonable value for any benefits received before the contract was avoided) (see Chapter Thirty-Two for a discussion of restitution).

E. **UNILATERAL MISTAKE DEFINED. [§11.4]** A unilateral mistake occurs when only one party to a contract has an erroneous belief as to the true facts present in an exchange [Restatement 2d §153].

   1. **ELEMENTS NECESSARY TO ESTABLISH UNILATERAL MISTAKE. [§11.41]** If only one party entered a contract under a mistake, it is relatively difficult for that party to avoid the contract due to his or her unilateral mistake. Under Restatement 2d §153, the party must show everything that a party seeking to void a contract under mutual mistake must show (see §11.31), plus **either** of the following:

      (1) the effect of the mistake is such that enforcement against the mistaken party would be unconscionable; **or**

      (2) the non-mistaken party either had reason to know of the mistake or caused the mistake.

      a. **Example of Mistaken Bid Cases. [§11.411]** By far the most common examples of unilateral mistake cases are those in which a general contractor submits a very low bid on a project which is accepted by a developer. After the contract has been awarded, the general finds that he or she has added up their figures incorrectly, and will end up losing money on the project (or perhaps, making much less than expected). To get relief in these situations, the general must show all the elements of a mutual mistake situation, i.e., the general contractor must establish that: (a) the mistake goes to a basic assumption of the contract; (b) the mistake has a material effect on the agreed exchange; and (c) he or she does not bear the risk of the mistake. In addition, because the mistake is only unilateral, the general must also prove that enforcement against it would be "unconscionable" or that the developer had reason to know of the mistake. Unconscionability is dealt with in Chapter Fifteen, but the idea is that the general must show that he or she would lose so much money on the deal that in good conscience a court could not force him or her to do that. If the general cannot establish unconscionability, then he or she must show that the developer knew of the mistake or caused it in order to get relief. For example, if all the other bids for a project were $10-13 million, and the bid of the general who was awarded the contract was $6 million, a case could be made that the developer had reason to know of the mistake.

      Several scholars have recently insisted that mistaken bid cases really present mutual mistake, not unilateral mistake, fact situations. That is, to assume in these cases that the contractor was mistaken, but that the developer was not, is to accuse the developer of acting in bad faith by accepting a bid he or she knew was mistakenly too low. It makes more sense, and is probably more accurate, to say that both parties were mistaken. However, these scholars note that requiring contractors to meet the more stringent unilateral mistake rules in mistaken bid cases may be justified as a matter of policy, given the nature of the contracting business and the contractor/developer relationship.

2. **LIMITATION ON WHEN A PARTY MAY VOID A CONTRACT BASED ON UNILATERAL MISTAKE: WITHIN A REASONABLE TIME AFTER DISCOVERY.** [§11.42] As with mutual mistake, the party seeking to rescind a contract based on unilateral mistake must do so within a reasonable time after discovering the mistake, or the contract will be deemed ratified by that party (see §11.33).

3. **LIMITATION ON WHEN A PARTY MAY VOID A CONTRACT BASED ON UNILATERAL MISTAKE: RELIANCE BY THE NON-MISTAKEN PARTY.** [§11.43] If the non-mistaken party has **substantially relied** by changing position based on the promises made by a party entering a contract under unilateral mistake, most courts hold that the adversely affected party loses his or her power to disaffirm the agreement. Note that this is not true with regard to mutual mistakes, i.e., with mutual mistakes an adversely affected party may always avoid the executory, i.e., unperformed, portion of a contract, no matter how much reliance by the other party has taken place (although the mistaken party will have to pay restitution).

4. **EFFECT OF UNILATERAL MISTAKE.** [§11.44] If a party can establish the requisites for relief under a unilateral mistake theory, the contract is voidable by that party. That is, the mistaken party can enforce it, or may disaffirm it, at that party's option.

   a. **Restitution Required upon Avoidance of Contract Entered into under Unilateral Mistake.** [§11.441] If the party who makes the unilateral mistake avoids a contract on that theory, he or she must make full restitution for (i.e., pay the fair value of) any benefits received under the contract up until the time of avoidance. Of course, that party may also be entitled to restitution for any benefits he or she provided as well (see Chapter Thirty-Two for a discussion of restitution.)

F. **THE "MISUNDERSTANDING" DOCTRINE.** [§11.5] A topic usually studied along with mistake, but distinguishable from it, is "misunderstanding." **Misunderstanding occurs when the parties agree to a term in their contract, but each has a different meaning of the term** [Restatement 2d §20]. For example, if the parties agree to the purchase and sale of ten tons of steel, but one party believes it to be metric tons and the other believes it to be English tons, the issue is one of misunderstanding, not of mistake.

   1. **DISTINGUISHING "MISUNDERSTANDING" FROM "MISTAKE".** [§11.51] Misunderstanding is a formation issue, i.e., the misunderstanding doctrine governs whether the parties in fact have a contract and, if so, what its terms are. The mistake doctrine, on the other hand, assumes the existence of a valid contract, and the issue is whether a party may avoid it due to a mistaken belief that is not in accord with the true facts.

   2. **EFFECT OF MISUNDERSTANDING.** [§11.52] The effect of the misunderstanding doctrine on a transaction depends on the understandings of the parties. **If neither party knows, or has reason to know, of the meaning of a material term attached by the other, then no contract is formed** [Restatement 2d §20(1)]. However, if the parties have different meanings of a material term, but one party knows of the misunderstanding and the other party does not, a contract is formed and the meaning of the disputed term is the

one believed by the party who did not know of the misunderstanding [Restatement 2d §20(2)]. Note that the misunderstanding must be as to a **material term** for the misunderstanding doctrine to apply.

a. **Example of *Raffles v. Wichelhaus*. [§11.521]** Buyer and seller agreed upon the sale of cotton to be sent on the ship *The Peerless* from Bombay, India. Unfortunately, there were two ships named *The Peerless*, and they each left Bombay a few months apart. The "1st *Peerless*" left in October; the "2nd *Peerless*" in December. The buyer believed the contract called for shipment on the 1st *Peerless*; the seller believed it called for shipment on the 2nd *Peerless*. **Held:** As neither party knew (or had reason to know) of the meaning attached to the term *"The Peerless"* by the other, no contract was ever formed since there was no mututal manifestation of agreement to go forward on the same terms, as is necessary for contract formation (see Chapter Two). Thus, while the seller was not in breach for sending the goods on the 2nd *Peerless*, the buyer was also not in breach for refusing to accept them when they arrived later than expected for no contract was ever formed between them. *Raffles v. Wichelhaus*, 159 Eng. Rep. 375 (1864).

b. **Example. [§11.522]** The facts are the same as in *Raffles*, except assume both buyer and seller knew there were two ships named *The Peerless*, and the buyer knew the seller meant the 2nd *Peerless*, but the seller knew the buyer meant the 1st *Peerless*. In that case, once again no contract would be formed, regardless of which ship the goods were eventually shipped on, for each party was aware of the other's misunderstanding, and chose to go ahead anyway without correcting it.

c. **Example. [§11.523]** The facts are the same as in, *Raffles*, except assume the seller (who is in Bombay) knows there are two ships called *The Peerless*. Seller intends to ship on the later departing ship, but is confident that buyer expects the goods to be shipped on the 1st *Peerless*. In that case a contract is formed, and it is for shipment on the 1st *Peerless* under the rule of Restatement 2d §20(2).

CHAPTER TWELVE: DURESS

A. THE PROBLEM OF DURESS. [§12.0] When a person enters a contract under duress, the principles of free choice and voluntary decision making inherent in freedom of contract are imperiled. As a consequence, such contracts are not enforceable. The effect of the duress doctrine on a particular contract depends on whether the contract is entered into under **physical compulsion**, or whether the contract is entered into under an **improper threat**. Each of these situations is discussed below.

B. DURESS BY PHYSICAL COMPULSION. [§12.1] If a party enters into a contract solely because he or she has been compelled to do so by the use of physical force, the contract is "**void**" (not voidable) [Restatement 2d §174]. This means that the "contract" cannot be enforced by either party. Thus, if Ed says to Bill "You had better sign this contract or I will stab you with the knife now pressed against your heart," the contract Bill signs cannot be enforced by Ed, or by Bill, even if Bill later wishes to do so. They have no legally enforceable agreement.

C. DURESS BY "IMPROPER" THREAT. [§12.2] If a party enters into a contract because of an improper threat that leaves the victim no reasonable alternative but to assent to the proposed deal, the contract is **voidable** by the victim [Restatement 2d §175]. Thus, the issue is to determine what threats are "proper" and which are "improper." This issue is discussed and explained below.

1. **WHAT CONSTITUTES AN "IMPROPER" THREAT. [§12.21]** Not all threats made in the bargaining process are improper, e.g., the statement, "If you do not promise to have the goods to me by November 10, I do not want to enter into a contract with you," is a threat of sorts, but it obviously is not improper when made during contract negotiations. The Restatement 2d provides two different sets of tests to determine when a threat is "improper," depending on whether the resulting exchange appears to be on fair terms or not. That is, perhaps surprisingly, sometimes duress results in an exchange that appears to be fair. The problem is that the contract is a "forced" sale, e.g., where Joe uses improper threats to get Mary to sell her house to him, when Mary does not want to, but where he agrees to pay her a fair price for it. On the other hand, sometimes duress results in an exchange on unfair terms, e.g., when Les uses duress to get June to sell her car to him at an unbelievably cheap price. Each situation is discussed below.

2. **IMPROPER THREAT WHEN TERMS OF THE EXCHANGE APPEAR FAIR. [§12.22]** Under Restatement 2d §176(1), a threat made to induce a party to enter a contract where the resulting exchange is fair is improper if:

   (1) what is threatened (or the threat itself) is a **crime or tort** (see §12.221);

   (2) what is threatened is **criminal prosecution** (see §12.222);

   (3) what is threatened is the **bad faith use of the civil process** (see §12.223); or

   (4) the threat is a **breach of the duty of good faith and fair dealing** (see §12.224).

Once again, recall that if a contract is made under the duress of an improper threat, it is voidable by the party against whom the threat was made.

a. **Example. [§12.221]** Larry badly wants to buy Bernice's car, but Bernice won't sell. Larry thereafter credibly threatens to poison Bernice's husband unless she agrees to sell the car to him at a fair price. Bernice agrees to sell. Bernice can disaffirm the contract based on duress, for Larry has threatened a criminal and a tortious act.

b. **Example. [§12.222]** Brenda, the Bank Manager, believes Cathy, a teller, has embezzled $10,000. Brenda threatens to report Cathy to the police as an embezzler unless Cathy signs an agreement to "repay" the $10,000 over time. If Cathy signs the agreement, she can avoid it under the duress doctrine, for the threat of criminal prosecution is an improper threat under contract law.

Note that this is true regardless of whether Cathy actually embezzled the money. The issue is whether she freely and voluntarily enter into the contract. Since contract law presumes she did not voluntarily enter into the agreement given the threat, the contract can be avoided.

c. **Example. [§12.223]** Norma is happy with the work done by Ted, a contractor she hired to build a room addition onto her home. However, she tells Ted that she will sue him for breach of warranty unless Ted agrees to install a fountain in her back yard. Ted does not want to build the fountain, even though Norma has agreed to pay him a fair price for his labors. Ultimately he agrees to do the work rather than go to the expense of fighting the suit. Ted can disaffirm that agreement, as Norma threatened the use of the civil process in bad faith. Note that if Norma really believed she had a claim against Ted, her threat would not be in bad faith. Thus, if Ted offered to build the fountain in order to settle the dispute, the promise would be enforceable.

d. **Example. [§12.224]** Ellen is an interior decorator. She has signed a contract to decorate one of Rick's homes for $50,000. When she is halfway through, she unambiguously threatens not to finish unless Rick enters into another contract with her allowing her to decorate his vacation home as well. If Rick signs the vacation home contract, he may avoid it, as Ellen's threat was a breach of her duty of good faith and fair dealing and therefore "improper."

3. **IMPROPER THREAT WHERE TERMS OF THE EXCHANGE APPEAR UNFAIR.** [§12.23] Under Restatement 2d §176(2), if a threat induces an exchange which is not on fair terms, that threat is improper if:

> (1) the threatened act would **harm the recipient and not really benefit the party making the threat** (see §12.231);
>
> (2) **prior dealing** between the parties significantly **increases the effectiveness of the threat** (see §12.232); or
>
> (3) the threatened action is a **use of power for illegitimate ends** (see §12.233).

a. **Example. [§12.231]** Ben tells Ted he will make public Ted's extra-marital affair unless Ted sells Ben his $15,000 stereo for $50, and Ted agrees to sell. Since the threatened act would harm Ted and not significantly benefit Ben, Ted can avoid the agreement.

b. **Example. [§12.232]** On the 10th of each month for the last two years, Ed's Food Company has delivered 20 pounds of ground coffee to Pete's Diner for $100. The coffee was a special blend made by Ed's and helped to make Pete's Diner popular. On June 11, the local gourmet club was to meet for the first time at Pete's. At 4:00 p.m.

on June 10, Ed's threatens not to deliver any coffee unless Pete's agrees to pay $800 for a normal 20 pound delivery. As Pete's was out of coffee and had the gourmet club coming the next day, he agreed. Pete's can avoid the agreement for the prior dealings between the parties increased the effectiveness of Ed's threat (i.e., Pete's relied on the delivery), and the terms of the exchange are unfair.

c. **Example. [§12.233]** Gas Company, a monopoly, typically charges developers $200 per home to connect houses in a new real estate development. However, they seek to charge Build Company $1,500 per home to hook up houses in Build Company Acres. Build Company can disaffirm any agreement to pay the $1,500 because Gas Company has used its monopoly power to supply gas for an illegitimate end [Restatement 2d §176, Ill. 16].

d. **REVIEW PROBLEM. [§12.234] Larry is in desperate need of money. Frank knows this and credibly tells Larry that unless Larry immediately accepts Frank's offer of $100 for Larry's $5,000 watch, the offer will be withdrawn. Question: Is the contract voidable on grounds of duress?**

> **Answer:** Even though the terms of the exchange are very unfair, if Larry accepts Frank's offer the contract will not be voidable on the grounds of duress. This is true even though Larry may legitimately feel he is under economic duress and that Frank is taking unfair advantage of him. The problem (for Larry) is that Larry's economic duress was not of Frank's making, and so none of the provisions of Restatement 2d §176(2) apply.

D. RESTITUTION RECOVERABLE UPON AVOIDANCE OF CONTRACT FOR DURESS.

[§12.3] When the victim of a contract entered into under duress avoids a contract, the victim is entitled to restitution. On the other hand, if appropriate, the victim may also have to make restitution to the party who made the improper threat. (See Chapter Thirty-Two for a discussion of restitution.)

CHAPTER THIRTEEN: UNDUE INFLUENCE

A. THE UNDUE INFLUENCE DOCTRINE. [§13.0] Undue influence occurs when a party suffering from some sort of mental weakness (short of incapacity) is subject to improper persuasion (short of duress) by someone who is in a "special relationship" with that party [Restatement 2d §177]. When it is determined that a party's assent to a contract has been induced by undue influence, the contract is **voidable** by the victim because it is deemed not to have been entered into with sufficient voluntariness.

B. ELEMENTS NECESSARY TO ESTABLISH UNDUE INFLUENCE. [§13.1] To establish a claim of undue influence, two elements must be proven:

(1) that there is a **special relationship** between the victim and the other party; and

(2) that there has been **improper persuasion** of the victim by the "stronger" party.

Each of these elements is discussed below. Note, however, that it is **not** a requirement that the ensuing contract be "unfair" to the weaker party. The idea behind the undue influence doctrine is that if the weaker party later objects to having entered into a contract under the improper domination of another, the legal system should not enforce that contract, regardless of whether the exchanged consideration is objectively "fair."

1. THE FIRST ELEMENT: A "SPECIAL RELATIONSHIP." [§13.11] The first element a plaintiff must prove to take advantage of the undue influence doctrine is the existence of a "special relationship" between the contracting parties. For purposes of undue influence, a "special relationship" occurs either when the victim is under the **domination of the other,** or when the relationship between the parties is such that the victim is **justified in assuming the other party will not jeopardize the victim's welfare.** The gist of this requirement is that if the circumstances surrounding the relationship of the parties make the victim particularly susceptible to influence by the other, a sufficient special relationship exists. Typical examples of such a relationship are: parent/child; lawyer/client; clergyman/parishioner; accountant/client; and physician/patient. However, these are not the only qualifying relationships. In addition, while typically the victim is weak, infirm, and/or aged, these characteristics are neither requirements nor limitations on who can be a victim of undue influence [Restatement 2d §177, Com. a].

The opposite of a situation giving rise to a special relationship is an arms' length transaction between two disinterested parties.

2. THE SECOND ELEMENT: IMPROPER PERSUASION. [§13.12] In addition to establishing a special relationship, a party seeking to avoid a contract based on undue influence must also show that the stronger party used "improper persuasion" to gain the victim's assent to a transaction. The test for when improper persuasion has been used is whether the stronger party **seriously impaired the free exercise of judgment by the victim.** Common features of a contract entered into by unfair persuasion are:

(a) an unfair exchange;

(b) the unavailability of independent advice given to the victim before assenting to the contract;

(c) the lack of time for reflection by the victim before assenting to the agreement; and

(d) a high degree of susceptibility to persuasion exhibited by the victim.

Note that these are simply features of such contracts. They provide circumstantial evidence that undue influence occurred. They are **not**, however, elements and thus, undue influence can be found even without them. (See Case Squibs section, *Methodist Mission Home v. N–A–B–*, for a classic application of the undue influence doctrine.)

C. **RESTITUTION RECOVERABLE UPON AVOIDANCE OF THE CONTRACT FOR UNDUE INFLUENCE. [§13.2]** When the victim of a contract entered into by undue influence avoids the contract, the victim is entitled to restitutionary recovery and must also make restitution to the stronger party. (See Chapter Thirty-Two for a discussion of restitution.)

CHAPTER FOURTEEN: MISREPRESENTATION

A. THE MISREPRESENTATION DOCTRINE. [§14.0] During the bargaining process, parties make representations to each other. When those representations turn out to be wrong, and when they have induced the other party to enter a contract, the process under which parties are free to make an informed bargain can be upset. Thus, in certain situations, contract law provides relief from bargains entered into as a result of misrepresentation. These situations are described below.

B. TYPES OF MISREPRESENTATIONS. [§14.1] Misrepresentation can be of three types:

(1) **innocent**, e.g., where the seller honestly and reasonably thought the property was 40 acres and not the 30 it turned out to be (for example, where the owner of the property hired an independent, licensed surveyor to tell her how large the property was, and the surveyor incorrectly stated it was 40 acres);

(2) **negligent**, e.g., where the seller honestly believed that the property was 40 acres, but "should have known" it was really 30 (for example, where she truly believed it was 30 acres because she personally, but carelessly, measured it); or

(3) **fraudulent**. Fraudulent representations are of three types:

    (a) where the seller **consciously lies**, e.g., where she knew the property was 30 acres but said it was 40 anyway just to close the deal;

    (b) where the seller **knows she does not know the true facts**, e.g., where she really had no idea of how big the property was and just made up the 40 acre figure to close the deal; or

    (c) where the seller has a **reckless disregard for the truth or falsity of the statement**, e.g., where she may have believed the property was 40 acres when she said so to the buyer, but such belief was based exclusively on a brief glimpse at a complicated map, and where she really had no expertise in reading maps.

As a matter of tort law, distinguishing among these different types of misrepresentation is quite important, for each can provide the innocent party with different remedies. However, in contract law these distinctions are not that important, for the only remedies available under contract law are avoidance of the contract and collection of restitution, if applicable.

C. EFFECT OF MISREPRESENTATION. [§14.2] The effect of an actionable misrepresentation during contract negotiations depends on what was misrepresented to the innocent party. If there was a misrepresentation as to the very nature of the agreement itself, the contract is "**void**." These "fraud in the *factum*" cases are discussed in §14.3.

If however, as is most often the case, the misrepresentation goes only to the inducement to enter into the contract, the resulting agreement is **voidable** at the option of the innocent party. These "fraud in the inducement" cases are discussed in §14.4.

D. FRAUD IN THE *FACTUM*. [§14.3] Typically misrepresentations, even fraudulent ones, merely go to the **inducement** to enter a contract, e.g., a party falsely tells another that a freezer will chill foods down to -20 degrees when it in fact will only chill them to 0 degrees. However, sometimes the "guilty" party will misrepresent **the very nature of the document**

presented to the innocent party. In that case, there is said to be fraud in the **factum**, and the agreement is never enforceable, i.e., it was a "void" contract from its inception [Restatement 2d §163].

1. **EXAMPLE. [§14.31]** Insurance agent tells customer that the form he is signing is only a release of medical records to the insurance company, which needs to be executed "just in case" the customer eventually decides to go ahead and purchase life insurance. In fact, the document is the life insurance contract, obligating the customer to $800 per year in premiums. The agreement is void because the very nature of the agreement was fraudulently misrepresented to the customer.

E. **ELEMENTS NECESSARY TO ESTABLISH FRAUD IN THE INDUCEMENT. [§14.4]** The **vast** bulk of misrepresentation cases involve fraud in the inducement. To establish that such an actionable misrepresentation occurred, and thereby **obtain the right to avoid the contract**, the innocent party must establish the following elements:

   (1) **a misrepresentation of fact** was made by the other party (see §14.4);

   (2) the misrepresentation was **either fraudulent or material** (see §14.42);

   (3) the misrepresentation was **actually relied upon by the innocent party** (see §14.43); and

   (4) such **reliance was reasonable** (see §14.4).

1. **MISREPRESENTATION OF "FACT." [§14.41] A misrepresentation is an assertion that is not in accord with the facts** [Restatement 2d §159]. To be actionable, the assertion giving rise to a claim of misrepresentation must be about a **fact in existence at the time the assertion was made**, as opposed to an opinion, a prediction of future events, statements of intention, puffery, etc.

   a. **Distinguishing "Fact" from "Opinion." [§14.411]** The general rule is that the assertion of an opinion cannot serve as the basis of a misrepresentation claim. The problem then is determining when a statement is a fact and when it is an opinion. There is no universally agreed upon definition of opinion in contract law, but the Restatement states that the more *verifiable* or *provable* an assertion, the more likely it is to be a fact. Conversely, the more the statement expresses only an unprovable or *unascertainable belief* about a good, the more likely it is to be an opinion [Restatement 2d §168(1)]. In other words, if a statement can be proven true or false, it is probably a fact. If it is incapable of being proven true or false, it is likely only an opinion.

      (1) **Exceptions When Even a Statement of Opinion Can Serve as the Basis for a Misrepresentation Claim. [§14.4111]** Contract law provides that when a party asserts even a "pure" opinion, the party also impliedly asserts at least one fact — namely that what the speaker says is truly the speaker's opinion (or at least that the speaker knows sufficient facts to justify forming the opinion). If this is not the case, i.e., if the speaker truly believes something different than what he or she opines, then such assertion is actionable, for it will be deemed the misrepresentation of a fact — the fact of what the speaker's opinion truly is [Restatement 2d §168(2)].

         (a) **Example. [§14.4111-1]** Frank is selling his home. He tells Bill that while the air conditioning system is "not perfect, in my opinion it works pretty well." In fact, Frank knows the air conditioning system is unworkable. Even though the

Sum & Substance QUICK REVIEW of Contracts

phrase "it works pretty well" generally is taken as only expressing a belief, without certainty, as to the quality of something (and therefore normally would be a non-actionable opinion), in this case Frank knew that his statement of opinion was not true, i.e., he misrepresented the "fact" of what his opinion truly was. As such, his assertion is actionable.

b. **Distinguishing "Fact" from "Prediction of Future Events."** [§14.412] A prediction of future events beyond the control of the speaker cannot serve as the basis for a misrepresentation claim. For example, assume the seller of a house says to a prospective buyer, "You should buy this house. It will only increase in value." Even if the buyer purchases the house based on the quoted statement, and even if a year later the house is worth less than what the buyer paid for it, the buyer still cannot avoid the contract based on misrepresentation. The reason is that the seller did not make a statement of existing fact about the house. Rather, the seller made only a prediction of future events beyond his or her control, which is not actionable.

c. **Distinguishing "Fact" from "Statement of Intention": The Difference Between Ordinary Breach and Misrepresentation.** [§14.413] An easy mistake students sometimes make is to assert that every time a contract is breached, there must have been fraud or some other kind of misrepresentation. That is, if the party promised to deliver 100 25-inch televisions on April 10, and did not do so, it is tempting to say that the seller has made an actionable misrepresentation. The misrepresentation doctrine is not that broad. Whether an ordinary breach rises to the level of misrepresentation depends on the intention of the promisor **at the time the promise was made.** If the promisor knew that he or she had no intention of carrying out the promise at the time it was made, then it is a misrepresentation, and the contract can be avoided by the innocent party. However, if the promisor intended to carry out the promise at the time it was made, but for one reason or another ended up not doing so, the failure to carry out the promise may be a breach of contract, but it cannot serve as the basis for a misrepresentation claim. Thus, in the latter case the innocent party can sue for damages as a result of the breach, but may not avoid the contract under the misrepresentation doctrine.

(1) **Example.** [§14.4131] Pam owns a lumber yard and promises Bob she will deliver firewood to his house in two weeks. She fails to deliver the wood without legal justification. Whether Bob can disaffirm the contract, or instead can only sue for breach, depends on what Pam's intentions were when she made the promise. If Pam never intended to deliver the wood, her promise is actionable as a misrepresentation of "fact," i.e., the fact of what her intention truly was. If, however, at the time she made the promise she intended to carry it out, then Bob's remedy is for breach, for there was no misrepresentation of a fact existing at the time the assertion was made.

d. **Distinguishing "Fact" from "Puffing" or "Trade Talk."** [§14.414] Today it is widely recognized that assertions adjudged to be mere "puffing" or "trade talk" are insufficient statements on which to base a misrepresentation claim. Once again, the key inquiry is how to determine whether a statement is a factual one or puffing. While there is no generally agreed upon definition of puffing, the main attribute of this kind of speech is that it is so amorphous and unprovable as to really be nothing more than opinion. Thus, phrases like "X brand of peanut butter is the *best*," or "This is a *superior* product," or "This deal is an *excellent value*" are not actionable. They are simply considered statements that puff up a product's or service's desirability without really promising anything concrete about the product. That is, there is no objective way to prove one brand of peanut butter is "the best," for the statement is full of ambiguity, e.g., is the speaker saying the product is the best value, the best tasting, the best for you, etc. As such, there is really no way of proving such claims true or false, and thus by definition, no way to establish that they are misrepresentations of **fact**.

Lately, the closest cases as to whether the assertion is non-actionable puffing or an actionable misrepresentation involve the word "good." For example, assume a seller says "This is a good car," and also assume the car completely breaks down while the buyer drives it home. Some courts hold that the words "good," "very good," etc. are too amorphous to mean anything concrete, and thus, are puffing only. However, the modern trend is to find that while it may be difficult to give those terms an exact meaning, it is not hard to find that the term means **something**, e.g., that the car was at least drivable for a little ways. Hence, if the car breaks down on the way home, a misrepresentation was made.

e. **When a Party's Silence Can Act as a Factual Misrepresentation: The Duty to Disclose. [§14.415]** It is almost never true that two parties to a contract have exactly the same information when negotiating a deal. Naturally, a party who lawfully and fairly obtains favorable information will be reluctant to disclose it, as it might make the bargain far less profitable for him or her. For example, a party who finds out where a road will be built because she was at the city council meeting the night the council approved the plans will not want to share that information with the owner of property next to the road who hasn't taken the trouble to find out about the city's plans. Most of the time the law allows a party to keep lawfully and fairly obtained information to himself or herself. However, there are five situations in which the **failure** to speak acts as a factual misrepresentation. In these cases it is said the party who is silent is under a "duty" to disclose the facts, and the failure to do so acts as an affirmative representation to the contrary. For example, if the woman who attended the council meeting was under a duty to disclose that a road was being built, then her silence would be taken as an affirmative statement that there were no plans by the city to build a road in that location.

The five situations in which a party's silence can act as a misrepresentation are:

(1) When a party has taken **affirmative action to conceal a fact**, with the intent to make it unlikely the innocent party will discover it [Restatement 2d §160] (see §14.4151);

(2) When, *before the contract is executed*, a party learns of **subsequent information** about which disclosure is necessary to prevent a previous assertion (which may have been true when made) from being a misrepresentation [Restatement 2d §161(a)] (see §14.4152);

(3) Where one party knows that disclosure of a fact is **necessary to correct a mistake of the other as to a basic assumption** on which the contract is based, so long as the non-disclosure would be a breach of good faith and reasonable standards of fair dealing [Restatement 2d §161(b)] (see §14.4153);

(4) Where **one party knows that disclosure of a fact is necessary to correct a mistake of the other** as to the *effect of a writing* which evidences the agreement of the parties [Restatement 2d §161(c)] (see §14.4154); and

(5) Where the innocent party is entitled to know of a fact due to the **relation of trust and confidence** between the innocent and misrepresenting parties [Restatement 2d §161(d)] (see §14.4155).

Each of these rules is illustrated in order by an example below.

(1) Example. [§14.4151] Jason's car had recently been in an accident which resulted in the front fender falling off. Jason glued it back on with house-hold glue and then offered it for sale to Jerry without saying anything about the fender. The active concealment of the fender problem will be treated as if there was an affirmative assertion by Jason that there were no problems with the fender. Accordingly, Jerry can avoid the contract based on the misrepresentation of the fact that no problem with the fender existed.

(2) Example. [§14.4152] In applying for life insurance, Kal truthfully tells the agent he has never been diagnosed as having cancer. However, in a physical taken a few days later, **before the life insurance contract is executed**, Kal learns he has cancer. He is under a duty to disclose the new diagnosis in order to prevent his previous assertion (which was true when it was made) from becoming an actionable misrepresentation. If he does not, the contract can be disaffirmed by the insurance company. Note that if Kal is diagnosed **after** having entered into the insurance contract, he is no longer under a misrepresentation duty to disclose that fact to the insurance company, for that is the kind of risk the company impliedly takes by entering into such a contract.

(3) Example. [§14.4153] Pete knows his television set does not have a picture tube, but does not disclose it to Sam, who buys the set. Pete does not say anything about the lack of a picture tube because Sam never asked about it, and Sam never asked about it because he figured when someone sells a television, it comes complete with a picture tube. Because a television having a picture tube is a **basic assumption** on which the contract is made, and because failing to disclose the problem would amount to a **breach of good faith and fair dealing**, Pete is under a duty to disclose the picture tube problem. Hence, his silence on the matter will be treated as an affirmative representation that the television has a picture tube, and that assertion can serve as the basis for a misrepresentation claim by Sam.

(4) Example. [§14.4154] Larry seeks to entice Sandra to sign a contract to purchase his home for $150,000. Although Larry does not say anything about it, Larry knows from what Sandra says that Sandra believes the contract provides that she can assume Larry's existing 7% mortgage. In fact, Larry's mortgage has a due-on-sale clause (meaning it is not assumable). If Sandra signs the contract, Larry's silence about the true nature of the assumability of his mortgage will be taken as a representation by him that the mortgage is assumable. Since it is not assumable, Larry's representation can serve as the basis for a misrepresentation claim by Sandra, and she is entitled to avoid the contract [Restatement 2d §161, Com. e, Ill. 12].

(5) Example. [§14.4155] Accountant has handled the business affairs of client for the past 30 years. Accountant learns that oil has been discovered on client's property, a fact unknown to client. Accountant offers client a fair price for the property without oil on it, which client accepts. Nothing is said or asked during negotiations about oil being discovered on the property, either by the accountant or the client. The accountant is under a duty to speak because the special nature of their relationship is one in which it is reasonable for the client to repose trust and confidence in accountant. The accountant's failure to disclose this information is thus actionable and will be taken as an implied representation that there was no oil on the property.

(f) Silence Does Not Act as an Actionable Misrepresentation When the Parties Are Dealing at Arm's Length and None of the Exceptions Apply. [§14.416] In truth, the five situations described in §14.415 and illustrated in §§14.4151-14.4155 occur relatively infrequently. Thus, the general rule is that when a party legally obtains information that would materially affect a transaction, and the transaction is made at arm's length (i.e., between parties who are not in a confidential relationship), the party with the information need not disclose it during negotiations with the other. That is, there is no duty of good faith or any other theory that makes silence in such a situation actionable. The party with the information cannot mislead the other, but as long as he or she says nothing, and none of the five situations set forth in §14.415 apply, no action for misrepresentation can be successfully pled. (See Case Squibs Section, *Laidlaw v, Organ*, for an example of a case in which the silence by a party who had obtained information lawfully and who was in an arm's length transaction was held not to be actionable in a misrepresentation claim.)

2. **THE MISREPRESENTATION MUST BE *EITHER* FRAUDULENT *OR* MATERIAL.** [§14.42] To recover under a theory of deceit in tort, a plaintiff must show that the misrepresentations were both fraudulent **and** material. To be entitled to relief in contract, however, a party need only establish that a misrepresentation is **either** fraudulent **or** material. Each of these terms is defined and discussed below.

   a. **Definition of "Fraudulent."** [§14.421] Under Restatement 2d §162(1), a statement is "fraudulent" if:

      (1) the deceiving party intended to induce the innocent party to enter a contract, or knew with substantial certainty that his or her actions would do so; and

      (2) the deceiving party acted with "scienter." Scienter is a word referring to the mental state of the deceiving party. The deceiving party can meet the scienter requirement in three different ways. That is, scienter is present if the deceiving party made the misrepresentation either:

         (a) knowing that what he or she represented was not true, i.e., the deceiving party told a conscious lie;

         (b) knowing that he or she did not have the basis to make the representation; or

         (c) knowing that he or she was being reckless in making the representation, because he or she did not have sufficient confidence in the truth of what was asserted.

      (1) **Example.** [§14.4211] Tom wants to sell his Acme Stereo receiver to Joe. During negotiations, Joe tells Tom that Acme made two types of receiver, one with copper internal wiring and one with silver internal wiring, and that he is only interested in buying Tom's if it is the silver wire model. Tom, who has no idea what wire is in his receiver, assures Joe his unit is a silver wire model so as to close the deal. If the wire turns out to be copper, Tom has made a fraudulent misrepresentation because: (a) he made the statement with the desire to induce Joe into making the contract; and (b) he made it with scienter, i.e., he knew he had no basis for making the claim.

      (2) **Example.** [§14.4212] See the 3 examples given in §14.1 paragraph "(3)" for further illustration of the different ways to achieve scienter.

b. **Definition of "Material".** [§14.422] A misrepresentation is "material" if it is likely to make a difference to a reasonable person in deciding whether to go through with the transaction [Restatement 2d §162(2)].

(1) **Example.** [§14.4221] Charles told his wife Helen that their car got, on average, 25 miles per gallon (m.p.g.). When selling the car, Helen repeated Charles's claim to Sally, the buyer. In fact, the car only got 17 m.p.g. Even though Helen's statement was not fraudulent, because she had no scienter, it is actionable in contract because it was material. That is, the correct number of miles per gallon of a car is something a reasonable person would want to know in deciding to purchase the car, and thus Helen's statement is a material falsehood, even though innocently made.

3. **THE MISREPRESENTATION MUST INDUCE ACTUAL RELIANCE.** [§14.43] The innocent party in a transaction induced by a misrepresentation must show actual reliance on the misrepresentation before he or she can disaffirm the contract. Such reliance is usually established by pointing to some change of position taken by the innocent party which was motivated, **even if only in part**, by the misrepresentation. Generally, the change of position is the buyer's payment of money, or signing of a contract, in reliance on the representations of the seller.

4. **THE RELIANCE MUST BE REASONABLE.** [§14.44] In addition to showing actual reliance on an erroneous factual assertion, a party seeking to avoid a contract based on misrepresentation must also show that such reliance was reasonable. The general rule is that reliance on a misrepresentation is reasonable, even if the innocent party is "at fault" in not knowing, or failing to discover, the true facts, so long as such fault does not amount to a failure to act in good faith [Restatement 2d §172].

a. **Example.** [§14.441] Libby is inspecting a house she is interested in purchasing and notices a water stain on the ceiling. She asks Dennis, the seller, about it and he says there used to be a leak in the roof, but that he has repaired it. She purchases the house without having the roof inspected. If she had inspected the roof, she would have clearly and easily seen that there were several roof tiles missing. Libby's reliance was nonetheless reasonable under the misrepresentation doctrine. Even if it can be argued that she was "at fault" in failing to inspect the roof, her actions did not constitute a breach of the duty of good faith. That is, even if it could be argued that the innocent party was, in tort terms, contributorily negligent in not discovering the true facts, such conduct is irrelevant to a contract-based recovery for misrepresentation unless the innocent party's actions amount to a breach of the duty of good faith.

b. **Example.** [§14.442] Phil asks a used car salesman whether a car he is considering purchasing has air conditioning, and is erroneously told that it does. Phil then takes the car on a test drive for two hours on a very hot day and ends up buying the car. He cannot avoid the contract based on the misrepresentation about the air conditioner for, given the situation, his reliance on the assertion that the car had an air conditioner was not reasonable and amounts to a violation of his duty of good faith.

F. **LIMITATION ON VOIDABILITY OF CONTRACT BASED ON MISREPRESENTATION: THE CLAIM MUST BE ASSERTED WITHIN A REASONABLE TIME AFTER DISCOVERY.** [§14.5] An innocent party seeking to disaffirm a contract on misrepresentation grounds must do so within a reasonable time after discovery of the misrepresentation. At the expiration of the reasonable time, the contract will be deemed ratified and the party's right to avoid it terminates.

G. RESTITUTION REQUIRED UPON AVOIDANCE OF CONTRACT BASED ON MISREPRESENTATION. [§14.6] A party avoiding a contract on the grounds of misrepresentation is entitled to restitutionary recovery upon the disaffirmance. In addition, the avoiding party may also be liable for restitution to the misrepresenting party as well. (See Chapter Thirty-Two for a discussion of restitution).

CHAPTER FIFTEEN: UNCONSCIONABILITY

A. THE UNCONSCIONABILITY DOCTRINE. [§15.0] As the term is used today, unconscionability is a flexible doctrine that largely prevents one party to a contract from taking undue advantage of the other and enforcing "too good" or "too one-sided" a deal. Some courts have suggested that unconscionability "incorporates a sense of business ethics and community morality into contract law," while others have said a contract is unconscionable if it sets forth a deal "no man in his senses . . . would make on the one hand, and no honest or fair man would accept on the other." In any event, the gist of the doctrine is that a court is directed to step in and correct a situation in which one party makes too good a deal for himself or herself, even in the absence of duress, undue influence, misrepresentation, etc.

Although most of our modern unconscionability jurisprudence comes from the UCC, somewhat surprisingly, the term is not defined there, nor is it defined in the Restatement 2d. The lack of a definition is intentional by the drafters of the UCC and Restatement 2d, for the idea is to give the courts as much flexibility as possible in deciding when to apply the doctrine and prohibit enforcement of unreasonably unfair transactions. Probably the most difficult part of learning about unconscionability is trying to understand a **structure** for analyzing the doctrine. Such structure is provided in §15.3.

B. UNCONSCIONABILITY APPLIES TO UCC AND NON-UCC TRANSACTIONS. [§15.1] The modern unconscionability doctrine emanates from §2-302 of the UCC. However, it has been routinely applied to non-UCC transactions and is now generally recognized as a limitation on the enforcement of unreasonably one-sided deals throughout contract law, and is also specifically included in the Restatement [Restatement 2d §208].

C. EFFECT OF A FINDING OF UNCONSCIONABILITY UNDER MODERN CONTRACT LAW. [§15.2] The decision as to whether a contract, or any part of it, is unconscionable is a decision for the court and not the jury [UCC §2-302; Restatement 2d §208]. Once a court determines unconscionability is present, it is empowered:

    (1) **to refuse enforcement of the entire contract;**

    (2) **to enforce the remainder of the contract without the unconscionable clause or clauses;** or

    (3) **to modify or limit application of any clause to avoid an unjust result.**

Note that the unconscionability doctrine thus proves an exception to the general rule that courts interpret contracts but do not get involved in re-writing them. Under the express provisions of UCC §2-302 and Restatement 2d §208, a court is authorized to change what the parties agreed to, and to re-write a contract to avoid its unconscionable features.

1. EFFECT OF FINDING OF UNCONSCIONABILITY UNDER COMMON LAW. [§15.21] Unconscionability was recognized at common law, but in a much different form. Essentially (although this puts it a bit too simply), unconscionability was a specialized application of the "unclean hands" doctrine and prevented a party from being granted equitable relief. That is, a party to a contract having an unconscionably good term in its favor was not entitled to an *equitable* remedy such as specific performance. The theory was that if a party did not proceed equitably in negotiating the contract, he or she was not entitled to an equitable remedy as a result of its breach. However, the "sharp" party was free to seek *legal* remedies, such as damages in the event the party that was taken advantage of did not perform under the contract. Note that the unconscionable provision did not have to be the provision breached for the prohibition on equitable relief to apply. So long as there was **any** unconscionable provision in a contract, the benefited party was not entitled to an equitable remedy. The following section provides a good illustration of how unconscionability was applied at common law. (See Case Squibs Section, *Campbell Soup Co. v. Wentz* for an example of a case applying the common law approach.)

D. ELEMENTS NECESSARY TO ESTABLISH UNCONSCIONABILITY. [§15.3] One of the frustrations resulting from the flexibility inherent in the modern unconscionability doctrine is that it is difficult to construct a structured analysis for when the doctrine should apply. However, while different courts may use different terms, **all clauses or contracts found to be unconscionable have some combination of:**

(1) **procedural unconscionability;** and

(2) **substantive unconscionability.**

1. **DEFINITION OF "PROCEDURAL" UNCONSCIONABILITY. [§15.31]** The essence of procedural unconscionability is the **absence of meaningful choice** provided a party to the contract. This absence of meaningful choice is, in turn, made up of:

   (1) **oppression,** i.e., unequal bargaining power between the parties; and

   (2) **surprise,** i.e., the fact that the unconscionable clause is typically hidden in the numerous terms and legal jargon of a written statement and is not really a bargained for, or dickered, term.

2. **DEFINITION OF "SUBSTANTIVE" UNCONSCIONABILITY. [§15.32]** The essence of substantive unconscionability is terms that are unreasonably favorable to one party.

3. **SOME COMBINATION OF BOTH PROCEDURAL AND SUBSTANTIVE UNCONSCIONABILITY IS NECESSARY FOR APPLICATION OF THE DOCTRINE. [§15.33]** For a court to find a contract or a particular clause of a contract unconscionable, there must be some combination of both procedural and substantive unconscionability involved in the making of the contract. It is probably fair to say the greater the presence of one type of unconscionability, the less the presence of the other is necessary before the doctrine applies, but nevertheless both types must be present in some degree. That is, a contract may be entered into without much meaningful choice on the part of one party, but if its terms are all scrupulously fair, no unconscionability will be found. Similarly, if the parties enter into a transaction that seems very much to favor one party over another, the courts will not upset that deal if both parties entered into it knowingly, by free choice, and after serious negotiation. It is only when the terms are unfair **and** one party's meaningful choices are limited that the doctrine applies.

SPECIAL CASE SQUIB

a. **Example of** *Williams v. Walker-Thomas Furniture Co.* **[§15.331]** Ms. Williams purchased several items of furniture and stereo equipment on several different occasions from Walker-Thomas. Each of these purchases was made on credit and each was "cross-collateralized." The cross-collateralization clause provided that until the outstanding balance for **each** piece of furniture was paid in full, the store retained a security interest or lien against **all** the pieces of furniture she had purchased. Thus, if she ever failed to make a payment on any one piece of furniture, the store could repossess any other piece of furniture previously purchased at the store so long as that previously purchased piece of equipment was not completely paid for at the time she bought the subsequent item. To illustrate this idea, assume she bought a couch for $1,200 in January of 1989 and agreed to pay $100 per month plus interest for it. Assume in December, 1989 (when only $100 principal remained on the couch), she bought a stereo for $600 and agreed to pay an additional $50 per month plus interest for the stereo. If she signed a cross-collateralization agreement during the stereo purchase, the store would retain its right to foreclose on the **couch** throughout 1990 should she default on making any of the **stereo** payments. This is true even though the couch would have been fully paid for under the original contract by January, 1990.

In May 1962, Ms. Williams defaulted on her credit obligation to the store, and Walker-Thomas sought to repossess everything she had purchased at the store including some items she had originally purchased as far back as 1958. **Held:** The cross-collateralization clause was unconscionable as applied to Ms. Williams, for both types of unconscionability were present. Procedural unconscionability was found because Ms. Williams had an absence of meaningful chance, i.e., due to Ms. Williams' poor financial situation and credit history, she did not have any real choice but to buy her furniture on credit from Walker-Thomas (or a store like Walker-Thomas) that insisted on cross-collateralization clauses in its credit sales. That is, there was no real or meaningful equality of bargaining power between Ms. Williams and the store for she could not have bargained for a contract without the cross-collateralization provision. Further, the court found that the cross-collateralization clause was not pointed out or explained to her, and was "hidden" in the contract. Additionally, the court held the clause substantively unfair, especially in light of the fact that the store was not seeking just to repossess the last goods purchased (the stereo) but all the goods she had bought there since 1958, many of which had been paid for. *Williams v. Walker-Thomas Fruniture Co.* 350 F.2d 445 (D.C. Cir. 1965).

(1) **Criticism of *Williams v. Walker-Thomas Furniture Co.*** [§15.3311] This case is a staple in most first year contracts classes and usually leads to spirited discussion. It has been criticized on the following grounds:

(a) The unconscionability doctrine should not apply where the lack of meaningful choice is derived from a party's own poor financial condition. In other words, if Ms. Williams was such a bad credit risk that Sears, Wal-mart, etc., would not extend her credit (thereby making her only choice Walker-Thomas or a like store that insisted on cross-collateralization), then she should not be able to claim she had no meaningful choice, for she did—she could have saved her money and paid cash, or she could have chosen not to purchase the goods. Those who find this criticism persuasive say that unconscionability should only apply when virtually everyone in an industry gives a buyer the same choice, e.g., if every manufacturer in the car industry only offered a 1 year/15,000 mile warranty on a new car, for it is only then that there truly is an absence of meaningful choice as to all purchasers;

(b) Even if the unconscionability doctrine is to have some effect on Walker-Thomas's contract with Ms. Williams, the doctrine should just apply for "necessities" e.g., beds, refrigerators, stoves, etc., and not for things like stereos;

(c) She apparently did not read the contract and thus should not be heard to complain about a provision she did not ask about or even try to understand; and

(d) Cross-collateralization clauses cannot be substantively unfair for purposes of unconscionability for they are expressly permitted by the UCC.

Some students (and professors) find these criticisms of greater weight than others, but from *Williams* came the idea that unconscionability consists of the absence of meaningful choice (procedural) and unfair terms (substantive) and thus, it is an important case from that perspective alone. Further, it has stood as the fountainhead for all unconscionability cases following it, and thus, its reasoning has been found persuasive by virtually all.

---

4. **UNCONSCIONABILITY APPLIES TO CONDITIONS PRESENT AT THE TIME OF MAKING THE CONTRACT.** [§15.34] The procedural and substantive aspects of unconscionability are examined at the time the contract was made, not at the time of its performance. Hence, an exchange that appeared fair at the time it was made, but in retrospect appears one-sided, will not be affected by the unconscionability doctrine.

5. **Note on Adhesion Contracts.** [§15.35] It is sometimes said that all adhesion contracts, i.e., contracts where non-negotiable terms are dictated by one party and the other party must agree to "adhere" to them or not enter a bargain, are unconscionable. This is not true. While the existence of an adhesion contract is evidence of a lack of bargaining power on one side, it is not evidence either that the terms were unfair or that the "weaker" party did not know, appreciate, and freely agree to be bound by those terms.

E. **UNCONSCIONABILITY NOT LIMITED TO CONSUMER TRANSACTIONS.** [§15.4] By far the most common application of unconscionability is to consumer transactions, like *Williams v. Walker-Thomas* (see §15.331). However, the doctrine is not limited to consumer transactions and has recently been applied with greater frequency in merchant-to-merchant business contracts. As long as an absence of meaningful choice, along with terms unreasonably unfair to one party can be demonstrated, the doctrine will apply. (See Case Squibs Section, *A&M Produce v. FMC Corp.* for an example of unconscionability in a merchant to merchant case.)

F. **UNCONSCIONABILITY APPLIED TO CLAUSES WHICH LIMIT REMEDIES OR DISCLAIM WARRANTIES.** [§15.5] In §§2-719 and 2-316 respectively, the UCC explicitly provides that a party's remedies upon breach can be limited, and that a buyer's warranties can be disclaimed. The argument is sometimes made that such clauses thus cannot be unconscionable when they appear in a contract as they are specifically permitted by the Code. This argument has not found much favor. While such clauses are specifically permitted by the Code, they are only enforceable if they are not unreasonably unfair under the circumstances, and if the other party is not the victim of oppression and/or surprise. (see §33.8) (Recall that a similar argument was made in *Williams v. Walker-Thomas*, (see §15.331). In that case, cross-collateralization clauses were specifically permitted by the UCC, but their inclusion in the contract at issue was nevertheless found to be unconscionable.)

CHAPTER SIXTEEN: ILLEGALITY

A. ILLEGALITY DISCUSSED. [§16.0] An agreement is illegal if either its formation or its performance is **criminal**, or otherwise **against public policy**. The general rule, subject to several exceptions, is that **such agreements are unenforceable by either party**, and thus are often said to be **"void"** contracts. (In some respects the term "void contract" is an oxymoron because if an agreement is void, it cannot be a contract.)

B. DEFINITION OF "ILLEGAL" CONTRACTS. [§16.1] The Restatement does not use the term "illegal" to describe these unenforceable agreements. Instead, it states that a contract is unenforceable if the societal interest in its enforcement is clearly outweighed by public policy [Restatement 2d §178]. While the broader idea of a contract being unenforceable because of public policy concerns has been adopted by the courts, the courts still use the term "illegal" to refer to such agreements. Note, however, that a contract need not call for a criminal act to be illegal. Rather, "illegal" is a kind of shorthand for agreements unenforceable because of public policy.

C. COMMON TYPES OF "ILLEGAL" CONTRACTS. [§16.2] Given the flexibility of the term "against public policy," there is no all-inclusive list of what kinds of contracts will be deemed illegal. However, what follows is a discussion of the most frequently litigated of such agreements.

1. **AGREEMENTS FOR THE PERFORMANCE OF CRIMINAL ACTS. [§16.21]** Any contract in which the promised or actual performance is a criminal act is an illegal contract. For example, contracts for prostitution, the purchase and sale of restricted drugs, contracts calling for the killing of someone, etc. are all void and cannot be enforced by either party.

2. **GAMBLING CONTRACTS. [§16.22]** In most states, contracts involving wagering or gambling are illegal, and thus void.

3. **BRIBERY. [§16.23]** Any agreement: (a) for the payment of a bribe; (b) procured by a bribe; or (c) performed by bribery, is "illegal" and thus unenforceable.

   a. **Example. [§16.231]** Bruce is a supplier of trees and Van is a landscape contractor. Van is working on a house owned by Elena. Bruce promises Van that he will pay Van $500 if Van can persuade Elena to buy the trees for her landscaping from Bruce. Van persuades Elena to order the trees from Bruce and she orders $5,000 worth of trees. Not only is the $500 bribery agreement between Van and Bruce illegal, under modern authority so is the $5,000 contract between Elena and Bruce because it was **procured** by a bribe.

4. **CONTRACTS IN WHICH A PARTY RELEASES ANOTHER FROM TORT LIABILITY. [§16.24]** The general rule is that any contract in which one party seeks to release another from liability for an intentional tort is illegal and will not be enforced. However, a release of liability for negligent torts will probably be upheld, if it is entered into knowingly and in good faith.

   a. **Example. [§16.241]** Leo owns a private race track. In order to race a car on the track, Leo requires the driver to sign a "Release and Waiver," releasing Leo from any liability due to his own, or his employees', negligence in operating the race track. Such a release will usually be upheld so long as the car owner is aware that he or she is releasing a potential cause of action. However, if Leo tried to get the car owner to sign a release from liability for his own, or his employees', intentional torts (e.g., battery), such an agreement would not be enforced. The reason is that society views the commission of an intentional tort as a much more heinous act, and thus will not allow parties (absent other factors) to contractually exonerate themselves for such conduct.

5. **AGREEMENTS FOR SERVICES PROVIDED BY PARTIES WHO SHOULD BE, BUT ARE NOT, LICENSED. [§16.25]** If the appropriate governmental agency requires that all persons engaged in a certain occupation must be licensed so as to control the skill and moral quality of persons engaged in that trade, then a contract for services with an unlicensed individual is illegal. However, if the reason for a government-granted license is principally as a revenue raising measure, a contract with an unlicensed person is not illegal and can be enforced.

   a. **Example. [§16.251]** Municipality requires all tradesmen with offices in the city to have a "Business License." Municipality does not test or screen those to whom it gives licenses, and enacted the business license statute as a way to raise revenues. Bob is a contractor whose office is in municipality but who does not have a business license. If Bob contracts with a church to install hardwood floors in the pulpit, the contract is not illegal, for the business license statute was not designed to control the quality of contractors.

   b. **Example. [§16.252]** Mary seeks legal advice from Mel, who is practicing as an attorney, but who in fact has never taken a bar examination. Any contract Mary enters into for Mel's services is "illegal," for the licensing statute serves to control the skill and moral quality of those who practice law.

6. **AGREEMENTS IN WHICH THE SELLER KNOWS OF BUYER'S ILLEGAL PURPOSE. [§16.26]** If a seller provides legal goods to a buyer who the seller knows will use them for an illegal purpose, the prevailing rule is that the agreement is illegal only if the buyer's intended purpose involves "serious moral turpitude," or if the seller acts to **assist** in the illegal purpose in some way in addition to merely supplying the goods.

   a. **Example. [§16.261]** The owner of an exterminator business sells Ralph rat poison knowing Ralph intends to poison his wife with it. The contract is illegal, for murder is a crime of serious moral turpitude.

   b. **Example. [§16.262]** It is illegal to trade with Country. Nevertheless, Frank sells 1,000 pairs of sunglasses to Jim, knowing that Jim intends to smuggle them to Country. The contract is enforceable because such smuggling is probably not a crime of "serious moral turpitude."

   c. **Example. [§16.263]** Same facts as above, except this time, in addition to supplying the sunglasses, Frank also fills out a false invoice and bill of lading indicating the glasses are to be shipped to the Philippines. The agreement between Jim and Frank is illegal and thus unenforceable, for Frank has now furthered the illegal enterprise by doing an act in addition to merely supplying goods.

C. **GENERAL RULE: IF AN "ILLEGAL" AGREEMENT IS WHOLLY EXECUTORY, NEITHER PARTY CAN ENFORCE IT. [§16.3]** If an "illegal" agreement is wholly executory, then, as a general rule, neither party can enforce it and a court will leave the parties as they find them. However, there are a few exceptions.

1. **EXCEPTION: IGNORANCE OF FACTS AT TIME CONTRACT MADE. [§16.31]** If one party is justifiably ignorant of the facts making the contract illegal at the time the contract is made, that party may treat the contract as **voidable** at his or her option within a reasonable time after learning of such facts.

   a. **Example. [§16.311]** Bill hires Irv to do plumbing work, and Irv does not have a license. Under the general rule, if the licensing provisions of the community are intended to do more than just raise revenue, the contract is illegal and neither Bill nor Irv may enforce it (see §16.25). However, if it is reasonable that Bill did not know that Irv did not have a license when he hired him, Bill may avoid the contract, or enforce it, at his option when he discovers the true facts. If he avoids it, he is entitled to restitution, but he may also have to make restitution to Irv. (See Chapter Thirty-Two for a discussion of restitution)

2. **EXCEPTION: STATUTES DESIGNED TO PROTECT A PARTICULAR CLASS. [§16.32]** If a statute that makes an agreement illegal is designed to protect a particular class, then the party so protected has the option of disaffirming or enforcing the contract.

   a. **Example. [§16.321]** State has a usury rate of 12%. Department store, subject to the usury statute, enters into a credit agreement with customer whereby customer promises to pay 18% interest on the outstanding balance. Customer has the option to enforce or to avoid the contract. That is, because the usury law was designed to protect a particular class of persons of which she is a part, i.e., consumers, the contract is voidable, not void. However, if the store were to try to enforce it, the store could not for as to it, the contract is illegal.

D. **WHERE "ILLEGAL" AGREEMENT IS EXECUTED IN WHOLE OR IN PART: NEITHER PARTY CAN ENFORCE IT. [§16.4]** Once again, the general rule regarding partially or fully executed illegal agreements is that neither party may enforce them, nor may obtain restitution, and the court will leave the parties as it finds them. For example, if Ed pays Don $10,000 to kill Noel, and Don fails to perform, Ed cannot sue Don seeking recovery of his payment. However, once again, this general rule is subject to several exceptions, discussed below.

1. **EXCEPTION: THE *IN PARI DELICTO* DOCTRINE. [§16.41]** A party to an illegal contract is entitled recovery in restitution for the value of the products or services provided if the party can establish:

   (1) **that he or she was not guilty of "serious moral turpitude;" and**

   (2) **that the other party was more blameworthy in the transaction.**

   The rationale for this rule is that since the less blameworthy party is not "in equal fault," i.e., the party is not *in pari delicto*, it should be entitled to at least restitutionary recovery.

   a. **Example of *Bateman, Eichler v. Berner*. [§16.411]** Stockbroker falsely claimed to have "inside" non-public information about a stock and told some of his customers about it. The customers in turn purchased the stock, thinking they were privy to information that would soon make the stock rise in value. When the information proved false, the customers sued the broker. The broker defended on the ground that the customers were *in pari delicto*, as they admitted trading only because they thought they were getting inside information. Held: The customers' wrongdoing was not as egregious or blameworthy as the broker's, and trading on inside information did not involve "serious moral turpitude." Accordingly, the customers could seek restitutionary relief. (See Case Squibs section, *Bateman*.) (See Chapter Thirty-Two for a discussion of restitution)

2. **EXCEPTION: THE *LOCUS POENITENTIAE* DOCTRINE. [§16.42]** If a party to an illegal agreement seeks to repudiate that agreement **before its illegal purpose has been either attempted or obtained**, he or she will be entitled to restitution, as long as the bargain is not one involving serious moral turpitude. In other words if the illegality is minor, the law allows a "place to repent," i.e., a *locus poenitentiae*, and if such repentance is forthcoming, restitution can follow. For example, assume Harry gives Tony $1,000 and asks that Tony use it to bribe a high school basketball player to throw a game. If Harry repents and tries to repudiate the deal before Tony has approached the player, Harry will probably be entitled to the $1,000 back from Tony in restitution. This is because bribery in such a case probably does not involve "serious moral turpitude" and because Harry's repentance came before the illegal purpose of the arrangement had been either **attempted or obtained**.

E. **DIVISIBILITY AND SEVERABILITY. [§16.5]** In all cases involving illegal contracts, if the contract does not involve serious moral turpitude, and if it is possible to sever, or divide out the illegal portion, a court is entitled to do so and enforce the remainder of the contract.

VII. THE PAROL EVIDENCE RULE AND INTERPRETATION

INTRODUCTORY NOTE ON THE PAROL EVIDENCE RULE AND INTERPRETATION:
This section deals with two related, but distinct, issues. The first is the determination as to what terms actually comprise the final, enforceable contract of the parties. This issue arises when a party to a written contract wants to show that one or more other terms were previously agreed upon, but somehow ended up not being included in the final writing that memorializes the contract. Whether the party seeking to establish these additional terms will be permitted to do so is governed by the **parol evidence rule,** which is discussed in Chapter Seventeen.

The second issue in this section is how to determine what a term means once it has been established that the term is part of the final enforceable contract. This topic includes both the question of how the courts are to construe language, and how much evidence should be allowed where one party asserts that the parties had a "special meaning" for a word that is contrary to the normal usage of that term. Contract law calls the rules governing the resolution of these issues "rules of **interpretation,**" and they are discussed in Chapter Eighteen.

The UCC combines the parol evidence and interpretation into a single section, **UCC §2-202,** which also contains slight twists to the common law versions of these doctrines. UCC §2-202 is thus treated separately in Chapter Nineteen.

CHAPTER SEVENTEEN: THE PAROL EVIDENCE RULE

A. THE PAROL EVIDENCE RULE GENERALLY. [§17.0] The parol evidence rule regulates when a party to a written contract may introduce evidence that the parties had reached an agreement as to a particular term when that term, for some reason, did not appear in the final version of the written contract. If the parties **both** agree that a term was left out, the parties are, of course, free to rewrite the contract and put the term back in. The parol evidence rule comes into play, however, when one party claims that a term was previously agreed to, and the other disagrees and claims that term was never part of any final agreement. **At the heart of this rule is a common sense preference held by contract law for only enforcing the final agreement of the contracting parties. When they cannot agree as to what their final agreement was, the parol evidence rule provides a way for a court to determine what terms the court will enforce.**

1. **THE REAL PROBLEM GIVING RISE TO THE PAROL EVIDENCE RULE. [§17.01]** One problem for students studying the parol evidence rule is that most of the time you are told what actually happened during the negotiation process. Thus, before you begin analyzing the problem, you already know which party is the "bad guy," i.e., which party is lying about a term being part of an agreement. Once that fact is known, there is a tendency to try to end up with a just resolution of the problem.

   However, to understand the dilemma the parol evidence rule seeks to solve, think of yourself for a moment as a judge with parties before you who are trying a breach of contract suit. The written contract calls for the seller to deliver her stereo to the buyer, and for the buyer to pay $750 for it. The seller says the buyer is in breach because she timely delivered her stereo to the buyer and the buyer refused to pay for it. The buyer says the reason he did not pay is because the seller did not live up to her bargain. That is, he says they orally agreed that he was to pay $750 for the seller's stereo **and** her compact disc collection. As the seller never delivered the discs, he claims he does not have to pay. The seller points to the written contract, which does not mention the disc collection, but the buyer is insistent that he and the seller spent a lot of time negotiating this point and that he ultimately agreed to pay $750 (for what he claims is only a $600 stereo) solely because the seller had agreed to include the compact discs. The seller says the compact disc conversations never took place and asserts the used stereo is worth at least $750. As the judge, how will you decide the case?

   If you decide this case in the seller's favor based on the written contract only, you may well be permitting fraud if the seller did in fact agree to include the discs. On the other hand, if you decide to let the buyer put on evidence of the alleged compact disc agreement, you also may be permitting fraud, for the seller may be right and the compact disc conversations may never have taken place. The parol evidence rule sets forth the approach contract law has determined should be used to resolve this kind of dispute.

2. **PAROL EVIDENCE CAN BE WRITTEN OR ORAL. [§17.02]** Often when students think of the parol evidence rule, there is an assumption that the previous agreement that is not included in the writings must be oral. This is usually, but not necessarily, the case. If a party has a draft written contract and wants to show that a particular term in the draft, but not the final version, of the written agreement was really part of the final deal, that written draft is analyzed the same way as if the alleged parol agreement was oral.

B. STATEMENT OF THE PAROL EVIDENCE RULE. [§17.1] The parol evidence rule operates whenever there is a writing evidencing an agreement, and when one party seeks to introduce evidence that the parties had agreed to other terms that are not now found in the written contract. The rule governing whether that party will be allowed to introduce evidence of those allegedly agreed upon, but excluded (from the final writing) terms, i.e., evidence of "parol" agreements, is in two parts:

(1) **If the writing is partially integrated, no evidence of a term agreed to prior to, or contemporaneous with, the writing, whether written or oral, can be introduced if such term will contradict a term of the writing; and**

(2) **If the writing is totally integrated, no evidence of prior or contemporaneous agreements, whether written or oral, can be admitted** [Restatement 2d §§210, 213, 215, and 216].

Stating the rule poses two questions: (a) when is a written agreement either partially or totally integrated; and (b) what kinds of terms "contradict" the writing. These are addressed below.

1. PARTIALLY INTEGRATED AGREEMENTS. [§17.11] A writing is "integrated" if it contains at least one term intended by the parties to be their final expression of agreement as to that term, i.e., the term is no longer meant to be part of negotiation, but rather is the term to which both parties have agreed to be bound [Restatement 2d §209]. A writing is "partially integrated" if the parties intended it to be the final expression of at least one of the terms it contains, but do not intend it to be a final expression of *all* terms of their agreement. That is, the writing contains some, but not all, of the final terms of their agreement [Restatement 2d §210(2)]. If a writing is found to be partially integrated, under the parol evidence rule a party may introduce evidence of other terms previously agreed to, but not now found in the writing, so long as they do not "contradict" any term found in the writing.

2. TOTALLY INTEGRATED AGREEMENTS. [§17.12] A writing is totally integrated if it is intended to be the complete and exclusive expression of *all* the terms of the deal [Restatement 2d §210(1)]. If a writing is found to be totally integrated, no evidence of **any** term not found in the writings is allowed. This makes sense, for if a writing is found to be a wholly integrated contract, by definition the parties have intended for it to be the **complete** statement of their final agreement.

3. HOW TO DETERMINE WHETHER AN AGREEMENT IS INTEGRATED, PARTIALLY INTEGRATED, OR TOTALLY INTEGRATED. [§17.13] Obviously, the decision whether an agreement is integrated at all, partially integrated, or totally integrated is crucial to the party seeking to introduce parol evidence. Essentially the issue is this: should contract law allow a party freely to put on evidence of the alleged prior agreements and see whether the jury believes or disbelieves the party's testimony; or should contract law be restrictive in allowing a party's ability to introduce such evidence, thereby expressing a preference for enforcing only the terms of a signed, written contract? Contract law's approach to this problem has changed over time.

a. **Williston View: Look only to "The Four Corners" of the Writing to Determine Integration. [§17.131]** Professor Williston's view, and that of most early American courts, was that a judge should examine the final writing to determine if the contract appeared complete on its face. If it did, Williston argued there was no reason to go beyond "the four corners" of the contract and it should be deemed totally integrated.

However, if it appeared from the writing itself that some, but not all, of the terms agreed to were found in the written document, then Williston believed it should be deemed partially integrated.

(1) **Williston View Today. [§17.1311]** The strict Williston view has fallen out of favor. Indeed, even those jurisdictions which purport to follow the Williston view today have softened it somewhat and allow the court to judge the completeness of the agreement based not only on the writings, but also on the "surrounding circumstances," e.g., the time frame under which it was made, how it was negotiated, by whom it was negotiated, etc. Thus, a judge may take into account these factors in determining whether an agreement appears complete on its face. However, proffered testimony by the parties of what was allegedly agreed to during the negotiations will usually not be permitted, even under the more modern adaptation of this view.

b. **Corbin and Restatement View: All Evidence Surrounding the Making of the Contract Should be Examined by the Court to Determine Integration. [§17.132]** Professor Corbin argued that the party seeking to introduce evidence of a parol agreement should be free to put on evidence tending to substantiate that claim, at least to the judge, out of the presence of the jury. Thus his view, which has been adopted by the Restatement 2d in §§210 and 214 and is the prevalent view today, is that a party can introduce all relevant evidence (at least to the judge) to show the circumstances surrounding the making of the writing in order to show the writing is not completely integrated or even that it is not integrated at all. The thought is that letting a judge hear the evidence out of the presence of the jury will not harm the fact finding process. If after hearing this testimony a judge decides that there is enough evidence so that a jury *could* find that the written document is not the complete and final agreement of the parties, it will be deemed partially integrated and evidence of non-contradictory parol terms can be admitted.

c. **Example Illustrating Difference Between Williston and Corbin/Restatement Views. [§17.133]** On October 1, Janet and Bob sign a written contract that states, in its entirety, "Seller, Janet, hereby agrees to sell her 1965 Mustang automobile, License No. ABC123, to buyer, Bob, for $8,000. Bob agrees to pay the purchase price at time and place of delivery, 1:00 p.m. on October 10, at Seller's house." Bob pays for and picks up the car on October 10, but later discovers that the car has not been given a polymer undercoating to protect against salt on the road during winter. Bob brings suit and wants to put on evidence that he and Janet agreed she would undercoat the car as part of the purchase price. Under the Williston view, Bob would not get to put on this evidence because the "four corners" of the contract seem complete and thus the contract would be deemed totally integrated. Under the Corbin/Restatement view, Bob would get to argue his point and put on evidence of the circumstances surrounding the making of the agreement to the judge. If after hearing that, and any other relevant, evidence (e.g., testimony from others that Bob made offers on three other cars and always demanded the undercoating be made part of the price), the court was persuaded that a jury **could** find that the written contract did not state the entire deal between Bob and Janet, the judge would find the agreement partially integrated. As such, Bob could then present his evidence to the jury, so long as the undercoating term was not deemed "contradictory," as per the test described in §17.14.

d. **Determination of Integration is to be Made by Court, Not Jury, and the Effects of Such Determination. [§17.134]** Under all views, the determination as to whether the writing is integrated at all, partially integrated, or totally integrated is to be made by the court outside the presence of the jury [Restatement 2d §210(3)]. If the court determines it is not integrated at all, the parol evidence rule does not apply and all relevant, competent, and material evidence about the contract and what its terms were may be introduced. If the writing is determined to be partially integrated, evidence of non-contradictory terms is admissible and can be presented to the jury. If the writing is determined to be totally integrated, no evidence of other terms will be admitted.

(1) **Effect of "Merger" or "Integration" Clauses.** [§17.1341] A "merger" or "integration" clause (the terms are synonymous) is usually found at the end of a written agreement and typically will say something like, "The parties to this contract hereby affirm that this writing expresses the final, complete and exclusive statement of the terms of their agreement. There are no inducements to enter this contract other than those appearing in this document, and all prior agreements, written or oral, are discharged and/or merged into this contract." The obvious intent of such clauses is to ensure that a court will find the document wholly integrated and permit no parol evidence of other terms. The general rule is that such clauses have persuasive, but not determinative, effect on the question of whether the parties intended the agreement to be totally integrated. Of course the greater the detail and specificity of such clause, the greater its persuasiveness. On the other hand, such a clause on the back side of a pre-printed form in small type has little persuasive effect in answering the question of whether the parties truly intended the agreement to be totally integrated.

4. **DETERMINATION OF WHETHER A TERM IS "CONTRADICTORY" AND THUS CANNOT BE INTRODUCED EVEN WITH A PARTIALLY INTEGRATED WRITING: THE "MIGHT NATURALLY" TEST.** [§17.14] If a court determines a writing to be only partially integrated, a party is entitled to present to the trier of fact evidence of a term which does not "contradict" a term in the writing. Under the Restatement 2d §216, a parol term does not "contradict" a term in the writing so long as it is a "consistent additional term." In other words, the term "contradictory" is not as broad as it sounds, for its antonym is "consistent additional term." Under the Restatement, **a term is a consistent additional term if, under the circumstances, it is one that "might naturally have been omitted from the writing."** In other words, the test is whether, if the parties had really agreed to such a term, it is the kind of term which might naturally have been left out when they finally reduced their agreement to writing [Restatement 2d §216(2)(b)]. If it might naturally have been left out, it is deemed a consistent additional term and can be introduced to supplement a partially integrated writing. However, if it is a term that, had the parties agreed to it, probably **would have been included** in the writings, i.e., it is a kind of term that naturally would **not** be left out of a final writing, then it is a contradictory term and cannot be introduced.

a. **Example of** *Mitchell v. Lath.* [§17.141] Purchaser of land attempted to show that, as a part of the purchase price, seller had orally agreed to remove an ice house from an adjacent piece of property that seller also controlled. The ice house interfered with the view from the piece of property buyer had purchased. The written contract of sale, however, made no mention of the removal of the ice house. **Held:** If the seller had really agreed to remove the ice house, it was the type of term which probably would have been included somewhere in the documents exchanged by the parties. As such, it was *not* the kind of term that "might naturally" be omitted from the writings. Hence, it was a "contradictory" term, and evidence of its having been agreed to could not be presented to the trier of fact, even if the contract was partially integrated. *Mitchell v. Lath*, 247 N.Y. 377, 160 N.E. 646 (1928).

b. **Example. [§17.142]** Jeff was interested in selling some property he owned for $7,500. Jeff was also about to undergo some plastic surgery and asked his doctor Elizabeth if she would be interested in purchasing it. She said she would and as Elizabeth's fee for the surgery was $7,500, they agreed to a barter exchange. However, for tax reasons, the conveyance documents recited that the price for the land was "$7,500" and said nothing about the barter agreement. Jeff now sues for $7,500 in cash. Elizabeth will be able to introduce evidence of the agreed barter payment term, for it is the kind of term that, under the circumstances, might naturally be omitted from the written embodiment of the agreement [Restatement 2d §216, Ill. 5].

C. **SITUATIONS IN WHICH THE PAROL EVIDENCE RULE DOES NOT APPLY. [§17.2]** There are recurring fact situations to which the parol evidence rule does not apply. That is, in the situations discussed below, the parol evidence rule does not in any way limit the introduction of evidence concerning any terms previously agreed to by the parties regardless of whether the final contract is fully, totally, and completely integrated.

1. **AGREEMENTS MADE AFTER THE CONTRACT HAS BEEN FORMED. [§17.21]** The parol evidence rule has no effect on agreements made after the contract has been established. Such agreements, whether oral or written, are **modifications** to an existing contract and are governed by the rules on modifications (see Chapter Twenty-Six). In other words, the cut off for when the parol evidence rule applies is the time of contract formation.

2. **WHERE A PARTY INTRODUCES EVIDENCE TO SHOW THERE WAS NO VALID AGREEMENT. [§17.22]** The parol evidence rule will not act to keep out any evidence of pre-contractual bargaining if the purpose of such evidence is to show that *no contract ever existed*. This is true even if, on its face, the writing appears to be completely integrated. Thus, if the evidence is intended to show the writing was a joke, a forgery, etc., it is freely admissible.

3. **EVIDENCE OF A CONDITION PRECEDENT. [§17.23]** The parol evidence rule will also not exclude evidence that the contract was subject to a parol condition precedent. The reason is that if such a condition was agreed to, and if it has not been fulfilled, no duty set forth in the written agreement would be enforceable (for a discussion of conditions, see Chapter Twenty).

4. **EVIDENCE OF A FAILURE TO PAY CONSIDERATION. [§17.24]** If a party wants to introduce proof that the purported consideration evidenced in the writing was never exchanged, the parol evidence rule will not keep such evidence from being presented.

   a. **Exception: Option Contracts. [§17.241]** Because option contracts can be enforced on the basis of purported, but unperformed, consideration, this exception does not apply to them. In other words, if the final written option contract states that the prospective purchaser paid consideration for the option, no parol evidence as to the fact that no such consideration was ever actually transferred will be permitted. [See also §4.4212]

5. **EVIDENCE OF FACTS ESTABLISHING THAT THE CONTRACT IS VOIDABLE. [§17.25]** A party who wants to introduce evidence that would entitle him or her to avoid the contract on the grounds of misrepresentation, duress, undue influence, illegality, mistake, or unconscionability will not be prohibited from doing so by the parol evidence rule for the rule does not apply to such situations.

D. **CONTEMPORANEOUS "SIDE" AGREEMENTS. [§17.3]** Parties with standardized contracts are sometimes reluctant to delete or amend them, even if the parties actually agree to a deal on terms different from those found in the standard agreement. In such cases, they will often enter into "side letter agreements" which specifically recite that contemporaneous with the signing of the standardized agreement the parties intended to change a provision of that agreement. The effect of such side letter agreements is that the "writing" to which the parol evidence rule applies consists of **both the standard form and the side letter agreement**, and the terms found in both such writings become the written contract.

E. **PAROL TERMS, EVEN WHEN ADMITTED, DO NOT AUTOMATICALLY BECOME PART OF THE CONTRACT. [§17.4]** A common misconception is that where a court permits the introduction of parol evidence, those terms automatically become part of the contract. This is **not** the case. All that happens when a judge allows the admission of parol evidence is that the party proffering the evidence has a **chance to convince** the trier of fact that the previous agreement existed. That is, he or she can put on evidence of a prior agreement as to a term. If the trier of fact does not believe the party seeking to prove the agreement, the parol term does **not** become part of the contract. If, but only if, the trier of fact believes the evidence, then those terms become part of the agreement, and any claim of breach is viewed in light of the final written contract plus the parol terms.

F. **RELATIONSHIP OF THE PAROL EVIDENCE RULE TO THE STATUTE OF FRAUDS. [§17.5]** The Statute of Frauds only regulates whether a contract may be enforced (see Chapter Nine). It has nothing to do with governing which terms are to be included in the contract, which is the function of the parol evidence rule. If the Statute of Frauds is satisfied, there is nothing in the Statute that will keep any and all evidence surrounding the contract, its making, its terms, etc. from being introduced. However, application of the parol evidence rule may keep such evidence from being admissible. That is, if the written contract is totally integrated, no such evidence can be introduced to supplement the writing, and only non-contradictory terms may be admitted if the written contract is partially integrated.

1. **EXAMPLE. [§17.51]** Buyer, the owner of a retail record store, receives a merchant's confirmatory memorandum from a record company confirming an order of specified rock videos for $12.50/video. Buyer does not object to the memorandum for ten days. The Statute of Frauds has thus been satisfied under §2-201(2) (see §9.63). Accordingly, under the Statute, Buyer can freely introduce evidence that she and record company had agreed that the videos would be recorded on professional-quality, rather than standard quality, video cassettes. However, under the parol evidence rule, whether or not Buyer can introduce evidence of the professional quality tape term depends or whether the written contract is totally or partially integrated, and if partially integrated, on whether such term contradicts the written contract.

G. **RELATIONSHIP OF THE PAROL EVIDENCE RULE TO MODIFICATIONS. [§17.6]** For an explanation of the difference between these two, see §§26.71;17.21.

H. **REVIEW PROBLEM. [§17.6] Student buys a computer at Computer America for $3,000. It does not come pre-loaded with any software. The sales draft, signed by student, specifies the correct amount of RAM, the size of the hard disc, the speed, etc. of the computer and has a pre-printed integration clause on it. However, the draft says nothing about software, and Student correctly claims the sales representative at the store promised her that the computer would come pre-loaded with Windows. Question: Is the Windows agreement enforceable?**

Answer: It depends. First, a court will have to determine whether the sales draft is a partially or totally integrated document. Under the modern Restatement view (§17.13), it will do this by listening to Student and deciding if a jury **could** believe student, taking into account the merger clause found in the draft. If the court decides a jury **could** believe her, it will judge the contract to be partially integrated.

The next step is to determine if the Windows agreement is "contradictory." The question here is whether it is the type of agreement that "might naturally" have been left out of the final contract (§17.14). If, for example, the sales draft form had only blanks for amount of RAM, size of hard drive, etc. that were filled in by hand, Student may have a good argument. On the other hand, if the sales draft form had a blank for "Included Software" which was blank, Student's argument is weaker.

If Student passes this test, i.e., if the court holds that the sales draft is only partially integrated and that the Windows term is not "contradictory" to the other terms of the agreement, she will be permitted to testify about the Windows agreement at trial. If the jury believes her evidence, Computer America will be in breach for failing to include the software. If the jury disbelieves her evidence, the Windows agreement will be deemed not part of the contract, and the store will thus not be in breach for failing to include it.

CHAPTER EIGHTEEN: INTERPRETATION

A. INTERPRETATION GENERALLY. [§18.0] The parol evidence rule helps courts decide which terms are included in the final agreement of the parties. Separate and apart from that inquiry is what **meaning** should be given to the terms found in the final agreement. Interpretation is the process a court uses to determine the meaning of those terms. Actually, when commentators speak of interpretation, they generally refer to two separate sets of rules:

> (1) **rules of construction**, which apply generally to any contract, and

> (2) **rules of interpretation**, which regulate how a court will discern the meaning to be given terms under a particular contract.

B. RULES OF CONSTRUCTION. [§18.1] Rules of construction are the generalized set of rules which apply to every contract. Often such rules are said to be "maxims" of law and provide at least a first step in determining how to interpret a contract. As generalized rules, they can be changed by the parties in any particular contract, and only apply in the absence of admissible proof that the parties intended a different construction for their agreement. The rules of construction are discussed below.

1. **AN INTERPRETATION THAT GIVES MEANING TO ALL TERMS IS PREFERABLE TO AN INTERPRETATION MAKING A PART OF THE AGREEMENT SURPLUSAGE. [§18.11]** If two meanings of an agreement are possible, the preferable one is the one that interprets the contract in such a way that each part of it has some meaning, rather than in a way that one or more terms are left meaningless [Restatement 2d §203(a)].

2. **IF TWO CLAUSES ARE IN CONFLICT, THE MORE SPECIFIC ACTS AS AN EXCEPTION TO THE GENERAL. [§18.12]** Where two terms in a contract are in conflict, the preferred approach is to find the more specific of the two an exception to the more general. [Restatement 2d §203(c)]. Thus, if one general clause in a contract says that buyers "shall be charged extra for delivery," but another very specific provision provides that the price for the particular shipment due on November 1, includes shipping charges, no extra shipping charge likely will be added for the November 1 shipment because the more specific term acts as an exception to the general.

3. **SEPARATELY NEGOTIATED TERMS ARE GIVEN GREATER WEIGHT THAN STANDARDIZED TERMS. [§18.13]** If a particular clause in a contract was a dickered, bargained for term, such term will generally be enforced even if it is in conflict with a more general, standardized, or pre-printed term. [Restatement 2d §203(d).]

4. **HANDWRITTEN TERMS GENERALLY CONTROL OVER TYPED OR PRINTED ONES; TYPEWRITTEN TERMS GENERALLY CONTROL OVER PRINTED ONES. [§18.14]** If a contract is printed but spaces are left to be filled in by hand, or if the parties agree to handwritten (or typewritten) changes to a printed form, generally such handwritten or typewritten clauses are to be enforced when in conflict with the preprinted terms.

5. **IF A TERM IS AMBIGUOUS, IT SHOULD BE RESOLVED AGAINST THE PARTY WHO DRAFTED IT. [§18.15]** Generally, an ambiguous term is construed against the drafter on the theory that the drafter could have made it clearer in the first place. This doctrine has had especial prominence in construing insurance contracts (i.e., construing such contracts against insurance companies), and is often used in adhesion contract situations as well.

6. THE EXPRESSION OF ONE THING IS THE EXCLUSION OF OTHERS. [§18.16] If the parties to a contract make a list as to certain items, it may be construed that if an item is not on the list, it is intended to be excluded. For example, in selling a house the buyer and seller agree that light fixtures are to be included in the sale. They then list the light fixtures in the contract. The general rule is that if a particular fixture is not on the list, it was intended to be excluded from the sale.

C. RULES OF INTERPRETATION. [§18.2] Rules of interpretation govern how a court derives the meaning to be given to a term in a particular contract [Restatement 2d §200]. As shown below, most of the time this is not difficult, for the parties usually mean the same thing when they use a word, and that meaning is usually the customary one generally understood in society. However, on occasion this is not the case. Sometimes the parties to the contract do not mean the same thing when they agree on the same word, e.g., "10 days" may be 10 calendar days to one party and 10 working days to the other. Also, sometimes one party to a contract claims that the parties had agreed on a special meaning for a term that is different from its generally understood meaning.

On occasion, the failure to agree on the meaning of a term can mean that there is no contract at all between the parties (see §15.5, Mistake). More often, however, the parties intend to be bound, and it is up to the court to determine their meaning. The rules of interpretation that follow set forth contract law's approach to determine the meaning of contract terms.

1. GENERAL RULES. [§18.21] The principal goal of contract interpretation is to give effect to the intent of the parties as to the meaning of words. However, most often the parties do not explicitly define a term or otherwise express their views as to the meaning of a particular word. Thus, courts must use presumptions to ascribe a meaning to the parties' chosen words. The following sections set forth these interpretative presumptions, which control the interpretation of a contract in the absence of admissible evidence showing the parties' contrary intention.

   a. Language Is to be Given its Generally Prevailing Meaning in Society. [§18.211] The general rule is that words are to be interpreted in light of their generally accepted societal meaning [Restatement 2d §202(3)(a)].

   b. Terms Are to be Interpreted in Light of their Meaning Within the Usage of Trade, Course of Dealing, Or Course of Performance. [§18.212] The concepts of usage of trade, course of dealing, and course of performance are principally at issue in transactions under the UCC and are defined and discussed in detail in §19.11. However, even in non-UCC transactions, absent any admissible evidence indicating a contrary interpretation by the parties, courts will give contractual terms the meanings they have in a particular trade or vocation (usage of trade), or the meanings they have been given by the parties themselves in prior contracts (course of dealing) or in their present contract (course of performance) [Restatement 2d §§219-223].

   (1) Hierarchy of Express Terms, Usage of Trade, Course of Dealing, and Course of Performance. [§18.2121] A court is directed, wherever possible, to construe the meanings of express terms, i.e., the terms that appear in the construct itself, **consistently** with the meaning given such terms in the usage of trade, course of dealing, or course of performance. However, **if there truly is a conflict** among those meanings, the following rules govern which meaning controls:

(i) the meaning of express terms shall prevail over any conflicting meaning given such terms in the course of dealing, course of performance, and usage of trade;

(ii) the meaning given a term in the course of dealing prevails over any conflicting meaning given that term in the course of performance or usage of trade; and

(iii) the meaning given a term in the course of performance controls over any conflicting meaning given that term in the usage of trade.

2. **ADMISSIBILITY OF EXTRINSIC EVIDENCE TO PROVE THE PARTIES HAD THEIR OWN SPECIAL MEANING FOR A TERM. [§18.22]** Sometimes a party will assert a breach of contract, but on the face of the contract the alleged breacher seemed to do nothing wrong. However, the party bringing the action will claim the parties had a special meaning for the term that is different from the one generally given to such a term. This special meaning can be a specialized application of a common term, **e.g.**, when the contract calls for delivery of 7,000 tons of asphalt it means 7,000 metric tons and not 7,000 English tons. In addition, the special meaning can be part of a secret code between the parties. For example, a famous hypothetical assumes a customer who believes people are spying on her agrees with her stockbroker that when the customer tells the broker to "sell," she really means "buy," and vice versa. One day the customer tells her broker to "buy" 1,000 shares of a certain stock, and her broker ends up buying, not selling, the shares. Obviously if the customer sues for breach, she would like to be able to introduce evidence (even if it is only her own testimony) of the secret meaning.

Note that this is not a parol evidence problem, because both parties agree that the term "buy" was in the contract. The dispute is over the *meaning* of the term used by the parties. The test for when such extrinsic evidence, i.e., evidence by a party of a term's meaning other than the normal definition of that term, is admissible has changed over time.

a. **Williston/Holmes View: The Plain Meaning Rule. [§18.221]** According to the approach set forth by Professor Williston and endorsed by Justice Holmes, a party cannot introduce extrinsic evidence to explain the meaning of a term unless the term is, on its face, ambiguous. If the term had a "plain meaning" as understood in society, that was the meaning it would be given. Thus, if the parties agreed to the delivery of 14 "dweeboids" of cotton at a price of 25 "units" per dweeboid, extrinsic evidence would be allowed to explain the parties meant a dweeboid to be 1,000 lbs. and that a "unit" was intended to be $1,000. However, in the stockbroker example given above, no evidence of the "buy-means-sell" agreement would be admitted under this view, for the words used in the contract, i.e., "buy" the stock, appeared clear on their face.

b. **Corbin/Restatement View: The "Reasonably Susceptible" Test. [§18.222]** The modern trend of cases, although probably not yet adopted in a majority of jurisdictions, sets forth a more liberal view regarding the admission of such extrinsic evidence. Under this view, if the contract term is "reasonably susceptible" to the proffered meaning urged by one party, that party may introduce extrinsic evidence tending to establish that the proffered meaning was the one actually shared by the parties. In determining whether the given term is reasonably susceptible to the ascribed meaning, a court is directed to examine all relevant circumstances outside the presence of the jury. Thus, in the stockbroker case, if the customer were prominent and could show with reasonable probability that she was being spied upon, under those circumstances a secret code where buy means sell is possible. Accordingly, because the term "buy" is reasonably susceptible of meaning "sell" under these circumstances, customer will be entitled to introduce evidence of the alleged secret agreement. Note that this does not mean that the trier of fact will necessarily believe the party asserting the secret meaning and must adopt the secret meaning as controlling. However, it does mean that the party will at least get a chance to introduce evidence of that meaning to the trier of fact.

CHAPTER NINETEEN: UCC §2-202

A. UCC §2-202: AN ATTEMPT TO COMBINE THE PAROL EVIDENCE RULE WITH INTERPRETATION RULES. [§19.0] In §2-202, the UCC has attempted to combine the parol evidence rule (Chapter Seventeen) with the rules of interpretation (Chapter Eighteen). That is, the rule attempts to regulate both what terms are included in the contract (the parol evidence rule) **and** when extrinsic evidence is admissible to show the parties' particular meaning of a term (interpretation). In the words of the statute, it governs both how terms in a written document may be "supplemented" and "explained."

B. HOW TO APPROACH A §2-202 PROBLEM. [§19.1] As with all UCC problems, the first step is to ensure that the transaction is one to which Article 2 of the UCC applies (see §34.1). The next step is to ascertain whether the writing is partially integrated, totally integrated, or not integrated at all. The rules governing this determination are the same as those for non-UCC transactions (see §17.13). Once that determination is made, the following rules govern when parol evidence may be introduced and what extrinsic evidence is admissible to explain the terms found in the agreement.

1. WHEN THE WRITING IS PARTIALLY INTEGRATED. [§19.11] If the writing is partially integrated, then no evidence of any supplementary term that **contradicts** any term in the writing will be admitted under §2-202. (Note, however, that under the UCC, terms made in a contemporaneous written agreement, e.g., a "side letter" agreement (see §17.3) are not subject to the parol evidence rule and are freely admissible.) In addition, evidence of course of performance, course of dealing, or usage of trade are freely admissible so long as they are introduced to **explain** a term found in the final agreement.

a. Evidence of "Contradictory" Terms Cannot be Used to *Supplement* the Contract. [§19.111] As under the common law parol evidence rule. [§17.1], evidence of a parol term that "contradicts" a term found in a partially integrated written agreement is inadmissible. The question then is how to tell whether a term is "contradictory."

(1) "Contradictory" Terms are Judged under the "Would Certainly" Test. [§19.1111] Under the common law parol evidence rule, the test for determining whether a term is "contradictory" or not is the "might naturally" test. (§17.14). Under the UCC, the test is similar, but different. It is known as the "**would certainly**" test. [UCC §2-202, Com 3.] Under the "would certainly" test, the question is **whether the proffered term is the type that *would certainly* have been included in the final agreement of the parties had it, in fact, been agreed to.**

(a) Example. [§19.1111-1] Although it is a non-UCC case (since it deals with real estate), to illustrate how the UCC's "would certainly" test applies, analyze *Mitchell v. Lath* as if it were a UCC case (the case is analyzed under the Restatement's "might naturally" test in §17.141). In *Mitchell*, a seller of property owned two adjacent lots. He sold one to the buyer, and the buyer later claimed that buyer and seller had made an oral agreement, not reflected in the final written contract, that the seller would remove an ice house from the property not sold, which blocked the view from the buyer's newly purchased lot. The seller claimed that agreement was never made.

Under the UCC the first step (assuming Article 2 applicability) would be to determine if the written agreement was partially integrated. Assuming it was, the next step would be to determine if the "move the ice house" term was a consistent additional term. If it was a consistent term, evidence of its making could be introduced. To determine if it is a consistent term the question is, had the parties agreed to it, is it of the type that they **would certainly** have made sure to include in the final written contract. As it likely would be the kind of term the parties "would certainly" have included in their contract if they had truly separately negotiated it, it will be deemed a contradictory term and evidence of its making would not be admissible by the buyer.

(b) Potential Limitation on the "Would Certainly Test. [§19.1111-2] Some scholars believe there is an inherent limitation on the application of the "would certainly" test, namely that it does not apply to a contract where it is facially obvious that a material term has not been inadvertently omitted from the final writing. For example, assume two companies have heavily negotiated a thirty page contract, and after it is signed, it is discovered that there is no price term in the contract. The seller would like to introduce evidence that the agreed-upon price was $1,800,000, a generous, but not unconscionably high, price for the goods involved. The buyer wants to introduce evidence that the agreed-upon price was $1,600,000, a low, but not unreasonable, price for the goods.

A court examining the agreement would doubtless find it only partially integrated given that it has no price term and is otherwise so heavily negotiated. But, under the "would certainly" test, evidence of either party as to the supposedly agreed-upon term would not be admissible. This is because a price term is the sort of term that **had** the parties agreed to one, it "would certainly" have been in the agreement. Since it is very unlikely in such a heavily negotiated agreement that the parties would not have made some arrangement as to price, the argument is that the would certainly test simply should not be applicable to such a case. That is, where it is reasonably apparent from the face of the written contract that a material term was inadvertently omitted from the final writing, these commentators hold that the parol evidence rule should not apply and all evidence of what the parties had agreed-upon concerning that term should be freely admissible.

Those that oppose this view state that if the term was important enough to a party, he or she should have ensured that it was included in the final draft of the contract before signing it. If such an effort was not made, then he or she should be subject to the parol evidence rule like everyone else, which in the hypothetical above means that the price term for the contract would be a "reasonable price" under the gap filler of UCC §2-305 (see §6.221).

b. **Evidence of course of performance, course of dealing, and usage of trade can be introduced to** *explain* **a term found in the contract. [§19.112]** As noted above, UCC §2-202 not only determines what terms can be added to the contract, but also what terms can be used to explain the terms that are admittedly found there. It sates that course of performance, course of dealing, and usage of trade can *always* be introduced to explain what the parties mean by a particular term. These terms are defined below.

(1) **Course of Performance. [§19.1121]** Course of performance consists of a sequence of consistent actions taken by two parties involving a term **under the particular contract at issue** [UCC §2-208]. For example, the present contract obligates the buyer to place 5 orders for widgets in a year, and obligates the seller to deliver them within "10 days" of the order. On the first 3 orders, seller delivered widgets, without objection, within 10 *working* days of the order, but not within 10 calendar

days. If the buyer attempts to refuse delivery of the fourth order because it was not made within ten calendar days (although it was delivered within 10 business days), the seller will be able to introduce evidence of the **course of performance** under the current contract to explain what the parties meant by the delivery term, and that evidence will likely be very persuasive.

> **(a) "Waiver" and Course of Performance. [§19.1121-1]** If the parties only act a particular way once in response to a particular fact situation, there is a real question as to whether it establishes a "course of performance" or whether one party simply "waived" its rights that one time as a favor to the other party. This is a question of fact to be determined on a case-by-case basis, but if the actions are judged to be a "waiver" and not a course of performance, such actions are inadmissible under the parol evidence rule to explain the parties' interpretation of the term. [See §20.41 for a further discussion of waiver]

(2) Course of Dealing. [§19.1122] Course of dealing consists of a sequence of consistent actions taken by the two parties in response to repeated situations involving a contractual term under **previous** contracts [UCC §1-205]. Again, the idea is that if the parties have had previous dealings where construction of the same term is at issue, how the parties acted is persuasive evidence of what they intended that term to mean in the present contract. For example, in three different contracts over the past two years with a "10 day" delivery term, the buyer has accepted delivery without objection so long as the goods were delivered within ten working days after the order was placed. Such conduct would amount to a **course of dealing** which is persuasive evidence of what the parties intended in the present contract by the "10 day" delivery term.

(3) Usage of Trade. [§19.1123] Usage of trade is any practice or method of dealing having such a regular occurrence in a particular place, vocation or trade that a party to the agreement should know of its existence [UCC §1-205(2)]. The meaning given a particular term in the trade can be introduced as evidence of what the parties to a contract must have meant when they used that same term. For example, if a neophyte buyer orders a "ton" of rock from a merchant seller, and if in the industry, a "ton" is a metric, not an English ton, that trade usage will be admissible to establish how the court should interpret the term in this contract. Note this is true regardless of the fact that the neophyte buyer may have subjective believed he was buying an English ton of rock.

(4) Hierarchy of Interpreting Express Terms, Course of Performance, Course of Dealing, and Usage of Trade. [§19.1124] When possible, a court is instructed to interpret express terms, course of performance, course of dealing, and usage of trade in such a way that they are consistent with each other [UCC §2-208]. However, when those terms are in conflict, the hierarchy as to which terms control are the same as for non-UCC transactions, [See §18.2121].

2. **WHEN THE WRITING IS TOTALLY INTEGRATED. [§19.12]** As under the common law parol evidence rule (§17.1) if the writing governed by Article 2 is totally integrated, no evidence of any supplementary terms is allowed UCC §2-202. However, under UCC §2-202 the **meaning** of the terms included in the writing may be explained by the course of performance, course of dealing, or usage of trade, even if the writing is totally integrated.

C. SITUATIONS WHERE UCC §2-202 DOES NOT APPLY. [§19.2] A list of situations in which the common law parol evidence rule does not apply are given in §17.2. Those same rules apply to UCC §2-202, i.e., the UCC parol evidence rule does not apply:

(a) to modifications agreed to after the contract has been made;

(b) when evidence is introduced to prove either that no contract was ever made, that a condition precedent has not been fulfilled, or that consideration has not been paid;

(c) to show the facts necessary to establish that the contract is voidable; or

(d) to contemporaneous **written** documents. Thus evidence of such writings typically "side letter" agreements (see §17.3), is freely admissible either to explain terms in the writing or to add terms to the writing, regardless of whether the writing is totally or partially integrated.

VIII. CONDITIONS

CHAPTER TWENTY: CONDITIONS

A. CONDITIONS GENERALLY. [§20.0] Conditions are devices that allow parties to a contract to be bound by a valid agreement, but to have the **duties** under that agreement **be (or become) unenforceable** either: (a) until an event occurs; or (b) because an event has occurred. For example, assume John agrees to buy Mary's house for $150,000 "on the condition that [John's] loan application at Central Bank is approved." While John and Mary have a viable contract, their duties under that contract (John's duty to pay and Mary's duty to transfer property), are not enforceable until a specified event occurs, i.e., loan approval. Similarly, assume that on April 10, Bill agreed to pay Sandra $150,000 for her house on June 1 "unless the Dow Jones Industrial Average has fallen below 2,500 points by then." The parties have a valid contract whose duties are enforceable until a specified event occurs, i.e., the Dow Jones average falling below 2,500 points by the specified date. Each of these situations describes a different type of condition. These types are discussed below.

B. THE DIFFERENT KINDS OF CONDITIONS. [§20.1]

1. THE DIFFERENCE BETWEEN A CONDITION PRECEDENT AND A CONDITION SUBSEQUENT. [§20.11]

a. Condition Precedent: Discussed and Defined. [§20.111] A condition precedent is: (a) an event, not certain to occur, which (b) must occur before performance under a contract is enforceable, unless (c) the non-occurrence of the event is excused. Most conditions are conditions precedent. In the John and Mary example given above in §20.0, the condition in the agreement to purchase Mary's home "on the condition that [John's] loan application at Central Bank is approved" is a condition precedent. This is because loan approval is: (a) an event, which is not certain to occur, but which (b) must occur in order for the duties under the contract to become enforceable, unless (c) John excuses the non-occurrence of the condition, i.e., unless John agrees to buy the house even if his loan is not approved. Note, however, that if a contract called for a payment of $10,000, "on the condition that 30 days pass," the promise would **not** be conditional in the contract law sense, for the passing of 30 days is an event that is certain to occur.

It is important to note that **the parties to a contract with an as yet unfulfilled condition precedent are in a valid, binding agreement. It is just that the duties subject to the conditions are unenforceable until the conditional event occurs** [Restatement 2d §225].

b. Condition Subsequent: Discussed and Defined. [§20.112] A condition subsequent is: (a) an event, the occurrence of which is not the result of a breach of the obligor's duty of good faith, which, (b) if it occurs, terminates a party's duty to perform, unless (c) its occurrence is excused. In the Bill and Sandra example given above in §20.0, the condition in Bill's agreement to purchase Sandra's home, "unless the Dow Jones Industrial Average has fallen to 2,500 points by June 1" is a condition subsequent. This is because the falling of the Dow Jones average is: (a) an event, the occurrence of which would not be a breach of Bill's duty of good faith, which (b) if it occurs, will terminate Bill's duty to perform, unless (c) Bill chooses to excuse it, i.e., unless Bill decides to go ahead and purchase the house even though the Dow Jones Average has fallen below 2,500 points.

Note that the **parties to a contract with an as yet unfulfilled condition subsequent are in a valid, binding agreement whose terms are enforceable but are subject to the condition being fulfilled. When the condition is fulfilled, the parties are still in a valid binding contract, but the duties under the agreement can no longer be enforced** [Restatement 2d §230(1)].

c. **Restatement 2d Rejects Terms "Condition Precedent" and "Condition Subsequent." [§20.113]** The Restatement 2d rejects the terms "condition precedent" and "condition subsequent." Instead, what at common law would be known as a condition precedent is simply called a "condition" under the Restatement [Restatement 2d §224]; and what at common law would be known as a condition subsequent is called an "event that terminates a duty" in the Restatement [Restatement 2d §230]. However, the Restatement terminology has not proven persuasive, and courts and commentators still tend to use the words "precedent" and "subsequent" as adjectives modifying the noun condition. Accordingly, this outline will use the term condition precedent to refer to the Restatement's "condition," and condition subsequent to refer to the Restatement's "event that terminates a duty."

d. **Effect of Classifying a Condition as "Precedent" or "Subsequent." [§20.114]** Besides the differences in operation described above (see §20.11), the only other legal effect of classifying a condition as precedent or subsequent is a procedural one in a breach of contract suit:

(1) **If the condition is a condition precedent, the party to whom a duty is now claimed to be owed bears the burden of proof to establish that the condition was satisfied.**

(2) **If the condition is a condition subsequent, the party who at one time owed the duty bears the burden of proof to establish that the condition has occurred.**

(1) **Example. [§20.1141]** In the John and Mary example in §20.0, loan approval by the Bank is a condition precedent to John's duty to pay becoming enforceable. Assume John's loan was approved, but he nevertheless refused to go through with the deal. In the ensuing breach of contract action, it is Mary, as the party claiming to be owed the duty of payment in a contract with a condition precedent, who must bear the burden to prove that the condition was met, i.e., that John's loan was approved, and thus he should have performed. The rationale for this rule is that if the loan was never approved, John's duty to pay would never become enforceable. Thus, to establish that the duty **was** enforceable and was **breached**, it is up to Mary to bear the burden of showing the condition was fulfilled.

(2) **Example. [§20.1142]** In the Bill and Sandra example in §20.112, the Dow Jones index falling to below 2,500 points is a condition subsequent. Assume the index timely fell below the 2,500 point threshold, but Sandra nevertheless brought suit for breach when Bill refused to pay. In that suit, it is Bill, as the party who at one time owed the duty to pay, who bears the burden to prove that the condition subsequent was satisfied in order to establish that his duty of payment was terminated. The rationale for this rule is that if the Dow Jones average had not fallen, Bill's duty to pay would be enforceable. Thus, as the party seeking to be **relieved** of the obligation, it is up to Bill to bear the burden showing his duty terminated.

2. THE DIFFERENCE BETWEEN EXPRESS CONDITIONS, IMPLIED-IN-FACT CONDITIONS, AND CONSTRUCTIVE (IMPLIED-IN-LAW) CONDITIONS. [§20.12]

a. **Express Conditions: Defined and Discussed. [§20.121] An express condition is a condition expressly agreed upon by the parties as evidenced by their words.** Typically, phrases like "on the condition that," "if, but only if," "unless," "in the event that," and "provided" are used to signify express conditions.

b. **Implied-in-Fact Conditions: Defined and Discussed. [§20.122] An implied-in-fact condition is a condition agreed upon by the parties as evidenced by their actions rather then their words.** Whether the actions of the parties constitute an implied-in-fact condition is judged under an objective test, i.e., whether a reasonable person would believe a condition had been agreed to by the parties. **Implied-in-fact conditions have the same legal effect as express conditions.** As a consequence, whenever a rule is given as to express conditions throughout the book, the rule applies equally to implied-in-fact conditions as well.

(1) **Example. [§20.1221]** Buyer says "I'll buy your autographed Mickey Mantle baseball card for $500, on the condition that the signature is authenticated by a handwriting expert." Seller says nothing, but hands over the card. The parties have entered into a valid contract with an implied-in-fact condition precedent. The condition of signature authentication is not "express" since there was no agreement to it in words, but to a reasonable person the parties' conduct would indicate that the condition was agreed to as a term of the contract.

c. **Constructive (Implied-in-Law) Conditions: Defined and Discussed. [§20.123] A constructive condition is a condition the parties have not expressly agreed upon, but which the court decides is necessary to imply in a contract to determine the parties' rights and duties under that contract** [Restatement 2d §226, Com. c]. In deciding whether to imply a condition, a court is directed to impose a constructive condition if it believes either that:

(a) such a condition would have been agreed to by the parties had they considered it; or

(b) whenever justice requires such a condition be imposed so the rights and duties of the parties under the agreement can be fairly ascertained.

Constructive conditions are, at best, distant cousins of express conditions. They operate differently and have wholly different purposes than do express conditions. Mostly they are important when analyzing performance and breach, and thus, except for a few times in this Chapter when they are mentioned to contrast a rule governing express conditions, constructive conditions are addressed separately in this book (see Chapter Twenty-One), and should be treated as analytically separate from express conditions.

(1) **Example of Constructive Condition. [§20.1231]** In a lease, landlord promises to make any necessary repairs in tenant's apartment, but reserves no privilege to enter the apartment. As there will be no way for landlord to know of the need for any repair without notice from the tenant of a problem, a court will "construct," i.e., imply as a matter of law, a condition requiring tenant to provide notice of the need for a repair before the landlord's duty to repair becomes enforceable. Thus, if there is a problem that needs fixing, tenant cannot sue landlord for breach without first fulfilling the implied condition and telling landlord of the problem.

(2) The Most Common Type of Constructive Conditions: Constructive Conditions of Exchange. [§20.1232] The most common form of implied-in-law conditions are known as **constructive conditions of exchange**. These conditions dictate:

(a) which party must perform first in a contract where both parties have remaining executory duties (see §21.1 et seq.); and

(b) when a party is in material, rather than only partial, breach of contract (see §21.2 et seq.).

d. Effect of Express Conditions: The Strict Construction (or Enforcement) Rule. [§20.124] If the parties enter into a contract with an express condition, that condition will be strictly construed. That is because if the parties go to the trouble of making their duties expressly conditional upon the happening of an event, a court will strictly enforce the agreement. This means that unless a condition precedent is fulfilled **in its entirety**, the duties subject to that condition will usually never be enforceable, no matter how insignificant the failure to fulfill it in its entirety seems, as explained below.

(1) Reasonableness and Materiality of Express Condition Usually Irrelevant. [§20.1241] In applying the strict enforcement rule, it is usually irrelevant whether a court determines the condition to be either reasonable or material. That is, if the parties expressly make a duty conditional upon the occurrence of an event, the failure to meet the condition completely will be strictly enforced.

(a) Example. [§20.1241-1] The parties agree that buyer will only have to accept delivery of goods and pay for them "on the condition they are delivered by 4:00 p.m. on October 1." The goods arrive at 4:05 p.m. on October 1. They are conforming goods, and the buyer has not been inconvenienced in the slightest by the five minute delay. Nevertheless, because express conditions are strictly enforced, buyer does not have to accept the goods or pay for them. This is because the duties to accept and pay never became due, since the express condition was never **entirely** fulfilled. (Note, however, that in the rather unique case where rejecting the goods would cause the seller to suffer a "disproportionate forfeiture" and the condition is determined not to be a "material" part of the bargain, failure to fulfill the condition completely can be "excused" by the court and performance of the duties to accept and pay for the goods may become enforceable despite the late tender (see §20.43)).

e. Effect of Constructive Conditions: Relaxation of the Strict Construction Rule. [§20.125] Constructive conditions are not subject to the strict enforcement rule, for a court is given some latitude in tailoring the enforcement of a term it has itself supplied to ascertain the parties' rights under a contract [Restatement 2d §226, Com. c].

(1) Example. [§20.1251] Bill promises to weed Della's garden by 4:00 p.m., in return for Della's promise to pay him $75.00. Della's duty to pay is not *expressly* conditioned on Bill's finishing by 4:00 p.m. Rather, Bill has merely promised to finish by 4:00. Nevertheless, a **constructive** condition exists (see §21.2 et seq.), stating that if Bill doesn't finish in a timely manner Della need not pay under the contract. That is, obviously if Bill walks away after only 5 minutes on the job, no one would think that Della's promise to pay him should be enforced. As such, her obligation to pay is said to be constructively conditioned on Bill's completing performance.

However, with constructive conditions, unlike with express conditions, if Bill finishes at, e.g., 4:05 p.m., Della will nonetheless have to pay him the full $75.00 contract price. True, Della will be entitled to sue Bill for any damages she may have suffered as a result of the five minute delay (which are likely nothing), but she cannot claim that her duty to pay never became due. This is because a court will not strictly enforce a constructive condition in the same way it does an express condition, and so will excuse slightly late performance in such circumstances. If their contract had said that Delia's duty to pay was "conditioned on" a 4:00 finish, Delia would not have to pay under the contract, although she would surely owe something to Bill in restitution (see Chapter Thirty-Two for a discussion of restitution).

C. EFFECTS OF CONSTRUING A PROMISE AS BEING SUBJECT TO AN EXPRESS CONDITION PRECEDENT AS OPPOSED TO BEING UNCONDITIONAL. [§20.2] We have already seen one effect of having a promise being expressly conditional rather than unconditional, namely the effect of the strict enforcement rule (see §§20.124 and 20.125). There are two other important effects of construing a promise as subject to an express condition precedent rather than being unconditional:

(1) **construing the promise as being subject to an express condition precedent shifts the risk of the non-fulfillment of the condition from one party to the other**; and

(2) **construing the promise as being subject to an express condition precedent means that so long as the event has not occurred, but is still capable of occurring, the promisor may suspend his or her performance.**

1. **EXAMPLE. [§20.21]** To best illustrate the different results occasioned by construing a promise as conditional as opposed to unconditional, examine the following transactions:

First, assume John has contracted to buy Mary's house and is applying for a $150,000 loan from Central Bank to finance the purchase. However, instead of making the sale expressly conditional on his receiving the loan, John simply promises to pay Mary $150,000 for her home on or before March 1 (an unconditional promise). The consequences of making the promise unconditional should John not obtain the loan are severe. First, John bears the financial risk if his loan is denied. That is, by making an unconditional promise in the contract, he has obligated himself to pay Mary $150,000 so long as she timely tenders the deed. Thus, if his loan is denied, he still has a duty to pay the $150,000 on March 1, and cannot walk away from the deal just because he doesn't have the loan. Second, if John hasn't heard one way or the other from the bank by March 1, he still has a duty to pay the money on that date for his promise to pay was unconditional.

Now assume that John agrees to purchase Mary's home for $150,000 on or before March 1, "on the condition that [his] pending loan application from Central Bank is approved." The consequences for John of his not obtaining the loan are far less drastic. First, the financial risk of the loan being denied has now shifted to Mary, for she is entitled to nothing from John if the loan does not come through. That is, if the loan is not approved, John can now walk away from the transaction without liability and Mary will not be entitled to the $150,000. Second, while the loan application is pending, John may suspend the performance of his duties under the contract and need not accept Mary's tender of the deed, for his duty to accept it is conditional on the bank approving the loan by March 1.

D. HOW TO DETERMINE IF A PROMISE IS CONDITIONAL OR UNCONDITIONAL.

[§20.3] Contract law has developed general rules on how to interpret contractual promises which are discussed below in §20.32. However, before the interpretation rules can be easily understood, the different ways conditional duties and unconditional duties can work together needs to be studied.

1. WAYS TO PHRASE A PARTY'S OBLIGATIONS: THE EFFECT OF INTERPRETING WHETHER AN OBLIGATION IS A CONDITIONAL PROMISE, AN UNCONDITIONAL DUTY, OR BOTH. [§20.31]

When a party wants to see to it that some event occurs, such as a buyer wanting to ensure that certain goods will be timely delivered, there are only three ways to phrase the seller's obligations:

(1) **as a conditional promise;**

(2) **as an unconditional duty;** or

(3) **as both a conditional promise and an unconditional duty.**

Each of these has important ramifications illustrated below.

a. Example. [§20.311]

A television station in California needs a special lens for one of its cameras as soon as possible. The lens is sold by a New York manufacturer. There are three ways for the buyer and seller to structure their transaction:

(1) They could agree that the manufacturer's delivery of the lens by overnight messenger was an express condition of the station's duties to accept and pay for the lens;

(2) They could make mutual promises to each other, the seller promising to deliver the lens by overnight messenger, the station promising to accept and pay for it upon its timely arrival. In this way, each party owes an unconditional duty to the other to perform; or

(3) They could agree **both** that the seller has an unconditional duty to deliver the lens by overnight messenger, **and** that the station's duty to accept and pay for the lens is expressly conditional on timely overnight delivery. In this way, the station has made a conditional promise **and** the seller has assumed an unconditional duty.

Assume the lens is shipped by regular mail, not overnight messenger, and arrives two days late.

(1) In the first scenario described above, the station can walk away from the deal and reject the late delivery. This is because the condition necessary to make enforceable its obligation to accept and pay for the lens was never fulfilled. However, the station will not be able to sue for damages resulting from late delivery because the seller never made any promise to deliver the lens. That is, the express condition term in the contract means the parties agreed only that if the lens was timely delivered via overnight messenger, the station would be obligated to accept and pay for it. If it were delivered late, the station's duty to accept it would not become enforceable. However, the manufacturer never promised to deliver it on time — it only agreed that if it did not, the station would not have to pay for it.

(2) In the second scenario, the station can sue for damages resulting from the delay in receiving the lens, for the seller breached its unconditional duty to deliver via overnight messenger. That is, by structuring the manufacturer's obligation as a duty rather than a condition, the parties have set up a situation whereby the failure to carry out the promised duty can serve as the basis for a breach. However, even though the lens is delivered late, the station may still have to live up to its promised duty to accept the lens and pay for it depending on whether seller's breach was material or not (see §21.2 for a discussion of material breach).

(3) In the third scenario, the station could reject the lens (for the condition to its duties to accept and pay for the lens was never fulfilled), but it can also sue the seller for breach of contract for any damages suffered as a result of the lens being tendered late, because the seller breached its unconditionally promised duty to deliver the lens via overnight messenger.

2. **GENERAL RULES OF INTERPRETATION FOR DETERMINING WHETHER AN OBLIGATION IS A CONDITIONAL PROMISE, AN UNCONDITIONAL DUTY, OR BOTH. [§20.32]** The principal determinant in interpreting a contractual term is, of course, the intention of the parties (see Chapter Eighteen). However, when the intent of the parties is unclear as to whether an obligation is intended to be a conditional promise, an unconditional duty, or both, contract law has adopted the following presumptions to govern a court's interpretation of such terms.

a. **Interpretation that a Promise is an Unconditional Duty Rather than a Conditional Obligation is Favored When the Event Necessary to Fulfill the Condition is Within the Obligee's Control. [§20.321]** If it is unclear whether a promise is intended as an unconditional duty or as a conditional obligation, it should be interpreted as a duty if the action necessary to fulfill the condition is within the obligee's control [Restatement 2d §227(2)].

(1) **Example. [§20.3211]** In April, Jed enters into a contract with Alice's Pet Shop calling for the purchase of a pedigree beagle from a specified litter currently in Alice's shop. The contract does not specify which puppy is Jed's. Rather, in the sales agreement Jed promised that he would "select which puppy he wished to purchase from the litter before June 1." Jed does not select a puppy by June 1 and refuses to pay for a dog. Alice's sues, claiming breach of contract. Jed's defense is that selection of a puppy by June 1 was a condition precedent to his obligation to pay for the dog, and since the condition was never fulfilled, his duty never became enforceable. Jed's promise to select the puppy will be interpreted as an unconditional duty on his part to do so, rather than as a condition to his duty to pay, for the selection of a puppy was an event within his (the obligee's) control. As Jed failed to perform an enforceable unconditional duty owed to Alice's, the pet store will prevail in the breach action [Restatement 2d §227, Ill. 9].

b. **Interpretation that Reduces Promisor's Risk of Forfeiture is Preferred. [§20.322]** If it is unclear whether or not a duty is conditional, an interpretation that reduces the promisor's forfeiture risk is preferred [Restatement 2d §227(1)].

(1) **Example. [§20.3221]** Subcontractor contracts with general contractor to do electrical work on a building. Under the contract, the general promises to pay the sub $70,000, "which shall be due five days after payment of general contractor by developer." If the developer does not pay the general contractor (and absent evidence of a contrary intention by the parties), the general will still have to pay

the subcontractor $70,000 within a reasonable time if the subcontractor completes performance. The reason is that the payment term in the contract will be interpreted as setting forth an unconditional duty of the general contractor to pay sub $70,000 for acceptable work. The "five days after payment of the general contractor by the developer" clause will be interpreted only as setting forth a suggested time for payment rather than as a conditional promise making the developer's payment to the general contractor a condition precedent of the general's duty to pay the sub. This is because interpreting the term as a condition would shift the risk of the developer's non-payment, i.e., the risk of **forfeiting** all the electrical work for nothing, to the subcontractor, and such a construction is disfavored.

E. **EXCUSE OF CONDITIONS. [§20.4]** As we have seen, if a party's duty under a contract is subject to a condition precedent, usually the party is not obligated to perform the duty if the condition is never satisfied. However, there are a number of situations in which the failure to perform the condition is "excused." The result of excusing a condition is that the promisor will be obligated to perform the duty anyway, **despite** the non-fulfillment of the condition. The most common reasons for conditions to be excused are:

(1) **waiver** (see §20.41);

(2) **breach** (see §20.42); and

(3) **disproportionate forfeiture** (see §20.43).

1. **EXCUSE OF A CONDITION BY WAIVER. [§20.41]** Sometimes a waiver is referred to as "the intentional relinquishment of a known right." While such a term is highly descriptive of what actually occurs, it is not technically accurate. More properly, **a waiver is one party's excuse of the non-occurrence of, or of a delay in the occurrence of, a condition**. For example, a buyer agrees to purchase goods "on the condition they are delivered by October 1." If the goods are delivered on October 9, but the buyer still accepts them, a waiver has occurred. In some respect the buyer has intentionally relinquished a known right, i.e., the right to reject the goods for lack of timely tender. However, the situation is more properly viewed as one where the buyer's duty to pay was conditioned on the seller's promise to deliver in a timely manner. By accepting the late delivery, the buyer is **excusing the delay in the occurrence of the condition**.

a. **When a Waiver Can Take Place. [§20.411]** A waiver can take place both before and after the contract is made, and both before and after the event that is the subject of the condition is due to occur. For example, assume a standardized contract entered into on October 15 says "delivery under this agreement is due on the first day of the month following execution of this agreement." The buyer can inform the seller that she will waive the November 1 delivery date for the first delivery under the agreement either: (a) before the contract is signed, e.g., during negotiations with the seller; (b) after it is signed, but before November 1, e.g., in an October 30 phone call from the seller asking for more time; or (c) after the non-occurrence of the event, e.g., on November 3, when the goods finally arrive.

b. **Establishing a Waiver. [§20.412]** A waiver may be established either by words or conduct. Most purported waivers take place after the contract has been signed, and in that situation evidence of waivers is pretty freely admissible. Unlike "modifications," a party seeking to show a waiver does not need to satisfy the Statute of Frauds (see Chapter Twenty-Six), does not need to show mutual assent to the waiver, (see Chapter Two) and does not need to satisfy any remnant of the pre-existing duty rule (see §7.63 et seq). However, if the condition is waived prior to entering into a written contract, there may be problems in establishing that the waiver was agreed to under the parol evidence rule if the waiver is not set forth in the final written agreement (see Chapter Seventeen).

c. **Retraction of a Waiver. [§20.413]** A party may retract a waiver as to executory portions of a contract: (1) so long as he or she gives reasonable notice of the retraction and; (2) so long as the other party has not *materially relied* on the waiver. Waivers of conditions made **after** the time for occurrence of the condition are called **elections** and are irrevocable. Once a party has elected to accept the other party's performance even though the other party has failed to satisfy the terms of a condition, the party accepting the performance cannot thereafter reject the performance and claim his or her own duties are not due because the condition has not been fulfilled.

(1) **Example. [§20.4131]** Dan has entered into a contract with Diane's Bakery whereby he agrees to deliver 150 pounds of flour each month for a year. Under their agreement, Dan is to deliver the flour on the first of the month. For the first four months, Dan has delivered the flour on the 15th, without objection from Diane. At this point, Diane has made an election to excuse the four late deliveries of the flour and cannot now revoke that election, i.e., she can no longer reject any of the four deliveries because of their late delivery. In addition, by course of dealing, Diane has also probably waived her right to demand delivery on the first of the month for the remaining eight deliveries. However, as the waiver regarding the remaining eight deliveries is a waiver as to executory duties owed under a contract, Diane may **retract** the waiver upon giving sufficient notice to Dan, and demand that Dan start delivering on the 1st, as he promised in the contract. However, if Dan can show that he has relied on the 15th as the new delivery date, Diane may not retract her waiver as to future deliveries. For example, if in reliance on the 15th as being the new delivery date under his contract with Diane, Dan has entered into a new contract with his own supplier calling for enough flour to complete Diane's order to be delivered monthly to Dan on the 12th of the month, then Diane's waiver would likely not be retractable.

d. **Waivers can be Made to Express or Constructive Conditions. [§20.414]** A party can waive both express or constructive conditions. For example, as noted in §20.41, if the contract states that the buyer's duty to pay is expressly conditional "on delivery of the goods on October 1," and if the goods are delivered and accepted without objection on October 9, the buyer has waived an express condition and that waiver is a valid election. However, assume the contract states only that "delivery is due on October 1." In this case the delivery term may set forth an express duty, but it is **not an express condition**, i.e., nothing is expressly stated that the buyer's duty to accept and pay for the goods is conditional upon the goods being timely delivered. Reasonably prompt delivery of the goods is nonetheless a **constructive** condition of the buyer's duty to pay. While this issue is covered in depth in §21.2, the idea is that if the seller never delivers the goods, the buyer never has to pay for them, i.e., payment is constructively conditioned on tender and reasonably timely delivery. If the goods are delivered on October 9, and are again accepted by the buyer, there has been an effective waiver of the constructive condition of timely delivery.

2. **EXCUSE OF A CONDITION BY BREACH. [§20.42]** If an obligor breaches a contract, and that breach causes the non-occurrence of a condition, the act of breaching the contract will excuse the non-occurrence of the event and transform that party's otherwise conditional duty into an unconditional enforceable promise. For example, assume (once again) that John makes an offer to purchase Mary's house for $150,000 "on the condition

buyer secures adequate financing for the purchase." In that case, John is under a good faith obligation at least to try to obtain financing (see §7.622). If John does not even try to get a loan, he has breached his obligation of good faith under the contract. In such a case, his otherwise conditional duty to purchase the house for the stated price is transformed into an unconditional enforceable promise to purchase the house, and John's duty to purchase the house will thereafter become enforceable.

3. **EXCUSE OF AN EXPRESS CONDITION TO AVOID DISPROPORTIONATE FORFEITURE. [§20.43]** As noted earlier (see §20.322), courts are directed to interpret ambiguous obligations in a contract as unconditional duties rather than conditional promises so as to avoid forfeitures. However, if the parties **unambiguously** intended for an obligation to be subject to an express condition, the general rule is that a court must follow the rule of strict enforcement and hold that the conditional duty is unenforceable if the condition is not completely fulfilled, even if it results in a forfeiture. Nonetheless, a court is entitled to excuse the failure to fulfill even an express condition if:

(1) **enforcement of the condition will lead to disproportionate forfeiture;** and

(2) **the condition is not as to a material part of the bargained for exchange** [Restatement 2d §229]. In determining whether a forfeiture is "disproportionate," a court is directed to balance how important the condition is to the obligor against the extent of loss to be suffered by the obligee should the condition be enforced. Note that if the court excuses the condition, the result is that the conditional obligation becomes an absolute duty.

a. **Example. [§20.431]** Sally agrees to build an addition to Bill's home for $50,000. However, the contract states that Bill's obligation to pay Sally is "on the condition all work on the addition is completed by March 1." Sally finishes on March 3. Bill is not inconvenienced by the delay, but refuses to pay her. A court is empowered to excuse the payment-only-if-completed-by March 1 express condition if it determines: (a) a "disproportionate" forfeiture will occur if Bill is allowed to enforce the condition; and (b) completion of the work by the March 1 deadline was not a material part of their bargain. If a court finds that both those elements are met, Bill will be deemed to have unconditionally obligated himself to pay $50,000 for the work, and Sally will be deemed to have made an unconditional promise to finish by March 1, which she breached. As a result, while Sally must pay for any damages suffered by Bill as a result of the two day delay, Bill must also pay her the $50,000 and cannot strictly enforce the condition [Restatement 2d §229, Ill. 3].

Note that if completion by March 1 was truly a material (important) part of their deal, e.g., because Bill was hosting an important party at his home on March 2, the condition would be enforced despite the forfeiture, and Bill would not be obligated under the contract to pay the $50,000. (However, Sally could seek restitutionary recovery. See Chapter Thirty-Two)

b. **Example. [§20.432]** Dave agrees to build an addition onto Larry's house and agrees that Larry need only pay him "on the condition Bob issues an Architect's Certificate certifying the work was done satisfactorily." After the work is done, but before the Certificate is issued, Bob dies or becomes incapacitated. The condition will be excused to avoid a disproportionate forfeiture.

IX. PERFORMANCE, NON-PERFORMANCE, AND MODIFICATION OF DUTIES

INTRODUCTORY NOTE REGARDING PERFORMANCE, NON-PERFORMANCE, AND MODIFICATION OF DUTIES. This section of the book discusses what can happen to enforceable duties under a contract. Absent a highly unusual situation, the following are the only things that can happen when one party owes the other an enforceable contractual duty:

(1) The duty may be **discharged by performance**, i.e. the party can do what he or she promised under the contract;

(2) The duty may be **breached**, because it was not performed and because there was no defense or other justification for such non-performance;

(3) The non-performed duty may be **discharged by subsequent agreement**, if the parties can agree to an enforceable **subsequent performance**, an **accord**, a **substituted contract (including novation)**, or a **mutual release**;

(4) The non-performed duty may be **discharged due to impossibility, impracticability, or frustration of purpose**, meaning that the party who does not perform can use one of these doctrines as a defense in the subsequent breach suit by the other over the non-performance;

(5) The non-performed duty may be **discharged by the other party's material breach**, meaning that if *one party* materially breached, all unperformed duties owed by the *other* party are cancelled and may go unperformed without incurring contractual liability; or

(6) The duty can be **waived or modified**.

Common law rules regarding *adequacy of performance*, how *constructive conditions* affect performance, and the crucial *differences between material and immaterial breach* **in common law (i.e., non-UCC) contracts** are discussed in **Chapter Twenty-One**.

The *adequacy of performance*, effect of *constructive conditions*, and the *differences between material and immaterial breaches* for **contracts governed by the UCC** are discussed in **Chapter Twenty-Two**. As will be seen, on a basic level, the rules for common law contracts and those governing UCC agreements are the same, with only the terminology slightly changed. Hence, a thorough understanding of Chapter Twenty-One, coupled with a knowledge of UCC terminology, should be sufficient for most students. However, for those Contracts courses whose Professor stresses knowledge of Article 2, the somewhat subtle changes between the UCC and common law regarding these doctrines are discussed in some detail.

Chapter Twenty-Three explains the process and effects of *anticipatory repudiation* (often, but mistakenly, called anticipatory breach) under **both common law and UCC rules**.

The different ways *duties under one contract can be exchanged for duties under a separate agreement*, and the effects of which device the parties choose to structure such an exchange of duties, are the subject of **Chapter Twenty-Four**.

The defenses of *impossibility, commercial impracticability, and frustration of purpose* are discussed in **Chapter Twenty-Five**.

The somewhat tricky rules regarding *modification and waivers* of contractual duties are explained and illustrated in **Chapter Twenty-Six**.

CHAPTER TWENTY-ONE: PERFORMANCE AND BREACH IN CONTRACTS NOT COVERED BY THE UCC

A. PERFORMANCE AND BREACH. [§21.0] Thankfully, most parties perform their duties under a contract. When they do, contract law holds that their duties are **"discharged" by performance**. However, it is important to note that to be discharged by performance, the duty must be fully and completely performed. If it is not *fully* and *completely* performed, the party owing the duty to the other will be deemed to have **breached** the contract, unless such non-performance is somehow justified or otherwise excused. This means that a contract will be breached even if there is only a slight deviation from full and complete performance as called for in the contract, and even if the failure to perform completely was unintentional. In this sense breach is a strict liability concept, for even if a party was reasonable in thinking he or she had completely performed all the required duties in the agreement, if it turns out that there has somehow been a lack of full and complete performance, a breach has occurred [Restatement 2d §235].

For example, suppose Larry contracts to paint Maria's kitchen lemon yellow. Larry goes to the paint store, buys a can of lemon yellow paint, and completes the job. However, unknown to Larry, the paint company made a mistake and the color in the can was really canary yellow, not lemon. Even though Larry acted in good faith, and even though he was reasonable in believing he was fully performing, he has still breached the contract with Maria for he has not provided completely what he promised.

This chapter deals with the concepts of performance and breach in non-UCC contexts. Chapter Twenty-Two sets forth and explains the rules governing these ideas in contracts covered by Article 2 of the UCC. As will be seen in the next chapter, the general ideas behind performance and breach under the UCC are not different in concept from those presented here, but the language and the application of the rules are specialized enough under the Code to warrant a separate discussion.

B. DETERMINING BREACH: CONSTRUCTIVE CONDITIONS OF EXCHANGE, TENDER, AND THE ISSUE OF WHICH PARTY MUST PERFORM FIRST. [§21.1]
Most of the time, determining when a party is under a duty to perform is fairly easily ascertained from the contract, e.g., Frank promises to show up on May 10 to tune the piano. However, in some cases this determination is not as easy as it sounds. For example, assume a contract in which Edna has promised to clean Elliot's swimming pool in return for Elliot's promise to pay her $50. When she arrives at Elliot's house, Edna says she won't clean the pool until she gets paid. Elliot says he won't pay until the pool has been cleaned. Nothing in their contract indicates who is to perform first. As a result, both parties walk away without performing and each sues the other for breach.

Contract law has solved the problem of determining who, if anyone, is in breach in such situations by **implying constructive conditions of exchange**. As noted earlier (see §20.123), constructive conditions are conditions implied by courts to ascertain the parties' rights and duties under a contract. In other words, even though the parties have not explicitly agreed on an express condition, a court will construct a condition and insert it into the parties' agreement so as to help ascertain their respective obligations. One of the principal uses of constructive conditions is to determine which party to a contract with executory duties on both sides must perform first. These rules are discussed below.

1. **CONSTRUCTIVE CONCURRENT CONDITIONS: IF PERFORMANCE OF EACH PARTY CAN BE RENDERED SIMULTANEOUSLY, TENDER OF SUCH PERFORMANCE IS DUE SIMULTANEOUSLY. [§21.11]** When there is no indication of the parties' intent as to the order of performance, and **where performance of each party can be rendered simultaneously, each party's duty to perform is constructively conditioned on "tender" of the other party's performance** [Restatement 2d §§234(1), 238]. That is, where both parties' performance can be rendered at the same time, a court will imply **constructive concurrent conditions** whereby each party's duties remain unenforceable until the other party fulfills the constructive condition of tender by actually tendering performance. The obvious question is what constitutes tender and this is discussed immediately below.

   a. **Definition of Tender. [§21.111]** "Tender" is not actual performance. Rather, it is an **offer** of performance coupled with a manifest **present ability** to perform [Restatement 2d §238].

   (1) **Example. [§21.112]** Frank has agreed to sell his house to Monica for $100,000. The exchange of the deed is due on May 1. They meet on May 1, but Monica says she is not prepared to proceed until Frank shows her the deed. Similarly, Frank says he will not proceed until he sees Monica's check. Both parties depart without performing. There is no breach in this situation by either party, for no duty under the contract ever became enforceable. The duties never became enforceable because each was subject to a constructive concurrent condition of tender by the other, and the conditions were never fulfilled. That is, Monica's duty to pay the $100,000 was constructively conditioned on Frank's "tendering" the deed. Thus to satisfy the condition of tender, Frank had to **offer** to perform and **manifest an ability** to perform, i.e., he had to show Monica he had the deed, and offer to exchange it upon her tender of the check. As Frank never tendered the deed, Monica's duty to pay never became enforceable, and thus her failure to pay was not a breach.

   Similarly, Frank's duty to give Monica the deed was constructively conditioned on Monica's tendering payment. That is, she had to show Frank the check and offer to exchange it upon Frank's tender of the deed. As she never tendered the check, the constructive condition as to Frank's duty was never fulfilled, and thus Frank's duty to transfer the deed never became enforceable. Accordingly, his failure to present the deed was not a breach.

   (2) **Example. [§21.113]** Same facts as in the previous example, except Monica now tells Frank that she has a check for $100,000, shows it to him, and tells him she will give it to Frank once he tenders the deed. Frank refuses even to show her the deed until he has her check in hand. Frank is now in breach, for his duty to transfer the deed became enforceable when Monica fulfilled the constructive condition by tendering payment.

2. **IF THE PERFORMANCE OF ONE PARTY REQUIRES A PERIOD OF TIME TO COMPLETE, AND THE OTHER DOES NOT, PERFORMANCE OF THE TIME-CONSUMING DUTY IS A CONSTRUCTIVE CONDITION OF COMPLETION OF THE NON-TIME CONSUMING DUTY. [§21.12]** In a situation where there is no indication of the parties' intent as to the order of performance, **and one party's performance will take some time to perform but the other's will not, complete performance of the time-consuming duty is a constructive condition of the duty to perform the non-time consuming duty.** In other words, wherever one party's

duty is to pay (which can be done instantaneously), and the other party's duty will take some time to complete (e.g., performing a service), the party whose performance will take some time must perform first in order to render the duty to pay enforceable.

a. **Example. [§21.121]** Assume the Elliot/Edna hypothetical described in §21.1, where Edna has promised to clean Elliot's pool for $50. Because Edna's performance will take time, and Elliot's will not, full and satisfactory completion of her duties is a constructive condition of Elliot's duty to pay. Meaning that if she doesn't clean the pool, Elliot's duty to pay never becomes enforceable. However, Edna is under a duty to clean the pool when promised, even if Elliot never first tenders her payment. So if she doesn't clean when promised, Elliot is entitled to sue her for breach.

b. **Rationale for Rule. [§21.122]** The rationale for this rule is rooted in both common sense and normative behavior. For example, examine again the Elliot/Edna pool cleaning problem. Under this rule, as soon as they enter into the agreement Elliot's duty to pay is constructively conditioned on Edna's cleaning the pool. Thus, if Edna never cleans it, she cannot validly demand that Elliot pay. Common sense would dictate no less, but note that, e.g., if Edna needed only **tender** performance to make Elliot's duty enforceable, she could offer to clean the pool, manifest an initial willingness to do so, later walk away, and still successfully sue Elliot for not performing **his** duty if Elliot never paid her. True, Elliot would also be able to sue her back in such a case, but by making performance of Elliot's duties conditional on Edna performing, Elliot's failure to pay when she walked off the job is not a **breach** by Elliot, for his duty never became enforceable.

C. **MATERIAL AND IMMATERIAL (OR PARTIAL) BREACH: ANOTHER APPLICATION OF CONSTRUCTIVE CONDITIONS OF EXCHANGE. [§21.2]** To the uninitiated, material breach seems a simple enough concept — if a breach is serious, it is material; if it is not very serious, it is immaterial. Unfortunately, the issue is much more complicated than that. To understand the doctrine sufficiently, it is important to comprehend:

(a) the definitions of material and immaterial breach (see §21.21);

(b) the different consequences that flow from finding a breach material versus finding it immaterial (see §21.22);

(c) when the doctrine of material breach applies, and when it does not (see §21.23); and

(d) how to determine when a material breach occurred (see §21.24).

1. **DEFINITIONS OF MATERIAL BREACH AND IMMATERIAL, OR PARTIAL, BREACH. [§21.21]** The definition of material breach under contract law is surprising because, on its face, it has nothing to do with the magnitude or seriousness of the breach. Rather, it is quite technical and is as follows:

A material breach occurs when a party fails to perform a duty due under a contract which results in the unexcused non-occurrence of a constructive condition of exchange.

Not surprisingly, the definition of an immaterial breach is similar, but different in one important respect:

An immaterial breach is a failure of a party to perform a duty due under a contract that results in the *excused* non-occurrence of a constructive condition of exchange.

(Some commentators disagree somewhat with this last definition and say that an immaterial breach is not an **excused** non-occurrence of a constructive condition, but rather is a breach of a duty due under a contract which does not result in the failure of an implied condition at all. Thus, instead of saying that there was failure of a constructive condition, but that such failure was excused, these commentators say that there was never a failure of a condition in the first place. As a practical matter there is little difference between these views, and for convenience's sake the definition set forth above in bold face will be used throughout the remainder of this outline.) Note that "immaterial" and "partial" breach are synonymous and are used interchangably. However, "material" and "total" breach are not synonymous, and should not be thought of as interchangable (see §21.241 for a discussion of how material and total breach differ).

Obviously, by themselves, these definitions do not explain all the ramifications of the material breach doctrine. In the following sections, the definitions are applied so that their significance can be appreciated.

2. **CONSEQUENCES OF DECIDING THAT A BREACH IS MATERIAL OR IMMATERIAL. [§21.22]** If you understand the consequences of declaring a breach to be material as opposed to immaterial, you should have no trouble understanding everything else about the material breach doctrine. The most important effects of deciding a breach material can be put like this:

1. **Upon a material breach, the non-breaching party is entitled immediately to** *suspend* his, her, or its duties under the contract without contractual liability.

2. If the material breach is not subsequently cured, or waived, the **material breach will become a** *total* breach.

3. Upon a total breach, the non-breaching party is entitled to terminate the contract, and his or her duties under the contract will be discharged, meaning the contract is over. In other words, **once the other party has** *totally* breached, the non-breaching party is under no continuing obligation under the contract to perform what he, she, or it promised, and thus may cease performance without contractual liability [see §21.2421, for a further discussion of how a material breach becomes a total breach, and the consequences of a breach being declared total].

4. However, **upon an** *immaterial* **breach, the non-breaching party must continue to perform or itself be in breach**. That is, the non-breaching party cannot suspend, or otherwise cease performance without incurring liability when the breaching party has only *immaterially* breached the agreement.

Thus, when there is a material breach, the non-breaching party need not continue under the agreement and can suspend performance. On the other hand, if there is only an immaterial breach, the non-breaching party is not "off the hook," and still must timely perform his or her own duties or be in breach.

Relating these consequences to the definitions given in §21.21 above, contract law accomplishes these results by making the non-breaching party's duties constructively conditioned upon the satisfactory completion of the breaching party's duties. Thus, upon a material breach, the event necessary to fulfill the condition (i.e., satisfactory performance by the breaching party) does not occur, and so the non-breaching party's duties are not enforceable. On the other hand, while an immaterial breach also results in the failure of the breaching party to satisfy the condition, the non-occurrence of the implied condition is **excused**. Thus the non-breaching party's duties must be timely performed, for at that point his or her obligations are enforceable, and thus the failure to perform them will itself be a breach. In summary the rule is this:

The performance of one party under a contract is constructively conditioned on there being no outstanding unexcused material breach by the other [Restatement 2d §237].

It is important to note that determining a breach to be immaterial does not deprive the non-breaching party of his or her right to sue for damages resulting from the breach. In this respect the non-breaching party's rights resulting from an immaterial breach are the same as those arising from a material one. That is, the non-breaching party in both an immaterial and a material breach situation is entitled to sue the other for breach of contract, and to collect full damages for the breach. It is just that when the breach is material, **in addition to the right to collect damages**, the non-breaching party is **also** entitled to suspend (and ultimately terminate) his or her performance obligations as well, because the material breach prevents the constructive condition relating to the non-breaching party's duties from being fulfilled.

a. **Example. [§21.221]** Pat enters into a bilateral contract with Cliff whereby Pat promises to pay Cliff $25,000 on May 1, in return for Cliff's promise to construct a pool at Pat's home by May 1. Cliff begins work on the appointed day, but walks off the job after only digging one shovel full of dirt. Naturally, Pat refuses to pay him any money on May 1. Obviously Cliff has breached, because he did not fulfill his promise. However, Cliff may try to argue that Pat has also breached, for her duty under the contract is to pay him $25,000 on May 1 and she did not do it. It would, of course, be unfair to make Pat pay the $25,000 when she did not get what she bargained for, but there are two ways of accomplishing that goal, given her express promise to pay Cliff $25,000 on May 1. One way is to make her live up to her promise and actually require her to pay the money on May 1, but then to give her the right to sue for its return (along with any other damages she might have) in a breach action against Cliff. The second is to say that she does not have to pay him the $25,000 in the first place, but that she is still entitled to sue Cliff for any damages suffered as a result of his breach. This latter approach is the one provided under the doctrine of material breach, but for it to work obviously Pat's duty to pay must somehow be made conditional on Cliff's full and complete performance in finishing the pool. Contract law does this by implying a constructive condition of exchange to the transaction. That is, Pat's duty to pay is constructively (not expressly, for she says nothing about it in the contract) conditioned on Cliff fully performing. As Pat's duty to pay is thus conditional on the occurrence of an event (the absence of material breach), and as the event did not occur (meaning there was a breach) and as the breach was neither not excused or justified, (meaning the breach was material) her duty to pay is not enforceable. Thus, the idea behind **material** breach is to give the non-breaching party a way to suspend and ultimately terminate duties under a contract by imposing an implied condition of exchange as to the enforceability of the non-breaching party's duties.

b. **Example. [§21.222]** Assume again the Pat/Cliff contract, except this time Cliff performs all his obligations under the contract by May 1 but he does not put in a light bulb for the pool light. Once again Cliff has breached, but this time, if Pat did not pay him the $25,000 due on May 1, it would be unfair to Cliff for Pat has received the vast majority of what she bargained for under the contract. This is not to say that Pat should not be able to sue Cliff for breach since he failed to perform his promises completely (meaning he breached), but it is to say that Cliff's slight deviation from delivering what he promised is insufficient to justify her not paying him at all on May 1. Contract law solves this problem by declaring Cliff's breach to be *immaterial*. That is, it says that while Cliff's breach resulted in the non-occurrence of a constructive condition (full and complete performance), the non-occurrence is **excused**. In this case, it is excused due to forfeiture, i.e., to make Cliff do all that work and to receive nothing for it would subject him to an unfair forfeiture (see §20.43). Thus, Pat's duty to pay is enforceable (for the non-occurrence of the condition precedent to her duty to pay has been excused), and she thus must pay $25,000 on May 1 or be in breach herself. However, she is entitled to sue Cliff for any damages she suffers as a result of Cliff's breach.

3. **THE ONLY SITUATION IN WHICH THE DOCTRINE OF MATERIAL BREACH APPLIES: BILATERAL CONTRACTS IN WHICH THERE ARE EXECUTORY DUTIES REMAINING ON BOTH SIDES AT THE TIME OF THE BREACH.**
[§21.23] There are many instances in which it is irrelevant whether a breach is "material" or "immaterial". In these cases, a breach is just a breach. The only time it matters whether it is material or not is when the parties have entered into a bilateral contract, and there are unperformed duties remaining on **both** sides at the time of the breach. This is because it is only in such a situation that whether the non-breaching party still has to perform is an issue. In any other case, by definition, one party has already completed performance, and thus the failure of the other can simply be treated as a "breach" and no reference to the effect of the occurrence or non-occurrence of implied condition need be made. In these situations the non-breaching party can just sue for "breach," and need not worry about having to prove whether it is material or not.

This idea is illustrated in the following sections.

a. **The Doctrine of Material/Immaterial Breach Does Not Apply to Unilateral Contracts.** [§21.231] The concept of a breach being material or immaterial, as opposed to just being a breach, has no relevance whatsoever in unilateral contract situations. This is because the only purpose of labelling a breach material is to allow the non-breaching party a way to suspend and ultimately terminate his or her duties under a contract without such action constituting a breach itself. In a unilateral contract, under the majority view, the contract is not formed until the offeree has completed performance for that is the only way an offer for a unilateral contract can be accepted (see §4.4134-1).

(1) **Example.** [§21.2311] In the Cliff/Pat swimming pool example set forth in §21.221, suppose Pat makes an offer for a unilateral contract to Cliff, promising to pay him $25,000 "upon completion of the pool." Assume that Cliff completely finishes building the pool, thereby accepting Pat's offer to enter into a unilateral contract. Assume also that Pat refuses to pay him. At this point her refusal to pay is simply a breach for which he can collect damages. Whether it is "material" or "immaterial" is irrelevant because the effect of those doctrines as to constructive conditions of exchange has no application to such a situation. This is because the non-breaching party only cares about a "material" breach finding when he or she has duties yet to be performed. That is, with a material breach, the non-breacher need not perform such executory duties, but with a immaterial breach, he or she must perform them or be in breach himself or herself (see §21.22). Here, Cliff does not need the protection of a material breach finding, entitling him to cease further performance, because he has already finished performing.

b. **The Doctrine of Material/Immaterial Breach Does Not Apply to Bilateral Contracts When All the Duties of One Party Have Been Completely Performed. [§21.232]** If one party fully completes all duties required under a bilateral contract, and the other party then breaches, once again it is irrelevant whether that breach is material or immaterial. Returning to the Cliff/Pat swimming pool problem where the parties have this time entered into a bilateral contract, assume Cliff has completely and timely built the pool, but Pat still refuses to pay him. It is irrelevant whether Pat's actions are classified as an immaterial or a material breach because there are no remaining duties left owing by Cliff that need to be made subject to an implied condition that Pat pay in order to protect Cliff's rights. Rather, Pat's failure to pay is simply classified as a "breach."

Note that if there were supposed to be **progress payments**, e.g., where Cliff was to get one-half the money when the hole was dug, and the remainder upon completing the pool, and Pat refused to pay half the money when Cliff finished digging the hole, then it would matter that her failure to pay is a "material" breach. It would matter because if it were material, Cliff would be excused from being in breach if he stopped working and failed to finish building the pool. In other words, to protect his rights in such a case it is important that the implied condition that accompanies a material breach be imposed.

4. **HOW TO DETERMINE WHETHER A BREACH IS MATERIAL OR IMMATERIAL. [§21.24]** Obviously, there is an enormous difference to the parties between classifying a breach of a bilateral contract with executory duties on both sides as material or immaterial. Basically, if the breach is serious enough so that it would be unjust to require the innocent, non-breaching party to perform, it is material. Conversely if the breach is minor enough so that it would be unjust to the breaching party to have him or her walk away with nothing under the contract, the breach is immaterial.

a. **The Common Law Test: Whether the Breach Was of an "Independent" Or a "Dependent" Promise. [§21.241]** At common law, the question of whether a breach was material or immaterial was determined by whether the non-breaching party's duties were "dependent" on completion of the breached promise, or "independent" of that promise. That is, if the non-breaching party would suffer a disproportionate forfeiture if he or she were required to perform in light of the breach, the duties of the non-breaching party were said to be **dependent** on the breaching party's unperformed duties, and thus the breach was material. In the Pat/Cliff pool building hypothetical referred to above in §21.221 where Cliff walked off after digging one shovel's worth of dirt, Pat's promise to pay Cliff was, in the contracts sense, "dependent" on Cliff's promise to build a functioning pool. That is, because Pat would suffer a huge forfeiture if she had to pay in light of Cliff's breach, performance of her promise to pay would be deemed **dependent** on performance of Cliff's promised duties. Therefore, because Cliff did not perform his duty, Pat's duty to pay, the enforceability of which was **dependent** on Cliff's finishing the pool, need not be performed.

If a common law court determined that the non-breaching party's promise was **independent** of completion of the breached duty, i.e., that the non-breaching party still would receive value for his or her promise even in light of the other party's incomplete performance, then the court would declare the breach immaterial. Thus, in the Pat/Cliff scenario in §21.222 where Cliff's breach was not installing the light bulb, Pat's promise to pay was almost certainly, in the contracts sense, "independent" of the bulb being installed. That is, even in view of the breach, Pat still will receive most of value she bargained for under the agreement. Thus, while she could sue for damages resulting from the breach, she still would have to perform her part of the bargain, for the enforceability of her promise to pay would be deemed **independent** of Cliff's failure to install the light bulb as promised.

Under the common law, whether a promise was considered dependent or independent was for a court to decide "from the evident sense and meaning of the parties." Thus, the decision was one of interpretation (see Chapter Eighteen), in which the court was given much latitude.

b. **The Modern Test: Whether the Breach Constitutes the Unexcused Non-occurrence, or Delay in Occurrence, of a Constructive Condition of Exchange. [§21.242]** As noted earlier (see §21.21), under modern contract law the test for whether a breach is material or not (assuming a bilateral contract with executory duties on both sides) is whether the breach results in an unexcused non-occurrence of a constructive condition of exchange. If it does, the breach is deemed material and the non-breaching party's duties are suspended and ultimately discharged if the breach becomes total. If the non-occurrence of the constructive condition is excused, the breach is deemed immaterial and the non-breaching party must perform or be himself or herself in breach.

In deciding whether a particular breach results in an unexcused failure of a constructive condition, Restatement 2d §241 states that the following factors need to be weighed:

(a) the extent to which the non-breaching party will be deprived of the reasonably expected benefit of his or her bargain;

(b) the extent to which the non-breaching party can be fully compensated for the breach if made to stay in the contract and complete performance;

(c) the extent to which the breaching party will suffer a forfeiture if the breach is declared material and the non-breaching party need not perform under the contract;

(d) the likelihood the breaching party will cure his or her failure; and

(e) the good or bad faith exhibited by the breaching party in breaching the contract.

(1) **The Test for When a Material Breach Becomes a *Total Breach*: When the Breach is Neither Cured nor Excused After a Reasonable Time. [§21.2421]** There is a distinction between a material breach and a total breach. Upon the occurrence of a material breach, the non-breaching party is justified in immediately **suspending** performance. However, in most instances the non-breaching party **may not terminate** the duties under the contract at the instant the material breach occurs. The non-breaching party may only **terminate** his or her duties under the contract when the material breach ripens into a **total breach**. This occurs at the end of a reasonable period of time if the breach has been neither cured nor excused [Restatement 2d §§241, 242 and 243]. ("Cure" is discussed in §§21.272, 21.2721; how the failure of the occurrence of a condition can be excused is discussed in §20.4 et seq.) In other words, the rule is as follows:

(1) Upon a material breach, the non-breaching party may suspend his or her performance under a contract, and may continue to do so for a reasonable period of time.

(2) Upon the expiration of a reasonable period of time, if the material breach is neither cured nor waived (§21.27), the material breach becomes a total breach. At that point, the non-breaching party's duties are discharged and the non-breaching party may sue for total breach. [See Part IX for the remedies obtainable for total breach; see also Restatement 2d §236, Com. a and b; §242; §243, Com. a]

(3) If the material breach is cured or waived within a reasonable period of time (§21.27), then the formerly material breach is transformed into an immaterial one, and the non-breaching party must continue performance or else that party will be in breach. Of course, the non-breaching party may sue for damages resulting from the beaching party's immaterial breach.

(a) **How to Determine What is "A Reasonable Time" for Purposes of Transforming a Material Breach into a Total Breach. [§21.2421-1]** There are no hard and fast rules regarding how much time needs to elapse before an uncured and unexcused material breach becomes a total one. The idea is that the more serious the breach, the more likely it was done intentionally, the more unlikely it is that substitute performance can be quickly found for the non-breaching party, etc., the shorter the time period between material and total breach. According to Restatement 2d §242, the following factors should be examined in determining the length of time before a material breach turns into a total one:

(1) The extent to which the non-breaching party will be deprived of the benefit of the bargain reasonably expected under the contract;

(2) The extent to which the non-breaching party can be adequately compensated for any losses suffered before the breach is declared total;

(3) The extent to which the breaching party will suffer a forfeiture if the breach is declared total;

(4) The good or bad faith of the breaching party;

(5) The likelihood of cure by the breaching party;

(6) The extent to which any further delay will prevent or hinder the non-breaching party from making substitute arrangements; and

(7) The extent to which prompt performance is part of the bargain of the parties.

(i) **Example. [§21.2421-1A]** Ent Co. purchased a dilapidated Amusement Park and had plans to renovate it. Ent Co. entered into a contract with Fix-It Corp. to do much of the renovation. Under the contract, Fix-It was to start work on March 1 and have the park in working order by the following February 1. No one from Fix-It showed up for work on March 1. At this point Fix-It is in material breach, and Ent Co.'s duty of payment is suspended.

The next day, the president of Fix-It calls Ent Co. and says that he wasn't going to send people to the construction site, but when he "slept on it," he had a change of heart. He says that Fix-It is now willing to perform under the contract, and that Fix-It will have its employees work the next Saturday at Fix-It's expense to make up for the one-day delay. Given the nature of the contract, its length, and the ability of Ent Co. to receive its bargained for benefits under the contract given Fix-It's proposed "cure" for its material breach, probably a "reasonable time" has not yet passed, and Fix-It's material breach has not been transformed into a total one. Thus, at that point, Ent Co.'s duties have not been discharged, and it will be unable to fire Fix-It without being in breach itself.

(ii) **Example. [§21.2421-1B]** Sports Arena enters into a contract with Clean-Up, Inc., ("Clean-Up") a janitorial service, whereby Clean-Up promises to clean the arena after a Saturday night basketball game to get the arena ready for a Sunday afternoon rock concert. On Saturday evening, just after the basketball game, the general manager of Clean-Up calls up the director of Sports Arena and says that Clean-Up will not send any employees to clean up the arena. At this point there is probably a simultaneous material and total breach given the nature of the contract, the fact that Sports Arena would be hindered in its ability to secure a replacement if the breach is not deemed total, etc. In other words, under these circumstances, the "reasonable time" given before the material breach ripens into a total breach is no time at all, and Sports Arena is entitled to fire Clean-Up and treat the contract as terminated without fear of contractual liability as soon the phone call was made.

(2) Alternative Way to Establish Total Breach: Partial Breach Accompanied or Followed by a Repudiation. [§21.2422] Section 21.2421 sets forth the general rule for ascertaining when a total breach occurs, namely upon the expiration of a reasonable time after a material breach, when the breach has been neither cured nor waived. However, there is another situation in which an innocent party can successfully sue for total breach. Under Restatement 2d §243(2), **it is also a total breach when the guilty party has immaterially breached the contract, and accompanies or follows the breach with a repudiation of any further willingness or ability to further perform under the contract.**

There is often much confusion between this doctrine and the doctrine of anticipatory repudiation (see Chapter Twenty-Three). Such confusion is understandable, but the two concepts are quite distinct. For a repudiation to turn an immaterial breach into a total one, the repudiation must either **accompany or follow** the breach, i.e., the breaching party must have failed to perform a duty that was due under the contract, and sent a repudiation either simultaneously with, or after the breach. In an **anticipatory** repudiation situation, the injured party gets a right to sue because of a repudiation made **before** performance is due. Further, for an **anticipatory** repudiation to be effective, the repudiated duty must be material, i.e., its non-performance must give rise to a material breach if it ultimately were not performed. In the rule given in this section, a simultaneous or subsequent repudiation turns a **partial** breach into a total one.

(a) **Example. [§21.2422-1]** Jill agrees to pay Lon $5,000 to paint her house, including the trim. Lon painted most of the house professionally but did not paint the rain gutters. Nevertheless, he submitted a bill for the full $5,000. Typically, the failure to paint the rain gutters would be considered only an immaterial breach. However, if such action is accompanied by a repudiation, i.e., a declaration by Lon that he refuses to perform his contract duties, Jill becomes entitled to sue for total breach [Restatement 2d §243, Com. b, Ill. 3]. (Note however, that even if Lon sent such a repudiation, he may be able to retract it, thereby reverting the breach to an immaterial one (see the rules governing retraction of a repudiation cure set forth in §23.4).)

(b) Exception: Failure to Make Payments, even when Accompanied by a Repudiation, Does Not Become a Total Breach. [§21.2422-2] Under Restatement 2d §243(3) if the guilty party's breach is simply a failure to make one or more payments when due, such actions do not revert into a material breach, even when accompanied by a repudiation.

(i) **Example. [§21.2422-2A]** Fred borrows $12,000 from Central Bank and promises to repay the loan at $1,000 per month plus interest starting August 1. Fred unjustifiably fails to make the August, September and October payments, and on October 10 writes to the bank stating that he will not be making any payments in the future. At that point, the bank has the right to sue only for the three missed payments, and may not treat the breach as total and sue for the remainder of the payments. It can only sue for the remaining missed payments after they become due and remain unpaid [Restatement 2d §243, Com. d, Ill. 4].

Note that this rule only applies in the absence of a contractual promise by the debtor to the contrary. Often to avoid such a result, lenders will include "acceleration" clauses in their contracts, stating that after one or more payments are missed, the remaining payments can be accelerated at the lender's option, and can be sued for immediatel [Restatement 2d §243, Com. d; UCC §1-208].

(3) Effect of "Time Is Of The Essence" Clauses. [§21.2423] The seventh factor listed in §21.2421-1 deals, in part, with "time is of the essence" clauses. When these clauses are negotiated as part of the dickered terms agreed to in a contract, they carry a substantial evidentiary weight, and thus, the period before a material breach becomes a total one is likely to be short. On the other hand, if the clause is part of the pre-printed standard boilerplate language in a contract, it is likely not to carry much evidentiary weight, and the reasonable period of time between material and total breach may be substantial. In other words, a viable time is of the essence clause makes what would otherwise be an immaterial breach (capable of being cured) (See §21.272) into a total breach, which ends the contract.

5. THE "FIRST" MATERIAL BREACH DOCTRINE. [§21.25]
Occasionally, the parties will find themselves in a situation where each party accuses the other of material breach, refuses to go forward with the deal, and sues the other for total breach. Contract law solves this dilemma such that **upon the first material breach**, the non-breaching party's duties under the contract are suspended. However, if the first party's breach is only immaterial, then the other party must perform or be in material breach.

Note that this obviously puts a lot of pressure on the non-breaching party (or more likely the non-breaching party's lawyer) in the first instance. That is, if the non-breaching party believes the other's breach to be material, probably that party will not perform. However, if the assumption was wrong, and the breach will ultimately be deemed partial, e.g., in a subsequent lawsuit, then the original non-breaching party's failure to perform will itself be a material breach, and the original breaching party may now cease further performance.

a. **Example. [§21.251]** Desmond hires Kathleen to paint his house for $2,000, with $1,000 due to be paid when the front of the house is completed. Kathleen paints most of the front, but does not do some of the trim. Desmond refuses to pay her, claiming he is entitled to suspend performance due to her material breach. If Desmond turns out to be right, and a court agrees that Kathleen's breach is material, he is entitled to suspend performance and withhold payment of the $1,000 without breaching the contract. However, if Desmond is wrong and Kathleen's breach is deemed to be only immaterial, then it is Desmond who will be in material breach by not paying the $1,000, and Kathleen need not finish the remainder of the house. Hence, under the first material breach doctrine, Desmond must weigh carefully the adverse consequences of his being wrong in characterizing her breach as material, for if it is not, it will be Desmond, not Kathleen, who will be judged in material breach.

6. **THE SUBSTANTIAL PERFORMANCE DOCTRINE: THE CLASSIC APPLICATION OF THE IMMATERIAL BREACH DOCTRINE. [§21.26]** The substantial performance doctrine states that so long as a party has "substantially performed" a duty under a contract, any discrepancy between the actual performance and the promised performance will be deemed an immaterial breach. Thus, the substantial performance doctrine is really only a specialized application of the general immaterial breach doctrine. It says that when there has been "substantial performance" (as opposed to full and complete performance) of the duties owed by the breaching party, the breach involved is only an immaterial one (see §21.22 et seq.). In theory, analysis under the substantial performance doctrine could be applied to every breach of bilateral contract with unperformed duties remaining on both sides. In practice, however, it is generally applied only to breaches of contracts involving services, especially those dealing with construction contracts [Restatement 2d §237, Com. d].

   a. **How to Determine Whether a Promise has been Substantially Performed. [§21.261]** The most important factors to be weighed in determining whether a party has substantially performed are:

   (1) How much of the reasonably expected benefit under the contract has the non-breaching party received under the contract at the time of the breach;

   (2) How great a forfeiture will the breaching party suffer if the breach is deemed material;

   (3) How completely will damages alone compensate the non-breaching party;

   (4) The good or bad faith of the breaching party; and

   (5) How likely is it that rectifying the breach will result in "economic waste," rather than actually providing a benefit for the non-breaching party.

SPECIAL CASE SQUIB

(1) **Example of *Jacob & Youngs v. Kent*. [§21.2611]** Kent entered into a contract with Jacob and Youngs, a contractor, to construct a house on Kent's property. The contract specified that all plumbing in the home was to be with "Reading" galvanized pipe, i.e., pipe made by the Reading Company. Through oversight, the

pipe actually used in approximately sixty percent of the home was of another manufacturer. However, the substituted pipe was of equal quality and price as Reading pipe. Further, by time the inadvertent breach was discovered, most of the pipe had been installed and was concealed within the walls of the house. Nevertheless, Kent's (and his architect's) argument was that the contractor had to rip out the walls and relay the Reading pipe, or Kent would not make the remaining payments due under the contract. In other words, Kent's argument was that if Jacob & Youngs did not fully perform the Reading pipe promise, the contractor would be in material breach, thereby suspending and ultimately discharging Kent's duty to make the remaining progress payments due under the contract. **Held:** The inadvertent use of the wrong pipe by Jacob and Youngs only amounted to an immaterial breach under the substantial performance doctrine. That is, because the contractor "substantially performed" its duties, the breach it committed was only an immaterial one. Nevertheless, because there was deviation from full and complete performance by Jacobs and Young, there was a breach, and Kent could sue for any damage he might have suffered as a result of the wrong pipe being installed (which likely would be nothing). However, because performance was substantial and the breach was thus immaterial, Kent was not excused from performing his remaining duties of payment under the contract. As Justice Cardozo put it, "The courts never say that one who makes a contract fills the measure of his duty by less than full performance" (hence, Jacobs and Youngs was liable for breach). "They do say, however, that an omission, both trivial and innocent, will sometimes be atoned for by allowance of the resulting damage, and will not always be the breach of a condition to be followed by forfeiture" (hence, the breach is an immaterial one). *Jacob & Youngs v. Kent*, 230 N.Y. 239, 129 N.E. 889 (1921).

An analysis of the factors set forth in §21.261 yields the same result. That is, the substantial performance doctrine applies here to make the breach an immaterial one because:

(1) Kent had received substantially all the benefit he could reasonably expect under the contract; i.e., he got a completed house for the price stated, with an equivalent quality of pipe throughout;

(2) To have the breach declared material would result in an unfair forfeiture to Jacob & Youngs, i.e., to deny the company relief under the contract for an inadvertent mistake that resulted in no objective detriment to Kent would be unjust;

(3) Damages could compensate Kent for any harm he might have suffered due to the breach;

(4) The breach was inadvertent, and thus was a "good faith" breach; and

(5) Having the breach declared material would result in economic waste, i.e., it would cost Jacob & Youngs a huge amount of money to rip out the walls and relay the pipe, with no corresponding benefit to Kent for doing so. Thus, any money spent remedying the breach (as opposed to paying for damages resulting from the breach) would be an economic waste. (Indeed, many have speculated that when Kent sued, he really was not all that concerned about having the Reading pipe installed. Rather, he just wanted leverage to get Jacob & Youngs to reduce their price on the house should the court find a material breach. That is, if it would have cost Jacob & Youngs $10,000 to rip out the dry wall and

relay Reading pipe, Kent would simply have offered to keep the pipe that was already in place if Jacobs & Young would accept something like $9,000 less than the agreed price for its work.)

---

(2) **Example.** [§21.2612] Bert contracted with Amy to paint Bert's living room "Robin's Egg Blue" so as to complement in a precise way Bert's couch and chairs. Through inadvertence, Amy paints the room in "Sky Blue." The colors are similar and the actual paint job is well done, but Bert is unhappy with the Sky Blue because it contrasts with rather than complements his furniture. In this case Amy's breach is a material one as the substantial performance doctrine does not apply. This can be seen again by using the factors given in §21.261:

(1) Bert has *not* received substantially all the benefits he reasonably expected under the contract, for the walls clash with the furniture;

(2) While it is true that Amy will have done a lot of work without benefit under the contract if the breach is declared material, it is also true that such action is **not** an *unfair forfeiture*, given that she has failed to provide much of the benefits Bert bargained for under the contract;

(3) Simply paying Bert for the discrepancy in colors, i.e., giving him the difference, if any, between the cost of painting the room with Robin's Egg Blue paint versus painting it with Sky Blue paint, will not adequately compensate Bert for the loss of bargain Amy's breach occasioned;

(4) While Amy's breach may have been in good faith, this factor is not determinative; and

(5) Repainting the room, i.e., rectifying the breach, will not result in economic waste. This is because while it will cost Amy some time and effort to repaint the room, Bert will reap a corresponding benefit from such efforts.

7. **DOCTRINES THAT TRANSFORM MATERIAL BREACHES INTO IMMATERIAL BREACHES.** [§21.27] There are three doctrines that, when applicable, transform a material breach into an immaterial one:

(1) **Divisibility,** or **part performance** (see §21.271);

(2) **Cure** (see §21.272); and

(3) **Waiver** (see §21.273).

a. **The Divisibility (or Part Performance) Doctrine.** [§21.271] Courts are empowered to "save" contracts when they can and prevent the suspension of duties and ultimate termination of agreements whenever possible. Accordingly, if a court can find that a discrete portion of a contract has been satisfactorily performed, while the remainder has not, a court may use the divisibility doctrine and declare that same portion of the non-breaching party's performance is due, while the remainder of the performance may be suspended and ultimately discharged.

(1) Requirements for Applying the Divisibility Doctrine. [§21.2711] According to the Restatement 2d, a court will declare a contract divisible upon a material breach whenever it is possible:

(1) to apportion the agreement into corresponding pairs of part performances; and

(2) to regard the parts of each pair as agreed equivalents [Restatement 2d §240].

    (a) Example. [§21.2711-1] Norma purchases three separate framed posters from Leroy's Art Shop. The posters are $150 each and are to be delivered next Thursday. On Thursday, Leroy's delivers only one of the posters and refuses to deliver the other two. The contract is divisible and thus, Norma is obligated to accept and pay for the one poster that was delivered. It is divisible because it is possible to apportion the agreement into three separate pairs of part performances, i.e., the performance of 3 separate $150 payments in exchange for each poster. Of course, Norma does not have to pay for the two posters that were not delivered, and may in addition sue for any damages she suffers as a result of the store's failure to deliver the two posters. However, she must pay for the one poster she got and cannot suspend her performance for that one claiming a material breach of the whole.

    (b) Example. [§21.2711-2] Same facts as above, except the three posters together make a triptych. Norma is not obligated to accept and pay for the one that was delivered, for the contract is not divisible. That is, it is impossible to separate the agreement into pairs of part performances. In effect, Norma bought one triptych, not three posters, and so delivery of only one part is a material breach of the whole.

b. Cure. [§21.272] Cure is the name given to the right of a breaching party to correct his or her failure of performance, thereby transforming what would be a material breach into a partial one. For example, a homeowner is scheduled to make a $10,000 progress payment to a contractor by 5:00 p.m. on Tuesday and fails to do so. The failure to make a progress payment is generally considered a material breach and at that point, contractor can suspend performance. Now, assume homeowner tenders a $10,000 check by 9:00 a.m. the next day. So long as the material breach has not turned into a total breach (see §21.2421), homeowner has the **right** to cure the material breach. Upon tender of the check Wednesday morning, the homeowner has thereby transformed the material breach into a partial one, and thus while contractor may sue for any damages resulting from the delay in getting the check, contractor must also continue performance after the check's tender or itself be in breach.

(1) A Breaching Party Has a *Right* to Cure Until the Breach Becomes Total. [§21.2721] A breaching party has a **right** to cure until the breach becomes total. That is, if the breaching party: (a) makes a conforming tender after the breach; and (b) establishes that the breach is not yet total, then the non-breaching party **must** accept the cure, and must thereafter timely perform any remaining duties under the contract or the non-breaching party himself or herself will be in breach. (In addition, some courts require that the proposed cure must also provide reasonable assurances that any damages resulting from the non-conforming tender will be paid by the breaching party to be effective.) (See discussion of cure in UCC contracts, §22.24).

c. **Waiver. [§21.273]** The doctrine of waiver is dealt with at length in §20.41. However, it is important to recognize that the non-breaching party may waive (excuse) a material breach, thereby transforming the breach into a partial one.

   (1) **Example. [§21.2731]** Jim contracts to show up at Janet's house to install a new hot water heater Janet bought. Under their agreement, Jim promises to be at Janet's house no later than noon on Monday, and Jim has agreed to a "time is of the essence" clause, meaning that if he is at all late, his breach will be a material and a total one (see §21.2423). Jim arrives at 2:00 Monday afternoon. Janet does not have to allow him to install the water heater and may treat the contract as terminated. However, if she decides she wants him to install the heater anyway, she will have waived her right to treat the breach (Jim's tardiness) as material and total, and will thereby have converted it into an immaterial breach. That is, she can still sue him for any recoverable damages resulting from the delay, but if she agrees to allow him to install the heater, she is liable for the agreed contract price, and may not suspend her performance without contractual liability.

8. **RESTITUTION AVAILABLE TO BOTH PARTIES UPON A MATERIAL BREACH. [§21.28]** In the event of a material breach, typically the non-breaching party will sue for breach of contract and seek to recover damages. However, the non-breaching party is also permitted to sue for restitution, which in some cases will produce a larger monetary recovery. In addition, the **breaching** party in a material breach situation is entitled to sue for restitution for benefits provided before the breach, even though he or she cannot sue the non-breaching party under the contract (see Chapter Thirty-Two for a discussion of restitution).

CHAPTER TWENTY-TWO: PERFORMANCE AND BREACH IN CONTRACTS GOVERNED BY THE UCC

A. PERFORMANCE AND BREACH IN CONTRACTS GOVERNED BY THE UCC, GENERALLY. [§22.0] Article 2 of the UCC is divided into seven "Parts." Part 5 (made up of the §2-500's) is entitled "Performance." Part 6 (made up of the §2-600's) is entitled "Breach, Repudiation and Excuse." In these provisions the UCC regulates the concepts discussed in the previous chapter for contracts governed by Article 2, i.e., for sales of goods contracts [UCC §2-102] (see also §34.1 for a discussion of Article 2 applicability). (In Chapter Thirty-Four it is noted that Article 2 arguably applies to transactions other than sales. However, since the vast bulk of transactions governed by Article 2 involve the sales of goods, this chapter will focus solely on those contracts.)

As you will note as you go through this chapter, the general concepts regarding tender, material breach, etc., discussed in Chapter Twenty-One are followed in contracts governed by the UCC. Hence, the material in this Chapter is presented on the assumption that the reader has already digested the material in Chapter Twenty-One, (and, if not, there is a fair amount of cross-referencing). However, the Code applies these doctrines somewhat differently, and thus the effects of those doctrines in Article 2 contracts need to be treated separately. These differences can be categorized as follows: (1) In certain cases the UCC uses different nomenclature to describe and define these concepts; (2) the Code has, in some cases, made it somewhat easier to establish material breach; and (3) the UCC is more detailed and specific in describing the rights and duties of the contracting parties.

Most Contracts Professors do not require their students to master the differences between common law and UCC performance in the detail presented in this Chapter. Hence, if you know the concepts presented in Chapter Twenty-One and learn the slightly different terminology of the UCC in this area, you should be fine. But for those courses where Article 2 is stressed, the UCC doctrines are explained in this chapter in some detail.

B. TENDER AND IMPLIED CONDITIONS OF EXCHANGE UNDER THE CODE. [§22.1]
As with non-UCC transactions, under the UCC, tender of performance by one party is necessary to make the other party's duties enforceable (see §21.11 et seq.). In the words of the Code, "[t]ender of delivery [by the seller] is a condition to the buyer's duty to accept the goods and . . . to his duty to pay for them" [UCC §2-507(1)]. Similarly, "tender of payment [by the buyer] is a condition to the seller's duty to tender and complete any delivery" [UCC §2-511 (1)]. In other words, just as in non-UCC transactions, tender by one party is a constructive condition precedent to the enforceability of the other's duties. Hence, if the buyer does not tender payment, the seller incurs no contractual liability for failing to provide the goods, because the condition precedent to the seller's duty to do so has not been fulfilled. Similarly, if the seller does not tender delivery, the buyer incurs no contractual liability in failing to pay for the goods because the condition precedent to the buyer's duty to do so has not been fulfilled.

Setting forth the rules of §2-507(1) and §2-511(1) leaves two questions: (1) what acts are necessary under the UCC to complete tender for each party; and (2) once tender has been made, what is the order of performance, i.e., which party must perform first or be in breach for not doing so.

1. **THE ACTS NECESSARY TO FULFILL A SELLER'S OBLIGATION TO TENDER DELIVERY. [§22.11]** As noted above, §2-507 states that a seller's "tender of delivery" is necessary to make the buyer's duty to pay enforceable. Section 2-503 states that to fulfill a seller's obligation to tender delivery, he or she must:

   (1) Put and hold **conforming** goods at the buyer's disposition;

   (2) Give the buyer reasonable notice so that the buyer may take delivery; and

   (3) Either: (a) make the goods available at a reasonable time and place if they are to be picked up by the buyer; or, (b) offer delivery of the goods at a reasonable time if they are to be delivered by the seller.

   a. **Example. [§22.111]** Electronics store orders 100 clock-radios from wholesaler, with delivery to be made at the wholesaler's place of business. Once the wholesaler notifies the buyer that it has the radios at its warehouse, and that the buyer can pick them up during regular business hours, tender has been made. Note, however, that if the radios are **non-conforming** goods, e.g., they are the wrong brand, they don't work, etc., then the seller's tender is ineffective, and the buyer's duty to pay for them is unenforceable.

2. **THE ACTS NECESSARY TO FULFILL A BUYER'S OBLIGATION TO TENDER PAYMENT. [§22.12]** Under UCC §2-511(1), tender of payment is a condition to the seller's obligation to complete delivery. Section 2-511(2) states that so long as the buyer demonstrates a willingness and ability to pay "by any means current in the ordinary course of business," the buyer's tender obligation is complete. Note, however, that if the seller does not want a check or other documentary forms of payment, and instead wants cash, the seller has the right to demand a cash payment under §2-511(2). However, if the seller makes such a demand, the seller must give the buyer a sufficient extension of time in which to obtain the cash.

3. **ORDER OF PERFORMANCE. [§22.13]** Surprisingly, the UCC does not provide rules governing which party must perform first once tender has been made. The general thought is that the non-UCC rule probably will apply even in UCC transactions, i.e., if one party's performance will take time to complete and the other's will not, the party who needs the time must go first. Generally, this means that the seller will need to perform first because the buyer's obligation is usually one of monetary payment only, which can be done immediately. If the performances of the buyer and seller can both be done immediately, then each party's tender is a concurrent implied condition of the other's performance (see §21.1 et seq. for a discussion of the non-UCC rules governing order of performance).

C. **THE PERFECT TENDER RULE UNDER THE UCC: EVERY SELLER'S BREACH IS, AT LEAST INITIALLY, A MATERIAL BREACH. [§22.2]** In its initial reading, the so-called "perfect tender rule" of the UCC seems relatively straightforward and pretty unremarkable. In some respects, all it does is require the seller to live up to his or her bargain, which is the reason the buyer entered into the contract in the first place. However, as discussed below, the rule changes substantially the analysis of breach in contracts to which it applies. The perfect tender rule is set forth in UCC §2-601 and provides:

In a "single lot" contract, i.e., a contract in which delivery of all the goods called for by the agreement is to be made in only one shipment, if either the goods or the tender of delivery fail in *any* respect to conform to the contract, the buyer may:

   (a) reject the entire shipment,

(b) accept the entire shipment, or

(c) accept any commercial unit or units in the shipment, and reject the rest.

Upon reflection, it can be seen why the perfect tender rule alters so dramatically analysis of breach in contracts governed by §2-601 versus those governed by common law/Restatement rules (see §21.2 et seq). Under the UCC rule, **every breach by the seller is a material breach**, for the failure of the seller to render promised performance "in *any* respect" gives the buyer the right to reject the shipment and relieves the buyer from having to pay for the goods. In traditional contract terms, under the perfect tender rule **any** non-performance by the seller, no matter how minor, discharges all remaining duties of the buyer under the contract. Thus, **for contracts subject to the Code's perfect tender rule, the immaterial breach and substantial performance doctrines are eliminated**, for the rule provides there is no breach minor enough to keep the buyer in the contract and make him or her pay for the goods sent by seller (see §21.21 et seq., and §21.26 respectively, for discussions of the immaterial breach and substantial performance doctrines). Note, this is true regardless of whether the result will cause the seller to suffer a substantial forfeiture, or regardless of whether the seller's breach was delivering 999,999 units when 1,000,000 were ordered. Under the rule, whenever the seller has failed to perform "in *any* respect" from what he or she promised, the buyer's duties to accept and pay for the goods are discharged.

Similarly, **the doctrine of divisibility is also eliminated for contracts subject to the perfect tender rule**, for upon any deviation from the seller's promised performance, the rule provides that the buyer is entitled to reject the **entire** shipment, and cannot be compelled to accept any conforming divisible unit of that shipment (see §21.271 for a discussion of the divisibility doctrine).

1. **EXAMPLE. [§22.21]** Betsy owns a hardware store and orders 300 faucets of a certain type from Sheila, a plumbing wholesaler. The goods arrive timely, but when Betsy counts them, she discovers that only 298 faucets were delivered. At that point there has been a material breach under the perfect tender rule and (subject to the limitations discussed §22.25 et seq.) Betsy is entitled to reject all 298 faucets, to accept all 298 faucets, or to keep, e.g., 100 (or any other number), and return the rest to Sheila.

2. **EXAMPLE. [§22.22]** Same facts as above, except this time 300 faucets are timely delivered by Sheila, but one of them is broken. Same results, for there is no divisibility doctrine under the perfect tender rule. Subject to the limitations discussed in §22.24 et seq., §2-601 provides that when there has been **any** failure of promised performance by the seller, there has been a material breach of the contract entitling Betsy to accept the 299 conforming faucets, to reject them all, or to accept some and reject the rest.

3. **EXAMPLE. [§22.23]** Benny ordered a custom-made couch from a furniture manufacturer. When he ordered it, the manufacturer showed Benny a sample color swatch for the couch, which Benny approved. When the couch was delivered, Benny felt the color was not exactly like the swatch, and it turns out that the manufacturer used 1% more blue dye in the couch fabric than in the swatch. There has been lack of perfect tender under §2-601, and Benny is thus entitled to reject the couch and need not pay for it.

4. **LIMITATIONS ON THE PERFECT TENDER RULE. [§22.24]** There are cases where application of the perfect tender rule unfairly punishes the seller. While it is true that the seller need not worry about the perfect tender rule if he or she completely performs what is promised under the contract, as a practical matter there will be times when a seller is going to make good faith mistakes during his or her performance. Workers on the loading

dock will misread a bill of lading and send the wrong goods; something will break during transit; someone will mistranscribe a number and the wrong quantity will be sent, or the right quantity will be sent but on the wrong date; a plane will crash and the delivery will be late, etc. Further, in some of these cases it may well be that the buyer is not very inconvenienced, or perhaps not inconvenienced at all, by the imperfect tender, and yet the perfect tender rule nonetheless permits the buyer to get out of his or her obligations under a contract. Thus, to combat instances of potential unfairness under §2-601, the courts and the Code limit application of the perfect tender rule in the following respects:

(1) While a buyer is initially entitled to reject a shipment for less than absolutely perfect tender, **a seller is granted fairly extensive rights to cure the imperfect tender** under the Code (see §22.241 for a discussion of cure under the Code);

(2) As noted earlier, the perfect tender rule applies only to "single lot" contracts. **In installment contracts, i.e., contracts where the goods are to be delivered in more than one shipment, the standards governing when a buyer can reject the goods and terminate the agreement in light of an imperfect tender are much more difficult for the buyer to meet** (see §22.242 for a discussion of installment contracts);

(3) By judicial decision, **some courts have held that the perfect tender rule does not apply when the breach is very minor**, i.e., they have engrafted a "*de minimus non curat lex*" exception to the perfect tender rule (see §22.243 for a further discussion of the *de minimus non curat lex* exception);

(4) Under the Code, **the perfect tender rule must be read in conjunction with usage of trade, course of dealing, and course of performance.** Thus, even if a seller's actions seem to constitute a "breach" based on one meaning of the words used in the contract, it may be that when those words are properly interpreted in light of trade usage or prior dealings of the parties, in fact no breach has occurred (see §22.244 for a further discussion of the operation of usage of trade, course of dealing, and course of performance in conjunction with the perfect tender rule); and

(5) **The perfect tender rule does not apply to situations where the buyer has already "accepted" the goods,** but later decides that he or she wishes to return them due to a defective tender. That is, the Code's standards under which a buyer can revoke his or her acceptance are more difficult for a buyer to meet than those standards governing when he or she can reject those same goods when they are initially tendered (see §22.245 for a further discussion of revocation of acceptance).

a. **The First Limitation on the Perfect Tender Rule: The Seller's Right to Cure under §2-508. [§22.241]** Probably the most significant limitation on the perfect tender rule is the right of the seller to cure certain imperfect tenders. Cure is the process by which the seller rectifies or "cures" the breach by, e.g., sending a replacement faucet if one is defective, or by shipping two more faucets if the promised quantity was not delivered in the original shipment. In colloquial terms, the effect of cure is to take an originally imperfect tender and repair it so that it is subsequently "perfect." In contract terms, the effect of cure is to take a material breach, and restore enough of the benefits under the contract to the injured party so that it is thereafter fair to treat the former material breach as an immaterial one. Thus, after an effective cure, the buyer is kept in the contract and must both accept and pay for the goods, but has the right to sue the seller for any damages caused by the breach [see §21.24 et seq].

To understand how cure works, the following questions need to be resolved:

(1) Under what circumstances is a seller entitled to cure? (This issue is discussed in §§22.2411 and 22.2412.);

(2) After it is determined that a seller has the right to cure, what kinds of actions constitute an effective cure? (This issue is discussed in §22.2413.); and

(3) What are a **buyer's** rights upon accepting a cure? (This issue is discussed in §22.2414.)

(1) **When a Seller Has the Right to Cure: If the "Time for Performance" under the Contract Has Not Passed, the Seller Has an Absolute Right to Cure under §2-508(1). [§22.2411]** Section 2-508(1) provides that **if the time for performance under the contract has not yet expired**, the seller has **an absolute right to cure**, so long as the seller provides adequate notice of his or her intention to do so. The idea behind giving the seller an absolute right to cure in this situation is that the buyer is not likely to suffer serious harm due to an imperfect tender so long as the seller ultimately delivers conforming goods to the buyer within the time the seller originally promised to perform under the contract. That is, because the buyer had no right to rely on having the goods before the seller's "time for performance" had expired, if the buyer ultimately receives conforming goods within that time anyway, it is only fair that the buyer be forced to accept and pay for them.

(a) **Example. [§22.2411-1]** A contract entered into on February 1 called for the delivery of 100 21-inch television sets in a single shipment to an electronics store on or before April 1. On March 16, seller delivered 100 televisions, but it turned out that one was defective. Under the perfect tender rule, the store is entitled to treat the breach as material and either send all the televisions back, or accept some and send the rest back. However, the seller has an absolute right for the next two weeks to cure the defective tender, because the seller's "time for performance" under the contract (April 1), has not yet expired. Hence, so long as the seller first gives timely notice of its intention to cure, the retailer must accept and pay for all 100 sets if the seller cures its imperfect tender by sending the retailer a replacement television by April 1. This is because once the replacement television set arrives, the imperfect tender will be made perfect, and the retailer thus has no basis on which to reject.

(2) **When a Seller Has the Right to Cure: After Expiration of the "Time For Performance," the Seller's Right to Cure is More Limited under §2-508(2). [§22.2412]** After the seller's "time for performance" has run under a contract, the seller's right to cure is more circumscribed. Section 2-508(2) provides that in such a situation, the seller has a right to cure only if:

(a) the seller had reasonable grounds to believe what was originally tendered would be acceptable to the buyer;

(b) the buyer would not be unduly inconvenienced by the delay in receiving the cured tender; and

(c) cure is made within a reasonable time under the circumstances.

The reason the seller's right to cure is more circumscribed in this situation is that, unlike the case where cure is made before the time for performance has expired, it may well be that the buyer could suffer a serious loss while waiting for the cured tender. That is, there are situations where if the promised delivery date is missed by the seller, the buyer simply cannot wait until the seller is able to procure replacement goods and send them to the buyer. In those cases, it is only fair to permit the buyer to reject a subsequently cured tender, and to declare a total breach of the contract. Thus, it is only when there is not an undue inconvenience to the buyer upon waiting for the cure, **and** where the seller made an inadvertent mistake in breaching the contract (or was otherwise reasonable in believing what he or she tendered was acceptable to the buyer), that the Code grants the seller the right to cure after the time for performance has expired.

(a) **Example. [§22.2412-1]** On March 15th, a retailer of televisions has twenty 21-inch televisions in stock. Because the store manager does not want to run low on inventory, she orders another 100 21-inch televisions from the manufacturer, to be delivered on or before April 1st. The televisions are delivered late in the day on April 1st, when the retailer still has a dozen 21-inch sets remaining in stock. The next day the manager begins unpacking the newly delivered sets, and discovers the manufacturer has sent 100 **15**-inch sets. At this point, the seller has materially breached under the perfect tender rule and so the buyer can reject all 100 sets. Because the time for the seller's performance under the contract has expired, the seller does not have the absolute right to cure under §2-508(1). Thus, if the seller is going to salvage the contract, it must establish that it has a right to cure under §2-508(2).

To do that it must prove: (1) that **it had reasonable grounds to think that its tender would be acceptable to the buyer** (e.g., that its shipping department made an honest mistake and the company thought it actually was sending 21-inch sets); (2) that **the buyer would not suffer too much of a commercial loss** in waiting for a new shipment of 21-inch sets (which the seller would likely be able to establish here, given that the buyer still has twelve 21-inch televisions in stock); and (3) that **it will effect the cure in a reasonably timely basis.**

(b) **Example. [§22.2412-2]** Ned is leaving on a European vacation on Friday the 10th and orders from an electronics store an electric shaver that will work in all the countries he will be visiting. Under the terms of the contract, the shaver is to be delivered to Ned no later than Thursday the 9th. The store does not have such a shaver in stock, but promptly orders one from a reputable manufacturer and it is delivered to the store on the 9th. Near the close of business on that day, Ned comes into the store to pick up the shaver. He tries it out at the store and it does not work. Even though the store had reasonable grounds to think that the shaver would be acceptable (because the manufacturer from which it ordered the shaver was reputable), nevertheless the store will **not** have the right to cure its defective tender because, under the circumstances, the buyer would suffer too much inconvenience waiting for the cured tender.

(3) **The Manner in Which a Seller May Cure: Cure by Replacement, Cure by Repair, or Cure by Cash Discount. [§22.2413]** Often a seller's imperfect tender is the delivery of an unworking good, e.g., a television whose picture is consistently green, or a new car whose transmission fails. In such cases, even assuming the seller has a right to cure under §2-508, there is often a disagreement between buyer

and seller as to how the cure should be effected. That is, usually the buyer will want a brand new television or a brand new car as a replacement, while the seller will want to try to repair the defective one (or, perhaps, even refund a portion of the purchase price) before it offers a brand new good to the buyer. The buyer, of course, usually does not want a repaired good and would rather have all his or her money back than to accept a repaired item.

The Code says nothing definitively about what manner of cure is effective. However, the courts have established the following general rules:

(a) A seller who has a right to cure under §2-508 is entitled first to attempt to cure by repair, so long as such repair, if successfully carried out, will result in the buyer ending up with substantially all of the benefit of his or her bargain.

(b) If cure by repair does not result in the buyer having the benefit of his or her bargain, it is an ineffective cure and the buyer must be given a new replacement good. If the seller does not tender a new replacement good in a cure situation, the buyer is entitled to reject the repaired one and sue for total breach.

(c) A seller, even one with a right to cure under §2-508, cannot require the buyer to accept a cure by refund of all or any portion of the purchase price. If the seller is unwilling either to repair or replace the defective good, the buyer is entitled to terminate the contract and sue for total breach.

Thus, if the seller of the television wants to fix the problem of a consistently green picture by installing a brand new picture tube, or if the seller of the car wants to install a brand new transmission to replace the defective one, generally the courts will allow it (assuming of course the problem is fixed), and the buyer cannot insist on a brand new television or a brand new car as a replacement. That is, in cases involving a successful cure by repair with brand new parts, the Code deems that the purchaser has received the benefit of his or her bargain, which the courts would define as a working television or car with all new parts. However, if the seller wants to cure by replacing the defective picture tube with a used one, or replacing the transmission with a rebuilt one, the buyer need not accept it, i.e., it is an ineffective cure. The reason is that in such cases the buyer is not receiving what he or she bargained for, i.e., the security of a good with all brand new parts in it.

(4) **Buyer's Rights and Duties When Seller Attempts to Cure. [§22.2414]** There are certain rules regarding a buyer's rights and duties in a cure situation that need to be understood in order to understand sufficiently how the doctrine of cure operates:

(1) Section 2-508 sets forth a seller's **right** to cure, which conversely means it is the **duty** of a buyer to allow a cure if the seller can meet the requisites provided in §2-508. Thus, if the seller is entitled to cure under §2-508, and timely tenders the cure in an effective manner, the buyer **must** accept the cured tender or be in breach himself or herself. However, if the seller is adjudged not entitled to cure under §2-508, or if the method of cure is not an effective one, then it is the seller who is in breach, and the buyer can reject the re-tendered goods without contractual liability.

(2) The effect of cure is to turn what would otherwise be a material breach into an immaterial one. Hence, even if the seller is entitled to cure and does so in an effective manner, the buyer is still entitled to sue the seller for breach and recover any damages suffered while waiting for the cure.

b. The Second Limitation on the Perfect Tender Rule: Installment Contracts. [§22.242] Section 2-601 itself provides that the perfect tender rule does not apply to installment contracts. An installment contract is one which either requires or authorizes the delivery of goods in more than one lot [UCC §2-612(1)]. When the seller's tender of a particular shipment under an installment contract is non-conforming, the buyer is faced with two issues: (1) is he or she entitled to reject **that particular shipment** due to the non-conforming tender of that shipment; and (2) is he or she entitled to reject **future shipments** and to **terminate the entire contract** due to the non-conforming tender of a particular shipment. UCC §2-612 sets forth the applicable standards governing the buyer's right of rejection in these situations, which are discussed below.

(1) A Buyer May Reject a Particular Shipment Due to a Non-Conforming Tender *of that Shipment* **only if the Non-Conformity Both Substantially Impairs the Value of the Shipment and Is Not Cured. [§22.2421]** Under §2-612(2), a buyer may not effectively reject *a particular shipment* of an installment contract due to a non-conforming tender of that shipment unless:

(a) the nonconformity **substantially impairs** the value of the shipment; and

(b) either: (1) the non-conformity **cannot be cured**, or (2) the seller **refuses to give adequate assurance** of cure.

Thus, for installment contracts under the UCC, the Code has adopted a kind of substantial performance doctrine to regulate a buyer's rights (see §21.26 for a discussion of the substantial performance doctrine). A minor breach by the seller in the tender of a particular shipment in an installment contract, i.e., a breach that does not "substantially impair" the value of the shipment, is treated as an immaterial breach. Hence, while the buyer is entitled to sue for any damages caused by the breach, the buyer cannot reject the shipment and refuse to pay for them without incurring contractual liability. In other words, the buyer is "stuck" with having to accept imperfect (or otherwise imperfectly tendered) goods, and cannot tell the seller to take them back when the seller makes an immaterial breach of a particular installment under §2-612. In such a case, the buyer's only recourse is to sue for the damages resulting from the breach. If the breach were serious enough that it did "substantially impair" the value of the shipment, then the buyer is entitled to reject the shipment and need not pay for the goods. However, even then the seller is entitled to cure such a breach if he or she can establish the right to do so under §2-508 (see §22.241 for a discussion of the seller's right of cure). If the seller effectively cures the substantial impairment breach, once again buyer cannot reject the shipment and must accept and pay for the goods, for his or her only recourse is to sue for damages caused by the imperfect tender.

(a) **Example. [§22.2421-1]** Betsy orders 300 faucets from Sheila, to be delivered in two lots of 150 faucets each. The first shipment was timely delivered, but when Betsy examined the faucets, she discovered that one was broken.

200

If this were a single lot contract for 150 faucets, Betsy would be entitled to reject all 150 faucets (or any portion thereof), and refuse to pay for them. However, because this is an *installment* contract, Betsy most likely would not be entitled to reject the shipment because the failure of one faucet to work out of 150 sent likely does not "substantially impair" the value of the shipment. As a result, Betsy must accept the shipment (although, of course, she doesn't have to pay for the broken one [See UCC §2-717]).

(b) **Example. [§22.2421-2]** Same as above, except this time 120 of the 150 faucets in the first shipment are broken. At this point, the magnitude of the breach "substantially impairs" the value of the shipment, and Betsy may reject the entire amount, or keep the 30 working models and reject the rest, subject to Sheila's right to cure.

(2) A Buyer May Terminate *the Entire Installment Contract* Due to a Non-Conforming Tender in a Particular Shipment only when the Non-Conformity in the Particular Shipment Substantially Impairs the Value of the Whole Contract. [§22.2422] Under §2-612(3), a buyer may not effectively terminate the remainder of an installment contract based upon the seller's non-conforming tender in one or more of the previously received installments unless the breach of the particular installment (or the sum of the breaches in the previous installments) **substantially impairs the value of the *whole contract***. In other words, once again the Code directs that the breach of an installment contract be treated as a partial breach until the substantial impairment test is met. Thus, if a breach of one delivery is so bad that the value of the **whole** contract is substantially impaired, the buyer is entitled to treat the entire contract as materially breached, and may suspend his or her own performance without liability. However, if the non-conformity as to one or more shipments does not seriously impair the value of the **whole** contract (even if the breach justifies rejection of that particular installment), then the buyer must perform the remainder of the agreement or be himself or herself in breach.

Note, however, that a seller's failure of perfect tender in one of more installments under an installment contract may give the buyer the right to demand reasonable assurances of future performance as provided in §2-609 (see §23.32 et seq. for a discussion of the requirements and effects of such a demand for reasonable assurances).

(a) **Example. [§22.2422-1]** A grocery store contract for the delivery of 100 pounds of apples per month over the next two years from Wholesaler. In the first shipment, 85 pounds of apples are spoiled and Wholesaler refuses to send any replacements, claiming any spoilage is not its fault. Clearly the store can reject that shipment (for there was a substantial impairment in the value of the shipment). Most likely the store management will have lost confidence in the wholesaler and will wonder whether the seller is going to deliver conforming goods in the future. Probably the store would like to cancel the contract at that point and find a new supplier. However, it is not entitled to do so. Under Comment 6 to §2-612, an insecurity as to the completeness of future performance based on a seller's past shipments is insufficient, in and of itself, to justify cancellation of the contract. It is only when the failure of tender in a particular shipment **substantially impairs the value of the whole** contract that the store will be entitled to declare a material breach of the whole, and cancel the remainder of the contract under §2-612(3). Obviously, if the wholesaler continues to send a large amount of spoiled fruit with each installment (and does not cure the defective shipments), at some point the aggregate effect of those acts will be to substantially impair the value of the whole contract to the store. However, note that it is rare that the imperfect tender in the first shipment of an installment contract can meet the "substantial impairment of the whole" standard of §2-612(3).

(3) Rationale for Different Treatment of Buyer's Right to Reject Goods in Installment and Single Lot Contracts. [§22.2423] As you no doubt have ascertained, in this area form controls substance under the UCC. That is, the same breach by the seller will enable a buyer to reject a shipment under the perfect tender rule if the contract calls for a single lot delivery, but will not allow the buyer to reject the shipment under the substantial impairment test if the contract calls for more than one shipment. There is some disagreement as to the rationale for this disparate treatment. While it does not explain the issue completely, the most frequently given reason is that it is more likely that merchants enter into installment contracts, whereas ordinary consumers enter into single lot ones. This theory holds that merchants are better prepared to deal with less than perfect tender than consumers. However, if this were truly the reason for the different treatment, it would seem likely the Code would simply provide separate rejection standards for merchant and consumer buyers.

c. The Third Limitation on the Perfect Tender Rule: *De Minimis Non Curat Lex*. [§22.243] Another limitation on the perfect tender rule is described by one of the few remaining Latin phrases that is mentioned occasionally in the case law, *de minimis non curat lex*. Loosely translated, the phrase means "the law does not deal in trifles." The idea is that if the breach is truly *de minimis*, i.e., truly trifling, some courts have found that the perfect tender rule should not apply even to a single lot contract despite the wording of §2-601. Thus, to these courts, a *de minimis* breach should be treated as an immaterial one.

(1) Example. [§22.2431] A car buyer was told by the dealer that the radio in his car would play up to 120 decibels ("db"). When the car was delivered, the radio played only to 119 db. A court accepting the *de minimis* exception would treat the breach as immaterial, thus requiring the buyer to accept and pay for the car. However, because the actions of the dealer constituted a breach, albeit a *de minimis* one, the buyer would be entitled to sue for damages, if any, resulting from the failure of the radio to perform as promised, i.e the difference between the value of a 120 db radio and a 119 db one.

d. The Fourth Limitation on the Perfect Tender Rule: Usage of Trade; Course of Dealing; and Course of Performance. [§22.244] Section 2-601 does not, on its face, use the words "perfect tender." Instead, it states that buyer has the right to reject any commercial unit of a single lot shipment if seller fails "to conform to the contract." Sometimes a usage of trade, course of dealing, or course of performance may modify the duties of the seller so that even though the seller's tendered performance fails to fulfill the express words of the contract, the performance nonetheless "conforms to the contract."

(1) Example. [§22.2441] Roger owns a golf shop and orders 10,000 tees from a golf supplier. Assume that in the golf industry it is a well known and accepted practice that a supplier need not count each tee separately to fulfill an order. Rather, tees are measured by weight and the custom is that 1,000 tees weigh 12 ounces. Accordingly, the supplier sends Roger ten 12-oz. packages. Roger is obsessive and counts the tees and it turns out that only 9,987 were sent. Roger will not be able to reject the shipment under §2-601 because given the usage of trade, the tender of the tees by the supplier "conformed to the contract."

e. **The Fifth Limitation on the Perfect Tender Rule: Revocation of Acceptance.** [§22.245] As explained in detail in §22.33, a party who "accepts" a good and later tries to revoke that acceptance cannot do so under the standards of the perfect tender rule. Once acceptance has taken place, a buyer cannot reject a good unless the non-conformity **substantially impairs the value of the good to the buyer, and either was: (a) difficult to discover when it was accepted, or (b) accepted knowingly by the buyer with the reasonable assumption the seller would fix it** [see UCC §2-608]. Thus, revocation of acceptance situations are also governed by a type of substantial impairment test, which limits the harshness to sellers of the perfect tender rule.

D. **PERFORMANCE IN CONTRACTS GOVERNED BY THE UCC: ACCEPTANCE, REJECTION, AND REVOCATION OF ACCEPTANCE.** [§22.3] When a buyer receives the seller's tender of goods under a transaction governed by Article 2 of the UCC, there are three things the buyer may do:

(1) **Accept** the tender;

(2) **Reject** the tender; or

(3) Accept the tender at first, but later **revoke his or her acceptance** of it.

1. **"ACCEPTANCE" OF GOODS UNDER THE UCC.** [§22.31] Once goods have been duly tendered to a buyer, most often the buyer accepts them. What constitutes acceptance is governed by §2-606, which says there are three ways a buyer may effectively accept a seller's tender:

(1) By informing the seller he or she will accept the goods after having a reasonable opportunity to inspect them [§2-606(1)(a)];

(2) By keeping them and saying nothing one way or another about acceptance, i.e., by failing to reject them effectively after a reasonable period of time [§2-606(1)(b)]; and

(3) By taking any act inconsistent with the seller's ownership of the tendered goods [§2-606(1)(c)].

It is important to note that mere possession of the goods by the buyer, or even payment for the goods by the buyer, does not necessarily constitute acceptance [UCC §2-606, Com. 3]. The buyer is entitled (absent an agreement to the contrary) to possess and inspect the goods for a reasonable period of time before "accepting" them [UCC §2-513]. "Inspection" in this context means more than just a quick glance at the goods; it means a reasonable chance to test them to see if they are conforming goods. As you might expect, the most common form of acceptance is under §2-606(1)(b), i.e., where the buyer receives the goods, inspects them, and simply keeps them without further communication with the seller. After a reasonable inspection period, acceptance by silence has taken place.

Note: There is sometimes an understandable confusion between the concepts of "acceptance" of an offer and "acceptance" of a good. However, you must keep them analytically separate, for they are completely different concepts. For example, while an offeree generally cannot accept an offer to enter into a contract by silence (see §4.56), "acceptance" of a tendered good by silence under §2-606(1)(b) is quite routine. As some commentators put it, there is a difference between "acceptance of the contract" and "acceptance of the good."

a. **Effect of Acceptance. [§22.311]** Acceptance is a significant event in the buyer-seller relationship. Upon a buyer's acceptance of goods, the rights and duties of the buyer and seller toward each other change. That is, upon acceptance of the goods:

(1) **The buyer must pay for the goods at the contract price [§2-607(1)].** Note that even if the goods later turn out to be defective, the buyer must still pay for them upon acceptance. Obviously the buyer can later sue for damages resulting from receiving the defective product, but the purchase price must nevertheless be paid after acceptance or the buyer will also be liable for breach.

(2) **The buyer can no longer reject the goods [§2-607(2)],** and so the buyer's right to rely on the perfect tender rule to reject a shipment is lost.

(3) **The burden of proof to establish that the seller's tender was non-conforming shifts from the seller to the buyer [§2-607(4)]** (i.e., if a buyer rejects a good as non-conforming before acceptance, it is up to the seller to prove his or her tender was conforming in the subsequent breach of contract suit. After acceptance, it is up to the buyer to prove that the seller's tender was **not** conforming); and

(4) **The buyer is obligated to notify the seller of any breach regarding the tender of the goods within a reasonable time,** or the buyer is barred from recovery [§2-607(3)]. Typically, this requirement is important in breach of warranty actions when reasonable notification to the seller is a condition precedent to allowing a breach of warranty claim to continue (see §36.41 for further discussion of this requirement).

2. **REJECTION OF GOODS UNDER THE UCC. [§22.32]** If a buyer does not accept goods tendered to him or her in a transaction governed by the UCC, by definition he or she "rejects" them. In other words, any non-acceptance under the Code is a rejection. However, for the rejection to be **effective**, certain things **must** be done and one thing **cannot** be done. If the buyer does not do one of the things he or she is obligated to do, or does the one thing he or she is not supposed to do, the attempted rejection is deemed ineffective, and the goods will be judged accepted under §2-606(1)(b). These things are discussed immediately below.

a. **Actions a Buyer *Must* Take in Order to Have an Effective Rejection. [§22.321]** Under the UCC, a buyer is under an obligation to do the following upon rejection:

(1) Reject the good **within a reasonable time** after delivery [§2-602(1)].

(2) **Seasonably** (i.e., within a commercially reasonable time under the circumstances) **notify the seller** of the rejection [§2-602(1)].

(3) **Hold and store the goods with reasonable care** if he or she has taken possession of them before rejection [§2-602(2)(b)]. (As noted earlier in §22.311), mere possession of a good does not signify acceptance of it. The buyer has a reasonable period within which to inspect the good before acceptance takes place. Thus, the buyer may well have possession of the good when the decision to reject it is made, and if so, the buyer must hold the good with reasonable care.)

(4) If the buyer is a merchant, **the buyer must try to sell any rejected perishable good as soon as possible**, assuming the seller or the seller's agent has no place of business "in the market of rejection" [UCC §2-603(1)]. That is, if the seller is in the same city or "market" as the buyer, the seller has to come and retake possession of rejected perishable goods and try to sell them if he or she can. If the seller is not in that market, however, the **buyer** has an obligation to attempt to sell them. However, the buyer is entitled to recover his or her costs in selling the goods, plus a reasonable commission [UCC §2-603(2)].

(5) **If the buyer is a merchant,** the rejected goods are not perishable, and the seller is not located in the "market of rejection," **the buyer must follow any reasonable instructions from the seller concerning the disposition of goods [UCC §2-603(1)].** Thus, if the seller asks the merchant buyer to ship back the goods the buyer has rejected, the merchant buyer must do so. However, the buyer may demand indemnity from the seller for any expenses incurred in shipping the goods back [UCC §2-603(1)].

b. **Action a Buyer *Cannot* Take in Order to Have an Effective Rejection. [§22.322]** Under §2-602(2)(a), if a buyer exercises any indicia of ownership over goods he or she has previously rejected, the rejection becomes ineffective and the buyer will be deemed to have accepted the goods. For example, suppose Megan purchased an electric lawn mower from Ralph's Hardware on Tuesday. Later that day Megan discovered it didn't work, and promptly notified Ralph that she was rejecting it. Ralph promised to pick it up from Megan's house on Friday. On Thursday, a worker repairing roof tiles at Megan's home drops a tile on the mower and destroys it. The worker immediately offers Megan a check to pay for the mower, which Megan accepts. By accepting the check made out in her name, Megan's rejection of the mower has become ineffective, for she exercised an indicia of ownership of the mower, i.e., accepting payment for its destruction. Thus, while she may keep the check, she must also pay Ralph the contract price for the mower as she has now "accepted" it under both UCC §2-602(1)(a) and §2-606(1)(c).

c. **Actions Which a Rejecting Buyer is *Permitted* to Take Which Do Not Render Acceptance Ineffective. [§22.323]** Upon rejection, the Code sets forth a series of options that a rejecting buyer is permitted, but is not required, to take. The most prominent of these are:

(1) If the rejecting buyer is a non-merchant, the buyer is permitted either to send rejected goods back to the seller, sell them for the seller's account, or store them reasonably until the seller picks them up (and can charge the seller for such storage). If the buyer in fact sells the goods for the seller, the buyer is entitled to withhold a reasonable commission from the amounts generated by the sale so long as such a sale is in good faith. Of course, the buyer must turn over any remaining proceeds from such sale to the seller [UCC §2-604]. In addition, if the rejecting buyer is a non-merchant, the buyer may, but is not required to, follow the instructions of the seller as to the disposition of the goods. This is true even if the

seller offers to pay the buyer for any inconvenience and expense [UCC §2-604]. (Note that while this approach follows from the explicit wording of §2-604, some courts and commentators disagree that it is what §2-604 means. They contend that a non-merchant buyer's deliberate refusal to follow a seller's reasonable and easily carried out instructions may constitute a breach of the duty of good faith.)

(2) If the rejecting buyer is a merchant, and if the goods are not perishable, and if the seller has not sent instructions regarding the disposition of the goods within a reasonable time, then the buyer is also entitled to sell the goods for the seller's account and keep a commission for his or her services, or may store them until the seller picks them up, and charge the seller a fee for such storage [UCC §2-604].

d. **Grounds for Rejection. [§22.324]** As a review, recall that in a single lot contract, the buyer is entitled to reject the goods upon any deviation from promised performance under the perfect tender rule [UCC §2-602]; (see §22.21). Under an installment contract, the grounds for rejection are more stringent [UCC §2-612]; (see §22.22).

e. **Rejection Against Remote Sellers [§22.325]** Most modern authorities permit a buyer to exercise a right of rejection against remote sellers. That is, if Joe bought a GM car from Sally's dealership, Joe could exercise his rejection rights against either Sally's or GM (the "remote" seller).

3. **REVOCATION OF ACCEPTANCE. [§22.33]** If a buyer initially accepts a good after sufficient inspection, but then later decides there are grounds to return it, the buyer's actions are no longer deemed a rejection, but rather constitute a **revocation of acceptance** [UCC §2-608].

a. **Elements of an Effective Revocation of Acceptance. [§22.331]** In order to establish that a buyer has sufficient grounds to revoke his or her previous acceptance effectively, the buyer must prove:

(1) The goods were accepted with knowledge of their non-conformity, but with a reasonable expectation that the non-conformity would be cured by the seller [§2-608(1)(a)]; or

(2) The goods were accepted without knowledge of their non-conformity, but the reason the non-conformity was not known was that it was difficult or impossible initially to discover it [§2-608(1)(b)].

In addition to **either** of the above grounds, the buyer must also establish **all** of the following:

(a) That the non-conformity on which the revocation is based **substantially impairs** the value of the goods **to the buyer** [§2-608(1)]. (Note two things about this requirement. **First**, as noted previously (see §22.2321), it acts as a limitation on the perfect tender rule, i.e., a buyer may not revoke his or her acceptance for **any** non-conformity, even when it was delivered under a single lot contract. Instead, to revoke effectively, the non-conformity must **substantially impair** the value of the good. **Second**, the test under §2-608(1) is subjective, i.e., the non-conformity need only substantially impair the value of the good **to the particular buyer**, and not to a hypothetical, ordinary reasonable buyer);

(b) Revocation must occur within a reasonable time after the buyer discovered or should have discovered the grounds for it [§2-608(2)]; and

(c) Revocation must occur before any substantial change in the condition of the goods not caused by the non-conformity [§2-608(2)].

(1) Example. [§22.3311] Ann buys a stereo system from a department store and when she gets it home, she discovers that the volume knob is not attached securely. She calls up the seller, who assures her the store will send someone out to her home in the next couple of weeks to fix it. On that representation Ann accepts and uses the stereo. If the repair is never made by the seller, Ann is probably entitled to revoke her acceptance based on §2-608(1)(a). To establish her right to revoke, she will need to establish that: (a) she accepted the stereo with knowledge of its non-conformity (i.e., she knew the knob was loose), but did so only on the reasonable assumption the defect would be cured; (b) the loose knob substantially impairs the value of the stereo to her; (c) her revocation occurred within a reasonable time after she realized the store was not sending someone out to fix it; and (d) there has been no substantial change in the condition of the stereo caused by anything other than the defect when she revokes her acceptance of it.

(2) Example. [§22.3312] Sam buys a television from Video, Inc., a retailer. The manufacturer of the set did not securely attach an internal wire. At first the television worked perfectly and Sam accepted it. After two weeks, however, the wire came loose and the set stopped working. Sam is likely entitled to revoke his acceptance against Video Inc. under §2-608(1)(b). That is, his acceptance of a defective good was reasonably made without discovery of the non-conformity given the difficulty of discovering the problem, and a non-working set substantially impairs the value of the contract to Sam. Assuming notice of Sam's revocation is timely made and that the revocation is done before there is any substantial change in the set not caused by the wire problem, Sam is entitled to revoke acceptance.

(3) Example. [§22.3313] Leonard, the conductor of the local symphony, buys a stereo. At first it sounds wonderful, just like it did in the store, and he accepts it. However, over time it develops, at least to his ears, a shrill quality that greatly disturbs him. No one else can hear this shrill quality, and indeed everyone who hears the stereo is quite impressed with the system. Nevertheless, assuming he does so in a timely fashion, Leonard may revoke his acceptance because the non-conformity (i.e., the difference between what the stereo sounded like in the store and what it sounds like now) substantially impairs the value of the stereo to him.

b. **Rationale for Having Different Standards for Rejection than for Revocation of Acceptance. [§22.332]** If a buyer wishes to send back a defective good delivered under a single lot contract, it is obviously easier to reject it (using the perfect tender rule of §2-601) than to revoke his or her acceptance of it (under the subjective substantial impairment test of §2-608). The principal reason (although there are others) for making it more difficult to revoke than to reject is that, by definition, a revocation must occur after the buyer has decided to accept the good. Thus, the buyer will almost surely have the good in his or her possession for a longer time in a revocation situation than in a rejection one. Hence, because it is more likely that the problem with the good which gives rise to the revocation was caused by the buyer (given the buyer's longer time of possession), the Code has made it somewhat more difficult for the buyer to establish the right to get out of the contract under revocation than under rejection.

c. **The Relationship Between Cure and Revocation of Acceptance. [§22.333]** There is a split of authority as to whether a seller has a right to cure a non-conformity giving rise to revocation of acceptance. Those who think a seller should have that cure right point to the general policy of the UCC to keep the parties in a contract, and to §2-608(3), which states that a buyer who revokes has the same "duties" as one who rejects. They argue that because one of the duties of a rejecting party is to allow the seller to cure, clearly the Code provides for a seller's right to cure in revocation situations.

Those who believe a seller does not have a right to cure upon revocation of acceptance point to the language of the cure provision itself. Under §2-508 there is no mention of a seller's right to cure in a revocation situation, only of a right to cure upon *rejection*. These commentators argue that if the drafters had meant for sellers to have a right to cure upon revocation, the drafters surely would have said so in §2-508. Hence, those who hold this view believe that by not mentioning it, the Code's drafters intended that a seller have the right to cure a defective tender only when a good was rejected.

d. **Typically No Restitution is Recoverable upon Revocation. [§22.334]** Assume Karen purchases a new car and after a few days begins to experience trouble with the ignition. She tries to reject the car, but the dealer assures her its service department will fix the problem. On those representations, she accepts it. Over the next six months the car is in for service numerous times, but the problem remains. Finally, Karen wants to revoke the acceptance of the car, which she is entitled do because while it was accepted with knowledge of the defect, she did so with a reasonable expectation that the problem would be fixed. Assume, however, that the dealership refuses to accept her revocation and Karen sues.

Most courts hold that Karen is entitled to the full amount of her purchase price back in addition to any other damages she can prove. Under the majority view she is **not** liable in restitution for the use of the car during the six months. Thus, the car dealership will receive nothing from Karen for the difference between the new car it gave her and the used car it gets back. Normal principles of restitution would seem to compel such recovery, but the Code does not specifically provide for it in revocation situations, and most courts do not grant it

e. **Revocation Against Remote Sellers. [§32.335]** As noted earlier (§32.325), there is little argument that an aggrieved buyer may exercise his or her *rejection* rights against a remote seller. However, there is a split among the courts whether a buyer may revoke his or her acceptance against a "remote" seller, i.e. a seller with whom the buyer was not in privity.

CHAPTER TWENTY-THREE: PROSPECTIVE NONPERFORMANCE OR ANTICIPATORY REPUDIATION

A. THE ANTICIPATORY REPUDIATION (ALSO INCORRECTLY CALLED THE "ANTICIPATORY BREACH") DOCTRINE. [§23.0] At first blush, it seems no one could credibly argue with the concept of anticipatory repudiation. After all, if Larry's Appliance Store has made a contractual promise to deliver a new television to Donna on May 15, and on May 1, Larry calls up Donna and says "The contract's over! We're not delivering the T.V.," it seems Donna should be able to take Larry at his word and immediately sue him for breach. However the doctrine, at least as we know it today, was not even fully articulated until the 1850's (in a case called *Hochster v. De la Tour*, see §23.1), and after *Hochster*, it still took decades before the doctrine was fully accepted and integrated into contract law. The facts and rationale of *Hochster* are presented below, along with a summary of the controversy surrounding the acceptance of the anticipatory repudiation doctrine.

SPECIAL CASE SQUIB

B. *HOCHSTER V. DE LA TOUR*: THE BEGINNING OF THE MODERN ANTICIPATORY REPUDIATION DOCTRINE. [§23.1] In April 1852, Hochster entered into a contract whereby he promised to accompany De la Tour as a courier throughout De la Tour's European trip. The trip was scheduled to start on June 1, 1852. In early May, De la Tour wrote to Hochster and said that because he had canceled his European trip, he was compelled to "decline" Hochster's services. When De la Tour refused to compensate Hochster for canceling the trip, Hochster brought suit for breach which was filed ten days before the date on which the trip was supposed to start. One of De la Tour's defenses was that the suit was premature. That is, he claimed he could not have "breached" the contract on the day the suit was filed since, on that date, he had not failed to perform an enforceable duty owed to Hochster. That is, he may have indicated that he was not going to perform such a duty, but on the day the suit was filed his breach was only a possibility and had not yet occurred. **Held:** The holding of *Hochster* is in two parts: (1) Upon the **unequivocal** repudiation of future performance from De la Tour, Hochster was entitled to treat his own duties under the contract as discharged, and was entitled immediately and lawfully to seek and to take other employment; and (2) Hochster was entitled to file suit immediately upon receipt of the repudiation, and need not wait until the date performance was due (in this case June 1), before instituting a breach action. *Hochster v. De La Tour*, 2 El. & Bl. 678, 118 Eng. Rep. 922 (Q.B. 1853).

The first part of the holding caused no controversy whatsoever. To make Hochster wait until June 1 before he was able to accept, or perhaps even to seek, other employment was manifestly unfair. Indeed, under the doctrine of mitigation of damages (see §31.43), it is arguable that Hochster would be penalized in the amount of his recovery if he did not seek and accept reasonably similar work soon after the repudiation.

However, the second part of the holding was met with much criticism. Those who argued against its adoption in the common law made the following points:

(1) As a matter of language, this part of the holding was illogical. A contract is not "breached" until there is a non-excused or unjustified failure to perform an enforceable duty. In this case no such duty existed until after June 1. There clearly

was a repudiation before then, but the cause of action filed by Hochster was for **breach** of contract, not repudiation of contract, and thus Hochster should not be entitled to sue for breach until after the date performance was due;

(2) Allowing a suit for breach before the date of performance could cause enormous problems in damage calculations. In *Hochster,* the potential problem was not likely to cause much confusion because there was only a 10-day difference between the date of suit and the date of performance. But suppose there was, e.g., a one-year or two-year gap between the filing of the lawsuit and the date on which the duty was to be performed. In such a case, trial might occur **before** the date of performance was due. If so, it might be impossible to know with certainty the dollar value of the non-breaching party's damages, as concepts such as mitigation, lost profits, the market value of replacement goods or services on the date of performance, etc., would be impossible to know with sufficient certainty.

(3) It is analytically unnecessary to find a "breach" in order to discharge the innocent party's obligations under the contract. Instead, the result could be achieved by holding that each party's unperformed duties under a bilateral contract are subject to a constructive condition that there be neither a material breach **nor a repudiation** by the other. That is, that a party to a bilateral contract need not perform such duties if the other party has either materially breached his or her duties (see §21.22) or the other party has anticipatorily repudiated his or her performance obligations. Thus, this view would hold that upon De la Tour's letter, the constructive condition precedent that no repudiation exist failed, and Hochster's duties were thereafter discharged.

Despite those arguments which, of course, have merit, the courts and commentators have nevertheless adopted the rule that **the innocent party is entitled to sue for total breach immediately upon the receipt of an anticipatory repudiation** [Restatement 2d §253(1); UCC §2-610]. They have formulated the following answers to the criticisms set forth above:

(1) It is not linguistically impossible to have a "breach" before performance is due. This is because implicit in a party's promise to do nothing that would substantially impair the good faith and fair dealing principles imputed in every contract is his or her promised performance before it is due. Thus, upon a repudiation there has, in fact, been a breach — a breach of the implied promise to do nothing to seriously impair a party's good faith performance obligation [Restatement 2d §205; UCC §1-203].

(2) As a practical matter, it is unlikely there will be so much time between anticipatory repudiation and promised performance that a case will actually get to trial before performance is due. If it does, however, problems regarding mitigation, consequential damages, and the like can be handled with normal allocations of burden of proof, i.e., it will be up to the plaintiff to prove the amount of his or her damages to the jury by a preponderance of the evidence, and if he or she cannot sustain that burden, then he or she will lose the suit, for establishing damages in an element of a breach of contract cause of action.

Further, because it is unlikely that many cases will come to trial before the date of performance, it would be unfair to the vast majority of innocent parties not to let them sue immediately. That is, a rule requiring innocent parties to wait until the date performance was due before filing suit would only delay their ability to obtain judicial relief from the other party's breach.

(3) It is simpler and more analytically consistent to say that the reason the innocent party's duties are discharged after a repudiation is because such action constitutes a material breach, the absence of which is a condition to the innocent party's performance.

As a result of these arguments, the doctrine **discharging prospective performance and allowing for immediate suit for total breach** is now well recognized by the courts, although the doctrine is now more accurately called **anticipatory repudiation** rather than anticipatory breach.

C. **ELEMENTS TO ESTABLISH A CLAIM FOR ANTICIPATORY REPUDIATION IN NON-UCC TRANSACTIONS. [§23.2]** If a non-repudiating party wishes to take advantage of the anticipatory repudiation doctrine, i.e., if he or she wants to be able to bring suit immediately and to have all of his or her duties under the agreement discharged in the face of a repudiation recieved before performance is due, the innocent party must establish the following elements:

(1) The repudiation was received under a **bilateral contract in which there were executory duties remaining** at the time of the repudiation (see §23.21);

(2) The repudiated duty would result in a **material**, and not an immaterial, **breach if it were not performed** when due (see §23.22); and

(3) The repudiation was **definite and unequivocal** (see §23.23) [Restatement 2d §§243, 250].

The elements of an effective repudiation in a contract governed by Article 2 of the UCC are similar, but the nomenclature and some of the analysis in such a situation are different enough to justify a separate discussion in §23.3 et seq.

1. **THERE MUST BE A REPUDIATION OF A BILATERAL CONTRACT WITH EXECUTORY DUTIES BY BOTH PARTIES FOR THE INNOCENT PARTY TO TAKE ADVANTAGE OF THE ANTICIPATORY REPUDIATION DOCTRINE. [§23.21]** Just as was true under the material breach doctrine (see §21.2 et seq.), the courts have held that the anticipatory repudiation doctrine will not apply unless the repudiation is of a duty owing under a bilateral contract in which both the repudiating and the innocent party still have unperformed duties at the time of repudiation. However, unlike material breach, there really is no satisfactory explanation for this rule. Nonetheless, it appears well established that in a unilateral contract, or in a bilateral contract where one party's performance is completed, a repudiation before performance is due will usually not result in the innocent party being able to sue the repudiator immediately (although there is one small exception to this rule, see §23.213).

a. **Example. [§23.211]** Shannon enters into a unilateral contract with Kelsey whereby she will pay Kelsey $3,000 in three weeks so long as Kelsey immediately turns over her Rolex watch to Shannon. Kelsey gives the watch to Shannon, and immediately Shannon says she will refuse to pay Kelsey in three weeks. Given the rules currently governing anticipatory repudiation, Kelsey may not bring suit to recover the $3,000 for three weeks, i.e., until Shannon's performance becomes due because the anticipatory repudiation doctrine does not operate in unilateral contracts.

b. Example. [§23.212] Sam borrows $25,000 from Bank and promises to repay the loan at a rate of $1,000 per month plus interest, starting January 15. Sam misses the January, February, and March payments, and on March 20 he sends a letter to the Bank stating that he is repudiating and will not be making any payments under the loan. In the absence of any clause to the contrary, Bank has a cause of action for the first three payments only, and may not use the anticipatory repudiation doctrine to sue immediately for the remaining payments due under the loan. This is because the repudiation was of a duty under a bilateral contract where one side (the Bank) had fully performed its duties at the time of the other's repudiation [Restatement 2d §243, Com. e, Ill. 4].

Note, however, it is because of this rule that most commercial lenders include "acceleration clauses" in their loan agreements. An acceleration clause provides that upon a specified breach of the borrower's promised payment schedule, the borrower's obligation to repay the loan is "accelerated" so that the full amount of the debt is due and payable immediately upon notice from the bank. Such clauses are specifically made enforceable under UCC §1-208.

c. Exception: Where Performance by the Innocent Party is a Condition of the Repudiated Duty. [§23.213] The only exception to the rule that anticipatory breach has effect only under a bilateral contract with each party having executory duties extant at the time of repudiation comes about **where performance by the innocent party is a condition precedent to the enforceability of the repudiated duty**. In those cases, which most often occur under option contracts, the innocent party may immediately bring suit for breach upon the repudiation, even if the innocent party is in a bilateral contract where one party's performance is already complete.

(1) Example. [§23.2131] Frank has entered into an option contract with Mary whereby Frank has the option to purchase Mary's home for $100,000 any time within the next three months. Frank has already completely paid Mary for the option. Mary calls Frank within the three month period and tells him that she has just sold her home to someone else and so Frank is out of luck. Even though performance by Frank under the option contract has been completely rendered, Frank may immediately bring suit for breach against Mary because Frank's performance, i.e., payment of the $100,000 for the house, is a condition of the repudiated duty, i.e., Mary's duty to tender the deed upon tender of payment.

2. THE REPUDIATED DUTY MUST BE IMPORTANT ENOUGH THAT ITS NON-PERFORMANCE WOULD BE DEEMED A MATERIAL BREACH FOR THE INNOCENT PARTY TO TAKE ADVANTAGE OF THE ANTICIPATORY REPUDIATION DOCTRINE. [§23.22] Not every repudiated duty allows the non-repudiating party to sue immediately for anticipatory repudiation and have his or her duties thereafter discharged. To take advantage of the doctrine, the innocent party must establish that the repudiated duty is important enough to the transaction that its non-performance when due would constitute a material breach (see §21.24 for a discussion of how to tell if a breach is material). If the duty is minor enough so that its non-performance would be only an immaterial breach, the innocent party's duties under the agreement are not discharged, and he or she must continue to perform under the contract and cannot bring suit for breach of that duty until it goes unperformed when due.

a. Example. [§23.221] A term of a construction contract requires the contractor to use Acme electrical outlets throughout the building. A month before construction is scheduled to begin, contractor writes developer stating that he will not be using Acme outlets as required, but will be using Watt-Man outlets instead, which are equivalent in size, style,

Sum & Substance QUICK REVIEW of Contracts

quality, and price. Developer cannot immediately sue claiming anticipatory repudiation because if the contractor in fact installed Watt-Man outlets, such conduct would only result in an immaterial breach. Hence, developer will have to wait until the Watt-Man outlets are actually installed before he can sue for breach (assuming he can prove damages), and his obligations to pay contractor are not discharged upon the repudiation.

3. **THE REPUDIATION MUST BE *DEFINITE* AND *UNEQUIVOCAL* FOR THE INNOCENT PARTY TO TAKE ADVANTAGE OF THE ANTICIPATORY REPUDIATION DOCTRINE. [§23.23]** The repudiation giving rise to an anticipatory repudiation claim may be communicated either by words or through actions. However, to be actionable, **the repudiation must be definite and unequivocal, meaning that it must indicate to a reasonable person in the position of the innocent party that the repudiator is unwilling or unable to perform under the contract.** The problems presented in analyzing whether an unequivocal repudiation has taken place differ depending on whether the repudiation is by words or by action, and each is discussed below.

a. **Repudiation by Words. [§23.231]** Because the consequences of an anticipatory repudiation are so great (i.e., cancellation of the contract, immediate suit for total breach, and a discharge of the non-repudiator's duties), contract law requires that a repudiation by words clearly and unambiguously indicate an unwillingness or inability to perform a promised duty [Restatement 2d §250(a)]. Obviously, when a party says, e.g., "I refuse to go forward with our deal and will not fulfill my promised duties," there is little doubt that a repudiation has occurred. However, most of the time it is a much closer call.

There are two recurring fact situations, discussed below, in which it is important to analyze carefully what is communicated, for if the innocent party declares an anticipatory breach and is subsequently found to be unjustified in doing so, it is the "innocent" party who ultimately will be liable if he or she does not perform. Once again, the guiding principle in each of these cases is to determine whether the allegedly repudiating party is clearly and unequivocally stating either an unwillingness or an inability to perform, as viewed by a reasonable person in the position of the innocent party. If so, an actionable repudiation has taken place.

(1) **Distinguishing Repudiation from a Request for Modification. [§23.2311]** Metal Co. has a contract with Electric Co. whereby it has agreed to provide Electric Co. with certain metal rods for use in generating electricity. The price is fixed at $12,000 per rod and delivery is to take place in two months. Near the time of delivery, the owner of Metal Co. calls up the president of Electric Co. and says, "The price of metal is going up. I don't think I can go forward with our deal at only $12,000. I really need $15,000." This is not a repudiation; it is only a **request for modification**, for the owner's statement is not a definite and unequivocal manifestation of an unwillingness or inability to perform under the contract. He is only asking if Electric Co. would be willing to re-negotiate the price term.

If, however, the president of Metal Co. had said, e.g., "I refuse to deliver for the paltry price of $12,000. Unless you agree right now to pay me $15,000, the deal is off!" then an actionable repudiation has occurred. In such a case, Electric Co.'s duties would be discharged, and it would be entitled to seek the rods elsewhere without contractual liability and sue immediately for breach.

(2) **Distinguishing Repudiation from a Good Faith Difference of Opinion as to the Meaning of the Contract. [§23.2312]** Service Co. has a contract to repair "all office equipment" at XYZ Corp. beginning October 1. In September, the president of XYZ mentions to the president of Service Co. how comforting it is to know

someone will be there to service the coffee maker at the office, which always breaks down. The president of Service Co. believes the contract only covers typewriters, computers, calculators, staplers, etc., and not coffee makers. Accordingly, she writes XYZ Corp. a letter noting that while Service Co. is able to service the coffee maker, it does not believe it is required to fix the machine under the contract and hence it refuses to service the machine unless it is found to be legally obligated to do so. Such a statement is not a repudiation; it is only the expression of **a good faith difference of opinion as to the rights and duties owed under the contract** [Restatement 2d §250, Com. b, Ill. 3].

If the president of Service Co. had said something like, "Under no circumstances will my employees fix a stupid coffee maker," then XYZ *might* be able to establish an anticipatory repudiation. To do so, however, it will have to establish that Service Co. is in fact obligated to fix the coffee maker and that such a duty is important enough that the failure to perform it when due would be a material breach.

b. **Repudiation by Conduct. [§23.232]** A party may also repudiate a contract by action. However, such a repudiation must also meet the "definite and unequivocal" standard, and thus, the act of the repudiator must render him or her unable, or apparently unable, to perform under the contract as viewed by a reasonable person in the position of the innocent party [Restatement 2d §250(b)]. Most often, repudiation by conduct occurs when a seller has sold or leased to a third party on a long-term basis the item that is the subject of the contract, and thus is no longer in a position legally to deliver the goods in accordance with the contract.

   (1) **Example. [§23.2321]** Fred has a contract with Gina whereby Gina is obligated to deliver her car to Fred on July 1. On June 15, Fred discovers Gina has sold her car to Lorraine. Gina's act of selling the car to Lorraine is a sufficiently definite act to constitute an anticipatory repudiation of the Fred/Gina agreement. Note that Gina may argue that she has not necessarily repudiated the contract because she could, after all, potentially repurchase the car from Lorraine and still deliver it timely to Fred on July 1. However, contract law provides that when a party has sold the good which he or she is contractually obligated to deliver to someone else, an actionable anticipatory repudiation has occurred.

   (2) **Example. [§23.2322]** Same as above, except this time Fred discovers on June 15 that Gina has leased her car to Lorraine for six months, starting June 1. Once again this is a sufficiently definite and unequivocal act so as to constitute an actionable repudiation of the Fred/Gina contract.

4. **AN EFFECTIVE REPUDIATION MAY ONLY REPUDIATE SOME DUTIES. [§23.24]** On occasion, a party will repudiate only some of the duties called for in the contract. Contract law holds that such a partial repudiation can still serve as the basis for the innocent party to take advantage of the anticipatory repudiation doctrine (meaning an end to the entire contract and an immediate suit for breach), so long as the duty or duties repudiated would give rise to a material breach if they were not performed, and so long as the repudiation is definite and unequivocal.

D. **ANTICIPATORY REPUDIATION IN CONTRACTS GOVERNED BY THE UCC. [§23.3]** The effect of anticipatory repudiation in contracts governed by the UCC is the same as that in non-UCC transactions, i.e., if the non-breaching party can establish the elements necessary for application of the doctrine, he or she:

Sum & Substance QUICK REVIEW of Contracts

(a) can immediately bring suit for breach;

(b) is discharged from all further duties remaining under the contract; and

(c) is entitled to declare the contract terminated.

There are two separate Code sections, §2-609 and §2-610, which provide different ways for a party to establish that an anticipatory repudiation has taken place under an agreement governed by Article 2. How to establish a valid anticipatory repudiation claim under each of these provisions is explained separately below.

1. **ANTICIPATORY REPUDIATION UNDER UCC §2-610. [§23.31]** The elements necessary to establish anticipatory repudiation under UCC §2-610 are quite similar to those necessary to establish anticipatory repudiation in non-UCC contracts (see §23.1 et seq.), but the nomenclature is changed in some respects. Under §2-610, the non-repudiating party is entitled to use the anticipatory repudiation doctrine if he or she can establish that:

   (a) the contract is a **bilateral** one with **unperformed duties remaining** on both sides at the time of the repudiation;

   (b) failure of the repudiating party to perform the repudiated duty would **"substantially impair"** the value of the contract to the innocent party (This is the UCC equivalent of the common law requirement that non-performance of the repudiated duty would result in a material breach.) (see §23.22); and

   (c) the repudiation, whether by words or by conduct, must **definitely and unequivocally indicate the repudiating party's unwillingness or inability to perform** his or her promised duties.

2. **ANTICIPATORY REPUDIATION BY FAILING TO PROVIDE REASONABLE ASSURANCES UNDER UCC §2-609. [§23.32]** In some ways, the common law anticipatory repudiation doctrine was not broad or strong enough. True, where the other party actually repudiated, the law gave the innocent party some powerful remedies. Still, the price for being entitled to use such extreme remedies was that there had to be a **definite and unequivocal** repudiation. As a practical matter, however, there are often times when a party may make statements which make the other party unsure about whether the party making the statements will perform, but where such statements do not rise to the level of an unequivocal repudiation of performance. While the innocent party may understandably be insecure as to the other party's ability or willingness to perform under these circumstances, there is little he or she can do to relieve such insecurity under the common law anticipatory repudiation doctrine. He or she cannot declare a breach given only an equivocal statement, but of course the innocent party does not want to perform or even prepare to perform, if the other will breach.

To illustrate this dilemma, suppose Machine, Inc., a manufacturer of custom machinery, had a contract to deliver an $800,000 carpet weaving machine to Carpets Co. on October 1. The machine will take four months to construct, and Machine, Inc. started the manufacture of it in late June. In mid-July, the owner of Machine, Inc. has a conversation with her counterpart at Carpet Co., in which the Carpet Co. officer says, only half jokingly, "Sure hope we'll be able to find the money to pay you for the machine." A week later, the president of Machine, Inc. reads in the *Wall Street Journal* that Carpet Co. is in deep financial trouble, is not paying its bills on time, and is likely to file for bankruptcy in the next three to four months. At this point Machine, Inc. is in an extremely vulnerable position. Carpet Co. has not repudiated its duties, and thus Machine, Inc. is not discharged from having to perform. Thus, if it chooses immediately to cease manufacture of the machine and, as a result, does not tender it as promised on October 1, Machine Inc. could well be in breach if Carpet Co. has not unequivocally repudiated before then. On the other hand, if Carpet Co. was really in poor financial condition, and will not pay Machine, Inc. for the machine when it is delivered, Machine Inc. might want to stop production of the carpet weaver now so as to cut its losses or try to sell the machine to someone else.

UCC §2-609 was designed to deal with this kind of situation and provide a remedy for a party who has reason to be insecure about the other's performance. Under §2-609, whenever one party has **"reasonable grounds for insecurity"** with respect to the other's ability or willingness to perform, he or she "may in writing demand adequate assurance of due performance." The party receiving such a demand must then provide assurances that its promised performance will be forthcoming. Thus, in the Machine, Inc./Carpet Co. contract above, after the troubling conversation and upon reading the *Journal* article, Machine, Inc. is entitled to demand reasonable assurances of Carpet Co.'s ability and willingness to pay for the machine on October 1. Once the letter is received, Carpet Co. must provide some sort of assurance of payment.

Stating the rule poses four questions:

(1) When does a party have "reasonable grounds for insecurity" (see §23.321);

(2) What kinds of things constitute "adequate assurances of due performance" by the responding party (see §23.322);

(3) What are the rights of the insecure party while waiting for assurances, i.e., can the insecure party suspend performance until such assurances arrive (see §23.323); and

(4) What are the consequences of failing to provide adequate assurances (see §23.324).

Each of these questions is addressed below.

a. **What Constitutes "Reasonable Grounds for Insecurity" under §2-609(1) and (2).** [§23.321] The Code provides no hard and fast test for ascertaining what gives one party reasonable grounds for insecurity about the other's ability and willingness to perform under the contract. However, the courts have generally agreed on such a test which is: **if innocent party would, in good faith, have a reasonable doubt as to the other party's willingness or ability to provide a substantial part of the bargain, reasonable grounds for insecurity exist.** [UCC §2-609, Com 1.]

While not an exhaustive list, some things that give rise to legitimate grounds for insecurity include:

(1) hearing a rumor from a reliable and knowledgeable source that the other party may be unwilling or unable to perform [UCC §2-609, Com. 4];

(2) a seller's receipt of a credit report from a commercial agency indicating the buyer is falling behind in paying his, her, or its bills;

(3) an article in a trustworthy publication indicating business difficulties for the other party;

(4) knowledge by the buyer that the seller has been making late deliveries to other purchasers [UCC §2-609, Com. 1];

(5) knowledge by the buyer that the seller has been delivering poorly performing products to others [UCC §2-609, Com. 3]; and

(6) previous imperfectly tendered deliveries by the seller to the particular buyer, including such deliveries in previous shipments under an installment contract (see §22.2322).

Note that §2-609 itself requires that if a party has sufficient grounds, he or she must make the demand for reasonable assurances in writing. Despite that language, a few courts have held that an oral demand is effective.

(1) The Grounds for Demanding Assurances Need Not Be True; They Need only Reasonably Appear to be True to the Insecure Party. [§23.3211] Suppose a reputable weekly financial magazine runs a lengthy article indicating that a buyer is in a perilous financial condition. A seller who is in a contract with that buyer sees the article and sends a demand for assurances. The article is mistaken and, in fact, the buyer is in excellent financial condition, is paying its bills on time, has a lot of cash in the bank, etc. Can the buyer ignore the demand for assurances since the source on which it is based is in error? **Answer: NO.** Under §2-609 the grounds on which the insecurity is based need not ultimately be true. Rather, all that is required is that the grounds **reasonably appear to be true** at the time the insecure party makes the request. If the demand is reasonably based, the party receiving it *must* respond to it and objectively establish its willingness and ability to perform under the contract or face the consequences if it does not (§21.324). The rationale behind this rule is that if in fact the information on which the demand is made is in error, it should not be difficult for the party receiving the demand to establish its ability and willingness to perform. On the other hand it would be burdensome for the demanding party to verify independently what appears to be a reliable report making questionable a party's ability or willingness to perform.

(2) Grounds for Insecurity must become Known to the Insecure Party *After* the Contract is Formed, and Not Before. [§23.3212] The idea behind §2-609 is that when a party in a contract with executory duties becomes concerned about the other's willingness or ability to perform, there should be a mechanism for alleviating that doubt short of taking a chance and declaring an anticipatory repudiation. However, if the seller knew **before** entering into the contract of grounds for such insecurity, the rationale behind §2-609 does not apply, and the party cannot legitimately demand assurances based on that information. If, for example, a seller knows prior to entering into a contract that the seller is in poor financial shape, contract law requires that the seller should protect himself or herself in other ways, e.g., by demanding security for the payment, negotiating for payment by letter of credit, raising the price to cover the risk of non-payment, choosing not to enter into the agreement at all, etc. Accordingly, it is only when the grounds for insecurity become known to the party **after** entering into the contract, when that party can no longer protect itself by demanding a change in the terms of the deal, that §2-609 permits a demand for adequate assurances.

(3) A Demand for Assurances Cannot Effectively Demand only a Particular Kind of Assurance. [§23.3213] Assume a seller has reasonable grounds to believe that a buyer may not pay when required under a contract and sends a demand for assurances. May the seller effectively demand a particular kind of assurance, e.g., "to satisfy me that you will perform, I demand to see an audited financial statement of your company" **Answer**: NO. If a party is entitled to demand assurance, it is up to the **receiving** party to provide such assurance and to determine what form the assurance will take.

b. **What Constitutes "Adequate Assurances" of Performance. [§23.322]** Once a party makes an effective demand for assurances, the question becomes what kinds of actions by the other party constitute "adequate" assurances. Once again, no precise test is given in the Code. However, the generally accepted formulation is that **so long as the responding party provides assurances that would indicate an ability and willingness to perform under the contract to a reasonable person in the position of the insecure party, the assurances will be adequate.** Sometimes (although rarely) even an unsubstantiated oral promise might be enough. For example, assume an electronics store has an installment contract with a reputable tube manufacturer calling for three deliveries of 500 tubes each. When the first shipment arrived, the store manager noticed that there were only 499 tubes included, and sent a written demand for assurances that the manufacturer take steps to ensure that the next delivery is complete. If in response to such a demand the manufacturer telephoned the store and told them that the defective shipment problem was being attended to and would not occur again, probably under such circumstances the manufacturer's oral representation would be an adequate assurance of performance [UCC §2-609, Com. 4].

However, in most cases more than just an unsupported oral intention to perform is necessary. For example, if a seller sends a request for assurances to a buyer expressing concern about the buyer's ability to pay based on a Dun & Bradstreet credit report showing that the buyer is paying its bills four months late, an oral (or even written) declaration by the buyer that "The company has plenty of money and we will pay you per the contract" will probably not be an adequate assurance of performance. In such a case, the buyer would have to provide some objective proof of its ability to pay in accordance with the contract, e.g., a financial statement, a bank statement, an explanation of its recent late payments, a reason why it expects to have funds in the future, etc.

c. **What an Insecure Party May Do While Waiting for a Response to a Justified Demand for Assurances. [§23.323]** Section 2-609(1) provides that an insecure party who has sent a justified demand for assurances may, if it is commercially reasonable to do so, **suspend performance** while waiting for the assurances. Thus, as soon as the request is sent the insecure party may, if it is commercially reasonable to do so, simply cease its own performance or preparations for performance, and wait for the other party to respond. If adequate assurances arrive, and if, because of the temporary suspension, the insecure party is late in performing, such lateness is excused.

d. **Consequence of Failing to Respond Adequately to a Justified Demand for Assurances. [§23.324]** A party in receipt of a justified demand for assurances under §2-609 must adequately respond to it within a **reasonable time not exceeding thirty days**. If that party either does not respond, or does not provide an adequate response within that time, **the failure to provide adequate assurances is treated as an anticipatory repudiation, and the innocent party may proceed under the remedies granted under UCC §2-610** (see §23.31).

There is an issue whether the failure to respond adequately to a legitimate demand for assurances about the performance of a minor duty under a contract, i.e., a duty whose non-performance would only give rise to an immaterial breach, gives the insecure party a right to declare an anticipatory repudiation. Most courts and commentators believe that it does not. That is, to use a failure to respond to an effective demand for assurances under §2-609 as a means to declare anticipatory repudiation under §2-610, the duty subject to the demand for assurances must be one whose non-performance when due would be a material breach.

In other words, most courts believe that failure to respond adequately to a legitimate demand for assurances does not give a right to anticipatory repudiation unless the requesting party is threatened with the loss of a substantial part of what was bargained for. [UCC §2-609, Com. 1.]

e. **Right to Demand Adequate Assurances in Contracts Not Governed by the UCC. [§23.325]** In theory, the right to demand reasonable assurances should not be restricted to UCC contracts. The Restatement 2d provides that an obligee has the right to demand assurances of future performance upon reasonable grounds to believe the obligor will totally breach the agreement. Further, it also provides that the failure to respond adequately to such a justified demand should be treated as an anticipatory repudiation [Restatement 2d §251(1), (2)]. However, this is another of the Restatement 2d provisions that has not been widely adopted in practice. Hence, the right to demand assurances is a right usually only exercised in Article 2 contracts.

E. **MECHANICS OF ANTICIPATORY REPUDIATION. [§23.4]** To completely understand the anticipatory repudiation doctrine, it is important to note that receipt of a repudiation does not necessarily terminate the contract. Rather, receipt of a repudiation only gives the innocent party a **conditional right to terminate** the agreement. To fulfill the condition, the innocent party **must do something which indicates he or she is treating the repudiation as final**. This can either be done by *informing* the repudiator of his or her intention to treat the repudiation as final, or by *materially changing his or her position* in reliance on the repudiation [Restatement 2d §256(1); UCC §2-611(1)]. Once such action is taken, the condition has been fulfilled; the innocent party is thereafter entitled to bring suit for total breach; and his or her duties under the contract are thereby discharged [Restatement 2d §253; UCC §2-610].

This means that a party who receives a repudiation is **entitled to ignore it** and, if he or she wishes, to urge the repudiator to retract the repudiation without giving up the right to later treat the repudiation as final [Restatement 2d §257; UCC §2-610(a) and Com. 4 to §2-610]; (see §23.5 for a discussion of retraction). If the innocent party chooses to **wait before treating the repudiation as final**, he or she is entitled to suspend performance or preparation for performance during that period. Thus, if the repudiating party later retracts the repudiation, and if the innocent party is late in performing under the revived contract due to the suspension in performance, such tardiness is excused [UCC §2-610(c)].

If the innocent party wants to **save the contract**, there are some obvious advantages to urging the repudiator to retract the repudiation and waiting before treating the repudiation as final. The repudiator may indeed have second thoughts and agree to continue under the contract. However, there are also risks with such a procedure. If the recipient of a repudiation made far in advance of the date performance is due under the contract does not treat the repudiation as final, the repudiator might retract his or her repudiation very close to the date on which performance was due. While in such a case the innocent party would not be required to perform on the promised date and would have a reasonable amount of time to complete performance, he or she could be hindered in such a situation because by having to perform a duty that he or she genuinely thought was discharged.

Furthermore, the innocent party is also taking a risk if he or she decides to **continue preparation for performance** after receipt of an anticipatory repudiation. (The innocent party may choose to continue preparation either because he or she thinks the repudiating party will retract the repudiation, because he or she does not believe the repudiation to be sufficiently unequivocal in its indication of an inability or unwillingness to perform, or for other reasons.) **In such a case, the innocent party will most likely not be entitled to recover the costs associated with any pre-performance preparation after the repudiation is sent if it is never retracted.**

F. **THE REPUDIATING PARTY'S RIGHT TO RETRACT THE REPUDIATION. [§23.5]** Both the Restatement 2d and the UCC provide that repudiations can be retracted [Restatement 2d §256; UCC §2-611]. That is, under certain conditions a party's anticipatory repudiation can be "taken back" or nullified. When a retraction is effectively made, both parties' duties under the contract again become enforceable (except that the aggrieved party must be entitled to more time to fulfill his or her duties than originally called for in the contract if the delay in fulfilling those duties is caused by a legitimate suspension of duties between the time of the repudiation and its retraction) [UCC §2-611]. There are two situations, however, in which a repudiation becomes **irrevocable**:

(1) When the non-repudiating party has given notice to the repudiator that he or she considers the repudiation final and the contract terminated; and

(2) When the non-repudiating party has materially changed position in reliance on the repudiation [Restatement 2d §256; UCC §2-611(1)].

In some ways, the revocation doctrine treats an anticipatory repudiation as a revocable "offer" by the repudiator to terminate the contract. As with all other revocable offers, the party making the offer is free to revoke it (i.e., by retracting the repudiation) unless it has been accepted. In this case, the "offer" to terminate the contract can be "accepted" either: (a) by notifying the repudiator that he or she considers the repudiation final (including filing suit for total breach); or (b) by materially relying on the repudiation in such a way that justice dictates it should be irrevocable.

1. **Example. [§23.51]** Ted is a retired carpenter and has agreed to make a custom couch for Laura, to be delivered and paid for on October 1. On August 10, Laura definitely and unequivocally repudiates. Ted writes Laura and asks her to reconsider, but Laura does not respond. Ted neither takes on any more work in the interim, nor relies on Laura's repudiation in any other way. However, he also never informs Laura of his intention to treat the repudiation as final. On September 29, Laura calls up and retracts her repudiation. The retraction is effective, because Ted has neither notified Laura that he is terminating the contract nor has he relied on her repudiation. Thus, while he does not have to tender the couch on October 1 (he has a reasonable time to complete it), he is under an obligation to supply her with the couch because he retraction came before the date on which Laura's performance was due under the original contract, and because Ted had not "accepted" her "offer" to terminate the contract.

CHAPTER TWENTY-FOUR: DISCHARGE OF DUTIES BY SUBSEQUENT AGREEMENT — SUBSTITUTED PERFORMANCES, SUBSTITUTED CONTRACTS (INCLUDING NOVATIONS), ACCORDS, MUTUAL RESCISSION, AND RELEASES

A. **DISCHARGE OF DUTY BY SUBSEQUENT AGREEMENTS, GENERALLY. [§24.0]** One way a party owing a duty under a contract can discharge it is by entering into a **new agreement** in its place. Contract law has categorized five types of such agreements:

(1) **Substituted performances**;

(2) **Substituted contracts** (including **novations**);

(3) **Accords**;

(4) **Mutual rescission**; and

(5) **Releases**.

B. **SUBSTITUTED PERFORMANCE. [§24.1]** "Substituted performance" describes a transaction in which a party owing a duty under a contract arranges to discharge it by making a different performance (as opposed to *promising* a different performance), than that called for in the original contract [Restatement 2d §278]. A substituted performance is itself a separate contract and thus, must be formed by means of an offer, an acceptance and consideration (or promissory estoppel) to be enforceable. A substituted performance is really a particular kind of unilateral contract, where the offer is a promise to discharge the duty in return for an act, the acceptance is the offeree's performance of the act called for in the offer, and the consideration constitutes the bargained for exchange of the offeror's promise to discharge a duty in return for the offeree's act.

Note that it is irrelevant whether the substituted performance is performed by the original obligor or by a third party. So long as the obligee agrees to accept a different performance as a substitute for the original duty, the original duty is discharged when the substituted performance occurs.

1. **EXAMPLE. [§24.11]** Larry is a veterinarian in a rural community who has performed professional services for Byron. Larry reasonably bills Byron $300 in accordance with their agreement, but Byron complains that he is short on cash at the moment. If Larry tells Byron something like, "If you deliver a cord of firewood to my home by 5:00 Tuesday, I will accept it in lieu of the bill," in essence he has made an offer to enter into a unilateral contract with Byron, whereby Byron's performance will act as the acceptance of the offer. Consideration is present as Byron's act in delivering the firewood, and Larry's promise to forego enforcing the debt, evidenced by the bill, are bargained for and sought in exchange, one for the other. Thus, if Byron timely delivers the firewood, a substituted performance has taken place and Byron's debt to Larry is discharged. If Byron does not deliver the wood, Larry may sue only to enforce the $300 debt evidenced by the bill, and may **not** sue to enforce the delivery of the wood, for Byron has not promised to make such a delivery. Their agreement is only that **if** Byron delivers the wood, the debt will be discharged.

Note that to be a valid substituted performance, the obligor (Byron) must agree to discharge the existing duty upon actual **performance only**. If the duty is discharged on the basis of a promised performance, e.g., if Byron had said to Larry "If you **promise** to deliver a load of firewood to my house by 5:00 p.m. Tuesday, I will accept it in lieu of the bill," it would be a substituted agreement or accord situation (addressed in §§24.2 and 24.3), not a substituted **performance** one.

2. **EXAMPLE. [§24.12]** Same situation as above, except this time Larry agrees to discharge the bill if Byron's sister, Gina, delivers a cord of firewood to Larry's house by 5:00 p.m. Tuesday. If the wood is timely delivered by Gina, Byron's duty to pay the debt is discharged. If it is not, Larry's only recourse is to sue Byron for payment of the original debt.

C. **SUBSTITUTED CONTRACTS, INCLUDING NOVATIONS. [§24.2]** A "substituted contract" is a transaction in which a party owing a duty under a contract discharges it by promising a different performance than that originally called for under the contract [Restatement 2d §279]. As its name suggests, a substituted contract is itself a separate contract and thus, must be formed by means of a separate offer, acceptance, and consideration (or promissory estoppel) to be enforceable. A substituted contract is really a special type of bilateral contract, where the offer is a promise to discharge the debt upon the promised performance of an act, the acceptance is the offeree's promise to do the act called for in the offer, and where each party's bargained for promise serves as consideration for the other.

There are two categories of substituted contracts depending on whether the original promisee, or a third party, promises to perform the new obligation. If the original obligor promises to perform the new duty, contract law calls it simply a "**substituted contract**;" i.e. the substitution of the duties under one contract for another. However, if the new contract is entered into between the original obligee and a third party, it is known as a "**novation**" [Restatement 2d §280].

1. **EFFECT OF SUBSTITUTED CONTRACT OR NOVATION. [§24.21]** Upon the valid formation of a substituted contract or novation, **the original debt is immediately discharged**. Thus, if the duty promised under the *new* contract is breached, the obligor is entitled to sue for damages resulting from *its* non-performance, **but cannot validly sue to enforce the original duty** [Restatement 2d §279(2)].

   a. **Example. [§24.211]** Jason owns a limousine service. One of his first clients was Rocker, a famous rock star. Jason drove Rocker for a week as Rocker made appearances on local talk shows, etc., before a big concert. At the end of the week, Rocker examines Jason's $5,000 bill and says, "If I promise to leave two front row tickets to the concert for you at the will-call booth, will you agree to accept my promise in exchange for payment of the bill?" Jason was a big fan of Rocker and so accepted Rocker's offer. Upon such acceptance, a substituted contract was formed, and Rocker's obligation to pay Jason $5,000 was immediately discharged. If Rocker does not leave the tickets, Jason may sue him for breaching **that** promise, but cannot validly sue him seeking to enforce payment of the $5,000 bill.

   b. **Example. [§24.212]** Sally lent Nancy $2,000, the repayment of which is due tomorrow. Nancy and her brother Pat, a carpenter, propose that Sally agree to discharge the debt in exchange for Pat's promise to deliver to Sally a custom made desk within 90 days. If Sally accepts the offer, she has entered into a novation. As such, Nancy's obligation to pay Sally is immediately discharged. Thus, if Pat does not deliver the desk, Sally's only recourse is to sue him for his failure to deliver as promised, because she can no longer enforce Nancy's promise to repay the $2,000.

Sum & Substance QUICK REVIEW of Contracts

D. ACCORDS. [§24.3] In some respects an accord is a hybrid made up of the attributes of a substituted performance agreement and a substituted contract. **An "accord" is a transaction in which a party owed a duty under a contract agrees to enter into what would otherwise be a substituted contract, except that the duty due under the original contract is discharged** *only when the duties promised under the accord are actually performed* [Restatement 2d §281(1)]. Until complete performance of the newly promised duties, the original obligation is only "suspended." If the newly promised duty in the accord is fully and completely performed, the obligations under **both** agreements have been discharged or, in the words of the doctrine, the obligations under both agreements have been "**satisfied**." Thus, upon performance of the accord, it is said the original duty has been discharged by **accord and satisfaction** [Restatement 2d §281(3)]. If the newly made promise in the accord is breached, the duty under the original contract is no longer suspended, and can thereafter be enforced. Thus, **upon the breach of the accord, the obligee has the option of either suing to enforce the original duty, or suing for the breach of the promises made in the accord** [Restatement 2d §281(3)].

As with substituted contracts, the obligor under an accord can be either the obligor under the original contract, or a third party. However unlike substituted contracts, no special name is given to an accord made between the original obligee and a third party.

1. **EXAMPLE. [§24.31]** Same facts as in the Jason/Rocker hypothetical set forth in §24.211, except this time Rocker looks at the bill and says, "If I promise to, and actually do, leave two front row tickets for you at the will call booth, will you promise to forego collecting the bill?" Jason says "O.K., I'll forget about the bill, but only if you actually follow through on your promise," and Rocker agrees. Jason has thus entered into an **accord** with Rocker for the front row tickets rather than a substituted contract. Thus, if Rocker leaves the tickets, the duties under the accord will be satisfied and the $5,000 debt will be discharged. If, however, Rocker breaches the accord by failing to leave the tickets, Jason will have the option of suing him either for breach of the promise to leave the tickets, **or** to enforce payment of the $5,000 debt.

2. **EXAMPLE. [§24.32]** Same facts as the Nancy/Pat/Sally hypothetical set forth in §24.212, except this time Sally enters into an **accord** with Pat, rather than a novation. If Pat breaches his promise to deliver the desk, Sally has the option of either suing Pat for breach of that promise, or suing Nancy to enforce her obligation to repay the $2,000.

   Note, however, that Sally could **not** legitimately sue Nancy for the $2,000 until Pat breached the promise made in the accord. By entering into the accord with Pat, Sally agreed to suspend the enforceability of the $2,000 debt until the accord was either satisfied or breached.

3. **RECURRING PROBLEMS UNDER THE MOST FREQUENT USE OF ACCORDS: OFFERS TO COMPROMISE A DISPUTED DEBT. [§24.33]** The most frequent use of accords in modern commerce is to settle disputed monetary obligations. These types of transactions raise a number of recurring issues, two of which are typically covered in a first year contracts course:

   (1) Whether a lack of consideration makes unenforceable a settlement agreement between a debtor and a creditor less than the creditor claims is due; and where the debtor agrees to pay.

(2) The effect of a debtor attempting to discharge a disputed debt by tendering a check "in full satisfaction" of the debt; and similarly the effect of the creditor crossing out the "in full satisfaction" language and cashing the check "without prejudice."

Each issue is discussed below.

a. **Consideration Issues when a Debtor Offers to Pay the Creditor Less Than the Full Amount the Creditor is Seeking. [§24.331]** Because an accord is itself a contract, traditional contract law holds that it must be supported by consideration to be enforceable to its full extent. This can present an issue when the accord consists of the debtor's promise to pay less than the full amount the creditor claims is owed. That is, under the pre-existing duty rule, an offer to pay $6,000 to discharge a $10,000 debt raises consideration concerns. However, if such agreements were unenforceable, debtors would have little reason to compromise and settle before trial, for there would be little enforceable benefit in doing so. In other words, the debtors of the world would not offer to pay the $6,000 as an accord to discharge the claimed $10,000 debt if the creditor could cash the check and still successfully sue the debtor for the remaining $4,000.

Even common law contract law was sensitive to the plight of the debtor in such a situation, and almost always found consideration when a debtor offered to compromise such a debt by paying less than the creditor claimed was owed. Under traditional rules, for consideration **not** to be present, the creditor would have to establish that: (a) the debt was for a liquidated (not a disputed) sum; (b) there was no **bona fide** dispute as to whether the debtor owed the full amount of the debt; **and** (c) the creditor did not receive some additional benefit from the accord than he or she had under the original contract. Thus, while there were a few situations in which an accord was found unenforceable due to the pre-existing duty rule, such as in the celebrated case of *Foakes v. Beer*, typically such agreements were enforceable (see §§7.634 and 7.6341, for a further discussion of the effect of the pre-existing duty rule on accords, and for an extended discussion of *Foakes v. Beer*).

Under modern commercial law, however, an accord to discharge a monetary debt by offering to pay the creditor less than the creditor demands need not be supported by consideration to be enforceable [UCC §1-107 (note that this is a provision under Article 1 of the UCC and not under Article 2; thus its application is broader than just to "transactions in goods"); Restatement 2d §277(1)]. Thus, under modern contract law even the accord reached in a case like *Foakes* would be enforceable against the creditor.

b. **The Effect of Attempted Settlement by Tender of a Check in "Full Satisfaction" of a Debt. [§24.332]** Another recurring issue in dealing with accords is determining what effect to give a debtor's attempted settlement of a debt where he or she tenders a check with the words, e.g., "This Check is in Full Satisfaction of our dispute" written on the back. This issue really presents two problems:

(1) If the creditor cashes the check without doing anything to the language on the back, has the creditor implicitly accepted the debtor's offer of an accord?; and

(2) If the creditor crosses out the language and writes, e.g., "Cashing of the check is without prejudice to my rights to enforce the full amount of the debt," can the creditor cash it and still sue for the remainder of the debt?

The resolution of these issues is discussed below.

(1) **A Creditor Who Cashes a Check Tendered "In Full Satisfaction" of a Debt is Typically Held to Have Accepted the Offer of an Accord. [§24.3321]** Traditional legal analysis holds that if a creditor cashes a check that was tendered "in full satisfaction" of a debt, the creditor has thereby accepted an accord to discharge the debt, and any duty of the debtor to repay the greater amount the creditor claims is owed is suspended. If the check is honored and the money paid to the creditor's order, there has been a satisfaction of the accord, and the duty to repay the original debt is discharged.

(2) **The Effect of a Creditor Who Crosses Out the "In Full Satisfaction" Language and Replaces it with "Without Prejudice" Language Instead. [§24.3322]** Of course, any offeree can reject an offer, and a creditor who simply returns a debtor's check with "in Full Satisfaction" language on it will be deemed to have rejected the offer to enter into an accord. However, most creditors would like to reject the accord offer **and** cash the check, **and** retain the right to sue the debtor for the remainder of the debt. Typically they attempt to accomplish these goals by crossing out the "in Full Satisfaction" language and writing "without prejudice" language in its stead.

Until 1990, there was a considerable split among courts and commentators as to whether such actions by a creditor should be effective. Those who held that a creditor should be entitled to reject the accord, cash the check, and still sue for the remainder of the debt when he or she crosses out the debtor's language and inserts the "without prejudice" language in its place, claimed that such a result was compelled by UCC §1-207. That provision states that a party who performs "with explicit reservation of rights" under a contract does not thereby prejudice the rights reserved. Those courts and commentators who disagreed with that view held that §1-207 was not intended to be read that expansively. They believed that a contrary rule would be unfair to debtors and a misapplication of traditional offer and acceptance principles. These commentators asserted that by writing the "in Full Satisfaction" language on checks, a debtor was offering only to pay the creditor the indicated sum if the creditor agreed to enter into an accord. They believed that a debtor in such a situation is not offering to give the creditor the option of taking some of the debtor's money and settling the entire claim, or of taking some of the debtor's money and still suing for the rest of the claimed amount.

(3) **UCC §3-311: Regulation of Accord and Satisfaction by Tender of a Check. [§24.3323]** To resolve the controversy set forth above, in 1990 the Permanent Editorial Board of the UCC adopted §3-311. That provision states that if a debtor tenders a check for the full satisfaction of an unliquidated claim, or a claim subject to a *bona fide* dispute, and if somewhere on the check the debtor has **conspicuously** stated that its tender is for the full satisfaction of that claim, then if the creditor cashes the check knowing that it was intended by the debtor to resolve the dispute, an accord has taken place even if the creditor crosses out the "in full satisfaction" language and writes "without prejudice" in its stead [UCC §3-311 (a), (b), (d)]. However, if the check does not conspicuously state that it is being tendered in full satisfaction of the claim, or if the creditor did not know that it was being tendered to compromise the disputed debt, then if the creditor returns the amount of the check to the debtor within 90 days after cashing the check, no accord and satisfaction has occurred, and the original debt is still enforceable by the creditor [UCC §3-311 (c)].

4. HOW TO DETERMINE IF A SUBSEQUENT CONTRACT IS A SUBSTITUTED CONTRACT OR AN ACCORD. [§24.34] Obviously the obligee receives greater protection when entering into an accord rather than a substituted contract. That is, if an accord is breached, the obligee can sue under either the accord or the original contract, whereas the obligee under a substituted contract or novation can only enforce the breach of the new agreement. Sometimes it is easy to tell whether the parties intended their subsequent contract to be an accord or a substituted contract because the agreement is explicit. However, unfortunately often it is not so easy to tell which type of agreement was intended from the language of the new agreement alone. In close cases, whether a subsequent agreement made to discharge a duty is an accord or a substituted contract is a question of **interpretation** for a court to be made from all the surrounding circumstances (see Chapter Eighteen).

E. MUTUAL RESCISSION. [§24.4] "Mutual rescission" is an agreement whereby each party in a bilateral contract agrees to discharge all the remaining unexecuted duties of the other [Restatement 2d §283]. A mutual rescission is itself a contract and thus must be formed by a separate offer, acceptance and consideration (or promissory estoppel) to be enforceable. A mutual rescission agreement is really a particular kind of bilateral contract, where the offer is a promise to discharge all remaining duties under the agreement upon a reciprocal promise from the offeree, the acceptance is the reciprocal promise by the offeree called for in the offer, and where consideration for the agreement is the bargained for exchange of such promises [Restatement 2d §283, Com. a]. In other words, when two parties to a contract want to "call off" the deal, they do so by means of mutual rescission. Note however, that to be effective as a mutual rescission, the parties must be in a bilateral contract with executory duties remaining on both sides at the time the rescission agreement is reached, otherwise there is no consideration for their promises.

1. **EXAMPLE. [§24.41]** Bill has promised to pay Judy $1,000 on Friday in exchange for Judy's promise to deliver to him on that day her Nolan Ryan rookie baseball card. On Thursday, both Bill and Judy agree to call off the deal. Whether they realize it or not, the means by which they have discharged each other's duty is by a mutual rescission.

2. **EXAMPLE. [§24.42]** Same as above, except this time Judy was obligated to give Bill the Nolan Ryan card a week before payment was due. She has given Bill the card, but now says, "I know you are in financial trouble. Don't worry, you need never pay me the $1,000." Even if Bill says, "Thanks, I accept!", there has been no enforceable mutual rescission because there were no unexecuted duties on Judy's part at the time the agreement was made. Accordingly, the obligation to pay the $1,000 is not thereby discharged on a mutual rescission theory. However, the obligation may be discharged if Judy's promise is deemed an effective release (see §24.5), or, possibly, under promissory estoppel if Bill reasonably relies on the promise.

3. **GENERAL RULE: MUTUAL RESCISSIONS CAN BE ORAL. [§24.43]** As a general rule, an oral mutual rescission is enforceable [Restatement 2d §283]

   a. **Exception: Rescission of a Duty to Transfer an Interest in Land Must be in Writing. [§24.431]** Rescission of a contract in which one party's duty is to transfer an interest in land must be in writing to be enforceable. [Restatement 2d §§148, 283, Com. b].

4. **DISTINGUISHING MUTUAL RESCISSION FROM SUBSTITUTED PERFORMANCE, SUBSTITUTED CONTRACTS, AND ACCORDS. [§24.44]** Mutual rescission differs from substituted performance, substituted contracts, and accords in that one party's agreement to discharge the duties of another is not given in exchange for some other performance or promised performance, but rather is given in exchange for the other party's promise to discharge the remaining duties under the contract.

F. **RELEASES. [§24.5]** A "release" is an enforceable promise by a party that he or she is discharging a duty owed him or her immediately or upon the occurrence of a condition [Restatement 2d §284]. Traditionally, to be effective a release needed either to be made under seal or supported by consideration [Restatement 2d §284, Com. a]. However, most states today provide by statute that a release is binding even in the absence of consideration. While the Restatement requires that a release be in writing to be effective, no special words need be used to constitute an effective release [Restatement 2d §284].

1. **EXAMPLE. [§24.51]** Fred owes Bill $10,000 for Bill's used car that was delivered to Fred last week. Fred is short on cash and so pleads with his friend Bill to let him keep the car and to release him from having to pay the debt. Bill has sympathy for his friend and decides that he will let Fred off the hook. As a consequence, he sends Fred a written document stating that Bill has released and discharged Fred from all payment obligations arising out of the contract for the car. While at common law such a release would not be enforceable by Fred (if Bill later tried to sue to collect) due to the lack of consideration supporting Bill's promise, under modern contract law the release will likely be enforceable.

2. **EXAMPLE. [§24.52]** Same as above, except this time Bill agrees to reduce the price of the car to $2,000, rather than to forgive the entire $10,000 debt. If he chooses to, Bill could effectively release Fred from payment of the $10,000 by sending him a written release discharging the debt upon fulfillment of a condition, i.e., payment of the $2,000.

   Note that the parties could structure such a reduction in payment as a substituted performance, a substituted contract, or an accord. However, structuring it as a release upon the fulfillment of a condition is also effective.

3. **DISTINGUISHING RELEASES FROM SUBSTITUTED PERFORMANCE, SUBSTITUTED CONTRACTS, AND ACCORDS. [§24.53]** A release differs from substituted performance, substituted contracts, and accords because the nature of the obligee's promise is different. In a release, the discharge of the obligor's duty takes effect immediately, or immediately on the occurrence of a condition. In the other situations mentioned above, the obligee has only made a **promise** to discharge the duty in the future in return for a specified performance or promised performance. That promise itself creates a new duty on the part of the obligee, which can later be discharged by the parties [Restatement 2d §284, Com. a].

CHAPTER TWENTY-FIVE: DISCHARGE OF DUTIES BY IMPOSSIBILITY, IMPRACTICABILITY, OR FRUSTRATION OF PURPOSE

A. IMPOSSIBILITY, IMPRACTICABILITY AND FRUSTRATION, GENERALLY. [§25.0] Every time parties enter into a contract, they do so with basic unstated assumptions. For example, when Sheila contracts to purchase Joe's racehorse, both assume the horse is alive when they sign the contract and will continue to be alive until its delivery, even if that fact is not actually spelled out in the contract. When a construction company contracts to build a swimming pool in a homeowner's backyard, both parties probably assume the soil in the homeowner's backyard is similar to the soil in the surrounding area, even if that assumption is unstated in their agreement. When Bernard agrees with a landlord to pay a premium price for a room offering a view to watch the coronation of a King of England, both parties assume the coronation will take place. However, things happen. The racehorse may die in its stable just after the contract is signed. The homeowner's property may unexpectedly contain a number of huge granite boulders hidden in the ground, making excavation of the property much more burdensome than anticipated. The King may be stricken with an ailment, and the coronation canceled.

There are two ways contract law can deal with these kinds of situations. It can take an absolutist position and say that if the seller of the horse cannot timely deliver as promised, if the construction company does not bear the extraordinary expense of digging the pool, and if Bernard refuses to pay for the room, each has breached his or her contract and is obligated to pay damages. On the other hand contract law could be more flexible and provide that in certain cases, i.e., when a basic assumption that both parties made when entering into a contract unexpectedly turns out not to be true, that a party's failure to perform is excused and no action for breach will lie. As you might guess from the title of this chapter, contract law has chosen the latter approach and has broken these kinds of cases into three categories:

(1) **Impossibility**, which applies when an unexpected event occurs which makes performance by a party objectively impossible, as in the case above where the horse died before it could be delivered;

(2) **Commercial impracticability**, which applies when an unexpected event occurs which makes performance by a party much more burdensome, as in the case above where the granite boulders were discovered in the homeowner's soil; and

(3) **Frustration of purpose**, which applies when an unexpected event occurs which renders virtually worthless the value of a party's bargain, as in the case above where the tenant can occupy the room, but will not be able to view the King's coronation due to its cancellation.

1. IMPOSSIBILITY, IMPRACTICABILITY, AND FRUSTRATION ARE CONTRACT DEFENSES. [§25.01] One thing that often gets overlooked in the study of these doctrines is the realization that, at bottom, they are nothing other than contract **defenses**. In contract theory, these doctrines are some of the ways an enforceable duty can be discharged other than by performance. But on a *practical* level, these are defenses. Let's say Contractor can establish the elements for impracticability (see §25.21) under a contract in which he is to build a swimming pool. As a result, he or she will not perform the duties called for under the contract. The other party to the contract may sue Contractor for failing to perform. In the breach action, Contractor will present the elements of impracticability as a defense, i.e., he or she will admit that the promised acts went unperformed, but will claim that such non-performance was justified or excused by the commercial impracticability. If the elements of the doctrine can be proven, he or she will have a defense to the breach claim.

B. IMPOSSIBILITY: DEFINED AND DISCUSSED. [§25.1] Impossibility of performance provides a defense to a breach of contract suit (see §25.01) whereby the party asserting the defense seeks a declaration that his or her duties under the contract have been discharged due to the occurrence of an unexpected event or series of events. A party is entitled to assert the defense when an unexpected event occurs, which both upsets a basic assumption of both parties about the contract and which makes subsequent performance by that party impossible (see §25.11 for a complete list of the elements of the defense). When the defense applies, it discharges a party's duty to perform and thus serves as an excuse justifying that party's non-performance. Of the three doctrines discussed in this chapter, impossibility was the most readily accepted at common law, which makes sense, for it is inherently unjust to hold someone liable for a breach when subsequent events made performance of the promised duty impossible.

Like "impracticability" (discussed in §25.2), impossibility is a defense mostly used by sellers as opposed to buyers. This is because the defense usually arises when some event occurs which renders a seller's promise to supply a good, land, service, etc., impossible to perform. On the other hand, a buyer's duty is usually only to pay money, and such payment is rarely "impossible" as defined by the doctrine.

Note that both the Restatement 2d and the UCC make no distinction between impossibility and impracticability [Restatement 2d §261; UCC §2-615]. These sources consider impracticability to flow from the impossibility doctrine and, in effect, find them to be part of a continuum whereby a party's duties should be discharged whenever performance becomes unexpectedly too difficult. Under this view, such performance can become too difficult either because it is too expensive to complete (impracticability), or because it is objectively impossible to execute (impossibility).

1. **ELEMENTS NECESSARY TO ESTABLISH DISCHARGE OF A DUTY DUE TO IMPOSSIBILITY. [§25.11]** A party seeking to use impossibility as a defense must prove the following:

    (1) The occurrence of an event which makes performance of a duty **impossible;**

    (2) the non-occurrence of the event causing the impossibility of performance was a **mutually shared basic assumption on which the contract was made;**

    (3) the event causing the impossibility of performance occurred **without fault of the party asserting the defense; and**

    (4) The party asserting the defense did not implicitly or explicitly **assume the risk of occurrence of the event** causing the impossibility of performance [Restatement 2d §261; UCC §§2-613, 2-615].

    a. **An Event Must Occur that Makes Performance of a Duty Impossible. [§25.111]** The first element of the impossibility defense is that an event must have occurred that makes performance impossible. While on its face this element seems straightforward, the term "impossible" can cause confusion and is subject to interpretation. For example, there is, a big difference between saying performance of a duty is impossible because **no one** can do it (e.g., when the horse dies), and saying it is "impossible" because only the person who made the promise cannot do it, while others can (e.g., when the reason Ted's Taxi Service does not take June to the airport on time is because Ted had a flat tire and no spare). Some commentators characterize this distinction as saying it is the difference between "objective" impossibility (when no one can perform) and "subjective" impossibility (when only the person who made the promise cannot perform), and note that only objective impossibility can serve to discharge a party's duties under the impossibility doctrine. The Restatement specifically declined to use "objective" to describe the type of impossibility needed [Restatement 2d §261, Com. e], but in any event the idea is that when performance is practicable by others, there has been an insufficient showing of impossibility. (See Case Squibs section, *U.S. v. Wegematic*.)

(1) **Example. [§25.1111]** Buyer is obligated to purchase $1 million worth of products. When the time for payment arrives, it has no money to pay for the goods and has used up every available credit source. While it might be "impossible" for the particular buyer to pay, its duty to pay is not excused, for there is insufficient impossibility as required by the doctrine.

(2) **Example. [§25.1112]** Tony is under a contractual duty to deliver his Rembrandt to Carol on Thursday. On Wednesday, Tony's house burns down through no fault of his own, destroying the painting. Tony's duty to deliver the painting is discharged, for delivery of the painting is sufficiently impossible.

b. **The Non-Occurrence of the Event Making Performance Impossible Must Have Been a "Basic Assumption" of Both Parties When They Entered into Their Agreement.** **[§25.112]** To fulfill this element, a party must establish that the non-happening of the event making performance impossible was an important, or basic, assumption when the contract was made. The assumption need not be (and usually is not) stated in the contract, **but it must be mutual.** That is, the purely unilateral assumptions of one party about performance under the contract are insufficient to give rise to an impossibility defense when those assumptions do not come to pass. (See Case Squibs section, *Taylor v. Caldwell*.)

(1) **Example. [§25.1121]** A car dealer ordered $2 million worth of automobiles from the manufacturer. Their contract stated that payment for the cars was to be made by a letter of credit issued by Central Bank. A few days before payment was due, Central Bank went out of business. Neither party's duties will be discharged due to impossibility. While it is probably true that the non-occurrence of the event, i.e., the continued existence of the Bank, was an unstated assumption of both parties when they entered the contract, the continued existence of the bank was almost surely not a **basic** assumption of the transaction. Any licensed bank could issue the letter of credit.

(2) **Example. [§25.1122]** Beverage Co. enters into a contract with Farmer for the delivery of 1 ton of apples to be made into apple juice. Beverage Co. does not care where the apples come from so long as they are of sufficient quality, but Farmer expects that they will come from her farm. An accidental fire destroys Farmer's crop. Farmer's duty to deliver is not discharged under the impossibility doctrine. This is because: (a) her performance has not been rendered sufficiently "impossible," for Farmer could buy someone else's apples and still perform under the contract; and (b) the non-occurrence of the event, i.e., the ability of Farmer to deliver the apples from her own crop, was not a **mutually shared** assumption under the contract.

Note that if the contract had specifically called for delivery of, say, grapes grown on a particular vineyard, and if the grapes were destroyed through no fault of Farmer, Farmer's duties would be discharged. In that case, performance of the delivery promise would be sufficiently impossible, and the assumption as to the continued existence of Farmer's grape crop would be a **mutual** assumption under the contract.

c. The Event Making Performance Impossible Must Have Occurred Without the Fault of the Party Asserting the Defense. [§25.113] In order for a party to successfully assert an impossibility defense, the event making performance impossible must have occurred without his or her fault. "Fault" here is given its tort meaning, and thus a party who is either the intentional or negligent proximate cause of the event giving rise to the impossibility cannot successfully use the defense thereafter to discharge his or her duty.

(1) Example. [§25.1131] A winery enters into a contract with Farmer calling for the delivery of three tons of grapes from a specific vineyard on Farmer's land. If the grapes are destroyed by fungus so that there is no crop to be delivered, whether Farmer's duties are discharged by impossibility depends on the reason the infection occurred. If it turns out that the reason grapes become diseased is because, e.g., the farmer intentionally failed to water adequately, thus substantially increasing the likelihood of fungal infection, the impossibility doctrine does not apply, and Farmer's duty to deliver is not discharged. Similarly, if the reason there is no crop to deliver is because Farmer negligently did not apply a fungicide to the grapes at the first sign of the disease as most growers would, Farmer again is not entitled to use the impossibility doctrine as a defense. However, if Farmer acted as a reasonable farmer in like circumstances in growing her crop, but the fungus nevertheless grew, Farmer's failure to deliver her grapes to the winery will be excused.

d. The Party Asserting the Impossibility Defense Must Not Have Assumed the Risk of the Occurrence of the Event Making Performance Impossible. [§25.114] The final element of the impossibility defense is a requirement that the party asserting the defense must not have assumed the risk that the event making performance impossible would occur. This element is not explicitly found in either the UCC or the Restatement 2d, but it has almost universally been adopted by courts in impossibility, impracticability, and frustration cases.

A party may assume the risk of the occurrence of an event either explicitly or implicitly under the contract. However, as a practical manner, it is rare for the parties to contest a case when a seller has explicitly assumed the risk. For example, if under a written agreement whereby Bill is obligated to sell his watch to Mary, Bill also promises to "assume the risk of destruction of the watch from any source, and will be strictly liable if he does not deliver for any reason," it is unlikely that Bill will contest liability if he does not deliver the watch. Hence, the typical litigation involving this element focuses on whether, under the circumstances, it is fair to say that the seller has impliedly promised to assume the risk that this type of contingency would occur.

(1) Example. [§25.1141] Larry promises to deliver a perpetual motion machine to Leo's Novelty Co., despite being cognizant of the fact that most physicists believe such a machine is impossible to build. Larry is not entitled to use the impossibility defense in a breach action stemming from his failure to deliver because, under the circumstances, he impliedly assumed the risk that he would not be able to perform.

Note that the implied assumption of the risk doctrine really has more application in impracticability situations than in impossibility situations. This is because it is relatively unusual to hold that someone implicitly accepts the risk that the subject matter of the contract will be destroyed, or that performance of the promise truly will be impossible (see §25.214 et seq., for examples of the implicit assumption of the risk doctrine as applied to commercial impracticability cases.)

2. **COMMON FACT SITUATIONS PRESENTING IMPOSSIBILITY ISSUES. [§25.12]** Over time, contract law has been able to categorize certain types of fact situations that recurrently present impossibility of performance issues, and these are discussed below. While the contours of the doctrine vary from fact situation to fact situation, the basic analytical framework for each case is the same, i.e., if the party seeking to assert an impossibility defense can establish the occurrence of an event making performance impossible; that the non-happening of that event was a basic assumption of both parties when the contract was made; that the event occurred without fault of the party asserting the defense; and that he or she has not assumed the risk of the event's occurrence, then the duty rendered impossible to perform by the event will be discharged.

a. **Death or Incapacity of a Particular Person Necessary for Performance ("Personal Service" Contracts). [§25.121]** Some contracts call not just for the performance of specified duties, but also require that specified persons perform them. These are known as personal service contracts. If a contract calls for a performance by a particular person, and that person dies or becomes incapacitated after the contract was entered into, but before performance is due, then the duty to perform is discharged by impossibility [Restatement 2d §262]. However, if performance of the contract does not call for a **particular** person to perform specified duties, then death or incapacity of the party will not discharge the promisor's duty. (Recall that the death of a person necessary for performance of a contract made while an offer is pending, but **before it has been accepted**, acts to terminate the offeree's power of acceptance, see §§4.415 and 4.416.)

(1) **Example. [§25.1211]** Carol is an art dealer. She enters into a contract with her customer, John, promising to deliver to John by December 1 a new painting by Lorenzo, a living artist. Shortly after the Carol/John contract is entered into, and before December 1, Lorenzo becomes incapacitated. Carol's duty to deliver the painting to John is discharged by impossibility.

(2) **Example. [§25.1212]** Same as above, except this time Lorenzo dies after the contract is entered into but before delivery is due. Same result.

b. **Death, Destruction, Deterioration, or the Failure to Come into Existence, of a Thing Necessary for Performance. [§25.122]** Some contracts call not just for the performance of specified duties, but also require that goods come from a specified place, or that a particular good be delivered. If the existence of a particular thing is necessary for performance of a duty under a contract, its death, destruction, deterioration, or failure to come into existence will discharge the duties remaining under a contract. Once again, however, for the defense to apply, the existence of a **particular** thing must be mutually assumed or agreed to under the contract [Restatement 2d §263].

(1) **Example. [§25.1221]** A grocery store contracts to purchase 200 gallons of whole milk daily from the Fresh Dairy Co. ("Dairy Co."). Dairy Co. expects that it will furnish such milk from its own cows, but there is no such requirement in the contract. The dairy accidentally burns down, through no fault of the dairy, and kills

all the cows. Dairy Co. now asserts its duty to supply the milk to the grocery store is discharged due to impossibility. It cannot successfully use the defense. While it may be impossible for the dairy to supply the milk from its own cows, it is freely able to go into the market, purchase 200 gallons of whole milk a day, and perform its delivery duties. Hence, because performance of the duties under the contract did not call for the existence of a particular thing, i.e., milk from cows owned by the dairy, their destruction does not give rise to impossibility.

Note that if the contract called for the milk to come only from the cows at the dairy, e.g., because they were supposed to produce sweeter milk, etc., then the fire would discharge the duties. This is because now the duty to supply what is called for by the contract is impossible, and the continued existence of the dairy's cows under the contract was obviously a basic assumption of both parties. (See also the example in §25.1123.)

(2) **Example.** [§25.1222] Tony agrees to sell to Laura a pedigreed dog from an upcoming litter of dogs born to Frieda. If Frieda dies before giving birth, the failure of the puppy to come into existence will discharge Tony's duty to deliver, assuming again Frieda's death occurred without Tony's fault.

c. **Impossibility Due to Government Regulation or Order Making Performance Illegal.** [§25.123] Usually, a basic assumption on which a contract is made is that there will be no law or regulation that will make performance illegal when due. In a strict sense, illegality does not result in "objective" impossibility, for the party under a duty could always perform and take the legal consequences for such action. However, as a matter of public policy, i.e., so as not to encourage people to violate valid laws and regulations, contract law holds that subsequent illegality of the duty called for in a contract discharges that duty under an impossibility theory [Restatement 2d §264; UCC §2-614(2)]. The law or regulation making the duty impossible can be either domestic or foreign. (Recall that when a law or regulation making illegal a requested performance in an offer becomes applicable while the offer is pending but **before the offer is accepted**, the power of the offeree to accept the offer is terminated. See §4.417.)

(1) **Example.** [§25.1231] Bob was a pioneer pilot for a major airline. Before FAA regulation, the airline contractually obligated itself to employ Bob as a pilot and let him fly the L.A. to N.Y. route "to age 70, so long as Bob continues to pass his annual physical examination." The FAA subsequently imposed a binding requirement on all airlines that no pilot could operate a commercial aircraft after reaching age 60. Bob was 65 when the regulation was enacted. The airline's duty to let him fly the L.A. to N.Y. route is discharged due to supervening illegality.

d. **Repair Contracts.** [§25.124] Another recurring situation involving the impossibility doctrine occurs when someone is hired to do repairs on a particular building. Sometimes, after the contract is signed, but before the repairs are completed, the building is destroyed without either party's fault. The duty of the laborer to perform the repairs in such a situation is discharged due to impossibility [Restatement 2d, §261, Com. d, Ill. 6; §263, Com. a, Ill. 3].

Note that while the Restatement analyzes this situation as one of impossibility, others disagree. They hold that it should more properly be analyzed as a failure of a constructive condition. That is, they claim that a constructive condition of the repair contract is that the building be in existence, and the failure of the building owner to fulfill the constructive condition (having the building available to be worked on) discharges the duties of the laborer. In either event the worker's duties are discharged, but this is a good example of how even contract experts cannot agree sometimes on why an outcome is proper.

e. **Labor Strikes. [§25.125]** Another recurring fact situation presents itself when a supplier's work force goes out on strike, thereby making it "impossible" for the supplier to perform in a timely fashion. The courts are split on how to treat such a case. Some hold that the impossibility defense does not apply, on the grounds that: (a) a labor strike is only a case of "subjective" impossibility for the employer can always hire new workers; or (b) that the employer is somewhat "at fault" in a strike, for the employer **could** have avoided the problem by acquiescing to the demands of its workers. However, other courts hold that if a labor strike prevents a party from timely performing under a contract, those duties are discharged due to impossibility.

f. **Land Sale Contracts. [§25.126]** At common law, upon execution of the land sale agreement the purchaser immediately became the equitable owner of the property and all its improvements, even if he or she did not have legal title at the time. Thus, the old rule held that any risk of destruction of the property was allocated to the buyer upon execution of the sales contract. Hence, if a building on the property burned before the purchaser had legal title, e.g., while the sale was in escrow, there was no discharge of the buyer's duty to pay for the property. A number of states have changed this rule today so that destruction of the property or of an improvement on the property after a land sale contract is executed, but before legal title passes, discharges the buyer's duty to accept title and pay for the property due to impossibility.

3. **PARTIAL IMPOSSIBILITY. [§25.13]** Sometimes impossibility can be partial, e.g. where only part of a crop is destroyed; or where a large shipment was divided in two lots and sent on two airplanes, and only one crashed. Under UCC §§2-615 and 2-616, contract law's responses to such a situation can be summed up as follows:

(1) If all the elements of impossibility can be established as to that portion of the goods destroyed, the seller will not be in breach for failing to supply the destroyed portion;

(2) The remaining portion must be offered to the customers of the seller on a *pro rata* basis; and

(3) If the buyer does not wish only a *pro rata* amount of his or her order, he or she may reject it without incurring contractual liability.

This concept is perhaps more easily visualized by example.

a. **Example. [§25.131]** Vinter owns some prized vineyards which produce, at a minimum, 30 tons of grapes per year. Vinter enters into a contract promising 20 tons of grapes from her vineyards to Buyer A, and 10 tons of grapes from her vineyards to Buyer B. Buyer B plans to make his 10 tons of grapes into 50,000 cases of a "single vineyard" wine, all of which he has pre-sold.

A blight, not at all Vinter's fault, destroyed half the crop so Vinter was left with only 15 tons of grapes. Under §2-615, Vinter is excused from having to provide the portion that was destroyed, i.e., neither Buyer A nor Buyer B can sue him for breach for failing to fulfill their orders completely.

Under §2-616, Vinter must offer the remaining grapes on a *pro rata* basis to Buyers A and B, i.e., he must offer Buyer A 10 tons and Buyer B 5 tons. At that point, either Buyer A or Buyer B can choose to accept the offer of a *pro rata* amount, or choose not to accept it without incurring contractual liability. For example, Buyer B would probably wish to decline the offer of only 5 tons and buy a full compliment of 10 tons from a single vineyard produced by another supplier to meet its orders. Hence, Buyer B may turn down Vinter's offer of a *pro rata* delivery without breaching the contract.

C. COMMERCIAL IMPRACTICABILITY: DEFINED AND DISCUSSED. [§25.2] Like impossibility, impracticability also provides a defense to a breach of contract suit (see §25.01) whereby the party asserting the defense seeks a declaration that his or her duties under the contract have been discharged due to the occurrence of an unexpected event or series of events. A party is entitled to assert the defense when an unexpected event occurs which both upsets a basic assumption of both parties about the contract and which makes subsequent performance by that party impractical (see §25.21 for a complete list of the elements of the defense). When the defense applies, it discharges a party's duty to perform and thus serves as an excuse justifying non-performance. The doctrine is recognized as a defense under both the Restatement 2d and the UCC [Restatement 2d §261; UCC §2-615].

Under impracticability, a party's duties are discharged due to the fact that performance turns out to be more burdensome than either party expected. Thus, while it cannot be said that the event triggering impracticability makes performance under the contract "impossible," if it nonetheless makes performance sufficiently "impractical," i.e., sufficiently more expensive, contract law provides that the party need not perform.

In truth, impracticability promises much but delivers little. Since its introduction into the UCC in 1952, there have been but a handful of reported cases in which the defense has been successfully asserted. The reason is that courts view an asserted impracticability claim on very different grounds than an impossibility claim. That is, while it is viewed as unjust to require a party to be liable in breach for not performing a duty which is impossible or illegal, it is viewed as quite a different matter to excuse a party from performing just because it will cost more than he or she expected it would. This flows from the axiom of modern contract law that contract making is risk allocation. That is, modern contract law generally states that once Lance contractually promises to build a garage for Susan at a fixed price, he bears the risk that the costs of construction may be more expensive than he thought they would be. Hence, while a court may excuse a party from performing if such performance will truly be **significantly** more expensive than either party thought, and for a reason the party **truly** should not have foreseen, in the vast majority of cases courts will deny a party's ability to assert the defense by holding that the party implicitly accepted the risk that a contract might not be as profitable as he or she unilaterally expected when the contract was signed.

Like impossibility, impracticability is almost always asserted by suppliers of goods or services, rather than by purchasers. The reason is that while there are a number of things that can make a seller's duties more burdensome, it is unlikely there is much that can make a buyer's duty to pay a contracted for sum more expensive.

1. ELEMENTS NECESSARY TO ESTABLISH AN IMPRACTICABILITY DEFENSE.
[§25.21] As noted earlier (see §25.1), the drafters of the Restatement 2d and of the UCC believed that impossibility and impracticability are in essence two sides of the same coin, i.e., they both describe a doctrine which provides relief from non-performance when such performance is unexpectedly difficult. As a result, the elements necessary to establish the impracticability defense are quite similar to those for impossibility.

Sum & Substance QUICK REVIEW of Contracts

To establish the defense, a party must prove:

(1) The occurrence of an event which makes performance of a duty **commercially impracticable;**

(2) The non-occurrence of the event making performance impractical was a **mutually shared basic assumption on which the contract was made;**

(3) The event making performance impractical occurred **without fault of the party asserting the defense; and**

(4) The party asserting the defense did not implicitly or explicitly **assume the risk** of the occurrence of the event making performance impractical [Restatement 2d §261; UCC §2-615].

a. **An Event Must Occur that Makes Performance of a Duty Commercially Impracticable. [§25.211]** The party asserting a commercial impracticability defense must establish the occurrence of an event that makes performance of a promised duty more expensive or "impractical." There are no hard and fast rules as to how much more expensive performance must be before the requisite threshold is reached, but there is some indication from the case law and elsewhere that the **minimum** amount of extra expense necessary to establish impracticability is a five or six times increase in cost (see, e.g., the Introductory Note to Chapter 11 of the Restatement 2d, which speaks in terms of a **tenfold** increase in cost for impracticability to occur).

In any event, certainly the fact that a party is not going to make quite as much of a profit as he or she thought when the contract was signed is not enough to trigger the defense. It is likely that even a showing that an unexpected event will turn a very profitable contract into one where the supplier will lose a little money will be insufficient to invoke impracticability. The courts really demand that the operable threshold of impracticability will not be triggered until a showing is made that performance of the promise would be very unjust and unconscionable before a party can meet this test.

(1) **Example. [§25.2111]** Laura hires Al, a contractor, to install a swimming pool in her home for $30,000. As Al begins digging the pool, he discovers that the soil a foot or so beneath the surface is so wet that the entire backyard will need to be drained, and extra steps will need to be taken to protect the pool's foundation against leakage. These procedures will triple the amount of labor needed for construction, and will cause Al to lose $4,000 on the deal. Al's duties will not be discharged due to impracticability.

(2) **Example. [§25.2112]** Same as above, except this time Al discovers huge granite boulders hidden a couple of feet below the surface. The cheapest way to remove them is by blasting, and the costs associated with such blasting and protecting Laura's and her neighbors' homes from the resulting debris will increase the costs of construction tenfold, and will mean that Al will lose $150,000 on the job if he has to perform for $30,000. Al can establish sufficient impracticability to fulfill the first element of the defense.

b. **The Non-Occurrence of the Event Making Performance Impractical must have been a Basic Assumption of both Parties When they Entered into their Agreement. [§25.212]** As with impossibility (see §25.112), to satisfy this element a party must establish that the non-occurrence of the event causing the impracticability was an important, or basic, assumption held by **both** parties when they entered into the contract. There is no test to determine whether the non-occurrence of an event was a "basic assumption" of the parties, but it is clear that the assumption must be an important one to both parties, and that it must be shared by them at the time they entered the contract.

(1) **Example.** [§25.2121] Assume the facts of the Laura/Al hypothetical set forth in §25.2113, where Al discovered huge granite boulders as he begins digging a swimming pool for Laura. It may well be that the absence of such boulders was a basic assumption shared by both parties when the contract was made. If so, Al has fulfilled the second element of the defense.

c. **The Event Making Performance Impractical Must Occur Without the Fault of the Party Asserting the Defense.** [§25.213] If the party asserting the defense of impracticability was at fault in causing the event giving rise to impracticability, the defense will fail. As with impossibility (see §25.113), fault is used here in the tort sense and thus includes either an intentional or a negligent act which proximately causes the event giving rise to the impracticability.

(1) **Example.** [§25.2131] Assume the facts of the Laura/Al hypothetical of §25.2121, where Al is to build a pool for Laura. This time, however, assume that Al did not take soil tests before beginning construction of the pool, and also assume that a reasonable pool builder would have performed such tests before making a fixed price offer to build the pool. If such tests would have disclosed the presence of the granite boulders, Al could not successfully assert the impracticability defense.

Note that Al might try to assert that the existence of the boulders was not his fault and thus try to argue that he did not cause the event making performance impractical. This is not a valid argument, for while Al was not at fault for the boulders being there, on these facts he **was** at fault for negligently failing to locate them before entering into the fixed price contract.

d. **The Party Asserting the Defense Must Not Have Assumed the Risk of the Occurrence of the Event Making Performance Impractical.** [§25.214] The last element a party asserting the impracticability defense must prove is that he or she did not assume the risk that the event which made performance impractical would occur. This element is also one that most parties seeking to use the doctrine cannot fulfill, for, as mentioned earlier (see §25.2), the idea behind mutuality of obligation under modern contract law is that contract-making is risk allocation. When a party makes a contractual promise to perform a task, he or she is taking a risk that the deal may be less profitable than expected. On the other hand, the party is also entitled to reap the benefits if the deal turns out to be more profitable than anticipated. Hence, freedom of contract and the "risk allocation" idea mandates that courts view with skepticism a party's plea that the courts impose a floor on the possible losses he or she may suffer under a contract which turned out to be an improvident deal. Indeed, recall that for every break given the party claiming impracticability, benefits are taken away from the other party. That is, a "bad" deal for one party is a "good" deal for the other, and often the party receiving the "good" deal claims that the chance to get such a profitable deal was the principal reason he or she entered into the contract in the first place. Thus, when a court grants a claim of impracticability, the party resisting application of the defense usually argues that the court is depriving that party of his or her bargained for expectations. As a consequence, courts are reluctant to find that the risk of a bad deal was not assumed by the party asserting the defense.

Another factor involved in assessing whether a party implicitly assumed the risk of the event making performance impractical is whether the event was foreseeable. While a party is not expected to protect himself or herself against every potential event that could make performance impracticable, it is fair to say that **the more foreseeable an event is, the more a party will be held to have impliedly assumed the risk of it occurring by failing to negotiate protection for himself or herself under the agreement.**

(1) Example. [§25.2141] Fusion Co. promises to supply uranium to Utility for operation of Utility's nuclear power plant. After the contract is signed, but before delivery is due, there is a price-fixing agreement among uranium suppliers throughout the world so that the cost of uranium on the open market increases tenfold. A court may well conclude that Fusion Co.'s duty to deliver the uranium is nevertheless **not** discharged due to impracticability despite the price fixing agreement.

A series of cases similar to this hypothetical arose in the 1970's and 1980's, and the courts consistently denied relief to the supplier of the uranium. The rationale was that while a supplier such as Fusion Co. may not have reasonably foreseen an illegal uranium cartel, it certainly was aware that the price of uranium might rise between the date of the contract and the date of delivery for any number of reasons. Thus, it could have negotiated a price term with a ceiling on it, or it could have agreed to supply the uranium on a cost plus basis (where it charges the buyer a certain percentage over its cost for the ore), or it could have structured the deal so that a condition precedent to its delivery obligations was that the cost of uranium not exceed a certain price, etc. By failing to protect itself, the courts held that a company such as Fusion Co. implicitly assumed the risk that the price of uranium would rise, regardless of the reason. As such, it was not entitled to successfully use the impracticability defense.

(2) Example of Construction Contracts When an Almost Completed Building is Destroyed. [§25.2142] A recurring fact situation raising impracticability issues occurs when, e.g., a contractor is hired to construct a building and, after it is largely (but not completely) finished, the building is destroyed through no fault of either party. The builders in these cases often attempt to assert that their duties under the contract should be discharged due to impracticability. The courts have consistently held that the defense is not available in such situations for two reasons. The first reason is because performance is usually not impractical enough since it will only result in a doubling of the cost (see §25.211). The second reason is because the builder is deemed to have assumed the risk of such an event by making an unconditional promise to finish a building by a certain date when it could have protected itself by negotiating conditional language in the contract, e.g., a clause like, "I will build at this price assuming there is no destruction of the building during construction that is not my fault." Also courts hold the availability of insurance to builders to protect against this type of loss is a factor that makes it reasonable to put the risk of destruction on the builder. So while the builder will have to finish construction, [Restatement 2d §263, Com. a, Ill. 4], the builder typically given a reasonable extension of time in which to perform.

SPECIAL CASE SQUIB

(3) Exception: Example of *Alcoa Co. V. Essex*. [§25.2143] The one famous case that analyzes impracticability differently from the approach set forth above is *Alcoa v. Essex*, 499 F. Supp. 53 (W.D. Pa. 1980). Alcoa agreed to convert specified amounts of alumina supplied by Essex into aluminum for Essex. The contract was heavily negotiated and was scheduled to run from 1968 through 1988. To protect against inflation, the price charged by Alcoa was subject to adjustment based, in part, on changes to a particular Wholesale Price Index ("WPI"). Indexing the price to the WPI was suggested by Alcoa and was the result of an enormous amount of study by various Alcoa experts who concluded that the change in WPI reliably tracked the changes in the actual cost of transforming alumina into aluminum.

After the contract was signed, the costs of transforming alumina into aluminum ran much higher than the corresponding rise in the WPI. As a result, Essex was getting below market prices for aluminum, and began selling aluminum on the open market, as well as using it for its own consumption. While there was nothing in the contract to prevent Essex from selling aluminum, by 1978 Essex was making a profit on the open market of around $.37/pound of aluminum, while Alcoa was losing about $.10/pound in processing the aluminum it delivered to Essex. Alcoa brought a declaratory relief action seeking to be discharged from its duties under the contract on the grounds, *inter alia*, of impracticability. Essex defended by saying Alcoa assumed the risk that the costs of production would not match the price increases for aluminum processing when it agreed to the WPI indexing formula, especially since the idea of WPI indexing was Alcoa's idea in the first place. **Held:** Alcoa was entitled to relief under the contract. In this case the court went farther than just discharging Alcoa's duties, and ended up actually rewriting the price term, ensuring that Alcoa would make a profit of at least $.01/pound of aluminum processed.

When *Alcoa* was first decided, it caused much stir in the commercial world. However, the case has proven but a single exception, albeit a famous one, to general impracticability rules. Hence if a case like *Alcoa* were to come along today, Essex would likely prevail on its argument that Alcoa impliedly assumed the risk that the WPI-adjusted price it charged for aluminum would not keep up with its costs when it signed the agreement, and Alcoa thus would either have to perform under the contract or be in breach for failing to do so.

---

2. CONTRASTING IMPOSSIBILITY AND IMPRACTIBILITY. [§25.22] Clearly the elements of impossibility and impractibility are quite similar (compare §25.11 with §25.21). However, there are reasons to treat them separately, as is done in this book. Impossibility is a defense all modern courts recognize and apply routinely; assertions of impracticability have not been very well received by modern courts. Moreover, there is a quantitative difference in the structure of the two defenses as well. That is, it is rare that the buyer will complain if he or she does not obtain a promised performance if such performance is truly impossible, i.e., if a one-of-a-kind painting is destroyed through no fault of the seller, there really is nothing that can be done and a buyer does not usually feel he or she is being taken advantage of if the seller does not perform. On the other

Sum & Substance QUICK REVIEW of Contracts

hand, if the seller's performance is merely impractical, i.e., more expensive, than the seller thought it would be, a buyer is much more likely to insist that the seller perform anyway. After all, the buyer did not promise the seller a profit when they made a contract. The buyer simply agreed to pay an agreed amount for a good, some land, or a service. Since performance is still possible, and the buyer is still willing to pay the agreed upon price, the buyer typically insists on performance.

D. FRUSTRATION OF PURPOSE: DEFINED AND DISCUSSED. [§25.3] Frustration of purpose is a defense to a breach of contract claim (see §25.01) whereby the party asserting the defense seeks a declaration that his or her duties under the contract have been discharged due to the occurrence of an unexpected event or series of events. As in impossibility or impracticability situations, frustration is triggered by the occurrence of an event, the non-occurrence of which is a basic assumption on which the contract is made. However, unlike impossibility or impracticability, in frustration situations performance of the promised duty is perfectly possible and is no more expensive or otherwise burdensome for the non-performing party. What provides the justification for the non-performance in frustration situations is that, because of the event, the principal **purpose** for which the non-performing party entered into the contract is largely gone. In other words, the **value** to one party of the other's promised performance is substantially eliminated. Thus, while the party asserting the defense can perform his or her duty, and can perform it without extra burden, contract law says he or she does not have to because the **reason** he or she entered into the contract is "frustrated."

As impossibility and impracticability are largely seller's defenses, frustration of purpose is largely a buyer's defense. That is, in the typical fact pattern giving rise to the assertion of a frustration defense, something happens which renders meaningless the purpose for which the buyer had agreed to pay money. The frustration defense is recognized by the Restatement 2d in §265, although, somewhat surprisingly, it is not specifically mentioned in the UCC. Nevertheless, most commentators believe that frustration is inherently included in §2-615, even if it is not specifically mentioned in the section, and one of the Official Comments to that provision seems to support the contention [see UCC §2-615, Com. 9].

As with impracticability, in close cases the frustration defense has received scant acceptance from the American courts. However, although the American courts continue to say that the frustration defense is a viable one, there are relatively few reported cases in which a defendant has successfully asserted the defense unless the need for it is almost too plain to be contested.

1. **ELEMENTS NECESSARY TO ESTABLISH THE FRUSTRATION OF PURPOSE DEFENSE. [§25.31]** A party wishing to justify his or her non-performance by use of the frustration defense must establish:

   (1) The occurrence of an event which **frustrates the party's principal purpose** for entering into a contract;

   (2) That the non-occurrence of the event causing frustration of purpose was a **mutually shared basic assumption** on which the contract was made;

   (3) That the event causing the frustration of purpose occurred **without fault** of the party asserting the defense; and

   (4) The party asserting the defense did not implicitly or explicitly **assume the risk** of the event causing frustration of purpose [Restatement 2d §265].

a. **An Event Must Occur that Frustrates the Principal Purpose for Entering into a Contract. [§25.311]** To establish the frustration defense, a party must show that as a result of an unexpected event, his or her **principal** propose for entering into the contract has been **substantially** frustrated. Buyers have had trouble convincing American courts that this element has been fulfilled for two reasons. First, courts have viewed the purpose of a party under a contract quite broadly. Hence, merely showing that a party cannot take advantage of a transaction in the particular way he or she thought would be available at the time the contract was made is insufficient to establish that the **principal** purpose has been frustrated so long as the party can realize **some** benefit from the contract. Second, even if a degree of frustration as to the principal purpose of the agreement is found, courts have insisted that the degree of frustration be quite substantial. Hence, just because the party would not receive **all** the benefits he or she expected under the contract, or cannot do with the goods exactly what he or she wants, does not mean frustration has been established.

(1) **Example. [§25.3111]** Myra contracted to purchase a vacant piece of property that was zoned for commercial development. Myra planned to use the site to build a mini-mall, a fact known to the seller. After she signed the contract to purchase the property, but before she took title, the land was re-zoned to allow only single family residences, apartment buildings, and condominiums. Myra's duties are not discharged under the frustration of purpose doctrine for two reasons. First, courts would likely hold that her principal purpose in entering into the contract was broad, i.e., to use the land for income-generation purposes, rather than narrow, i.e., to build a mini-mall. Hence, they would hold that her principal purpose is not frustrated at all by the re-zoning, because she can build an apartment building or a condominium complex on the site and generate income from the property.

Second, even if she could establish some degree of frustration in the realization of her principal purpose, it would almost surely not be substantial enough to trigger the doctrine. That is, the fact that she can use the property to generate some amount of income, even if it is not as much as the mini-mall would provide, shows that the zoning change did not cause a **substantial** frustration of her purpose in purchasing the property.

b. **The Non-Occurrence of the Event Frustrating Performance Must Have Been a Basic Assumption of both Parties on Which the Contract Was Made. [§25.312]** The second element of a frustration defense is that the non-occurrence of the event causing the frustration must have been an important, or basic, assumption on which the contract was based. Once again, there is no set test to determine whether this element is met, but the party seeking to assert the defense must show that the non-occurrence of the event was an **important** and **mutually held** assumption when the contract was entered into.

(1) **Example of Leased Premises Destroyed During Term of Lease. [§25.3121]** Peter agrees to rent an apartment from Kristen, and they enter into a one-year written lease. Two months after the contract was signed, the apartment building burns down through no fault of either Peter or Kristen. In such a case, Kristen's duty to provide an apartment is discharged due to impossibility. Similarly, Peter's duty to pay rent is discharged through frustration, as the continued presence of the apartment was certainly a shared basic assumption on which the contract was made, and Peter's principal purpose in entering into the contract would be substantially frustrated by the absence of the building.

c. **The Event Causing Frustration of Purpose Must Have Occurred Without the Fault of the Party Asserting the Defense. [§25.313]** As with impossibility and impracticability, a party may not validly use the frustration of propose defense if he or she was at fault in causing the event giving rise to the frustration. Once again, the term fault under this doctrine is given its tort meaning, and thus includes both intentional and negligent acts of the defendant.

    (1) **Example. [§25.3131]** Take the Peter/Kristen example set forth in §25.3121 where Peter is a tenant of Kristen's. If the fire that burns down the apartment building was caused by Peter's negligence, then his duty to pay rent would not be discharged due to frustration, although Kristen's duty to provide an apartment would still be discharged due to impossibility.

d. **The Party Asserting the Frustration Defense Must Not Have Assumed the Risk of the Occurrence of the Event Frustrating Performance of the Duty. [§25.314]** As noted above, the American courts have largely been unsympathetic to frustration of purpose claims. This has occurred in part because of the strictures of the requirement that a party must establish that the principal purpose of the contract must be substantially frustrated. However, it is also, because of the fourth element of the defense, i.e., that the party asserting the defense has not implicitly or explicitly assumed the risk of the frustrating event's occurrence. As with impracticability, the courts have in effect held that if the kind of event that frustrates performance is relatively foreseeable, the failure of a party explicitly to guard against its occurrence in the contract means that he or she has implicitly accepted the risk that the event will occur.

    (1) **Example. [§25.3141]** Assume the facts of the hypothetical set forth in §25.3111 where Myra purchased a piece of property that was zoned for commercial purposes at the time the contract was signed. Assume this time that before she took title, the City Council zoned her parcel so that she had to keep it as vacant land. Obviously this would be a severe frustration of her principal purpose to purchase income generating property, which is why she entered into the contract in the first place. However, if, e.g., it was known that the City Council was debating zoning changes at the time she purchased the property, she probably would **not** be entitled to the frustration defense because she would be deemed to have assumed the risk of the zoning change (a foreseeable event) by not providing for such an occurrence in her contract (e.g., by making her obligations conditional on there being no zoning change).

2. **EXAMPLES OF FRUSTRATION CASES. [§25.32]** The following are examples of relatively famous cases arising under the frustration doctrines.

    a. **Example of *Krell v. Henry (The Coronation Cases)*. [§25.321]** *Krell v. Henry*, 2 K.B. 740 (C.A.) (1903), the most famous of "*The Coronation Cases*," was the first significant case to allow the frustration of purpose defense. (All of the *Coronation Cases* arose on similar facts.) In *Krell v. Henry*, Krell owned a flat which provided a good view of the planned coronation of King Edward VII of Great Britain. Krell advertised that he would rent the flat to anyone who wished to view the ceremony for £75. Henry agreed to sublease the flat, paid £25 immediately upon executing the contract, and promised to pay the remaining £50 on the day of the coronation. Unfortunately, King Edward suffered appendicitis on the day of the coronation, and the ceremony was indefinitely postponed. Henry refused to pay the remaining £50, and Krell sued. The gist of Krell's argument was that because there was nothing preventing

Henry from paying the £50, his failure to do so was an unexcused breach. **Held:** Henry did not have to pay the £50 as his duty to do so was discharged due to frustration of purpose. That is:

(1) The principal purpose for which Henry let the rooms, i.e., to watch the coronation, was substantially frustrated. While it was true Henry could still take occupancy, his purpose in doing so was not to see the normal street traffic; it was to see the coronation. Accordingly, the value to him of his tenancy became non-existent when the King postponed the event;

(2) Cancellation of the coronation was an event, the non-occurrence of which was a mutually shared basic assumption on which the contract was based;

(3) Cancellation of the coronation was certainly not due to any fault of Henry; and

(4) The risk of the coronation being canceled was not fairly assumed by Henry.

For an example of an earlier case reaching the opposite decision from *Krell v. Henry*, see Case Squibs Section, *Paradine v. Jane*.

b. **Example of *Lloyd v. Murphy*.** [§25.322] Murphy leased commercial space from Lloyd in August 1941. Under their agreement, Murphy's use of the property was initially restricted "for the sole purpose of conducting thereon the business of displaying and selling new automobiles" in Beverly Hills. The United States entered World War II shortly after the lease was signed, and the government thereafter issued restrictions on the sale of new cars. These regulations essentially meant Murphy would not be able to get any (or very few) new cars to sell. As a consequence, Murphy vacated the premises and refused to pay rent. Lloyd eventually agreed to remove the "car dealership only" restriction of the lease, and even lowered the rent, but Murphy nonetheless would not occupy or pay for the space. In the subsequent breach action for failure to pay rent, Murphy asserted frustration as a defense. **Held:** Frustration was not shown here for two reasons. **First**, to the extent there was any frustration at all, there was an insufficient showing of **substantial** frustration, given Lloyd's offer to allow the premises to be used for any legal purpose, and given the prime location of the premises. That is, since the property could be used to sell any lawfully traded goods, the broad propose of the lease, i.e., retail commercial space, was not frustrated, even if Murphy's personal expectations as to the use of the property to sell cars were frustrated. **Second**, Murphy, as lessee, was deemed to have assumed the risk of the wartime regulations. At the time the lease was signed, automobile sales were brisk because the consuming public anticipated production might be restricted in the future. Given those facts, Justice Traynor concluded that Murphy was on notice that such restrictions were foreseeable, and that by failing to include a provision in the lease making the absence of such restrictions a condition of his duty to pay rent, Murphy had assumed the risk that the regulations might be imposed. *Lloyd v. Murphy*, 25 Cal.2d 48, 153 P.2d 47 (1944)

E. THE EVENTS GIVING RISE TO CLAIMS OF IMPOSSIBILITY, IMPRACTICABILITY, AND FRUSTRATION MAY EITHER BE IN EXISTENCE AT THE TIME THE CONTRACT IS SIGNED, OR BE SUPERVENING. [§25.4] The occurrence of the events giving rise to impossibility, impracticability, or frustration may either occur after the contract is signed but before performance is due (i.e., where the horse dies after the sales agreement is made) [Restatement 2d §264], or they can be in existence at the time the contract is signed, but unknown to the parties (e.g., the boulders are already in the ground making pool construction more burdensome) [Restatement 2d §265]. The elements for the defenses in both cases are the same, except that *if the event is already in existence at the time the agreement is signed,* **the party asserting the defense must neither know of it, nor have reason to know of it, when he or she signs the contract** [Restatement 2d §265].

F. **TEMPORARY IMPOSSIBILITY, IMPRACTICABILITY, OR FRUSTRATION. [§25.5]** There may be occasions in which the event making performance impossible, impracticable, or frustrated is only temporary. Contract law holds that in such situations, the aggrieved party's duties under the contract are initially only suspended. The duties do not become discharged until and unless performance after cessation of the impossibility or frustration would be materially more burdensome than if the event had not occurred [Restatement 2d §269; UCC §2-615(c)].

  1. **EXAMPLE. [§25.51]** A producer has leased a theatre for a six-month run of a play. Two months into the lease, a fire breaks out in the theatre, through no fault of either the producer or the landlord. The fire does relatively extensive damage to the balcony, and the theatre must be closed for two days while repairs are made. During those two days, the duties of the landlord to provide a theatre, and the duty of the producer to pay rent, are temporarily suspended. However, since it will likely not be materially more burdensome for either party to continue once the theatre reopens, the contract is not discharged, and the lease will run for two days past the original expiration date.

  2. **EXAMPLE. [§25.52]** Same as above, except this time the fire is severe enough to cause the theatre to close for two months. This time the theatre is leased by another production company a week after the expiration of the first producer's six-month lease term; hence, to extend the run of the play's production at the theatre when the fire occurred would result in the theatre's having to break its lease with the next production company. The duty under the contract to provide a theatre for six months are discharged because extending them would be too burdensome to the theatre owner.

G. **RESTITUTION AVAILABLE IN CONTRACTS DISCHARGED DUE TO IMPOSSIBILITY, IMPRACTIBILITY, AND FRUSTRATION. [§25.6]** While a party who successfully asserts an impossibility, impracticability, or frustration defense has his or her duties under the agreement discharged and thus, cannot be liable under the contract for such excused non-performance, he or she may still be liable in restitution for any benefits already conferred. Hence, while the other party who did not suffer the event giving use to the defense may not recover expectation or reliance damages in a breach action, he or she is not completely without remedy for a restitutionary recovery is available (see Chapter Thirty-Two for a discussion of restitution).

CHAPTER TWENTY-SIX: MODIFICATION AND WAIVER (WITH A FOCUS ON UCC §2-209)

A. MODIFICATION, GENERALLY. [§26.0] A modification occurs when the parties to an already existing contract agree to add or change the terms of that contract. At first there seems to be nothing controversial about enforcing contract modifications. After all, if a supplier is contractually obligated to deliver goods on May 1, but the parties later agree that the seller should deliver them on May 5, there would seem no problem in a court's holding the parties to their words and making May 5 the operatative delivery rate. In truth, when **both** parties agree that a modification has taken place, **and** agree as to its terms, enforcing the contract as modified presents no unusual problems. However, issues abound when one party says a modification took place and the other disagrees; or when the parties agree that a modification took place but disagree as to its terms; or when one party tries to retract a previously made modification.

Modern contract law has changed significantly the common law rules regulating whether a party will be able to enforce an asserted modification, i.e., modern law has changed the requirements that the party seeking to prove a modification took place must meet before the contract, **as modified**, will be controlling. The rules regulating modifications are substantially the same under both the UCC and the Restatement 2d, but because most Contracts professors seem to teach modifications with reference to UCC §2-209, that provision will serve as the principle source throughout the Chapter, with reference made to the Restatement when its rules differ from those in §2-209.

1. THE REAL ISSUE REGARDING MODIFICATIONS. [§26.01] Like the parol evidence rule (see §§17.01; 26.6), one problem in learning the issues giving rise to the modification doctrine is that usually you are told up front in a hypothetical whether a modification actually took place and if it did, its terms. With that knowledge, it is tempting to try and make sure the case comes out the "right" way and reward the innocent party.

To realize the complexity of the issues surrounding modification, assume you are a judge. Two contracting parties, Ed, the President of Boutique (a clothing store), and Sally, the owner of Sweaters-R-Us (a clothing manufacturer). They have a written contract calling for the delivery of 200 sweaters — 50 each of blue, green, red, and yellow. They both agree there was timely delivery of the sweaters, and both agree that there were no green sweaters in the delivery; instead there were 100 yellow ones. Sally claims this was not a breach, however, as she telephoned Ed a few days before delivery was due, and he told her it was OK to substitute the extra yellow sweaters for the green ones called for in the contract. Sally says that in the phone call, she told Ed that she was temporarily out of green sweaters, and was willing to work her factory overtime to produce the green sweaters if Ed really wanted them, but if Ed could live with the extra yellow ones, she'd appreciate it. She says Ed agreed. Ed denies that such a conversation ever took place.

As judge, if you go by the contract only, and say that Sally's company is in breach for not delivering the green sweaters, you may be fostering fraud, because what Sally said may well have happened. However, if you allow Sally to testify about this alleged oral modification, you may also be perpetuating fraud, for Sally may just be trying to cover up a breach on her part by making up this whole conversation.

The modification rules discussed in the remainder of this Chapter set forth contract law's process for dealing with such modification issues.

B. THE STRUCTURE OF UCC §2-209. [§26.1] UCC §2-209 has five sections, which can be summarized as follows:

(1) An agreement to modify a contract is **enforceable** even in the **absence of consideration** [UCC §2-209(1); see §26.2];

(2) If the parties include **a "no modification except in writing clause,"** in their contract, all attempted oral modifications by the parties are without effect, and **any modification must be in writing to be enforceable** [UCC §2-209(2); see §26.3];

(3) If the parties modify a contract, **the modified agreement must satisfy the statute of frauds to be enforceable.** If it does not, the terms of the original contract control, assuming the original contract satisfied the Statute [UCC §2-209(3); see §26.4];

(4) **If an oral modification is unenforceable** because it does not satisfy the statute of frauds, or because the parties had previously agreed to a no modification except in writing clause, **no evidence of the attempted modification is admissible. However, the attempted modification can nevertheless operate as an enforceable** *waiver* [UCC §2-209(4); see §26.5];

(5) **A party who has waived the right to enforce an executory portion of the contract may** *retract the waiver* **with reasonable notice,** so long as the other party has not made a material change of position in reliance on the waiver [UCC §2-209(5); see §26.6].

C. A MODIFICATION NEED NOT BE SUPPORTED BY CONSIDERATION TO BE ENFORCEABLE. [§26.2] UCC §2-209(1) provides that **contract modifications are enforceable even if not supported by consideration.** This is a change from the common law which required that modifications had to be supported by consideration to be enforceable under the pre-existing duty rule (*see* §7.633). For example, assume Richard, the president of a sporting goods manufacturing company, is under a duty to deliver 100 volleyballs to Karyn, the owner of a retail sports shop, on May 10. On May 6, Richard calls Karyn and they agree that Richard can deliver the volleyballs on May 15 without being in breach. At common law, Karyn's promise to accept delivery on the 15th might be unenforceable because Richard gave no new consideration for the changed delivery date. That is, he did not promise anything more than he was already contractually obligated to do, i.e., deliver the volleyballs. Hence, in the absence of promissory estoppel or another theory that would make enforceable Karyn's promise to accept a later delivery, Karyn could reject the volleyballs if they were delivered after May 10, and could sue Richard for breach. However, under UCC §2-209(1), Karyn's promise is enforceable by Richard despite the fact that it is not supported by consideration.

1. RESTATEMENT'S CONSIDERATION RULE SOMEWHAT MORE NARROW. [§26.21] The Restatement 2d also provides that modifications can be enforceable in the absence of consideration. [Restatement 2d §89]. However, the Restatement's rule in this regard is not quite as broad as the UCC's. Under the Restatement, a modification unsupported by consideration will be enforceable only if:

(a) it is **fair** in view of **circumstances not reasonably foreseen** when the contract was made;

(b) a state **statute provides for such enforceability**; or

(c) **justice otherwise requires** that it be enforced.

a. **Example. [§26.211]** Contractor agrees to build an enclosed parking structure for Developer at a cost of $500,000. Contractor performs all standard soil tests before making the bid. After a week of excavation, an underground pool is discovered, which will require an extra $300,000 worth of work to drain and divert. Developer agrees to pay Contractor the $300,000 if she'll finish. *Question*: Is the promised $300,000 payment enforceable? *Answer*: **YES.** This situation is governed by the Restatement (as it's not a contract for the sale of goods) and thus a modification will only be upheld on the grounds given in §26.21. Here, the amount of the modification is **fair**, and the promise was made in light **circumstances not reasonably foreseen when the contract was made.**

D. **AN ORAL MODIFICATION IS UNENFORCEABLE IF THE PARTIES HAVE AGREED TO A "NO MODIFICATION EXCEPT IN WRITING" CLAUSE. [§26.3]** On occasion, buyers and sellers will enter into an agreement in which both parties agree that no modification may be effectively made to their contract unless the terms of the modification are reduced to a writing signed by both parties. There is an obvious evidentiary advantage to requiring that no provision of a contract can be altered unless it is in writing, and such a clause is also useful to stop a company's lower level employees from making promises to customers that company management does not wish to perform.

UCC §2-209(2) provides that "no modification except in writing" clauses (or, as they are sometimes known, "private statute of frauds" clauses) are enforceable. Thus, while a modification need not have consideration to be binding under §2-209(1), if the parties have agreed to a no modification except in writing clause, the modification itself must be in a signed writing or it is unenforceable.

E. **IF THE CONTRACT, AS MODIFIED, IS WITHIN THE STATUTE OF FRAUDS, THE MODIFIED AGREEMENT MUST SATISFY THE STATUTE OR IT WILL BE UNENFORCEABLE. [§26.4]** Section 2-209(3) provides that the statute of frauds set forth in UCC §2-201 must be satisfied if the contract, **as modified**, is within the statute. Thus, if the parties' amended contract is for the sale of goods for $500 or more, the modified agreement must satisfy UCC §2-201 or it is unenforceable. If the modified contract is unenforceable, then the original contract's terms are binding. Thus, here again, while the modification need not be supported by consideration under UCC §2-209(1) to be enforceable, the modified agreement must satisfy the statute of frauds under §2-209(3) to be effective.

The rule under Restatement 2d §149 is also that the contract as modified must satisfy the applicable statute of frauds in order to be enforceable (see §7.633). Recall that while usually the statute of frauds under §2-201 is satisfied by the existence of a signed writing, there are other ways to satisfy it, e.g., by a merchant's confirmatory memorandum, by the sending of specially made goods, by court-related admission, or by performance (see §§9.63 and 9.64). Hence, if the contract as modified can satisfy any portion of §2-201, it will be enforceable. However, if it cannot, the terms of the original unmodified contract will control, assuming the original contract satisfied the Statute.

Note that a distinct minority of commentators have espoused a very different view of what §2-209(3) means. To them, the provision means that the modified contract must be in writing only if the **modification itself is for the sale of goods for $500 or more**; otherwise, oral modifications are freely enforceable. That is, they claim that if the modification was, e.g., to change the agreement from three sets of golf clubs at $600 each to four sets of clubs at that price, the modification would have to satisfy §2-201 to be enforceable because the **modification itself** concerned the sale of goods for $500 or more. However, if the modification was only, e.g., to change the delivery date, then evidence of its making would be freely admissible and enforceable under §2-209(3) because the **modification itself** did not deal with a sale of goods for $500 or more, but rather only with a change in dates.

1. **EXAMPLE. [§26.41]** Bob and Janet have signed a contract whereby Bob has agreed to sell his Poussin painting to Janet for $100,000. Under the contract, Bob is to deliver the painting on September 1. Bob claims that he and Janet modified their agreement in a telephone conversation made after the contract was signed so as to allow Bob to deliver the painting a month later, on October 1. Janet denies she ever agreed to a later delivery. Even if the telephone conversation occurred the way Bob said it did, under the majority view Janet's promise to accept the painting is unenforceable under §2-209(3) because the contract as modified, i.e., the contract with the October 1 delivery date, did not satisfy the statute of frauds under §2-201. That is, there is no signed writing evidencing a contract with an October 1 delivery date. As such, the enforceable terms of Bob and Janet's agreement are those found in the original contract which calls for the September 1 delivery. Hence, if Bob delivers the painting after September 1, he has breached.

   Although such an agreement cannot be enforced as a *modification* under §2-209(3), note that there is the possibility Bob may prevail by means of *waiver* as set forth in §26.5.

2. **EXAMPLE. [§26.42]** Larry and Gina have a written contract calling for Larry to sell his stereo to Gina for $550. Gina claims they orally modified the price term to $490. Evidence of the alleged modification is freely admissible because the contract, as assertedly modified, is not within the UCC's statute of frauds since it is for the sale of goods for less than $500.

F. **A MODIFICATION THAT IS UNENFORCEABLE BECAUSE IT IS NOT IN WRITING MAY STILL OPERATE AS AN ENFORCEABLE WAIVER. [§26.5]** Section 2-209(4) is probably the most complicated provision in Article 2, although it does not seem so at first glance. The provision says that if an attempted oral modification is unenforceable, either because the contract as modified does not satisfy the statute of frauds under §2-209(3), or because there is a valid "no modification except in writing" clause under §2-209(2), the attempted modification nonetheless "can operate as a waiver." The interpretive problems concerning this provision have centered around two questions:

   (1) What is it that can be "waived" under §2-209(4); and

   (2) How can an otherwise unenforceable oral modification "operate" at all?

The courts have developed four theories as to how this provision operates and what it means.

1. **THE FIRST INTERPRETATION OF HOW §2-209(4) OPERATES: THE ONLY WAY A NO MODIFICATION EXCEPT IN WRITING CLAUSE, OR THE STATUTE OF FRAUDS, MAY BE "WAIVED" IS BY WRITTEN AGREEMENT OF THE PARTIES. [§26.51]** This view holds that §2-209(4)'s "waiver" provision means that the parties are permitted, if they so choose, to waive the effects of either a no modification except in writing clause, or the statute of frauds. That is, §2-209(4) gives permission to the parties to vary the operation of an otherwise binding writing requirement. However, the only effective way to make such a waiver, according to this interpretation, is in a signed writing which, by its own terms, specifically authorizes the parties to make subsequent binding oral modifications.

2. THE SECOND INTERPRETATION OF HOW §2-209(4) OPERATES: AN ATTEMPTED ORAL MODIFICATION CAN ACT AS AN IMPLIED WAIVER OF BOTH A NO MODIFICATION EXCEPT IN WRITING CLAUSE AND THE STATUTE OF FRAUDS. [§26.52] This interpretation of §2-209(4) provides that every time one party asserts that an oral modification took place, the court should initially examine the testimony and other evidence of that party concerning the alleged modification out of the presence of the jury. If the court finds such evidence sufficiently credible, i.e., evidence from which the jury could believe the modification occurred, the court is instructed to let the party present that same evidence before the jury.

The rationale for allowing the introduction of evidence of an oral modification even when the contract as modified does not satisfy the Statute, or when there is a no modification except in writing clause, is that **by agreeing to an oral modification, both parties simultaneously, but implicitly, agreed to a waiver of any writing requirement that formerly bound them.** That is, if the parties truly agreed to an oral modification, obviously the presence of a writing requirement such as the statute of frauds was of no concern to them. Hence, upon their making such an agreement, there must have been a mutual, but implied, waiver of the Statute. That being so, this view holds that since courts are directed to enforce the contract in such a way as to effectuate the parties' intentions whenever possible, the modification, if truly agreed to, should be enforced and all credible evidence surrounding its making should be allowed in.

3. THE THIRD INTERPRETATION OF HOW §2-209(4) OPERATES: THE TERMS OF A BILATERAL ORAL MODIFICATION ARE INADMISSIBLE, BUT EVIDENCE OF ONE PARTY'S UNILATERAL WAIVER IS ADMISSIBLE. [§26.53] There are several "background" concepts that must be discussed before this theory can be completely understood.

The first such concept is the difference between a waiver and a modification in traditional contract terms. As noted earlier, a waiver is sometimes defined as the intentional relinquishment of a known right, but is more properly defined as the excuse in the non-occurrence of, or delay in the occurrence of, a constructive condition (see §20.41). The important things about a waiver for §2-209(4) purposes are: (a) that a waiver is the result of unilateral action, whereas a modification requires the agreement of **both** parties to a substitution of terms; and (b) a waiver focuses solely on the choice not to enforce a particular duty, whereas a modification concerns both the old term that the parties have canceled **and** the new term they have substituted in its place.

The second concept that needs to be understood is that inherent in any bilateral modification is one party's waiver. For example, assume a written contract calls for delivery of certain goods on August 10, and that the parties orally agree to modify that date to September 1. While a modification has occurred, so has a waiver. That is, there has been a modification since both the parties agreed to substitute the September 1 date for the August 10 date. Inherent in that transaction, however, is also the buyer's **waiver** i.e., the intentional relinquishment of of his or her right, to declare a breach if the goods are not delivered on August 10.

Putting those ideas together, this interpretation of §2-209(4) holds that while evidence of what **both** parties orally agreed to in their modification is inadmissible, evidence of one party's waiver of a particular term is admissible. That is, evidence that the parties got together and orally changed the August 10 delivery date to September 1 would be inadmissible. However, evidence that the buyer unilaterally relinquished his or her right to insist on an August 10 delivery **would be** admissible.

4. **THE FOURTH INTERPRETATION OF HOW §2-209(4) OPERATES: EVIDENCE OF THE MODIFICATION IS FREELY ADMISSIBLE IF THE PARTY SEEKING TO ESTABLISH THE MODIFICATION CAN SHOW RELIANCE ON THE MODIFIED AGREEMENT. [§26.54]** Under this interpretation of §2-209(4), a party seeking to establish a modification will not be allowed to do so unless he or she can establish reliance on the alleged modification. If such reliance can be shown, then evidence of the entire oral modification is freely admissible.

The proponents of this view note that one of the reasons behind the common law requirement that consideration be present to enforce a modification was that consideration provided evidence that the modification had, in fact, occurred. In other words, if Joe paid Rebecca $50, and now says the reason he did so was to move the delivery date of the contract back 10 days, the check itself provides some evidence that a modification did, in fact, occur. (Of course the $50 could have been for the re-payment of an independent loan, but at least it provides some basis to believe Joe other than just his unsupported testimony.) Since reliance is often used to enforce a contractual promise in the absence of consideration, this view posits that when the drafters of the Code removed consideration as a requisite for enforcing modifications in §2-209(1), it is reasonable to assume they intended to include reliance in its place in §2-209(4). Further, as noted earlier, in many jurisdictions reliance is a common law exception to the statute of frauds (see §§9.2;9.7).

5. **EXAMPLE OF *WISCONSIN KNIFE WORKS V. NATIONAL METAL CRAFTERS*.** [§26.55] Wisconsin Knife Works ("Wisconsin") entered into a series of contracts with National Metal Crafters ("National") calling for National to deliver spade bit blanks. Each contract had a "no modification except in writing" clause. National appeared to miss several delivery deadlines under these contracts, and eventually Wisconsin terminated the contracts, declaring the cumulative effect of the late deliveries amounted to a material breach. Wisconsin thereafter sued National seeking damages for that material breach. In its defense, National claimed that it had not missed the **operative** delivery deadlines of the contract because the original delivery dates had been orally modified. As a consequence, National counter-claimed against Wisconsin, asserting that Wisconsin breached by anticipatorily repudiating the agreement in its termination letter. The trial court admitted the evidence proffered by National that changes had been made to the delivery dates, and the jury apparently believed National, for it awarded National $30,000 on its counter-claim, and awarded Wisconsin nothing.

Judge Posner wrote the majority opinion for the Seventh Circuit, reversing the trial court and adopting the "fourth interpretation" of §2-209(4)'s operation. He stated that unless National could establish reliance on the alleged modifications (which it had not done at the earlier trial), it could not introduce evidence of the alleged modifications. Therefore, he remanded the case to allow National the opportunity to prove some sort of reliance. Judge Easterbrook dissented, holding that National's evidence of the changed delivery dates was properly received. He stated that the "third interpretation" was the proper one, and hence National was freely entitled to introduce evidence of Wisconsin's unilateral waiver of the original delivery dates. *Wisconsin Knife Works v. National Metal Crafters*, 781 F.2d 1280 (7th Cir. 1986).

G. **RETRACTION OF WAIVERS. [§26.6]** An enforceable **modification** made under §2-209 cannot be unilaterally retracted, for it is the result of the agreement of both parties. Of course, it can be mutually rescinded, released, further modified, etc., but it cannot simply be rendered a nullity just because one party later changes his or her mind.

However, a **waiver** of an executory duty can be unilaterally retracted, for a waiver concerns the rights of only one party to enforce an obligation. The rules governing when such waiver can be retracted are set forth in §2-209(5), and are identical to the rules as stated earlier for non-UCC contracts (see §20.413). That is, upon reasonable notice, a waiver of executory duties due under a contract is freely retractable **unless** such retraction would be unjust under the circumstances due to a material change of position by the other party in reliance on the waiver.

1. **EXAMPLE. [§26.61]** Alex purchased a boat and was obligated to make payments to the Boat Yard of $1,000/month for 48 months. Six months into the contract Alex asked Julie, the owner of Boat Yard, if she would be willing to take $800/month for 60 months rather than insist on forty-eight $1,000 payments. Julie orally agreed, and for a year accepted the $800 payments. However, she thereafter changed her mind and demanded that Alex go back to making $1,000/month payments. As Julie's initial waiver of the right to insist on $1,000 payments was only as to executory portions of the contract, i.e., as to future unmade payments, she is entitled unilaterally to rescind the waiver and demand $1,000 payments from now on, **unless** Alex can show some sort of changed position in reliance on Julie's waiver, e.g., he took a lesser paying job, incurred another $200/month obligation, etc.

H. **DISTINGUISHING MODIFICATION FROM THE PAROL EVIDENCE RULE. [§26.7]**
A frequently made mistake by first year students is to confuse analysis under modification rules with analysis under the parol evidence rule. The standard is this:

If the alleged oral agreement of the parties was made **before**, or **contemporaneous with**, execution of the written contract, it is a parol evidence rule issue.

If the alleged oral agreement of the parties was made **after the contract was signed, it is a modification issue.**

That is, the key to determining which set of rules applies is to determine **when** the alleged oral agreement was made.

1. **EXAMPLE. [§26.71]** Fred negotiated with Computer Co. over the sale of a XT-100 computer. Fred thought he and the salesman had reached an agreement during the bargaining process that Computer Co. would include an extra 1 Megabyte ("Mb") of RAM in his computer at no extra charge, but that term did not appear in their final written and signed contract. In addition, the final contract called for delivery of the computer on September 30, but after the contract was executed Computer Co. says it asked, and claims Fred agreed, to extend the delivery date to October 15.

The issue of whether Fred can enforce the promise to install an extra 1 Mb of RAM is a parol evidence question, for it concerns agreement as to a term assertedly made prior to execution of the contract. Resolution of the proper delivery date is a modification issue, for it concerns an alleged agreement made after the contract was signed.

X. RIGHTS AND OBLIGATIONS IN CONTRACTS INVOLVING MORE THAN TWO PARTIES

INTRODUCTORY NOTE TO RIGHTS AND OBLIGATIONS OF CONTRACTS INVOLVING MORE THAN TWO PARTIES: Until this point, this Book has focused almost exclusively on contracts involving only two parties. However, most contracts involve, either directly or indirectly, numerous third parties. This Part of the Outline details the rights and obligations under a contract when third parties are involved. Contract law has categorized third party involvement with various contracts into three basic categories:

(1) Agreements in which, as part of the bargaining process, one party to a contract promises to perform an act benefiting someone who is not a party to the contract. Such agreements are known as **third party beneficiary contracts**, and are discussed in Chapter Twenty-Seven.

(2) Agreements in which one party already in a contract transfers the right to receive the other party's performance under that contract to a third person. Such transactions are known as **assignments**, and are discussed in Chapter Twenty-Eight.

(3) Agreements in which one party already in a contract transfers the obligation to perform a contractual duty under that contract to a third person. Such transactions are known as **delegations**, and are discussed in Chapter Twenty-Nine.

CHAPTER TWENTY-SEVEN: THIRD PARTY BENEFICIARY CONTRACTS

A. THIRD PARTY BENEFICIARY CONTRACTS GENERALLY. [§27.0] Third party beneficiary contracts are contracts in which one of the two parties to the agreement makes an enforeable promise benefiting someone who is not a party to the agreement.

Almost all contracts between two parties benefit a third party in one way or another. Sometimes these benefits are direct; sometimes indirect. When they are sufficiently direct, the third party benefited by a contract can sue to enforce it, i.e., even though they are not a party to the contract, they nevertheless sue for its breach. To fully analyze this and other issues associated with such contracts, the nomenclature used to describe the parties must be learned, and is explained below.

B. TERMINOLOGY OF THIRD PARTY BENEFICIARY CONTRACTS. [§27.1] The three parties involved in third party beneficiary contract analysis are:

(1) The **Promisor**. The promisor is the party who is contractually bound to perform an act that will benefit a third person. That is, the promisor makes a contract with someone, and in that contract he or she promises to perform an act that benefits a third party.

(2) The **Promisee**. The promisee is the party who bargained for the promisor's promise to perform the act which will benefit a third person. In other words, the promisee is the other party who is in the contract with the promisor, and it is the promisee who bargains for the promisor's agreement to do something to benefit the third party.

(3) The **Beneficiary**. The beneficiary is the person who is not a party to the promisor/promisee agreement and who stands to benefit from performance of the promisor's promise [Restatement 2d §302, Com. a].

1. **EXAMPLE. [§27.11]** Mark wants to help his sister financially. Accordingly, he enters into a contract promising to sell his record collection to Janet in return for Janet's promise to pay Mark's sister $500. In this case, **Janet is the promisor**, for she is in a contract with the promisee (Mark), and she is the one making a promise, the performance of which will benefit a third person. **Mark is the promisee**, because he is the one who bargained for the promise which benefits the third party. **Mark's sister is the beneficiary**, for she is the one who benefits from the promisor's (Janet's) performance.

C. ISSUES ARISING UNDER THIRD PARTY BENEFICIARY CONTRACTS. [§27.2] The good news is that there are five, and only five issues surrounding third party beneficiary contracts. If you know the answers to these five questions, and how to analyze them, you will know all you need to know in this area. The five issues are:

(1) **When is the beneficiary entitled to sue the promisor for breach if the promisor does not perform?** (See §27.3.)

(2) Assuming the beneficiary can sue the promisor, **what defenses will the promisor be able to assert**? (See §27.4.)

(3) **Is the beneficiary entitled to sue the *promisee* if the *promisor* does not perform?** (See §27.5.)

(4) **Is the *promisee* entitled to sue the *promisor* if the promisor does not perform?** (See §27.6.)

(5) **May the promisor and promisee effectively modify (or even recind) the third party beneficiary contract to the detriment of the beneficiary?** (See §27.7.)

D. WHEN CAN SOMEONE WHO IS NOT A PARTY TO A CONTRACT SUE TO ENFORCE PERFORMANCE UNDER THAT CONTRACT: THE RIGHTS OF THE BENEFICIARY TO SUE THE PROMISOR. [§27.3] The test for when a beneficiary is entitled to sue a promisor for damages arising from a promisor's failure of performance in a third party beneficiary contract has changed over time.

1. EARLY AMERICAN LAW AS EXEMPLIFIED BY THE FIRST RESTATEMENT: "CREDITOR" AND "DONEE" BENEFICIARIES COULD ENFORCE THE PROMISOR'S PROMISE; "INCIDENTAL" BENEFICIARIES COULD NOT. [§27.31] From the early days of American contract law, certain kinds of beneficiaries have been entitled to enforce a promisor's promise (with the notable exceptions of those suing in Massachusetts, which did not allow recovery under a third party beneficiary theory until 1979; and of New York, which had certain restrictions on the doctrine until 1985). (For the early English common law view, see Case Squibs section, *Dutton v. Poole*.) However, the nomenclature and categorizations of which kinds of beneficiaries could sue the promisor has changed somewhat over time.

The early American courts, as exemplified by the First Restatement, divided beneficiaries into three categories:

      (i)   "**donee**" beneficiaries;

      (ii) "**creditor**" beneficiaries; and

      (iii) "**incidental**" beneficiaries [Restatement 1st §133].

Of these, donee and creditor beneficiaries were entitled to enforce promises of the promisor, whereas incidental beneficiaries were not. That is, donee and creditor beneficiaries, even though they were not a party to the contract and made no promises under it, would nevertheless be able to sue the promisor for breach of contract if the promisor failed to perform without a sufficient reason.

This categorization raises the question of what characteristics gave a beneficiary "donee", "creditor," or "incidental" status? These issues are discussed below.

    a. "Donee" Beneficiaries: Defined and Discussed. [§27.311] Under the First Restatement, a donee beneficiary was a beneficiary of a contractual promise made by a promisor, the **purpose** of which was either:

        (i)   to make **a gift** to the beneficiary; or

        (ii) to confer on the beneficiary **a right against the promisor to performance that was not already owing, nor supposed to be owing, nor asserted to be owing,** from the promisor to the beneficiary [Restatement 1st §133(1)].

When a beneficiary could establish the elements to become a "donee" beneficiary, he or she was entitled to enforce the promisor's promise and thus to recover damages from the promisor for its breach. That is, when the promisor initially made his or her contractual promises to the promisee, he or she was also deemed to have undertaken an enforceable duty to a donee beneficiary as well [Restatement 1st, §133(1)(a)].

SPECIAL CASE SQUIB

(1) **Example of** *Seaver v. Ransom.* [§27.3111] Mrs. Beman wished to leave her home to her niece, Ms. Seaver, when she died. However, Mrs. Beman's husband had already drawn up a will for her which left the house to him. As Mrs. Beman was quite ill when the will was drafted, she and her husband entered into a contract whereby she agreed to sign the will as it was, leaving the house to Mr. Beman. In return, Mr. Beman promised to leave Ms. Seaver enough money in **his** will to make up for Ms. Seaver's not getting the house in Mrs. Beman's will. When Mr. Beman died, he left no money to Ms. Seaver. Ms. Seaver sued his executor, Ransom, to enforce the promise Mr. Beman made to Mrs. Beman. **Held**: Ms. Seaver was a donee beneficiary of the Mr. Beman/Mrs. Beman contract, and was thus entitled to enforce Mr. Beman's promise by suing his estate for breach of Mr. Beman's promised performance.

Recall that to analyze any third party beneficiary situation, the parties must first be characterized. **Mr. Beman was the promisor**, since it was performance of his promise to leave money in his will that would benefit a third person, Ms. Seaver. **Mrs. Beman was the promisee**, since she bargained for the promise benefiting the third party. **Ms. Seaver was the beneficiary**, since she was the party outside the promisor/promisee contract who would benefit by performance of Mr. Beman's (the promisor's) promise.

The next issue is to determine what kind of beneficiary Ms. Seaver was. Ms. Seaver met the test to be a **donee beneficiary** under Section 133(1) for two reasons. First, the purpose of Mrs. Beman in bargaining for her husband's promise to leave money in his will was to make a gift to Ms. Seaver. Second, Ms. Seaver also met the test for a donee beneficiary because Mr. Beman's promise conferred in Ms. Seaver the right to a performance (i.e., the payment of money), that was neither owed to her by Mrs. Beman, nor was supposed by Mrs. Beman to be owing her, nor was asserted by Ms. Seaver to be owed to her. Hence, Ms. Seaver was entitled to sue to enforce the promise even though she was not a party to the contract between Mr. Beman and his wife.

Note that while Mrs. Beman's intention to benefit Ms. Seaver was a gift, that does not mean that the contract failed for lack of consideration as a gift promise (see §7.51). This is because for consideration purposes the relevant question is whether the promise made by Mr. Beman, the promisor, in the contract he entered into with his wife was supported by consideration. Since his promise to leave Ms. Seaver the money was clearly bargained for and given in exchange for receipt of the house, it is amply supported by consideration. The fact that his performance is promised to someone other than the one who provided the consideration is irrelevant (see also §7.4). *Seaver v. Ransom*, 224 N.Y. 233, 120 N.E. 639 (1918).

b. "Creditor" Beneficiaries: Defined and Discussed. [§27.312] A "creditor" beneficiary under the First Restatement was the beneficiary of a contractual promise, the **purpose of which was to satisfy an actual, supposed, or asserted debt the promisee owed the beneficiary**. Once again, the effect of a beneficiary being able to establish "creditor" status was that he or she was entitled to sue the promisor for breach if the promisor did not perform. That is, when the promisor made an enforceable promise in his or her contract with the promisee, the effect was also to create an enforceable duty owing to the creditor beneficiary [Restatement 1st §133(1)(b)].

(1) Example of *Lawrence v. Fox*. [§27.3121] Holly owed Lawrence $300. Holly had the money to re-pay Lawrence, but instead decided to lend the $300 to Fox in return for *Fox's* promise to re-pay the $300 to Lawrence directly to discharge Holly's obligation. Fox ended up paying no one, so Lawrence sued Fox for re-payment of Holly's debt. **Held**: Lawrence was a creditor beneficiary, and was thus entitled to sue Fox to enforce the re-payment promise Fox made to Holly. *Lawrence v. Fox*, 20 N.Y. 268 (1859).

Once again, the first step in analyzing the case is to identify the parties. **Fox was the promisor**, for he contractually promised to do an act (pay $300) which benefited a third party. **Holly was the promisee**, for she bargained for Fox's promise. **Lawrence was the third party beneficiary**, for performance of Fox's promise would benefit him and he was not a party to the promisor/promisee contract.

The next issue in the case is whether Lawrence could be classified as a "creditor" beneficiary so that he would be able to sue Fox for not paying him. (Note, he could not be a "donee" beneficiary for Holly was clearly not bargaining to make a gift of the $300 to Lawrence.) Lawrence satisfies the test of a creditor beneficiary under §133(1)(b) because Holly's purpose in seeking Fox's promise was **to satisfy a duty** that the promisee (Holly) already owed the beneficiary (Lawrence). Hence, Lawrence was entitled to sue Fox when he did not repay the $300.

c. "Incidental" Beneficiary: Defined and Discussed. [§27.313] "Incidental" beneficiaries under the First Restatement were **all** third party contract beneficiaries **who were neither donee nor creditor beneficiaries**. That is, it was a "catchall" category consisting of all the third party beneficiaries in the world who might be benefited by a contract but who were neither creditor nor donee beneficiaries. The effect of being an incidental beneficiary, as opposed to a creditor or donee beneficiary, was that an incidental beneficiary could not enforce the promisor's promise, i.e., a merely incidental beneficiary could not sue the promisor for breach if the promisor failed to perform the contractual promise made to the promisee. A promisor simply owed no duty to an incidental beneficiary as a result of his or her contract with the promisee. This is because any benefit that would come to an incidental beneficiary as a result of the promisor's performance was deemed too indirect or "incidental" to be enforceable by the beneficiary [Restatement 1st §133(1)(c)].

(1) Example. [§27.3131] Bob lived next door to Nancy. His yard was full of unkept weeds, so Bob contracted with Candice to landscape his house. If Candice performed as promised, the value of Nancy's house would increase. Candice breached, however, and did not perform the landscaping. Nancy is not entitled to sue Candice for her breach, for Nancy is only an incidental beneficiary.

Candice was the promisor (making a contractual promise whose performance would have benefited Nancy), **Bob was the promisee** (he bargained for the promise), and **Nancy was the beneficiary.** Nancy is not a donee beneficiary, for the **purpose** of Bob's landscaping his house was not to make a gift to Nancy of the appreciation in the value of her house. Similarly, Nancy is also not a creditor beneficiary, for the **purpose** of Bob's promise was not to satisfy a debt that Bob owed Nancy. Hence, as she is neither a donee nor creditor beneficiary, under the Restatement 1st formulation she is only an incidental beneficiary. As an incidental beneficiary, Nancy is not entitled to sue Candice to enforce her duty to landscape Bob's house, for Candice owed Nancy no duty arising out of the promisor/promisee contract.

2. **MODERN CONTRACT LAW AS EXEMPLIFIED BY THE SECOND RESTATEMENT: "INTENDED" BENEFICIARIES CAN ENFORCE THE PROMISOR'S PROMISE; "INCIDENTAL" BENEFICIARIES CANNOT. [§27.32]**
The drafters of the Second Restatement rejected the three-tiered categorization of third party beneficiaries found in the First Restatement. In its place, the drafters provided that there are only two types of beneficiaries:

(a) "**intended**" beneficiaries; and

(b) "**incidental**" beneficiaries [Restatement 2d §302].

Intended beneficiaries are entitled to enforce the promisor's promise by directly suing the promisor for breach, whereas incidental beneficiaries cannot enforce that promise [Restatement 2d §§304, 315].

a. **"Intended" Beneficiaries: Defined and Discussed. [§27.321]** Section 302(1) of the Restatement 2d defines intended beneficiaries as follows:

[A] beneficiary of a promise is an intended beneficiary if **recognition of a right** to **performance in the beneficiary is appropriate to effectuate the intention of the promisor and promisee, and either**:

(a) the performance of the promise will satisfy an *obligation of the promisee to pay money* to the beneficiary; or

(b) the circumstances indicate that the *promisee intends to give the beneficiary the benefit of the promised performance.*

Hence, there is a two-part test to achieve intended beneficiary status under §302. The first part requires a determination of whether designation as an intended beneficiary is "appropriate to effectuate the intention of the parties." The issue is whether the **promisor and promisee intended to grant the beneficiary a right to enforce the promises** made by the promisor when they entered into their contract. This question is one that can be answered only by a fact finder's sifting through all the circumstances surrounding a particular transaction, but the idea is to determine whether the promisor and promisee were bargaining **directly to provide a benefit to the beneficiary,** or whether the promisor and promisee did not **intend to create an enforceable duty in the beneficiary** when making their contract. If the promisor and promisee did not intend to create such a duty, it would not be "appropriate to effectuate" their intentions to grant the third party intended beneficiary status.

Once it is established that the parties' intent will be furthered if intended beneficiary status is awarded a third party, the second step is to see whether the beneficiary can meet one of the two alternative tests of Restatement 2d §302(1)(a) or (b); that is, to determine whether performance of the promise will satisfy an antecedent *obligation* of the promisee to pay money [§302(1)(a)], or whether the promisee intended to *make a gift* to the beneficiary [§302(1)(b)].

Obviously the definitions given in §§302(1)(a) and (1)(b) are very close to the definitions of creditor and donee beneficiary under the First Restatement (see §§27.311 and 27.312). To use the language adopted by many commentators throughout the remainder of this chapter, intended beneficiaries under the Restatement 2d will be designated as either "creditor-like" intended beneficiaries under §302(1)(a), or "donee-like" intended beneficiaries under §302(1)(b).

(1) Example of *Seaver v. Ransom*. [§27.3211] (The facts of *Seaver* are given in §27.3111.) Under Restatement 2d §302(1)(b), Ms. Seaver would still be able to enforce Mr. Beman's promise, for Ms. Seaver would be classified as a "donee-like" intended beneficiary of the Mr. Beman/Mrs. Beman contract. This is because: (a) recognition of her right to sue Mr. Beman (via his estate) to enforce the promise he made to his wife is appropriate to effectuate the contracting parties' intentions (i.e., Mr. and Mrs. Beman intended to confer a benefit on Ms. Seaver when they entered into their contract); and (b) the circumstances indicate a desire by Mrs. Beman to make a gift of the promised performance to Ms. Seaver.

(2) Example of *Lawrence v. Fox*. [§27.3212] (The facts of *Lawrence* are given in §27.3121.) Under the Restatement 2d §302(1)(a), Lawrence would be classified as a "creditor-like" intended beneficiary, and thus entitled to sue Fox for Fox's failure to repay the loan. This is because: (a) recognition of Lawrence's right to enforce Fox's promise is appropriate to effectuate the contracting parties' intentions (i.e., Holly and Fox intended to benefit Lawrence when they entered into their loan agreement); and (b) performance of Fox's promise will satisfy an antecedent obligation of Holly to pay money to Lawrence.

b. **"Incidental" Beneficiary: Defined and Discussed. [§27.322]** Incidental beneficiaries under the Restatement 2d are defined almost exactly the way incidental beneficiaries were defined under the Restatement 1st (see §27.313). Namely, under Restatement 2d §302(2), "An incidental beneficiary is a beneficiary who is not an intended beneficiary." Once again, it is a catchall category. The effect of being an incidental beneficiary under the Restatement 2d is also identical to being such a beneficiary under the Restatement 1st — namely, incidental beneficiaries cannot sue the promisor for breach of the promisor's contractual duty.

(1) Example. [§27.3221] John was due to be paid by his employer on Friday. He had planned to use the money from his paycheck to pay off his Visa credit card bill. John's employer unjustifiedly fails to pay him. Visa may not enforce the duty of the employer to pay John under the provisions of Restatement 2d §302(2), for Visa is only an incidental beneficiary of the employment contract. This is because:

(a) it is not appropriate in this case to give Visa a right to enforce the promise, for in entering into the employment agreement, neither John nor his employer intended that Visa be given a right to enforce the agreement; and

Sum & Substance QUICK REVIEW of Contracts

(b) performance of the employer's promise would not have satisfied John's obligation to pay money to Visa (i.e., had the employer done what it promised, i.e., paid John, John's debt to Visa would still be owing until John paid the company); thus Visa is not a "creditor-like" intended beneficiary; and

(c) John certainly did not intend a "gift" of his paycheck to Visa — thus Visa is also not a "donee-like" intended beneficiary.

Since it is not an intended beneficiary under §302(1), Visa must be an incidental beneficiary under §302(2), and is thus ineligible to enforce the promisor's promise.

c. **Situations in which Analysis under the First and Second Restatements Would Yield Different Results Regarding When a Beneficiary is Entitled to Enforce a Promisor's Promise. [§27.323]** As noted earlier, the Restatement 2d's alternative tests for attaining intended beneficiary status seem almost identical to the First Restatement's definitions of creditor and donee beneficiary. In fact, the tests for donee beneficiaries under the two Restatements **are** very close and any donee beneficiary under the Restatement 1st would be a "donee-like" intended beneficiary under the Restatement 2d.

There are, however, a few important differences between a creditor beneficiary under the Restatement 1st and a "creditor-like" intended beneficiary under the Restatement 2d. Under §133(1)(b) of the First Restatement, a third party is a creditor beneficiary whenever performance of the promisor's promise would "satisfy an actual, or supposed, or asserted duty of the promisee to the beneficiary." Under Restatement 2d §302(1)(a), a third party is a creditor-like intended beneficiary only when performance of the promisor's promise "will satisfy an obligation of the promisee to pay money to the beneficiary." Hence, these provisions differ in two respects:

(1) Under the Restatement 2d, the obligation of the promisee to the "creditor-like" beneficiary **must be to pay money**. Under the Restatement 1st, the obligation could be to perform any duty; and

(2) Under the Restatement 2d, the monetary obligation owed by the promisee to the creditor-like intended beneficiary **must be an actual one**. Under the Restatement 1st, the obligation could be actual, or one that is merely "supposed" to be owed by the promisee, or one that is only "asserted" to be owed by the beneficiary.

(a) **Example. [§27.3231]** Dave is a gardener who is contractually obligated to mow Steve's lawn twice a month for a year. Dave enters into a contract with Jane, where in return for supplying and planting 3 large trees at Jane's house, Jane promises to perform Dave's obligation to mow Steve's lawn twice a month for the next year.

Dave and Jane have entered into a third party beneficiary contract. **Jane is the promisor; Dave is the promisee; and Steve is the beneficiary.** Under the First Restatement, Steve would be a creditor beneficiary under the Dave/Jane contract and hence entitled to enforce Jane's promise and sue her for breach if she failed to mow his lawn. However, because the obligation Dave (the promisee) owed to Steve (the beneficiary) is not one to pay money, Steve cannot be a "creditor-like" intended beneficiary of the promisor/promisee agreement under Restatement 2d, §302(1). As such, he will be merely an incidental beneficiary under modern contract law, and thus unable to sue Jane if she should breach.

(Note, however, Steve is also a "delegate" and so while he cannot enforce Jane's promise under a third party beneficiary theory, he would be entitled to enforce Jane's promise under a delegation theory [see gen. Chapter Twenty-Nine for a discussion of delegation; and see §29.5, for a discussion of the relationship between third party beneficiary contracts and delegations].

(b) **Example. [§27.3232]** Ryan, an 18-year old high school senior, receives in the mail an unsolicited Fruitomatic fruit slicer. Ryan keeps the product in the box and does not wish to accept it. Under traditional rules of contract formation, of course he is under no obligation to pay for it and his silence cannot be deemed an acceptance of Fruitomatic's offer to have Ryan purchase the machine. [see §4.56]. However, Ryan does not know this and 30 days later he receives an invoice from the Fruitomatic company. Thinking he has to pay the bill, Ryan thereafter enters into a contract with his parents whereby they will pay the $150 invoice if he paints the living room the next weekend. Under the First Restatement, Fruitomatic would be a creditor beneficiary of the Ryan/Ryan's parents agreement, and thus could enforce Ryan's parents' promise to pay the invoice by suing them directly if they did not pay the $150. Fruitomatic could **not** enforce Ryan's parents' promise, however, under Restatement 2d §302(1), because Ryan only "supposed" he owed, but did not actually owe, a monetary debt to Fruitomatic.

d. **Important Principles in Analyzing Third Party Beneficiary Contracts under Modern Contract Law. [§27.324]** There are certain principles which need to be understood in order to completely analyze third party beneficiary contracts. These are discussed below.

(1) **Performance of the Promisor's Promise Need Not be Made Directly to the Third Party in Order for the Third Party to be an Intended Beneficiary. [§27.3241]** For a third party to be an intended beneficiary under modern contract law, most often the promisor's promise will be rendered directly to the beneficiary. However, this is not a necessary requirement. For example, assume Dorothy instructs her lawyer to make sure her will includes a bequest of $10,000 to her nephew Bob. Performance of the promisor's (the lawyer's) duty is to be rendered directly to Dorothy, i.e., the making of the will with an appropriate clause benefiting Bob. However, Bob is nevertheless an intended beneficiary of the lawyer/Dorothy contract, and the lawyer owes a duty to Bob to ensure the bequest is made. Thus, if the lawyer does not include a provision for Bob in Dorothy's will, Bob may sue the lawyer for breach of the duty owed him even though performance was to be rendered to the promisee.

(2) **The Identity of The Intended Beneficiary Need Not be Known at the Time the Promisor/Promisee Contract is Made. [§27.3242]** It is not necessary that the identity of a beneficiary be known at the time the promisor/promisee contract is entered into in order to make the beneficiary an intended one [Restatement 2d §308]. For example, assume a radio station contracts with an airline to fly the winner of a station-sponsored contest to Australia. Even though the identity of the beneficiary is not known at the time of the making of the radio station/airline contract, the winner of the contest, whoever it ultimately turns out to be, is nonetheless an intended beneficiary who can sue the airline if it breaches its contract with the radio station by refusing to fly the contestant to Australia.

(3) An Intended Beneficiary Need Not Manifest any Agreement to the Promisor/Promisee Contract in Order to Gain Enforceable Rights Against the Promisee. [§27.3243] Perhaps surprisingly, a third party can become an intended beneficiary without even knowing it. In other words, once the promisor and promisee make the contract that confers intended beneficiary status on a third party, the third party is a viable intended beneficiary regardless of whether he or she knows it.

Note, however, that if for some reason the beneficiary does not want to be an intended beneficiary, he or she has the right to disclaim such status within a reasonable time after learning of the promisor/promisee agreement (see §27.3244).

(4) A Beneficiary May Disclaim His or Her Rights to Enforce the Promisor's Promise. [§27.3244] A third party need not acquiesce in, or even know about, the promisor/promisee agreement to become an intended third party beneficiary to that contract (see §27.3243). However, sometimes when the beneficiary finds out about the agreement, the beneficiary will not find its terms acceptable. In that case, contract law provides that the beneficiary has the power to "opt out" of having to accept satisfaction of the debt by the promisor, and may continue to insist on satisfaction by the promisee only. The formal name for such a choice is **disclaimer by the beneficiary,** and it is effectively accomplished when:

(i) the beneficiary gives **notice** of his or her decision to disclaim any obligation owing from the promisor;

(ii) such notice is given **within a reasonable time** after learning of the existence of the third party beneficiary contract; and

(iii) such **notice is not received after the beneficiary has already assented** to the contract [Restatement 2d §306].

If the beneficiary says nothing one way or another after learning of the contract's terms, he or she is deemed to have impliedly ratified the arrangement by silence after the expiration of a reasonable time, and may not thereafter disclaim it [Restatement 2d §306, Com. a].

(a) Example. [§27.3244-1] Ted is obligated to repay Larry $100 on August 1. On June 1, Ted enters into a contract with June whereby June promises to repay Ted's debt to Larry. At that point, whether Larry knows it or not, he is an intended creditor-like beneficiary of the Ted/June contract and is entitled to sue June if she does not pay him.

A week later, on June 7, Larry learns of the Ted/June agreement. If for some reason it is important to Larry that **Ted** repay him, Larry is entitled to notify June and Ted that he (Larry) is disclaiming his intended beneficiary status, and demanding that Ted re-pay the debt as promised on August 1. If Larry does not give such notice within a reasonable time after learning of the Ted/June contract, he will be deemed to have ratified his status as an intended beneficiary and will not thereafter be able to disclaim it.

3. **RECURRING FACT SITUATIONS CONCERNING WHETHER A BENEFICIARY IS INTENDED OR INCIDENTAL. [§27.33]** Over time, certain recurring fact situations have arisen which present the issue of whether the beneficiary is entitled to sue to enforce the promisor's promise, i.e., whether the beneficiary is intended or incidental. The most significant of these are discussed below.

a. **A Citizen's Right to Enforce a Government's Contract with a Private Party to Perform a Municipal Service. [§27.331]** One recurring third party beneficiary issue has to do with the rights of citizens as beneficiaries when the government enters into a contract with a private company to perform a municipal service. For example, assume that under the city charter a local government is under a duty to keep the streets in good repair. The city thereafter enters into a contract with Repair Co. to keep the streets in good order, but Repair Co. breaches. The issue is whether the citizens of the town are entitled to sue Repair Co. as intended beneficiaries of the Repair Co./City contract. The answer given by most courts is that **citizens are not entitled to sue** to enforce the promises of a private company such as Repair Co. In other words, most courts hold that citizens are only incidental, not intended, beneficiaries of such contracts with private companies performing traditionally municipal functions.

The rationale for these decisions is as follows: The citizen is an incidental beneficiary unless he or she can meet the tests of Restatement 2d §302(1). To become an intended beneficiary under §302, the citizen first must establish that the city and the private company **intended** to confer on the citizen an enforceable right to the private company's promised performance. Courts generally find that such an intention was not present.

Second, even if such intention could be found, the citizen would also have to establish that he or she was either a "donee-like" or "creditor-like" intended beneficiary. The citizen cannot be a "creditor-like" beneficiary, because the government's duty to the citizen is not one to pay money (see §27.32). The citizen is not a "donee-like" beneficiary, because typically there is no evidence that the municipality wanted to make a "gift" of the road repair to the citizen. Hence, the citizens must be incidental beneficiaries and thus, not entitled to sue to enforce the contract [Restatement 2d §313].

Many commentators have expressed the view that a neutral application of third party beneficiary rules to these kinds of situations would, in fact, allow the citizen to recover against the private company on a donee-like beneficiary basis. These commentators thus believe that the real reason for the rule discussed above is policy-based. That is, if contract law permitted citizens to sue private companies such as Repair Co., it would create an excessive financial burden for them, i.e., if **every** citizen had a right to sue when the road was not fixed properly, it would be incredibly expensive for the private company. In turn, this would lead to a decrease in the number of private companies willing to do such work, which would eventually produce an overall decline in services available to the public [Restatement 2d §313, Com. a]. (See Case Squibs section, *Moch v. Rensselaer Water Co.*)

b. **Construction Contracts. [§27.332]** The second type of recurring fact situation involving third party beneficiary issues arises out of a developer/general contractor/subcontractor relationship. As explained previously (see §8.342), after a developer selects a general contractor for a large construction project, the general contractor enters into contracts with one or more subcontractors to perform discrete parts of the construction project. The third party beneficiary issue arises upon the subcontractor's breach. The question is whether the **developer** can bring suit against the subcontractor on the theory that the developer is an intended beneficiary of the subcontractor's promises made in the subcontractor/general contractor contract. The answer usually given is **developers are not entitled to sue contractors**. Once again, the courts typically find that the developer in such cases cannot establish the elements to prove he or she is an intended beneficiary and thus, as an incidental beneficiary, the developer is owed no duty by the subcontractor.

E. **RIGHTS OF THE PROMISOR IN A SUIT BROUGHT BY THE BENEFICIARY. [§27.4]** Over time, contract law has developed rules governing the rights of the promisor in suits by the beneficiary.

1. **AN INTENDED BENEFICIARY IS SUBJECT TO ANY DEFENSE THE PROMISOR HAS AGAINST THE PROMISEE. [§27.41]** An intended third party beneficiary of a promisor/promisee agreement receives no more rights against the promisor than those enjoyed by the promisee. Hence any defense that could be asserted by the promisor if he or she were sued by the promisee can also be asserted against the intended beneficiary. As some courts and commentators put it, "the intended beneficiary stands in the shoes of the promisee," and is thus subject to any defenses that the promisor could assert against the promisee if it was the promisee who sued instead of the beneficiary.

   a. **Example. [§27.411]** Eileen is contractually obligated to pay $1,000/month to Central Bank on her mortgage. Eileen is strapped for cash and so offers to sell her car to Judy, receiving in return Judy's promise to make the next three mortgage payments. Eileen neither delivers the car nor makes the mortgage payments herself. Because she did not receive the car, Judy of course did not make the mortgage payments either. The issue is whether Central Bank, as a creditor-like intended beneficiary of the Judy/Eileen contract, can successfully sue Judy (as the promisor) for breach? Contract law holds it cannot.

   Judy has a complete defense to any such suit brought by the Bank. That is, because the beneficiary "stands in the shoes of the promisee," Central Bank's right to enforce Judy's promise is subject to any defense Judy could assert against Eileen if Eileen had sued Judy for her failure to pay. Obviously if Eileen (the promisee) sued Judy, Judy would have a material breach defense (Eileen never delivered the car), and thus, she is entitled to raise that same defense against the Bank because a beneficiary (the Bank) stands in the shoes of the promisee and is subject to the same defenses as the promisor would have against the promisee if the promisee brought suit. (Of course, the Bank can still sue Eileen for the payments (see §27.5 for a discussion of the promisor's rights against the promisee.)

SPECIAL CASE SQUIB

   b. **Example of *Rouse v. United States*. [§27.412]** Ms. Winston contracted with Associated Contractors to install a furnace in her home. She financed the purchase by signing a $1,008.37 promissory note, payable to Associated Contractors at the rate of $28.01/month. Under a program then in existence, the U.S. Government guaranteed payment in full of the promissory note if the obligor stopped paying, i.e., if there was a "default" in the note's repayment. Thereafter, Associated Contractors sold the note to Union Trust Co., and the government's guarantee in case of default was also transferred to Union Trust.

Ms. Winston made the required monthly payments under the note until she sold her house to Rouse. In the sales contract for the house, Rouse specifically promised to make the $28.01 monthly payments, but never did so. Accordingly, Union Trust sought payment of the entire outstanding balance of the note from the government under the government's guarantee against default. The government paid Union Trust, and thereafter brought suit against Rouse to recoup its payment. One of Rouse's defenses was that Ms. Winston had misrepresented to him the condition of the furnace.

One issue in the case was whether Rouse was entitled to assert the misrepresentation defense against the government, when it was Ms. Winston who made the representation. **Held**: Rouse was entitled to use the defense to defeat the government's claim. (See Case Squib section, *Rouse v. United States*.)

To understand the decision, the parties must first be categorized. **Rouse was the promisor**, for he promised to make payments for the benefit of Union Trust Co. (and thus for the benefit of the government as guarantor of the note). **Ms. Winston was the promisee**, for she initially owed the money and bargained for Rouse's promise to relieve her of a debt. **The Union Trust Co., and thereafter the United States, were intended "creditor-like" beneficiaries**, for performance of Mr. Rouse's promise would inure to their benefit. Hence, the legal question in the case was whether the promisor (Rouse) could assert a defense in a suit brought by a beneficiary (the United States) that he could have asserted had the suit had been brought by the promisee (Ms. Winston). Since Mr. Rouse clearly could have used Ms. Winston's misrepresentations as a defense had Ms. Winston tried to sue him, he was entitled to use her misrepresentations as a defense in the suit brought by the government. That is, the United States, as an intended beneficiary, merely "stepped into Ms. Winston's shoes," and was thereby subject to the defenses that could be asserted against her had she sued Rouse.

---

2. **AN INTENDED BENEFICIARY'S RIGHT TO SUE THE PROMISOR IS SUBJECT TO ANY LIMITING TERMS OF THE PROMISOR/PROMISEE CONTRACT. [§27.42]** An intended beneficiary's right to enforce the promisor's promise is subject to any limiting terms in the promisor/promisee contract. Thus, for example, if the promisor's duty is conditional upon the occurrence of an event, and that event does not occur, the beneficiary cannot bring suit for a failure of the promisor to perform. This is because the promisor's duty in such a case never became enforceable by either the promisee or the beneficiary.

   a. **Example. [§27.421]** Leo wanted to make a gift to his friend Bill. He entered into an agreement with his stockbroker Margaret whereby Margaret was contractually obligated to deliver $1,000 to Bill "on the condition that Leo's IBM stock was worth more than $200/share at any time before Dec. 1." The stock price never broke $200/share before Dec. 1. While Bill is clearly an intended "donee-like" beneficiary, he may not successfully sue Margaret to enforce payment of the $1,000, for his rights as beneficiary are subject to the terms of the Leo/Margaret contract.

3. **AN INTENDED THIRD PARTY BENEFICIARY'S RECOVERY AGAINST THE PROMISOR IS SUBJECT TO OFFSET BY THE AMOUNT OF ANY DAMAGES THE PROMISOR SUFFERS AS A RESULT OF AN IMMATERIAL BREACH BY THE PROMISEE. [§27.43]** An intended beneficiary has no more rights to enforce the promisor's promise than does the promisee. This is another way of saying the beneficiary

only "stands in the shoes of the promisee." Hence, if the promisor would be entitled to an offset in the damages owed due to an immaterial breach by the promisee in a suit brought by the promisee, the beneficiary's recovery is subject to that same offset.

a. **Example. [§27.431]** Maxine owes Keith $5,000. She enters into a contract with Tom whereby Tom promises to pay Maxine's debt to Keith in return for Maxine's promise to paint Tom's house, including the wooden windows. Maxine paints the house but fails to paint the windows. Tom reasonably hires another painter to paint them for $400. At that point, Tom is only obligated to pay Keith $4,600, because Keith (the beneficiary) can only enforce the contract to the extent Maxine could. Since Maxine's recovery would be subject to a $400 recoupment due to her immaterial breach, Keith's recovery is offset by that same amount.

Note, however, that while the beneficiary is said to "stand in the shoes" of the promisee, this is only true to a point. If the promisee materially breached the contract so that the promisee in fact owes the promisor damages, the promisor must sue the **promisee** to recover, not the beneficiary. For example, if Maxine had done no work on Tom's house, and Tom reasonably ended up paying another painter $5,500 to do the work, the extra $500 in damages would be due from Maxine alone. That is, Tom could not sue Keith seeking $500 in damages just because Keith "stood in Maxine's shoes" regarding his rights as an intended beneficiary.

F. **RIGHTS OF AN INTENDED BENEFICIARY TO SUE THE PROMISEE. [§27.5]** The focus of this chapter to this point has been on the right of the beneficiary to sue the **promisor**. However, often beneficiaries would rather sue the **promisee**. This is especially true in "creditor-like" beneficiary cases where it is the promisee that the beneficiary knew in the first place, for it was the promisee who was already indebted to the beneficiary before formation of the promisor/promisee contract. The rule regarding a beneficiary's right to sue the promisee is simple: **An intended beneficiary retains whatever rights he or she had to bring suit against the promisee before the promisor/promisee agreement was made.**

In a "creditor-like" intended beneficiary situation, this rule means that an intended beneficiary can choose to enforce **either** of the two duties owed him or her: (i) the antecedent duty to pay the debt, owed by the promisee; or (ii) the new duty to pay the debt, owed by the promisor. Hence, the beneficiary is entitled to bring suit and recover a judgment against either the promisee, or the promisor, or both; but, of course, the beneficiary is limited to only one satisfaction of that judgment.

In a "donee-like" intended beneficiary situation, the beneficiary likely will be able to enforce only the **new** duty of the promisor. That is, creation of the promisor/promisee contract does not create a duty where none existed before. It only fails to discharge whatever duty already existed between the promisee and the beneficiary. If all the promisee intended was to make a gift to the beneficiary, then the beneficiary cannot enforce the gift promise of the promisee (see §27.3211 for an explanation of why the **promisor's** duty is nonetheless enforceable even when the **promisee** is only intending to make a gift).

1. **EXAMPLE. [§27.51]** Betty owes Earl $10,000 and enters into a valid contract with Ralph in which Ralph promises to repay her debt to Earl. If the debt is not repaid, Earl, the beneficiary of the Ralph/Betty contract, can either sue Betty (the promisee) on her old promise to pay, and/or Ralph (the promisor) to enforce his new promise to pay arising from the Ralph/Betty contract. However, Earl is only entitled to one complete satisfaction.

2. **EXAMPLE. [§27.52]** Kelly takes out a life insurance policy naming his sister Tara as his beneficiary. Kelly dies and the insurance company does not pay Tara. Tara as "donee-like" intended beneficiary, may not bring suit against Kelly's heirs to enforce the gift promise, for Kelly was under no obligation to name Tara as his beneficiary when he took out the insurance contract. That is, Kelly's decision to enter into a third party beneficiary contract with the insurance company does not create a duty where none existed before. Hence, Tara's only claim for breach is against the promisor, the insurance company.

G. **RIGHTS OF THE PROMISEE AGAINST THE PROMISOR. [§27.6]** If a promisor under a third party beneficiary contract breaches the agreement, he or she is liable to **both** the promisee **and** to the beneficiary. Hence, the promisee and the beneficiary may both bring suit, although of course the promisor is liable for only one recovery.

1. **EXAMPLE. [27.61]** Recall the Maxine/Keith/Tom hypothetical from §27.431, whereby Maxine owes Keith $5,000, but agrees to paint Tom's house in return for Tom's promise to repay Maxine's debt to Keith. This time assume Maxine does all the painting competently, but Tom nevertheless fails to pay either Keith or Maxine. Both Keith, as an intended beneficiary, and Maxine, as promisee, are entitled to sue Tom for his non-payment, although Tom is only required to pay a total of $5,000.

H. **RIGHTS OF THE PROMISEE AND PROMISOR TO MODIFY THEIR CONTRACT TO THE DISADVANTAGE OF AN INTENDED BENEFICIARY. [§27.7]** Once a promisor and promisee have entered into a contract making a third party an intended beneficiary, a question often arises whether promisor and promisee can later modify (or even rescind) their agreement to the disadvantage of the beneficiary. All courts agree that at some point the rights of the beneficiary vest and the promisor and promisee cannot thereafter enforceably modify their agreement. However, there is a split of opinion as to **when** the beneficiary's rights vest. The major views are set forth below.

1. **VIEW OF THE RESTATEMENT 2D: AN INTENDED BENEFICIARY'S RIGHTS VEST UPON HIS OR HER RELIANCE ON THE PROMISOR'S PROMISE. [§27.71]** The Restatement 2d sets forth what is probably the majority view on this issue, which is that the beneficiary's rights vest upon a material change of position in justifiable reliance on the promisor's promise [Restatement 2d §311(3)]. Hence, the promisor and promisee can freely modify or terminate the promisor's duty to the beneficiary until the beneficiary both **knows** of the promisor's promise, and **relies on it** to some extent.

Note that the promisor and promisee may not be aware of the beneficiary's reliance, and thus they may modify their contract to the beneficiary's detriment in good faith. However, under the Restatement 2d view, such a modification is not enforceable after the beneficiary's reliance, regardless of whether the modification was done in good faith.

a. **Example. [§27.711]** Ned and Sara have entered into an enforceable contract whereby Ned promised to pay $1,000 to Ashley, in settlement of an antecedent monetary debt Sara owes Ashley. Hence, **Ned is the promisor; Sara is the promisee;** and **Ashley is an intended third party beneficiary.** Under the contract, Ned's performance (i.e., payment of the $1,000 to Ashley) is due August 10. On August 1, Ned and Sara meet and modify their agreement so that Ned will now pay the $1,000 directly to Sara. The issue is whether Ned and Sara (the promisor and promisee) are entitled to make an enforceable modification of their contract to Ashley's detriment.

The answer to that question under the Restatement 2d view depends on whether Ashley both: (i) knows that she is an intended third party beneficiary; and (ii) can establish some change of position in reliance on Ned's promise. **Both** must occur before Ashley's rights are vested, i.e., before her rights as a beneficiary are irrevocable and unmodifiable by the promisor and promisee. Thus if, for example, Sara has broken a business appointment so that she can meet Ned at a particular time and place on August 10 to receive the payment, her rights as an intended beneficiary have vested. If she only knows of the Ned/Sara contract but can show no reliance on it, or if she does not know of the contract, Sara and Ned's modification is enforceable. Note that even if the modification is enforceable, it really is not all that unfair to Ashley, for she still retains her right to sue Sara to repay the original debt.

Note also that Ashley may have canceled her business appointment to make time to meet Ned without letting either Ned or Sara know. That is, Ned and Sara may have modified their agreement in good faith, before becoming aware of Ashley's reliance on Ned's promise. It does not matter. Once there has been reliance, an intended beneficiary's rights are irrevocable and unmodifiable under this view.

2. **MINORITY VIEW: AN INTENDED BENEFICIARY'S RIGHTS VEST IMMEDIATELY UPON EXECUTION OF THE PROMISOR/PROMISEE CONTRACT. [§27.72]** A minority of courts hold that an intended beneficiary's rights vest immediately upon execution of the promisor/promisee contract. This is true regardless of whether the beneficiary knows at the time that he or she is a beneficiary. Hence, under this view, once the promisor/ promisee contract is formed, the promisor and promisee may not thereafter validly modify their agreement to the beneficiary's detriment.

3. **MINORITY VIEW: THE BENEFICIARY'S RIGHTS VEST UPON KNOWLEDGE OF THE PROMISOR'S PROMISE. [§27.73]** Another minority view holds that the beneficiary's rights vest as soon as he or she learns of the promisor/promisee contract which makes him or her an intended beneficiary. Hence, under this view the beneficiary's rights can be changed so long as he or she does not know that he or she is a beneficiary. However, once the third party learns of his or her status as an intended beneficiary, no modifications to the detriment of the beneficiary may validly be made by the promisor and promisee, regardless of whether the beneficiary relies on the promise.

I. **DISTINCTION BETWEEN CREDITOR-LIKE INTENDED THIRD PARTY BENEFICIARY CONTRACTS AND ACCORDS OR NOVATIONS. [§27.8]** It is important to be able to explain the differences between third party beneficiary contracts with a creditor-like intended beneficiary, and an accord or a novation transaction (partly because it is a favorite question of Contracts professors). While the doctrines are related, there is one big difference between them. In novations and accords, the creditor must **agree** that performance (or promised performance) by a third party will discharge the antecedent debt (see §§24.2 and 24.3 for an explanation of accords and novations). In a creditor-type third party beneficiary situation, the beneficiary (i.e., the creditor) need not agree to the promisee's performance of the promisee's obligation. In fact, the beneficiary need not even know about it, and once he or she **does** know of it, he or she can disclaim it (see §§27.3243, 27.3244).

1. **EXAMPLE. [§27.81]** Bart owes Homer $1,000. Because Bart does not have the money to repay Homer, he enters into negotiations with Homer and his friend Jennifer, hoping he can sell his watch for the necessary $1,000. After a good deal of negotiation, Homer agrees to discharge Bart's duty to pay him $1,000 and replace it with Jennifer's promise to pay Homer $1,000 upon Bart's tender of the watch to Jennifer. Depending on how they structure the deal, it can be either an accord or a novation, but in either event Homer is

not an intended third party beneficiary of the Jennifer/Bart contract. That is, by agreeing to accept Jennifer's performance *in lieu* of Bart's debt, Homer's rights are are those of an obligee in a novation or accord which are quite different from those of an intended beneficiary.

2. **EXAMPLE. [§27.82]** Same situation, except this time Bart and Jennifer have entered a contract whereby Bart agrees to sell his watch to Jennifer in return for Jennifer's promise to pay $1,000 to Homer. Homer is not involved in the negotiations. This time, Homer is a third party creditor-like intended beneficiary, even if he does not know it at the time the contract is made. When he finds out about it, he is entitled to disclaim his status as beneficiary, or he is entitled to remain silent and implicitly ratify it. However, Homer's rights are only those of an intended beneficiary. For Homer's rights to become those of an obligee in an accord or a novation situation, **Homer would have to affirmatively agree** to accept Jennifer's performance (or her promised performance) in satisfaction of Bart's antecedent obligation to Homer.

J. **DISTINCTION BETWEEN A THIRD PARTY BENEFICIARY CONTRACT SITUATION AND AN ASSIGNMENT SITUATION. [§27.9]** See §28.3.

Sum & Substance QUICK REVIEW of Contracts

CHAPTER TWENTY-EIGHT: ASSIGNMENTS

A. ASSIGNMENTS GENERALLY. [§28.0] When a party enters into a bilateral contract, he or she obtains the right to the promised performance of another. While not discussed in this Outline until now, the right to receive that promised performance is a type of intangible property (see §31.0 for a further elaboration of this principle). One of the attributes of property is that it is transferable. When one contracting party validly transfers the right to receive the promised performance of the other to a third person, contract law calls the transfer an **assignment**.

B. DEFINITION, TERMINOLOGY, AND MAJOR EFFECTS OF ASSIGNMENTS. [§28.1] As with third party beneficiary situations, the threshold concept to understanding assignments is to understand the terminology contract law uses in analyzing such transactions. This terminology is described and defined below.

An assignment is a transfer of contractual rights [Restatement 2d §317]. (The transfer of contractual **duties** is known as a **delegation**; see Chapter Twenty-Nine.)

There are typically three parties in an assignment:

(1) The **Assignor (or Obligee)**. The assignor (sometimes called the "obligee") is the party who transfers a right under a contract to a third party. That is, the assignor is already a party to a contract before the assignment occurs. It is the assignor who transfers the right to *receive* the other contracting party's performance to a third person.

(2) The **Obligor**. The obligor is the party who initially owes a contractual duty of performance to the assignor but who, after the assignment, owes that duty to a third person.

(3) The **Assignee**. The assignee is not a party to the initial assignor/obligor contract. The assignee is the third party who receives from the assignor the enforceable right to performance by the obligor.

The principal consequence of an effective assignment is that the assignee acquires the right to enforce the obligor's promise. That is, the duty that the obligor had previously promised and owed to the assignor is now owed to the assignee. Further, it is the assignee, and **only** the assignee, who is entitled to sue the obligor for breach if the obligor unjustifiably fails to perform.

1. **EXAMPLE. [§28.11]** Lorenzo is under a contractual duty to sell his watch to Lori next week for $500. Lorenzo would like to make a gift of the $500 to his sister, Darla. Accordingly, he instructs Lori to pay the $500 for the watch directly to Darla.

   An assignment has taken place. **Lorenzo is the assignor**, for it was he who had a contractual right to receive performance from Lori (payment of $500), and who transferred that right to a third party (Darla). **Lori is the obligor**, for she was under a duty to render performance to Lorenzo, but as a result of the assignment, she is now obligated to render that performance to a third person (Darla). **Darla is the assignee**, for she is the person who was not originally a party to the assignor/obligor contract, and who is now owed performance by the obligor (Lori). If Lori does not perform it is Darla, and only Darla, who can sue to enforce the promise.

C. TYPES OF ASSIGNMENTS. [§28.2] Contract law has categorized assignments into two types: "gratuitous assignments" and "assignments for value."

1. **"GRATUITOUS ASSIGNMENTS": DEFINED AND DISCUSSED. [§28.21]** A gratuitous assignment is one in which the assignor's **purpose** in making the transfer of the contract right is **to confer a gift** on the assignee.

   a. **Example. [§28.211]** Uncle Joe would like to give his niece Penny $5,000. Joe is owed $5,000 under a loan he made to Jill, a friend of his. If Joe validly transfers his right to receive the $5,000 to his niece, an assignment has taken place. **Joe is the assignor** (because he has transferred a right to performance under a contract to a third party); **Jill is the obligor** (for she was obligated to pay Joe and, as a result of the transfer, is now obligated to pay Penny); and **Penny is the assignee** (because she was not a party to the Joe/Jill contract and now has a right to enforce Jill's re-payment promise).

   This is a **gratuitous assignment**, because Uncle Joe's purpose in making the assignment to Penny was to make a gift of the money to her. Upon the assignment it is Penny, and only Penny, who is owed the obligation of payment. Hence, if Jill does not re-pay the $5,000 when due, only Penny is entitled to sue her for breach.

   Note that the promise to pay Penny does not fail for lack of consideration because Jill's promise to pay is supported by whatever consideration she received for it in the loan from Uncle Joe. That is, so long as her promise to pay **Uncle Joe** was supported by consideration, Uncle Joe's transfer of his right to receive payment to someone else does not make the promise unenforceable. In other words, the fact that the identity of who Jill is supposed to pay does not change the fact that her promise to repay the loan is supported by consideration and thus enforceable.

2. **"ASSIGNMENT FOR VALUE": DEFINED AND DISCUSSED. [§28.22]** An assignment for value is one in which the assignee has given consideration to the assignor in order to receive the benefits of the obligor's performance. One of the most common types of assignments for value used in business transactions (and typically covered in first year Contracts courses) is accounts receivable financing.

   a. **Example. [§28.221]** Dennis owns a wine shop and sells wine to a number of restaurants on 60 days credit. The total amount he is owed by these restaurants at any one time varies, but it averages approximately $300,000. Most small businesses (and many large ones) do not like to keep such credit accounts on their books. They would prefer to sell the rights to collect the accounts to a financial institution, thereby getting cash immediately (rather than waiting the 60 days before the account is paid), and transferring the risk of the debtor's non-payment to someone else. Of course, a bank willing to purchase the right to collect such receivables will not pay Dennis the full amount of the debt, given both the risk of non-payment and the time value of money (i.e., getting $100 today is more valuable than getting $100 sixty days from now, because the $100 paid today can earn interest and thus be worth more than $100 in sixty days). Hence, banks and other financial institutions will typically discount the amount of the receivables by about 20-30%. A bank thus would pay Dennis $225,000 today (using a 25% discount), for the right to collect $300,000 from Dennis's customers in the future.

   In the transaction giving Dennis the $225,000, an assignment has taken place. **Dennis is the assignor, the restaurants are the obligors, and the bank is the assignee.** This type of assignment is an "assignment for value," since the **assignee (the bank)** gave consideration **to the assignor** (Dennis) for the assignment. Specifically, it is an "accounts receivable financing" type of assignment for value because Dennis has assigned the right to receive payments from his credit account customers as a way to finance his business.

D. ELEMENTS NECESSARY TO MAKE AN EFFECTIVE ASSIGNMENT. [§28.3] In order to make an **effective** assignment, the following elements must be satisfied:

(1) The assignor must manifest a **present** intention to transfer an existing contractual right to the assignee without further action by the assignor;

(2) The assignment must be "permissible," i.e., there must be no prohibition against the assignment of that type of contract right; and

(3) In most cases, the assignee must also manifest his or her acceptance of the assignment.

1. THE ASSIGNOR MUST MANIFEST A PRESENT INTENTION TO TRANSFER AN *EXISTING* CONTRACTUAL RIGHT. [§28.31] The first element of an effective assignment requires the assignor to manifest an intention to transfer an *existing* contractual right to the assignee [Restatement 2d §324]. Perhaps surprisingly, an assignment can be effective if the assignor manifests his or her intention to **anyone**, but of course, usually such manifestation is made to the assignee and/or the obligor. No special words are required for an assignment, and in close cases it is for the court to determine from an examination of all the surrounding circumstances whether the words of the purported assignment actually manifest the requisite intent.

To meet this test, the assignment must be an actual present transfer of the contractual right and **not require any further action by the assignor**. If any further action is required, that may constitute a separate contract by the purported assignor, the subject of which is his or her promise to transfer rights in the future. However, it is not an assignment, for that requires the **present** transfer of **existing** contractual rights [Restatement 2d §330]; (see §28.371).

a. Example. [§28.311] Linda is under a contractual duty to pay Margaret $1,000 on May 15. Margaret owes Brian $900 on May 10. Brian expresses to Margaret his concern as to whether she will have the money to pay him. Accordingly, she promises Brian that if she does not repay Brian the $900 on May 10, on May 14 she will make an assignment to him of her right to Linda's $1,000 payment. Brian agrees to this proposition. **There has been no assignment,** for Margaret has made only a promise to assign in the future. That is, while Margaret has an existing contractual right to performance from Linda, she did not transfer that right to Brian. She only promised that she **would** transfer the right in the future. Because the assignor would have to take further action before the assignee has an enforceable right to the obligor's (Linda's) performance, no assignment has occurred. Hence, if neither Margaret nor Linda pays Brian, Brian's rights are only against Margaret.

If Margaret and Brian had agreed that in lieu of her paying him $900 on the 10th, she would presently assign to him her right to collect the $1,000 from Linda on the 15th, then a valid assignment would have taken place. In that case, Brian would immediately acquire rights against Linda, and could sue her if she did not perform.

b. Example. [§28.312] Sally owed David $10,000 on Monday, but did not have the cash to pay him. She asked for one day's extension, promising David that she would go to the pawn shop the next day, obtain a loan on her heirloom bracelet, and assign her rights to receive the loan proceeds to David. The next day the pawn shop offered to lend her $10,000 with her bracelet as security, and Sally told the pawn shop owner to mail the check to David.

There has been no assignment. On Monday, Sally only bound herself to make an assignment to a contract not yet in existence. On Tuesday, she did not enter into a contract and thereafter assign rights to it to David. Rather, she entered into a third party beneficiary contract whereby David became a creditor-type intended beneficiary of the pawn shop owner's promise (see §28.37 for a further discussion of the difference between third party beneficiaries and assignments). Hence, David is entitled to enforce the pawn shop owner's promise to mail him the check, but as a third party beneficiary, not as an assignee.

c. **Special Rule under Article 9 of the UCC: After-Acquired Property Clauses.** **[§28.313]** Recall the Dennis/restaurants/bank example of accounts receivable financing discussed in §28.221. There, Dennis is a wine shop owner and has $300,000 in accounts receivable from various restaurants which he assigns for value to the bank for $225,000. A practical problem that arises in such financing is that every day Dennis sells more wine to the restaurants. Contract law could require that Dennis go to the bank every night and fill out more forms for each account receivable assignment he makes, but that would be cumbersome. Hence, Article 9 of the UCC specifically permits Dennis to assign all the accounts receivable he presently has, and all "after acquired" accounts in a single transaction [UCC §9-204].

In return, the bank will set up a line of credit that Dennis may draw upon every time he transfers a new account receivable to the bank. As such, this arrangement avoids a lot of complications and paperwork. While some claim that after-acquired property clauses are an **exception** to the rules against assignment of future rights, that really is not true. After-acquired property clauses are only promises to assign contract rights in the future. It is just that the promise to assign is self-executing, i.e., as soon as the account comes in, it is automatically assigned to the bank. However, the assignment is not effective until an actual contract right is transferred. Before that, the bank merely has Dennis's promise to assign an account.

2. **THERE MUST BE NO PROHIBITION AGAINST ASSIGNMENT OF THE PARTICULAR RIGHT. [§28.32]** Even if the manifestation of the assignor's present intent to transfer an existing contractual right can be established, a purported assignment may still not be effective. This is because contract law has established several limitations as to what rights can be assigned. While these rules have changed somewhat over time, the current rules are as follows:

Generally all contract rights may be assigned [Restatement 2d §317(4)]. A contract right may not be assigned only when:

(1) The assignment **violates public policy** [Restatement 2d §317(2)(b)] (see §28.321);

(2) The assignment would **materially and adversely affect the obligor's rights, duties or justified expectations** under his or her contract with the assignor [Restatement 2d §317(2)(a)] (see §28.322); or

(3) An assignor's right to assign duties is **specifically and enforceably prohibited under the assignor/obligor** contract [Restatement 2d §317(2)(c)] (see §28.323).

Each of these limitations is discussed and illustrated below.

a. A Purported Assignment that Violates Public Policy is Ineffective. [§28.321] Courts and legislatures are empowered to nullify any purported assignment if they believe it would violate public policy [Restatement 2d §317(2)(b)]. By far the most common example of the use of such power is the prohibition against an employee's ability to assign future wages. That is, **in almost every state an employee cannot assign the right to collect future wages due the employee to a creditor**.

The reason for voiding such an assignment on public policy grounds is, in part, based on the belief that when an employee does not receive the full value of his or her employment, there may be a lack of incentive for the employee to work as hard as he or she would otherwise do. For example, assume Doug was supposed to receive a net $1,000 per week from his employer. However, because of previous debts, Doug has entered into multiple assignments whereby he will only receive $300/week from his employer, and his creditors will split the remaining $700. In such a case, there is a worry that Doug may look at his duties differently when he only personally receives $300 as opposed to when he gets $1,000.

b. A Purported Assignment that Materially and Adversely Affects the Obligor's Rights, Duties, and Justified Expectations as to Return Performance is Ineffective. [§28.322] It is one thing for an assignor to say to an obligor, "You are under a contractual duty to pay me $1,000. I would rather you pay that money to my nephew, Adam, instead." It is quite another for the assignor to say, "You are under a contractual duty to paint my 2,000 square foot house for $3,000. I am assigning the right to have you paint a house for $3,000 to my rich Uncle Montesque, who lives in a 15,000 square foot mansion." Hence, for common sense reasons, contract law invalidates purported assignments that have a materially adverse consequence to the obligor. There are two ways such adverse consequences can occur:

(1) When the assignment results in a **material increase** in either the **burden of**, or the **risk to**, the obligor; or

(2) When the assignment results either in a **material impairment of the obligor's chance of obtaining return performance**, or in a **material reduction of the value of the return performance** due the obligor [Restatement 2d §317(2)(a); UCC §2-210(2)].

(1) Example. [§28.3221] The hypothetical case given above with the painter and Uncle Montesque is an example of when a purported assignment would be invalid because the obligor's **burden** in performing his or her duty is **materially increased** by the assignment. There is no hard and fast test for determining when the duty of the obligor has changed enough to make it a materially greater burden, but it is fair to say the courts have been more solicitous of obligors in these cases than of assignors. Hence, when an obligor will have to expend a reasonably greater amount of effort to perform the assigned duty than he or she would have under the obligor/assignor contract, the assignment is likely to be invalid.

(2) Example. [§28.3222] Daryl takes out an automobile insurance policy with Ins. Co. Daryl is 45 years old, owns a 6 year old car, drives less than 12,000 miles per year and has neither been issued a ticket nor been in an accident for the past 10 years. His premium is $400/year. If Daryl tries to assign the right to be insured for $400/year to Tom, an 18-year old driver who has had two accidents last year, 3 speeding tickets in the last month, and who drives 30,000 miles per year in his new

Corvette, the attempted assignment will be invalid. This is because as a result of the assignment, Ins. Co.'s (i.e., the obligor's) **risks** under the insurance contract have been **materially and adversely changed**.

(3) Example. [§28.3223] A concert promotor has booked Loco, a popular heavy metal group, to play at a concert for $15,000. Loco assigns its rights to receive the $15,000 to the Vienna Boys Choir. Such an assignment may be invalidated if the circumstances make it likely that what is really happening is that Loco is planning both to assign to the Vienna Boys Choir the right to receive the money, **and** to have the Vienna Boys Choir take its place at the concert. This is because such an assignment will materially impair the promotor's right to receive its bargained for performance. That is, it seems likely concert goers who wanted to see Loco would demand their money back when the featured band turns out to be the Vienna Boys Choir. As such, the obligor (the promoter) faces a "material reduction of the value of the return performance due the obligor."

c. A Purported Assignment that Violates a Valid "No Assignment" Provision in the Assignor/Obligor Contract is Ineffective. [§28.323] Historically, a specifically negotiated "no assignment" clause in an assignor/obligor contract was rather strictly enforced by the courts [Restatement 2d §317(2)(c)]. However, in the last 30 years or so there has been a steady decline in the courts' willingness to enforce such clauses, and a simultaneous increase in contract law's desire to promote the free assignability of contractual rights. Hence, while a fully negotiated, explicit clause **may** still act as a bar to an assignment, courts analyze even such fully negotiated clauses carefully and with the following points in mind:

First, all courts interpret such clauses as narrowly as possible. Thus, if there is a way to find the "no assignment" clause limited in time, in subject matter, or to a particular class of persons, the courts will do so.

Second, courts generally hold that such clauses operate only for the **benefit** of the obligor. Hence, if the obligor consents to the assignment, it is effective [Restatement 2d §322(2)(c)].

Third, courts tend to construe a term in an agreement prohibiting "assignment of the contract" as prohibiting only **delegation** of performance, and not assignment of rights, absent evidence of the parties' contrary intention [Restatement 2d §322(1); UCC §2-210(3)]. That is they will interpret the phrase as denying the part, the power to designate another to *perform* a promised duty under the contract, but not as prohibiting a party's right to transfer the right *to receive* a promised benefit to another.

Fourth, many courts now interpret such clauses as creating only a contractual **duty** not to assign, and not a total bar to assignment. That is, if there is a "no assignment" clause in the assignor/obligor contract, but the assignor nevertheless assigns an otherwise transferable right, these courts hold that the only recourse of the obligor is to sue the assignor to collect damages for breach of the duty not to assign. However, **the assignment itself is valid**, meaning the obligor must render performance to the assignee or be in breach for failing to do so despite the "no assignment" clause [Restatement 2d §322 (2)(b)]. In other words, these courts hold that "no assignment" clauses deprive the assignor of the **right** to assign, but not of the **power** to do so effectively.

Fifth, a number of courts have interpreted "no assignment without obligor consent" clauses to mean that an assignment under such a clause is effective despite the obligor's refusal to give his or her consent if the obligor's refusal is objectively unreasonable or made in bad faith. This is a common ground for interpreting no assignment clauses in leases. That is, if there is a "no assignment without the consent of the landlord" clause in a lease, many courts hold that so long as the new tenant is objectively acceptable, the landlord (i.e., the obligor) **must** accept the assignment and rent to the assignee (i.e., the sub-lessee). (See §28.34.)

Sixth, the UCC has gone even further to restrict the efficacy of certain types of no assignment clauses. UCC §9-318(4) provides that any clause prohibiting the assignment of a right to payment for goods sold or services rendered is *per se* ineffective. That same provision also renders *per se* ineffective any clause requiring the obligor's consent for such an assignment. In addition, the Code provides that a clause attempting to prohibit the right to assign damages for breach of the whole contract is similarly *per se* ineffective [UCC §2-210(2); Restatement 2d §322(2)(a) makes such clauses presumptively ineffective, but does not adopt a **per se** rule against their validity].

3. **GENERALLY THE ASSIGNEE MUST AGREE TO THE ASSIGNMENT TO MAKE IT EFFECTIVE. [§28.33]** The general rule is that the assignee must manifest assent to the assignment to render it effective. That is, before the assignment becomes effective and the obligor thereafter becomes bound to render performance to the assignee instead of the assignor, usually the assignee must somehow signify his or her acceptance of the arrangement [Restatement 2d §327(1)]. Once again, no special words are necessary, and whether such a manifestation of assent has been made will be judged under an objective theory, i.e., whether a reasonable person would find that a manifestation of assent to the assignment has been made as judged from all the circumstances. There are exceptions to this general rule, however, which are discussed immediately below.

   a. **Exceptions to the General Rule that the Assignee Must Agree before the Assignment is Effective. [§28.331]** There are two situations in which an assignee does **not** have to manifest acceptance before an assignment is deemed effective:

      (1) When a third party other than the assignee has given the assignor consideration for the assignment; or

      (2) When the assignment is irrevocable because of the delivery of a writing to a third party [Restatement 2d §327(1)].

   Note, however, that while an assignment without the assignee's consent is effective in these types of cases, when the assignee learns of the assignment he or she has the right to **disclaim** any rights under it within a reasonable time [Restatement 2d §327(2)]. If no disclaimer is made after a reasonable time, the assignee may not thereafter validly disclaim it.

      (1) **Example. [§28.3311]** Lisa owes Beverly $1,000. Dan's father contracts to paint Beverly's kitchen in return for Beverly's promise to assign her right to receive the $1,000 to Dan. If Beverly makes the assignment by objectively manifesting her intent to do so, the assignment is effective notwithstanding Dan's lack of knowledge or assent to the transfer. This is because consideration for the assignment has come from someone other than the assignee. However, when Dan finally learns of the assignment, he is entitled to disclaim his right as an assignee if he wishes, so long as he does so within a reasonable time [Restatement §327, Com. a, Ill. 1].

      (2) **Example. [§28.3312]** Valerie gives her savings bank book to John, saying "I know your brother Tony needs some money, so I am making him a present of the funds in my savings account. To show you I am serious, I am now giving you my

passbook to the account." Despite the fact that Tony does not know of the assignment and has not manifested his assent to it, the assignment is effective. This is because there has been a delivery of a writing to a third party making irrevocable the assignment of Valerie's contract right to withdraw her money from the bank (see §28.8 for a discussion of the irrevocability of assignments). If Tony wishes to disaffirm the assignment when he learns of it, he may do so if he sufficiently notifies Valerie within a reasonable time [Restatement 2d §327, Com. a, Ill. 2].

(3) **REVIEW PROBLEM. [§28.3313] Darrin is owed $1,000 from Pam. He would like to make a gift of that money to Bob, and so tells Pam he is assigning his right to receive the $1,000 to Bob. Question: When is the assignment effective?**

Answer: The assignment is not effective until Bob manifests his acceptance of the assignment, for neither of the exceptions to the general rule set forth in §28.331 apply.

4. **NOTIFICATION TO THE OBLIGOR OF THE ASSIGNMENT IS NOT NECESSARY FOR THE ASSIGNMENT TO BE EFFECTIVE. [§28.34]** While usually the **assignee** must be notified and agree to the assignment before it is effective, the same is **not** true for the obligor. **That is, absent a contractual obligation to do so, the obligor need not be notified of the assignment before it becomes effective.** This means that once the assignment is made, the obligor is under a duty to render performance to the assignee instead of to the assignor even if the obligor does not know that! Further, once the obligor finds out about the assignment, there is no requirement that the obligor assent to the transfer. That is, contract law gives the obligor no grounds to object to, or otherwise disclaim, such an assignment, assuming that there is no prohibition against assignments (see §28.32). The point is that an assignment is effective from the moment the assignor manifests his or her interest to transfer a permissible right and the assignee agrees to the assignment, even if the obligor does not yet know about it.

5. **AN EFFECTIVE ASSIGNMENT CAN BE PARTIAL. [§28.35]** The assignor can make an effective assignment of only part of the duties owed by the obligor under the assignor/obligor contract [Restatement 2d §326]. The result is that the obligor thereafter owes duties both to the assignor and the assignee.

a. **Example. [§28.351]** Ted owes Kevin $100. Kevin owes Samantha $25. Kevin can validly assign one-quarter of his rights to receive the $100 from Ted to Samantha. As a result of the assignment, Ted (the obligor) will owe a duty to pay Kevin (the assignor) $75, and a duty to pay Samantha (the assignee) $25.

6. **AN EFFECTIVE ASSIGNMENT CAN BE CONDITIONAL OR OTHERWISE LIMITED. [§28.36]** The assignor is entitled to make an effective assignment where the assignee's rights are expressly conditional on the occurrence of a particular event, or are otherwise limited [Restatement 2d §331].

a. **Example. [§28.361]** Ryan is entitled to receive $1,000 from Sue. Ryan assigns his right to the $1,000 payment to David, "on the condition Judy gets an 'A, on her Contracts midterm." Such an assignment is effective but limited in scope by the terms of the assignment, and thus, David's entitlement to the $1,000 is dependent on Judy's performance on the midterm.

7. **DISTINCTION BETWEEN AN ASSIGNMENT AND A THIRD PARTY BENEFICIARY CONTRACT. [§28.37]** The principal difference between an assignment situation and a third party beneficiary situation is that it takes **two** transactions to make a

third party an assignee, and only one transaction to establish someone as an intended third party beneficiary. That is, for an assignee to receive an enforceable duty arising from an assignment, **first** there must be an existing contract between the assignor and obligor, and **second** the assignor must make a transfer of rights under that contract to the assignee. On the other hand, for an intended beneficiary to receive an enforceable right arising from a third party beneficiary contract, there is only **one** transaction, namely the one contract between the promisor and promisee which benefits a third person.

a. **Example. [§28.371]** Bill enters into a contract with Mary Lee whereby he offers to sell her his watch in return for Mary Lee's promise to pay Bill's daughter Christina $500. This is a third party beneficiary situation because Christina's receipt of an enforceable duty arose out of the promises made in only one transaction — the contract between Bill (the promisee) and Mary Lee (the promisor).

b. **Example. [§28.372]** Bill is under a contractual duty to sell his watch to Mary Lee for $500. Bill is obligated to deliver the watch on May 5, and Mary Lee is obligated to pay the $500 on delivery. On May 1, Bill validly transfers his right to receive the money to his daughter Christina. This time there has been an assignment, for Christina's receipt of an enforceable duty arose from two transactions: (i) the original contract between Bill (the assignor) and Mary Lee (the obligor); and (ii) the subsequent transfer of the right to payment to Christina.

8. **INTERPRETATION OF THE PHRASE "ASSIGNMENT OF THE CONTRACT" OR "...OF ALL MY RIGHTS UNDER THE CONTRACT." [§28.38]** Contract law has established that unless the parties evidence a different intention, when a party assigns "the contract" or "all my rights under the contract" to an assignee, such a transfer acts as both an assignment of rights **and** a delegation of any executory duties of that party under the agreement [Restatement 2d §328; UCC §2-210(4)]; (see also §29.211).

a. **Example. [§28.381]** Louise wants to order a new book from Rich's Book Shop. She agrees to pay the $22.00 cover price upon delivery. Rich "assigns the contract" to Ed's Book Store. In the absence of a contrary intention, Ed has both been assigned the right to collect the $22 from Louise, and has been delegated the obligation to deliver the book to Louise as well.

9. **ORAL ASSIGNMENTS ARE EFFECTIVE UNLESS THE SUBJECT MATTER OF THE ASSIGNMENT IS WITHIN THE STATUTE OF FRAUDS. [§28.39]** Oral assignments are usually effective. An oral assignment is **not** effective only when the subject matter of the assignment itself is within the statute of frauds [Restatement 2d §324, Com. b]. As a practical matter, a writing requirement typically becomes an issue in two types of assignments:

(1) When the subject matter of the assignment is a right to receive an interest in land, the original transfer of which had to be in writing under the statute of frauds (see §9.2); or

(2) An assignment of a right within the scope of Article 9 of the UCC, such as a security agreement [UCC §9-302].

Recall that failure to satisfy the statute of frauds only makes a contract **voidable**, not void. That is, the only effect of the Statute is to deny one party to a contract the right to enforce it against the non-signing party. In the case of an assignment, it means that if the Statute applies and is not satisfied, the assignee may not enforce the assignment against the obligor. However, if the obligor wishes to go ahead with the transaction or otherwise fails to raise the Statute as a defense, failure to satisfy the Statute does not render the transaction void.

   a. **Example.** [§28.391] Karen is contractually bound to pay Selina $100,000 for Selina's house. Karen is subsequently offered $10,000 by Loye to assign her rights under the Selina/Karen contract. Karen accepts Loye's offer, but the assignment is oral. The effect of the oral assignment is to render the assignment unenforceable by Loye, the assignee. That is, Loye is not entitled to sue Selina if Selina does not transfer title to the house to Loye upon tender of $100,000. In other words, the oral assignee of an obligation subject to the statute of frauds cannot enforce an orally transferred contract right. However, if Selina wished to go ahead with the transaction and sell her house to Loye for $100,000, the fact that there was only an oral assignment between Loye and Karen will not render the sale void.

E. RIGHTS OF ASSIGNEE, AND DUTIES OF AN OBLIGOR AFTER VALID ASSIGNMENT. [§28.4] One of the principal effects of a valid assignment is that once the assignment occurs, the obligor no longer owes a duty to the assignor, and now owes the duty to render the promised performance to the assignee. That is, the assignee is deemed to have "stepped into the assignor's shoes" upon an assignment. After the assignment, it is the assignee, **and only the assignee**, who can enforce the obligor's duty to render the assigned performance. That also means that once the obligor receives notice of the assignment, the obligor can no longer discharge his or her duties by rendering performance to the assignor, and must render that performance to the assignee.

As mentioned earlier (see §28.34), occasionally a situation arises whereby the obligor learns of the assignment only after he or she has rendered performance to the assignor. Because it would be unfair to the obligor to make him or her perform twice, contract law provides that if he or she does not have notice of the assignment, performance to the assignor will discharge his or her duty [Restatement 2d §338].

   1. **EXAMPLE.** [§28.41] Fred purchases a stereo on credit from Leroy's Stereo Shop ("Leroy's"). Under the terms of the credit sale, Fred must make monthly payments of $100 to Leroy's on the 1st of every month for a year, starting October 1. On September 28, Leroy assigns the right to receive Fred's payments over the next year to Finance Co. Finance Co. immediately sends notice of the assignment to Fred.

   If Fred mailed the first $100 payment to Leroy's before he received notice of the assignment, his duty to make that month's payment has been discharged by performance, and Finance Co.'s only recourse is to get the $100 from Leroy's. However, if Fred had received notice of the assignment and nevertheless went ahead and paid Leroy's, thinking he was "safe" to pay the company that sold him the stereo rather than obey the dictates of some letter which told him to make his payment elsewhere, **he still is obligated to make a $100 payment to Finance Co.** If he does not make it, Finance Co. is entitled to sue Fred to recover the $100 payment. In other words, good faith does not discharge the obligor's mistaken performance after the obligor has actual notice of the assignment. (Of course, in the case described above, Fred is entitled to sue Leroy's in restitution for return of the $100 mistakenly paid to Leroy's.)

F. CLAIMS AND DEFENSES THE OBLIGOR CAN ASSERT AGAINST ASSIGNEE. [§28.5] As noted earlier, upon a valid assignment, the rights of the assignor are simply transferred to the assignee. As contract law puts it, "the assignee stands in the shoes of the assignor." Hence, any defenses or other claims arising out of the assignor/obligor contract that could be asserted by the obligor against the assignor had there been no assignment can be asserted by the obligor in a suit brought by the assignee after an assignment has been made [Restatement 2d §336(1)]. In other words, the assignment does not deprive the obligor of any defense or claim he would have had without the assignment. Hence, if an obligor could have asserted a statute of frauds, duress, undue influence, lack of consideration, fraud, or other defense had there been no assignment and he or she been sued by the assignor, those same defenses are equally available after the assignment in a suit brought by the assignee. Further, this rule holds true regardless of whether either the assignor or the assignee was aware of any such defenses at the time of the assignment (see §28.52 for an important exception to this rule).

1. **EXAMPLE.** [§28.51] Sara purchased a used refrigerator on credit from Ted on January 25. Ted told her the appliance was "in perfect shape" and that he had "no problems with it whatsoever." As part of the purchase transaction, Sara signed a contract calling for 10 monthly payments of $40, the first of which was due on March 1. On February 1, Ted assigned to Peter the right to collect Sara's payments under the contract. Peter promptly gave notice to Sara of the assignment, which was received by Sara before she made her first payment.

   The refrigerator was delivered to Sara on January 31 and it did not operate. Sara later found out that Ted had lied to her, and that he knew the refrigerator was inoperative at the time of the sale. Not surprisingly, Sara refused to make any of the payments for the inoperative refrigerator. When her payments under the contract were not forthcoming, Peter brought suit against Sara.

   Obviously there has been an assignment. **Ted is the assignor** (assigning a right to payment to a third person); **Sara is the obligor** (she initially owed a duty to Ted and, after the assignment, owed that same duty to a third party); and **Peter is the assignee** (for after the assignment he is owed performance by the obligor).

   The question is whether Sara is entitled to assert her misrepresentation defense in a suit brought by Peter, when after all it was Ted, not Peter, who actually made the misrepresentations. That is, can an obligor assert a defense in a suit by the assignee that she would have had if the suit had been brought by the assignor? The answer is yes, she can assert such a defense. The assignee (Peter) "stands in the shoes" of the assignor (Ted), and any defense assertable against Ted is fully assertable against Peter. Note that this is true even if Peter was absolutely unaware of the misrepresentations when the assignment was made, and in all other respects acted in good faith.

2. **"HOLDER IN DUE COURSE" EXCEPTION.** [§28.52] In some ways it is unfair that an assignee, like Peter in the hypothetical immediately above, is subject to defenses he did not know about when he agreed to the assignment. After all, he was an innocent party as well. Thus, contract law has developed a limited exception to the general rule that assignees are subject to defenses that could be asserted against assignors, namely the "holder in due course" exception.

   a. **Definition of "Holder in Due Course".** [§28.521] A holder in due course is a special kind of assignee for value. It is an assignee who purchases an assignor's rights to receive payments under something called a "negotiable instrument." While deciding exactly what is and what is not a "negotiable instrument" can be the subject of an entire law school course, first year Contracts courses generally analyze only two types of "negotiable instruments": (i) checks; and (ii) negotiable promissory notes.

To become a holder in due course, the assignee who purchases the rights to collect monies under a check or negotiable promissory note must make the purchase:

  (i)   of an instrument that does not bear objective evidence of forgery, alteration, irregularity, or incompleteness so as to call its authenticity into question;

  (ii) in good faith;

  (iii) for value;

  (iv) without personal notice of defenses to its enforcement such as alteration, forgery competing claims, etc. [UCC 3-305]

In essence, this means that an assignee for value of a negotiable instrument becomes a holder in due course of that instrument so long as he, she, or it acts in good faith when buying the note or check, and was unaware of any defenses the obligor might have to defeat a suit brought by the assignor.

b. **Effect of "Holder In Due Course" Status. [§28.522]** A "holder in due course" assignee receives substantial benefits over ordinary assignees. Specifically, under UCC §3-305, holders in due course are **not** subject to any defenses that could be asserted by the obligor against the assignee (with the exception of the rarely encountered so-called "real" defenses" set forth in that provision).

  (1) **Example. [§28.5221]** Joe's Appliance Shop ("Joe's") orders 100 refrigerators from Manufacturer. To finance the purchase, Joe's executes a negotiable promissory note, promising to pay Manufacturer $4,500/month for a year. Manufacturer "negotiates," i.e., assigns for value, its right to receive Joe's payments under the negotiable promissory note to Credit Bank. Credit Bank purchases the note: (i) for value; (ii) in good faith; (iii) without knowledge of any defenses against Manufacturer; and in all other ways becomes a holder in due course.

  When the refrigerators arrive, they prove defective, and so Joe's refuses to make payments on the note. If Credit Bank brings suit against Joe's for its failure to pay, Credit Bank will win. As a holder in due course, Credit Bank is not subject to any defenses an obligor such as Joe's could assert against Manufacturer. Hence, Joe's (the obligor) must continue to pay Credit Bank (the holder in due course assignee) $4,500/month for a year or be in breach for failing to do so. To recoup its losses, Joe's must seek its recovery from Manufacturer (the assignor) for breach of warranty, misrepresentation, etc.

  Compare this result with the Ted/Sara/Peter refrigerator transaction described in §28.51. Where an assignee is just an ordinary assignee, as was Peter in the §28.51 hypothetical, his rights against the obligor are subject to all the defenses that the obligor could assert against the assignee. However, when the assignee is a "holder in due course," the assignee takes free and clear from almost all of the defenses that can be caused by the assignor's conduct.

c. **Limitation on Holder in Due Course Doctrine. [§28.523]** Due to various abuses practiced by assignors and holders in due course in consumer transactions, the FTC passed a regulation in the early 1970's stating that a purchaser of a negotiable instrument could not attain holder in due course status when the obligor was a consumer. Hence, today the holder in due course doctrine is alive and well in

merchant-to-merchant situations. However, when a consumer is involved, the assignee for value is still subject to any defenses the consumer could assert against the assignor.

G. RIGHTS OF THE ASSIGNEE TO SUE THE ASSIGNOR: THE IMPLIED WARRANTIES INHERENT IN ASSIGNMENTS FOR VALUE. [§28.6]

Until this point, most of the focus in this chapter has been on the rights of the assignee to sue the obligor. However, there are occasions in which the assignee would like to bring suit against the **assignor** for interfering with his or her right to receive performance from the obligor. For example, suppose the assignee tries to sue the obligor for non-performance, and then finds out that the obligor has a defense to the action based on the assignor's misrepresentation, undue influence, etc. In such cases, the assignee typically feels entitled to sue the assignor for the actions which resulted in the obligor's defense.

Contract law provides that the assignee can, in fact, sue the assignor in such cases. The theory on which the suit is based is breach of warranty. That is, contract law provides that whenever an assignment for value is made, the assignor impliedly makes certain warranties to the assignee. While the scope of those warranties varies slightly among jurisdictions, the Restatement 2d provides that the assignor warrants:

(1) that he or she will do nothing to impair the value of the assignment; and

(2) that the assigned right in fact exists, and is subject to no limitations or defenses other than those either told to the assignee, or those that are reasonably apparent to the assignee, at the time of assignment [Restatement 2d §333(1)].

Note that Restatement 2d §333(2) specifically provides that in making an assignment for value an assignor does **not** impliedly warrant to the assignee that the obligor is solvent, or is either willing or able to perform his or her obligations after the assignment is made. Those risks are assumed by the assignee in purchasing the rights of the assignment, and presumably are reflected in the price the assignee is willing to pay for the assignment.

1. **EXAMPLE. [§28.61]** Assume again the facts of the hypothetical involving the sale of a refrigerator to Sara by Ted described in §28.51. When Ted sells his rights to collect payment under the promissory note to Peter, he is impliedly warranting to Peter that he will do nothing in the future to impair the value of the assignment, and that there are no defenses to the assigned payment obligation that can be asserted by Sara. Hence when Sara successfully asserts Ted's fraud as a defense to Peter's suit, there has been a breach of Ted's warranty to Peter that no such defense exists. As a result, Peter (the assignee) can recover from Ted (the assignor) whatever damages he suffers from the breach of that warranty.

2. **EXAMPLE. [§28.62]** Hobby Shop sells a 50-inch television to Ken on credit. Ken signs a promissory note to finance the purchase, promising to pay Hobby Shop $100/month for 2 years. Hobby Shop assigns its rights to Ken's payments to First Bank for $1,800. The television works well, but Ken nevertheless refuses to make any payments to First Bank. The bank's only recourse is to sue Ken. This is because when Hobby Shop assigned the accounts receivable to First Bank, it made no implied warranty as to the solvency, ability, or willingness of Ken (the obligor) to make the payments. The risk of Ken not performing is part of what went into the price the bank was willing to pay Hobby Shop for the assignment, and thus it may only look to Ken for payment.

H. ASSIGNEE'S RIGHTS UPON ATTEMPTED MODIFICATION OF ASSIGNMENT BY THE ASSIGNOR AND THE OBLIGOR. [§28.7]

Sometimes after an assignment is made, the obligor and assignor attempt to modify (or even retract) the assignment, to the detriment of the assignee. The rules regarding the rights of the obligor and assignor to make an effective post-assignment modification depend on whether the assignment is gratuitous or is for value, as explained below.

1. **MODIFICATION RULES REGARDING ASSIGNMENTS FOR VALUE. [§28.71]** Assignors and obligors have **no right to modify the assignment after an assignment for value** has been effectively made. That is, an assignment for value is *irrevocable* once validly made, and the assignee's rights vest immediately. This makes sense, for an assignment for value arises out of a separate contract between the assignor and assignee. That agreement should not be alterable by the subsequent agreement of the assignor and obligor.

2. **MODIFICATION RULES REGARDING GRATUITOUS ASSIGNMENTS. [§28.72]** The rules as to the rights of the assignor and obligor to modify a gratuitous assignment are different from, and more complex than, the rule regarding such modification rights under an assignment for value. **The general rule is that gratuitous assignments are fully revocable and modifiable.** Under §332(1) of the Restatement 2d, a gratuitous assignment is **not** modifiable, i.e., it becomes irrevocable, **only** when:

   (1) the assignment is **in writing and is signed by the assignor**;

   (2) the assignment **is accompanied by delivery of a customary symbol** or so-called "token chose." For example, when a party wishes to assign the rights to money in a savings account, delivery of the bank pass book to the assignee will make the gratuitous assignment irrevocable because the book is a customary "symbol" of assignment;

   (3) **the assignee has relied on the assignment;** or

   (4) **the assignee has received performance by the obligor of the assigned duty.** That is, once the obligor has rendered performance to the assignee, the assignor and obligor cannot go back and rescind or otherwise modify the assignee's rights in the hopes of making the assignee pay back the value of what he or she has already received.

I. **RIGHTS OF THE ASSIGNEE AMONG COMPETING CLAIMS OF OWNERSHIP. [§28.8]** While the number and complexity of issues potentially falling under this section heading are enormous, generally first year Contracts courses focus on only one aspect of the potential problems. That is, what happens when a single assignor attempts to assign the **same** right to **two or more** different assignees. The question is which of the assignees has priority over the others. Contract law has developed four different approaches to this issue, each of which is discussed below.

1. **THE "NEW YORK" RULE: THE FIRST ASSIGNEE ALWAYS HAS PRIORITY. [§28.81]** Under the so-called "New York" rule, the first assignee automatically has priority over all later assignees. Sometimes this rule is also known as "the rule of latent equities," for in equity "first in time is first in right."

   a. **Example. [§28.811]** Jerome owes Leslie $1,000 under a contract. The money is due to be paid on October 15. On September 1, Leslie makes an assignment for value of the right to collect the $1,000 to John. John does not notify Jerome of the assignment. On September 30, Leslie again makes an assignment for value of the same right to collect Jerome's payment, this time to Karen. Karen immediately notifies Jerome of the assignment and Jerome pays Karen the $1,000 on October 15. Under the New York rule, John's claim to the payment nonetheless has priority over Karen's, for he was the first assignee of the right. Hence, Karen will be deemed to have received the money "in trust" for John, even though she neither knew John nor of the first assignment to him. As a result, John is entitled to sue Karen for the $1,000 since she is holding the money "in trust" for him, and Karen's relief, if any, will have to come from Leslie.

2. **THE ENGLISH RULE: THE FIRST ASSIGNEE TO NOTIFY THE OBLIGOR HAS PRIORITY. [§28.82]** Under the so-called "English Rule," the determinative factor as to which of two competing assignees has priority is which assignee first gave notice of the assignment to the obligor. This rule has the advantage of encouraging prompt obligor notification.

   a. **Example. [§28.821]** Using the Jerome/Leslie hypothetical set forth in §28.811, under the "English Rule" Karen would prevail, for she was the first to *notify* Jerome of the assignment. Hence, it would be John, not Karen, who would have to sue Leslie in a jurisdiction adopting this view.

3. **THE MASSACHUSETTS/RESTATEMENT 2D RULE: THE FIRST ASSIGNEE GENERALLY PREVAILS, SUBJECT TO FOUR EXCEPTIONS. [§28.83]** Under the so-called "Massachusetts Rule," which has been adopted by the Restatement 2d in §342, the first assignee prevails, unless a later assignee can establish one of four exceptions:

   (1) that the later assignee has already received satisfaction of the obligation from the obligor;

   (2) that the later assignee has already obtained a judgment against the obligor resulting from the obligor's failure to perform;

   (3) that the later assignee has already entered into a novation with the obligor (see §24.2); or

   (4) that the later assignee obtained possession of a symbolic writing from the obligor.

   a. **Example. [§28.831]** In the Jerome/Leslie hypothetical set forth in §28.811 Karen would also prevail under the Massachusetts/Restatement 2d view. This time Karen would prevail because she actually received satisfaction of the obligation from Jerome before John brought suit. Thus, she would have a greater entitlement to the payment than would John, and John would again have to sue Leslie for breach of the implied warranty in making the assignment.

4. **ARTICLE 9 OF THE UCC RULE: FIRST TO FILE OR PERFECT GETS PRIORITY. [§28.84]** Article 9 of the UCC sets forth very specialized and elaborate rules regarding the function and priorities of "security interests." A security interest is an interest, akin to a lien, in personal property or fixtures which secures a payment or some other performance obligation [UCC §1-201 (37)]. While this puts it too simply, a security interest is an intangible ownership interest that the lender has in collateral that secures a loan. For example, Jerry buys a new car with the proceeds of a car loan from a bank. Jerry gets to keep the car and drive it, and he has an ownership interest in it. However, so does the bank. The bank has a kind of lien or "security interest" in the car which serves as collateral for the loan. One effect of the security interest is that if Jerry defaults on the loan, the bank may foreclose on its security interest and repossess the car. That is, rather than just suing Jerry for breach of contract and waiting for its money until the case comes to trial, the bank can repossess the car after default, sell it, and get its money back relatively quickly. That's why a secured loan, i.e. a loan with collateral, is usually favored by lenders.

Under Article 9, a secured creditor can "perfect" his, her, or its security interest in personal property by, among other things, filing a "financing statement" with the appropriate governmental body, usually the Secretary of State's office for a particular state. Once filed, the financing statement gives any other interested party notice that the bank has a prior security interest in the car. Accordingly, anyone else who may wish to lend money to Jerry and use the car as collateral can determine whether an assignment of a security interest has already been made by checking with the Secretary of State [UCC §§9-302 to 9-306]. Under the Code, the first assignee to file or perfect the security interest has priority over any other assignees of that property [UCC §9-312(5)].

CHAPTER TWENTY-NINE: DELEGATION

A. DELEGATION GENERALLY. [§29.0] Just as a party may transfer the right to receive benefits under a contract via an assignment, a party may also transfer the obligation to perform a **duty** called for in a contract. When a party effectively transfers a contractual obligation of performance to a third party, it is known as a **delegation**. The terminology, mechanics, and effect of delegation are discussed in the remainder of this chapter.

B. TERMINOLOGY OF DELEGATION. [§29.1] A delegation is the transfer of a contractual duty of performance to another [Restatement 2d §318]. There are typically three parties involved in a delegation:

> (1) The **Delegating Party**. The delegating party (sometimes known as the "obligor" or even the "delegator") is the party who transfers the duty of performance under a contract to a third party. That is, the delegating party is already a party to a contract before the delegation occurs and is under an obligation to undertake executory duties in that contract. By means of the delegation, the delegating party transfers to someone else the obligation to perform some or all of those duties.

> (2) The **Obligee**. The obligee is the party who is in a contract with the delegating party before the delegation occurs, and who is owed performance of the duty the delegating party is trying to transfer. Hence, it is the obligee who, before the delegation, was expecting performance by the delegating party, and who, after the delegation, must allow a third party to perform that duty.

> (3) The **Delegate**. The delegate is not a party to the original delegating party/obligee agreement. The delegate is the party to whom the delegating party transfers the obligation to perform a duty owed the obligee.

1. EXAMPLE. [§29.11] Sam entered into a contract with Bill's Ticket Agency to get him a front row ticket to a rock concert. Bill's then enters into an agreement with Lorraine's Hot Tix, transferring to Lorraine's the obligation to procure Sam's ticket. A delegation has occurred. **Bill's is the delegating party**, for it owed a contractual obligation to Sam and is now trying to transfer that obligation to another. **Sam is the obligee**, for the delegating party (Bill's) originally owed him a duty and, as a result of the delegation, Sam must now allow a third party to perform that duty. **Lorraine's is the delegate**, for it is to Lorraine's that the delegating party (Bill's) is transferring a contractual obligation.

C. ELEMENTS OF AN EFFECTIVE DELEGATION. [§29.2] There are only two requirements to establish an effective delegation:

> (1) The delegating party must manifest an intention to delegate a particular duty or duties under a contract (discussed in §29.21); and

> (2) The delegation must be "permissible," i.e., there must be no prohibition against the delegation of that particular duty (discussed in §29.22).

Note that there is **no** requirement that the delegate "accept" the delegation. While initially this is surprising, it is nevertheless true that the delegate need not even know of the delegation for it to be effective. However, this is not unfair to the delegate because, as discussed later, if the delegate does not objectively "assume" the delegated duty (which would of course be the case if the delegate did not know of the delegation), he or she is not liable to anyone for its non-performance (see §29.34).

1. **THE DELEGATING PARTY MUST MANIFEST AN INTENTION TO DELEGATE A DUTY. [§29.21]** In order to make an effective delegation, the delegating party must manifest an intention to transfer the obligation to perform a duty under an existing contract to a third party. No particular language is necessary to establish such an intention, and in close cases courts are directed to examine a party's intent from all surrounding circumstances.

   a. **Construction of a Clause "Assigning the Contract." [§29.211]** Contract law has established that, absent evidence of a contrary intention by the parties, when a party assigns "the contract," or "all my rights under the contract" to someone else, such a transfer acts as both an assignment of rights **and** a delegation of any executory duties owed by that party under the contract [Restatement 2d §328; UCC §2-210(4)]; (see also §28.38).

      (1) **Example. [§29.2111]** Jim has a contract with Vergie, a travel agent, to secure him tickets for a cruise at a price of $1,500. Vergie thereafter "assigns the contract" to another travel agency. Absent evidence of a contrary intention, Vergie's act both delegates the duty to provide Jim with a ticket on the cruise for $1,500, and assigns the right to receive Jim's $1,500 payment to the other travel agency.

2. **THERE MUST BE NO PROHIBITION AGAINST DELEGATION OF THIS PARTICULAR DUTY. [§29.22]** The second requirement for an effective delegation is that there be no prohibition against the delegation of that particular duty. The rules governing when a particular duty is delegable are as follows:

   Generally, duties in a contract are freely delegable. They are only NOT delegable when:

      (1) Delegation of that particular duty **violates public policy** [Restatement 2d §318(1)] (see §29.221);

      (2) The obligee has a **substantial interest in having the original obligor perform the duty** [Restatement 2d §318(2)] (see §29.222); and

      (3) There is an **enforceable "no delegation" clause** in the original delegating party/obligee contract [Restatement 2d §318(3)] (see §29.223).

   Each of these limitations is discussed and illustrated below.

   a. **A Purported Delegation that Violates Public Policy is Ineffective. [§29.221]** Courts and legislatures are empowered to nullify purported delegations that violate public policy [Restatement 2d §318(1)]. While courts and legislatures do, in fact, use their power to nullify purported **assignments** on public policy grounds on a regular basis (see §28.321), there are relatively few cases where a **delegation** has been voided on such grounds. In those few cases where a court has exercised this power, it has typically nullified a municipality's attempt to delegate performance of a municipal service to a private company, e.g., running a jail. Despite the fact that there are only a handful of such cases, however, both the courts and the commentators continue to claim that the public policy nullification doctrine is still valid as applied to delegations, and that, in a proper case, the doctrine could serve to void a particular delegation.

   b. **A Purported Delegation of a Duty that the Obligee Has a "Substantial Interest" in Having the Delegating Party Perform is Ineffective. [§29.222]** Common sense dictates that not all duties can be delegated. If, for example, a movie producer agrees to pay Jack Nicholson several million dollars to star in a movie, Mr. Nicholson cannot delegate the duty to appear in the film to someone else. The reason is because performance of such a duty is too personal to be delegated effectively. The test for when a duty is too personal is nearly identical in both the UCC and the Restatement 2d:

A duty may not be delegated if the obligee has a "substantial interest" in having a particular person perform the promised acts [Restatement 2d §318(2); UCC §2-210(1)].

This test is intentionally flexible so as to give the courts discretion in applying it, but the courts have established the following as general criteria:

      (1)   The more the performance depends on the **particular skills, character, training, taste, discretion, etc., of the delegating party,** the less likely the duty may be validly transferred. On the other hand, the more the performance is ministerial, calling for little discretion by the delegating party, the more likely it is such a delegation will be upheld; and

      (2)   In certain contracts, the more the **delegating party retains control over the delegate,** the more likely it is that the delegation will be upheld.

Of course, if the obligee agrees to having the obligor delegate the duty, even a "personal one," the obligor is entitled to do so. This rule does not prohibit an obligee from accepting a delegate's performance. Rather it only protects the obligee from being **forced** to accept a substitute performance of a personal duty when the obligee does not wish to do so.

(1) Example. [§29.2221] Law School hires Bob to teach Contracts during the next academic year. Bob cannot delegate his duties, no matter how competent the delegate may be, for the school has a "substantial interest" in seeing to it that Bob will perform [Restatement 2d §318, Com. c, Ill. 5].

(2) Example. [§29.2222] Steve owes Jamie $100. He delegates his duty to repay the money to Ron, who tenders the $100 to Jamie. As there is no discretion or skill involved in the repayment of money, the delegation is valid. Thus, if Jamie does not accept Ron's payment to discharge Steve's debt, she will thereafter be precluded from suing either Ron or Steve for non-payment. [Restatement 2d §318, Com. a, Ill. 1].

(3) Example. [§29.2223] Peri hires Ann, a sole practitioner, to be her attorney and Ann promises to do all legal-related work for Peri personally. Ann subsequently hires John, a paralegal. Some of the work Ann is doing for Peri is of a type that can be handled by a paralegal under professional standards. So long as Ann (the delegating party) retains **sufficient control** over John's (the delegate's) performance of such duties, she may validly delegate them to John.

c. **A Purported Delegation that Violates a Specific "No Delegation" Clause In a Contract is Ineffective. [§29.223]** As noted earlier, anti-assignment clauses are not favored by the courts, and in the last 30 years, **anti-assignment** clauses have been strictly and narrowly construed (see §28.323). However, anti-delegation clauses face no such hostility. Thus, a "no delegation" clause in the delegating party/obligee contract that is freely bargained for and sufficiently detailed will generally be enforced.

3. **THE OBLIGEE NEED NOT ASSENT TO, OR EVEN BE AWARE OF, THE DELEGATION FOR IT TO BE EFFECTIVE. [§29.23]** The obligee originally enters into a contract with the delegating party. He or she looks to the delegating party for

performance. Hence, it may be somewhat surprising that, so long as the duty is properly delegable (see §29.22), a delegation is effective even if the obligee does not know of it, or even if the obligee protests it.

a. **Example. [§29.231]** Denise has entered into a one year contract with Grocery Store, whereby she is under a duty to deliver 20 lbs. of Washington Delicious apples per week to the store. The contract calls for the apples to be certified Grade A-1 by the local produce board. Denise wishes to delegate her duties under the contract to Rob, another wholesale produce vendor who buys apples from the same supplier as does Denise, and who thus can supply Grade A-1 Washington Delicious apples to Grocery Store on the same terms as Denise. Accordingly, Denise delegates her delivery duties under the contract to Rob in a procedurally effective manner. Even if the owner of Grocery Store does not like Rob, and tells him she does not wish Rob to make the delivery, Rob has a right to make the deliveries, for a valid delegation can be made without the knowledge of, or even over the objections of, the obligee.

D. PRINCIPAL CONSEQUENCES OF AN EFFECTIVE DELEGATION. [§29.3] Contract law identifies five principal effects of a valid delegation:

(1) The delegate acquires a **right** to perform the delegated duty (see §29.31);

(2) The duty of the delegating party to render performance to the obligee is **not** discharged (see §29.32);

(3) Performance by the delegate of the transferred duty **discharges** the duty the delegating party owed the obligee (see §29.33);

(4) The delegate generally acquires no **duty** to perform the delegated tasks. He or she obtains an enforceable obligation to perform those delegated duties **only if** the delegate manifests **an express assumption** to undertake them (see §29.34); and

(5) If the delegation occurs as a result of a contract between the delegating party and the delegate (as is typically the case), the right of the delegating party to sue the delegate upon non-performance is the same as the right of the promisee to sue the promisor for non-performance under a third party beneficiary contract (see §29.35).

1. **UPON A VALID DELEGATION, THE DELEGATE ACQUIRES A *RIGHT* TO PERFORM THE DELEGATED DUTY. [§29.31]** Once a delegation becomes effective, the obligee **must** allow the delegate to perform the duty or else either be in breach for not allowing such performance or forfeit the right to sue for non-performance of the duty. In some ways this rule may seem unfair since the obligee originally entered into a contract with the delegating party, not the delegate, and probably looks to the delegating party for performance. Nevertheless, if the duty is one that can be delegated, and if the delegation is done effectively, the delegate thereafter has a right to perform it.

a. **Example. [§29.311]** Neil owes Mary $1,500 under a contract. Neil is strapped for cash, so he enters into an agreement with Letticia whereby Letticia is delegated the duty to pay Mary $1,500 in return for Neil's CD collection. A delegation has occurred. **Neil is the delegating party,** for he is transferring the obligation to perform a contractual duty to another. **Mary is the obligee,** for she was owed performance of a duty by Neil, and as a result of the delegation, Mary must now allow another to perform the payment obligation. **Letticia is the delegate,** because Neil's contractual obligation has been transferred to her. (Note, the Neil/Letticia contract is also a third party beneficiary contract, but the delegation aspects of the transaction will be analyzed here; see §29.35.)

As a consequence of the delegation, if Letticia timely tenders $1,500 to Mary, Mary must accept it or she forfeits he rights to sue either Neil or Letticia for non-performance. That is, since the obligation to pay money is a type of duty that can be delegated (see §29.22), and since the delegation is otherwise effective, Mary may not insist on Neil making the payment, and must allow Letticia to do so if she timely performs. (See also §29.341)

2. **DELEGATION DOES NOT DISCHARGE THE DUTY OF THE DELEGATING PARTY TO RENDER PERFORMANCE TO THE OBLIGEE. [§29.32]** If the delegate does not perform the transferred duty after an effective delegation has taken place, the obligee still retains the right to sue the delegating party for breach [Restatement 2d §318(3); UCC §2-210(1)]. That is, a delegation carries with it no implied release of the delegating party's obligations. Hence, after a delegation, the delegating party is still "on the hook," and liable to the obligee in the event of the delegate's non-performance.

Note that this rule is somewhat different from the rule governing assignments. Recall that upon an effective assignment, the assignor immediately loses his or her right to receive performance under the contract (see §28.1 et seq.). In other words, once the assignment is made the assignor is "out of the picture". However, upon a delegation the delegating party is still "in the picture," i.e., is still liable for his or her promised performance. (See §29.341 for an example illustrating this rule)

The reason usually given for the different treatment of assignors and delegating parties has to do with the potential for abuse. That is, assume Drew, who is solvent, owes Brad a contractual payment of $500. If an effective delegation ended Drew's obligations, there is a fear that Drew would simply delegate his performance (i.e., his duty to pay the $500) to an insolvent person or entity, leaving Brad with no recovery. Hence, to avoid this problem, the delegating party is still liable for the promised performance, even after an effective delegation has been made.

3. **FULL PERFORMANCE BY THE DELEGATE DISCHARGES THE DUTY OWED BY THE DELEGATING PARTY. [§29.33]** As mentioned above, upon an effective delegation the delegate acquires the **right** to perform the transferred duty (see §29.31). If the delegate exercises that right and tenders complete performance to the obligee, the corresponding duties owed by the delegating party to the obligee are discharged. In other words, even though one person (the delegate) renders performance, it discharges another person's (the delegating party's) duty.

4. **A DELEGATE HAS AN ENFORCEABLE OBLIGATION, AS OPPOSED TO A RIGHT, TO PERFORM THE TRANSFERRED DUTY ONLY WHEN HE OR SHE SPECIFICALLY ASSUMES SUCH A DUTY. [§29.34]** Whether or not a delegate has an **obligation**, as well as a **right**, to perform the delegated duty depends on whether he or she objectively manifests an assumption of the obligation. That is, in a delegation transaction where the delegating party simply delegates a duty and the delegate makes no acknowledgment of any obligations arising from the delegation, the delegate obtains only a right to perform the duty, and not an obligation to do so (see §29.341). This means that if the delegate does not perform the delegated duty **in such a case, the obligee is entitled only to sue the delegating party for breach.**

Most of the time, however, a delegation is the result of a contract between the delegating party and the delegate. In those kinds of cases, or in any other situation where the delegate objectively manifests an intention to assume the obligation to perform the delegated duties, the obligee may enforce that promise by suing the delegate for breach upon the delegate's non-performance. That is, a manifestation by the delegate of his or her assumption of the transferred duties creates in the delegate a duty to perform those obligations which can be enforced by the obligee. The manifestation by the delegate of his or her assumption of the transferred duties need not be express. So long as a reasonable person would find under the circumstances that the delegate had manifested such an intention, an assumption will be found.

Note that even when there has been an "assumption" of the duties by the delegate, such action does **not** discharge the duty of the delegating party (see §29.4, however, for a discussion of when a delegation becomes a novation, in which case the delegating party is released from his or her performance duties). In a delegation followed by a delegate's assumption of the transferred duties, the obligee is thereafter owed two enforceable duties: (i) the original one, owed by the delegating party; and (ii) the new one, owed by the delegate. If neither the delegate nor the delegating party perform, the obligee is entitled to sue **either** the delegating party, **or** the delegate, **or both** for breach; but, of course, the obligee is entitled to only one complete satisfaction.

    a. **Example. [§29.341]** Dan writes a letter to his Bank notifying them that he is delegating the duty to pay his outstanding Visa bill to the President of the United States. This is an effective delegation. Note, however (before all the readers of this book try to do the same), that all such delegation means is that the Bank must *allow* the President to pay Dan's Visa bill **if the President submits payment** (§29.31). That is, the President has the **right** to make the payment on Dan's behalf, but NOT the **duty** to do so. Only if the President says that he is **specifically assuming the duty to pay Dan's bill**, a highly unlikely prospect, will the President have the *obligation* to make the payment as well as the right to do so, meaning that the Bank could sue the President if the payment was never made.

    Note also that if the President assumed the obligation to pay the bill, the Bank is entitled to sue either the President or Dan, or both, for a delegation (as opposed to a novation, see §29.4) does not release the delegating party, i.e., the original party owing the contractual duty.

    b. **Example. [§29.342]** Gail is contractually owed $1,000 by Ira. Ira enters into a written contract with Dennis wherein Dennis agrees to assume Ira's obligation to pay Gail $1,000 in return for Ira's watch. Ira transfers his watch to Dennis, but Dennis does not pay Gail. Gail is not aware of the delegation until after the payment was due. Gail is nonetheless entitled to sue either Ira, or Dennis, or both. That is, the manifestation by the delegate to assume the transferred duty need **not** be made **to the obligee**. As long as there is an objective manifestation of the delegate's assumption of the obligation made to **anyone**, the delegate thereafter owes an enforceable duty of performance to the obligee. As the terms of the contract between Ira and Dennis make manifest Dennis's assumption of the payment obligation, Gail thereby acquired the right to sue Dennis for non-payment even if she did not know it at the time.

5. **RELATIONSHIP BETWEEN DELEGATIONS AND THIRD PARTY BENEFICIARY CONTRACTS. [§29.35]** When the delegation results from an enforceable contract between the delegating party and the delegate, that agreement is also an **enforceable third party beneficiary contract**, and the right of the delegating party to sue the delegate upon non-performance is the same as the right of the promisee to sue the promisor for non-performance under third party beneficiary contract principles. Most delegations occur as a result of a valid contract between the delegating party and the delegate. Typically, the delegating party gives some sort of consideration to the delegate in order to secure the delegate's promise to perform the transferred duty. Such a contract is a third party beneficiary contract since the delegating party and the delegate have made an agreement,

the performance of which will benefit the obligee, i.e., a third person who is not a party to the delegating party/delegate contract. In third party beneficiary terms, the delegating party is the promisee, the delegate is the promisor, and the obligee is the beneficiary.

An issue sometimes arises as to whether the delegating party (as well as the obligee) can sue the delegate if the delegate does not perform. Where the delegating party and the delegate have entered into a third party beneficiary contract as part of the delegation, the delegate may be sued by the delegating party for non-performance in the same manner as the promisor can be sued by the promisee for breach under a third party beneficiary contract (see §§27.6, 29.352). However, where the promise of the delegate to assume the delegating party's duties is only a gift promise, the delegating party has no right to sue the delegate upon the delegate's non-performance.

a. **Example. [§29.351]** Lorna is contractually owed $5,000 from Michael. Michael thereafter makes a contract with Chris, promising to sell Chris his car in return for Chris's promise to assume Michael's duty to pay Lorna.

There has been a delegation. **Michael is the delegating party**, for he transferred an obligation under a contract to Chris, a third party. **Lorna is the obligee**, for she was owed a duty by Michael and, after the delegation, a third party acquired the obligation to perform the duty. **Chris is the delegate**, for Michael's duty of payment is being transferred to him.

The agreement between Michael and Chris is also a third party beneficiary contract. In third party beneficiary language, **Chris is the promisor**, for he has undertaken a contractual promise to perform an act that will benefit a third person. **Michael is the promisee**, for he bargained for Chris's promise. **Lorna is the beneficiary**, for she is not a party to the Chris/Michael contract and will be befited by its performance.

Suppose Chris does not pay Lorna as he promised. The issue here is whether *Michael*, as well as Lorna, can sue Chris for his non-performance. The answer is **YES**. Michael, as the promisee under a third party beneficiary contract, has the right to sue a breaching promisor for the promisor's breach (see §27.6). Of course Chris does not have to pay twice; he is liable for only one complete satisfaction. Nonetheless, both Lorna and Michael have a valid claim against him.

b. **Example. [§29.352]** Sam owes Leo $1,000 under a valid contract, the payment of which is due on Wednesday. On Tuesday, Sam calls his rich Aunt Freida and asks whether she will pay Leo for him as a favor. Freida agrees to do so, and Sam immediately calls Leo and tells Leo that Sam's payment obligation has been "delegated" to Aunt Freida. Aunt Freida does not pay the $1,000 on Wednesday.

Leo is certainly entitled to sue Sam, the delegating party, for breach when Aunt Freida does not pay. Leo is also entitled to sue Aunt Freida, the delegate, assuming that what she said in her conversation with Sam was a sufficient objective manifestation of her intention to assume Sam's payment obligation. However, **Sam** may **not** sue Aunt Freida for her failure to pay, for Aunt Freida's promise to Sam was only an unenforceable gift promise. Accordingly, Sam acquired no right to enforce her promise. Thus, since Sam is not a "promisor" with third party beneficiary contractual rights against a "promisee," but merely a delegating party attempting to sue a delegate for non-performance of an unenforceable gift promise, he has no valid claim for breach resulting from Aunt Freida's failure to make the payment.

E. DISTINCTION BETWEEN NOVATION AND DELEGATION. [§29.4] A novation occurs when a party who is owed a duty agrees to accept the promised performance of another in **satisfaction of that duty** (see §24.2). Hence, a delegation differs from a novation in that an effective delegation does not carry with it a discharge of the delegating party's duties. That is, if all that occurs is a delegation, the delegating party still remains liable to the obligee for non-performance. However, if: (i) the delegate offers to perform the delegating party's duty **in return for the obligee's promise to release the delegating party from having to perform that duty**; and (ii) **the obligee agrees to such a transaction**, then a novation has occurred and the delegating party's duty is discharged.

1. **EXAMPLE. [§29.41]** In the Vergie/Jim hypothetical discussed in §29.2111, assume that the new travel agency writes Jim just after the delegation, but this time the letter says "Vergie has retired and has asked us to look after her accounts. If you are willing to accept our agency as your exclusive travel consultant and to let us provide you with the cruise ticket for $1,500 instead of Vergie, please sign below." If Jim signs, there has now been a novation, not a delegation, and the result of which is that Jim has discharged the obligation Vergie owed him and now is entitled to enforce the promise to provide him with a ticket only against the new travel agency.

XI. REMEDIES

INTRODUCTORY NOTE REGARDING REMEDIES FOR BREACH OF CONTRACT: Contracts professors generally hold one of two views as to where in the course remedies should be studied. Some teach it in the first month or so, on the theory that students need to know what the litigants in breach actions are really fighting about before concepts of formation, defenses, and performance, etc. make sense. Others teach it near the end of the course, on the theory that students cannot fully comprehend the intricacies of remedies until they already have a good understanding of formation, breach, and defenses. In either case, students learn that contracts remedies are categorized into three types: (i) equitable remedies; (ii) money damages; and (iii) restitution. As a consequence, this part of the Book is organized as follows:

Chapter Thirty contains a discussion of the two most common forms of **equitable relief**: *specific performance* and *prohibitory injunctions*.

Chapter Thirty-One discusses the "legal" remedy of **money damages**, which is the most common form of remedy awarded in breach actions under American law. This Chapter focuses on damages for breaches of common law (i.e., non-UCC) contracts, but the basics of breaches under contracts governed by Article 2 are also discussed.

Chapter Thirty-Two discusses **restitution**, which provides a remedy when one contracting party unjustly enriches another.

Chapter Thirty-Three discusses how these remedies are specifically applied in the **UCC**. The basics of UCC breach remedies (usually sufficient for most contracts courses) can be gleaned from Chapters Thirty through Thirty-Two. But for those Contracts classes whose Professors stress the UCC, the remedies under the UCC are set forth in some detail in this Chapter.

CHAPTER THIRTY: EQUITABLE REMEDIES

A. EQUITABLE RELIEF GENERALLY. [§30.0] Early common law jurisprudence was administered by two separate court systems — courts of law and courts of equity (the latter also known as ecclesiastical courts). While the civil procedures governing legal and equitable claims are now "merged" into one set of rules, one vestige of the split jurisprudential system continues to be evident in the different substantive rules contract law maintains for determining when a non-breaching party is entitled to equitable relief, as opposed to "legal" relief (the payment of money damages) upon the other party's breach. This Chapter deals with the two most significant kinds of equitable relief, specific performance and injunctions. (Note that equitable remedies in Article 2 contracts are governed by these same general principles. The differences are discussed in §§33.1;33.4.)

B. THE TWO COMMON TYPES OF EQUITABLE REMEDIES FOR BREACH OF CONTRACT: SPECIFIC PERFORMANCE AND PROHIBITORY INJUNCTION. [§30.1] The two most common types of equitable relief granted for breach of contract claims by American courts are:

(1) **Specific Performance**, where a court orders a party actually to perform the very duty that he or she promised to perform in the contract; and

(2) **Prohibitory Injunctions**, where a court orders a party to refrain from doing something that would interfere with his or her ability to carry out the performance promised under the contract.

1. EXAMPLE. [§30.11] In a written and signed contract, Janet freely and voluntarily promised to sell her Rembrandt painting to the County Art Museum for $1,500,000. However, on the day she is supposed to deliver it, she calls the Museum and says she has changed her mind and will no longer go through with the deal. The Museum is entitled to seek an order of specific performance, requiring Janet to perform specifically what she promised to do in the contract, namely to deliver possession of, and title to, the painting to the Museum upon the Museum's tender of $1,500,000 [Restatement 2d §360, Com. b, Ill. 1]. If she disregards the court's specific performance order, the court may enforce it by holding Janet in contempt until she turns over possession of the painting.

2. EXAMPLE OF *LUMLEY V. WAGNER*. [§30.12] Ms. Wagner, an opera singer, signed a contract agreeing to sing exclusively for Mr. Lumley, the producer of an opera company in London, for a three-month period. However, Mr. Gye, the producer of a competing London company, induced Ms. Wagner to sing at his theatre instead during this three-month period. **Held:** Mr. Lumley was entitled to obtain an injunction prohibiting Ms. Wagner from appearing at any other concert during the three months she had agreed to sing with Mr. Lumley's company. *Lumley v. Wagner*, 1 DeG. M. & G. 604, 42 Eng. Rep. 687 (Ch. 1852).

An order for specific performance is not appropriate to enforce a personal service contract (such as the one Ms. Wagner signed), partly because such an order could perpetuate a system of involuntary servitude. In other words the court would not require Ms. Wagner to sing at Lumley's theatre. However, it would grant the equitable remedy of a prohibitory injunction restraining her from singing at Mr. Gye's theatre or from undertaking any similar employment which would interfere with her ability to perform under the original personal service contract. As with specific performance, courts are entitled to enforce such injunctions through their contempt powers (see §30.223).

C. REQUIREMENTS FOR OBTAINING EQUITABLE RELIEF FOR BREACH OF CONTRACT. [§30.2]

As contract law developed, common law judges were faced with the decision whether to award equitable relief as the normal remedy for contractual breach (making the recovery of money damages the exception), or whether to award money damages as the norm (making specific performance and injunctive relief the unusual remedy). Having equitable relief as the typical remedy is, in some sense, the more moral approach, for it would ordinarily force a party to live up to his or her promises and actually perform what he or she said she would do. However, that approach also has significant costs for the legal system. If a court orders that some task be performed, a court must engage in some supervision of the task, not only to ensure it is done, but also that it is done acceptably well, or else its orders will become meaningless. Partly because of this administrative burden, and partly for other reasons, contract law has opted for money damages as being the typical remedy for a breach (see §31.0). Hence it is only in the extraordinary case where equitable relief will be granted.

As a consequence, the elements a non-breaching party must meet in order to obtain an order for equitable relief are fairly stringent. To obtain an order for equitable relief, the non-breaching party must establish:

(1) That an award of **money damages** is "**inadequate**" to give the innocent party the benefit of his or her bargain [Restatement 2d §359] (see §30.21);

(2) That there are **no undue "practical limitations"** on a court's ability to grant equitable relief [Restatement 2d §§362, 366, and 367] (see §30.22); and

(3) That an award of equitable relief will **not itself be unfair** by violating one of the "equitable principles" governing the grant of equitable relief [Restatement 2d §§364, 365] (see §30.33).

1. EQUITABLE RELIEF WILL NOT BE AWARDED UNLESS AN AWARD OF DAMAGES WOULD BE "INADEQUATE" TO PUT THE NON-BREACHING PARTY IN THE POSITION THE PARTY WOULD HAVE BEEN IN HAD THE CONTRACT BEEN PERFORMED. [§30.21]

As noted above (§30.2), American contract law provides that an award of money damages is the presumptive remedy granted in breach of contract cases. Hence, the first requirement a non-breaching party seeking equitable relief must establish is that an award of damages would somehow be "inadequate" to compensate fully. In contract law, a non-breaching party is considered fully compensated when a remedy awarded by a court puts the party in the position he or she would have been in had the contract been performed [UCC §1-106; Restatement 2d §347, Com. a]; (see §31.3). If an award of money damages can possibly fulfill that goal, contract law dictates that money damages should be awarded. However, when money damages are "inadequate" to meet this goal, equitable relief may be appropriate.

The Restatement 2d sets forth three factors a court must weigh in determining whether money damages are adequate to give the non-breaching party the benefit of the contract, i.e., to put the non-breaching party in the position he or she would have been in had the contract been performed:

(1) **The difficulty in proving damages with reasonable certainty;**

(2) **The difficulty of procuring a suitable substitute performance upon an award of monetary damages; and**

(3) **The likelihood that an award of damages could not be collected** [Restatement 2d §360].

a. The Difficulty of Proving Damages with Reasonable Certainty. [§30.211] Sometimes it is reasonably easy to establish a breach, but very difficult to establish with any kind of certainty what damages will flow from that breach; e.g., the breach has prevented a new business from starting and no one can predict with certainty how much money the new business owner would have realized; or where the breach is a repudiation of a future performance, where the value of the performance in the future is likely subject to a number of variables; or where the breach is a requirement or output contracts where precise quantity levels are unknown before performance has actually taken place (see §7.623). In these kinds of situations, there is simply no accurate way to come up with an amount of money damages that would put the non-breaching party in the same position as he or she would have been in had the contract been performed. *Any* amount would be too speculative. Accordingly, contract law deems money damages "inadequate" to appropriately compensate the non-breaching party in these types of cases, thereby fulfilling the first requirement for awarding equitable relief [Restatement 2d §360(1)].

SPECIAL CASE SQUIB

(1) Example of *Laclede Gas Co. v. Amoco Oil Co.* [§30.2111] Laclede's predecessor entered into a long-term requirements contract with Amoco, whereby Amoco was to provide the former company, and now Laclede with its needs for propane. After operating under the agreement for some time, Amoco stated that it would be making no further deliveries. Laclede brought suit, seeking an order for specific performance compelling Amoco to continue supplying its requirements of propane. **Held:** Laclede was entitled to an order of specific performance. *Laclede Gas Co. v. Amoco Oil Co.*, 522 F.2d 33 (8th Cir. 1975).

The court held that specific performance was proper because of the difficulty in proving with reasonable certainty damages that would flow from the breach. Amoco argued that money damages would be sufficient to give Laclede the benefit of the bargain. That is, Amoco's argument was that propane gas was plentiful from other suppliers in the area, and so even if Amoco were found to be in breach, the only damages Laclede would suffer would be the difference between the price at which Amoco had agreed to supply the gas, and the price charged Laclede by another supplier.

The court stated that while an award of money damages would probably be an adequate remedy if the contract called for a one-time, fixed amount delivery of propane, such was not the case under the Amoco/Laclede contract. This was a long term requirements contract, and so it is not possible to know exactly how much gas Laclede would order in the future, thus making a precise award of damages hard to calculate. In addition, while gas from alternative sources was plentiful now, no one could predict whether that would continue, or would continue at any particular price, again making damages difficult to approximate. Further, a one-time award of damages would not really give Laclede what it bargained for, since part of the reason Laclede entered into a long-term requirements contract was to secure the peace of mind that came from assurances of a long-term adequate supply of propane. Accordingly, Laclede was entitled to equitable relief [Restatement 2d §360, Com. b, Ill. 4 and 5].

---

(2) Example. [§30.2112] Shelly was awarded a fried chicken franchise by a national company in a brand new location. Her contract provided that she was to receive 30% of the net profits from the franchise. Without justification, the company breached its agreement with Shelly and awarded the franchise to Gary instead. Shelly can satisfy the first element necessary for an award of specific performance, i.e., that it would be difficult to prove with reasonable certainty an amount of damages that would compensate her for the breach.

(3) Example. [§30.2113] First Bank is contractually obligated to lend $30 million to a producer for the production of a new movie. The Bank unjustifiedly refuses to fund the loan, and upon hearing that First Bank would not lend the producer money, no other financial institution would lend the producer money either. In such a case, an award of specific performance would be appropriate, since it would be difficult to estimate what profits, if any, the producer would make from the movie.

Note that if the producer was able to secure a loan from another bank, but at a higher interest rate, First Bank would only be liable in money damages measured by the difference in interest charges the producer has to pay for the new loan versus the First Bank loan.

b. The Difficulty of Procuring Suitable Substitute Performance. [§30.212] The second factor a court will weigh in determining whether an award of money damages is "inadequate" in a particular case is the amount of difficulty the non-breaching party will have in obtaining suitable substitute performance from a third party if an award of damages is made. That is, if the goods, services, etc., which are the subject matter of the contract are fungible, or otherwise can easily be purchased elsewhere, an award of damages is appropriate. In such a case, the non-breaching party can go into the market, purchase the goods, services, etc., from a third party, and require the breaching party to pay the difference, if any, between what he or she paid in the market for the product or service and the contract price (see §33.21). That way the non-breaching party is put in exactly the same position he or she would have been in had the contract been performed.

If the goods or services are not readily available elsewhere, however, an award of damages would not result in the non-breaching party ending up in the position he or she would have been in had the contract been performed. This is because, by definition, it would be sufficiently difficult for the injured party to buy substitute goods or services promised under the contract from anyone, no matter how large an award of damages. Accordingly, **the more unique a good or a service promised to be provided under a contract is, the more likely equitable relief will be awarded for breach of that agreement** [Restatement 2d §360(2)]. Many years ago, courts demanded that to fulfill this requirement the good truly be a one-of-a-kind item. However, today the party seeking equitable relief need only show the item to be *fairly unique,* or as some courts put it, that there "would be undue difficulty in procuring a suitable replacement."

One intractable rule governing "uniqueness" in this context is that **land is always considered unique,** and so a buyer under a contract for the purchase of land will always be able to meet this part of the test for equitable relief. (See Case Squibs Section, *Hilmor Sales Co v. Neushaefer Div. of Surponics Corp.* for the argument that a low price can make an item "unique"

(1) **Example. [§30.2121]** The Janet/County Art Museum hypothetical concerning the Rembrandt painting discussed in §30.11 is an example of a "unique" good situation. That is, an award of damages to the Museum as a result of Janet's refusal to turn over the particular painting would not allow the Museum to replace what it bargained for. As such, equitable relief is appropriate.

(2) **Example. [§30.2122]** Mary Lee contracts to sell her house to Bill. Later, she changes her mind, decides to stay in her house, and cancels the contract. She offers to pay Bill the difference, if any, between the price Bill was going to pay for her house and the price of the house next door, which has the identical floor plan to Mary Lee's house and is presently for sale. Bill is entitled to specific performance of his contract with Mary Lee. As noted above, each piece of land is considered unique, and even if the house next door has the identical floor plan, etc., contract law holds there will be enough differences between the two properties to make Mary Lee's property unique. Hence, an award of damages will not be "adequate" to obtain Bill the benefits to which he was contractually entitled, and so he is empowered to have Mary Lee's promise to sell him her house specifically performed.

(3) **Example. [§30.2123]** Gail owns a Dusenberg automobile in pristine condition. There are only seven other known models of this type of Dusenberg in pristine condition, none of which are currently for sale. Gail contracts to sell it to Bob for $1,000,000, but later also contracts to sell it to Dick for $1,500,000. Bob is probably entitled to specific performance. While the car is not "unique" in that it is not a "one-of-a-kind" car, it is unique enough that Bob would have sufficient difficulty procuring a suitable substitute, even with an award of damages.

(4) **REVIEW PROBLEM. [§30.2124] Leslie contracts with a car dealership for a new car with specified equipment. The car dealership calls her later and refuses to deliver at the contract price. Question: What kind of relief can Leslie obtain?**

> **Answer:** Leslie is not entitled to specific performance, for she can procure a substitute car with the same equipment at another dealership. If the car at the other dealership costs more than she was obligated to pay the first dealer, an award of damages covering the difference will give her the benefit of her bargain with the breaching dealer, i.e., the car she wants at the price she agreed to pay.

c. **The Likelihood that an Award of Damages could not be Collected. [§30.213]** Courts do not want to issue orders that cannot be fulfilled by the parties. If a breaching party has no money, a court's award of money damages to the non-breaching party is likely not going to do that party much good. Thus, the inability of a breacher to pay a damage award is one factor a court will weigh in deciding whether to order equitable relief [Restatement 2d §360(3)].

Note that Restatement 2d §360(3) does not set forth a rule that any time a breaching party is in poor financial health an award of equitable relief will automatically be forthcoming; nor does it say that a non-breaching party is always entitled to specific performance if the breaching party is in bankruptcy. Rather, this provision only states that a court will look at the likelihood of the non-breaching party's ability to collect an award of damages as **one factor** in deciding whether to exercise its discretion to award equitable relief.

(1) Example. [30.2131] Dorothy contracts to sell her bicycle shop to Maury for $80,000. Shortly before the transfer of ownership is to take place, Dorothy becomes insolvent and repudiates the contract. Dorothy's insolvency is a factor indicating specific performance should be granted, as there is a genuine likelihood that an award of damages could not be collected [Restatement 2d §360(3), Com. d., Ill. 9].

2. EQUITABLE RELIEF WILL NOT BE AWARDED IF THERE ARE UNDUE PRACTICAL LIMITATIONS ON A COURT'S ABILITY TO GRANT SUCH RELIEF. [§30.22] Whenever a court grants equitable relief, there are administrative burdens involved in supervising a party's compliance with the court's order. When those burdens get too great, a court will decline to order specific performance or an injunction, even if a damage award would not reliably put the innocent party in the position he or she would have been in had the contract been performed. In other words, the decision to grant equitable relief is discretionary with the court, and one of the factors a court may weigh in deciding to use its discretion is how burdensome supervising the equitable decree will be. A non-exhaustive but typical list of the practical problems of enforcement that courts consider in deciding whether to order equitable relief includes:

(1) Whether the terms of the contract are sufficiently certain so as to provide a basis for an appropriate court order [Restatement 2d §362] (see §30.221);

(2) Whether the nature and magnitude of the performance promised in the contract would impose a supervisory burden on the court that is disproportionate to the advantages to be gained from specific enforcement and to the harm to be suffered from its denial [Restatement 2d §366] (see §30.222); and

(3) Whether the contract calls for personal services [Restatement 2d §367(1)] (see §30.323).

a. Whether the Terms of the Contract Are Too Uncertain to Provide a Basis for a Specific Performance Order. [§30.221] A court is entitled to refuse equitable relief if the standards set forth in the contract are insufficiently detailed to allow the court to formulate a clear order, or to allow the court to monitor in any meaningful way whether the breaching party is complying with an order for equitable relief [Restatement 2d §362]. The idea is that if a court orders specific performance, it wants to make its order clear enough so that the party subject to the order knows what he or she has to do to avoid being in contempt for violating the order. Further, the order must be detailed enough so that the court can easily monitor whether its order is being followed. Hence, when the terms of the contract at issue are insufficiently detailed to allow the court to issue a reasonably specific order, a court is disinclined to grant equitable relief.

Note there is a fine line between a contract that is so indefinite that it cannot be enforced (see Chapter Six), and one that is definite enough to be enforced, but too indefinite to support an award of equitable relief. While the line may be fine, there are some contracts that fall between those boundaries, and so when the parties contract in very general terms, often courts will decline to specifically enforce their agreements.

(1) Example. [§30.2211] Darryl owns a piece of prime downtown property. He enters into a contract with Construct Co. to develop the property. Under their contract, Construct Co. will furnish the plans and eventually construct a 30-story high rise on the premises, which Construct Co. promises will be a "first class building, equivalent to other prime office space in the downtown area." Construct Co. breaches, failing either to submit the plans or build the building.

Darryl would probably not be entitled to an order of specific performance because his contract with Construct Co. is too uncertain to allow the court to fashion a sufficiently detailed specific performance order. That is, the most a court could do would be to order Construct Co. "to build a first class building equivalent to other prime office space . . . ." Issuing such an order would probably not provide Construct Co. with enough direction as to what it had to do to avoid being in contempt. In addition, it would be difficult for the court to monitor the order and to decide whether its order had been violated. Hence, such a contract is too uncertain to support a specific performance order [Restatement 2d §362, Com b., Ill. 1].

b. **Whether the Supervisory Burden on the Court Outweighs the Advantage to be Gained by an Order for an Equitable Remedy. [§30.222]** There are occasions when a court will decline to issue an order for equitable relief simply because enforcement and supervision of the order will be far more burdensome than the advantages the non-breaching party will receive from the issuance of such an order [Restatement 2d §366]. This will occur when difficult questions will be raised as to the quality of performance under the decree, when the court's supervision will have to continue for a long period of time, or when the court will have to supervise a very complex operation. This is not to say that any time a complex contract comes before the court there cannot be a specific performance decree. However, it is to say a court is entitled to weigh the supervisory burdens involved in issuing an equitable remedy against the advantages gained by the non-breaching party from such an order. If the former are disproportionate to the latter, a court is entitled to use its discretion and decline to issue equitable relief, even if a damage award to the innocent party would otherwise be considered "inadequate."

(1) **Example. [§30.2221]** An airplane manufacturer promises United Air Lines that it will design, test, and have certified a new jet airplane to fulfill United's needs for such a plane in 1999. In 1996, the manufacturer still has not produced a prototype. The manufacturer estimates that to meet its promised deadline, it will have to employ 300 more engineers and take additional steps to speed up the work. United will be unable to get a decree of specific performance, for the burden to the court involved in enforcing such an order outweighs the advantages to be gained from specifically enforcing the manufacturer's promise [Restatement 2d §366, Com. a, Ill. 1].

(2) **Example. [§30.2222]** Build'em is a real estate developer who sells a house to Baxter, promising Baxter that before escrow closes, there will be a sewer system in place. Build'em never constructs the sewer system. While an order of specific performance would require some supervision by the court, the administrative burden is not disproportionate to the health and safety benefits Baxter would receive from the installation of a working sewage system and thus equitable relief would be available. [Restatement 2d §366, Com. a, Ill. 3].

c. **If the Contract Calls for the Performance of "Personal Services" it Will Not be Specifically Enforced. [§30.223]** A court will not issue an order requiring that a contract for personal service be specifically enforced [Restatement 2d §367(1)]. This rule leads to three questions: (1) what are "personal service" contracts?; (2) why won't courts order that they be specifically performed?; and (3) what rights does the innocent party have upon the breach of such a contract if he or she cannot obtain a specific performance decree? Each of these questions is answered below.

In a general sense, a "personal services" contract is any contract that calls not only for performance of a specific duty, but also for a particular person to do it. However, for purposes of the doctrine denying specific performance in "personal service" contracts, that definition is too broad. That is, there are some contracts that will meet the general definition given above, but are still be capable of being specifically enforced (see §30.2231).

While there is no universally agreed upon definition for the subset of personal service contracts that will be subject to the specific performance bar, the idea is that the more the contract calls for the performance by a particular person based on that **particular** individual's skills, character, training, talents, etc., the more likely it is to be subject to this rule. In other words, the more the performance in the contract would be non-delegable (see §29.222), the more likely it is that the party promising to perform the service will not be ordered specifically to perform it.

To say that such contracts will not be **specifically** enforced does not mean they will not be enforced at all. The non-breaching party is, of course, free to seek a damage award. Further, the non-breaching party may also seek a prohibitory injunction preventing the breaching party from engaging in any competitive work during the period he or she was supposed to be working for the non-breaching party. However, there are limitations on when the non-breaching party is entitled to such an injunction, and these limitations are discussed below.

Under Restatement 2d §367(2), a non-breaching party is **not** entitled to a prohibitory injunction for breach of a personal service contract when either:

(a) the probable result of such an order will be to compel an undesirable personal relationship; or

(b) the breaching party will be left without a reasonable means of making a living if such an order were issued.

(1) **Example. [§30.2231]** Ted occasionally supplies air taxi service to remote regions in Alaska. On Jan. 10, a scientific research team visited Ted and explained that they were just about to leave for an extended study of weather patterns in a remote area of the Alaskan tundra. They explained that while their project was to last for four months, they could only carry two months worth of supplies with them. Accordingly, they signed a contract with Ted whereby he unconditionally and personally promised to fly food and other provisions to the team on March 15 to replenish their supplies. In early March, Ted decides the trip is not worth the hassle, and anticipatorialy repudiates the agreement. There is no other way to get the supplies to the research team. Even though this is a personal services contract in the general sense of the term, i.e., it calls for a particular person to do a particular task, it probably can be specifically enforced. That is, the contract was not awarded to Ted based on any particular skill, training, etc., that separates him from any other pilot. Any reliable air carrier would have been acceptable to deliver the supplies for the research team. Accordingly, Ted could be subject to a specific performance order compelling him to fulfill his promised performance.

(2) Example. [§30.2232] A prominent actor is hired to star in a movie and contractually promises the producer his exclusive services for the next four months. A few days after signing that contract, the actor signs another contract to appear in a second movie, the filming of which would entail some overlap with his four-month exclusive commitment in the first movie. The producer of the first movie is not entitled to an order of specific performance, for acting is a "personal service" which could not be delegated. That is, the contract was awarded based on the skills and training which separate this particular actor from all other actors. However, the producer is entitled to an injunction prohibiting the actor from taking on potentially competitive work during the four-month period [Restatement 2d §367, Com b, Ill. 1].

(3) Example. [§30.2233] Same as above, except this time it is the producer who unjustifiably fires the actor shortly after beginning production of the movie. As is true for producer, the actor would similarly not be entitled to a specific performance order compelling the producer to hire him back, for the producer has breached the type of "personal services" contract which is not subject to a specific performance decree. Such an order would end up with an undesirable personal relationship between the actor and the producer.

Note, however, the actor would **not** be entitled to an injunction prohibiting the producer from hiring anyone else to take his place. The reason is that the likely result of such an order would also be "an enforced continuance of an undesirable personal relationship" under §367(2). That is, if the court issued an injunction prohibiting the producer from hiring any one else to take the actor's place, the producer probably has only two realistic choices: (i) to use the actor to complete the film (which she does not want to do); or (ii) to abandon the movie. Since she would likely end up using the actor, the effect of an injunction would be the same as an order of specific performance forcing people to work together who do not want to work together, and under the Restatement 2d, equitable relief should not be issued if the likely result will be the compelled continuance of an undesirable personal relationship [Restatement 2d §367, Com. b, Ill. 4].

(4) Example of Personal Services Contract With Covenant Not to Compete. [§30.2234] An industrial tool manufacturer enters into employment contracts with its sales force. The contract provides, in part, that if a member of the sales force voluntarily leaves the company, "he or she will not take a position in which the employee will compete with the company for a period of two years." This type of clause is known as a "covenant not to compete" and the validity of such clauses have been the subject of much commentary.

Employers want to enforce covenants not to compete so as to prevent employees from taking the trade secrets, customer lists, and other knowledge, the employee has learned while working for the employer and "selling" that knowledge to the employer's competitor upon an offer of a higher salary. Further, the employer has typically invested time and effort into the training of the employee and wants to insure a competitor will not be freely able to purchase the fruits of that training. On the other hand, if such covenants are enforced, the employee ends up being economically tied to his or her employer, and cannot earn a living in his or her chosen profession from anyone else, at least for the period of time he or she has promised not to compete. Hence, because there are reasonable arguments on both sides, contract and labor law have struggled to find the proper approach to such covenants.

The general rule regarding such clauses today is that if a covenant not to compete is freely negotiated and voluntarily assumed by the employee, and if a court finds that the employee did in fact have access to the original employer's trade secrets, such clauses will be enforced by prohibitory injunction. That is, if an employee agrees to such a clause but nevertheless accepts a position with a business rival of the employer, a court will enforce the covenant and issue a prohibitory injunction enjoining the employee from competing with his or her original employer.

However, **courts will only issue such orders if the covenant not to compete is reasonably limited in time, in geography, and in scope.** In other words, a court will not issue an injunction prohibiting an employee: (i) from working for a competing firm if the covenant is supposed to run for an unreasonably long time (probably three to five years is approaching the outside limit in this regard for most kinds of jobs under modern law); or (ii) from doing the same job for a company located in a different geographical market from that in which his or her old employer competed; or (iii) from taking **any** job (not just one which would require divulging trade secrets) with another employer.

3. **EQUITABLE RELIEF WILL NOT BE GRANTED IF CERTAIN "EQUITABLE PRINCIPLES" ARE VIOLATED. [§30.23]** Yet another series of limitations on a court's discretion to make an equitable decree is the presence of certain equitable principles limiting the availability of equitable relief. When equity was its own branch of jurisprudence, the ecclesiastical courts required that the non-breaching party could be guilty of no unfairness in order to qualify for equitable relief. Sometimes this was phrased "to seek equity a party must do equity," or that "a party must not come into equity with 'unclean hands.'" The broader idea was that the hallmark of equity was fairness, and hence before a court would invoke its discretion to grant equitable relief, it had to be convinced that the party seeking such relief had acted fairly in the negotiation and operation of the contract, so as to ensure that the court was not being used to further an injustice. Today, courts consider the following equitable principles in deciding whether to issue an order for specific performance or an injunction:

(1) Whether the act or forbearance compelled by the grant of equitable relief would be **contrary to public policy** [Restatement 2d §365] (see §30.23);

(2) Whether specific enforcement of the contract would be unjust because the breaching party's assent to the contract was **induced by an unfair business practice** [Restatement 2d §364(1)(a)] (see §30.232);

(3) Whether specific enforcement of the contract would **cause unreasonable hardship** to the breaching party [Restatement 2d §364(1)(b)] (see §30.233); and

(4) Whether the court is satisfied that specific enforcement of the contract **would not result in the non-performance** of a substantial part of the agreed exchange [Restatement 2d §363] (see §30.234).

a. **Whether Such an Order Would Violate Public Policy. [§30.231]** Sometimes public policy will prevent an order of specific performance, even though an award of money damages would not be adequate to place the innocent party in the same position as if the contract had been performed, and even though there are not an undue number of practical considerations weighing against the granting of equitable relief. The idea is that a court in equity should not issue an order that itself would be inequitable by violating some other aspect of public policy [Restatement 2d §365].

Sum & Substance QUICK REVIEW of Contracts

(1) Example. [§30.2311] Judy is a trustee, holding a piece of property in trust for Larry, a minor. Judy enters into a contract promising to sell the property, but does so in her own name, not as trustee for Larry. In fact, she plans to abscond with the money and live on a Caribbean island. At the last minute her conscience gets the better of her and she decides she cannot go through with the deal. The purchaser is not entitled to an order of specific performance even though the subject of the contract is real property and even though, as trustee, Judy has the power to sell the property (see §30.21). This is because ordering Judy to go through with the contract as it is written would violate public policy since she is breaching a trust. Courts will not issue an equitable order forcing her to sell the property if such an order will lead to an inequitable result.

b. Whether Such Order would be Unjust Because the Breaching Party's Assent to the Contract Was Induced by Unfair Practices. [§30.232] A court will not issue an order of specific performance if the breaching party was induced to enter the contract by means of an unfair business practice [Restatement 2d §364(1)(a)]. Once again, the idea is that a court in equity wants "to do equity," and thus, will not issue an order compelling someone to live up to their contractual promises when these promises were not made as a result of fully informed, voluntary decision making. Hence, if it turns out that the non-breaching party seeking equitable relief has secured the breaching party's consent to the contract by means of "unclean hands," or "sharp" practices, equitable relief will not be granted.

Note that if the actions of the non-breaching party give rise to one of the contract defenses, e.g., duress, undue influence, etc., no relief of any sort will be granted because the non-performing party is, by definition, not liable for breach. Thus, the rule of Restatement 2d §364(1)(a) covers those situations where the practices of the **non-breaching** party during the negotiation of, or operation under, the contract are deemed "sharp" or sufficiently "unfair." In such cases, if a court determines that it would be unjust to specifically enforce the contract against the breaching party, **equity** will provide no relief, although the breaching party may well be liable in money damages arising from his or her non-performance.

(1) Example. [§30.2321] Sally makes an offer to purchase Bob's home for $200,000. Bob knows comparable homes in his neighborhood are selling for $140,000, and correctly suspects that Sally believes that unfenced the backyard of Bob's house is an acre. In truth, it is only 200 sq. feet. Bob accepts Sally's offer and when she finds out the true facts, she refuses to go through with the transaction. Assuming Bob's acts do not give Sally a defense to the contract such as mistake, or misrepresentation, or that they do not give rise to a successful unconscionability claim, specific performance of the contract can be refused on the ground of unfairness [Restatement 2d §364, Com. a, Ill. 1].

c. Whether Such an Order would be Unjust as Causing Unreasonable Hardship or Loss to the *Breaching* Party. [§30.233] When requiring a breaching party to specifically perform a promise would result in an unjust hardship to the breacher, a court is entitled to use its discretion to deny equitable relief and require the breaching party to pay an award of money damages instead [Restatement 2d §364(1)(b)].

(1) Example based on *Peevyhouse v. Garland Coal & Mining Co.* [§30.2331] Larry owns property in a desolate part of the state which lies fallow. Mining Co. acquires from Larry the right to strip mine for copper on the land, promising in its contract that it will refill the hole after it is done mining and will restore the land so that it will be indistinguishable from the surrounding countryside. After finishing mining, Mining Co. discovers it will cost over $3,000,000 to fill the hole and otherwise perform its promise. The decreased fair market value of the land as a result of having a large hole in it (disregarding the coal taken out), is only $30,000 (i.e., the fair market value of the desolate land without a hole in the middle of it minus its fair market value with such a hole is $30,000). Mining Co. does not fill the hole. Larry is probably not entitled to an order of specific performance given the disproportionate economic hardship such an order would cause to Mining Co. (Note this hypothetical is based on the facts of *Peevyhouse v. Garland Coal & Mining Co.*, 383 P.2d 109 (Okla. 1962)

Note that some commentators defend this kind of decision using a combination of economic policy grounds and a fear that the non-breaching party may be guilty of unclean hands. To them, making a party spend $3,000,000 to convey only a $30,000 monetary benefit is an example of "economic waste," and as such should not be ordered by a court. Also, these commentators suspect that the non-breaching party such as Larry really does not want Mining Co. to specifically perform. They argue that plaintiffs in these cases simply **want a court to issue an order requiring the promisor to perform**, which they will later agree not to enforce upon a payment of an amount less than the cost of performance. That is, in the above case the fear is that Larry is seeking a court order of specific performance just so he can later offer to relieve Mining Co. of its $3,000,000 obligation upon payment to him of, e.g., $2,500,000. Accordingly, these commentators believe that a plaintiff such as Larry is coming into court with "unclean hands" and should be denied equitable relief for that reason as well.

d. **Whether there is Sufficient Security to Believe the Non-Breaching Party Will Perform. [§30.234]** A court will not order the breaching party to specifically perform a promise if the court is worried that the party ordered to perform will not thereafter receive his or her benefits under the contract. For example, a court will not order Joe to deliver his Picasso to Ellyn as he contractually promised if it does not appear that Ellyn will be able to pay Joe upon delivery. Hence, contract law provides that no order of specific performance will be issued unless a substantial part of the return performance due to the breaching party **has already been rendered**, or unless the court determines to its satisfaction that such **return performance is likely** [Restatement 2d §363]. In older cases, this rule was sometimes put that the court will not grant equitable relief unless there is "mutuality of remedy," but this phrase is inaccurate and no longer has any validity. The idea, however, is that a court will not order the breaching party to perform if the non-breaching party has not already substantially performed, or if it does not appear likely that the non-breaching party is in a position to perform.

(1) **Example. [§30.2341]** Sara contracts to sell a piece of land to David for $100,000. Sara refuses to tender the deed, and David seeks an order compelling specific performance. Such an order will not be issued unless David can satisfy the court that he has the money to pay for the land once the deed is tendered. If he cannot establish such ability to the court's satisfaction, he may still be entitled to damages, but not to equitable relief. That is, the court will not order Sara to perform specifically if, as a result, Sara will end up both without her land and without David's payment.

CHAPTER THIRTY-ONE: MONEY DAMAGES

A. THE "INTEREST" ANALYSIS OF CONTRACT LAW AND THE CONCEPT OF ECONOMIC BREACH. [§31.0] As a general rule, contract law does not require parties actually to **perform** their promises. Instead, contract law usually requires only that a party who breaches a contractual promise pay some money to the party injured by the breach. As pointed out in the last chapter, it is the unusual fact situation which permits a court to order a breaching party specifically to perform a contractually undertaken promise (see §30.2).

This phenomenon can be explained by understanding the "interest" analysis of contract law. When a party enters into an enforceable contract, he or she does not receive a protected right to performance by the other party. Instead, he or she is given only a protected economic "interest" in the other party's performance. Hence, when a contract is breached, contract law typically does not order performance. Instead, it generally awards damages based on the extent of the interference with the non-breaching party's protected economic "interest." In other words, when a contract is made, each party gets a kind of property right in the other's performance which contract law protects. The value of the property right is equal to the economic value of performance, i.e., a dollar amount is calculated for the value of the performance promised by each party. When the contract is breached, the injured party can thus recover money damages based on the extent to which he or she failed to receive the complete amount of the economic value of the breaching party's performance.

1. THE "EFFICIENT BREACH" DOCTRINE DEFINED AND EXPLAINED. [§31.01] One result of the "interest" analysis is that, in certain cases, traditional contract law actually **encourages** breach and dictates that a party should **not** render performance. This is known as the doctrine of "efficient breach." The efficient breach doctrine provides that so long as a breaching party is willing to pay for any damages caused by the breach, he or she **should** breach if the end result, after the breacher pays contract damages, is that the breacher will be economically better off. The doctrine is perhaps better explained by example:

Jim's Tool and Die ("Jim's") has a contract with National Hardware Co. to manufacture and deliver one million drywall nails of assorted sizes on or before March 31. Producing one million nails in a month is the limit of Jim's production capacity. The contract price for the nails is $15,000, which was the market price for a million nails the previous October when the contract was signed. However, as of February 15 (approximately six weeks before delivery is due, and before Jim's has started production), the $15,000 contract price appears to make this a good deal for National Hardware, for on that date other manufacturers were charging $17,000 for identical nails. In late February, International Builders ("International") has just received a large building contract on a rush schedule and, as a result, offers Jim's Tool and Die $25,000 for one million assorted drywall nails, also conditioned upon delivery on or before March 31.

The efficient breach doctrine says Jim's should breach its contract with National Hardware and sell the nails to International Builders, for the end result would be a more economically efficient allocation of resources than if it performed. That is, if it is worth $8,000 above the current fair market value to International Builders to acquire the nails, economic efficiency dictates that such money should be allocated to a supplier such as Jim's. Hence, if Jim's breaches its contract with National Hardware so that it can supply International Builders, the end result will be that International Builders will be satisfied, for it will get what it bargained for, a million nails for $25,000. Jim's will be better off, because it will have received $10,000 more for the same goods than it would have from National Hardware.

This, of course, leaves National Hardware without nails. Obviously it is not better off after the breach by Jim's. Recall, however, that one of the principles of the efficient breach doctrine is that the breaching party must be willing to pay damages to the injured party. For National Hardware to receive what it bargained for under its contract with Jim's, Jim's will have to pay National $2,000. That is, since other nail manufacturers are now charging $17,000 for identical nails, to allow National Hardware to receive its bargain, i.e., a million nails for $15,000 out of its own pocket, Jim's will have to pay National $2,000. Jim's will do that because it will still be better off because of the breach.

Hence, in this case the efficient breach doctrine counsels that Jim's breach the contract. This is because by virtue of the breach both National Hardware and International Builders will obtain the benefit of their bargains, i.e., a million nails at the prices they were willing to pay. Jim's, the breaching party, will be a net $8,000 better off as a result of the breach, even after paying the damages caused by the breach.

B. DEFINING, IDENTIFYING, AND VALUING THE ECONOMIC INTERESTS RESULTING FROM CONTRACT FORMATION. [§31.1]

As noted above (see §31.0), the amount of damages an injured party is awarded upon a breach depends on the extent the breach interferes with the non-breaching party realizing the full value of the protected economic interest contract law providing a party upon contract formation. Over time, contract law has arrived at three different ways of calculating the full value of this protected economic interest, which could potentially result in the same or different dollar figures. The amount of the non-breaching party's recovery may well depend on which valuation method is used to ascertain the protected economic interest. The rule is that the unjust party is entitled to pick whichever valuation method he or she wishes, so long as the value of the interest can be adequately proven [Restatement 2d §344].

Rather than referring to these different approaches as different valuation methods, contract law has instead chosen to say that each approach really describes its own kind of "interest." Each party receives contract law's protection for three different types of economic interests. These three different "interests" are really only three different approaches to calculating the value of performance by the breaching party.

The three interests protected by contract law are:

(1) The **expectation interest**;

(2) The **reliance interest**; and

(3) The **restitution interest**.

1. THE EXPECTATION (OR "BENEFIT OF THE BARGAIN") INTEREST. [§31.11]

The economic value of a party's expectation interest is the dollar amount that would place the non-breaching party in as good a position as he or she would have been in had the contract been performed. The expectation interest is also sometimes known as the "benefit of the bargain" interest.

a. **Example. [§31.111]** Barbra is a wholesaler of furniture. That is, she is a "middleman," buying furniture from manufacturers and re-selling that same furniture to retailers. On March 1, Barbra entered into a contract to purchase a dining room set from Manufacturer. Delivery was due April 15, and the price, $5,000, was to be paid 30 days after delivery. Manufacturer knew that Barbra had a retail buyer for the dining room set at the time she placed her order. Nevertheless, Manufacturer failed to deliver the dining room set, and Barbra sued Manufacturer for breach. At trial, Barbra will be able to demonstrate by competent evidence that the retail buyer had agreed to pay $8,000 for the dining room set.

Leaving aside (for the present) concerns about shipping costs, interest, etc., Barbra's expectation interest arising from this contract would be valued at $3,000. That is, to put her in the position she would have been in had Manufacturer performed, she is entitled to $3,000 in damages. That sum is the "benefit of her bargain" for she had a contract to purchase a good at one price ($5,000), and would have been able to sell it to another for a higher price ($8,000). The value of this lost "expectation," i.e., the lost "benefit of the bargain," caused by Manufacturer's breach is thus $3,000 (see §31.3).

2. **THE RELIANCE (OR "OUT-OF-POCKET") INTEREST. [§31.12] The economic value of a party's reliance interest is typically the dollar amount of whatever out-of-pocket costs (including labor) were incurred by the non-breaching party up to the time of the breach in reliance on the breaching party's performance.** In most instances, the amount of a party's reliance interest is thus fairly easily valued, since a party usually knows how much he or she has spent in performance (or preparing for performance) under a contract.

Note that the goal in protecting a party's expectation interest is "forward looking," i.e., an award of expectation damages is designed to put the non-breaching party in the position he or she would have been in had the contract gone forward (see §31.11). On the other hand, the goal in protecting a party's **reliance** interest is "backward looking," i.e., an award of reliance damages is designed to put the non-breaching party back in the position he or she was in before the contract was entered into by making the breaching party refund any money the injured party has spent in reliance on the breaching party's performance.

a. **Example. [§31.121]** Betty contracts with Archie, promising to build him a custom house for $100,000. Betty promptly begins construction and within a few days has poured the foundation and has erected the house's frame. At this point, Archie breaches by unjustifiably ordering Betty to stop construction and to leave his property. At the time of the breach, Betty has incurred costs of $20,000 (including labor) in pouring the foundation and erecting the frame. The value of her reliance interest is therefore $20,000.

3. **THE RESTITUTIONARY INTEREST. [§31.13] A contracting party's restitutionary interest is valued by the dollar amount one party has unjustly enriched the other at the time of the breach.** The value of a party's restitutionary interest is the reasonable value of the benefits that party has actually received from the other up to the time of the breach (see Chapter Thirty-Two for a discussion and examples of the restitutionary interest).

4. **WHICH TYPE OF DAMAGES CAN THE NON-BREACHING PARTY RECOVER: THE INTERESTS PROTECTED IN PARTICULAR CONTRACTS. [§31.14]** One of the interesting things about modern contract law is that, **in every contract**, a party has an expectation, a reliance, *and* a restitutionary interest. In other words, these interests are really just three different *methods* used to place a value on the economic value of the other party's promised performance. Hence, upon a breach, the non-breacher has a choice of which method he or she wishes to use in seeking monetary recovery for the breach. That is, in every case, the innocent party has the option to seek recovery of either expectation damages, of reliance damages, or in restitution. It is up to that party and his or her lawyer to figure out which valuation method would provide the largest recovery in that particular situation, and it under that theory a monetary recovery will be sought. But,

again, the main point is that the non-breaching party may seek recovery under any of the theories in every breach of contract case, and should proceed under the theory that provides a maximum award.

C. **A GLOSSARY OF DAMAGES TERMINOLOGY: TYPES OF CONTRACT DAMAGES DEFINED AND DISCUSSED. [§31.2]** One difficulty students often have in beginning their study of contract damages is that the subject carries with it its own, rather extensive, vocabulary. Hence, the major types of contract damages are listed, defined, and illustrated below.

1. **BENEFIT OF THE BARGAIN DAMAGES. [§31.21]** Benefit of the bargain damages are synonymous with **expectation** damages (see §31.24).

2. **CONSEQUENTIAL DAMAGES. [§31.22]** Consequential damages are damages which a reasonable person, present at the time of contract formation, would **not** foresee occurring as a natural result of the breach. The injured party must not only prove that the loss occurred and its amount, but **also** that there was some reason the party in breach should have known that such a loss would follow from a breach of their particular contract. The injured party will only be able to recover his or her "consequential" damages if he or she can prove that something happened to put the breaching party on notice at the time of contract formation that the injured party would suffer an otherwise unforseeable kind of damage upon a breach, and that the breaching party would be responsible for this reasonnably unforseeable kind of damage. Most damages deemed consequential are lost profits (however, not all lost profits are consequential damages; see §31.423). The point is that a "consequential" damage can be **any** kind of damage, so long as its occurrence would not be foreseeably incurred by the non-breaching party as judged by a reasonable person present at contract formation.

The rationale for consequential loss and the strictures for its recovery eminated from *Hadley v. Baxendale* (see §31.421 et seq).

a. **Example. [§31.221]** Greg, a law student, buys a stereo from a retailer for $1,000. Although the retailer does not know it, Greg intends to re-sell the stereo to his friend Ann for $1,500. When the retailer does not deliver the stereo, Greg loses the sale to Ann and sues the retailer for the lost $500 profit.

The $500 is a "consequential damage." This is because a reasonable person in the position of the retailer at the time the contract was made would not foresee that the failure to deliver the stereo would naturally result in a lost profit in a subsequent re-sale transaction. That does not mean that such a loss would be inconceivable, but it does mean that a retailer would not reasonably foresee that its failure to deliver the system would cause Greg a lost profit.

Labelling the loss "consequential" does not mean it cannot be recovered. However, it does mean that it can only be recovered if Greg can prove the retailer was somehow put on notice that such a loss would ensue upon non-delivery. Since the facts indicate that no such notice was given, Greg cannot meet the proof requirements under the foreseeability doctrine to recover the real, but consequential, loss he suffered (see §31.42).

3. **DIRECT DAMAGES. [§31.23]** Direct damages are damages that may fairly and reasonably be considered as arising naturally from a breach of contract, as viewed by a reasonable person at the time of contract formation. Thus, they are the kind of damages the injured party may recover without having to make the special showing of foreseeability necessary to recover consequential damages (see §31.42).

The rationale for "direct" loss and the requirements for its recovery eminated from *Hadley v. Baxendale* (see §31.421 et seq).

    a. **Example. [§31.231]** Manufacturer is under a contractual obligation to deliver 100 clock-radios to a retailer. Manufacturer breaches the contract, and fails to cure. The retailer goes into the open market and reasonably purchases 100 identical radios for $3/radio more than Manufacturer's price. The $300 price differential (100 radios x $3/radio) is a direct damage, for it is the type of damage a reasonable person in the position of Manufacturer at the time of contract formation would foresee the injured party suffering as a natural result of its failure to deliver the radios. That is, a price differential in securing replacement goods is certainly the kind of damage that flows in the ordinary course of events from a failure of a manufacturer to deliver promised goods. Accordingly, such loss may be recovered without the special showing of foreseeability necessary for the recovery of consequential damages.

4. **EXEMPLARY DAMAGES. [§31.24]** Exemplary damages are synonymous with **punitive** damages (see §31.2-11).

5. **EXPECTATION DAMAGES. [§31.25]** Expectation damages are damages awarded as a result of the breaching party's interference with the injured party's expectation interest (see §31.11 for a discussion of the expectation interest). Expectation damages are measured by the dollar value necessary to put the injured party in the position he or she would have been in had the contract been performed. Note, however, an award of expectation damages is subject to three important limitations: certainty, foreseeability, and avoidability (see §31.4).

6. **GENERAL DAMAGES. [§31.26]** General damages are synonymous with **direct** damages (see §31.23). Note that the term "general damages" is also used in tort law to denote things like pain and suffering and general emotional distress. The term does **not** have that meaning in contract, where its meaning is limited to those damages that a reasonable person present at the time of the contract's making would foresee as naturally flowing from the breach, and thus, are recoverable without the special foreseeability showing necessary for consequential loss.

7. **INCIDENTAL DAMAGES. [§31.27]** Incidental damages are costs incurred by the **non-breaching** party, **after** the breach, in an attempt to avoid increased loss to the breaching party. Often these damages are out-of-pocket costs, but they also include things like reasonable charges for storing the non-conforming goods that are stored at the non-breaching party's plant. The term "incidental damage" was first used by the UCC in §2-715, but it is now accepted as a measure of contract damage in non-UCC situations as well [Restatement 2d §347(b)]. Typical incidental costs are the expenses borne in the storage, receipt, or transportation of improperly tendered goods, interest costs, etc. Note that so long as the decision of the non-breaching party to incur a cost in an attempt to avoid further damages to the breacher was reasonable, and so long as the amount of the expenditure was reasonable, the loss is recoverable. (See §33.312 for additional explination of incidental damages under the UCC.)

    a. **Example. [§31.271]** Larry has been unjustly fired by his employer. He spends $300 hiring a search firm to help him find a new job. The $300 is a recoverable incidental damage, for it is expense incurred after the breach by the injured party (Larry), in a reasonable attempt to lessen the damages owed by the employer. That is, if Larry could find a comparable job, the amount of his salary would be offset from the damages owed by the breaching employer. Note that the $300 incidental damage is recoverable

regardless of whether the search firm actually finds Larry a new job. Since Larry would not have borne this expense absent his employer's breach, and since the decision to hire the firm is a reasonable one in an attempt to mitigate the employer's loss, and because the amount of the expenditure was reasonable, Larry is entitled to the $300 in his breach action regardless of the search firm's success. Moreover, the majority view is that Larry is entitled to the $300 even if the search firm finds him employment that pays him more than his old job. That is, even if he is economically "better off" because of the breach, he still can recover his incidental damages.

8. **LIQUIDATED DAMAGES. [§31.28]** Liquidated damages are damages, the amount of which are fixed by the parties in advance as the amount due upon a breach of their contract. That is, as part of their contract, the parties stipulate how much one will have to pay the other upon a breach of the contract.

   Contract law does not look with favor on liquidated damages. They are only recoverable if: (i) the amount of actual damages resulting from a breach is hard to calculate with precision; **and** (ii) where the amount of the liquidated damage is a reasonable estimate of what the actual damages would be [Restatement 2d §356; UCC §2-718 (1)]; (see §31.7).

9. **NOMINAL DAMAGES. [§31.29]** In every successful breach of contract action, the non-breaching party is entitled to damages. Usually, these will be in the form of expectation damages, reliance damages, or in restitution. However, when the non-breaching party either has not been damaged or cannot sufficiently prove the amount due him or her, the non-breaching party is still entitled to collect "nominal damages" [Restatement 2d §346(2)].

   A nominal damage is a small sum which has nothing to do with the actual amount of damage suffered. Today a typical nominal damage award is $1.00. The reason contract law provides an award of nominal damages for breach of contract is that a breach is considered a serious enough act that it should not go unpunished, even if the non-breaching party is otherwise not injured, or cannot sufficiently prove the extent of his or her injuries. Additionally, some contracts provide that the prevailing party in a breach action is entitled to attorneys' fees. By awarding nominal damages, an innocent party who can establish that the other party breached can still be the "prevailing party" under such a clause, even if he or she cannot otherwise establish any other contract damage.

10. **OUT-OF-POCKET DAMAGES. [§31.2-10]** Out-of-pocket damages are synonymous with **reliance** damages (see §31.2-12).

11. **PUNITIVE DAMAGES. [§31.2-11]** Punitive damages in contract have the same meaning as they do in tort law — they are damages awarded as punishment for behavior that falls below certain normative levels. However, they are awarded far less often in breach of contract suits as they are in tort actions. That is, there are only a few situations in which the court will even consider an award of punitive damages for a contractual breach (see §31.8).

12. **RELIANCE DAMAGES. [§31.2-12]** Reliance damages are damages awarded to compensate for the breaching party's interference with the injured party's reliance interest (see §31.12). Reliance damages are measured by the dollar value of whatever out-of-pocket costs (including labor) were incurred by the innocent party up to the time of the breach in reliance on the breaching party's performance (see §31.5).

a. **Example.** [§31.2-12-1] Stephanie contracts to build a garage on Mark's property. After she begins, Mark unjustifiably orders her off the job. At the time she is fired, she has invested $14,500 in labor and materials in the job. Her reliance damages (out-of-pocket costs) would be $14,500.

13. **SPECIAL DAMAGES.** [§31.2-13] Special damages are synonymous with **consequential** damages (see §31.22).

14. **STIPULATED DAMAGES.** [§31.2-14] Stipulated damages are synonymous with **liquidated** damages (see §31.28).

D. **EXPECTATION DAMAGES: THE GENERAL MEASURE OF CONTRACT DAMAGES.** [§31.3] The most typical measure of contract damages is an award of expectation damages. To fulfill the goal of expectation loss recovery, the amount of such damage should be an amount that will put the non-breaching party in the position he or she would have been in had the contract been performed [Restatement 2d §347, Com. a; UCC §1-106]. The amount of an expectations damage award is thus the amount which will compensate the non-breaching party completely for the economic interference to his or her expectation interest caused by the breach. Note, however, that expectation recovery is limited by three important doctrines: certainty, foreseeability, and avoidability. These doctrines are discussed in §31.4.

1. **EXPECTATION DAMAGES AND "LOSING" CONTRACTS.** [§31.31] A non-breaching party in a "losing" contract, i.e., an economically improvident contract where the party would lose money had the contract been carried out, will not seek expectation damages. That is, because the goal of expectation damages is to put the party in the position he or she would have been in had the contract been carried out, an expectation damages recovery would be no recovery at all. Instead, a party to a losing contract will typically seek a restitutionary recovery (see §32.231), or, perhaps, a reliance damages recovery (see §31.522).

NOTE ON CALCULATING EXPECTATION DAMAGES: There are two basic methods for calculating the level of expectation damages arising from a breach. One is by way of mathematical formula. Such a formula is set forth below, and if you understand how to apply it, damages should not be a difficult subject area for you. The other way is to try to figure out, without resorting to a formula, how much money it would take to put the non-breaching party in the position he or she would have been in had the contract been performed. This latter method will, if analyzed properly, arrive at the same damage figure as the formula, and also uses the same data to achieve that result. However, many students find it both difficult conceptually, and confining intellectually, to be tied to a formula, and prefer the more informal approach of using their common sense to dictate what amount would allow the injured party to reap the benefit of the bargain. Accordingly, in many of the examples given in this chapter, the damage computations are analyzed both ways, i.e., by means of the formula, and by means of analyzing the problem to arrive at the correct damage total without using an equation. Most students will benefit from reading through both approaches. Nevertheless, if you know you are, or are not, a "formula" person, you should follow the method that best helps you learn the material.

In both approaches, however, you must learn the terminology and components that go into such calculations. Section 347 of the Restatement 2d identifies five factors that need to be accounted for in calculating expectation damages:

(1) **Lost Value**. When a party performs a contractual promise, that performance renders value to the other party. When there is a breach, some or all of that value is not received, and is thus "lost." Hence, one component of expectation damages takes into account the economic value that was never received by the innocent party as a result of the breach. This is done by calculating a dollar amount for the economic value that full performance by the non-breaching party would have rendered, and subtracting from that figure the amount of value actually received by the non-breaching party up to the time of the breach.

(2) **Incidental Loss**. The second type of harm recoverable by the injured party as part of his or her expectation damage recovery is the incidental damages suffered by the party as a result of the breach. (See §31.27, incidental damages).

(3) **Consequential Loss**. The third type of harm recoverable by the injured party as part of his or her expectation damage recovery are the consequential damages suffered by the injured party as a result of the breach (see §31.22, consequential damages; see §31.42, recovering consequential damages).

(4) **Cost Avoided.** Recall that one consequence of another party's material breach is that the non-breaching party need not continue performance (see §21.22). Hence, if an injured party ceases his or her own performance due to the other party's material breach, the injured party saves whatever monies it would have taken him or her to finish performance. These "**costs avoided** due to the breach" need to be accounted for in determining the injured party's expectation damages. That is, if as a result of the breach certain monies are not spent by the innocent party, the breaching party must get "credit" for those costs avoided, or else he or she will be made to pay a sum greater than necessary to put the non-breaching party in the position he or she would have been in had the contract been performed.

For example, assume Charles was contractually obligated to purchase Delores's necklace for $1,000 and that payment was due upon delivery. Delores unjustifiably failed to deliver the necklace to Charles, and Charles, of course, did not pay her the $1,000. This $1,000 is thus a "**cost avoided** due to the breach." As a consequence, while Charles is entitled to sue Delores for breach and recover any lost value resulting from Delores's failure to deliver, Delores must also get credit for the $1,000 avoided cost when ascertaining Charles's expectation damages, or else Charles will be overcompensated. That is, let us suppose Charles had made a "good" deal, because the fair market value of the necklace was really $1,250. Delores's breach thus caused Charles to suffer a lost value of $1,250 (i.e., because of her breach he was deprived of owning a $1,250 necklace). However, if he were awarded $1,250 in damages he would be put in a better position than he would have been in had the contract gone forward, for to get the $1,250 worth of benefit (i.e., to get the necklace), he would have had to spend $1,000. Hence, the true measure of his expectation loss because of Delores's breach was only $250. It is that amount, not $1,250, that reflects his lost benefit of the bargain, and which is needed to put him in the same position he would have been in had the contract gone forward. To arrive at that figure, contract law holds that Charles had a "lost value" of $1,250, but subtracts from that figure the $1,000 "cost avoided" he "saved" due to Delores's breach.

(5) **Loss Avoided**. When a non-breaching party can make substitute arrangements for the materials or other resources which were supplied under the breached contract, the breaching party must get credit for the value of these materials or resources in

ascertaining expectation damages. That is, if a non-breaching party can salvage the materials or resources purchased for use in the breached agreement, contract law requires that the breaching party cannot be saddled with their cost, for such a result would end up giving the non-breaching party a windfall, i.e., putting him or her in a better position than the position he or she would have been in had the contract gone forward.

For example, suppose a builder has a contract to build a garage on a homeowner's lot. The builder purchases $5,000 worth of lumber to be used in the job. The homeowner breaches before construction begins. If the builder can use that lumber on another job, the builder cannot recover the $5,000 for the lumber from the breaching homeowner. If the homeowner had to pay for the lumber, the contractor would end up in a **better** position than he or she would have been in had the contract been performed for he or she would have both the $5,000 **and** the lumber.

Accordingly, if materials or resources available for performance under one contract can be salvaged, but **only** if they **can** be salvaged, the fair market value of the salvaged materials must be subtracted from other damages as a "loss avoided" to calculate accurately the injured party's expectation recovery.

Expectation Damages Determined by Formula

Expressed mathematically, the proper formula for calculating expectation damages using the criteria in Restatement 2d §347 is:

Expectation Damages = Lost Value + Incidental Loss + Consequential Loss - Cost Avoided - Loss Avoided.

Hereafter, this formula will be abbreviated: E.D. = L.V.+ I + C - C.A. - L.A.

Expectation Damages Not Determined by Formula

In determining the proper amount of expectation damages due the non-breaching party without reference to the formula, the key is to keep in mind the goal of expectation relief, i.e., to give the injured party enough money so as to put him or her in the same position he or she would have been in had the contract been completely performed.

Several examples of breaches in the most common type of non-UCC contracts follow as illustration of how these principles are applied (see §31.8 and Chapter Thirty-Three, for discussions of the operation of damage remedies in contracts governed by the UCC).

2. **EXAMPLE OF WRONGFUL TERMINATION BY AN EMPLOYER. [§31.32]** Nora is the Head of Surgery at Mercy Hospital ("Mercy"). Nora and Mercy have entered into a written employment agreement which calls for Nora to receive $240,000 in salary over the next year, plus another $36,000 in benefits. Nora and Mercy operate under the contract for 5 months, but then Mercy breaches by wrongfully firing Nora. Nora hires a physician search firm to find her a position, which costs her $400. A few weeks later, the search firm finds her a position as a staff surgeon at a large hospital in another state. Her salary at this new position is $180,000/year, and the benefit package is worth $12,000/year less at the new facility than it was at Mercy. She starts at the new position exactly one month after being fired from Mercy. To take the position, Nora incurs a moving expense of $6,000.

The components of Nora's damages are valued the same way:

Lost Value - The lost value to Nora due to the breach is relatively easy to compute. The total value to Nora of her salary at Mercy for the year-long contract was $240,000, or $20,000/month. She was paid for five months, so she has already received $100,000 of that value. Thus, the lost value of the salary part of her compensation due to Mercy's breach is $240,000 - $100,000 or $140,000. Similarly, the total value of her benefits was $36,000 for the year, or $3,000/month. She has received $15,000 worth of her benefits under the contract (5 months x $3,000/month), and thus, she has a lost value in benefits due to the breach of $36,000 - $15,000 or $21,000. Hence, the total objective "lost value" as a result of Mercy's breach is $140,000 + $21,000 or $161,000.

Incidental Loss - Nora suffered two separate kinds of incidental damages in this hypothetical: (i) the fee Nora paid to the medical search company of $400; and (ii) Nora's moving expenses of $6,000. Both are recoverable in the breach action. That is, both are expenses borne by Nora **after** the breach, and reasonably spent in an attempt to mitigate the breaching party's losses, i.e., they were expenditures reasonably made while searching for, and taking, other employment. These expenditures mitigate Mercy's damages because the salary and benefits of Nora's other employment must be subtracted from Nora's damages as losses avoided. The only question as to their recoverability by Nora is whether those amounts are "reasonable." As it appears they are, Nora is entitled to recover these amounts in her breach action against Mercy.

Consequential Loss — There are no consequential damages on these facts.

Costs Avoided — There are no costs avoided on these facts.

Loss Avoided — Nora's salary and benefits for 6 months at the other hospital are losses avoided for purposes of her expectation damages, for she is making a substitute use as to the value of the services that were the subject of the employment agreement. That is, she is "salvaging" those services and selling them to someone else. Nora earned $15,000/month in her new job, and thus there is a 6 x $15,000 or $90,000 loss avoided as to the salary component of Nora's damages. Similarly, Nora will be able to earn 6 x $2,000/month or $12,000 in benefits at her new job during the period of time she would have been paid by Mercy if Mercy had not breached. Accordingly, her total "loss avoided" is $90,000 + $12,000 or $102,000, which must be accounted for in computing Nora's expectation recovery.

Expectation Damages Determined by Formula

Using the E.D. = L.V. + I + C - C.A. - L.A. formula (see §31.3), Nora's expectation damages due from Mercy as a result of its breach are: $161,000 + $6,400 + $0 - $0 - $102,000, or **$65,400**.

Expectation Damages Not Determined by Formula

Had her employment contract been fully performed, Nora would have received $240,000 in salary and $36,000 in benefits from Mercy, for a total of $276,000 in salary and benefits. This figure represents the benefit of her bargain with Mercy, and thus any award of expectation damages must see to it that she will recognize the total value of that benefit.

At the time of the breach she had already received $115,000 from Mercy ($100,000 in salary + $15,000 in benefits), so that amount must be subtracted from the $276,000. In her new job, she will earn $102,000 in the six months which overlap the time period under her contract with Mercy ($90,000 in salary and $12,000 in benefits). Hence, this amount also must be subtracted from the $276,000 figure. Accordingly, Mercy must pay her $59,000 just to compensate her for lost salary and benefits due to its breach, i.e., [$276,000 - ($102,000 + $115,000)] = $59,000. In addition, Nora would not have had to have spend the $400 she paid to the search firm and the $6,000 in moving expenses if Mercy had lived up to its contract. Accordingly, because they are reasonable expenses incurred as a result of the breach in an attempt to mitigate Mercy's loss, they are expenses Mercy must pay for. Hence, Nora is "made whole" by receiving $59,000 (in salary and benefits) + **$6,400 (in incidental damages) or $65,400** from Mercy.

Note that the rule regarding whether salary from another job should be accounted for as a loss avoided in cases when an employer has breached an employment contract is:

(1) any salary **actually earned** in substitute work during the time period of the original contract must be accounted for as a "loss avoided" regardless of whether it is "comparable" to the work from which the emplyee was unjustly terminated in calculating expectation damages;

(2) if an offer of **comparable** substitute work is not accepted, any salary that **could** have been earned in such a comparable position during the time period must also be accounted for as a loss avoided in calculating expectation loss; and

(3) if an employee is offered **non-comparable** work that he or she rejects, any salary that *could* have been made at the non-comparable position does NOT have to be counted as a loss avoided.

Note also that in wrongful discharge cases, there is also the possibility that the employer may have to pay emotional distress and punitive damages in addition to expectation damages (see §§31.62 and 31.82).

3. **EXAMPLE OF BREACH OF EMPLOYMENT CONTRACT WHERE THE BREACH IS COMMITTED BY THE EMPLOYEE. [§31.33]** Sid is a party to a written employment contract in which he promised to serve as a sales representative of XYZ Corp. at an annual salary of $36,000. The contract called for Sid to work for a year, but Sid breached and left XYZ for another job after just one month. Sid had collected his salary for the month before he left. XYZ ran an ad in the paper seeking a replacement for Sid, which cost XYZ $500. As a result of the ad, XYZ was able to hire Pam as a suitable replacement for Sid. Pam started a month after Sid left and XYZ reasonably agreed to pay her $39,000/year.

Lost Value — In employee breach cases, the lost value to the employer is equal to the salary the employer has to pay the person hired to replace the breaching employee. Here, XYZ is obligated to pay Sid's replacement $3,250/month for the ten months remaining on Sid's contract, and thus the lost value to the company is 10 x $3,250 or $32,500.

Incidental Loss — XYZ has suffered an incidental loss of $500, measured by the cost to run the advertisement in the paper. That is, the $500 is a reasonable expense incurred by the injured party after the breach in an effort to avoid the breaching party's damages, namely to find someone who could give the company whatever benefits Sid could have given. Note that XYZ would have been entitled to recover this money regardless of whether the advertisement actually resulted in XYZ finding a replacement for Sid (see §31.27).

Consequential Loss - In theory, any profits that Sid would have made for XYZ under the contract are recoverable by the company as a consequential loss. However, recovering the lost profits would be subject to the usual limitations of being proven with reasonable certainty (see §31.41). Because it would be almost impossible to prove, the amount of profits Sid did not earn, it is very unlikely any consequential loss of this type could actually be recovered by XYZ. (Note this conclusion is buttressed by the fact that there are only a very few reported cases in which such consequential damages have been awarded to an employer in employee-breach cases). Accordingly, as a practical matter, there will be $0 in consequential loss recoverable by XYZ.

Cost Avoided - Due to Sid's breach, XYZ did not have to pay Sid for 11 months under the contract. Sid was to make $3,000/month under his contract, and thus XYZ avoided a cost of having to pay 11 months of his salary, or $33,000.

Loss Avoided - There are no losses avoided on these facts.

Expectation Damages Determined by Formula

Under the E.D. = L.V. + I + C - C.A. - L. A. formula, XYZ's expectation damages due from Sid as a result of his breach are:

$32,500 + $500 + 0 - $33,000 - 0 or **$0**. Hence, XYZ is entitled only to a recovery of nominal damages (see §31.29).

Expectation Damages Not Determined by Formula

A nominal damage recovery may at first seem surprising, but it does make sense if the goal of expectation damages is kept in mind. That is, the goal of such damages is to put XYZ in as good a position as it would have been in had Sid fulfilled his contract. XYZ was harmed by Sid's leaving, because it had to find a replacement for him. It had to agree to pay Pam $250 more per month than it paid Sid, and it chose to run a $500 ad in the paper. However, as a result of the breach the company did not have to pay **anyone** in Sid's position for an entire month. This one month's savings offsets any increased salary and other expenses incurred by XYZ. Hence, while XYZ was in some ways economically worse off because of the breach (because it paid an extra $2,500 in salary to Pam and $500 to the paper), it was also economically better off (because it saved having to pay $3,000/month worth of Sid's salary) in other ways. Here, the offsets happen to cancel completely the detriments, and so XYZ is owed nothing but nominal damages.

4. **EXAMPLES OF BREACHES OF CONSTRUCTION CONTRACTS WHERE THE BREACH IS COMMITTED BY THE BUILDER. [§31.34]** Before discussing examples of problems illustrating an expectation damage recovery in builder breach cases, it must be noted that there are **special rules governing the calculation of "lost value" in these cases.** The reason for the special rules has to do with the fact that there are two reasonable ways of calculating lost value in a construction contract when the builder breaches. That is "lost value" could reasonably be calculated either:

(i) by the diminution in fair market value of the property caused by the breach; or

(ii) by the amount of money necessary to finish the job (if the builder never starts construction or quits part way through), or the amount of money necessary to remedy any problems with the construction (if the builder finished the work, but did not perform it well).

Accordingly, in a rather complicated series of rules set forth in §§347, 348, and 350, the Restatement 2d has adopted the following rules to compute "lost value" for the breach of construction contracts where the breach is caused by the builder:

Rule No. 1: If the diminution in the fair market value of the property caused by the breach is greater than the cost of completion or repair, the injured party may only use the cost of completion or repair as the "lost value." (See §31.341).

Rule No. 2: If the cost of completion or repair is greater than the diminution in the fair market value of the property caused by the breach, the injured party is **still** *generally* entitled to the cost of completion or repair as the "lost value" [Restatement 2d §348, Com. c]. In other words, even where the cost to fix a contractor's poor workmanship, or the cost to complete a project unjustly left unfinished by a contractor, may cost more than the decrease in fair market value to the property caused by the poor workmanship or unfinished work, contract law still generally allows the owner to recover the amount of money which will allow the injured party to receive what he or she bargained for, namely an adequately constructed, completed project. This is accomplished by awarding the home owner the cost of repair (see §33.342).

Rule No. 3: When the cost of completion or repair is so much greater than the diminution in fair market value to the property caused by the breach **so that it is "clearly disproportionate"** to the amount of diminution in market value, the injured party may **only** use the decreased fair market value as the "lost value" and is not entitled to use the disproportionately greater amount of the repair or completion cost in computing expectation damages [Restatement 2d §348(2)(b)]. This Rule is thus a limited exception to Rule No. 2 above. It applies where the cost to repair the poor construction or to finish the construction would be **far** more expensive than the loss in market value occasioned by the breach. When that is so, only the lesser amount may be recovered (see §33.343).

Note that while there is no hard and fast test for how great the disparity between the repair/completion costs and the fair market value diminution must be to have Rule No. 3 apply instead of Rule No. 2, it is clear that the disparity must be **very** large, e.g., on the order of **at least** 5-10 times more expensive (if not more) to repair or complete, as compared with the loss in market value. Some authorities limit the applicability of Rule No. 3 to those situations where the breach is non-willful. That is, if the contractor's breach is willful, these authorities would allow the land owner to use the full cost of repair or of completion as the lost value component of his or her expectation recovery even if such amount turns out to be "clearly disproportionate" to the lost market value.

a. Example. [§31.341] Barry hires Andrea to build a pool at his house for $40,000. Andrea completes the work, and is paid the contract price. Soon thereafter, however, cracks start appearing in the sides and bottom of the pool. It will cost $5,000 to repair the cracks. At trial, competent evidence demonstrates that the diminution in the fair market value of Barry's house due to the breach, i.e., the fair market value of the house with a watertight pool minus the fair market value of the house with a cracked pool, is $10,000.

The "lost value" component of Barry's expectation damages is $5,000 under Rule No. 1 above. That is, since the cost of repair ($5,000) is less than the diminution in fair market value caused by the breach ($10,000), Barry must use $5,000 as his lost value. This makes sense, for with an expenditure of $5,000, he can get everything he bargained for, i.e., a fully-completed watertight pool. Thus, if he were awarded $10,000, he would be put in a better position than if the contract had not been breached in that he could repair the pool, **plus** be left with $5,000 in cash.

b. **Example.** [§31.342] Same as above, except this time the cracks are more extensive and it will cost $15,000 to repair the pool, but the fair market value diminution resulting from the breach is still $10,000. Barry is nevertheless entitled to use $15,000 as his "lost value" under Rule No. 2 above. That is, even though the cost to repair or complete construction is somewhat greater than the diminution in the fair market value of the property, the injured party is still entitled to use the costs of repair or completion in computing his "lost value," so long as such costs are not "clearly disproportionate" to the lost fair market value. As the $5,000 difference between the cost of repair and the loss is fair market value is plainly not "clearly disproportionate" (as the term is used in Restatement 2d §348), and since the only way to award Barry the full benefit of his bargain is by awarding him enough money to repair the pool, he is entitled to use $15,000 as his "lost value" in computing expectation damages.

c. **Example of *Jacob & Youngs, Inc. v. Kent*.** [§31.343] Kent hired Jacob & Youngs, Inc., a contracting firm, to build a home. In their contract it specified that Jacob & Youngs would use copper pipe made by the Reading company when installing the plumbing. Shortly before construction was complete, and after most of the pipe had been covered by drywall, it was discovered that some of the pipe installed in the house was made by the Cohoes company. It was clear that the use of Cohoes pipe instead of Reading was inadvertent, and it was uncontroverted that the Cohoes pipe was functionally equivalent to the Reading pipe in quality, cost, market value, and appearance. Significantly, installation of the Cohoes pipe did not reduce the fair market value of Kent's house appreciably, if at all. However, tearing out the drywall and inspecting and replacing all the pipe would have been very expensive. *Jacobs & Young, Inc. v. Kent*, 230 N.Y. 239, 129 N.E. 889 (1921).

Under Rule No. 3 above, Kent was only entitled to use the diminished fair market value of his home caused by the breach as the "lost value" component of his expectation damages calculation, and not the cost to repair the construction mistake caused by using the wrong pipe. This is the type of case where the cost of completion or repair is "clearly disproportionate" to the loss in fair market value due to the breach, and hence the owner is only entitled to use the diminished fair market value as the "lost value" component of his expectation damages [Restatement 2d §348(2), Com. c, Ill. 4]; (see also §21.2611).

Recall that if the breach had been willful, i.e., had Jacob & Youngs deliberately used Cohoes pipe instead of Reading, there are some authorities that would have allowed Kent to recover the full cost of repair.

5. **EXAMPLE OF BREACH OF CONSTRUCTION CONTRACT WHERE THE BREACH IS COMMITTED BY THE LAND OWNER.** [§31.35] Wayne agrees to construct a home for Mary for $100,000. The contract calls for progress payments to be made after certain

parts of the project are completed, and Wayne has appropriately been paid $20,000 in such progress payments. Mary thereafter breaches and orders Wayne off her property. At that point, Wayne has incurred costs of $25,000 in labor and materials and he can establish that it would have cost him another $65,000 to finish the job. At the time of the breach, Wayne has also purchased $2,000 worth of 2 x 10 lumber for work on Mary's house that has not yet been used in the construction, and which can be used by Wayne on other jobs.

The components of Wayne's expectation damages are:

Lost Value — Had the contract been completed, Wayne would have been paid $100,000. He has already been paid $20,000, so the objective **lost** value as a result of the breach is $80,000.

Incidental Loss — There are no incidental damages on these facts.

Consequential Loss — There are no consequential damages on these facts.

Cost Avoided — As a result of the breach, Wayne will not have to spend the remaining $65,000 to finish construction. Therefore, Mary's breach has resulted in a $65,000 cost avoided to him.

Loss Avoided — The $2,000 in lumber that can be used on other jobs is the kind of substitute use of resources that make up loss avoided. That is, because Wayne can salvage that lumber for work on other jobs, Mary cannot be charged for paying for it (see the discussion of "loss avoided" in §31.3).

Expectation Damages Determined by Formula

Under the E.D. = L.V. + I + C - C.A. - L.A. formula (see §31.3), the amount of Wayne's expectation damages recoverable against Mary as a result of the breach are: $80,000 + $0 + $0 - $65,000 - $2,000 or **$13,000**.

Expectation Damages Not Determined by Formula

Awarding Wayne $13,000 makes sense for that amount leaves him in the same position he would have been in had the contract been performed. Had Mary not breached, Wayne would have realized a $10,000 profit from the job. That is, he would have received $100,000 in payment from Mary, and would have spent $90,000 to build the house (i.e., he has already spent $25,000 and would have had to spend another $65,000 to finish).

At the time of the breach, he has spent $25,000, but has only received $20,000 in progress payments. Hence, at the time of the breach he is $5,000 "in the hole." To allow him to realize his $10,000 profit (thereby giving him the benefit of his bargain), and to compensate him fully for the $5,000 materials he has not already been paid for, Mary would have to pay him $15,000. However, this $15,000 figure must be reduced by the value of the lumber he can use on another job, $2,000, or else he will be better off because of the breach, i.e., he'd have the money **and** the lumber. Accordingly, if Mary pays Wayne **$13,000**, he will be in exactly the same position he would have been in had the contract been performed.

6. **EXAMPLE OF BREACH OF CONTRACT TO SELL REAL ESTATE WHERE THE BREACH IS COMMITTED BY THE BUYER. [§31.36]** Connie was under a contract to sell her house to Bernie for $100,000 on March 1. At the last minute Bernie breached, and

it took Connie six months to find a new buyer. The demand for real estate declined somewhat during the six-month period, and she was only able to sell her house to the new buyer for $98,000.

The components of Connie's expectation damages are as follows:

Lost Value — Connie lost $100,000 in value from Bernie as a result of Bernie's breach.

Incidental Loss — Connie lost the value of 6 months interest on $100,000 due to Bernie's failure to pay. Hence, at a 10% rate (which is a typical statutory rate of interest in breach of contract cases, see §31.9), Connie has $500 in lost interest as an incidental damage.

Consequential Loss — There are no consequential damages on these facts.

Cost Avoided — There are no costs avoided on these facts.

Loss Avoided — Connie was able to make substitute arrangements for the house that was the subject matter of the contract by re-selling it to another for $98,000. Hence, there is a $98,000 loss avoided which must be factored in when calculating Connie's expectation recovery.

Expectation Damages Determined by Formula

Under the E.D. = L.V. + I + C - C.A. - L.A. formula (see §31.3), the amount of Connie's expectation damages due from Bernie as a result of his breach are: $100,000 + $500 + $0 - $0 - $98,000 or **$2,500**.

Expectation Damages Not Determined by Formula

A $2,500 recovery puts Connie in the position she would have been in had the contract been performed. That is, had Bernie not breached, Connie would have received $100,000 on March 1. As a consequence of the breach, she will now receive $98,000 from the new buyer on September 1. Accordingly, to be "made whole," i.e., to realize the benefit of the bargain, she will need to recover $2,000 from Bernie to make up the difference in the two sales prices, and $500 from Bernie to compensate her for the loss of use of the $100,000 during the March 1 - September 1 period.

7. **EXAMPLE OF BREACH OF CONTRACT TO SELL REAL ESTATE WHERE THE BREACH IS COMMITTED BY THE SELLER. [§31.37]** Typically, when a seller breaches a contract to transfer an interest in land, the buyer will sue for an order of specific performance, and thus force the seller actually to transfer the property to the buyer as promised in the contract (see §30.212). However, if for some reason the buyer does not wish to sue for equitable relief, or is not entitled to do so because such an award would violate principles of equity (see e.g., §30.2311), then an award of damages is available.

The courts have developed two theories of how to calculate the amount of expectation damages recoverable in these cases:

(i) The **"American Rule,"** where the purchaser is entitled to recover the full amount of his or her expectation damages, i.e., the buyer can recover the difference between the contract price and the fair market value of the property, plus any down payment and any incidental damages; and

(ii) The "**English Rule**," where the purchaser is only entitled to recover his or her reliance damages, i.e., the buyer can recover any down payment, plus any out-of-pocket costs spent in acquiring title, e.g., a title insurance policy, house inspection, etc. However, no benefit of the bargain damages are permitted. That is, the buyer is not entitled to damages resulting from a "good" deal, and thus, cannot recover the difference between the fair market value of the property and the contract price under this view.

Perhaps surprisingly, the "English Rule" is still probably the rule followed in a majority of the jurisdictions in the United States. However, as noted above, the issue does not frequently arise because buyers generally obtain a specific performance decree upon a seller's breach in these cases.

a. **Example. [§31.371]** Don signed a contract to purchase a piece of property sold due to foreclosure at a price of $80,000, the price of the unpaid mortgage at the time of default. This was a good deal for Don, for competent evidence can establish that the fair market value of the property was $95,000. At the time he signed the contract, Don paid $8,000 as a down payment, and later incurred expenses of $1,000 for title insurance reports, termite inspections, etc. Shortly thereafter, just before title was to be transferred to Don, the seller breached and refused to deliver the deed.

Most likely, Don would sue for specific performance, and thus would seek an order giving him title. However, if for whatever reason such a recovery was unavailable to him, or if he chose to seek damages instead, the extent of Don's recovery would depend on whether he was in an "American Rule" jurisdiction or an "English Rule" jurisdiction.

If he were is an "American Rule" jurisdiction, Don would be entitled to a $23,000 expectation damage recovery, i.e., the difference between the purchase price and the fair market value of the property ($95,000-$80,000), plus the return of his $8,000 down payment. Note, he would not be entitled to the $1,000 he spent on title insurance, termite inspections, etc. because he would have had to spend that money anyway had the contract not been breached. That is, the $15,000 benefit of the bargain ($95,000 - $80,000) would not have been pure profit to him had the contract gone forward. Don would have to have spent the $1,000 on the reports regardless. Since he would have to have spent $1,000 had the contract gone forward to obtain the property so as to realize its $15,000 benefit in value over what he paid for it, he cannot be awarded the $1,000 as contract damages because it would put him in a better position than he would have been in had the contract gone forward.

Note the $1,000 cannot be classified as an "incidental" damage because it was money spent before the breach, and it was not money spent to avoid further loss.

If Don were in an "English Rule" jurisdiction, he would only be entitled to a recovery for the $1,000 he spent in reliance on the transfer of the property, along with the return of his $8,000 down payment.

8. **NOTE ON EXPECTATION DAMAGE RECOVERY UNDER CONTRACTS GOVERNED BY THE UCC. [§31.38]** The various formulas for recovering damages resulting from breaches in contracts governed by Article 2 are designed to allow the recovery of expectation damages. These formulas are explained in detail in Chapter Thirty-Three, but the basics are given below.

a. **Buyer's Damages. [§31.381]** The basic UCC formula a buyer uses in a suit against a breaching seller who fails to tender a conforming good is:

Buyer's Recovery = [(Cost of substitute good from another seller) - (Contract price of good from the breaching seller)] + Incidental damages + Consequential damages. [UCC §§2-712; 2-713]

(Note that the buyer is also entitled to the recovery of any deposit, down payment, or full payment already made to the seller under UCC §2-711)

As can be seen, such a formula is really just a specialized application of the more general E.D. = L.V. + I + C - C.A. - L.A. formula used previously (see §31.3), where:

L.V. = the cost of acquiring the substitute good from another;

I = has the same meaning of incidental damages as in non-UCC contracts (see §31.27);

C = has the same meaning of consequential damages as in non-UCC contracts (see §31.22);

C.A. = the contract price (cost) that the buyer no longer has to pay to the breaching buyer (and thus avoids); and

L.A. doesn't come into play because a *buyer* typically has no salvage value or other loss avoided.

Note that the Code provides that the above formula should be applied slightly differently depending whether the buyer actually purchases replacement goods versus whether the buyer doesn't buy the goods but wants to recover the benefit of the bargain, i.e., the appreciated value of the goods, anyway (see §§33.51 and 31.52 for a detailed discussion of these issues). But, **the point is that the basic Code formula granting damages to buyers is a derivative of the more general expectation damage recovery formula used in non-UCC transactions and that the Code formula is thus designed to allow recovery of expectation damages.**

(1) **Example. [§31.3811]** Ben wants to buy some in-line skates from Sports Store. Sports Store is out of stock in Ben's size, but promises to back order a pair for him from the manufacturer and promises delivery in a month. The price of the skates is $125 and Ben puts down a $50 deposit. That brand of skates turns out to be particularly popular, and so when "Ben's" pair comes into Sports Store, the Store ends up selling them to another for $200 — the going price around town. It tells Ben they haven't arrived yet, and keep putting him off. After 3 months of no skates and no refund, Ben files suit.

Under the Code, Ben is entitled to his deposit back under UCC §2-711. He is also entitled to the difference between the price for replacement skates from another store minus the contract price from Sports Store, or $200 - $125 = $75 [UCC §§2-712; 2-713]

Such recovery makes sense for $75 is the value of Ben's "expectation" under the contract. That is, he made a "good" deal by contracting to pay $125 for an item valued by the market at $200 at the time of promised delivery. That is, he had a protected expectation interest valued at $75. So he can either pocket the $75 and realize the benefit of his bargain, or buy replacement skates for a net $125 to him, i.e., pay the purchase price of $200 to another, less the $75 recovered from Sports Store. In that way, he will be in exactly the same position as he would have been had the contract been carried out — he has his bargained for skates for $125 — which, after all, is the idea behind expectation damages (see §31.3). (See also §§33.21 and 33.22 for further, and more detailed examples and discussion of buyers' remedies under the Code).

(2) Different Formulation for Buyer's Warranty Damages. [§31.3812] If a buyer is tendered a non-conforming good and decides to keep it and sue for breach of warranty, rather than reject it or revoke his or her acceptance of it and sue for money damages, the formula for a buyer's recovery is quite different, but the idea behind the formula is still the same — to put the buyer in the position he or she would have been in had the contract been carried out. (See Chapter Thirty-Six for a discussion of the substantive law regarding warranties under the Code and §33.3 for a the damages formula used in a breach of warranty suit.]

b. Seller's Damages. [§31.382] The formulas for a seller's damages recovery under Article 2 also are designed to allow the seller to recover expectation damages. The basic formulation is essentially the reciprocal of the buyer's damages formulation given in §31.381, namely:

Seller's recovery = [(Contract price from the breaching buyer) - (Price to be realized upon reasonable sale of the goods to another) + Incidental Damages [UCC §2-706; 2-708(1)]

This formula is really a specialized application of the more general E.D. = L.V. + I + C - C.A. - L.A. formula used to calculate expectation damages explained previously previously (see §31.3), where:

L.V. = the contract price the seller was to receive from the buyer, i.e. the "value" of the contract that has now been "lost;"

I = has the same meaning of incidental damages as in non-UCC contracts (see §31.27); and

L.A. = the price the seller can receive from another buyer for the improperly rejected goods.

Note that neither consequential damages ("C" in the formula) nor costs avoided ("C.A." in the formula) are part of the seller's damage formulation given above. When a seller tries to claim a lost profit (a consequential damage) or has to account for the salvage value or other cost avoided, the Code directs that another formula be used, that in §2-708(2), which accounts for such items (see §31.3822; 33.53).

As was true regarding the general formula for buyer's damages (§31.381), the Code states that the above formula should be applied slightly differently depending whether the seller actually sells the replacement goods to another versus whether the seller doesn't sell the goods but wants to recover the benefit of the bargain, i.e., the depreciated value of the goods, anyway (see §§33.51 and 31.52 for a detailed discussion of these issues). But, **the point is that the basic Code formula granting damages to sellers is a derivative of the more general expectation damage recovery formula used in non-UCC transactions and the Code formula is thus designed to allow recovery of expectation damages.**

(1) Example. [§31.3821] Sam contracts to sell his car to Betty for $5,000. Betty breaches, and Sam runs an ad in the paper (for $20), and eventually finds a few other buyers willing to pay him $4,800 for the car. He sues Betty.

Under the Code, he is entitled to the contract price from Betty minus the amount he could receive from another buyer, plus any incidental damages (the newspaper ad), or $5,000 - $4,800 + 20 = $220.

Such a recovery makes sense, for it protects his legitimate expectations under the Code. He made an economically good deal by contracting to sell a $4,800 item (as valued by the market) for $5,000. He can either pocket the $200 (plus the reimbursement for the ad) and keep the car, or he can sell it — which puts him in the exact position he would have been in had the contract been performed, i.e. he has a net $5,000 — $4,800 from the new buyer, $200 from Betty, and a reimbursement from Betty of the $20 he had to pay for the ad.

(2) Different Formulation for Lost Volume Sellers. [§31.3822] The formula in §31.382 works well for a seller who has only one item to sell. But for commercial sellers with a large supply of goods, a buyer's breach typically costs them a sale. That is, if a buyer unjustifiably backs out of a purchase of a microwave from an appliance store, the store probably can sell that same microwave to another. But had the first purchaser not breached, the store would have been able to sell another microwave from its inventory to the second buyer, i.e. it would have had two sales, and hence two profits, instead of one. So the breach actually cost it a sale, even though the particular microwave that was the subject of the breached contract was eventually sold at the contract price to another.

In such situations, the Code permits the seller to recoup the profit lost because of the buyer's breach, i.e., the profit it would have made by selling the second microwave, under the formula in UCC §2-708(2). [See §33.53 for a more extensive discussion of lost volume sellers and for the formula used in such cases]

Once again, however, realize that the idea behind such a doctrine is the recovery of expectation damages, i.e., to put the retailer in the position it would have been in had the contract been performed. In other words, it would have had 2 profits had the contract not been breached — one from the purchase of the first microwave by the breacher, and a second from the sale of another microwave to the second buyer. Since it now has only one profit, it can seek the "lost profit" from the breaching buyer and be "made whole."

E. THREE LIMITATIONS ON THE RECOVERABILITY OF EXPECTATION DAMAGES: CERTAINTY, FORESEEABILITY, AND AVOIDABILITY. [§31.4] The recoverability of expectation damages is limited by three significant doctrines:

(1) To be recoverable, **damages must be proven with "reasonable certainty,"** i.e. the amount of the damage suffered cannot be speculative and the non-breaching party must put on proof to establish to the jury the amount of his or her losses with some degree of certainty [Restatement 2d §352] (see §31.41);

(2) To be recoverable, the party in breach **must have reasonably foreseen**, at the time the contract was formed, that **the type of damage** sought by the injured party would follow from the breach [Restatement 2d §351] (see §31.42); and

(3) To be recoverable, the damages sought by the injured party **must not have been avoidable** by him or her without undue risk, burden, or humiliation, i.e., the non-breaching party may not recover damages from the breacher that could easily have been **mitigated** or avoided by the non-breaching party [Restatement 2d §350] (see §31.43).

1. **THE "CERTAINTY" LIMITATION: Damages May Not be Recovered for Breach of Contract Unless They are Proven with "Reasonable Certainty."** [§31.41] Generally, American courts have refused to allow an injured party to recover damages for a breach of contract unless the damages can be proven with reasonable certainty. **This rule is not limited to expectation damages,** i.e., all contract damages must be proven with sufficient certainty to be recoverable [Restatement 2d §352]; (see also §31.521). However, when the reasonable certainty limitation is applied to expectation damages, it is almost always in the context of denying an injured party's attempt to recover lost profits as a consequential damage [Restatement 2d §352, Com. a]; (see §31.4111).

   a. **Modern Rules Governing the Test as to How "Certain" a Damage must be Proven to be Recoverable.** [§31.411] There is no precise test as to how certain proof of the amount of damages must be before they can be recovered. Indeed, the reasonable certainty doctrine is intended to be flexible so that a court can apply it more or less stringently as the facts warrant. However, over time the following rules have developed as a guide in determining whether a particular loss has been proven with enough certainty to be recoverable:

   Rule No. 1. In a close case, any doubts as to whether a loss is sufficiently certain are to be resolved against the breaching party [Restatement 2d §352, Com. a]. That is, once a court has determined that the injured party has suffered a real loss and that the breaching party caused it, any doubts about whether the loss is proven with sufficient certainty in a close case are resolved against the breacher. This is because where the choice is to deny an injured party recovery, or to deny a breacher a windfall by not having to pay for the damages that he or she caused because the magnitude of the harm cannot be precisely established, the breacher should lose.

   Rule No. 2. The requirement of certainty is less strictly applied when the breach is deliberate than when it is not. That is, courts tend to give more leeway in allowing the injured party to recover for damages which can only be approximated (rather than proven with certainty) when the breach is a willful one. Once again, this is not to say that upon a deliberate breach the certainty requirement no longer applies. But it is to say that the certainty standards are relaxed in such a case as a penalty for intentional **malum in se** conduct.

   Rule No. 3. So long as the injured party provides a "reasonable basis" for his or her damage calculations, those calculations are likely to be accepted as sufficient under the reasonable certainty test. Recently, courts have required much less precision in the proof of damages. In other words, modern courts place more emphasis on the modifier "reasonable" than they do on the object "certainty" in applying the rule of Restatement 2d §352. Hence, modern courts tend to be receptive to the idea that in some cases a particular kind of loss simply is incapable of being quantified with precision, and thus, reasonable assumptions need to be made and numbers need to be approximated in order to come up with any kind of proof of loss [UCC §1-106, Com. 1; Restatement 2d §352, Com. a].

(1) The Reasonable Certainty Test Typically Limits Recovery of Damages Only Where a Non-Breaching Buyer is Suing for Lost Profits Resulting from a "Collateral" Transaction. [§31.4111] By far the most frequent application of the reasonable certainty test as a limitation on the recovery of contract damages takes place in cases where the non-breaching purchaser of land, goods, or services is suing for lost profits resulting from a "collateral" transaction that never took place because of the supplier's breach. These "collateral" transactions are of three types:

(1) Cases where the buyer planned to re-sell to another the land or good that was never delivered due to the seller's breach. In these cases, it is the lost profits from the re-sale that never took place for which the injured buyer seeks recovery;

(2) Cases where the buyer planned to use the goods or services that were never delivered due to the breach as raw materials in the manufacture or assembly of another product. In these cases it is the lost profits from the sales of these other never fabricated products for which the injured party seeks recovery; and

(3) Cases where a breach by the supplier of services causes a delay in the opening of, or in the continued operation of, the purchaser's retail establishment. In these cases the injured party seeks recovery of lost profits from the retail sales that never took place because the store was closed.

The certainty problems in these types of cases stem from the fact that there is often no proof that these other sales transactions would ever have taken place even if the supplier had not breached; or if they would have taken place, there is no solid proof as to what the terms or frequency of those sales would have been. For example, suppose a furniture manufacturer never delived a dining room set to a retailer. To recover lost profits from the sale of the dining room set that never occurred, the retailer faces problems under the certainty rule. That is, there is no uncontentable proof as to how much the retailer would have charged for the set; **when** it would have been sold; whether the retailer would have lowered the price if it did not sell right away; whether the retailer would have financed the sale rather than making it for cash, etc.

Because courts view it as unfair to the breaching party to make him or her pay an amount which has little or no basis in fact and is simply a guess by the injured party as to the amount of any harm suffered, contract law has developed the following considerations to help resolve the question of whether lost profits from collateral transactions that never took place should be recoverable:

(a) **When a retailer seeks to recover profits lost due to a delay in the opening, or re-opening, of commercial premises, the newer the business of the injured party, the less likely it is that a court will find that lost profits can be proven with reasonable certainty.** The converse of this rule is that the longer a party seeking lost profits in such cases has been in business, the more likely a court is to accept historical sales figures as sufficient proof of lost profits caused by the supplier's breach. However, it should be noted that even with newer businesses modern courts are increasingly willing to use subsequent sales figures, showing profits made by the business when it finally did open, as sufficiently certain proof of what the profits would have been had the business opened on time. Obviously, the trier of fact need not accept these subsequent sales figures as conclusive proof of what the lost profits would have been while the premises were closed, but the point is that at least the injured party can make the argument on that ground to the jury and is not precluded from trying to recover lost profits from the speculative collateral transactions under the reasonable certainty rule.

(b) **The more the non-breaching party's lost profits depend on uncertain tastes and preferences of the public, the more unlikely it is that such lost profits can be established with reasonable certainty (see §31.4113).**

(c) **The longer the period of time between the breach and the expected collateral sale, or the more tenuous the connection between the breach and the anticipated collateral sale, the less likely it is that such lost profits will be established with enough certainty to be recoverable.** For example, if a supplier did not provide a chemical that the buyer says was supposed to be used in experiments for the possible development (if feasable) of a new non-dairy creamer, that, even if developed would not have been on the market for three years, it is unlikely the supplier will be held liable for lost profits from the creamer.

(d) **The more an injured party's claim for lost profits can be supported by expert economic testimony, the more likely it is a modern court will accept that proof as meeting a party's claim for lost profits under the reasonable certainty requirement.**

(2) **Example. [§31.4112]** Smith Construction Co. ("Smith") agrees contractually to build a supermarket for A & B, Inc. in a small rural community. The store would be the first supermarket in the community. Smith promised to complete construction by April 1 in the contract, but did not actually finish until September 15.

It is possible that A & B can recover for lost profits from the sales that did not occur during the April 1 through September 15 period. A & B would try to establish the amount of such lost profits by its subsequent sales history, by the profits made by similar supermarkets in comparable areas around the country, by expert economic testimony as to expected profits during that time, etc. A modern court **may** find that such proof can establish A & B's lost profits with reasonable certainty. However, because the supermarket is a new enterprise and the first of its kind in the community, it is also possible that any proof as to its lost profits would not, even today, be found to be established with enough certitude to be recoverable [Restatement 2d §352, Com. b, Ill. 5]. Note that if the store had been in operation for ten years or so, its sales constant, one month to the next, and Smith's breach had been the failure to finish a **re-modeling** project on time, A & B could surely recover its lost profits based on historical sales figures under modern contract law.

(3) **Example. [§31.4113]** Jack's Publishing contracts to publish a novel written by Christie. It is to be Christie's first published book. Christie is to be paid only on a royalty basis, i.e., she is entitled only to a percentage of the purchase price of each book sold. Jack's breaches, deciding that it does not want to publish the book. Despite diligent efforts, Christie can find no other publisher willing to publish the book. Christie probably cannot recover her lost profits. This is because it is unlikely Christie can prove what her royalties would have been with **any** degree of certainty given that this is her first book and that her compensation for the book is dependent totally on the uncertain tastes of the public. [Restatement 2d §352, Com. a, Ill. 1.]

2. **THE "FORESEEABILITY" LIMITATION: Damages may not be recovered unless the breaching party either foresaw or should have foreseen at the time the contract was made that such a damage would follow from a breach. [§31.42]** The second limitation

on recovery of expectation loss is the "foreseeability" doctrine. It is this principle which both defines consequential damages and limits the recovery of such damages. The modern rule regarding foreseeability is relatively straightforward. As stated in Restatement 2d §351(1):

Damages are not recoverable for loss that the party in breach did not have reason to foresee as a probable result of the breach when the contract was made.

What proves difficult about the foreseeability doctrine is not stating it, but applying it. Specifically, the difficulties in application of the rule are of two related, but distinct types: (i) deciding what makes a loss sufficiently foreseeable to the party in breach so that it will be recoverable *without* a special proof of foreseeability; and (ii) deciding what kind of showing must the innocent party must make if it is determined the injured party must make a showing of forseeability.

The origin of the doctrine is the most famous case in contract law, the English decision *Hadley v. Baxendale*, 9 Ex. 341, 156 Eng. Rep. 145 (1854), which is the "*Palsgraf*" of contracts. Before explaining and discussing completely the modern day applications of the rules governing foreseeability, an examination of *Hadley* is appropriate.

SPECIAL CASE SQUIB

a. *Hadley v. Baxendale.* [§31.421] Mr. and Mrs. Hadley owned a mill that produced flour in Glouster, England. The crankshaft of their mill broke, shutting down production at the plant. There was apparently no feasible way to repair the shaft, so the Hadleys quickly made arrangements with W. Joyce & Co. ("Joyce"), to manufacture a new crankshaft as soon as possible. Joyce was located several hundred miles away, in Greenwich, England, which was significant because Joyce told the Hadleys that its engineers needed the old shaft to serve as a model before they could manufacture a new one.

Accordingly, the Hadleys sent one of their employees to Pickford & Co. ("Pickford"), which was owned by Mr. Baxendale, and was a common carrier (i.e., the U.P.S. of its day). The Pickford employee behind the counter promised the Hadley employee a two-day delivery of the shaft. Mr. Hadley had the old shaft delivered to Pickford the next day. Unfortunately, delivery of the shaft to Joyce took a week, not two days. As a result, the Hadleys' mill was shut down five days longer than it should have been.

The reason for the delay in shipping turned out to be a simple mistake. Pickford had included instructions with the shaft that it should be transported by railway whenever possible. When it got to the last stage of its journey, Pickford's agent either ignored (or did not see) the instructions to ship the shaft by rail, and instead included it with some other items that also happened to be shipped to Joyce, but which were being shipped by canal rather than by rail. The canal trip, as opposed to shipment by rail, accounted for the five day delay.

When Mr. Hadley discovered what had happened, he brought suit against Baxendale, as the owner of Pickford, for breach. As part of his damages he sought five days' worth of lost profits at the mill, which he (at least initially) asserted was £300.

Held: Hadley was **not** entitled to recover for the lost profits from the mill's being shut down an extra five days. He was not denied such recovery on "certainty" grounds, but rather on "foreseeability" grounds. *Hadley v. Baxendale*, 9 Ex. 341, 156 Eng. Rep. 145 (1854).

Hadley set forth two rules regarding the recoverability of expectation damages:

(1) A non-breaching party may recover "direct" ("general") damages without having to prove specially that such damages were a foreseeable consequence of the breach (because, by definition, any reasonable person viewing the contract at the time it was negotiated, would foresee that such direct damages would naturally follow if the contract was breached); and

(2) Any damage that was not a direct damage was, by definition, a "consequential" damage. To recover consequential damages, the non-breaching party must **prove** that the breaching party either foresaw, or should have foreseen, them as following from the breach. Hence, because consequential damages were, by definition, not the kind of damages a reasonable person would foresee as resulting from a breach, the burden was on the injured party to prove that in the case at hand there was some notice given the breaching party that this unusual "consequential" damage would follow from the breach of the particular contract at issue. If such a showing could be made, then the loss would be sufficiently foreseeable, and its recovery posed no special problems.

The first question in deciding the case presented in *Hadley* was thus to determine whether the lost profits due to the mill's being shut down were "direct" or "consequential" damages. That is, would a loss of profits from a business having to close down production "arise naturally, according to the usual course of things" from the failure to deliver a package promptly. If so, the lost profits would be a direct damage and thus recoverable without a special showing of foreseeability on Hadley's part. If not, then the loss would be consequential, and thus recoverable only if Hadley (or his employee) had somehow put Baxendale's company on notice that a delayed delivery would result in lost profits for the mill. That is, only by proving that Baxendale's company was put on such notice could Hadley prove that lost profits were a sufficiently foreseeable result of the breach so as to be recoverable should the profits be judged consequential.

Hadley held that the lost profits from Hadley's mill due to the delayed delivery were consequential rather than direct. Hence, they were only recoverable if Hadley could prove that "they were in the contemplation of both parties at the time they made the contract as the probable result of the breach." Since there was no evidence in the case that Pickford had been made aware that the mill would be losing profits while the package was in transit, and thus such loss could not have been in Pickford's contemplation at the time the contract was made as being a probable result of the breach, Hadley's lost profits were not recoverable under the foreseeability limitations.

b. **Analysis of *Hadley v. Baxendale* and the "Foreseeability" Limitation of Contract Damages. [§31.422]** While not expressly stated in the opinion, the rationale of the *Hadley* foreseeability doctrine is that for our system of contract formation to work correctly, it is necessary that the parties know when they are negotiating a contract what risks they are being asked to take should the contract be breached. That is, freedom of contract requires that a party's decision to enter into an agreement, and to do so for a particular price, be fully informed. If a party will later be required to pay for a loss about which he or she did not reasonably know when the decision was made to enter the contract, then, by definition, his or her decision to enter the transaction in the first place was neither fully informed nor completely voluntary.

To illustrate this idea, let's update *Hadley*. Assume a woman came to Federal Express and contracted with the company to deliver a package to a computer manufacturer in Palo Alto. It turns out that package contained a defective computer chip which General Motors was returning to the manufacturer. The chip was crucial to running a GM production plant, and the plant has to be shut down until a working chip is sent as a replacement. Each day the plant is shut down costs GM $1,000,000. Federal Express does not know any of these facts, other than it contracted to deliver overnight a package to a computer manufacturer. If it fails to do so, it has no way of knowing whether its breach will cause a minor inconvenience, a $50,000 loss, or a or $1,000,000 plant closure. The foreseeability doctrine holds that before Federal Express can be asked to pay $1,000,000 for one day's delay in delivery, it must be apprised that such a result is a risk it is taking by promising overnight delivery. Knowing of that risk, it may decide it does not want to enter into the contract at all; or it may decide to do so, but charge a higher price for its service; or it may negotiate with its customer a damage limitation clause, etc. Whatever it may do, the point is that voluntary decision making, which is at the heart of modern contract doctrine, requires that a party cannot be forced to pay for a kind of loss upon his or her breach that it could not have reasonably foreseen would occur when the contract was made.

The two rules of *Hadley* thus set forth the two ways a loss can be sufficiently foreseeable to be recoverable under the doctrine. If the loss is "direct," then it is, in effect, foreseeable as a matter of law. That is, because such a loss is a kind which can "fairly and reasonably be considered as arising naturally from the breach," contract law assumes that any reasonable person would foresee such a loss as occurring upon a breach, and thus factored the risk of having to pay for it upon a breach in deciding to enter the contract. Accordingly, the injured party can recover that loss without having to prove specially its foreseeability.

On the other hand, if the loss is unusual enough that a reasonable person would not foresee it as a natural result of the breach, then the injured party must prove that the breacher was aware (or at least should have been aware) of the risk of having to pay for such loss if he or she breached. Only with such proof can contract law be sure that the breaching party voluntarily entered the agreement knowing of what risks loomed if he or she should fail to perform what was promised. If the injured party cannot make such a foreseeability showing, then the consequential loss he or she suffered, no matter how real the loss may be, cannot be recovered because the foreseeability doctrine states that unless it is reasonable to assume that the party is breach factored in the risk of having to pay that loss when he or she entered the contract, he or she cannot be liable for it.

---

c. **The Modern Test for Whether a Loss is "Direct" or "Consequential." [§31.423]** In *Hadley*, the test for a direct damage was whether it "may fairly . . . be considered arising naturally, i.e., according to the usual course of things, from [a] breach." Under both the Restatement 2d and the UCC, this test has been changed to state that:

damages are direct if they follow " in the ordinary course of events" from the breach [Restatement 2d §351(2)(a); UCC §2-714(1)]. All other damages are consequential.

There are several rules that have developed in determining whether a loss is direct or consequential.

(1) Generally, the only time there is any question at all regarding whether a loss was sufficiently foreseeable to be "direct" arises in **the recovery of lost profits**. That is, while the principles of foreseeability and consequential loss are not theoretically limited to lost profits (i.e. they apply to any damage that is reasonably unforseeable at the time of contract formation), probably 90% of the time in real life (and 98% of the time in first-year Contracts courses), a loss that is deemed consequential will be a lost profit.

Note this does not mean that every time a party tries to recover a lost profit, he or she will only be able to do so upon proving the foreseeability of that damage. There are a number of situations where a lost profit so clearly will follow in the ordinary course of events after a breach that such losses will be judged direct damages. For example, suppose Copymart leased a coin-operated photocopier to University, which placed it in its law library. As part of the lease, Copymart promised that it would repair any problem with the copier in 12 hours or less. If it takes Copymart three days on one occasion to repair the copier, certainly it is foreseeable that in that context there could be lost profits. (Obviously, University might run into certainty problems in trying to quantify those losses, but there would be no problem in holding that the loss is *foreseeable*.) Hence while (virtually) all consequential losses arise upon an attempt to recover lost profits, not all lost profits are consequential losses. Whether they are or not depends upon the reasonable foreseeability of the loss as determined by application of the remaining factors discussed below.

(2) **The foreseeability of the loss is to be judged at the time the contract was made, not at the time the contract was breached** or any other time. Hence it is irrelevant if circumstances subsequent to the execution of the contract make it likely that a lost profit will (or will not) occur. The only relevant inquiry is whether such a loss was reasonably foreseeable at the time the contract was entered into.

(3) **The test of foreseeability is an objective one**. The test is whether a **reasonable person**, looking at the contract when it was made, would have foreseen that the injured party would lose profits in the ordinary course of events if the other party breached. If so, such lost profit is a direct damage. If not, it is consequential.

(4) **It is only necessary that such loss foreseeably be "a probable result," not a certain result, of the breach**. In other words, it need not appear certain, or almost certain, that a particular kind of loss would occur upon a breach before such a loss is deemed direct. Rather, it is only necessary that a reasonable person would see such a loss as a **probable** result of the breach.

d. **The Showing the Non-Breaching Party Must Make to Recover Consequential Damages under Modern Contract Law. [§31.424]** Just as modern contract law has changed *Hadley's* test somewhat for judging when a loss is direct (see §31.423), it has also changed the test as to the showing the non-breaching party must make in order to collect consequential damages. In *Hadley*, consequential damages were recoverable upon a showing that such damages "may reasonably be supposed to have been in the contemplation of both parties, at the time they made the contract, as the probable result of the breach of it." From this language arose the **"tacit agreement test,"** which stated that consequential losses were recoverable only when the injured party could prove that **both parties** to the contract had **tacitly agreed** that the consequential loss would be recoverable upon a breach. This test proved difficult for injured parties to meet. This is because, under the test, the injured party did not just have to show that the breaching party was **aware** that such a loss would be suffered by the non-breaching party as a result of the breach. Rather, the injured party also had to **prove** that the other party had tacitly **agreed** with the injured party that he or she would be liable for the loss upon a breach.

Because of the inherent difficulty of prevailing under the tacit agreement test, at least when it was strictly applied, modern contract law has specifically rejected it [UCC §2-715, Com. 2]. In its place, both the Restatement 2d and the UCC have adopted a "reason to foresee" test, applicable only to the breaching party. Thus, no longer must the injured party show any sort of mutual tacit agreement about the payment of consequential damages. Instead, **to recover a consequential loss, modern contract law requires only that the injured party prove that, at the time of contract formation, the breaching party either *knew or had reason to know* that such loss would follow as a probable result of the breach.** [Restatement 2d §351(2)(b); UCC §2-715 (2) (a)].

e. **Example. [§31.425]** Ted purchases a brand new mini-van from Dealer. Unknown to Dealer, Ted planned to use the van in his automobile repossession business. A few months after Ted purchased the van, while it is still under warranty, the van stops working. Ted has it towed to Dealer's, and it takes Dealer two days to find and fix the electrical problem. During those two days, Ted does not work, and his company loses the profits it would have made on repossessing cars for those two days.

While Ted has a valid breach of warranty case against the dealer, he will not be able to recover for his lost profits due to the foreseeability doctrine. That is, the lost profits suffered by Ted are not "direct" damages, for a reasonable person viewing the contract at the time it was negotiated, would not foresee that if the van had electrical problems, the purchaser would probably suffer a loss of business. That is not to say that such a possibility was inconceivable, but "conceivability" is not the test. The test is would a reasonable person have foreseen that such a result was probable. Since it is impossible to know whether the van's not working would cause a minor inconvenience or a major lost profit, the risk of paying for the purchaser's lost profits was not reasonably in the contemplation of Dealer when it entered into the contract. Accordingly, the lost profits from Ted's business is a consequential damage on these facts.

As a consequential loss, the lost profits can only be recovered by Ted if he somehow put Dealer on notice so that Dealer knew, or should have known, that one result of a breach would be that Ted would suffer lost profits. Since Ted did not declare his purpose in using the van to Dealer, Dealer had no reason to foresee that it would be liable for such a loss, and hence Ted would not be able to meet his burden for recovering such real, but consequential, damages under the foreseeability limitation.

3. **THE AVOIDABILITY LIMITATION. [§31.43]** Under the rule stated in §350 of the Restatement 2d, a party may not recover damages that the injured party could have avoided or mitigated without undue risk, burden or humiliation. That is, even if it is stipulated that the injured party has actually suffered foreseeable damage that can be proven with reasonable certainty, he or she is not entitled to recover such damages if they

could have been easily avoided. Thus a party cannot increase his or her own recovery when taking steps to avoid or reduce damages that would not involve any unreasonable risk, burden, or humiliation.

Two points are worth noting. First, if an injured party has taken reasonable steps in an attempt to avoid a loss, but those steps in fact prove unsuccessful (or ultimately prove not to be the most inexpensive way of avoiding the loss), he or she is still entitled to recover the full amount of the loss suffered [Restatement 2d §350(2)].

Second, while some courts and commentators state that the avoidability doctrine really sets forth a "duty to mitigate," that phrase is somewhat misleading. That is, the avoidability limitation sets forth no "duty" to do anything. Stating that the injured party has a "duty" suggests that if he or she somehow violated this "duty," the breaching party would have a right to sue the injured party for breach of the duty. That is not the case. Rather, if the injured party fails to avoid a loss that he or she could have avoided without undue risk, burden or humiliation, the only consequence is that the damages resulting from the failure to act may not be recovered. Hence, the worst possible case for the injured party under the avoidability principle is that he or she will not be entitled to recover anything due to the other party's breach of contract. It is never the case that the injured party will be liable for the breach of his or her "duty" to mitigate.

a. **Example. [§31.431]** Tim contracts to build a vacation home on property Cindy owns 1,000 miles from her principal residence. Tim promptly begins construction, but after a week he receives a telegram from Cindy unequivocally telling him to stop construction, as she has decided not to go forward with the building project. At the time Tim receives the telegram, he has spent $5,000 in labor and materials. Tim nevertheless spends another two weeks working on the house in the hopes that Cindy will change her mind. During these extra two weeks he incurs another $7,500 in labor and materials costs. The extra $7,500 is not recoverable under the avoidability doctrine, for Tim could have avoided those damages without undue risk, burden, or humiliation.

b. **Limits on the Avoidability Principle: An Injured Party Need Not Take Steps to Avoid Damages if Doing So Would Cause the Injured Party Undue Risk, Burden or Humiliation. [§31.432]** While a party injured by a breach must take appropriate steps to avoid a loss, this does not mean he or she must take all possible steps to do so. When avoiding the loss would force the injured party to undertake an undue risk or burden, or to undergo unreasonable humiliation, the failure to take such steps will not limit the amount of recoverable damages.

(1) **Example. [§31.4321]** Harry hires Gina to supervise his workers as they harvest crops on his farm. He agrees to pay her $30,000. A few days before the harvest is scheduled to begin, Gina breaches. Harry tries to find someone with Gina's qualifications to replace her, but because it is harvest time, all the experienced supervisors are employed elsewhere. Bill, who has little experience either as a grower or manager, and was otherwise unknown to Harry, nevertheless hears of Harry's plight and offers to take Gina's place at a salary of $20,000. Harry declines to hire Bill, and harvests his crop with no supervisor. Because there was no one in charge, some of Harry's crops did not get harvested in time and were spoiled.

Harry's recovery against Gina will not be affected by the avoidability doctrine, even though he could have, but chose not to, hire Bill. Thus, Gina is liable for the full amount of Harry's provable damages resulting from the crop failure. The reason the avoidability doctrine will not decrease his recovery is that hiring an inexperienced supervisor who Harry knew nothing about right before the harvest would have required

Harry to undertake an **unreasonable risk**. Note that this result would be true even if Gina can introduce evidence indicating that had Bill been hired, some of the losses Harry suffered potentially could have been avoided. The point is that contract law will not penalize an innocent party's recovery when he or she does not take **unreasonably risky** steps to avoid a loss, even if those steps may have been successful.

(2) **Example. [§31.4322]** Ron contractually agrees to build an addition onto Jennifer's house for $20,000. Just before he is scheduled to begin construction, Ron breaches. Jennifer calls five contractors in the area to bid on the job. Jennifer ends up selecting the cheapest bid of the five, a $23,000 bid from Delores, to build the addition. Thereafter, Jennifer brings suit against Ron for breach. At trial, Ron would like to offer testimony from Sam, yet another contractor from the same town who will testify that had Jennifer called **him** when she was soliciting new bids, he would have quoted her a price of $20,000 to build the addition. As such, Ron would like to assert that he owes Jennifer nothing, for she could have avoided having to pay the extra $3,000 by just calling Sam.

Jennifer is still entitled to a $3,000 recovery against Ron. An injured party need only take reasonable steps in mitigation. In other words, contract law will not require Jennifer to bear the risk that **somewhere**, there may be **someone**, who was willing to provide replacement services for a cheaper price than the one she found. To do so would be to place an **unreasonable burden** on her. Accordingly, so long as Jennifer acted reasonably (and it appeared she did so by calling five contractors), the amount of her recovery is not limited by the avoidability limitation.

SPECIAL CASE SQUIB

(3) **Example of *Parker v. Twentieth Century - Fox Film Corp.* [§31.4323]** The actress Shirley MacLaine (then Shirley MacLaine Parker) had a contract with Twentieth Century-Fox ("Fox") to star in a musical entitled Bloomer Girl for $750,000. Her contract provided that in addition to her salary, she also had the right to approve both the final screenplay and the choice of director. Shortly before filming was scheduled to begin, Fox breached by deciding not to produce the picture.

In the letter informing Ms. MacLaine of that decision, Fox offered to employ her to star in a western called Big Country, Big Man ("Big Country"). Big Country was scheduled to be shot on roughly the same time schedule as Bloomer Girl, and she was again offered $750,000 to appear in the movie. However, Big Country was a straight dramatic role, whereas in Bloomer Girl, Ms. MacLaine would have had the chance both to sing and dance. Moreover, she was given neither screenplay nor director approval in Big Country (although 31 of the 34 terms in the Bloomer Girl contract were identical to the terms offered her in the Big Country contract).

Ms. MacLaine refused to accept the offer to star in Big Country, and sued for her lost $750,000 salary. Fox was willing to admit the breach, but claimed her damages were subject to avoidability limitations. That is, Fox was willing to admit its actions resulted in a $750,000 loss, but also asserted she could have avoided such loss completely without undue burden, risk, or humiliation by accepting its offer to star in Big Country. As such, the studio claimed she was only entitled to a nominal damages recovery. **Held:** Ms. MacLaine was entitled to recover the total amount of her lost salary. *Parker v. Twentieth Century - Fox Film Corp.*, 3 Cal.3d 176, 474 P.2d 689 (1970).

This case is another example of the principle that the injured party need only act reasonably to escape penalty under the avoidability limitation. In employment contracts, the rule is that the salary a non-breaching employee would have earned from a substitute job that he or she did not accept triggers the avoidability limitations of contract damages **only** if the substitute employment offers reasonably comparable work (see §31.31). (Requiring anything else would be **unreasonably burdensome**, or perhaps, **unreasonably humiliating**, for the injured party for purposes of Restatement 2d §350(2).) Hence, the question in this case was whether starring in a dramatic western without script and director approval was reasonably comparable to starring in a musical with director and script approval rights. The court's answer was no, and hence Ms. MacLaine was entitled to recover all the damages she suffered without having that recovery limited by the avoidability principle.

F. **RELIANCE DAMAGES. [§31.5]** Reliance damages are damages based on the amount of interference with the injured party's reliance interest caused by the breach (see §31.12). The value of reliance damages is typically equal to the amount of out-of-pocket costs, including labor, incurred by the injured party at the time of the breach either in preparation for performance, or in actual performance, under the contract.

The most significant difference between reliance and expectation damages is that in the former, there is no recovery for lost profits — only for out-of-pocket costs. In this respect, expectation damages are "forward looking," i.e., they attempt to put the injured party in the position he or she would have been in had the contract been performed, and that includes recovery of any foreseeable and reasonably certain profit or benefit of the bargain. Reliance damages, on the other hand, are "backward looking," i.e., they try to put the injured party in the position he or she was in before the contract was signed. In other words, an award of reliance damages is designed to leave the injured party just as he or she was before the contract's execution — a position in which he or she has not realized any profit from the as yet- unsigned contract, but also a position in which he or she has not incurred any expenses in performing under the contract.

1. **THE AVAILABILITY OF RELIANCE DAMAGES. [§31.51]** Reliance damages are always available to an injured party as an alternative to expectation damages [Restatement 2d §344]. Typically, however, reliance damages are sought only when the injured party is unable to prove his or her expectation damages with reasonable certainty (see §31.41), or when such damages are not sufficiently foreseeable to be recovered (see §31.42).

   a. **Example. [§31.511]** Dick contracts to build a swimming pool for Edna. The contract price is $40,000 and Dick begins construction promptly. Two weeks into the project, Edna breaches by unjustifiably ordering Dick to cease building the pool. At the time of the breach, Dick had spent $8,000 in materials and labor.

   Dick would ordinarily sue for expectation damages, which would allow him to recover for any profit he would have made in building the pool. However, if Dick cannot prove with reasonable certainty how much it would have cost him to finish, and thus cannot sufficiently establish how much his profit would have been, he is still entitled to recover his reliance damages, i.e., the $8,000 he spent in reliance on Edna's promise to pay him.

2. LIMITATIONS ON RELIANCE DAMAGE RECOVERY. [§31.52] There are four limitations on an injured party's recovery of reliance damages:

(i) any damages claimed must be proven with **reasonable certainty** [Restatement 2d §352] (see §31.521);

(ii) if the breaching party can prove that **the injured party would have lost money** on the contract if it had been performed, i.e. it was a "losing contract," the amount of **the loss must be subtracted** from any reliance damage recovery (see §31.522);

(iii) the **value** of any materials purchased by the non-breaching party in performance or preparation for performance that **can be salvaged must be subtracted** from any reliance damage recovery (see §31.523); and

(iv) any damages claimed must **not have been avoidable** by the non-breaching party without undue burden, risk, or humiliation (see §31.524) [Restatement 2d §350].

a. **Reliance Damages Must be Proven with Reasonable Certainty. [§31.521]** As noted previously, (see §31.41), the reasonable certainty limitation on contract damages is not limited to expectation damages. It is a limitation on recovery of reliance damages as well [Restatement 2d §§349, 352]. However, as a practical matter, the reasonable certainty requirement rarely serves to limit an injured party's recovery of reliance damages. This is because reliance damages are typically valued in an amount equal to the out-of-pocket costs incurred by the non-breaching party in reliance on the breaching party's performance under the contract. Hence, it is the rare case where a non-breaching cannot prove with reasonable certainty the amount of his or her out-of-pocket costs.

b. **Limitation on the Recovery of Reliance Damages in "Losing Contract" Situations. [§31.522]** The principal goal of contract damages is to put the non-breaching party in the same position he or she would have been in had the contract been performed. A necessary corollary of this goal is that contract damages should not put the party in a **better** position than he or she would have been in had the contract been performed. Accordingly, if the party in breach can prove that the non-breaching party would have lost money on the contract had it been performed, the amount of such loss must be subtracted from any reliance recovery [Restatement 2d §349].

It is because of this rule that a party in a losing contract will usually opt for restitutionary recovery instead of a reliance damage recovery. (see §32.231)

(1) **Example. [§31.5221]** Glenda contracted to build a swimming pool for Don at a price of $35,000. About a week after Glenda began construction, Don unjustifiably fired her. At the time of the breach, Glenda can establish she had spent $7,000 in materials and labor on the project, which Don refuses to pay. Accordingly, Glenda files suit seeking to recover her reliance damages.

During discovery, Don obtains Glenda's internal profit and loss figures for the job. As a result, Don can competently establish at trial that Glenda underbid the pool project and would have lost $5,000 had the project been completed. As a result, Glenda's reliance damage recovery would only be $2,000 (i.e., the $5,000 loss subtracted from the $7,000 she has already spent). Note that if she were awarded the full $7,000 she has spent in reliance up to the time of the breach, she would be in a better position than she would have been in had the contract been performed. That is, she would be "even," whereas had the contract been performed she would have been $5,000 "in the hole." Hence, the amount of such provable losses must be subtracted from her reliance damages recovery in keeping with the general goal of contract damages.

c. **The Value of Any Salvageable Materials must be Subtracted from a Recovery of Reliance Damages as a Cost Avoided. [§31.523]** As with expectation damages, the value of any salvageable materials purchased by the non-breaching party in performance or preparation for performance under the contract must be subtracted from any reliance damage recovery. As with expectation recovery, the reason for this requirement is that without deducting the amount of such salvageable materials from the damages recovered, the non-breaching party would end up with an unbargained for windfall, and would once again be in a better position than he or she would have been in had the contract gone forward (see §31.3).

d. **Damages Must Not be Avoidable Without Undue Risk, Burden, or Humiliation. [§31.524]** Reliance damages are also subject to the Restatement 2d's rules regarding avoidability or mitigation in §350. Hence, to be recoverable, a damage must not have been avoidable by the non-breacher without undue risk, burden, or humiliation (see §31.43).

3. **RECOVERY BASED ON THE RELIANCE INTEREST IN OTHER SITUATIONS. [§31.53]** In addition to being available as an alternate means of recovery for breach of contract, recovery based on the reliance interest is also the exclusive means of recovery in other situations previously covered in this outline. In other words, the only recovery available to the innocent party in these situations, is an award based on the amount of his or her reliance [Restatement 2d §349, Com. b]. These situations include:

   (i) recovery based on promissory estoppel [Restatement 2d §90]; (see §8.4);

   (ii) recovery based on contract modifications where the rule of Restatement 2d §89 is applied (see §7.633);

   (iii) recovery based on pre-performance preparation by the offeree which does not rise to the level of acceptance [Restatement 2d §87(2)]; (see §§4.21, 8.34);

   (iv) recovery based on actions taken in reliance on promises that are unenforceable under the statute of frauds [Restatement 2d §139]; (see §§8.32, 9.7); and

   (v) recovery based on actions taken in reliance on promises made in pre-offer, preliminary negotiations (see §8.35).

G. **EMOTIONAL DISTRESS DAMAGES ARE GENERALLY NOT AVAILABLE IN BREACH OF CONTRACT SUITS. [§31.6]** Virtually every breach of contract causes some kind of emotional distress to the non-breaching party. This is true even in merchant-to-merchant contracts. For example, assume a retailer has ordered 50 television sets from a manufacturer which are due to be delivered on Friday. If the sets do not come, the retailer is likely to be at least exasperated, about having to deal with the breaching manufacturer, find replacement sets if necessary, and perhaps lose a sale or two if the retailer is out of inventory and cannot obtain replacement televisions quickly.

Nevertheless, contract law has been particularly unyielding in its view that emotional distress damages are not recoverable in contract [Restatement 2d §353] and should only be available in tort. Partly this is a reflection of the separation of tort and contract, i.e., on the whole, tort damages are much more "personal" and designed to compensate the injured party for all personal harms (such as emotional distress), whereas contract damages are more "economic" and designed to compensate only for the lost monetary value resulting from the breach. In addition, it is also a reflection of the idea that the amount the injured party should recover from a breach should not greatly exceed the value of the consideration promised the breaching party [Restatement 2d §351(3), Com. f]. That is, awarding a non-breaching party lost value, lost profits, incidental loss, **and** emotional distress damage could result in the amount of recoverable contract damages being far in excess of the value of the non-breaching party's performance that was expected by the breaching party.

There are two exceptions to the general bar on emotional distress recovery arising from a breach of contract suit:

> (i)   when the breach also results in tangible personal injury; and

> (ii) when emotional distress is "**particularly likely**" to result from breach of a specific contract [Restatement 2d §353].

1. **EXCEPTION: EMOTIONAL DISTRESS DAMAGES ARE AVAILABLE WHEN THE BREACH OF CONTRACT ALSO RESULTS IN TANGIBLE PERSONAL INJURY.** [§31.61] When a breach of contract results in personal injury, contract law permits the non-breaching party to recover his or her emotional distress damages from the breacher. The rationale for this exception is that in such cases the interest invaded by the breach i.e., injury to the person, is a kind of interest that civil law values very highly and thus is willing to reward to a greater degree than when the interference is only a loss to the injured party's economic interest. Moreover, providing recovery for losses accompanying personal injury is the kind of interest that tort law protects. Obviously if the injured party sued in tort, recovery of emotional distress would be permitted in such situations. Hence, contract law does not deny emotional distress recovery in such cases just because a party chooses to sue in contract rather than tort.

There are two typical ways a breach of contract can result in personal injury. One is where the breach is a breach of warranty involving a machine or other product which, even though used foreseeably, nevertheless causes an injury. The second is where the contract is one for services involving a physician (or other health provider), where the breach is of a promise either to use reasonable care in treating a patient, or to achieve a particular result. In these types of cases, often the result is personal injury to the patient.

a. **Example.** [§31.611] Joe buys a power mower, relying on the promise on the front of the package guaranteeing that the mower is "perfectly safe when used as directed." Joe uses the mower as directed, but it turns out the blade assembly is not bolted on tightly, and the blades came off injuring his foot. If Joe sues the manufacturer for breach of express warranty, he is entitled to recover for any emotional distress he suffers as a result of his injury.

b. **Example of** *Sullivan v. O'Connor.* [§31.612] Ms. Sullivan contracted with Dr. O'Connor to perform plastic surgery on her nose. Ms. Sullivan claimed the doctor had promised her that the surgery would enhance her beauty and improve her appearance. However, the surgery (actually three surgeries) ended up disfiguring her nose. Because the breach of the contract between Dr. O'Connor and Ms. Sullivan resulted in a physical injury, the court allowed Ms. Sullivan to recover for the pain and suffering and mental distress she suffered with respect to her third operation.

2. EXCEPTION: RECOVERY OF EMOTIONAL DISTRESS DAMAGES IS PERMITTED WHEN SUCH HARM IS "PARTICULARLY LIKELY" TO RESULT FROM A BREACH. [§31.62] Contract law also allows emotional distress damages to be recovered if the nature of the contract is such that mental anguish is "particularly likely" to result from a breach of that agreement [Restatement 2d §353]. This exception is very limited. Its principal application has been to three types of cases:

(i)   where a mortuary mishandles a corpse;

(ii) where a telegram company mistakenly delivers a telegram informing the wrong person of a death of their loved ones; or

(iii) where an insurance company is guilty of a "bad faith" breach (see §31.81).

Note that a few judges have suggested that some wrongful termination of employment contracts also meet this test. That is, that the argument is that the employer should know that being fired wrongfully, and in violation of the terms of the employment contract, is "particularly likely" to cause emotional distress in the employee. While this argument has some currency, to date it is very much a minority position.

H. LIQUIDATED DAMAGES. [§31.7] As a general rule, parties can enforce whatever lawful promises they voluntarily agree to in their contract. Indeed, this is largely what freedom of contract means. One of the biggest exceptions to this general rule, however, is liquidated damages. As will be seen below, liquidated damages are frequently held unenforceable [Restatement 2d §356; UCC §2-718].

Liquidated damages are damages the parties have agreed to in advance. That is, as part of their contract negotiations, they agree as to how much one will owe the other upon a breach (see §31.28). To examine why liquidated damage clauses are so rarely enforced, study the following hypothetical:

Ruth and Sam entered into a contract whereby Sam promised to sell his record collection to Ruth for $7,000. Both parties were very anxious that the transaction actually be performed, i.e., neither wanted to have the bother of enforcing his or her expectation interest by means of a lawsuit. Hence, they agreed that if either of them breached the agreement, the breaching party would owe the other $100,000 as a liquidated damage.

Contract law would not enforce their liquidated damage provision. At first thought, it might seem that the legal system would be happy to enforce liquidated damages. After all, by stipulating in advance to the amount of a loss one party will owe the other upon a breach, the only question in a breach of contract suit would be whether there was a breach. Accordingly, enforcing such provisions would save a court time, for there would be no need for the injured party to prove the actual amount of his or her damages, whether those damages were foreseeable, avoidable, etc., for the amount of recovery has been fixed in advance.

The reason contract law will not enforce such a liquidated damage clause has to do with the twin ideas that a party should not be better off as a result of a breach than he or she would have been had the contract been performed, and that a party should not be penalized for breaching a contract. That is, if Ruth breached the agreement to pay $7,000 for Sam's records, and if as a result of that breach Sam ended up with $100,000, Sam is obviously in a far better position than he would have been in had the contract been performed.

Morever, such a result would also penalize Ruth because the liquidated damage clause makes it too expensive for her to breach under the principles of the efficient breach doctrine (see §31.01). For example, suppose Ruth decided she would rather spend her money some other way than by giving it to Sam in exchange for his records. The efficient breach doctrine says that so long as Ruth is willing to pay the Sam's expectation damages, she should be able to breach when it is more efficient for her to do so, i.e., whenever she will be better off after breaching and paying damages. Here, if Ruth is willing to pay the difference between the price she was willing to pay for the records and the price someone else may offer Sam for his records, the efficient breach doctrine says she should be able to do so. However, under the liquidated damage clause, Ruth will be liable for $100,000 upon breach, not the difference between $7,000 and whatever other price Sam can get for his record collection. Hence, Ruth would be **penalized** because of her breach because she will have to give Sam $100,000 to compensate him for what is, at maximum, a $7,000 loss [Restatement 2d §356, Com. a].

Accordingly, there are only a limited number of situations in which contract law does not view the enforcement of a liquidated damage clause as extracting a penalty on the breaching party and thus will allow a party to collect a liquidated amount. Those situations are described in the next section.

1. **REQUIREMENTS FOR AN ENFORCEABLE LIQUIDATED DAMAGE PROVISION.** [§31.71] In order to enforce a liquidated damage provision, the injured party must prove the following:

> (i)   that the amount of the liquidated damage is **reasonable in light of the anticipated harm** to the injured party that was foreseen at the time of contract formation, or that the amount is **reasonable in light of the actual harm** suffered by the injured party; and

> (ii)   that there is some reason to believe that there will be **difficulties in proving the actual loss with precision**. [UCC §2-718(1).]

a. **The Amount of the Liquidated Damage must be Reasonable in Light of the Anticipated or Actual Loss.** [§31.711] As noted above, it is only when a liquidated damage is considered a "penalty" that contract law will not enforce it. Hence, if the amount of the liquidated damage in a contract is reasonable in light of the amount of the injured party's expectation loss that was either anticipated at the time the contract was signed, or was actually suffered by that party as a result of the breach, then by definition the liquidated amount does not extract penalty from the breaching party [Restatement 2d §356(1); UCC §2-718(1)].

Note that the common law test was slightly more limited. At common law, the amount of the liquidated damage had to be a reasonable estimate of the **anticipated** harm only. If it was not, the fact that it might be reasonable in light of the actual harm suffered even irrelevant and the clause would not be enforceable.

(1) **Example. [§31.7111]** Bill was an attorney who was asked to perform legal services for Laura in 1970. Bill and his wife had just become parents of a baby boy, and Bill wished to provide for his future. Accordingly, he and Laura agreed that in consideration of Bill's legal work for Laura, she promised to transfer the deed of her beach front property to Bill's son when he turned 21. The fair market value of the

property in 1960 was $10,000, but Bill and Laura nevertheless agreed that if she breached the agreement by not turning over the deed in 1991, she would owe Bill $300,000. By 1991, the property had become extremely valuable and various appraisers valued it between $280,000 and $350,000. However, Laura refuses to transfer the property.

Under the rule set forth in §356(1) of the Restatement 2d, the liquidated damage clause would be enforceable, since it calls for payment of a reasonable amount in light of the actual harm caused by Laura's breach. Under the older rule, however it is unlikely that the provision would be upheld because by 1970 standards, having someone pay $300,000 for the breach of a promise to transfer a $10,000 piece of property in the future, even with inflation taken into account, would almost certainly have been thought a penalty.

b. **Actual Damages must be Somewhat Difficult to Prove in Order for a Liquidated Damage Provision to be Enforceable. [§31.712]** While contract law generally allows parties to make reasonable estimates of actual damages in creating an enforceable liquidated damage provision, it will not do so if the precise amount of damages suffered by the breaching party can be easily determined. That is, if the precise amount of damages can be easily proven, there is no need to estimate it by means of a liquidated damage clause. In such a case, the theory of contract damages requires that the non-breaching party be compensated for the exact amount of his or her loss, and not for an estimated value of that loss.

There is an obvious tension between the two parts of the test for a liquidated damage. In other words, if the amount of a party's actual damages must be somewhat difficult to prove, then it is obviously difficult to establish that the amount of the liquidated damage is a "reasonable" amount in light of the anticipated or actual loss. While there is some truth to the argument that the two parts of the test are incompatible, it is also true they can be harmonized. That is, once it is determined that the **precise** amount of damages will be somewhat difficult to prove, then contract law will uphold a liquidated damage amount if it is a reasonable estimate of that loss.

(1) **Example. [§31.7121]** Dale hires Ned's Construction Co. to build a small commercial office building on some property she owns. The contract calls for construction to be completed by September 1, and that if it is not, Ned's will be liable to Dale for $3,000/day thereafter until it is finished.

Depending on the circumstances, such a liquidated damage clause may or may not be enforceable. It is likely that it will be difficult to prove the exact amount of Dale's damages with precision, because her profits would depend on how much of the office building would be rented, what the exact terms of the leases would be, etc. Hence, Dale would fairly easily pass the second part of the test.

The real issue is whether she could pass the first part, i.e., whether she could prove that $3,000/day is a reasonable estimate of her actual damages in light of her real or anticipated harm. If from all the circumstances it appears that $3,000 is reasonable and is not extracting a penalty from Ned's, then it will be enforced. If $3,000 is in excess of the profit Dale reasonably would have made, then the liquidated damages clause will be judged void as a penalty.

2. ALTERNATIVE PERFORMANCE CLAUSES DISTINGUISHED FROM LIQUIDATED DAMAGE CLAUSES. [§31.72]

Compare the following two contract provisions:

Contract No. 1

Steel Co. agrees to purchase at least $300,000 of pure oxygen during the next calendar year from Gas Co. In the event of a breach of this promise, Steel Co. will pay to Gas Co. $50,000 on December 31 as a liquidated damage.

Contract No. 2

Steel Co. agrees that during the next calendar year it will either: (a) purchase at least $300,000 worth of pure oxygen from Gas Co.; or (b) pay Gas Co. $50,000 on December 31.

Contract No. 1 is a standard liquidated damage clause and will only be upheld if the amount is reasonable in light of the actual or anticipated harm and if the exact amount of damages are somewhat difficult to calculate. However, there is no problem whatsoever in enforcing Contract No. 2.

The difference between the two contracts is that the $50,000 payment in Contract No. 1 is triggered by a **breach**, whereas such a payment in Contract No. 2 is an alternative means of **performance**. Thus, there is no fear in Contract No. 2 that the Steel Co. will be penalized by breaching the contract in that it will be forced to pay an unreasonably high amount over and above the actual loss suffered by Gas Co. as a result of the breach. In other words, Contract No. 2 is really no different from a contract that said "Upon payment of $15, Joe is entitled to receive, at his option, either: (a) my U2 compact disc, or (b) my Miriah Carey video." Obviously in that case no one would say selection of the video presents any liquidated damage concerns, and the same holds true for Contract No. 2 above. Where the parties grant two alternative means of **performance**, as opposed to one means of performance and a liquidated damage figure for **breach** of that performance, then the contract is generally enforceable.

I. PUNITIVE DAMAGES ARE GENERALLY NOT RECOVERABLE IN BREACH OF CONTRACT ACTIONS. [§31.8] As in tort law, punitive damages in contract are damages awarded over and above any compensatory loss suffered by the injured party as punishment for conduct that falls below societally defined norms. Because a recovery of punitive damages for breach of contract would end up putting the non-breaching party in a better position than he or she would have been in had the contract been performed, the almost universal rule is that such damages are **not** recoverable in breach of contract actions [Restatement 2d §355].

Despite this long-standing and relatively inflexible doctrine, over the past thirty years or so a number of commentators, plaintiff's lawyers, and some judges have tried to make a case for the recovery of punitive damages in certain contract actions. They claim that when there has been a "bad faith" breach of contract, as opposed to an "ordinary" breach, punitive damages are warranted. Under this view, an "ordinary" breach is one where a party is ultimately found to have breached a substantive term of the contract, but that the party's reasons for doing so were legitimate, e.g., it had a different, but reasonable, interpretations of what the clause meant. A "bad faith" breach is one where a party both breaches a substantive term of the contrast, **and** does so in such a way, or for such a reason, that the breacher's conduct

352

also violates the implied duty of good faith and fair dealing included in every contract [Restatement 2d §205; UCC §1-203]. In those cases, so the argument goes, punitive damages are warranted as punishment for socially reprehensible conduct.

Under the Restatement 2d, punitive damages are only available when the breach of contract also turns out to be a tort. That is, the fact that tort occurred in the context of a contractual breach does not somehow deprive the court from its ability to award punitive damages for the tort (e.g., where a seller fraudulently misrepresents something as part of a sales transaction) [Restatement 2d §355]. In all other cases, the Restatement 2d provides that no punitive damages are permitted, the "bad faith" motives of the breacher not withstanding.

This is one area, however, where the courts have not completely followed the Restatement 2d. As will be seen in the next few sections, in selected areas modern courts are willing to allow for punitive damage recovery against particularly egregious "bad faith" breachers.

1. **EXCEPTION TO GENERAL RULE: PUNITIVE DAMAGES CAN BE RECOVERED FOR "BAD FAITH" BREACHES OF INSURANCE CONTRACTS. [§31.81]** Many states allow punitive damages to be awarded for the bad faith breach of an insurance contract, especially a life insurance contract. The doctrine became established in cases like the following hypothetical:

A husband and wife take out a life insurance policy on the husband's life for $100,000 and faithfully pay premiums on the policy for 30 years. When the husband dies, however, the insurance company does not pay the widow the $100,000. Knowing they have no real basis for saying so, they assert that the husband committed suicide (or did some other act which would allow it to avoid coverage). While, of course, this happens in only a minority of cases, when it does occur, the insurance company has been found to have made the bogus claim denying coverage for the following reasons:

(1) It knows that the maximum extent of its contractual liability will be $100,000, i.e., there are no lost profits or consequential damages flowing from the breach that increase as time goes on. Hence, if it can keep the $100,000 for a few more months in its bank rather than paying it to the widow, it can earn interest on the funds. In other words, given the choice between having to pay $100,000 in January of year 1, or in January of year 3 (after a lawsuit, appeals, etc.), it is in the economic interest of the insurance company to pay in year 3 given the time value of money. Besides, with the interest it makes off the $100,000, it can offset some or all of the attorneys' fees needed to fight the expected suit of the widow.

(2) It may never have to pay the $100,000 at all. While it is likely the widow may see a lawyer and file suit for breach of contract, there are a few who will not, and so it may be able to keep all the money.

(3) Even when the widow does file suit, if she desperately needs the insurance money to pay her bills after her husband dies, she might be willing to settle for less than the $100,000 just to receive some amount of money immediately. In other words, a widow badly in need of money might be willing to settle for an immediate $70,000 payment to have the matter over with, rather than wait three years or so for a trial and an appeal. If so, the insurance company has "saved" $30,000.

Hence, given the unique factual situation of the innocent party found in such a case, coupled with the particularly reprehensible nature of the breacher's acts, most states allow a jury to award punitive damages for the "bad faith" breach of an insurance contract. Initially, this doctrine was limited just to life insurance contracts, and it is with those agreements that courts still award punitive damages with the greatest frequency. However, currently, most states that recognize the bad faith doctrine allow for punitive damages whenever an insurance company makes a bad faith denial of coverage, no matter what kind of policy it is. (Recall also that most states allow for the recovery of emotional distress damages as well in "bad faith" breach cases against insurance companies (see §31.62). (See Case Squibs, *Seamen's Direct Buying Service v. Standard Oil*, regarding whether there should be a further exception to the "no punitive damages" rule in contract actions for bad faith breaches in commercial contracts.)

J. **THE INJURED PARTY'S RECOVERY OF PRE-JUDGMENT INTEREST IN BREACH OF CONTRACT CASES IS USUALLY ALLOWED IF THE AMOUNT IN CONTROVERSY IS LIQUIDATED. [§31.9]** In every jurisdiction, interest is awarded on a **judgment** from the date the award is officially entered in the courts "judgment book." However, a separate question is whether interest should be awarded to the non-breaching party **from the date of the breach (or the repudiation) until the day of judgment.** Restatement 2d §354 sets forth the majority rule on this issue, which is that so long as the breach consists of the failure to pay a **fixed sum of money**, or to **render a performance with a fixed or ascertainable monetary value**, the non-breaching party is entitled to prejudgment interest on the debt, *beginning on the date performance was due* [Restatement 2d §354 (1)]. In all other cases, the awarding of interest is discretionary with the court [Restatement 2d §354 (1)]. In other words, so long as the amount of damages involved in the dispute is a liquidated amount, i.e., a "sum certain," or can readily be calculated into a sum certain, interest is recoverable by the injured party as a matter of right. If the amount of damages is not liquidated, however, prejudgment interest in only awarded to the injured party when the court believes is just to do so [Restatement 2d §354 (2)].

The rate of prejudgment interest varies form jurisdiction to jurisdiction. Presently the rate granted by most states is in the range of 6% to 10%. Typically it is a simple interest award (not compound), and the actual calculations are done by the court, not left to the jury.

CHAPTER THIRTY-TWO: RESTITUTION

A. RESTITUTION GENERALLY. [§32.0] The crux of restitution can be fairly easily stated: a person who has been *unjustly* enriched by another must account for that enrichment, usually by restoring the value of the benefits received through a payment of money. In other words, the amount of restitutionary recovery due an aggrieved party is equal to the value of the benefits the benefited party has thus far received and not yet paid for.

Before discussing its application to contracts, there are a few general concepts that need to be understood:

(1) **Recovery in Restitution is Based on the Value of the Enrichment Received by the benefited Party, and Not on the Value of the Aggrieved Party's Promises**. Recovery of money damages for breach of contract is based on the value of the promises made by the breaching party. As explained earlier, the idea behind expectation damages is that each party's promised performance is given a dollar value, and an injured party's recovery is based on the extent to which the breach prevented that party from receiving the full value of the breacher's promised performance (see §31.0).

On the other hand, in restitution the measure of the aggrieved party's recovery has nothing directly to do with the economic value of the other's promised performance. Rather, it is based on the value of the **benefits** that have been *actually received* by the benefited party. If those benefits turn out to be worth more than the value of the promised performance, the aggrieved party may recover **more** than the value of the contractual promise. If they are worth *less* than the value of the promised performance, then the aggrieved party is entitled to the *lesser* amount. The point is that the promises made under the contract are largely irrelevant for restitution purposes. What is relevant is the amount of benefits actually received by a party, for it is on the value of those benefits that restitutionary relief is awarded.

(2) **Recovery in Restitution is Based on the Value of the Enrichment Actually Received by the benefited Party, and Not on the Value of the Efforts Undertaken by the Aggrieved Party**. It is important to realize that restitutionary recovery is only based on the extent to which one party **actually receives** benefits provided by the other. That is, sometimes one party spends much time and effort in preparing to perform and in beginning performance. If those efforts produce no tangible benefits to the other, there has, by definition, been no enrichment of the other. Accordingly, since there has been no benefit received, there is nothing for that party to restore, and thus no action for restitution can be successfully brought.

For example, assume that Maria's Machine Shop contracts to manufacture a drill press for Butler's Tool Company for $100,000. Maria's begins building the machine and has spent $40,000 in time and labor to the point at which Butler's breaches by telling Maria's to discontinue performance. Maria's $40,000 worth of expenditures are probably recoverable in a suit for reliance damages, and she may be able to sue for expectation damages as well. But she is entitled to **no** restitutionary recovery from Butler's because her $40,000 in expenditures conferred no tangible benefit on Butler's. That is, Butler's company has not been enriched by Maria's efforts in constructing a half-built machine at her factory. Because there has been no benefit received by the company that it can restore to Maria's, it owes Maria's nothing in restitution.

As can be seen, restitutionary recovery is thus different from recovery of reliance damages. An award of reliance damages attempts to put the **innocent party** in the position he or she was in before the contract was signed (see §31.5). An award of restitution, on the other hand, attempts to put a **benefited party** in the position he or she was in before the contract was signed. Restitution does this by making a benefited party pay for the value of any enrichment provided him or her by the other party that the benefited party did not have before the agreement was made. The interesting thing is that the **benefitted party** can be the innocent party or *the breaching party* (see below and §32.3)

(3) **Restitution is Potentially Available as a Remedy for Both the Breaching and the Non-Breaching Parties.** Because restitutionary recovery focuses only on the value of any benefits received, and not on a party's promises, it does not matter whether those benefits were received by the non-breaching party or by the breaching party. That is, long as the non-breaching party has received unpaid-for benefits, and so long as it would be unjust for the non-breaching party to retain those benefits without paying for them, the *non-breaching* party will be liable to the breacher in restitution (see §32.3 et seq.).

B. **RULES COMMON TO ALL RESTITUTION ACTIONS. [§32.1]** Restitution is a separate branch of the law, but it has been used frequently as the basis for a remedy in contracts and contracts-related cases. There are two rules that are applicable to **all** restitution actions:

(1) The value of the benefits conferred on the benefited party must be properly valued under the appropriate theory; and

(2) When a party seeks restitution, he or she must make restitution. That is, there must be mutual restitution or there can be no restitution.

1. **THE TWO METHODS OF VALUING THE RESTITUTION INTEREST: THE "COST AVOIDED" AND THE "NET BENEFIT" METHODS. [§32.11]** As noted above, a party's restitutionary recovery is equal to the value of the tangible benefits he or she has provided that have been received by the other party. Thus, an important question is how the benefits received by the other party are valued. Restitution recognizes two different, but reasonable, methods to calculate the dollar amount of these received benefits: (1) The "Cost Avoided" Method; and (2) The "Net Benefit" Method.

The **"Cost Avoided"** method holds that the benefits received by the benefited party should be valued as the dollar amount it would have cost the benefited party to obtain those same benefits from another [Restatement 2d §371(a)]. That is, under the cost avoided method the question is what is the fair market value of the benefits received by the benefited party, **as measured by how much it would have cost the benefited party to hire someone else to provide those benefits.**

The **"Net Benefit"** method holds that the benefit to the enriched party should be valued as the dollar amount of the extent to which the benefited party's property has been increased in value, or his or her other interests advanced, by the actions of the aggrieved party [Restatement 2d §371(b)]. That is, under this approach the measure of the benefits received by the enriched party is **the difference in the fair market value of his or her property, or his or her net worth, before and after the actions of the aggrieved party.**

Sum & Substance QUICK REVIEW of Contracts

Sometimes the dollar value of the restitutionary recovery due under these two methods yields the same result. This is especially the case if the benefit conferred by the aggrieved party is a cash payment. For example, suppose Larry contracted to purchase a piece of land from Trish for $50,000. He pays Trish the money, but she never delivers the deed. If he sues her in restitution for return of the benefits provided to her, those benefits will be valued at $50,000 regardless of whether they are calculated under the "cost avoided" or the "net benefit" method. That is, the reasonable value of the amount of the enrichment given Trish as measured by what it would cost someone else to give her those benefits (i.e., the "cost avoided" method) is $50,000. Similarly, the increased value of her net worth due to the benefits provided by Larry (i.e., the "net benefit" method) is also $50,000.

Where the benefits provided are *services*, however, it is **very unlikely** the two valuation methods will yield the same results. For example, assume that Alysia hired Lance to build a custom home for her. Lance timely began construction and had done quite a bit of work on the house when Alysia breached and ordered him off her property. Lance brings suit against Alysia seeking to recover for his restitutionary interest. Competent evidence will show that the reasonable value of the work performed by Lance was $70,000 at the time of the breach, and that the market value of Alysia's property increased by $30,000 as a result of having a partially completed structure on it. That is, the fair market value of the property with the structure on it, minus the fair market value without the structure, is $30,000.

Using the "cost avoided" method, Lance's actions benefited Alysia by $70,000, for this is the amount it would have cost her to hire someone else to provide those benefits, and thus it is also the *cost* she *avoided* by not having to pay someone else for those services. Using the "net benefit" method, however, Lance benefited Alysia by only $30,000, for this figure constitutes the extent to which the fair market value of her property increased by Lance's actions.

Which of the two valuation methods should be used in determining the amount of an aggrieved party's restitutionary recovery is answered immediately below.

a. **Determining Which Method of Valuing the Restitutionary Interest should be Used in Ascertaining an Aggrieved Party's Restitutionary Recovery. [§32.111]** In all cases, a court has the discretion to choose either the cost avoided or net benefit valuation method in calculating the aggrieved party's restitutionary award depending on which one seems the most "just" in that particular situation [Restatement 2d §371]. However, contract law has developed presumptions as to which method should be used:

(1) When a **non-breaching party is seeking restitutionary recovery against the breacher**, the presumption is that the non-breaching party will be entitled to recover using the method which yields **the most generous restitutionary recovery** [Restatement 2d §371, Com. b]; and

(2) When a **breaching party is seeking restitutionary recovery against a non-breacher**, the presumption is that the breaching party will be entitled to recover using the method which yields **the least generous recovery** [Restatement 2d §374, Com. b].

These rules are only presumptions, and a court may choose not to follow them if it would not be "just" to do so. However, in a vast majority of cases courts adopt these presumptions in calculating the value of restitutionary awards.

2. THE "MUTUAL RESTITUTION" REQUIREMENT. [§32.12] An aggrieved party who seeks restitution of a benefit he or she has conferred on another must offer to return whatever benefits he or she has received from the other party as part of a final restitutionary judgment. In other words, unless there is a mutual restitution of benefits, a court will not allow any restitutionary recovery [Restatement 2d §384].

Sometimes, of course, the aggrieved party has received no benefits, e.g., Bill gave Darla $50,000 for a piece of property and she has not tendered the deed to him. In such cases, obviously no mutual restitution is possible, for Darla gave Bill nothing to return. But where, e.g., Ted gave Ann $25,000 in progress payments for a construction job, and Ted later breaches, Ann will have to make restitution of the $25,000 before she can obtain restitution for her services from Ted. The ideal is to return the very benefit received if that is possible. Thus, if the aggrieved party has received land or goods, he or she is expected to offer to return that same land, or those very same goods (and not a cash payment in lieu thereof) before restitution will be awarded. If the benefits obtained by the aggrieved party cannot be returned intact, e.g., when they are services or when the goods are damaged or lost, the value of those services or goods, as calculated by the appropriate method (see §32.11), must be subtracted from the net amount owing that party in ascertaining the correct amount of restitutionary recovery [Restatement 2d §384(2)].

a. **Example. [§32.121]** Millie hires Frank to build an addition onto her house. Under their contract, Millie was obligated to make monthly progress payments to Frank. Frank began construction and had both laid the foundation and put up two walls when Millie unjustly fired him. At that point, Millie had paid Frank $15,000 in monthly progress payments. To be entitled to sue Millie in restitution, Frank will have to offer to return the $15,000 in progress payments under the rule of Restatement 2d 384(1), and will have to be prepared to pay that money, or at least account for it as an offset, in any restitutionary recovery.

b. **Example. [§32.122]** Same as above, except this time it was Frank who breached, and Millie sued Frank in restitution for the $15,000 in progress payments. Obviously Millie could not "return" the foundation and the walls. In cases like this where return of the exact benefits provided by the non-breaching party is either impossible or unavailing, the aggrieved party must at least offer to offset the value of such benefits in any restitutionary recovery [Restatement 2d §384(2)].

C. RESTITUTIONARY RECOVERY FOR BREACH OF CONTRACT AND THE NOTICE OF RESCISSION REQUIREMENT. [§32.2] There is a scholarly debate as to whether restitution can be thought of as a remedy for breach of contract or whether it is only an extra-contractual remedy, i.e., a separate kind of recovery unto itself, with its own rules. This is not really an "academic" question, for if it is truly a remedy for breach of contract, then the party injured by the breach need only establish the existence of the contract and its breach to be entitled to enforce his or her restitutionary interest. On the other hand, if restitution is an extra-contractual remedy, the injured party will be required to send some sort of notice to the breacher rescinding the contract before a restitutionary recovery is permitted. That is, the aggrieved party will have to renounce his or her intention to sue under the contract by rescinding it, and only then will he or she be entitled to sue in restitution.

Those who feel the contract must be rescinded before a restitution action can successfully be alleged believe that, as a matter of logical consistency, restitution must be viewed as extra-contractual. They note that restitution provides the basis for recovery in a great number of situations, including recovery by the **breaching** party and recovery by aggrieved parties under voidable agreements, and thus assert that restitution cannot be thought of as a remedy for breach itself. However, most contracts scholars now agree that restitution, like the recovery of money damages, is a remedial right based on the contract itself [Restatement 2d §344(c)]. Hence, most (but not all) jurisdictions no longer require a formal rescission notice from the aggrieved party in a breach situation before that party is entitled to restitution.

Note that even though restitution is a remedy for contract breach, a recovery based on restitutionary principles should not be thought of as "damages." Hence, any reference to "restitution damages" is incorrect. It is more accurate to say the aggrieved party has a "restitutionary recovery."

Also note this means that the non-breaching party in a breach suit thus has three choices as to the theory on which to base his or her claim for damages: (1) expectation damages (see §31.31); (2) reliance damages (see §31.5); or (3) restitutionary recovery. The non-breaching party is free to choose whichever method will maximize recovery (see §31.14).

1. **LIMITATIONS ON THE AVAILABILITY OF RESTITUTION AS A REMEDY FOR BREACH OF CONTRACT. [§31.21]** There are two limitations on a non-breaching party's right to seek restitution for a breach of contract:

    (1) Restitution is only available if the injured party would be able to sue the breaching party for total, as opposed to partial, breach [Restatement 2d §373, Com. a]; and

    (2) A party injured by the other's breach is **not** entitled to restitution if he or she has performed all of his or her duties under the contract, and the only remaining performance due under the agreement by the breaching party is payment of a definite sum of money [Restatement 2d §373(2)].

    These limitations are discussed below.

    a. **Restitution is Available Only if the Breach Would Give Rise to Damages for Total, and Not Just Partial, Breach. [§32.211]** Before a party can recover in restitution, the breach involved must be serious enough to give rise to damages for a **total** breach [Restatement 2d §373, Com a]; (see also §21.24 et seq.). If the breach is only a partial one, no restitution is recoverable.

        (1) **Example. [§32.2111]** Terry contractually agrees to build a house for Geri, and promises to use electrical wire made by Power Co. throughout the house. Geri agrees to make monthly progress payments to Terry. After two months, Terry has been paid $40,000 in progress payments, but it is then discovered that he inadvertently used nearly identical wire made by Electric Co. in various places throughout the house instead of Power Co. wire. While Geri is entitled to sue Terry for whatever damages she can prove has been caused by the partial breach, she is not entitled to recover the $40,000 that she has paid Terry in restitution [Restatement 2d §373, Com. a, Ill. 2].

    b. **Restitution is Not Available if the Non-breaching Party Has Performed All of His or Her Duties Under the Contract, and No Performance by the Breaching Party Remains Owing Other Than the Payment of a Definite Sum of Money. [§32.22]** If a non-breaching party has fully performed, and the other party has simply not paid the non-breaching party, restitution is not available to the non-breacher [Restatement 2d §373(2)]. The rationale for this is two-fold: (1) in such cases, a court should not be put to the burden of determining a value for the benefits of the goods, land, or services the non-breaching party has provided the breacher because the parties themselves have already set such a value of how much the goods, land, or services were worth when they made their contract, i.e., the value of the unpaid sum of money; and (2) where a supplier's expectation damages can be so easily calculated with reference to the contract price, there is no need to resort to restitution.

(1) Example. [§32.221] Vince has agreed to paint a portrait of Darla for $7,000. Vince paints the portrait and finally delivers it to Darla, who keeps it but refuses to pay for it. Under the rule of Restatement 2d §373(2), Vince is not entitled to a restitutionary recovery even though he has clearly conferred a benefit on Darla, and even though Darla will be unjustly enriched if she fails to pay for it. That is because Vince (the non-breaching party), has performed all of his duties under the contract, and the only performance remaining is for Darla (the breacher), to pay of a fixed sum of money. As such, Vince must sue to recover the contract price as part of his expectation damages. This is exactly the kind of case where the court should not be burdened with trying to decide the value of the painting, i.e., the objective value of the benefit Vince has conferred on Darla, when the parties themselves established that value when they made the contract, and where the extent of Vince's expectation loss is so easily calculable from the contract price.

(2) Example. [§32.222] Marge has contracted to sell Steve a painting for $100,000. Steve makes the payment, but Marge never tenders the painting. Steve is entitled to recover $100,000 in restitution. In this case, while Steve has fully performed all of his duties under the contract, Restatement 2d §373(2) does not bar restitutionary recovery because Marge's remaining duty is to deliver a good, not to pay a fixed sum of money. Accordingly, Steve would be entitled to the value of the benefit he conferred on Marge, in this case $100,000.

2. **VALUING THE RESTITUTIONARY INTEREST WHEN THE NON-BREACHING PARTY SEEKS A RESTITUTIONARY RECOVERY FROM THE BREACHER.** [§32.23] As noted earlier, a court is directed to select, based on what justice requires, either the "cost avoided" or the "net benefit" method in determining the value of the benefits received by the breacher [Restatement 2d §371]; (see also §32.111). However, there is a presumption that the court should use the method yielding the most generous recovery when a non-breaching party seeks restitution from the party in breach [Restatement 2d §371, Com. b]. Examples of how the rule is applied are given below.

a. **Example of Losing Contract Situation. [§32.231]** James's construction company is hired to construct an office building on Developer's property for $1 million. James starts construction in a timely fashion and spent $600,000 in labor and materials when developer breaches by telling him to stop. Internal profit and loss documents show that James would have needed to spend another $500,000 to finish construction. The reasonable value of James's services was $600,000, for that is the amount most other contractors in the area are prepared to testify that they would have charged to perform the services James did before the breach. The market value of Developer's property increased by $350,000 as a result of the partially constructed building.

In a suit for breach, James would not want to sue for his expectation or reliance damages. This is because the facts show that James underbid the contract and would have lost money had the contract been performed, i.e., he had already spent $600,000 and would have needed another $500,000 to finish, and he was only entitled to $1 million from Developer under the contract. Recall that the amount of any provable loss from the contract had it been performed must be subtracted from any reliance or expectation damage recovery (see §§31.31, 31.5221), and thus James would end up losing money if he sought a money damages recovery for breach of contract.

Accordingly, James would want to recover in restitution for the breach. As the non-breaching party, he is entitled to the greater of the two methods of valuing the benefits received by Developer. Those benefits are valued at $600,000 under the cost avoided method, for this is the cost the developer has avoided by not paying James, as measured by what other contractors would have charged to provide those same benefits. The benefits provided the Developer are valued at $350,000 under the net benefit method, for that is the net increase in the value of Developer's property as the result of James's efforts. Hence, James would be entitled to recover $600,000 in restitution.

Note that a non-breaching party almost always seeks restitution in a losing contract case (see §31.31). Because restitution focuses on the value of the benefits received, and not on putting the party in the position he or she would have been in had the contract been performed, the amount of the contract loss that would be expected from complete performance is irrelevant.

b. **Example When the Value of the Benefits Provided Exceeds the Contract Price.** [§32.232] Stuart hires Mary to paint his house for $800. Mary has almost finished when Stuart fires her. As this was Mary's first commercial painting job, she priced her services well under market. Most other painters is the area would have charged at least $1,500 for doing the work Mary did before the breach, and her efforts in almost completely painting Stuart's house have increased its market value by $1,000.

Mary would seek a restitutionary recovery against Stuart for Stuart's breach. This is because, once again, restitution only focuses on the value of the benefits actually received, not on the value of a party's promised performance. Hence, the contract price does not provide a ceiling for restitutionary recovery, and so Mary is entitled to recover for the **value** of the enrichment her services provided to Stuart. As she is the non-breaching party seeking restitution, she is presumptively entitled to the greater of the amounts calculated under the cost avoided or net benefit methods (see §32.11). Under the cost avoided method, the amount of benefits received by Stuart is $1,500, for that is the cost Stuart avoided by not having to pay another painter to do the work Mary did. Under the net benefit method, the value of the services retained by Stuart was $1,000, for that is the net increase in the fair market value of Stuart's property caused by Mary's services. Hence, Mary will recover $1,500 in restitution for the breach of a contract for which she only would have been paid $800 had it been performed.

Note that if Stuart had waited until Mary had finished, and then simply not paid her, Mary would **not** have been entitled to sue in restitution for the value of her services under the rule of Restatement 2d §373(2) (see §32.22). In that case, she would have been limited by the contract price for her recovery.

c. **Example When the Value of the Benefits is Less than Contract Price.** [§32.233] Phil has a contract to build a custom-made wall unit for Jackie. He is to build it in place at Jackie's house. The contract price is $3,500. Phil timely began construction and is partially completed when Jackie breaches and orders him to stop. At that point Phil has spent $2,000 in labor and materials, and his partially constructed wall unit has increased the value of Jackie's home by $300. It turns out that Phil is an expensive carpenter for the area, as most other carpenters would charge only $1,750 to do the work Phil did prior to the breach.

Phil's restitutionary recovery would be limited to $1,750. This is, once again, because recovery in restitution focuses only on the value of the benefits received by the other party, and not on the cost to provide those benefits. Hence, the question is what is the fair market **value** of the benefits conferred by Phil. Under the cost avoided method, the value is $1,750, for that is the cost Jackie avoided by not having to pay a reasonable carpenter in the area to do the work. Under the net benefit method, the value of Phil's services were $300, for that is the total appreciation of Jackie's home due to Phil's efforts. As the non-breaching party, Phil is presumptively entitled to the greater of these two figures (§32.111). Hence, even though Phil claims to have spent $2,000 in labor and materials on the job, he will only be able to collect $1,750 in restitution. Obviously, under these facts Phil would prefer suing at least for his reliance (§31.5), if not for his expectation damages (§31.3), assuming it was not a losing contract.

D. **RESTITUTIONARY RECOVERY IN FAVOR OF THE PARTY IN BREACH. [§32.3]** As noted earlier, one of the unique features of restitution is that a party can be entitled to a restitutionary recovery even though he or she is the one who breached the contract [Restatement 2d §374]. This can be explained once again by the fact that restitution focuses on the value of benefits conferred on a party and when it would be unjust for the benefited party to retain the benefits without paying for them. Since often a breaching party will have rendered benefits to the non-breacher before the contract was breached, it only makes sense that when it would be unjust for the non-breacher to retain those benefits without paying for them, an action in restitution should be allowed in favor of the breaching party.

1. **REQUIREMENTS FOR BREACHING PARTIES TO SEEK RECOVERY IN RESTITUTION. [§32.31]** Unlike the special rules that govern whether a non-breacher can sue in restitution (see §32.2), there are no special requirements for a breaching party to institute such a suit. Hence, so long as the breaching party offers to restore any benefits he or she has received under the contract as part of the final restitution (see §32.12), such a claim can be brought.

2. **CALCULATING THE VALUE OF THE RESTITUTIONARY AWARD IN CASES BROUGHT BY THE BREACHING PARTY. [§32.32]** As noted in §32.11, to calculate the proper amount of the breacher's restitutionary award, the value of the benefits received by the non-breaching party from the breacher must be calculated on both a "cost avoided" and a "net benefit" basis (see §32.11). Once again, a court is entitled to use whichever calculation method justice dictates should be used in the particular case to calculate the award, but there is a presumption that the method yielding the **least generous** valuation measure be used for the breaching party.

Selecting the proper valuation method does not end the award calculation. Because it is the breaching party who is seeking recovery, **any damages suffered by the non-breacher must then be subtracted from the value of the benefits received by the non-breacher to arrive at the proper amount for the breaching party's restitutionary award.** That is, calculation of the breacher's recovery in these cases is a two-step process. First, the value of the service received by the non-breaching party must be calculated, and the least generous measure is presumptively selected. From that value, the amount of any losses the non-breaching party suffered due to the breach must be subtracted to arrive at the proper net restitutionary award.

a. **EXAMPLE. [§32.21]** Dave is in the business of making repairs to office buildings damaged by fire. He contracts to repair a commercial building that was severely damaged for a price of $60,000, which is to be paid on completion of the work. Dave works on the building for a few weeks, reasonably incurring $20,000 in labor and materials costs. At trial, it can be established that other builders in the area would have charged a similar amount to perform the services provided by Dave up to the point of the breach. However, Dave breaches and leaves the work site to take another, more lucrative job. The owner of the building hired someone to replace Dave, who finished the repairs for $45,000. In addition, since it took a week longer to finish the clean-up due to the delay in finding Dave's replacement, the building owner lost $2,000 in rent. Cleaning up the building from the fire damage increased its fair market value by $55,000.

The building owner would likely not bring suit against Dave, for she only had to spend $45,000 (plus $2,000 in lost rent) to get the benefits of a job for which she had contracted to pay Dave $60,000. However, **Dave** will bring suit, for he has received nothing for the benefits provided the owner. Because Dave is the breaching party, he can only sue in restitution.

The next issue is to determine the value of the benefits he provided the building owner. Under the cost avoided method of valuing the benefits received, Dave provided $20,000 in benefits, for that is the reasonable value of the services for which the owner did not have to pay, as measured by the cost others would have charged to provide those same services. Under the net benefit method, the value received by the landowner from Dave's efforts was only $10,000. That is, due to the clean-up she received a $55,000 increase in the fair market value of her property, but that $55,000 increase in value was as a result of the work of both Dave and his replacement. We know that the services of Dave's replacement were worth $45,000 (for that is how much the replacement was paid), and so the "**net** benefit" to the landowner of **Dave's** work in repairing the building would be $55,000 minus $45,000 or **$10,000**.

Because Dave is the breaching party, he is presumptively limited to using the valuation method yielding the least generous amount of recovery, or $10,000. In addition, the $2,000 lost rent suffered by the landowner must also be subtracted from Dave's recovery, so the net restitutionary relief due to Dave under these facts is **$8,000**. Note that Dave will likely consider this award unfair since he is "out-of-pocket" $20,000 in labor and materials. However, as the breaching party, contract law believes he should not be heard to complain about receiving the least generous measure of recovery. In other words, he could have ensured that the deal went forward. When he chose to breach, one of the consequences he had to suffer was the least generous method of restitutionary recovery for his work thus far.

E. **RECOVERY IN RESTITUTION FOR QUASI-CONTRACT. [§32.4]** A party seeking to recover in "quasi-contract" must use restitution (see §1.35). That is, a quasi-contract, or implied-in-law contract, describes a situation in which there is no contract at all, i.e., there is no offer, acceptance, or consideration. Rather, the aggrieved party in such cases is seeking to recover for the benefit of some services provided another in a situation where it would be unjust for the benefited party to have been enriched by such services without paying for them. In these cases, while it is theoretically possible to calculate the value of the service using either the cost avoided or net benefit method (see §32.11), contract law has universally held that the aggrieved party is limited to a cost avoided recovery [Restatement 2d §371, Com. b].

1. **EXAMPLE. [§32.41]** Roberta is a surgeon who comes across Lou, a car accident victim, lying injured and unconscious on the road. She realizes that Lou immediately needs life-saving surgery, has Lou rushed to the hospital in an ambulance, and performs surgery on him which saves his life. Lou remained unconscious until the next day.

If Lou refuses to compensate Roberta, she is entitled to sue him in restitution. Under the "cost avoided" method of value calculation, the value of the benefit Roberta provided Lou would be equal to the reasonable value for such surgery as measured by what other surgeons in the area would charge for that procedure (this value may be more or less than the fee Roberta usually charges. That is, Roberta does not automatically receive her customery fee in restitution; rather she is only entitled to the reasonable value of her service as measured by what other surgeons charge for that service.). Under the net benefit method, the value of the benefit Roberta provided Lou would be equal to the net economic benefits Lou would earn over the remainder of his life. That is, without Roberta's services, Lou would not have earned any more money. Hence, his interests were advanced in an amount equal to any salary or other income he would earn for the rest of his life. For obvious reasons, recovery in quasi-contract is thus limited to the value of the benefits received as calculated under the cost avoided method.

F. **RESTITUTIONARY RECOVERY IN OTHER CONTRACTS — RELATED SITUATIONS. [§32.5]** Generally, restitutionary recovery is available to a party who, for one reason or another, either could not enforce the other party's contractual promises, or who decided to exercise his or her right to avoid the agreement. In these situations the idea is that one party provided another a benefit under a contract that later could not be enforced, or was avoided, due to:

(1) the statute of frauds (see §9.93); (2) incapacity by minority for cash sales and necessities (see §10.13); (3) incapacity due to mental defect (see §10.2); (4) mutual mistake (see §11.341); (5) unilateral mistake (see §11.441) (6) duress (see §12.3); (7) undue influence (see §13.2); (8) misrepresentation (see §14.6); (9) illegality under certain circumstance (see §16.25 and §16.26); (10) the failure of the occurrence of a condition (see §20.124); and (11) impossibility, impracticability, and frustration of purpose (see §25.6); [see gen, Restatement 2d §§375-377].

The application of restitution to these cases follows standard analysis. That is, if one party provides benefits that are received by the other, and if it would be unjust to allow the benefited party to retain those benefits without paying for them, a restitutionary recovery is warranted. In such cases, the benefits reserved by the other party must be valued under both the cost avoided and net benefit methods (see §32.11), and a court is directed to allow "justice" to determine which method is the appropriate one to be used in calculating the aggrieved's restitutionary award under the circumstances [Restatement 2d §371]. There is no presumption favoring one method over another in these kinds of cases. Of course, as with all restitutionary recoveries, restitution must be mutual, and the party seeking restitution must offer to return, or at least account for, any benefits he or she has received as part of the final restitutionary judgment [Restatement 2d §384]; (see §32.12).

CHAPTER THIRTY-THREE: REMEDIES FOR BREACH UNDER THE UCC

A. **UCC REMEDIES GENERALLY. [§33.0]** The remedies for breach of contract governed by Article 2 of the UCC do not differ in kind from the types of equitable relief, money damages, and restitution remedies discussed in the last three chapters. However, the Code organizes these remedies somewhat differently and applies them uniquely. [See, however, §33.38 for a discussion comparing the basic UCC damage formulations with the common law damage formulations.]

NOTE TO STUDENTS: For most Contracts courses, an understanding of the material in Chapters Thirty and Thirty One will be almost all your Professor will expect you to have with regard to equitable and money damage remedies (see, e.g., §31.8 for a basic discussion of UCC money damage remedies). Hence, reference to this Chapter will largely be unnecessary, except, perhaps, to learn the exact formulas and terminology for damage calculations under Article 2 (see §§33.21-33.53). However, for those classes where Article 2 plays an extremely important part of the curricula, this Chapter sets forth the rules of Article 2 regarding remedies for breach in some detail.

B. **EQUITABLE REMEDIES AVAILABLE TO BUYERS. [§33.1]** There are two equitable remedies specifically available to the non-breaching buyer under UCC §2-716: (1) specific performance; and (2) replevin.

1. **SPECIFIC PERFORMANCE. [§33.11]** Specific performance is an order by a court that requires a party to actually perform a promise he or she made in a contract. As in non-UCC contexts, the court enforces a specific performance order through the use of its contempt powers (see §30.1). At early common law, specific performance was available to a buyer only when the goods involved in the contract were highly unique, one-of-a-kind items. However, the Code "seeks to further a more liberal attitude than some courts have shown in connection with the specific performance of contracts for sale." [UCC §2-716, Com. 1.] The Code has tried to further this "more liberal" attitude by stating that a court may order specific performance "where the goods are unique **or in other proper circumstances**." [UCC §2-716(1).]

   While the Code provides no definition for "other proper circumstances," case law has established that a court should order specific performance under §2-716(1) whenever it would be "unreasonably burdensome" to require the buyer to locate and acquire comparable goods upon a breach.

   a. **Example. [§33.111]** Ira contracted to buy a particular Ming vase from Jane. Jane refused to deliver possession of the vase, even though Ira timely tendered the amount of the agreed payment. Under both common law and UCC rules, a particular Ming vase is unique enough that Ira would be entitled to an order of specific performance.

   b. **Example. [§33.112]** Dennis is under a contractual duty to deliver a bottle of 1811 Chateau Lafite Rothschild to Lydia. At the last minute, however, Dennis decides to keep the bottle himself and does not deliver it as promised. There are probably 350 or so bottles of the wine in the world, almost all in the hands of a few restaurants and an unknown number of private collectors.

It is questionable whether such a bottle would be considered unique enough under early common law equity rules to justify specific performance. However, under §2-716(1), specific performance would be ordered so long as Lydia can establish that it would be unreasonably difficult or burdensome for her to procure a substitute bottle from another. She can establish this fact either by testifying as to her unsuccessful efforts to obtain another bottle, or by proving that such efforts would likely be unavailing.

c. **REVIEW PROBLEM. [§33.113] Art has contractually agreed to purchase a case of 1988 Chateau Lafite Rothschild from a big wine store in town. The wine store owner refuses to deliver the wine. Art cannot obtain the wine from any other store in town, for the other stores have completely sold their supply. However, the wine is available from a store across the state line, about 20 miles away. Question: Can Art get specific performance?**

> Answer: Even under the more liberal rules of UCC §2-716(1), Art would not be entitled to an order of specific performance on these facts, because procuring a substitute would not be **unreasonably** difficult or burdensome under the circumstances.

2. **REPLEVIN. [§33.12]** Replevin is typically a pre-judgment remedy whereby a non-breaching buyer can have the sheriff (or marshal) take possession of the goods which are the subject matter of a breached contract and hold them during the pendency of a breach of contract lawsuit. That is, after a buyer files an action for breach, he or she can file a motion requesting an order from the court directing the sheriff to seize certain property which is the subject of the contract. If the court grants the motion, the sheriff is empowered to go to wherever the goods are kept, take possession of them, and hold onto them throughout the pendency of the lawsuit. (Indeed, some states even permit the sheriff to deliver the goods to the buyer, to be kept by him or her until the lawsuit is over.) The reason for seeking an order of replevin is that once the goods are in the hands of the sheriff, the buyer knows that the goods are safe and cannot be sold or harmed by the seller until the lawsuit is over.

Under UCC §2-716(3), a buyer is entitled to replevin in cases where the goods which are the subject of the contract are reasonably difficult to obtain from another source. In other words, a buyer is entitled to a pre-judgment order of replevin in cases where he or she would be entitled to a **final** judgment of specific performance. Note that in some jurisdictions what might be more properly called a final judgement of specific performance is known as a final judgment of replevin, i.e. an order to the sheriff to turn the good over to the buyer.

Replevin sounds like a good idea for the non-breaching buyer when he or she is worried about the seller's intentions and wants assurances that the good will be available for delivery should the court order specific performance. However, most states in their replevin (or "claim and delivery" as it is sometimes called) statutes provide that the seller can take possession of the goods from the sheriff upon posting a bond. That is, once the sheriff takes possession, the seller is entitled as a matter of right to post a bond in an amount set by the court, and upon the posting of the bond, the sheriff must re-deliver the goods to the seller. The bond gives the buyer an assurance that there will be money available to pay a judgment if the buyer should prevail in the lawsuit, but of course the whole idea behind replevin is that the buyer does not want money; the buyer wants the specific goods that are the subject of the contract. Hence, because a buyer cannot guarantee that the seller will be deprived of possession of the goods throughout the pendency of the breach action even if his or her motion for a replevin order is granted, most buyers choose not to go to the bother and expense of filing such a motion.

C. BUYER'S RIGHT TO SUE FOR DAMAGES IN CASES WHERE HE OR SHE DOES NOT HAVE THE GOODS. [§33.2] This section covers the Code's treatment of those situations in which a non-breaching buyer sues the breaching seller for damages where the buyer does not have the goods. There are three reasons why a non-breaching buyer may not have the goods when a suit for breach is filed:

(1) The seller breached by never tendering the goods to the buyer;

(2) The buyer rightfully and effectively rejected non-conforming goods provided by the seller, and the seller breached by not adequately cureing (see §22.2 et seq.); and

(3) The buyer rightfully and effectively revoked his or her acceptance of non-conforming goods provided by the seller, and the seller breached by not adequately curing (see §22.3 et seq.).

In these cases, the UCC provides the buyer with two related, but distinct, remedies:

(1) The buyer can go into the market, purchase replacement goods ("cover"), and sue for the difference between the cover price and the contract price, along with other related damages [UCC §2-712]; or

(2) The buyer can choose not to purchase replacement goods, and instead simply sue for the difference between the market price (i.e., the price pending if the buyer had covered) and the contract price, along with other related damages [UCC §2-713].

Each of these remedies is discussed below.

1. UCC §2-712: COVER DAMAGES. [§33.21] A buyer who ends up without goods due to a seller's breach (see §32.2) is entitled to go in the market and "cover" by purchasing substitute goods. If the cost of cover is more than the contract price, the buyer is entitled to sue the breaching seller for that price differential.

It is crucial to note that under §2-712(1) a party is allowed to effect "reasonable cover" by acting "in good faith and without unreasonable delay." This means that if the replacement goods are a little different, and perhaps a little more expensive, than the goods that are the subject of the breached contract, the buyer can recover for the increased price it takes to cover for the breach as long as the buyer acts in "good faith." Similarly, if the buyer waits a few days before purchasing substitute goods, and during that period the price of replacement goods goes up, the buyer is entitled to seek damages based on the increased price so long as there was no "unreasonable delay" in securing replacement goods. That is, the seller cannot claim the increased price should be ignored due to mitigation (see §31.43)

For example, suppose a large department store placed an order for 5,000 2-speed blenders from a manufacturer, to be delivered on October 15, just before the start of the store's Christmas season. The manufacturer unjustifiably fails to deliver the blenders, and the store tries to find replacements. However, it proves difficult to find 5,000 2-speed blenders which can be delivered in time for the Christmas rush. Another manufacturer can immediately deliver 5,000 5-speed blenders, but the 5-speed blenders cost $3/per blender more than the buyer was obligated to pay for the 2-speed models. Because cover need only be reasonable to be recoverable, so long as the store acted in good faith in purchasing the 5-speed models, i.e., it did not do so just to increase damages to the breaching seller, it is entitled to recover the differential between the cover price and the contract price if it actually goes into the market and purchases the 5-speed models.

Similarly, assume instead that the store began looking for replacement blenders 5 days after they learned of the breach, and on that day the store's buyer located some 2-speed blenders that were comparable to those scheduled to be delivered under the breached contract. However, between October 15 (the promised delivery date) and October 20 (the date the store began looking), the price for the replacement blenders increased $2/blender. So long as the store did not engage in "unreasonable delay" before buying the blenders, it will be entitled to collect from the manufacturer the difference between the new cover price and the contract price.

Accordingly, the idea of cover in UCC §2-712(1) allows the non-breaching buyer some flexibility in proceeding after a breach. Rather then having his or her damages fixed on the day of the breach as the difference between market price for identical goods pending that day and the contract price, the buyer is entitled to spend some time looking for reasonably comparable goods. So long as the buyer acts reasonably and in good faith in purchasing replacement goods, he or she is entitled to recover the full amount of his or her cover damages.

a. **The Formula for Recovery of Cover Damages.** [§33.211] The formula provided in UCC §2-712 for the recovery of cover damages is:

Buyer's Cover Damages = [(Cost of Cover) - (Contract Price)] + Incidental Damages + Consequential Damages - Costs Avoided as a Consequence of the Breach.

Note that the relationship between this formula and the more general formula for recovering expectation damages is discussed in §31.381

Also note that in addition to cover damages under §2-712, **a buyer in these types of cases is also entitled to recover any money he or she has already paid to the breaching seller as part of a down payment, deposit, etc., under UCC §2-711(1).**

(1) **Example.** [§33.2111] CDarama placed an order with Billy's Electronics for 100 single play CD players at $200/player. Billy's does not deliver as promised on November 1, in time for CDarama's Christmas rush. As a result, CDarama's president spends nearly ten hours on the phone over the next couple of days trying to find replacement units. She finally locates 100 5-play CD players immediately available for $207/player, and has them express shipped to her store. The express shipping cost $400 more than regular freight shipment. One of the reasons she had the new players express shipped is that she was out of stock of CD players and had already lost two sales because she could not provide immediate delivery. At trial, she can prove she could have sold the players for $350/player to the two buyers. Additionally, she can prove that when she does consulting work for clients about their stereo systems, she charges $30/hour.

Under the formula set forth in UCC §2-712, CDarama's recovery is determined as follows:

Cover Price — 100 units x $207/unit = $20,700. (Note that the $207/unit price is recoverable even though it is for a 5-play unit. This is because, on these facts, CDarama's decision to purchase 5-play units was neither in bad faith nor made with unreasonable delay.)

Contract Price — 100 units x $200/unit = $20,000.

Incidental Damages — A buyer's incidental damages under the Code are governed by §2-715(1) and are defined the same way as in non-UCC contracts (see §31.27 and §33.312 for a discussion of incidental damages). Accordingly, CDarama can recover for two types of incidental loss:

(1) the time spent by the CDarama President in finding replacement units. Since $30/hour seems a reasonable figure to use for the value of her time, CDarama is entitled to collect $300 for the ten hours she spent tracking down replacement units; and

(2) The $400 extra in express shipping charges. Given the season, it was reasonable to foresee the need for someone like CDarama to get the units quickly. Hence, because the shipping charges represent reasonable expenses incurred after the breach in an attempt to cover, they are recoverable.

Consequential Loss — CDarama lost two sales due to Bill's breach in not getting the units to the store as promised. The profits on those units were ($350 - $200) or $150 each. This loss was plainly foreseeable, for if a seller does not provide a **retail** store with merchandise, it is certainly sufficiently foreseeable that the store can lose sales. Hence, CDarama also has $300 in recoverable consequential damages. (See §33.313 for a definition and discussion of consequential damages under Article 2).

Costs Avoided — There are no costs avoided as defined by UCC §2-712 to be accounted for in this fact pattern.

Accordingly, CDarama's recovery under §2-712 would be: $20,700 - $20,000 + $700 + $300 - $0 or **$1,700.**

2. **UCC §2-713: MARKET DIFFERENTIAL DAMAGES. [§33.22]** To be entitled to cover damages under UCC §2-712, a non-breaching buyer must go into the market and actually purchase replacement goods. Finding such goods and coming up with the money to purchase them may be such a hassle for the buyer that he or she does not wish to do it. UCC §2-713 holds that the buyer may avoid that hassle and still recover the full extent of his or her expectation loss. That is, §2-713(1) allows the buyer to sue for the difference between the fair market price of replacement goods and the contract price, together with associated other damages. (See §31.381 for a discussion of how this formula is really just a specialized formulation of the more general formula for recovery of expectation damages

a. **The Formula for Recovery of Market Differential Damages. [§33.221]** The formula for recovering market differential damages provided in §2-713 is:

Buyer's Market Differential Damages = [(Market Price of the Goods) - (Contract Price for the Goods)] + Incidental Damages + Consequential Damages - Costs Avoided Due to the Breach.

Note that in addition to market differential damages under §2-713, **a buyer in these types of cases is also entitled to recover any money he or she has previously paid the breaching seller as a down payment, deposit, etc., under UCC §2-711(1).**

(1) **Determining the "Market Price." [§33.2211]** The formula for market differential damages under §2-713 requires that the contract price for the goods be subtracted from the "market price" for the goods. An issue in applying the formula is that the

market price for the goods may be volatile, and change day to day. Similarly, if the buyer and seller are in different cities, it may well be that on the same day the market price for the goods in those different cities is different. Hence, a decision must be made as to which of the potentially different market prices should be selected as the proper "market price" for purposes of §2-713 damages.

Section 2-713(1) states that the temporal market price that should be used in the formula is the market price pending "at the time the buyer learned of the breach" (not the price on the day delivery was due). Section 2-713(2) provides that the proper geographical market price to be used depends on the nature of the seller's breach. *If the seller breaches by never tendering goods*, the **"market price"** for purposes of §2-713 is the one pending *at the place for tender. If the seller breaches by sending non-conforming goods*, and the buyer rightfully either rejects or revokes his or her acceptance of them, then the **"market price"** that should be used is the *one pending at the place where the goods arrived.*

(2) **Example. [§33.2212]** Roberta, a retail buyer in California, ordered 100 dozen Grade AA eggs from a seller in New York. The contract price was $10/dozen. Under their contract, tender of the eggs was to take place in New York on May 15. Hence, Roberta planned to hire a carrier to pick up the eggs on that day in New York and transport them to California. If the contract had gone forward, the eggs were scheduled to be delivered to Roberta on May 18. On May 15, however, the seller calls Roberta and tells her that he will not deliver. The fair market value for such eggs on May 15 was $10.50/dozen in New York, and $11/dozen in California. On May 18, the expected date of delivery in California, the market value for the eggs was back to $10/dozen in New York, and it was $10.75/dozen in California.

If Roberta chooses **not** to cover, she is entitled to recover market differential damages under §2-713. To do so she must select the appropriate market value for use in calculating her damages. Under §2-713(1), she must use the price pending "at the time she learned of the breach" as the temporal market value. Hence, she will have to use either the $10.50/dozen New York price, or the $11/dozen California price, which were the prices pending on May 15 (the date she learned the seller would not deliver the eggs) and not the prices pending on May 18, the delivery date under the contract. The nature of the seller's breach was that he never tendered the goods. Hence under §2-713(2), the geographical market to be used is the place where the goods were to be tendered. Since eggs were due to be tendered in New York, Roberta must use the $10.50/dozen price pending in New York on May 15 in determining her market differential damages.

Under the formula set forth in UCC §2-713, Roberta's recovery is determined as follows:

Market Price - $10.50/dozen x 1,000 dozen = $10,500.

Contract Price - $10/dozen x 1,000 dozen = $10,000.

Incidental Damages - There are no incidental damages on these facts.

Consequential Damages - There are no consequential damages on these facts.

Costs Avoided - There are no costs avoided on these facts.

Accordingly, Roberta's recovery under §2-713 would be: $10,500 - $10,000 + $0 + $0 - $0 or **$500**.

D. BUYER'S RIGHT TO DAMAGES UPON BREACH OF GOODS HE OR SHE KEEPS: WARRANTY DAMAGES. [§33.3]

A buyer is entitled to accept non-conforming goods and still bring an action against the seller based on the extent to which he or she is economically injured by the non-conformity. Similarly, a buyer may at some point discover that he or she has the right to revoke his or her acceptance of the goods, and decide not to exercise it. Nevertheless, the buyer is still entitled to sue the seller for the difference in value between the good he or she was promised and the good he or she received. These types of cases, i.e., where the buyer decides to keep non-conforming goods and sue the seller for the diminished value of the goods due to their non-conformity, are breach of warranty claims, the damages for which are governed by UCC §2-714 (see Chapter Thirty-Six for the substantive law of warranty).

Once a party accepts a good, he or she is liable for its full contract price [UCC §2-607(1)]. Hence, in breach of warranty cases, the buyer is liable to the seller for the full contract price, but is also entitled to sue the seller for the difference between the value of the conforming good he or she was promised and the non-conforming good he or she decided to keep.

1. THE FORMULA FOR BREACH OF WARRANTY RECOVERY UNDER UCC §2-714. [§33.31]

The general formula for a buyer's recovery breach of warranty actions set forth in §§2-714(2) and (3):

Buyer's Warranty Damages = [(Value of Goods as Warranted) - (Value of Goods Received)] + Incidental Damages + Consequential Damages.

a. The Difference Between the Value of the Goods as Promised and the Value of Goods Received. [§33.311]

There are two points that need to be discussed about the value differential portion of the formula regulating the amount of a buyer's recovery for breach of warranty.

First, the focus of the recovery is on the fair market **value** of the goods as promised and as received, and **not on the contract price**. As a result, it is entirely possible that a buyer's recovery in warranty can be **greater** than the contract price he or she is obligated to pay the seller upon the decision to accept the good.

> For example, suppose Kathy is told by a sales representative in a computer store that the processor of a computer she is thinking of purchasing is fast enough to spell check a 50-page document in 90 seconds. Accordingly, she buys the computer for $3,500. When she gets it home, she discovers it takes 9 minutes to spell check a 50-page document.
>
> Subsequent investigation establishes that a computer with a processor capable of spell checking a 50-page document in 90 seconds would cost at least $15,000. Similarly, most computer companies would charge no more than $3,000 for a computer with the features Kathy's computer has.
>
> Assuming she decides to keep the computer, the value differential to which Kathy is entitled under §2-714(2) is $15,000 - $3,000 or $12,000, i.e., the **value** of the computer she was promised minus the **value** of the computer she actually received. Accordingly, while Kathy is still obligated to pay the purchase price of $3,500

because she has accepted, rather than rejected (or revoked her acceptance of) the computer, §2-607(1), she is entitled to at least a $12,000 warranty recovery from the store plus any incidental or consequential damages she can establish.

The second point that needs to be mentioned about the value differential portion of the §2-714 formula for recovery of breach of warranty damages is that it is often measured by the cost to repair the non-conforming good. That is, a reasonable way to estimate the difference between the value of the good as warranted and the value of the good as received is to ascertain how much it would cost to repair the good received to make it into the good promised.

b. **Incidental Damages under the Code. [§33.312]** Incidental damages under the Code are governed by UCC §2-715(1). Code-based incidental damages are no different than incidental damages recoverable under common law contracts damage principles (see §31.27). That is, they are reasonable costs incurred by the buyer, **after** the seller's breach, in an attempt to mitigate the seller's damages. Typically, they include things like expenses incurred in the inspection, receipt, transportation, and storage of rightfully rejected goods, and damages associated with the time and expenses spent in effecting cover.

c. **Consequential Damages under the UCC. [§33.313]** The recovery of consequential damages in Article 2 contracts is governed by UCC §2-715(2). In general, the principles for recovery of consequential loss in Code-based transactions is no different than those used for the recovery of such damages in contracts governed by common law principles (see §31.42). However, §2-715 presents two issues that merit discussion.

First, §2-715 divides consequential loss into two types: (i) consequential **economic** loss, as described in UCC §2-715(2)(a); and (ii) consequential **personal injury and personal property** loss, as described in UCC §2-715(2)(b). The chief difference between these two types of consequential loss is in the level of foreseeability the buyer must prove before he or she is entitled to their recovery. That is, recall that what distinguishes consequential loss from direct damage is that to recover for consequential loss, the injured party must make a special showing that such loss was foreseeable to the breaching party at the time the contract was made (see §31.42). In dividing consequential loss into two types in §2-715(2), the Code has formulated different foreseeability requirements that must be established by the buyer to recover for each type of consequential damage.

The foreseeability rules governing the recovery of consequential economic loss under the Code are identical to the foreseeability rules for the recovery of consequential damages under common law contract principles based on *Hadley v. Baxendale*. (§31.4) That is, before a buyer can recover for any type of loss that was not reasonably foreseeable at the time the contract was entered into, the buyer is required to show that "the seller at the time of contracting had reason to know" that such loss would follow from the breach. [UCC §2-715(2)(a).]

To recover for consequential personal injury or personal property loss under the Code, however, the buyer need only show that such losses "proximately resulted" from any breach of warranty. In sum, the foreseeability test for recovery of consequential personal injury or personal property damage loss is not the fairly stringent foreseeability test of contract (i.e., did the seller have reason to know at the time of contracting that he or she would be liable for that type of loss upon a breach), but rather is the far more lenient foreseeability test of tort (i.e., was the breach a proximate cause of the damage). Hence, if the good kept by the buyer caused personal injuries, or personal property damage, a seller will likely not be able to avoid paying for those damages on the basis that they were consequential and the seller had "no reason to know of the possible harm to the particular injured party.

The second issue regarding consequential loss under the Code that needs to be discussed is whether damage to the good itself should be classified as economic loss, and thus subject to the more stringent foreseeability test of §2-715(2)(a), or should be regarded as personal property loss, and thus recoverable under the more lenient proximate cause standard of §2-715(2)(b). That is, suppose an airline purchases new jet engines for one of the airplanes in its fleet. The first time the engine is engaged after delivery it implodes, due to faulty construction. The accident caused much harm to the engine, but not to anything else. The question is thus whether harm to the good itself, i.e., harm solely to the non-conforming engine, is economic consequential loss, or is personal property damage. The universal answer is that **injury to the good itself is considered economic loss** for purposes of UCC §2-715(2). Hence, such loss would be governed by the contract-based foreseeability principles of §2-715(2)(a).

d. **Offset of Damages under §2-717. [§33.314]** Consider the following case. Colleen examines two televisions in a department store, a 25-inch model for $400, and a 21-inch model for $350. She decides on the 25-inch one, arranges for 30 days deferred billing, and for delivery the following week. When the television arrives, however, the store mistakenly delivered the 21-inch model. Obviously Colleen could reject it, but she decides to keep it and pocket the extra $50. When her bill comes, she is charged $400, i.e., she was charged the price for the set she ordered, not the one she received.

Under the rules of §2-607(1) and §2-714, Colleen would be obligated to pay the store the full $400 contract price, but then would be entitled to sue the store in small claims court for the difference between the value of the good she was promised ($400), and the value of the good she received ($350). Obviously such a two step process is inefficient. Accordingly, under UCC §2-717, a buyer is entitled to deduct from the purchase price all or any part of the damages due the buyer resulting from the seller's breach, as long as the buyer gives adequate notice of his or her intentions. Accordingly, Colleen is entitled to pay the store only $350 in response to its $400 bill, so long as she explains why she is doing so.

E. **SELLER'S RIGHT TO SUE FOR THE FULL CONTRACT PRICE UPON BUYER'S BREACH: SELLERS "SPECIFIC PERFORMANCE". [§33.4]** When a seller is entitled to sue the buyer for the full contract price, the action is the equivalent of specific performance (see §33.1). That is, the seller is seeking an order requiring the buyer actually to perform in full what the buyer promised to do under the contract. Accordingly, just as it is the unusual case where the buyer is entitled to get specific performance from the seller (see §33.1), it is also the unusual case where the seller is entitled to receive the full contract price from the buyer in a breach action. It is much more likely that the seller will only get damages for breach, i.e. a lower recovery than the full contract price.

The Code provides that a buyer is entitled to bring an action for the price in only four cases:

(1) when the buyer has **accepted** the goods [UCC §2-709(1)(a)] (see §33.41);

(2) when a seller sends conforming goods to the buyer **after the risk of loss has passed to the buyer,** and when the goods are thereafter lost or destroyed before acceptance [UCC §2-709(1)(a)]; (see §35.0 for a discussion of risk of loss; §33.42 for a discussion of the effect of risk of loss on the seller's action for the full price);

(3) **when the seller reasonably tries to re-sell the goods** to another after the buyer's breach, **but is unable to re-sell them for a reasonable price** [UCC §2-709(1)(b)] (see §33.43); and

(4) **when the seller does not attempt to re-sell the goods** to another after the buyer's breach **because such efforts will be unavailing** [UCC §2-709(1)(b)] (see §33.44).

Note that a successful action for price is really a forced sale of the goods. That is, in such cases the seller has performed and tendered conforming goods to the buyer. For whatever reason, the buyer refuses to pay for them and does not want to go through with the sale any longer. However, if the seller is successful in the suit and can collect the full purchase price from the buyer, he or she will have attained all the benefits due the seller under the contract. Hence, upon payment of the final judgment, the buyer is entitled to possession of the goods because in paying the seller the full contract price, he or she has "purchased" them. Accordingly, upon the full satisfaction of a judgment for the price, the seller must turn the goods over to the buyer, i.e., it truly is a "forced sale."

Each of the situations in which a seller is entitled to sue for the price is discussed below.

1. **WHEN THE BUYER HAS ACCEPTED THE GOODS. [§33.41]** One of the consequences of acceptance under the Code is that a buyer must pay the contract price for goods when he or she accepts them [UCC §2-607(1)]; (see also §22.31). Hence, when a party accepts goods and does not pay for them, the seller is entitled to bring an action for the full contract price [UCC §2-709(1)(a)].

Note that the seller has the right to sue for the contract price regardless of whether the buyer keeps the goods he or she has accepted, or whether the buyer ships them back to the seller. So long as there has been an acceptance, the buyer is liable for the full contract price. If the buyer does ship the goods back to the seller, however, that act has two consequences:

(1) in addition to the purchase price, the buyer will also be liable for storage and other incidental expenses incurred by the seller as long as he or she cares for the goods [UCC §§2-703; 2-710]; and

(2) the buyer has implicitly given the seller permission to sell the goods for a reasonable price. Hence, at any time prior to the satisfaction of a final judgment in such a case, the seller is entitled to sell the goods to another for a reasonable price. Upon such a sale, any proceeds must be credited to the breaching buyer, meaning that the damages for which the buyer is liable must be reduced by the amount of the re-sale.

2. **WHEN THE GOODS ARE LOST OR DESTROYED AFTER THE RISK OF LOSS HAS PASSED TO THE BUYER. [§33.42]** Risk of loss is covered in some detail in Chapter Thirty-Five, but the idea is that when goods are shipped, at some point they become the buyer's responsibility. That is, if they are lost or destroyed during transit, the buyer must nevertheless pay for goods he or she has not received because he or she bears their "risk of loss." UCC §2-709(1)(a) codifies this concept and provides that if a buyer refuses to pay for goods that are lost or destroyed after the buyer has assumed the risk of loss, the seller is entitled to sue the buyer for the full contract price.

3. **WHEN THE BUYER ATTEMPTS TO RE-SELL GOODS WRONGFULLY REJECTED BY THE BUYER, BUT CANNOT OBTAIN A REASONABLE PRICE UPON RE-SALE. [§33.43]** Suppose a seller tenders absolutely conforming goods to the buyer, but the buyer nevertheless breaches by rejecting the goods and returns them to the seller. At that point the buyer is not obligated to pay the purchase price for the goods, for there has been no acceptance of them [UCC §2-607(1)]; (see also §33.41). Further, normal principles of avoidability dictate that the seller try to re-sell the goods to another, thereby reducing the buyer's damages (see §31.43).

Sometimes, however, a seller will make reasonable efforts to re-sell merchandise, but will not be able to find anyone willing to pay a reasonable price for the goods. This often happens when the good involved is custom-made, e.g., an especially long couch made to fit in a particular area in a particular buyer's home, such that there is no real market for the goods other than the breaching buyer. In such cases, when a seller is unable to re-sell wrongfully rejected goods for a reasonable price after reasonable efforts, the seller is entitled to sue the buyer for the full contract price [UCC §2-709(1)(b)].

4. **WHEN THE SELLER CAN ESTABLISH THAT RE-SALE OF THE WRONGFULLY REJECTED GOODS WOULD BE UNAVAILING. [§33.44]** Every once in awhile, a good ordered specifically for a particular buyer is so unusual that a reasonable person would conclude that any attempt to re-sell it to another would be unavailing. If the seller can establish that the buyer wrongfully rejected such a good, and can carry the burden of proof to establish that any efforts to re-sell the goods would be unavailing, the seller is entitled to bring an action for the full purchase price [UCC §2-709(1)(b)].

F. **SELLER'S RIGHT TO SUE FOR DAMAGES OTHER THAN THE FULL CONTRACT PRICE UPON BUYER'S BREACH. [§33.5]** As noted in §33.4, it is the relatively rare case where a buyer who breaches an Article 2 contract before acceptance will be liable for the full contract price. Most of the time breaching buyers in such cases breach by wrongfully rejecting conforming goods which can be re-sold to others. The Code provides three potential remedies for the non-breaching seller in such cases:

(1) The seller can re-sell the goods to another, and collect from the buyer any difference between the re-sale price and the contract price, along with other related damages under §2-706;

(2) The seller can keep the goods, but still sue the breaching buyer for the difference between the market price at the time and place for tender and the contract price, along with other related damages under §2-708(1); or

(3) In cases where a buyer's breach causes injury to a "lost volume" seller, the seller is entitled to sue for lost profits and related damages under §2-708(2).

Each of these methods of recovery are discussed below.

1. **RECOVERY UNDER §2-706: SELLER'S "COVER" DAMAGES. [§33.51]** Most of the time when a seller tenders conforming goods to the buyer and the buyer wrongfully rejects them, the seller will want to re-sell the goods to another as quickly as possible so as to realize at least some cash for the goods, and not choose to wait until a lawsuit is concluded to receive any recovery. UCC §2-706 permits a seller to re-sell the goods and thereafter be entitled to recover from the breaching buyer the difference, if any, between the re-sale price and the contract price. Since this procedure is analogous in many respects to the non-breaching **buyer's** right to cover under UCC §2-712 (see §33.31), recovery

under §2-706 is sometimes referred to as "seller's cover." (See §31.382 for a discussion of how seller's cover is really the Code's formula for the recovery of expectation damages.)

a. **The Formula for Calculating a Seller's "Cover" Damages. [§33.511]** Under UCC §2-706(1), when the seller has re-sold goods wrongfully rejected by the buyer and has done so in good faith and in a commercially reasonable manner [see UCC §§2-706(2) to 2-706(4)], he or she is entitled to damages computed as follows:

Seller's Cover Damages = [(Contract Price for the Goods) - (Re-Sale Price for the Goods)] + Incidental Damages.

A seller's recoverable incidental damages are governed by UCC §2-710. Like other types of incidental damages, recoverable incidental losses under §2-710 are expenses incurred by the seller, after the buyer's breach, in an attempt to preserve the goods or otherwise mitigate the buyer's loss (See §31.27). Hence, they include costs incurred in stopping delivery, storage charges until the goods are sold, out-of-pocket costs associated with the re-sale, etc.

Note that there is no provision for recovery of consequential loss in the §2-706 formula. If a seller is claiming such loss, i.e. a lost profit resulting from the buyer's breach, the seller must proceed under §2-708(2) (see §33.53).

(1) **Example. [§33.5111]** Manufacturer has contracted to sell 1,000 VCRs to Retailer for $200/unit. The VCRs are timely delivered and are conforming, but Retailer nevertheless rejects. Manufacturer pays to have the sets shipped back to its plant, and one of its employees spends a good deal of time trying to find a substitute buyer, which she finally does. The substitute buyer is willing, in good faith and after notice to Retailer, to purchase the VCRs at $190/unit, a commercially reasonable price given the circumstances.

Under §2-706(1), Manufacturer is entitled to recover ($200/unit) - ($190/unit) x 1,000 units, plus whatever incidental costs it incurred in shipping the goods back to its factory, the time spent by its employee in arranging the re-sale, and any other costs associated with the re-sale.

2. **RECOVERY UNDER §2-708(1): SELLER'S MARKET DIFFERENTIAL DAMAGES. [§33.52]** Just as a non-breaching buyer who choses not to bear the costs of cover is still entitled to recover market differential damages upon a seller's breach [see UCC §2-713]; (see §33.22), a non-breaching seller is also entitled to choose not to re-sell wrongfully rejected goods and recover instead for market differential damages. Under §2-708(1), upon a buyer's wrongful rejection or repudiation a seller may recover the difference between the contract price and the market price for the goods, along with other associated damages. (See §31.382 for a discussion of how recovery under §2-708(1) is a specialized application of general contract law's formulation for recovering expectation damages.)

a. **The Formula for Calculating a Seller's Market Differential Damages. [§33.521]** Under UCC §2-708(1), when a seller opts to hold onto goods that could be re-sold after a wrongful rejection or repudiation by the buyer, the seller is entitled to damages computed as follows:

Seller's Damages = [(Contract Price for the Goods) - (Market Price for the Goods)] + Incidental Damages.

Note that there is no provision for the recovery of consequential loss in §2-708(1). A seller seeking lost profits as a result of the buyer's breach must proceed under §2-708(2) (see §33.53).

(1) **Determining the "Market Price".** [§33.5211] The formula for market differential damages under UCC §2-708(1) requires that the "market price" for the goods be subtracted from the contract price for those goods. Just as with a **buyer's** market differential damages (see e.g., §33.2211), there may be occasions when the market price for the goods is volatile, and thus will change from day to day. Further, on the same day the market price for the goods may be different in the buyer's city and the seller's city. Hence, a determination must be made as to which of the potentially different market prices should be selected as the proper "market price" for purposes of §2-708(1) damages. Under §2-708(1), the rule is that the "market price" for purposes of the formula is always **the market price pending at the time and place for tender** regardless of when it learned of the breach.

(a) **Example.** [§33.5211-1] Can Co., a manufacturer of aluminum cans in California, contracts to sell 100,000 cans at $0.20/can to Food Co., at Food Co.'s Cleveland, Ohio plant. Under their contract, tender of the cans was to take place in California on May 1, and delivery was expected in Cleveland on May 5. Due to world-wide economic uncertainty, the price of aluminum is fluctuating. On April 25, Food Co. breached by canceling its order and telling Can Co. not to bother tendering the cans, for no one would be there to pick them up. Can Co. had already finished making the cans. On May 1, the date of expected tender under the contract, the fair market value of aluminum cans was $0.17/can in Cleveland and $0.16/can in California. On May 5, the date of expected delivery under the contract, the value of aluminum cans was $0.14/can in Cleveland and $0.15/can in California.

In determining its §2-708(1) damages, Can Co. must use the market price of the cans pending at the time and place for tender. Hence, it must use the $0.16/can price that was pending in California on May 1, i.e., the date and place where tender was to take place under the contract. Hence, Can Co.'s damages under §2-708(1) would be ($0.20/can) - ($0.16/can) x 100,000 cans, plus any incidental damages it can establish.

3. **RECOVERY UNDER §2-708(2): SELLER'S LOST PROFIT RECOVERY.** [§33.53] A seller is entitled to recover under UCC §2-708(2), "[i]f the measure of damages provided in [§2-708(1)] is inadequate to put the seller in as good a position as performance would have done." If the seller can establish that recovery under §2-708(1) would not provide the benefit of his or her bargain, then under §2-708(2) the seller's measure of damages is the "profit the seller would have made from full performance by the buyer, together with any incidental damages . . . due allowance for costs reasonably incurred and due credit for payment or proceeds of resale." The question is thus under what circumstances will a seller's resort to damages under §2-708(1) be inadequate to put the seller in as good a position as full performance would have done? A discussion how §2-708(2)'s formula applies to lost volume sellers follows.

a. **Recovery of Profits for "Lost Volume" Sellers.** [§33.531] The idea behind the "lost volume" doctrine stems from the fact that sometimes a seller is not made whole even by selling a wrongfully rejected good to another for its full contract price. This occurs when the seller has an excess supply of the goods that were the subject of the breached contract, and thus, the buyer's breach has really cost the seller a profit from a lost second sale. While this may seem a little hard to grasp in the abstract, the idea is much clearer when illustrated.

A department store has thirty 25-inch color televisions in stock, and can easily and quickly get more if necessary. Devin contracts to buy one of the sets for $500, and arranges for delivery next week. Devin later changes his mind, and breaches the contract by telling the store not to deliver the television. Later that same day, the store sells the very television to Kim that it was going to deliver to Devin, and sells it to her for $500. Devin would like to argue that the store has been made whole. That is, his argument is that the store had a right to expect $500 for that set from him, and it ended up getting $500 for that set from Kim. Devin is right if the store's recovery is limited to either §2-706 or §2-708(1), for the result of either the (contract price) - (re-sale price) formula of §2-706, or the (contract price) - (market price) formula of §2-708(1), would result in a $0 recovery for the store.

The store, on the other hand, would argue that it has lost the **profit** from one sale. That is, if Devin had taken delivery of his set, the store still would have made the sale to Kim, for it would have sold her another set out of its inventory. Therefore, if Devin had not breached, it would have had the profits from **two** sales — Devin's and Kim's. As a result of Devin's breach, it only has the profit from **one** sale, i.e., Kim's. Thus, to be made whole it must be able to recover from Devin the amount of the profit it lost from the second sale that never occurred. (See also §31.3822 for a discussion of the lost profit problem).

Contract law accepts that argument, and UCC §2-708(2) gives the store the right to collect the lost profit from Devin in such a situation.

Note that in order to be a "lost volume" seller, and thus entitled to recover under §2-708(2), the seller must truly have excess supply so that the "second" sale can take place. For example, suppose Ed had a contract to sell his Van Gough painting to Barbra for $1,000,000. Barbra breaches, but that same day Ed was able to sell it to the Getty Museum, also for $1,000,000. In this case Ed is not damaged by the breach for he has obtained all the benefits to which he was entitled under his contract with Barbra. That is, because there is no second sale possible given the limited supply of the goods, Ed did not lose a profit from the second sale, and thus is not a "lost volume" seller.

Note also that the concept of lost volume is not limited to UCC cases governed by §2-708(2), although it is in this context that the doctrine has its most frequent application.

(1) The Formula for Lost Volume Seller's Recovery of Lost Profits under UCC §2-708(2). [§33.5311] It is now fairly well accepted that there is a drafting error in UCC §2-708(2), at least when that provision is used to calculate the recovery due a lost volume seller. The formula given in the statute states that a lost volume seller is entitled to recover the following:

Seller's Damages = The Profit From the Contract That was Breached + Incidental Damages + Costs Reasonably Incurred In Performance - <u>Due Credit For the Payments or Proceeds of Any Re-Sale</u>.

It is the underscored provision which is in error. That is, the whole idea of lost volume recovery is that the proceeds from the re-sale of the wrongfully rejected or repudiated goods should **not** be used to offset the seller's recovery. Hence, courts and commentators simply ignore the "due credit for the payments or proceeds of the re-sale" clause when applying §2-708(2) in lost volume seller cases.

G. **LIQUIDATED DAMAGES UNDER ARTICLE 2. [§33.6]** Liquidated damages are damages, the amount of which the parties have agreed in advance that will be owed upon a breach of their contract. The ability of the parties to agree to an enforceable liquidated damage provision under the Code is governed by UCC §2-718(1). The rules of §2-718(1), however, are the same as those governing the enforceability of liquidated damage clauses in non-UCC agreements (see §31.7). That is, the parties' agreement on liquidated damages will only be enforced if the amount of the liquidated damages is reasonable in light of the anticipated or actual harm caused by the breach, and where the actual amount of damages is difficult to ascertain with precision.

H. **EMOTIONAL DISTRESS DAMAGES, PUNITIVE DAMAGES, AND RECOVERY OF PRE-JUDGMENT INTEREST UNDER THE UCC. [§33.7]** The Code has no special rules governing the recovery of emotional distress damages, punitive damages, and pre-judgment interest. Hence, the rules regarding those subjects discussed in §§31.6, 31.8 and 31.9 are applicable to Article 2 contracts as well.

I. **LIMITATION ON, OR MODIFICATION OF, CONTRACT REMEDIES. [§33.8]** Under the principles of freedom of contract, UCC §2-719 provides that contracting parties of roughly equal bargaining power may validly modify the remedies for breach provided in the Code. Indeed, they may even eliminate them entirely should they choose to do so. However, this general rule is subject to two limitations:

(1) The parties' ability to substitute liquidated damages for the remedies of the Code is limited by the rule set forth in §33.6 [UCC §§2-718(1) and 2-719(1)]; and

(2) Limitation of consequential damages for injury to the person is *prima facie* unconscionable [UCC §2-719(3)].

Note, however, that UCC §2-719 provides that a limitation on **economic** consequential loss is **not** presumptively unconscionable, and is, in fact, specifically permitted by the Code (see §33.313, economic and personal injury consequential loss).

1. **WHEN A LIMITED REMEDY "FAILS OF ITS ESSENTIAL PURPOSE" UNDER UCC §2-719(2): REPAIR OR REPLACEMENT CLAUSES. [§33.81]** A recurring issue in commercial law is the effect of a seller's breach of a clause which limits the buyer's remedies under the Code. For example, assume Felicia buys a car and in her sales agreement she agrees to an exclusive "repair or replacement" clause. That is, she agrees that if there are any mechanical problems with her car, her exclusive remedy against the dealer is to take the car back to the dealer, who in turn promises Felicia it will either repair the problem, or replace the car, at its option. Repair or replacement clauses are quite common, are expressly permitted by the Code [UCC §2-719(1)(b)], and are examples of clauses that limit and modify the Code's otherwise - applying remedies available for breach.

With a repair or replacement clause, a buyer like Felicia receives a benefit, but also loses a benefit. Felicia gets the benefit of the dealer's promise to repair the car. Otherwise, if the car has mechanical problems, her remedies would be things like rejection, revocation, or a breach of warranty lawsuit. Because of the dealer's repair or replacement promise, however, she now has the benefit of a promise from the dealer that any problem with her car will be taken care of relatively promptly. However, because she agreed to the repair or replacement clause as an **exclusive** remedy, she has lost the benefit of being able to resort to any other Code-based remedy should the seller breach by tendering a car that needs repairs. In other words, for the benefit of getting the seller's repair promise, she traded her rights to seek all other Code-based relief.

Assume that Felicia has mechanical problems with her car. She takes it to the dealer a number of times with the same complaints, but it is never fixed. The recurring question in these types of cases is whether the dealer's breach of its repair or replacement promise now frees Felicia to resort to **any** Article 2 remedy, or whether she is limited to suing only for money damages resulting from the dealer's breach of the *limited remedy clause*. In other words, does breach of the clause negate the limitation of remedies entirely, or does it not. The dealer's argument, of course, is that by agreeing to an exclusive repair or replacement clause, Felicia forever waived her rights to recover under the panoply of Article 2 remedies and is now limited to suing for breach of that clause only.

The dealer's position in this regard is rejected by the Code. UCC §2-719(2) makes it clear that Felicia is entitled to sue under **any** Article 2 provided remedy in such a case. Section 2-719(2) provides that whenever an exclusive or limited damage provision **"fails of its essential purpose,"** the buyer is thereafter entitled to recover under **any** provision of Article 2. In other words, once the car dealership has breached its repair promise so thoroughly that there has been a failure in the essential purpose of such a clause, i.e., to give the purchaser comfort in knowing that her car will be repaired, *the limitation of remedy provision is thereafter void and without effect*. Hence, at that point there is nothing limiting Felicia from suing for breach of warranty, revoking her acceptance, etc.

a. **When a "No Consequential Damages" Clause is Linked with a "Repair or Replacement" Clause. [§33.811]** Another recurring issue in commercial transactions under §2-719 is what happens when there is not just one limitation of remedy clause, but two. For example, suppose Doug's machine shop had a contract to sell a computerized drill press to Andrea's manufacturing plant. In their contract, there is **both** an exclusive repair or replacement clause, **and** a limitation on Andrea's ability to collect consequential damages upon a breach. Once again, assume there has been a failure of the essential purpose of the repair and replacement clause, as Doug has not fixed a recurring problem with the press. The issue is whether the breach of one limited damage provision acts as a breach of both of them, or whether the breach of the repair and replacement clause is independent of the consequential damages limitation. That is, if there were only a repair and replacement clause, when it failed of its essential purpose Andrea would be entitled to recover under any UCC provision, including ones allowing for consequential loss [§2-719(2); see §33.81]. However, in her contract Andrea also agreed to a consequential damage limitation. Hence, Doug would argue that breach of the repair and replacement clause means that Andrea is entitled to recover under any UCC provision **except** those allowing for recovery of consequential damages. He will say that Andrea separately agreed that he would **never** be liable for such damages under their contract when she agreed to the consequential damage limitation clause. Andrea, on the other hand, would argue that the clauses were linked, i.e., that they are dependent on each other. She would allege that the only reason she agreed to the consequential damage limitation is because Doug had provided a repair or replacement guarantee. Hence, her view would be that the breach of the repair or replacement promise should also render the consequential damage limitation unenforceable.

It is fair to say there is no uniform treatment of this issue by the courts. Increasingly, however, courts are seeking to discover the parties' true intentions in agreeing to these clauses, i.e., did the parties consider them dependent or independent. If a court finds that the parties intended to link them together, then breach of the repair or replacement provision will also result in the breach of the consequential damages limitation as well, and someone such as Andrea can thus recover for her provable consequential losses. On the other hand, if the parties intended for the clauses to be independent, then they will be interpreted independently. In such a case, Doug's breach of the repair or replacement promise will not effect the consequential damage limitation and will thus supercede the effect of §2-719(2).

2. **DISTINCTION BETWEEN LIMITATION OF REMEDY UNDER UCC §2-719 AND DISCLAIMER OF WARRANTY UNDER UCC §2-316.** [§33.82] Students sometimes get confused as to when the rules of §2-719 relating to limitations of remedies apply, and when the rules of §2-316 relating to disclaimers of warranty are operative (see §§36.13, 36.23, and 36.33). When the clause in question **completely eliminates the warranty** so that it is impossible to breach that kind of warranty under the contract, the clause is a **warranty disclaimer**, and UCC **§2-316's provisions govern**. However, if a contract provision provides that a breach of warranty can still occur, but that the *range of remedies for such breach is limited*, e.g., instead of a lawsuit the buyer is limited to repair or replacement remedy, then the *rules of §2-719 are operative*.

XII. MISCELLANEOUS UCC PROVISIONS

CHAPTER THIRTY-FOUR: APPLICABILITY OF ARTICLE TWO OF THE UCC

A. APPLICABILITY OF ARTICLE TWO GENERALLY. [§34.0] One of the first issues a student or a lawyer has to confront when analyzing a contract is whether it is governed by the UCC or by common law contract principles. If Article 2 applies, then its language and doctrines need to be used in evaluating whether a contract was formed, what the parties' performance obligations are, the enforceability of its terms, and the remedies to be applied upon a breach. Hence, determination of whether a transaction is governed by Article 2 or not is a crucial one, and sometimes may be outcome determinative for a party seeking to establish his or her right to judicial relief. The rules for deciding whether Article 2 applies to a transaction are discussed in the remainder of this chapter.

B. ARTICLE TWO IS NOT LIMITED TO MERCHANTS. [§34.1] One of the biggest misconceptions that seems to plague a good number of students is that Article 2 is limited to merchants. It is **NOT**. The distant origins of the UCC are found in the merchant law of England, and many of the cases in Contracts textbooks deal with merchants. Thus, it is understandable why some students at first believe there is a merchant limitation on the applicability of the Code. This is not the case, however. While there are 19 provisions which set forth special rules governing merchant rights and obligations under Article 2, you must realize that the remaining sections apply to a contract in which a friend of yours sells you her watch, just as they do to an agreement where IBM sells computers to General Motors.

C. UCC §2-102: ARTICLE TWO APPLIES TO "TRANSACTIONS IN GOODS." [§34.2] UCC §2-102 provides that Article 2 "applies to transactions in goods." Hence, the general rule is simple enough to state — **anytime there is a "transaction in goods," the rules of the UCC govern the agreement; when there is no "transaction in goods," common law contract rules apply**. This general rule, of course, leaves two questions: (1) What sorts of "transactions" are intended to be included within §2-102; and (2) What are "goods" for purposes of Article 2 applicability. These questions are discussed below.

    1. THE MEANING OF "TRANSACTION." [§34.21] One of the most surprising omissions in Article 2 is its failure to define the term "transaction." Since the question of Article 2 applicability is so important, and since applicability turns on whether the contract is a "transaction in goods," the absence of any indication as to what transactions are meant to be included is puzzling.

    While lawyers have asserted that various kinds of transactions merit Article 2 applicability, as a practical matter the courts routinely have to deal with only two types of "transactions" for Article 2 applicability purposes: (1) sales; and (2) leases. The rules governing Article 2 applicability for each of these transactions follow.

        a. Sales. [§34.211] There is no question that a "sale of goods" is a "transaction in goods" for purposes of Article 2 applicability. Indeed, the title of Article 2 is "Uniform Commercial Code — Sales" [UCC §2-101]. Hence, a pure sales of goods, i.e., a transaction where title and possession of a good is transferred from the seller to the buyer, is clearly covered by Article 2 (see §§34.3, and 34.4 however for a discussion of whether Article 2 applies when the same transaction has within it both a sale of goods and a sale of a service, or where the transaction involves the sale of a good attached to real estate).

b. Leases. [§34.212] For many years, the question of whether a lease of goods was a "transaction in goods" for Article 2 applicability purposes has yielded conflicting answers. The rationale for the various viewpoints can be seen by examining a typical lease case where a party is seeking UCC applicability.

John leases a car for the day from a car rental facility at the airport and later gets into an accident which he claims was caused by an insufficient level of brake fluid in the car he rented. John would like Article 2 to apply to his lease so that he could validly assert a breach of warranty claim against the car rental agency (see Chapter Thirty-Six). Obviously, John's claim could also be brought in tort, but it is typical in these cases that the consumer is also trying to take advantage of the UCC's rather generous 4-year statute of limitations [UCC §2-725(1)], instead of perhaps being time barred by the usual one-year statute of limitations that applies to personal injury tort claims.

Those courts and commentators who believe that Article 2 should apply to lease transactions point to the plain reading of UCC §2-102. That is, they state that a lease is certainly a "transaction" under anyone's definition of the term, and when a consumer such as John leases a "good," a "transaction in goods" has taken place and thus Article 2's provisions must apply.

Those who do not believe leases were intended to be governed by Article 2 point out that while UCC §2-102 speaks in terms of transactions in goods, the substantive provisions of Article 2 do not. That is, §2-725(1) (the statute of limitations provision), says "[a]n action for breach of any **contract for sale** must be commenced within four years . . ." Similarly, §2-314 (the implied warranty of merchantability provision), states that, "a warranty that the goods shall be merchantable is implied in a **contract for their sale** . . ." Moreover, the other warranty provisions also speak in terms of "seller" rather than "lessor" or "transactor" [UCC §§2-313; 2-315]. Hence, this view holds that the more specific language of the substantive provisions of the Code makes it clear that leases should be excluded from Article 2 coverage.

Thankfully, the different treatment of this issue seems about to end. In 1990, the Permanent Editorial Board of the UCC enacted Article 2A, which is entitled "Uniform Commercial Code — Leases" [UCC §2A-101]. In those states which have adopted it, the provisions of Article 2A will govern the formation, operation, performance obligations, etc. regarding leases. Article 2A has already been adopted in about 30 states. It is thus likely that within a few years, Article 2A will be applicable everywhere, and there will then be a uniform answer as to whether a lease is a "transaction" for Article 2 purposes.

2. THE MEANING OF "GOODS." [§34.22] Unlike the word "transactions," the word "goods" is defined in UCC §2-105. That statute states that "goods" for purposes of Article 2 are "all things . . . which are movable at the time of identification to the contract . . ." Before discussing exactly what is meant by that definition, it is perhaps useful to get a general understanding of what is, and is not, meant by "goods." In general, a good is personal property, i.e., something which is "movable." A contract for services is clearly not governed by Article 2, for services are not movable. Hence, when someone makes a contract with a mechanic to tune a car, there may be a transaction, but it is not a transaction in **goods** and such a contract is thus governed by common law contract principles and not the UCC. Similarly, a contract for real estate is also clearly not governed by Article 2, for real estate is also not "movable."

UCC §2-105 does not just say that a good is anything "movable," however. It says that to be a good, a thing must be "movable *at the time of identification to the contract.*" The concept of "identification" is peculiar to the Code and is set forth in §2-501. Essentially, something is "identified" to the contract when the **particular object** that is to be provided to the **particular buyer** under the contract is determined. Depending on the type of contract involved, identification can occur either at the time of contract formation (see §34.221) or after the contract has been executed (see §34.222). A few examples should make this clearer.

a. **Example. [§34.221]** Dan enters a grocery store, selects an apple from the display, and approaches the check-out counter. By selecting the particular apple which he will buy, Dan has thereby "identified" the particular good to the contract [UCC §2-501(1)(a)]. Hence, because at the time of the identification to the contract the apple is movable, and because Dan will get possession of the apple by a means of a sales transaction, the contract between Dan and the store is a "transaction in goods" governed by Article 2.

b. **Example. [§34.222]** Mary buys a 50-inch television from a large department store, and arranges for delivery the following Wednesday. At the time she pays for it, her television set is not "identified" to the contract, for no one knows which particular set in the department store's inventory will be Mary's. Probably her particular set will not be "identified" until the following Wednesday morning when someone from the store will select a set from the store's inventory and designate it as the one to be delivered to Mary [UCC §2-501(1)(b)].

The fact that Mary's television was not identified at the time the contract was made does not mean that such a sale is not an Article 2 transaction, however. Recall that to be a "good" under §2-105, the television set does not have to be identified at the time the contract is made; rather §2-105 says that to be a good the object must be movable **when** it is identified. Since the television is movable on Wednesday morning when the store designates the particular set as Mary's set, it is surely a good. Thus, her purchase satisfies the "transaction in goods" standard of §2-102 for Article 2 applicability even though her good was not identified to the contract until after its making.

D. **ARTICLE TWO APPLICABILITY TO SALES/SERVICES "HYBRID" TRANSACTIONS. [§34.3]** Sometimes a transaction is neither purely the sale of a good nor purely the sale of a service — it is a "hybrid." For example, suppose Martin bought a water heater from a department store for $400. Included within that price, however, was installation of the heater at Martin's house. Obviously the transaction involves the sale of a good, i.e., the water heater, but it also involves the sale of a service, i.e., the installation. Two theories have developed as to whether such a sales/service hybrid transaction should be governed by Article 2: (1) the "predominant purpose" test; and (2) the "gravamen" test.

1. **THE "PREDOMINANT PURPOSE" TEST. [§34.31]** Under the predominant purpose test, whether Article 2 applies to a sales/service hybrid transaction depends on which part of the transaction predominates. That is, the court must determine whether the principal purpose of the buyer in deciding to enter the transaction was really to acquire goods or to obtain services. If it is the former, then **all** parts of the transaction are governed by Article 2 under this theory; if it is the latter, **no** part of the transaction is subject to Article 2.

For example, use the Martin/Department Store hypothetical of §34.3, where Martin purchased a water heater and its installation for $400. Most likely Martin's predominant purpose in the transaction was the acquisition of the good. Accordingly, Martin's rights arising from the contract are exclusively governed by the UCC, regardless of whether the water heater blew up because the heater itself was defective or because the installer was negligent (in the tort sense) in not tightening certain valves. Hence, on occasion, application of the predominant purpose tests results in what probably should be a tort negligence claim (failure to tighten valves) being judged under the UCC. (At least under a strict application of the predominant purpose test.)

2. **THE "GRAVAMEN" TEST. [§34.32]** Within the past 15 years or so, another test for Article 2 applicability in hybrid situations has developed, the "gravemen" test. Under this test, the court asks what is the **gravamen of the cause of action**. That is, it determines whether the buyer is complaining about a problem with non-conforming goods, or whether the buyer is complaining about negligent service. If it is the former (the heater was defective), Article 2 would apply; if it is the latter (the valve was negligently tightened), the suit is decided under tort principles regardless of the "predominant purpose" of the transaction.

The trend of modern decisions is towards adoption of the gravamen test, but the predominant purpose test is probably still the majority rule.

E. **ARTICLE TWO APPLICABILITY WHEN THERE IS A SALE OF SOMETHING ATTACHED TO REALTY. [§34.4]** Sometimes a contract calls for the sale of something that is attached to realty, but could be severed from it. For example, suppose a cereal maker makes a contract for the wheat growing on Farmer's land. In some senses, the wheat is identified when the contract is made, and at that point it is not movable because it is in the ground. Thus, a strict application of §2-105 would hold that the wheat was not a "good." On the other hand, when the wheat is delivered to the cereal maker it certainly will be movable, which argues for the application of Article 2 to such a transaction.

UCC §2-107 governs these kinds of cases. That provision set forth two situations as to whether Article 2 governs contracts where goods are attached to, but capable of severance from, realty.

(1) The sale of minerals (including oil and gas), and the sale of a structure attached to real estate but due to be severed from its foundation, **are Article 2 transactions only if the contract calls for the seller to do the severance.** That is, if the contract calls for the buyer to mine the minerals or remove the house, then the contract is considered one for the transfer of real estate and is not governed by Article 2 [UCC §2-107(1)].

(2) A sale apart from the land of crops, timber, and anything else attached to realty which is capable of severance without material harm to the property (but which is also not governed by the rule in part (1) above), is an Article 2 transaction **regardless of who severs the goods** [UCC §2-107(2)]. Thus, regardless of whether it is the cereal company or the farmer who harvests the crop, so long as the contract is for sale of the wheat apart from the land, Article 2 applies.

CHAPTER THIRTY-FIVE: RISK OF LOSS AND MERCANTILE TERMS

A. RISK OF LOSS. [§35.0] Risk of loss principles determine which party to a contract still has the obligation to perform when goods are lost, damaged, or destroyed during transit. If the seller has the risk of loss, and replaceable goods are lost, damaged, or destroyed before they reach the buyer, the seller must still timely tender another delivery of his or her goods, or else be in breach for failing to do so. If the buyer has the risk of loss, and the goods are lost, damaged, or destroyed in transit, the buyer must still pay for the goods, even though the buyer will never obtain the benefit of his or her bargain, or be in breach for failing to do so.

For example, suppose a manufacturer in New York sells 100 television sets to a retailer in California. As the goods are being transported across country, through no apparent fault of either party, the sets are stolen. If the risk of loss is on the seller, the seller is under a duty to ensure another 100 sets will timely be delivered to the buyer to collect payment. If the risk is on the buyer, the buyer will have to pay for all 100 sets, even though it will never receive them.

The rules regarding risk of loss under the Code are set forth in §§2-509 and 2-510. The rules differ depending on whether the parties have performed or breached their duties prior to the loss, damage, or destruction of the goods. These rules are set forth below. When the goods are in the control of buyer's agent, the buyer has the risk from then on because the buyer has control over them. So in every contract, at some point (unless the goods are destroyed before then) the risk shifts to buyer.

1. **RISK OF LOSS IN THE ABSENCE OF BREACH. [§35.01]** Unless the parties have agreed otherwise, when the seller first acquires goods, he or she has the risk of loss; if they are destroyed at that instant, the seller still is required to perform by timely tendering replacements. Assuming neither party has breached, when the risk shifts to the buyer depends on whether the contract is a "shipment" contract or a "destination" contract.

   a. **Shipment Contract. [§35.011]** A shipment contract is one in which the contract does not require the seller to ship the goods to any particular location [UCC §2-509(1)(a)]. In other words, it is a contract where the **buyer** agrees to make all the delivery arrangements, and will send someone to pick up the finished goods from the seller, usually at the seller's plant. **In shipment contracts, where the seller has tendered conforming goods in a conforming manner, the risk of loss passes to the buyer when the goods are transferred to the buyer or to the buyer's agent** [UCC §2-509(1)(a)]. That is, typically the risk will pass to the buyer at the loading dock of the seller's plant when the seller gives the goods to the carrier hired by the buyer to transport the goods.

   b. **Destination Contract. [§35.012]** A destination contract is one in which the contract requires the seller to deliver goods to a particular place, usually to the buyer's home or place of business. In other words, it is a contract where the seller's price includes shipping charges and under which the seller makes all the shipping arrangements [UCC §2-509(1)(b)]. **In destination contracts, where the seller has tendered conforming goods in a conforming manner, the risk of loss passes to the buyer only after the goods are delivered to the destination called for under the contract in a manner that enables the buyer to take delivery** [UCC §2-509(1)(b)]. That is, typically the risk will pass only after the carrier hired by the seller transfers possession of the goods to the buyer at the buyer's home or place of business.

For example, when a consumer orders something from a catalogue, typically the contract formed will be a destination contract. The company putting out the catalogue will promise to deliver the goods to a particular destination, usually the buyer's home. The price paid by the buyer thus includes a shipping charge. Hence, if the good is destroyed before it reaches the particular destination, the risk of loss is on the seller, and the seller is then obligated to re-tender another conforming shipment to the destination called for in the contract, or be in breach for failing to do so.

2. **EFFECT OF BREACH ON RISK OF LOSS. [§35.02]** UCC §2-510 sets forth three changes to the risk of loss rules that apply when one of the parties has breached before the goods have been delivered.

   a. **When a Seller Breaches in Such a Way to Give the Buyer a Right of Rejection. [§35.021]** Under §2-510(1), if a seller has breached the contract either by sending sufficiently non-conforming goods, or by tendering goods in a sufficiently non-conforming way, so that the buyer would have a right of rejection of the goods if they were received, then the risk of loss stays with the seller until the seller cures any problem and/or the buyer accepts goods under the contract (see §22.22); [UCC §§2-601; 2-612].

   Suppose Ralph purchases a blue couch from Veronica's Furniture Store by means of a shipment contract. Ralph hires a carrier to pick up the couch at Veronica's and ship it to him. However, when the carrier Ralph hires arrives at Veronica's, it is given a green couch to deliver to Ralph. Along the way, the couch is severely damaged, through no apparent fault of anyone. Under normal risk of loss rules in the absence of a breach, the risk of loss in such a case would be on Ralph (the buyer), because Veronica's contract with Ralph was a shipment contract, and the risk of loss in such contracts shifts when the seller (Veronica's) tenders the good to the buyer's carrier [UCC §2-509 (1) (a)]; (see §35.011). However, because Veronica's breached by sending the wrong color couch, and because the breach would have given Ralph a right of rejection had it been delivered, the risk of loss is deemed to have stayed with the breaching seller from the beginning, and Veronica's is still obligated to deliver a conforming blue couch, or be in breach for failing to do so.

   b. **UCC §2-510(2): When a Seller Breaches and the Buyer Revokes Acceptance. [§35.022]** Under UCC §2-510(2), if a seller breaches and a buyer later validly revokes acceptance due to that breach, the buyer is entitled to treat the loss as having rested on the seller from the beginning, but only "to the extent of any deficiency in his [or her] insurance coverage." That is, if a buyer validly revokes acceptance and later, before the goods are returned to the buyer, something happens to them, the buyer must first try to recover under his or her insurance policy. If the buyer has no policy, or if the insurance policy does not pay the full amount of the loss, e.g., there is a deductible, then the buyer may recover from the store for any deficiency in his or her insurance proceeds.

   c. **UCC §2-510(3): When a Buyer Repudiates or Otherwise Breaches Before the Risk Has Shifted to Him or Her. [§35.023]** Under UCC 2-510(3), when a buyer has repudiated under a contract, or is otherwise in breach before the risk of loss has passed to him or her, the seller may treat the risk as having rested on the buyer for a commercially reasonable time, but again "only to the extent of any deficiency in his [or her] effective insurance coverage." Hence, in such a case, the seller must first try to recover against his or her own insurance, and only if a deficiency still remains may he or she recover the remainder of the purchase price from the buyer.

B. MERCANTILE TERMS. [§35.1] Mercantile terms are shorthand expressions of various terms of a contract. In other words, they are abbreviations used in commercial law to denote a lengthy series of terms in an economical way. It is the unusual Contracts course that spends a lot of time studying those terms, but they are mentioned in first year cases and can occasionally be important to the outcome of a suit. Accordingly, they are briefly defined and discussed below.

1. **F.O.B. [§35.11]** F.O.B. means "Free On Board," and is shorthand for describing whether the contract is a shipment contract or a destination contract [UCC §2-319]; (see §35.011 and §35.012). Whether the F.O.B. term connotes a shipment or a destination contract depends on whether the term is followed by the place of shipment or the place of destination.

   For example, suppose a seller in Cleveland made a contract with a buyer in Atlanta:

   (a) If the mercantile term of the contract was **F.O.B., Cleveland**, it would mean: (i) the contract was a shipment contract, and thus the risk of loss shifts to the buyer when the seller tenders the goods to the carrier in Cleveland; (ii) the seller's price does not include shipping charges; and (iii) it is up to the buyer to select, hire, and pay the carrier for shipping the goods to Atlanta [UCC §2-319(1)(a)];

   (b) If the mercantile term in the contract was **F.O.B., Atlanta**, it would mean: (i) the contract was a destination contract, and thus the risk of loss does not pass to the buyer until the goods are duly delivered in Atlanta; (ii) the seller's price includes the cost of shipping; and (iii) it is the seller who must select, hire, and pay the carrier for shipping the goods to Atlanta [UCC §2-319(1)(b)].

2. **F.A.S. [§35.12]** F.A.S. means "Free Along Side," [UCC §2-319 (2)]. The term is usually followed by the name of a ship, e.g., F.A.S., S.S. Normandie. When used in this way, it means: (i) the risk of loss passes to the buyer when the goods are brought along side the ship, e.g., to the dock or port; (ii) the selling price only includes delivery to the dock or port; and (iii) the seller only selects and pays the carrier to get the goods to the dock; it is the buyer who selects and pays for the ship on which the goods are to be transported [UCC §2-319(2)].

   Hence, if the mercantile term was F.A.S., S.S. Normandie, and if the goods were damaged or destroyed while being loaded from the dock into the cargo hold of the Normandie, the risk of loss would be on the buyer, for the goods become the buyer's risk as soon as they were safely delivered to the dock.

3. **C.I.F. [§35.13]** The term C.I.F. stands for Cost of Goods, Insurance, and Freight [UCC §2-320]. By common designation, it only has meaning if it is followed by the place of destination. However, that does **not** mean it is a destination contract. To the contrary it is a shipment contract. [UCC §2-320, Com. 1.]

   For example, a seller in New York contracts with a buyer in Oregon. If they agree to use C.I.F. as the mercantile term in their agreement, it must be set forth as C.I.F., Oregon, i.e., the destination of the shipment.

   A **C.I.F., Oregon** term means: (i) the contract is a **shipment** contract (even though it is the destination point which follows the "C.I.F." term), and thus the risk of loss passes to the buyer upon the seller's delivery to the carrier; (ii) the seller's price includes the cost of goods, the cost of insurance for those goods during transit, and the cost of shipping the goods; (iii) the seller must select, hire, and pay for the carrier; and (iv) the seller must obtain insurance on the goods, but the beneficiary of that insurance is the **buyer** [UCC §2-320 (1)].

Thus, if goods are lost during shipment from New York to Oregon, the risk of loss is on the **buyer** (which makes sense, because C.I.F. contracts are shipment contracts). Recall, however, that as part of the contract the seller was required to procure insurance on the goods, with the proceeds of that insurance payable to the buyer as the beneficiary. Hence, while the buyer may have to pay the seller for the goods that are destroyed, the buyer will be reimbursed for such payment by the insurance provided by the seller.

4. **C. & F. [§35.14]** The term C. & F. means the same as C.I.F., except that the seller's price does not include insurance, and the seller, therefore, need not procure it [UCC §2-320 (3)]. Hence, if a buyer agrees to buy his or her own insurance to cover the risk of loss, but still wants the seller's price to include both the cost of goods and of the cost of shipment as well, a C. & F. term should be used.

CHAPTER THIRTY-SIX: WARRANTIES

A. **WARRANTIES UNDER THE UCC GENERALLY. [§36.0]** Article 2 of the UCC contains three warranties that are often studied in first-year Contracts courses:

    (1) Express warranty, found in UCC §2-313;

    (2) The Implied Warranty of Merchantability, found in UCC §2-314; and

    (3) The Implied Warranty of Fitness for a Particular Purpose, found in UCC §2-315.

Note that the Code also provides for a warranty of title in UCC §2-312, but this provision is not typically taught in Contracts courses, and thus will not be discussed here.

B. **EXPRESS WARRANTIES. [§36.1]** A buyer seeking to prove that an actionable express warranty was made to him or her must establish that: (1) the seller made a sufficiently factual promise about the qualities or attributes of the goods which were the subject matter of the contract; and (2) the factual promise was part of the "basis of the bargain."

Each of these elements is discussed below.

1. **AN EXPRESS WARRANTY IS CREATED BY AN AFFIRMATION, PROMISE, DESCRIPTION, OR SAMPLE. [§36.11]** A buyer seeking to prove the existence of an actionable express warranty must show that the seller made a sufficiently factual promise to him or her relating to the qualities or attributes of the goods that were sold. Under UCC §2-313(1), an actionable express warranty can be made in three separate, but related, ways:

    (i) by means of an "**affirmation of fact or promise** made by the seller which relates to the goods" [UCC §2-313(1)(a)];

    (ii) by means of "a **description of the goods**" made by the seller [UCC §2-313(1)(b)]; and

    (iii) by means of "**a sample or model**" shown to the buyer as representative of the goods the buyer will receive under the contract [UCC §2-313(1)(c)].

The Code makes clear that not every statement relating to a product's attributes becomes actionable. While there is no requirement that the word "warranty" or "guarantee" be used to create an express warranty, the Code does require that any representation made to the buyer must be **factual** before it can be actionable [UCC §2-313(2)]. The rules used to determine whether a particular statement is sufficiently factual to create an enforceable warranty are the same as they are for determining when a statement is sufficiently factual to serve as the basis for a misrepresentation claim (see §14.41). That is, the more verifiable and provable a statement is, the more likely it will be held to be an actionable affirmation of fact. The more it is an unprovable, amorphous statement about the qualities of a good, the more likely it is to be found to be an unactionable opinion or a "puffing" statement. Hence, statements like "this car will get 25 miles per gallon" clearly will be actionable as an express warranty, whereas statements like "this car is a honey" clearly will not.

2. THE AFFIRMATIONS MADE BY THE SELLER MUST BECOME PART OF "THE BASIS OF THE BARGAIN." [§36.12] Once a buyer has established that a sufficiently factual statement has been made by the seller, the buyer must next prove that the statement was part of "the basis of the bargain" between the buyer and seller. There are two views as to what "basis of the bargain" means:

> (1) the first view holds that basis of the bargain is simply a synonym for reliance, i.e., that it sets forth a requirement that the buyer must have relied on the seller's factual promise in deciding to purchase the product before a buyer can recover for breach of warranty;

> (2) the second view holds that "benefit of the bargain" means only that the factual affirmations of the seller were made sometime before the sale took place.

Part of the reason different courts come to different conclusions on this issue stems from the fact that they have different views as to the purposes of the express warranty protections in the Code, as explained below.

a. Theory One: "Basis Of The Bargain" Means "Reliance." [§36.121] Those courts and commentators who hold that basis of the bargain is only a synonym for reliance believe that the express warranty protections of the Code are principally designed to protect the reasonable expectations of the buyer in a sales transaction. That is, they hold that if a buyer hears or reads something the seller has said about the product, and relies on that representation in making the decision to purchase the good, then the seller should be liable if the good does not have those promised qualities, for the basis on which the bargain was made has been upset.

This view also holds, however, that if the buyer did **not** rely on the seller's statements in making the decision to purchase the good, e.g., because he or she did not see or hear them before deciding to purchase the good, or because he or she would have purchased the good anyway, regardless of what the seller said, than no express warranty claim should be allowed. This is because if the buyer did not rely on the seller's promises, then the fact that the goods do not conform to what the seller promised about them caused the buyer no harm, since it resulted in no disruption of the buyer's bargain. In other words, this view holds that if the seller's statements played no role in the buyer's decision to buy the goods, those statements could not have been part of the basis of the buyer's bargain and thus there is no interest of the buyer justifying protection.

One rationale for this view is that reliance has long been a requirement for fraud and misrepresentation claims (see §§14.43 and 14.44). While a claim for breach of express warranty is not identical to a tort claim for misrepresentation, the two are related. That is, in each type of case a buyer is suing for damages resulting from a statement made by a seller about the qualities of goods. Hence, as a matter of consistency, it is thought that reliance should be an element of a §2-313 claim. Moreover, many commentators believe that a buyer truly is not deserving of recovery if he or she was not aware of, or did not rely on, the seller's warranty, for the seller's promises in these cases were, by definition, irrelevant to the bargain.

Note that there is a split even among those jurisdictions which believe that basis of the bargain means reliance. Some feel that the burden of proving reliance should be on the buyer, whereas others believe it should be on the seller to prove the absence of reliance as a defense. That is, this latter view holds that a buyer can prove his or her **prima facie** case for breach of express warranty without showing reliance, for reliance will be presumed. However, a seller is entitled to rebut that presumption by establishing that the buyer did not see, hear, and/or rely on the seller's affirmations in deciding to purchase the good.

b. **Theory Two: "Basis Of The Bargain" Means the Affirmation was Made Before The Sale Took Place. [§36.122]** This theory holds that basis of the bargain is really only a timing requirement, i.e., that it only requires proof that the seller made the factual affirmation before the sale took place. The rationale for this view is that the Code's express warranty provisions were not designed to protect the expectations of a buyer so much as they were to punish a seller for not living up to the promises he or she made about goods. That is, this view holds that contract law does not require the seller to make any representations about his or her goods; so if the seller says nothing about them there will be no express warranty liability. However, once the seller does voluntarily say something about the qualities of his or her goods, he or she should be prepared to face the consequences when the goods fail to perform as promised. Hence, under this view it is irrelevant whether the buyer saw, heard, and/or relied on the warranty, it is only relevant that the seller made it before the sale, and that the goods did not perform as promised.

There are two justifications given for this view. First, Comment 3 to §2-313, states that "[i]n actual practice affirmations of fact made by the seller about the goods during a bargain are regarded as part of the description of those goods; **hence no particular reliance on such statements need be shown in order to weave them into the fabric of the agreement.**" The second justification is that, whether the buyer was aware of the promise or not, the price he or she paid for the goods probably reflected the costs of the warranty. That is, typically when a company makes a warranty, it will increase its price somewhat to cover the costs of having to live up to it in the future. Thus, even if the buyer did not know about the warranty, it is likely he or she paid for its protection.

At the present time, the view that basis of the bargain means reliance is still probably the majority, but there appears to be growing acceptance of the view that the term only means that the statement must be made before the sale takes place.

3. **DISCLAIMING AN EXPRESS WARRANTY. [§36.13]** Somewhat surprisingly, an express warranty can be disclaimed under the Code. That is, a seller can make an express warranty by making some affirmation of fact to the buyer that was part of the basis of the bargain, but then before the contract is made, the seller can "take it back" and disclaim the previously made express promise.

Obviously the idea of disclaiming an express warranty is not troubling if both buyer and seller are aware that the seller's representations about the product are no longer intended to be part of the transaction. That is, if a sales representative at a car dealership tells the buyer that a car gets 25 m.p.g., but then before the car is purchased the sales representative recants, informs the buyer he or she was mistaken, and tells the buyer that he or she really cannot say what the gas mileage of the car will be, there is no dispute about whether a gas mileage warranty exists regarding the car if the buyer later purchases it. Such is not the typical scenario, however. Typically, the issue arises when a sales representative makes an oral express warranty to the buyer, and thereafter there is an attempt to disclaim that warranty in a written purchase agreement the parties sign to close the deal. The problem is that the buyer may not read and/or understand the written contract, and certainly does not expect that the oral warranty he or she has just been given 10 minutes before is effectively disclaimed in such a writing.

The Code regulates the disclaimer of express warranties in §2-316(1). That provision is syntactically somewhat difficult to understand, but its approach is as follows:

(1) If it is reasonable to do so, the words of the warranty and the words of the warranty disclaimer should be construed as consistent with each other. That is, the warranty and the disclaimer should try to be harmonized so that they both can be found valid and enforceable. For example, if the oral warranty made by the sales representative was that the car got 25 m.p.g., and the warranty disclaimer disclaimed all warranties as to the quality of workmanship on the car, it might be possible to construe them as reasonably harmonious, i.e., there may be no warranty as to things like the fit and finish of the car, but there is warranty regarding its mileage.

(2) If the express warranty and the disclaimer cannot be read consistently, as is usually the case, then the buyer's rights are circumscribed. At first the language of §2-316(1) makes it seem as though the oral express warranty should prevail over the written disclaimer, for §2-316(1) states that when the warranty and the disclaimer cannot be harmonized, "the negation or limitation [of the warranty] is inoperative." However, application of this rule is specifically subject to the parol evidence rule, UCC §2-202 (see Chapter Nineteen). By making the "negation is inoperative" term subject to the parol evidence rule, §2-316(1) makes it almost impossible for an oral warranty ever to be enforceable when paired with a valid written warranty disclaimer. Obviously this is a difficult area, which perhaps can be better understood by illustration.

Susan buys a computer from Mega Byte, Inc. The Mega Byte sales representative tells Susan that the computer she is interested in will run the "DataPro" program that Susan likes to use. Relying on the representation that the computer will run DataPro, Susan buys it. When she gets home, she discovers both that the computer will not run the DataPro program and that her bill of sale provides that "Mega Byte makes no representation or warranty that its computers will be compatible with any software program on the market, and any indication to the contrary by any sales representative should be disregarded. Buyer must test the compatibility of any program **prior to** purchasing this computer."

In evaluating whether the disclaimer is effective under UCC §2-316(1), the analysis is as follows:

(1) Can the warranty and the disclaimer be read consistently? Here they cannot, for an oral warranty providing that Data Pro can be run on the computer cannot be harmonized with a disclaimer providing that Mega Byte makes no enforceable warranty as to whether its computers can run any program.

(2) If the disclaimer and the warranty cannot be read consistently, then the disclaimer is inoperative, **subject to the parol evidence rule**. However, recall that under the UCC's parol evidence rule, no evidence of an oral term that "contradicts" a term in a writing can be introduced (see §19.1). Here, the oral term that the computer will run DataPro certainly contradicts the written term that no representations are made as to the compatibility of any program with a Mega Byte computer. Thus, if, somehow, evidence of the warranty and of the disclaimer could both be introduced at trial, the warranty would prevail and the disclaimer would be inoperative. However, because most such oral warranties will be found as "contradicting" the

written disclaimer, evidence of the oral warranty will almost never be admitted. As such, the only operable provision that will be in evidence in such cases will be the disclaimer, and the disclaimer will thus control.

Note that such a result, while faithful to the language of §2-316, is unfair to someone in Susan's position. Accordingly, courts often decide that written express warranty disclaimers will not be enforced either on unconscionability grounds [UCC §2-302]; (see also Chapter 15), or on the grounds that a seller's conduct in such cases constitutes a breach of the covenant of good faith and fair dealing [UCC §1-203].

C. IMPLIED WARRANTY OF MERCHANTABILITY. [§36.2] A buyer seeking to establish breach of the implied warranty of merchantability under §2-314 must prove that: (1)the seller of the good was a "merchant"; and (2)the goods sold by the seller were not "merchantable."

1. THE BUYER MUST ESTABLISH THAT THE SELLER WAS A "MERCHANT." [§36.21] Not surprisingly, only **merchant** sellers are subject to liability for breach of the implied warranty of **merchantability**. Under UCC §2-104(1), a "merchant" is someone who deals in goods of the kind, or otherwise holds himself out as having skill or knowledge peculiar to the practices or goods involved in the transaction by virtue of his or her occupation. Thus, to be liable for a breach of the merchantability warranty, the seller must be more than just an occasional seller. Rather, the seller must be someone who, by virtue of his or her occupation, regularly deals in goods of the kind involved in the sale.

2. THE BUYER MUST ESTABLISH THAT THE GOODS WERE NOT "MERCHANTABLE". [§36.22] After proving that the seller is a merchant, the next element a buyer must establish to prove a breach of the implied warranty of merchantability is that the goods sold were not "merchantable." In UCC §2-314(2), the Code gives six examples of what "merchantable" means, the most common of which are:

UCC §2-314(2)(a) — goods are merchantable if they "**pass without objection in the trade**;"

UCC §2-314(2)(b) — fungible goods are merchantable if they "**are of fair average quality**"; and

UCC §2-314(2)(c) — goods are merchantable if they are "**fit for the ordinary purposes for which such goods are used**."

The idea behind these definitions, and the rationale behind the implied merchantability doctrine, is that the common law doctrine of **caveat emptor**, i.e., "buyer beware," no longer prevails, at least where the seller is a merchant. Because this is an **implied** warranty, it attaches to goods sold by a merchant seller automatically upon the sale. Hence, even if a merchant seller says absolutely nothing about the qualities of his or her product, §2-314 provides that a buyer in contemporary society has a right to expect that goods sold by a merchant are of "fair average quality," and "are fit for the ordinary purposes for which such goods are used." That is, when a party walks into a merchant's retail store, a buyer has an enforceable right to expect the merchant's goods will be usable and average versions of what they are supposed to be.

3. DISCLAIMER OF IMPLIED WARRANTY OF MERCHANTABILITY. [§36.23] There are two ways to disclaim the implied warranty of merchantability:

(1) If the seller wishes to disclaim only the implied warranty of merchantability, he or she may effectively do so *either in writing or orally*, but such disclaimer **must mention** the word "**merchantability**" to be effective. If this disclaimer is in writing, its provisions must be *conspicuous* [UCC §2-316(2)]; and

(2) If the seller wishes to disclaim **all** implied warranties, including the implied warranty of merchantability, he or she may do so by using expressions like "Goods are sold '*as is*,' or '*with all faults*,'" or any other language that makes it plain that no implied warranty is contemplated in the transaction [UCC §2-316(3)(a)]. Note that while on its face §2-316(3)(a) does not require the "as is," "with all faults," or like language to be conspicuous, courts have read such a requirement into the provision as a matter of fairness. Furthermore, as a matter of conscionability, many jurisdictions also forbid a merchant seller to sell new goods on an "as is" basis. Rather, they hold that such broad disclaimers of all implied warranties are only enforceable in connection with the sale of used goods.

D. THE IMPLIED WARRANTY OF FITNESS FOR A PARTICULAR PURPOSE. [§36.3]
To establish that the implied warranty of fitness for a particular purpose under UCC §2-315 has been made, a buyer must prove that: (1) the buyer had an unusual or particular purpose in mind for the goods; (2) the seller had reason to know of this particular purpose (usually because the buyer has told the seller of this purpose); (3) the seller has reason to know that the buyer is relying on the seller's skill or judgment to select or furnish goods that will meet the buyer's needs; and (4) the buyer in fact relied on the seller's skill or judgment in selecting suitable goods.

1. EXAMPLE. [§36.31]
Jason goes into a sporting goods store and explains to Margaret, the owner of the store, that he has just been invited along on a mountain climbing expedition and needs to purchase shoes that are suitable for repelling down sides of mountains and thick enough to give some comfort when walking along jagged peaks. The owner of the shoe store gives him a pair of ordinary tennis shoes, which cause him injury while on the mountain climbing expedition. Jason has a valid implied warranty of fitness for a particular purpose claim against the store, for he: (1) had a need for goods to perform a particular purpose; (2) informed the seller of his needs so that the seller had reason to know of it; (3) gave the owner reason to know he was relying on her skill and judgment in selecting the shoes; and (4) did in fact rely on the store owner's skill and judgment in selecting the goods.

2. EXAMPLE. [§36.32]
Same as above, but this time Jason simply walks into a store and selects the sturdiest looking and most expensive pair of shoes in the "outdoor hiking" section of the store, and figures they will satisfy his needs. No implied warranty of fitness for a particular purpose has taken place.

3. DISCLAIMING THE IMPLIED WARRANTY OF FITNESS FOR A PARTICULAR PURPOSE. [§36.33]
There are two ways to disclaim the implied warranty of fitness for a particular purpose:

(1) If the seller wants to disclaim only the implied warranty of fitness for a particular purpose, he or she **must do so in writing** to be effective. While there is no requirement that the phrase "fitness for a particular purpose" be used in the disclaimer, the disclaimer itself must be conspicuous and make plain that the implied warranty of fitness is being excluded from the transaction [UCC §2-316(2)].

(2) If the seller wants to exclude all implied warranties, including the implied warranty of fitness for a particular purpose, the rules are the same as those discussed above in the merchantability context (see §36.23).

E. DOCTRINES APPLICABLE TO ALL WARRANTY CLAIMS. [§36.4] There are three issues that affect all types of breach of warranty claims:

(1) The extent to which a buyer must notify the seller of the breach of warranty before he or she brings suit (see §36.41);

(2) Whether other sellers in the vertical distribution chain other than the retailer, i.e., the manufacturer and any wholesaler/distributors can be sued successfully for breach of warranty (see §36.42); and

(3) Whether persons other than the buyer are entitled to recover for breach of warranty (see §36.43).

Each is discussed below.

1. THE NOTICE REQUIREMENT UNDER UCC §2-607(3). [§36.41] UCC §2-607(3) provides that a buyer must notify the seller of the breach of warranty within a reasonable time after the breach was either discovered or should have been discovered. If no such notice is provided, the buyer is "barred from any remedy" for breach.

2. WHO IS A PROPER DEFENDANT: VERTICAL PRIVITY. [§36.42] Privity in contract law means that the parties had direct contractual dealings. For example, if Sally buys a Magnavox television from Sears, she is in privity with Sears, but not with the Magnavox, for she had no direct dealings with the "remote" manufacturer.

At early common law, privity was a requirement in breach actions because, understandably, it was thought improper to allow one party to sue another for breach of contract when there was, in fact, no contract between them. Hence, in the above hypothetical, Sally would have no breach rights against Magnavox using strict privity rules, for no offer, acceptance, or consideration passed between her and Magnavox, and thus there is nothing on which she could base a suit for breach.

Modern warranty law, however, has almost completely eliminated the vertical privity requirement in warranty cases. It is thought that since everyone in the vertical distribution chain of the goods benefits from the sale of the goods to the consumer, everyone in that chain should also share liability for goods that do not perform as are warranted. Moreover, in express warranty claims, it is often the remote manufacturer who makes the representations about the qualities of the goods, e.g., in an advertising campaign, or on the package of the good itself. Further, in a merchantability claim, it is again the remote manufacturer who is almost surely responsible for the good not being "merchantable" due to a defect in its manufacture or design. Moreover, to deny liability for a remote manufacturer would mean the injured buyer could not recover for injuries caused by the manufacturer when the retailer is either out of business or insolvent. Hence, for all these reasons privity is no longer required, and today a proper plaintiff is entitled to bring suit against anyone in the vertical distribution chain against whom the elements of a warranty can be established.

Note that some courts and commentators suggest that privity still exists when a party seeks to collect consequential damages from a remote seller for breach of the implied warranty of merchantability. Such a statement is not technically correct. The reason consequential damages are usually not awarded against remote manufacturers is that it is rare the plaintiff can establish the requisite foreseeability on the part of the remote manufacturer to recover for such loss. That is, recall that before a non-breaching party is entitled to recover for consequential loss, he or she will have to establish that the breacher knew that such otherwise unforeseeable type of loss was, in fact, sufficiently foreseeable to this particular defendant (see §§31.42 and 33.313). It is rare that a remote manufacturer would ever be in a position to have some reason to know that an otherwise unforeseeable kind of damage would follow from the breach of a warranty regarding a good it has produced. That is, while Sally may tell Sears that she is intending to use the television as part of a pay per view network in her sports bar, and thus if it does not operate she will lose profits, it is unlikely that Magnavox will ever know of that arrangement. Hence, while it is true that consequential damages are rarely awarded against a remote manufacturer in merchantability cases, this is not because of a privity requirement, but because the buyer is usually unable to prove the elements necessary to recover such damages.

3. **WHO IS ENTITLED TO SUE: HORIZONTAL PRIVITY. [§36.43]** The previous section discussed the privity requirement in the vertical distribution chain. There is another type of privity, i.e., "horizontal" privity, that is an issue in breach of warranty cases. The horizontal privity issue involves what kinds of third parties can recover in breach of warranty when their injuries are due to a breach of a warranty promise given another. That is, no one disputes that a buyer can sue in warranty for his or her injures. However, suppose the by-stander is injured because a good was improperly manufactured and thus unmerchantable. The question is whether the by-stander can recover for breach of the warranty promises given the **buyer**, not the by-stander.

There is universal agreement that warranty protections are not limited only to the buyer. There is disagreement, however, as to how far those protections should extend. There are currently four views as to what kinds of third parties should be entitled to bring actions for breaches of a warranty not made to them:

(1) UCC §2-318 — **Alternative A,** provides that the only third parties who should be able to recover in warranty are **members of the buyer's household and guests in the household.** By-standers, people outside the home, etc., should not be able to recover under this view.

(2) UCC §2-318 — **Alternative B,** provides that the range of third parties entitled to sue for injuries caused by a breach of warranty include **"any natural person who may reasonably be expected to use, consume, or be affected by the goods."** However, these individuals are only entitled to recover for *personal injury* under this test.

(3) UCC §2-318 — **Alternative C,** is much like UCC §2-318 Alternative B, except that **a third party reasonably expected to use, consume, or be affected by the good** may recover *for both economic as well as personal injuries.*

(4) Some jurisdictions have intentionally refused to adopt any of the three alternatives listed in §2-318 discussed above. Instead, their rules regarding when third parties are entitled to sue for breach of warranty are the same as those used to govern when third parties in that jurisdiction can sue in tort for negligence or strict products liability.

F. **WARRANTY DEFENSES. [§36.5]** While the rule varies somewhat among jurisdictions, it is fairly well agreed that there are two complete defenses to a breach of warranty claim: (1) Assumption of the Risk; and (2) Unforeseeable Misuse of the Product.

1. **ASSUMPTION OF THE RISK. [§36.51]** In those jurisdictions where assumption of the risk remains a valid defense, i.e., where it has not been eliminated by comparative negligence, it provides a complete defense to a breach of warranty claim. Hence if a seller can prove that the plaintiff knowledgeably and voluntarily undertook a known risk in using the product as he or she did, understanding the magnitude of the risk at the time it was taken, then the seller has a complete defense to the warranty suit.

   a. **Comparative Negligence. [§36.511]** In those jurisdictions which have eliminated assumption of the risk through comparative negligence, there is a split in the courts as to whether comparative fault principles will be allowed to offset a warranty recovery.

2. **UNFORESEEABLE MISUSE OF THE PRODUCT. [§36.52]** If a seller can establish that a buyer was using a product in an unforeseeable manner, and that it was *such use* that caused his or her injury rather than a defect in the goods or promised attribute about the goods, once again a seller has a complete defense to a breach of warranty claim.

G. **DAMAGES FOR BREACH OF WARRANTY. [§36.6]** Damages recoverable for breach of warranty are governed by UCC §2-714 and are discussed in §33.3 et seq.

XV. PRACTICE MULTIPLE CHOICE QUESTIONS AND ANSWERS

SUBJECT MATTER TABLE OF MULTIPLE CHOICE QUESTIONS

Questions 1 - 3 are based on the following fact situation:

Priscilla was a plumbing contractor. Allan and Brenda each owned an apartment building. Allan explained to Priscilla the plumbing work that was needed for his building. Brenda also explained to Priscilla the plumbing work that was needed for her building.

On January 15, Priscilla mailed offers to Allan and Brenda. Priscilla offered to do the work on Allan's building for $2,000 and offered to do the work on Brenda's building for $4,000. In each case, Priscilla's offer stated that it would be open until January 30.

On the morning of January 20, Allan mailed a properly addressed letter to Priscilla stating, "We've got a deal." That afternoon, Allan spoke to Xerxes, another plumber, who said he would do the job for $1,500. Allan immediately sent a letter by express mail to Priscilla, stating, "Please disregard my other letter. I am going to have someone else do the plumbing work."

On January 21, Priscilla received the letter Allan sent by express mail. Priscilla received Allan's other letter on January 22. Priscilla demanded that Allan permit her to do the work for $2,000, but Allan refused.

On January 24, Brenda mailed a letter to Priscilla, stating, "$4,000 is too much. I will agree to pay you $3,000 if you will agree to do the job." On January 25, Brenda spoke to Xerxes, who said he would not do the job for less than $5,000. That afternoon, Brenda sent a letter by express mail to Priscilla, stating, "Disregard my letter of 1/24. I accept your offer." Priscilla received both of Brenda's letters on January 27. Brenda thereafter spoke to Yolanda, another plumber; Yolanda said she would do the plumbing work on Brenda's building for $3,500. Brenda immediately telephoned Priscilla and said (before Priscilla could say a word), "This is Brenda. The deal is off." Priscilla then demanded that Brenda permit her (Priscilla) to do the work for $4,000. Brenda refused.

1. If Priscilla sues Allan for breach of contract, Priscilla will:

(A) **Lose**, because Priscilla received the letter Allan sent by express mail before Priscilla received Allan's first letter (the one not sent by express mail).

(B) **Lose**, because the offer in Allan's first letter (the one not sent by express mail) could be retracted up until the time Priscilla received it.

(C) **Win**, because the letter Allan sent by express mail did not have legal effect until Priscilla received it.

(D) **Win**, because the offer in Allan's first letter (the one not sent by express mail) had legal effect when it was sent, even though it was not received first.

2. Assume Brenda's first letter (the one not sent by express mail) was received on the morning of January 26, and Brenda's letter sent by express mail was received on the afternoon of January 26. If Priscilla sues Brenda for breach of contract, Priscilla will:

(A) **Lose**, because Priscilla received Brenda's first letter before Priscilla received the letter Brenda sent by express mail.

(B) **Lose**, because Brenda's first letter had legal effect when it was sent.

(C) **Win**, because Brenda's first letter did not have legal effect until Priscilla received it.

(D) **Win**, because the letter Brenda sent by express mail had legal effect when it was sent, even though it was not received first.

3. Assume the letter Brenda sent by express mail was received on the morning of January 26, and Brenda's first letter (the one not sent by express mail) was received on the afternoon of January 26. If Priscilla sues Brenda for breach of contract, Priscilla will:

(A) **Lose**, because the letter Brenda sent by express mail did not have legal effect when it was sent.

(B) **Lose**, because Brenda's first letter had legal effect when it was sent, even though it was not received first.

(C) **Win**, because Priscilla received the letter Brenda sent by express mail before Priscilla received Brenda's first letter.

(D) **Win**, because the letter Brenda sent by express mail had legal effect when it was sent.

Questions 4 - 6 are based on the following fact situation:

Professor Jones was out for a walk with his family. He heard a sudden squeal of brakes and was horrified to see that his neighbor Quigley had been run over by an automobile driven by Jones's nephew Newton. Quigley was lying in the street, unconscious. Dr. Fiscus, who happened to be driving by, stopped, gave aid to Quigley, and accompanied Quigley to the hospital. Despite Dr. Fiscus's prompt and expert medical attention, Quigley never regained consciousness; Quigley died a week later. Jones was noticeably bothered by these events; to cheer him up, three of his students washed and waxed his automobile early one morning before Jones awoke. (Jones had parked the auto on the street.) The next day, out of gratitude, Jones promised the students that he would pay each of them $10. (The reasonable value of the wash and wax job was $45.) Although Jones was not legally responsible for Newton's negligence in driving over Quigley, Jones told others he felt responsible since Newton was coming to see him. For that reason, Jones promised Quigley's widow that he would pay her $10,000.

4. Who, if anyone, is obligated to pay Dr. Fiscus for his services?

(A) Jones.

(B) Quigley's estate.

(C) Both Quigley's estate and Jones.

(D) Neither Quigley's estate nor Jones.

5. Under the Restatement 2d of Contracts, Jones would:

(A) Be obligated to pay $10 to each of the students.

(B) Be obligated to pay $45 to each of the students.

(C) Not be obligated to pay anything to the students because, in washing and waxing his car without asking him first, the students deprived him of the opportunity of declining the benefit.

(D) Not be obligated to pay anything to the students because the students washed and waxed his car as a gift to him.

6. Under the Restatement 2d of Contracts, Jones would:

(A) Not be obligated to pay $10,000 to Quigley's widow.

(B) Be obligated to pay $10,000 to Quigley's widow, assuming her loss due to the death of her husband is at least equal to the $10,000 Quigley promised to pay her.

(C) Be obligated to pay $10,000 to Quigley's widow under the doctrine of promissory estoppel, assuming the jurisdiction accepts that doctrine.

(D) Be obligated to pay $10,000 to Quigley's widow under the doctrine of consideration, assuming Jones obtained some peace of mind as a result of making the promise.

Questions 7 - 10 are based on the following fact situation:

Rita operated a retail computer store in the State of Washegon. Diane operated a wholesale distribution business (also in Washegon) which specialized in computers and computer monitors, such as the Sony XYZ monitor. Rita telephoned Diane on February 1 and said, "I need a Sony XYZ monitor. Can you get me one?" Diane replied, "Sure, but it will take a month . . ." At that point Rita interrupted Diane to say "I have to go now; an important customer just walked in. You will deliver the monitor in a month for sure?" Diane responded "Yes," and Rita ended the conversation by saying, "I'll be waiting for it. Good-bye."

The next day Diane sent Rita a brief note (with Diane's initials at the bottom) that said, "Per agreement with Rita: one Sony XYZ monitor to be delivered on March 1." Rita received Diane's note on February 4. Rita later sent Diane a letter that stated, "I never agreed to buy a monitor from you. We didn't even agree on a price."

Diane sued Rita; in Diane's complaint all of the foregoing facts were alleged.

Consider the following possible facts:

I. Rita sent her letter to Diane on February 16.

II. The wholesale price for the Sony XYZ monitor was $750.

III. The wholesale price for the Sony XYZ monitor was $400.

7. Which of those possible facts would be helpful to Diane in countering Rita's statute of frauds argument?

(A) I only.

(B) II only.

(C) I and III.

(D) III.

8. Was a contract formed?

(A) No, because Rita never promised to pay for the monitor.

(B) No, because Diane and Rita did not manifest mutual assent to the sale of the monitor.

(C) No, because Diane and Rita did not agree on a specific price.

(D)   Yes, because the contract is definite enough to enforce.

9.   Assume Diane's complaint also alleges (1) that XYZ monitors typically sold at wholesale for $1,500 and (2) that Rita sent her letter to Diane on February 4, the same day Rita received Diane's note. In *Diane v. Rita*, should the court grant Rita's motion to dismiss (the equivalent of a demurrer)?

(A)   No, because Diane should have an opportunity to take Rita's deposition.

(B)   No, because the complaint does not show that the contract is within the statute of frauds.

(C)   Yes, because the complaint shows the contract is within the statute of frauds.

(D)   Yes, because Rita objected to the contents of Diane's note.

10.   Assume that a contract was formed, that Rita did not send any letter to Diane, that Diane failed to deliver the XYZ monitor, that the monitor's reasonable wholesale value was $1,500, that Rita sued Diane, instead of Diane suing Rita, and that Diane has asserted the statute of frauds defense. Consider the following statements:

I.   Rita is the "party to be charged" for purposes of the statute of frauds.

II.   The contract is enforceable because there is an adequate memorandum signed by "the party to be charged."

III.   The contract is enforceable because there is a confirming memorandum that satisfies the statute of frauds as against the recipient of the memorandum.

Which of those statements are true?

(A)   I only.

(B)   I and III.

(C)   II only.

(D)   III only.

Questions 11 and 12 are based on the following fact situation:

Sally orally contracted to sell her home (consisting of a two story house and the surrounding quarter acre of land in the State of Arivada) to Bert. Sally owned no other real

property. Their written agreement provided that "The price for the home is $100,000, which Bert agrees to pay." The written agreement described the home as "Sally's home, 4029 Smithson Street," but said nothing about the $45,000 mortgage that was on the home. During oral negotiations before the written agreement was signed, Sally and Bert had agreed that Bert could pay Sally $55,000 cash (in the form of a cashier's check) and assume the $45,000 mortgage; as they signed the written agreement they remarked to each other that the $55,000 cashier's check Bert was supposed to obtain for Sally would be the largest check either of them had ever seen. (It was much easier for Bert to come up with $55,000 cash rather than $100,000 cash, so Bert preferred to pay $55,000 cash and assume the mortgage rather than paying $100,000 cash. Of course, if the deal were for payment of $100,000 cash, Sally would have to use $45,000 of the cash to pay off the mortgage, so she could deliver title to her home to Bert unencumbered by the mortgage. Sally would have preferred an all cash deal so she could pay off the mortgage. If Bert assumes the mortgage, Sally will still be liable on the mortgage debt if Bert does not make the payments, so she is safer if the mortgage debt is paid off.)

11.   Is Bert's promise to make the mortgage payments unenforceable under the suretyship section of the statute of frauds? Consider the following responses to that question:

I.   Yes, because there is no writing signed by Bert that evidences the promise.

II.   Yes, because there is no writing signed by both parties that evidences the promise.

III.   No, because the promise was made to Sally.

IV.   No, because Bert is not a surety for Sally.

Which of those responses is correct?

(A)   I only.

(B)   II only.

(C)   III and IV.

(D)   IV only.

12.   If Bert refuses to purchase Sally's home, and Sally then sues Bert, alleging that he was obligated to pay the $100,000 price for the home by giving her a $55,000 cashier's check and assuming the $45,000 mortgage, Bert's best argument in defense will be:

(A)   The alleged agreement is unenforceable because the description of the home in the written agreement does not include a city or state.

(B)   The alleged promise to pay part of the price by assuming the mortgage is an essential term of the alleged agreement.

(C)   The alleged agreement for him to assume the mortgage cannot be proved because of the parol evidence rule.

(D)   The alleged agreement is too indefinite to enforce.

Questions 13 - 16 are based on the following fact situation:

Morton Manufacturing contracted in writing to sell 250 "400 day, key-wound anniversary clocks" to Store for $12,500. Delivery was due June 1. The written agreement provided that "Morton Manufacturing must provide one sample clock for Store to inspect on or before May 1." (That was so Store could decide how it wanted to advertise and display the clocks.) That is, Morton did not have to "deliver" the clocks then, but it did have to allow Store to photograph and examine a model by that date.

On April 1, Morton wrote Store to say that Morton was having difficulty obtaining parts to make all 250 of the clocks and to ask if the contract could be reduced to 200 clocks for $10,000. Store replied by phone on April 5 that the change was acceptable. The next day Store telephoned Morton to ask that the price for the 200 clocks be decreased to $9,000; the Store representative truthfully pointed out that other retail stores had recently reduced their prices on similar clocks and that Store therefore could not sell the clocks for as much as they had expected. The authorized Morton representative agreed on the phone to the price reduction.

On May 1, Morton did not provide the sample clock because the Morton employee responsible for providing it thought it was supposed to be provided on May 2. When the Morton employee showed up at Store's offices on May 2, he was unceremoniously told to get out and the President of Store told the Morton employee to pass on the word to Morton's management that, "as result of this late and sloppy practice" Store would not buy **any** of the clocks.

On May 5, after cooling off a bit, Store's President wrote to Morton and reaffirmed Store's commitment to purchase "250 clocks for $12,500, as specified in our contract." When the General Manager of Morton got the letter, she first checked to see if it was still possible for Morton to purchase the parts for 250 clocks (instead

of 200) and to manufacture and deliver them on time. She was told that Morton could make the 250 clocks, but that it would need to start immediately making the additional 50 units to have them finished by June 1. After debating the issue, she finally concluded that Morton was only obligated to deliver 200 clocks. Accordingly, she instructed her manufacturing facility not to make the additional clocks, and only tendered 200 on June 1. Store rejected the delivery of 200 clocks, insisting on delivery of all 250.

All of these events took place in State which allows neither admissions nor reliance to satisfy the statute of frauds.

13.   The court will most likely construe the requirement of delivery of a sample clock on May 1 as:

(A)   A promise.

(B)   An express condition.

(C)   A promise and an express condition.

(D)   Neither a promise nor an express condition.

14.   The delay in delivery of the sample clock will probably:

(A)   Prevent Morton from enforcing the contract against Store.

(B)   Entitle Store to recover any damages caused by the delay.

(C)   Prevent Morton from enforcing the contract against Store and entitle Store to recover any damages caused by the delay.

(D)   Neither prevent Morton from enforcing the contract against Store nor entitle Store to recover any damages resulting from the delay.

15.   As of May 3, what is the best characterization of the parties?

(A)   Morton was entitled to declare the contract canceled and cease its performance.

(B)   Both Morton and Store were entitled to declare the contract canceled and cease their performance.

(C)   Store was entitled to declare the contract canceled and cease its performance.

(D)   Neither Morton nor Store were entitled to declare the contract canceled and cease their performance.

16. As of June 1, what is the best characterization of the parties?

(A) Morton has materially breached by tendering only 200 clocks.

(B) Morton has immaterially breached by tendering 200 clocks.

(C) Store has materially breached by refusing to accept and pay for 200 clocks.

(D) Store has immaterially breached by refusing to accept and pay for 200 clocks.

Question 17

On April 1, Sy, the owner of a very well known art gallery, had the following telephone conversation with Bob, one of his most valued customers:

S: Bob, I just procured "The Blue City" by Chagall. I know it would go nicely with your collection and I will let you have it for $25,000.

B: I'm tempted, but I couldn't begin thinking about making such a purchase until my CD matures at the end of July.

S: For you, my friend, I will hold my offer open until August 10.

The best description of Bob's right to purchase the Chagall is:

(A) Bob has an irrevocable right to purchase the Chagall for $25,000 until August 10.

(B) Bob has a power to purchase the Chagall for $25,000 until June 30, but that power is revocable by Sy.

(C) Bob has an irrevocable right to purchase the Chagall for $25,000 until June 30.

(D) Bob has only a power to purchase the Chagall for $25,000 until August 10, and that power is revocable by Sy.

Questions 18 and 19 are based on the following fact situation:

Betty Buyer owned Bower Records, a retail record store in Sacramento. On behalf of Bower, Betty ordered 150 copies of the latest 45 r.p.m. hit from Sorrygram Records, Luciano Pavatotti's "Boys Just Want To Have Fun," at the

price listed in Sorrygram's catalogue, $1/record. A few days later, Bower received a shipment from Sorrygram which also contained the following cover letter:

SORRYGRAM RECORDS, INC.
Los Angeles, California
Ms. Betty Buyer
Bower Records
Sacramento, Calif.

Dear Betty:

Due to unprecedented demand, we are presently sold out of the 45 r.p.m. "Boys Just Want To Have Fun," and thus we can neither accept nor fill your latest order. However, because you are such a valued customer, we have sent instead 150 copies of Pavarotti's new album, "Luciano Rides the New Wave," which has "Boys Just Want To Have Fun" on the front side. As you know, we usually charge retailers $2.50 for our albums, but because of the inconvenience we have already caused you, we will only charge you our special accommodation price of $1.25/album and consider the matter closed.

Sincerely,
/s/Sam Seller
Sorrygram Records

As indicated in the letter, Sorrygram shipped 150 albums to Bower instead of the requested 45 r.p.m. records.

Variation One

18. The best description of the legal relationship between Bower and Sorrygram is:

(A) They have a contract for 150 "Boys Just Want To Have Fun" 45 r.p.m. records at $1/record, which has been breached by Sorrygram.

(B) They have no contract.

(C) If Sorrygram had reasonable grounds to believe that shipment of the albums instead of the 45 r.p.m. records would be acceptable by Bower with the indicated money allowance, they have a contract for 150 "Pavarotti Rides the New Wave" albums at $1.25/album.

(D) They have a contract for 150 "Boys Just Want To Have Fun" 45 r.p.m. records at $1/record, but Betty has the right to accept the albums as a substituted performance for the 45 r.p.m. contract.

Variation Two

Betty considered keeping the albums, but in good faith determined that her tiny store did not have sufficient shelf space at the time to display them. Accordingly, she called Seller and told him she did not want the shipment. The next day, Betty received the following Mailgram:

Mrs. Betty Buyer
Bower Records
Sacramento, Calif.

Dear Betty:

Sorry to hear you won't be able to take the albums. Please send them back to us within the next week or so, and we will credit any shipping cots you incur to your next order from us.

/s/ Sam Seller

19.   The best description of Bower Records's duties with respect to the return of the albums is:

(A)   So long as Bower stores the albums with reasonable care, Bower is under no duty to send the albums back to Sorrygram and can charge Sorrygram a fee for storing the records until Sorrygram arranges to pick up the records.

(B)   So long as Bower stores the albums with reasonable care, Bower is under no duty to send the albums back to Sorrygram, but cannot charge Sorrygram a fee for storing the albums.

(C)   Bower is under a duty to send the albums back to Sorrygram, but may do so freight collect.

(D)   Bower is under a duty to send the albums back to Sorrygram, but cannot do so freight collect. Rather, Bower is bound by the terms of Seller's letter and must take the shipping costs as a credit against Sorrygram's next shipment.

Questions 20 - 22 are based on the following fact situation:

On June 1, Owner orally offered to pay Andy $1,000 if Andy would repair the roof at Owner's beach cottage. Andy requested time to think it over. Owner told Andy that he would give Andy a couple of days to think about it, but that he had to know Andy's decision no later than June 3.

On June 3, Owner, impatient at waiting for word from Andy, offered Brenda $1,000 if Brenda would promise

to repair the roof at the cottage. Brenda stated that she would take her equipment to the cottage tomorrow and, if the job looked worth it, she would start right in. Brenda also stated that if it appeared not to be worth it, she would contact Owner and give an estimate of her price. Owner consented to such an arrangement.

When Brenda arrived at the cottage on June 4, she saw Andy working on the roof. Andy truthfully explained to her that he decided to accept the job, and that he had begun working on the project on the afternoon of June 3, and that he had dispatched a letter to Owner that at about 9:30 p.m. the previous night stating he would undertake the work.

20.   If Owner's offer to Andy is considered an offer looking towards an unilateral contract, which of the following is true?

(A)   Andy had to notify Owner of his acceptance before he started work on the roof, or else his acceptance was ineffective.

(B)   Andy's dispatch of the letter on June 3, properly addressed to Owner, was a valid acceptance of Owner's offer.

(C)   Andy may cease, without breach, if he has started to perform; but Owner must hold his offer open for a reasonable period of time.

(D)   Andy may not withdraw without breach once he has started to perform because by starting to work on the roof, Andy has made an implied promise to finish the work.

21.   If Owner's offer to Andy is considered an offer looking towards a bilateral contract, which of the following is true?

(A)   A contract was formed when Andy commenced work on the roof.

(B)   A contract was formed when Andy dispatched the letter of acceptance, properly addressed, on June 3.

(C)   A contract would be formed when Andy's letter is received by the Owner.

(D)   They have no contract.

22.   If Owner's offer to Brenda is considered an offer looking towards a bilateral contract, which of the following is true?

(A)   A contract would be formed when Brenda communicated her promise of acceptance to Owner.

(B) Brenda could no longer effectively accept the offer because the offer was effectively revoked when Brenda saw Andy repairing the cottage and heard of Andy's acceptance.

(C) Brenda can no longer validly accept the offer because, as a matter of law, there cannot be a valid contract between Brenda and Owner if there is a prior valid contract for repair of the same cottage roof between Owner and Andy.

(D) The consideration for Owner's promise to pay Brenda $1,000 would be Brenda's actual performance of the roof repair in a satisfactory manner.

Questions 23 - 25 are based on the following fact situation:

Writer agreed to write a book on a then-topical subject for Publisher within twelve months. Writer was to receive $1 per page, but if he completed the book in six months, he would receive a bonus of an additional $1 per page. However, if Writer drank alcoholic beverages while under the contract, Writer would get only 50 cents per page, regardless of when the book was completed, but assuming it was completed. After four months, Writer telephoned Publisher and demanded $3 per page if he should meet the six month deadline. When asked why, the writer stated that he just felt he was worth it. Publisher agreed to such change and Writer continued working as before.

23. If Writer meets the six month deadline:

(A) Publisher owes Writer $3 per page.

(B) Publisher owes Writer $2 per page.

(C) A new modified contract has been formed for $3 per page, the old contract having been partially rescinded by mutual agreement.

(D) Writer has relied upon the new promise of Publisher by meeting the deadline and Publisher is, therefore, estopped from revoking it.

24. Writer does not meet the twelve month deadline and does not expect to finish in less than an additional twelve months. Which of the following best describes the consequence of this fact?

(A) Publisher must accept the book when it is completed, but is entitled to damages resulting from the breach.

(B) Publisher may waive the deadline, in which event Publisher has waived his right to damages resulting from the breach.

(C) Writer is excused from meeting the deadline if the reason he is late in producing the material is unexpected difficulty in learning how to operate his new word processor.

(D) Publisher may agree to an extension, receive the book, and still hold the Writer liable in breach of contract.

25. If Writer completed the book in six months, but drinks during the contract period, which of the following best describes the situation?

(A) Writer is entitled to receive only 50 cents per page.

(B) Writer is entitled to receive $2 per page if Publisher knew of his drinking while it was going on, but said nothing at the time.

(C) Writer is entitled to recover $2 per page if he could show that he only drank after Publisher had told him that the "no drinking" provision was designed solely to insure that Writer finished the book within a year and that, otherwise, it did not matter to Publisher whether or not Writer drank.

(D) Publisher may not enforce the no drinking condition as such a clause violates public policy.

Questions 26 - 28 are based on the following fact situation:

Hotel advertised in the paper that it would rent rooms to delegates to the Republican Convention for $20 a night, a drastically reduced rate, for the seven day period the convention is in progress. Delegate read such ad and wrote for a room for seven days, mentioning the ad. As specified in the ad, Delegate enclosed a non-refundable $50 deposit. Hotel answered that a room was reserved for the time requested but stating no purpose for which room was reserved.

26. If the Hotel is destroyed by fire just before the day of the convention:

(A) Delegate, assuming she comes to the convention, is entitled to sue the Hotel for the price difference between their rate and the rate she is forced to pay at another hotel, regardless of who or what is responsible for the fire.

(B) Hotel will escape liability to Delegate because performance is impossible, regardless of who or what is responsible for the fire.

(C) Delegate is entitled to damages from Hotel if Hotel's own carelessness caused the fire.

(D) The risk of the Hotel burning is upon Hotel, not Delegate, because Hotel can safeguard itself by insurance and is in control of the premises.

27. If Delegate becomes very ill the day before and cannot attend the convention, she is entitled to:

(A) Recover the $50 deposit from Hotel, subject to an offset for any loss suffered by Hotel due to its inability to rent the room under a frustration of purpose/restitution theory.

(B) Recover the $50 deposit from Hotel with no offset for any loss suffered by Hotel in failing to rent the room under a frustration of purpose/restitution theory.

(C) Recover nothing from Hotel, because Delegate can establish the elements of neither impossibility nor frustration of purpose.

(D) Recover the $50 deposit from Hotel, subject to a deduction for any loss suffered by Hotel due to its inability to rent the room, under temporary impossibility/restitution theory.

28. If the Republican Convention is moved suddenly to another city, which is the most accurate description?

(A) Delegate is entitled to cancel and recover the $50 deposit under an impossibility/restitution theory.

(B) Delegate will still be liable for the week's room rate, because the parol evidence rule will not permit Delegate to introduce the special propose of the contract with the Hotel.

(C) Delegate cannot cancel or recover her deposit because Hotel did not expressly restrict use of the room to any particular purpose.

(D) Delegate is entitled to cancel and recover the $50 from the Hotel under a frustration of purpose/restitution theory.

Questions 29 - 31 are based on the following fact situation:

Dealer, a retailer of automobiles, advertised that it will provide a "free" one-year insurance policy protecting the purchaser of one of its cars from loss due to theft. Dealer thereafter contracts with Insurance Company for a "blanket coverage policy" wherein Insurance Company promised to provide coverage on any car sold by Dealer, so long as Dealer paid the monthly premium.

Later, a car is sold by Dealer to Buyer, who receives a written statement from both Dealer and Insurance Company explaining one-year "free" coverage. Buyer did not procure insurance on her car.

29. In the contract between Dealer and Insurance Company, what is the best categorization of Buyer under the Restatement 2d:

(A) A donee-like intended beneficiary.

(B) A creditor-like intended beneficiary.

(C) An incidental beneficiary.

(D) Not a third party beneficiary at all because Buyer's identity was unknown at the time of contract formation.

30. If Buyer's car is stolen within the year, and both Dealer and Insurance Company refuse to pay Buyer for her loss, which is the most accurate statement?

(A) Buyer is only entitled to recover from Insurance Company for breach of the Dealer/Insurance Co. contract.

(B) Buyer is only entitled to recover from Dealer for breach of the Dealer/Insurance Co. contract.

(C) Buyer is entitled to recover from either Dealer or Insurance Company for breach of the Dealer/Insurance Co. contract.

(D) Only Dealer can bring suit against the Insurance Company for breach of the Dealer/Insurance Co. contract.

31. Dealer cancels the insurance policy six months after Buyer purchases the car, and stops paying the premiums, all without telling Buyer. The car is stolen one month later, and once again, neither Dealer nor Insurance Company pays Buyer for her car. Which of the following best describes Buyer's rights?

I. Buyer may sue Dealer for breach of the Dealer/Insurance Co. contract.

II. Buyer may sue Insurance Co. for breach of the Dealer/Insurance Co. contract.

III. Buyer may sue Dealer for breach of warranty that follows a third party beneficiary contract.

(A) I only.

(B) II only.

(C)   I and II.

(D)   I, II, and III.

Questions 32 - 35 are based on the following fact situation:

Alexandra has a bilateral contract with Owen to paint Owen's house this year for $500. Alexandra assigns for value the contract to Roger, a competent painter. Alexandra thereafter informs Owen that she has "assigned the contract" to Roger because she (Alexandra) is moving out of the state and, therefore, must divest herself of rights and obligations under the painting contract.

32.   Which is the most accurate statement?

(A)   Owen must accept if Roger tenders performance, but Owen can hold either Alexandra or Roger liable for any defects in Roger's performance.

(B)   Owen is entitled to refuse to accept the tender of performance by Roger, because Alexandra could not have assigned her rights under this contract.

(C)   Owen is entitled to refuse to accept the tender of performance by Roger because there can be no valid delegation of a personal service contract.

(D)   If Owen allows Roger to perform, and Roger performs acceptably well, such performance terminates Alexandra's duty.

33.   Alexandra and Owen, after the assignment but before performance, agree that the house should not be painted by Roger because they just found out Roger is an anarchist. Which of the following best describes Roger's rights?

(A)   Roger's rights and duties are extinguished.

(B)   Roger may sue either Alexandra or Owen, or both, if Owen does not permit him to paint the house due to the subsequent "anarchist" agreement by Alexandra and Owen.

(C)   Roger may sue only Owen if Owen does not permit him to paint the house due to the subsequent "anarchist" agreement by Alexandra and Owen.

(D)   Roger may sue only Alexandra if Owen does not permit him to paint the house due to the subsequent "anarchist" agreement by Alexandra and Owen.

34.   Assume Roger told Owen he "was taking over the contract" from Alexandra shortly after Alexandra "as-

signed" him the contract. If Roger fails to paint Owen's house after the assignment, Owen may sue:

(A)   Alexandra only.

(B)   Roger only.

(C)   Either Alexandra or Roger, or both.

(D)   Either Alexandra or Roger, but not both.

35.   Roger paints Owen's house. Owen:

(A)   Can discharge by performance his duties under the Owen/Alexandra contract by paying either Alexandra or Roger.

(B)   Is only liable for the reasonable value of Roger's performance, if that is less then the contract price.

(C)   Must pay Roger the contract price to discharge by performance his duties under the Owen/Alexandra contract.

(D)   Must pay Alexandra the contract price to discharge by performance his duties under the Owen/Alexandra contract.

Questions 36 - 39 are based on the following fact situation:

Bill and Emily entered into a contract whereby Bill promised to build an apartment building for Emily for $100,000, with progress payments of $9,000 a month. Honest differences arose after five months over whether landscaping was extra or within the contract terms. Emily suggested that the issue be resolved by her promising to pay Bill an additional $5,000 upon Bill's current promise to do, and eventual completion of, the landscaping as set forth in the plans. Bill agreed.

36.   Assume that Bill does the landscaping. If Emily can prove that landscaping was within the terms of the original contract:

(A)   She need not pay the extra $5,000 for her promise to do so is unenforceable.

(B)   She must pay Bill the extra $5,000 because she entered into a valid accord with Bill.

(C)   She must pay Bill the extra $5,000 because she entered into a valid novation with Bill.

(D)   She must pay Bill the extra $5,000 because she entered into a valid substituted performance agreement with Bill.

37. Assume that Bill does not do the landscaping. If Emily can prove that landscaping was, in fact, within the terms of the original contract, which is the most accurate statement?

(A) She may recover only for breach of the original contract.

(B) She can recover only for breach of Bill's second promise.

(C) She can recover for Bill's breach of the original promise or for Bill's breach of the second promise.

(D) She can withhold payment due under both agreements until Bill honors his second promise.

38. Emily withholds the seventh progress payment because of an honest dispute as to the amount of progress Bill has made at the end of the seventh month. Which of the following best describes Bill's rights?

(A) Bill may suspend performance, but he will be liable for breach of contract if Emily is ultimately found to be correct.

(B) Bill must continue performance until the honest dispute is resolved, but is entitled to recover damages if he is ultimately found to be correct.

(C) Bill is discharged from any further obligation to build by Emily's unilateral decision to withhold payment.

(D) Bill may consider himself discharged from any further obligation to build, in which event his recovery, if he is ultimately found to be correct, is the amount due under the contract at the time of suspension of work.

39. Emily now asserts that Bill also orally and separately agreed that the contract price would also include a sidewalk surrounding the structure after the structure was completed. Which of the following scenarios would most likely allow Emily to enforce such an agreement.

(A) The oral agreement was made just before they signed their written construction contract.

(B) The oral agreement was made just after the written contract was signed. Emily asserts that she had just forgotten about asking Bill about it during contract negotiations, and when she remembered (about 30 minutes after the contract was signed), Bill said no problem — I'll put it in for the same price.

(C) The oral agreement was made just after the written contract was signed, as part of a conversation in which Emily agreed to extend the completion date given that pouring and hardening of the sidewalk would take time.

(D) The oral agreement was made just before the written contract was signed as part of a conversation in which she promised not to hold Bill to the completion date in the written contact, given the amount of time it would take to make the sidewalk.

Question 40

On May 26, Jones says to Smith, "I will sell you my Chevy for $1,500 or my Dodge for $1,700. Just let me know which one by next Friday, June 1." Smith replies, "I will definitely buy one of your cars. I'll let you know which one before June 1." Which is the most accurate statement?

(A) There is no contract as of May 26, because Smith cannot accept until he designates which car he will buy; otherwise there would be a lack of mutuality.

(B) There is a contract as of May 26, with Jones guaranteeing, in return for Smith's promise to buy that Smith has a choice that can be made as late as June 1.

(C) There is no contract as of May 26, because it would be unfair to require Jones to have both cars encumbered until Smith designates which car he will buy.

(D) Smith's reply is only a counter-offer; Jones now must decide whether to accept this counter-offer, in which case he must encumber both cars until Smith decides which car he wants.

Question 41

Martha, in Maine, wrote to Daisy, her daughter who lived in Missouri, saying, "I am in bad shape. Promise me you will come and take care of me for the rest of my life and you can have my home when I'm gone. Write me your plans at once, because if you can't come I want to get someone else."

This letter was posted on June 1 and received by Daisy on June 4. On the morning of June 5, Daisy sent a letter to Martha saying, "Don't worry. You can depend on me. I am coming right away." On June 6, Martha became suddenly and violently insane. On June 7, Daisy resigned her job and boarded a train bound for Martha's home.

When Martha received Daisy's letter on June 8, she tore it up, and telegraphed Daisy, "Stay away from me. You are trying to hex me." Daisy was then en route, and did not receive this message. When Daisy arrived at Martha's home on June 11, Martha refused to receive her, and died the next day, June 12.

No provision was made for Daisy in Martha's will, which left everything to Martha's sister in San Diego. Daisy demanded that Martha's executor convey the home to her. On his refusal, Daisy brings suit for breach of contract by Martha. Which of the following arguments best supports Daisy's position?

(A) Daisy reasonably and detrimentally relied on Martha's promise at a time when she did not know Martha had become insane.

(B) Since Martha was insane at the time she attempted to revoke the offer, the revocation is without legal effect, and the original offer stands.

(C) Daisy gave the promise requested, and thereby entered a bilateral contract that was not lacking in mutuality or legal efficacy.

(D) A revocation is effective only on receipt, and here Martha's revocation was not received by Daisy, since she was en route to Maine as her mother had requested.

Question 42

The rule that the death of the offeror terminates the offeree's power of acceptance is:

(A) Consistent with the objective theory of contracts, but inconsistent with the subjective theory.

(B) Consistent with the subjective theory of contracts, but inconsistent with the objective theory.

(C) Equally consistent with both the objective and subjective theories of contracts.

(D) Equally inconsistent with both the objective and subjective theories of contracts.

Questions 43 - 44 are based on the following fact situation:

Bernice, the owner of an advertising agency, had the following conversation with Sheila, the owner of a 1929 Model T Ford with the license No. PIK/FAIR, on October 1:

B: You are positive that this was the car in which Douglas Fairbanks proposed to Mary Pickford?

S: Yes, it is. I bought the car at an auction from Christie's Auction House last month, and I have a letter

from Christie's authenticating the car. I wouldn't ask $150,000 for it otherwise.

B: That's important to me, because we have an advertising campaign for Le Pew perfume that revolves around re-living the elegant lifestyles of Fairbanks and Pickford. We plan to feature the car as authentic in our T.V. ads, and to send the car around the country to shopping malls and the like to increase the volume of our department store sales. However, Le Pew is willing to go forward with our agency only if we are able to secure the authentic car.

S: I understand. However, I would not have bought it from Christie's if I wasn't sure it was the right car.

B: Well, O.K., I'll take it. Shall we say delivery of the car on November 1.

S: That will be fine.

Variation One

The next day, Sheila telephoned Bernice and they had the following conversation:

S: When we spoke yesterday we neglected to set any payment terms. Is it acceptable if we agree that you will pay $15,000 down by October 15, and the remainder on delivery?

B: That will be no problem at all.

On October 15, Sheila received a check from Bernice's agency for $15,000, which had the following phrase typed on the check's "Memo" line: "Dn. Pymt. for PIK/FAIR Model T." Sheila immediately deposited the check in her account.

On November 1, Bernice came to Sheila's house with a cashier's check in the amount of $135,000. However, Sheila appeared at the door and said she had changed her mind and no longer wished to sell the car. She offered Bernice $15,000 in cash and said: "We never really had a deal anyway. Our agreement was never reduced to writing."

43. In a suit by Bernice against Sheila for breach, which of the following accurately describes how the court should rule on Sheila's statute of frauds defense?

I. The defense should succeed because of the part performance exception to the statute of frauds.

II. The defense should fail because of the part performance exception to the statute of frauds.

III. The defense should fail because the notation on the "Memo" line of the $15,000 check is sufficient to satisfy the UCC's statute of frauds, assuming the check was signed by Bernice.

IV. The defense should succeed because no evidence of the October 1 conversation, or of the $15,000 check, will be admissible under the parol evidence rule.

(A) I only.

(B) II only.

(C) I and IV.

(D) II and III.

Variation Two

On November 1, Sheila tendered the keys and certificate of title to Bernice, and Bernice gave Sheila a check for $150,000. However, on December 1, the man who furnished the Model T to Christie's confessed that he had perpetrated a fraud, and that the Model T with the PIK/FAIR license plates that he had auctioned through Christie's was not the authentic car in which Douglas Fairbanks had proposed to Mary Pickford. The authentic car was, in fact, owned by another antique car collector, Reginald Jackson. Subsequent investigation revealed that neither Christie's nor Sheila nor Bernice had any idea that the PIK/FAIR Model T was not authentic.

44. Which of the following warranties, if any, has Sheila breached?

I. Express Warranty.

II. Warranty of Merchantability

(A) I and II.

(B) I only.

(C) II only.

(D) Sheila has breached neither of the listed warranties.

Question 45 is based on the following fact situation:

Bruce Buyer owned a large electronics store and placed an order for 75 Sony XB-100 Cassette Decks, which were timely delivered by Sony. Upon inspecting the decks the next day, Bruce determined that none of the tape counters worked and thus told Sony he was rejecting the shipment.

45. The best description of the parties' rights and duties is:

I. Sony has a right to cure so long as the time for performance under the contract has not passed and it seasonably notifies Bruce of its intention to do so.

II. Sony has a right to cure even if it only establishes that it had reasonable grounds to believe that the cassette decks were acceptable when shipped and seasonably notifies Bruce of its intention to do so.

III. Sony has no right to cure if the time for performance under the contract has passed.

IV. Sony has a right to cure even if the time for performance under the contract has passed, but only if it can establish that it reasonably believed the decks were acceptable when shipped, seasonably notifies Bruce of its intention to do so, and the delay in getting new decks to Bruce does not cause him any commercial hardship.

(A) I only.

(B) I and III.

(C) I and IV.

(D) III only.

Question 46 is based on the following fact situation:

Sid Seller owns a wine shop in Beverly Hills. Buford Buyer lives in San Francisco and regularly purchases wines from Sid.

In 1982, Sid and Buford entered into a "wine futures" contract for 1 case of 1982 Chateau Margaux, a very popular wine. Under this agreement, Buford committed to purchase the wine at a fixed price and gained the right to obtain possession of the wine in the summer of 1986, shortly after its arrival in the United States. Under their contract, Buford had to leave a $200 deposit on placing the order (which he did), and was obligated to pay the remaining $400 when the wine was tendered to him.

On April 1, 1984, the *L.A. Times*'s Business Section featured an article entitled, "San Francisco Mogul Hits the Skids—Buford Buyer in Serious Financial Trouble," which set forth a long list of Buford's business troubles.

Sid immediately sent Buford a telegram stating, "Saw article in *L.A. Times*. Please advise whether you are willing and able to pay for the Ch. Margaux when it arrives. Buford timely dispatched the following reply:

April 5, 1984

Sid Seller
Beverly Hills, Ca.

L.A. Times article in error. I am doing fine. I will be
able to pay the $400 in 1986.

/s/ Buford

Buford did not communicate further with Sid.

46.   If Sid sued Buford for anticipatory repudiation on
May 15, 1984, Sid should:

(A)   **Lose**, because Buford responded to Sid's request for
assurances within a commercially reasonable time.

(B)   **Lose**, if Buford can establish that the L.A. Times article was inaccurate and that he was very well off
financially in April.

(C)   **Lose**, because Buford has expressed no definite and
unequivocal refusal to perform as is required before an anticipatory breach action can successfully be brought under the UCC.

(D)   **Prevail**, because Buford did not provide sufficient
reasonable assurances in his April 5, 1984 telegram.

ANSWERS TO THE MULTIPLE CHOICE QUESTIONS

Answer to Question 1.

(D) is the correct answer.

Under the "mailbox rule," an acceptance is generally valid upon dispatch so long as it is properly addressed and acceptance by mail is an authorized method of acceptance. However, one exception to this principle is that when an offeree sends an acceptance which is followed by a rejection, it is the **rejection** that is effective so long as the rejection arrives first **and the offeror changes position in reliance on the rejection** [Text §4.64]. Here, Allan's 1/20 letter was an effective acceptance. However, his 1/20 (express mail) rejection overtook it in the mail. Hence, if Priscilla had relied on the rejection, e.g., by taking another job during the same time period she had offered to work for Allan, the rejection would have become the operative response from the offeree. However, no reliance is shown on these facts, and thus the correct choice is D. A and B are incorrect because the express mail rejection was received first and takes precedence over the 1/20 regular mail acceptance. Thus, there is no contract on which Priscilla can successfully sue. C is incorrect because it is an incorrect statement of the substantive law under the mailbox rule.

Answer to Question 2.

(A) is the correct answer.

Under the mailbox rule, when a rejection is followed by an acceptance, the first to arrive becomes the operative response [Text §4.63]. Brenda's 1/24 letter is a counter-offer, which, of course, also serves as a rejection. Her 1/25 letter (the one sent by express mail) is an acceptance. The 1/24 letter arrived first, so it is the operative document. Thus, A is the only correct choice. B is incorrect for it misstates the substantive rule set forthe above. C and D are incorrect because for Priscilla to prevail, Brenda's acceptance letter would have had to arrive before her counter-offer/rejection letter, under the mailbox rule, which it did not.

Answer to Question 3.

(C) is the correct answer.

As noted above in the Answer to Question No. 2, in cases where an offeree first sends a rejection and follows that with an acceptance, the first to arrive is operative [Text §4.63]. Here, the 1/25 acceptance arrived first, hence the contract was made at that point. Once an offer has been effectively accepted, it can no longer be rejected, and thus Priscilla's receipt of the 1/25 counter-offer/rejection has no effect. A and B are thus incorrect, because for Priscilla to lose, Brenda's counter-offer/rejection must have been the operative document. However, as noted above, since the counter-offer arrived after the acceptance, the acceptance took precedence. D is incorrect because it misstates the substantive law under the mailbox rule.

Answer to question 4.

(B) is the correct answer.

This is an implied-in-law contract, or quasi-contract. That is, it is a situation in which it would be unjust for a party to receive benefits from another without paying for such benefits. The fact that Dr. Fiscus's efforts were ultimately unsuccessful in saving Quigley's life is irrelevant to the question of whether Quigley's estate is responsible in restitution for Dr. Fiscus's services [Text §§1.35; 32.4]. A is not correct for two reasons. Jones cannot be liable in contract to Dr. Fiscus because he never entered into a contract with Dr. Fiscus. He cannot be liable in restitution for quasi-contract, because Dr. Fiscus never performed any services that benefitted him (Jones). C is incorrect because A is incorrect. D is incorrect because B is correct.

Answer to Question 5.

(D) is the correct answer.

The Restatement 2d has relaxed the common law rules relating to the adequacy of past consideration to be effective consideration. Under §86, a promise based on past consideration will be enforceable to the extent necessary to avoid injustice unless: (a) **the promisee intended the benefit received by the promisor as a gift**, or (b) the value of the promise is disproportionate to the benefits received. [Text §7.522] Here, the students intended to make a gift of the car wash and wax to their professor, thus, Professor Jones's promise to pay them for it is unenforceable. Thus, A is incorrect for it is based on Jones's unenforceable promise. B is incorrect for it is based on the fair market value or quasi-contractual value of the student's efforts. However, because Jones was not unconscious or otherwise unavailable to bargain with the students before they began work on his car, and because there was no emergency that called for immediate car washing action by the students, this is not a quasi-contract situation [Text §1.35]. C is incorrect because it inaccurately states the Restatement's rules regarding past consideration.

Answer to Question 6.

(A) is the correct answer.

Jones's promise to Quigley's widow is only a gift promise and thus unenforceable. B is incorrect because, although it accurately states one part of the rule of Restatement 2d §86 (see the Answer to Question 5, above), §86 cannot be used to enforce Jones's promise since Quigley's widow provided no benefit to Jones as is required under that provision [Text §7.522]. C is incorrect because, on these facts, there is no evidence that Quigley's widow relied on Jones's promise. D is not correct because, even if Jones obtained some peace of mind, that benefit is not "bargained for" as the term is used in the Restatement 2d's formulation of consideration [Text §7.13; 7.51].

Answer to Question 7.

(C) is the correct answer.

The contract is for the sale of goods, and thus governed by the UCC. The UCC's statute of frauds must be satisfied if the contract is for $500 [Text §9.6]. Of the three choices, both I and III help Diane in overcoming Rita's assertion of the statute as a defense. Under UCC §2-201 (2), if a merchant buyer does not object within 10 days after the receipt of a memorandum form the seller that, *inter alia*, confirms the transaction, the buyer loses his or her right to assert the Statute as a defense. [Text §9.632] Under Choice I, Rita's memorandum was untimely, for it was sent 12 days after its receipt, and thus such a fact would be helpful to Diane. Choice III is also helpful to Diane because if a contract was formed, the price for the monitor would be a "reasonable price" under UCC §2-305, the gap filler on price [Text §6.221]. It is likely that the price other wholesalers in the area charged for the monitor would become the "reasonable price," and thus the contract, if it existed, would be for the sale of goods for less than $500. As such, the UCC's statute of frauds would not apply to it [Text §9.6], and that fact is also helpful to Diane. Thus II would not be helpful, because if the monitor typically sold for more than $500, the UCC statute of frauds would apply, and that would be helpful to Rita, not Diane.

Answer to Question 8.

(D) is the correct answer.

This is a fairly close call, but under the relaxed formation rules of the UCC, a contract was formed. Under §2-204(a), a contract may be made in any manner sufficient to show agreement [Text §6.2]. Here, Rita gave objective indications that she was willing to be bound to purchase the monitor and Diane gave objective indications that she was willing to sell Rita a monitor. Accordingly, since the parties have agreed as to subject matter (the monitor) and quantity (one) and have indicated an intent to contract, the contract is definite enough to be enforced under the UCC, by use of the gap fillers. [Text §6.22] For these reasons, A and B are incorrect. Similarly, C is also incorrect because under the UCC, when the parties evidence an intent to contract but do not reach agreement in the price, UCC §2-305 states that the price will be a "reasonable price." [Text §6.221]

Answer to Question 9.

(A) is the correct answer.

While some courts disagree, the majority rule is that a party seeking to enforce an agreement governed by the UCC has a right to take deposition testimony of the party asserting the defense for purposes of eliciting an "admission" of the elements of a contract by that party, and thereby satisfying the Statute under §2-201(3)(b) [Text §9.642]. B is not right, because the contract is within the Statute if the reasonable price for the monitor is $1,500 (see the answer to Question 8, above). C and D are correct statements of law, but the principles set forth in each of those answers is subject to the rule discussed above, namely that a party opposing assertion of the Statute has the right to elicit an admission, under oath, under §2-201(3)(b).

Answer to Question 10.

(C) is the correct answer.

Choice I is incorrect, because under the statute of frauds, the "party to be charged" is the party who is asserting a statute of frauds defense and claims that his or her promise cannot be enforced, i.e., "charged." Choice III is an incorrect statement of the law. UCC §2-201(2) states that to be effective, the confirming memorandum must satisfy the statute under §2-201 (1) as against **the sender**, not the recipient [Text §9.635]. Choice II is true because Diane is the party to be charged and she sent an adequate memorandum [Text §9.63]. Note that while she did not "sign" the memorandum, her initials are a sufficient "signature" for statute of frauds purposes under §1-201 (39) [Text §9.6224].

Answer to Qustion 11.

(C) is the correct answer.

A surety is someone who promises a third party to pay the debt of another [Text §9.51]. To be a surety, the party must only be secondarily liable on the debt, and thus called on to perform his or her promise only if the principal, who is primarily liable, does not pay the obligation [Text §9.52]. While a suretyship promise, with some exceptions, must be in writing to be enforceable, here Bert is not a surety. He is not secondarily liable on the mortgage, for the facts say that upon assumption of the debt it is he who must make the payments and it is Sally who remains liable only if **he** defaults. Hence, Choice IV is correct. Additionally, on these facts Bert is also not a surety because he did not promise the Bank that he would be secondarily liable for Sally's debt. He only made Sally the promise that he would assume the mortgage. Accordingly, Choice III is correct as well. Choices I and II would be correct only if Bert **were** a surety, which he is not.

Answer to Question 12.

(C) is the correct answer.

A modern court will use its interpretive powers to fill in gaps in an agreement, even in contracts not specifically governed by the UCC's gap fillers [Text §6.23]. Here, given that Sally owned only one piece of property, and that the property was located at 4029 Smithson Street, a court would be able to determine sufficiently the subject matter of the contract, even in the absence of the state and city. Hence A is incorrect. B and D are also incorrect for the same reason. That is, a court would be able to use the custom of the area or the usage of trade, e.g., full payment due at the close of escrow, to interpret the proper payment terms under the contract [Text §18.212]. C is correct. Recall that a written contract will either be considered totally or partially integrated for purposes of the parol evidence rule [Text §17.1]. If it is considered totally integrated, then no evidence of any other term can be admitted, which, in this case, means that no evidence of the mortgage assumption could be introduced [Text §17.1]. If it is partially integrated, evidence of any consistent term can be admitted, but the test for whether a term is consistent is the "might naturally" test for this kind of contract. That is, whether, if the parties really agreed on the term, is it the kind of term they might naturally omit from their final written agreement. [Text §17.14] A mortgage assumption clause, if it were agreed to, would be considered such an important clause that a court would not conclude that it is the kind of term the parties might naturally have left out of their sales agreement, and thus the parol evidence rule would serve as Bert's best argument.

Answer to Question 13.

(A) is the correct answer.

The language creating the duty to provide the sample clock evidences a promise, not a condition. A condition is created with phrases like "if but only if", "on the condition that", "provided that", or any other language indicating that the entire transaction will not be enforceable until or unless something happens (i.e., occurrence of the condition is either fulfilled or excused) [Text §20.31]. Here, the sample clause is merely a promise by Morton that it would supply one clock by a certain date. There is absolutely no evidence that the parties intended that their deal was contingent on the strict enforcement of that provision. B, C, and D are thus incorrect for the clock delivery term is a promise and not a condition.

Anwer to Question 14.

(B) is the correct answer.

By failing to do what it promised, Morton has breached and thus, at the very least, must pay for damages caused by the breach [Text §21.0]. Hence D is incorrect. The question is whether the breach could be classified as material or immaterial. If material, Store would be entitled to cease its own performance and to sue Morton for damages. If immaterial, Store would be obligated to continue performance and the only effect of the breach would be its suit for any damages caused by the one day delay [Text §21.22]. The Restatement has identified various factors that go into the determination of whether a breach is material or partial [Text §21.242]. These factors all point to Morton's breach as being immaterial, i.e., the breach did not deprive Store of most of the benefits of its bargain; Store can be fully compensated for its damages if the breach is declared only immaterial; Morton would suffer a fairly severe forfeiture under the contract if the breach were ruled material; Morton cured the breach within a day; and Morton acted in good faith. Hence, because the breach is only a partial one, B is the correct answer. A and C are both incorrect because they presume a material breach, i.e., one that would prevent Morton from enforcing the contract against Store [Text §21.22].

Answer to Question 15.

(A) is the correct answer.

There was an anticipatory repudiation by Store when its President unequivocally told the Morton's employee that Store was not going to proceed under the contract and buy any clocks [Text §§23.2; 23.3]. At that point, Store was entitled to declare the contract over, cease its own performance, and sue Morton for material breach. As noted above (see the Answer to Question 14), because the failure to deliver the single clock on April 1 was only an immaterial breach [Text §21.22], Store had no right to terminate the contract and cease its own performance at that point. Hence, A is the correct answer and B, C and D are incorrect.

Answer to Question 16.

(A) is the correct answer.

The May 5 letter by Store's President had the effect of retracting the anticipatory repudiation and reinstating the contract [Text §23.5]. Hence, the question is whether Morton had a right to deliver only 200 clocks given the April 5 and April 6 telephone conversations, or whether it was obligated to deliver all 250 clocks. Morton would not be able to introduce evidence of the oral modification to 200 units. Under UCC §2-209(3), if the contract as modified is within the statute of frauds (which this was), then the Statute must be satisfied before evidence of the modification is allowed [Text §26.4]. Store did not sign anything indicating the reduced quantity, and there are no other facts that suggest the Statute had been satisfied. However, there was the possibility that the reduction might be enforced as a waiver [Text §26.5]. That is, under §2-209(4), modifications rendered unenforceable due to a lack of writing can be enforced as waivers. However, under §2-209(5), waivers can be retracted so long as the party benefiting from the waiver has not detrimentally relied on it. [Text §26.6]. Here, besides retracting the repudiation, Store's May 5 letter also retracted the waiver to 200 units. Because Morton still could have performed at the time it received the retraction (and thus did not detrimentally rely on it), upon receipt of the May 5 letter the contract once again became one for 250 clocks. Hence, under the perfect tender rule [Text §22.2] Morton's tender of only 200 clocks was therefore a material breach, and A is the correct response. B is thus incorrect because it states that Morton immaterially breached the contract. C and D are incorrect because they state that it is Store, not Morton, who has breached the contract.

Answer to Question 17.

(D) is the correct answer.

The difference between a power to accept and a right to accept turns on whether the offer is a revocable or an irrevocable one [Text §4.4211]. UCC §2-205 rejects the common law rule that an offer may be made irrevocable only when consideration passes between the parties, i.e., when there is an option contract, and allows a merchant seller to make an enforceable irrevocable offer even in the absence of consideration [Text §4.422]. However, to accomplish this "firm offer" effectively, the merchant seller must do so in writing. Here, the promise of the seller to hold open the offer was made orally, so the offeree (Bob) has only the power of acceptance under it, not the right to accept. A and C are thus incorrect for they state that Bob has a right to purchase the painting, and not merely a power to do so. D is incorrect for it states that Bob's power to purchase the painting only lasts to June 30, when Sy promised to hold his offer open until August 10.

Answer to Question 18.

(B) is the correct answer.

Under the "unilateral contract trick" of the UCC, a seller who is entitled to accept an offer by shipment, and who ships non-conforming goods, has simultaneously accepted and breached the contract [Text §4.55]. However, if the seller who sent the non-conforming goods notifies the buyer that the goods are non-conforming and are being sent to the buyer as only an accommodation, the sending of such goods acts only as a counter-offer and not a breach [Text §4.551]. The last sentence of the substantive paragraph of Sam's letter makes clear that this is an accommodation shipment, and thus since Betty has not accepted the tender of the records, their present status is that they do not have a contract. Thus A and D are incorrect.

Answer to Question 19.

(C) is the correct answer.

Upon a rightful rejection of goods under the UCC, a merchant buyer such as Bower's must follow any reasonable instructions of the buyer to return the goods [Text §22.321]. However, it is entitled to be indemnified for any costs it has expended in doing so, which includes return the goods freight collect. Thus, A, B, and D are incorrect.

Answer to Question 20.

(C) is the correct answer.

Under §45 of the Restatement 2d, beginning performance in response to an offer to enter into a unilateral contract creates a unilateral option contract exercisable by the offeree [Text §4.4134-1B]. Hence, as soon as Andy started repairing the roof, the offer became temporarily irrevocable and Owner had to allow Andy a reasonable time to finish performance. A is not correct, for while Andy has an obligation to notify Owner within a reasonable time **after** beginning performance, he has no obligation to make such notice **before** beginning performance [Text §4.5432]. B is not correct, for a promissory offer in response to an offer for a unilateral contract is not a valid acceptance [Text §4.51]. D is not correct under Restatement 2d §45, although it is a minority position [Text §4.4134-1C]. That is, under §45, the option contract is unilateral only, and beginning performance does not obligate him or her to finish.

Answer to Question 21.

(D) is the correct answer.

A is not correct, because acceptance by beginning performance is only an acceptable method of acceptance in response to an ambiguous offer, or to an offer seeking a unilateral contract. [Text §§4.54; 4.542] B is also not correct. Generally, under the "mailbox rule," an acceptance is effective upon dispatch [Text §4.61]. However, for that rule to apply, acceptance by mail must be an authorized method of acceptance [Text §4.612]. Here, Owner made it clear that Andy's power of acceptance would lapse unless Andy told Owner of his decision by June 3. In that situation, mailing an acceptance late in the day on June 3 is not an effective method of acceptance, and thus B is incorrect. C is incorrect because the Owner would not receive the acceptance until after the offer lapsed by its own terms, i.e., after June 3 [Text §4.4121].

Answer to Question 22.

(B) is the correct answer.

Under the indirect revocation doctrine, when an offeree learns from a reliable source that an offeror has taken a definite act inconsistent with an intention to enter into the contract with the offeree, the offer is effectively revoked [Text §4.4133]. A is incorrect, because Brenda lost the power to accept the offer when it was revoked as explained above [Text §4.413]. C is incorrect as a matter of law. That is, a careless offeror can indeed have made a contract to sell the same thing to two or more different offerees. All that means is that the offeror will be liable in breach to one or more parties if the offerees accept and the seller doesn't perform. D is incorrect, for the consideration that supports a bilateral contract is the mutual promises, not performances by each party [Text §7.3].

Answer to Question 23.

(B) is the correct answer.

The pre-existing duty rule regarding the consideration needed to enforce a contract modification has been relaxed, but not eliminated in non-UCC contracts. (It **has** been eliminated for UCC contracts, see UCC §2-209(1). [Text §26.2]) Under §89 of the Restatement, parties can make an enforceable modification to any executory duties under a contract only if the modification is fair, equitable, and either: (i) is made due to circumstances unanticipated at the time of contract formation; or (ii) has induced reliance by a party benefited by the modification [Text §§7.633; 26.21]. Here, the modification is not made due to unanticipated circumstances, nor has it induced reliance by Writer. Accordingly, the $3/page modification is unenforceable, so A is incorrect. C is wrong because the elements of a mutual rescission have not been established [Text §24.4]. D is factually incorrect, i.e., there is no showing of reliance on these facts.

Answer to Question 24.

(D) is the correct answer.

The first question here is whether Writer's breach is material or immaterial. If material, Publisher is entitled to cease performance under the contract and need not accept it when it is tendered 12 months late [Text §21.22]. If immaterial, Publisher cannot cease performance, and thus must accept its late delivery (although it will, of course, have the right to sue for any damages caused by the breach). Doubling the time agreed upon to tender a book on a then-topical subject is a material breach, and thus A is incorrect, and the Publisher need not accept the book when tendered [Text §21.242]. B is incorrect, for when a non-breaching party waives the material breach of the other, the former material breach becomes an immaterial one [Text §21.273]. That is, such a waiver is not a waiver of the right to sue for damages; rather it is a waiver of the right to cease performance due to the material breach. C is incorrect, for it is an example of "subjective" not "objective" impossibility/impracticability [Text §25.111].

Answer to Question 25.

(C) is the correct answer.

One party's breach with the knowledge of the other does not amount to a "waiver" of the non-breaching party's right to sue for damages. To constitute a waiver, there must be some affirmative statement or action by the waiving party establishing the relinquishment of a right, or the affirmative excuse in the occurrence of, or delay in the occurrence of, a condition [Text §21.273]. Accordingly, B is incorrect. A is a plausible answer, but it is only true if you assume facts not given, i.e., you assume that Publisher told Writer that the "no drinking" clause was important to Publisher regardless of when the book was finished. D is incorrect as a matter of law. A contract wherein someone agrees to forego a legal activity is not an "illegal" contract [Text §16.1].

Answer to Question 26.

(C) is the correct answer.

A party's duties under a contract are discharged under the impossibility doctrine only if, **inter alia**, the impossibility-causing event occurred without the fault of the party asserting the defense [Text §25.113]. Accordingly, A and B are incorrect, for they are too broad, i.e., they allocate liability to one party or the other regardless of who was at fault in causing the fire. D is incorrect because the contract between Delegate and Hotel did not allocate the risk of fire [Text §25.114]. Both clearly contemplated the continuing existence of the hotel as a basic assumption of their contract [Text §25.112].

Answer to Question 27.

(C) is the correct answer.

The fact that Delegate cannot attend the convention due to illness is an insufficient reason to trigger the impossibility, impracticability, or frustration doctrines. Her performance is not impossible of being performed by anyone, and thus, at most is only a case of "subjective" impossibility, which is insufficient to establish impossibility as a defense [Text §25.11]. For the same reasons, her performance is not rendered impractical, for it will not cost her any additional money to perform [Text §25.211]. There is no frustration here, for the fact that the deposit was labelled non-refundable demonstrates that the financial risk of Delegate's non-attendance, for whatever reason, was on Delegate, and not Hotel, under the contract [Text §25.314]. A, B, and D are incorrect for they state that Delegate is entitled to her money back under either a frustration or an impossibility theory.

Answer to Question 28.

(D) is the correct answer.

The facts of this hypothetical are drawn almost exactly from *Krell v. Henry*, the classic case on frustration of purpose [Text §25.322]. Here, Delegate's reference to the ad when the reservation was made, together with the timing of the reservation and the request for the special price, demonstrate that both parties knew the purpose for which Delegate entered into the contract. A is wrong because this is not an impossibility of performance case, for Delegate can still perform, and can perform for the agreed upon price [Text §25.1]. Rather, the problem is that the value of the return performance has been frustrated. B is incorrect, for the parol evidence rule does not apply to situations giving one party the power to avoid an agreement [Text §17.25]. C is incorrect because the value of the return performance to Delegate is sufficiently frustrated to invoke the frustration defense [Text §25.21]. Hence, D is the correct choice, with frustration giving Delegate the power to cancel the contract, and restitution providing the theory by which she can recover her deposit [Text §§25.6; 32.5].

Answer to Question 29.

(A) is the correct answer.

As with any potential third party beneficiary situation, first identify the parties. Insurance Co. is the promisor, for it is obligated to do an act (provide coverage) that will benefit a third party. Dealer is the promisee, for it bargained for the promisor's promise. Buyer is the beneficiary, for she will benefit from performance of Insurance Co.'s promise [Text §27.1]. D is incorrect because a valid third party beneficiary contract can be formed even if the precise identity of the beneficiary is not known at the time the contract is made. [Text §27.3242] C is incorrect, because granting Buyer a right to enforce Insurance Co.'s promise of coverage surely will effectuate the intentions of Insurance Co. and Dealer when they entered into their third party beneficiary contract, thereby making Buyer an intended, rather than an incidental beneficiary. [Text §27.321] B is wrong, because to be a creditor-like intended beneficiary under Restatement 2d §302, performance of the promisor's promise must satisfy an obligation of the promisee to pay money to the beneficiary. That is, for Buyer to be an intended creditor-like beneficiary, the third party beneficiary contract would have to have been entered into to satisfy an obligation of **the Dealer** to pay money to Buyer [Text §§27.321; 27.323]. As this was not the case, the correct choice is A.

Answer to Question 30.

(A) is the correct answer.

The key to this question was the focus in each of the responses on who the beneficiary (Buyer) could sue "**for breach of the Dealer/Insurance Co. contract.**" In other words, what rights does a donee-like intended beneficiary have against the promisor and promisee solely arising out of that contract, and that contract alone. An intended beneficiary (Buyer) has the right to sue the promisor, Insurance Co., for breach of his, her, or its promise [Text §27.3]. Indeed, that is often the central issue arising from such agreements. However, an intended donee-like beneficiary acquires no rights **against the promisee** (here, Dealer), arising from the formation of such a contract [Text §27.5]. Hence, while Buyer may have some rights against Dealer for breach of the direct promise made to Buyer that the Dealer would provide insurance, those rights did not arise from the Dealer/Insurance Co. agreement. Accordingly, since the only entity an intended donee-like beneficiary can sue for breach of a third party beneficiary contract alone is the promisor, the correct answer is A. Thus, B and C are incorrect. D is incorrect because Buyer, as an intended beneficiary, is entitled to bring suit against the promisor, Insurance Co [Text §27.3].

Answer to Question 31.

(B) is the correct answer.

The issue in this question turns, in part, on the rights of the promisor and promisee to modify the third party beneficiary contract to the detriment of the intended beneficiary [Text §27.7]. While there are three tests, reflecting different views, as to when the beneficiary's rights vest under such a contract, all three are satisfied here. Accordingly, Dealer and Insurance Co. were without power to modify the contract to the detriment of Buyer. As such, Buyer retained whatever rights she had prior to the attempted modification which, as set forth in the Answer to Question 30 above, means she could only sue Insurance Co., the promisor, for its breach of the third party beneficiary contract. Note that Choice III is incorrect because there are no warranties that follow from the creation of a third party beneficiary contract (although there are warranties that follow an assignment for value [Text §28.6]). Thus, choice I is incorrect.

Answer to Question 32.

(A) is the correct answer.

Absent evidence to the contrary, the phrase "assigning the contract" includes both an assignment of rights under the agreement and a delegation of the assigning party's duties [Text §§28.38; 29.211]. Hence, upon the "assignment of the contract," Roger acquired both a right to receive the $500 payment for the job from Owen, and the right to perform the painting, so long as the duty was validly delegable. A duty is not delegable when its performance requires the special training, skills, abilities, etc., of the delegating party, in this case Alexandra, i.e., when it is a "personal services" contract within the meaning of the term used in delegation situations [Text §29.222]. A contract to paint a house is not a "personal services" contract in that sense, for the task is one any competent painter can accomplish. Accordingly, C is incorrect and the delegation was valid. Upon a valid delegation, the obligee, in this case Owen, must allow the delegate, Roger, to perform the duties called for in the obligee/delegating party contract. That is, Owen must allow Roger to do the painting or be in breach for failing to do so [Text §§29.31; 29.32]; accordingly B is an incorrect choice. Upon a simple delegation, the delegating party (Alexandra) is still liable to the obligee (Roger) for breach by the delegate. The only way the delegating party can be "off the hook" is if the delegating party and the obligee enter into a novation, whereby the obligee specifically agrees to accept the delegate's performance in satisfaction of the duty owed by the delegating party [Text §§29.4; 24.2]. Because no novation occurred here, D is wrong and A is the correct response.

Answer to Question 33.

(B) is the correct answer.

The assignor and the obligor have no power to modify or terminate an assignment for value [Text §28.71]. Accordingly, A is incorrect. Upon the delegation, Roger acquired the right to perform the painting duties on Owen's home. If Owen will not allow him to paint the house, Owen is in breach [Text §§29.31; 29.32]. Upon an assignment for value, the assignor makes an implied warranty *inter alia*, that he or she will do nothing to impair the value of the assignment [Text §28.6]. If Alexandra conspires with Roger to terminate the assigned right, and Roger is thereby prevented from doing the acts necessary to receive the benefits of the assignment, Alexandra is also liable to him. Hence, B is the correct answer, since both Owen and Alexandra may be sued, and so C and D are incorrect.

Answer to Question 34.

(C) is the correct answer.

After a valid delegating with an express assertion by the delegate that he will assume the obligation, an obligee such as Owen has the right to sue either the delegating party or the delegate, or both, for the delegate's breach [Text §29.34]. Of course, the obligee is only entitled to one recovery, but he or she is freely entitled to bring suit against both parties. Thus, A, B, and D are incorrect.

Answer to Question 35.

(C) is the correct answer.

After a valid assignment *with notice to the obligor*, the only way the obligor may discharge his or her duties by performance is by rendering such performance **to the assignee** [Text §28.4]. Here, the assignment was valid, and the obligor (Owen) had notice of the assignment. Accordingly, his tender of payment to anyone other than Roger, the assignee, will not discharge his duties under the Alexandra/Owen contract. Thus, A and D are incorrect. B is incorrect for if Owen prevails, he prevails because of the contract and is thus entitled to the contract price for the painting, regardless of its fair market or restitutionary value.

Answer to Question 36.

(B) is the correct answer.

The issue is whether there is sufficient consideration to enforce the promise to pay $5,000, and if so, whether their resulting agreement can be called a novation or a substituted performance. An agreement to surrender a claim under a contract is supported by consideration when the existence and/or amount of the claim is the subject of a **bona fide** dispute between the parties [Text §§7.634; 24.331]. Accordingly, A is incorrect. B is correct, and C and D are incorrect, because the subsequent agreement between Emily and Bill is an accord, and neither a novation nor a substituted performance agreement. A novation occurs when a party who is owed a duty under a contract agrees to discharge that duty in return for a promised performance by a third party [Text §24.2]. Here, no third parties entered into agreements with Emily so it is not a novation. A substituted performance agreement is one in which a party who is owed a duty under a contract agrees to discharge that duty upon the actual performance of another duty [Text §24.1]. Here, Emily's promise to discharge the debt was made in return for Bill's **promise** of completing the landscaping, and she made it clear that the duty she was compromising would not be discharged until the landscaping was completed. The promise constituted an accord, and the discharge upon completion of the landscaping would be a satisfaction [Text §24.3].

Answer to Question 37.

(C) is the correct answer.

Upon breach of an accord, the non-breaching party is entitled to sue for breach of the original contract duty or of the accord [Text §24.3]. Thus, A and B are incorrect. D is incorrect for Emily would only be entitled to cease performance under the contract upon a material breach by Bill. Here, the failure to provide $5,000 worth of landscaping in a $100,000 apartment building construction contract would most likely be considered only an immaterial breach under the substantial performance doctrine [Text §21.22].

Answer to Question 38.

(A) is the correct answer.

Typically, an unjustified failure to provide progress payments in a construction contract acts as a material breach, which would allow Bill to cease (or at least suspend) performance. However, under the "first" material breach doctrine, if Emily was **justified** in withholding the progress payment and Bill nevertheless walked off the job, it would be Bill who has breached the agreement, not Emily [Text §21.25]. In other words, the fact that Bill has an honest dispute with Emily will not shield him from being a breaching party if the facts ultimately prove he was in the wrong. B is wrong because Bill is not obligated to continue performance if Emily's withholding of the progress payments was unjustified. C is incorrect because Bill will only be discharged from performance if Emily's withholding of progress payments was unjustified. D is incorrect because the amount of recovery he would be entitled to if Emily were found to be the breaching party would not be fixed at the amount then due under the contract at the time of the breach. (Text §31.34.)

Answer to Question 39.

(C) is the correct answer.

An agreement on a term like putting in a sidewalk is the kind of term that the parties would not naturally leave out of their written agreement. Accordingly, A and D are incorrect because the parol evidence rule, which applies to terms allegedly agreed upon prior to the making of the contract, would provide an obstacle to Emily in trying to prove that the sidewalk agreement was part of the contract [Text §17.14]. B and C deal with modifications, which are not subject to the parol evidence rule, i.e., to agreements made after the contract was established [Text §§17.6; 26.7]. In §89, the Restatement 2d has relaxed somewhat the pre-existing duty rule dealing with contract modifications, providing that parties can make an enforceable modification to any executory duties under a contract only if the modification is fair, equitable, and either: (i) is made due to circumstances unanticipated at the time of contract formation; or (ii) has induced reliance by a party benefited by the modification [Text §7.633; 26.21]. Here in, B the modification is not made due to unanticipated circumstances (Emily says she just forgot about it), nor do the facts reveal that it has induced reliance by Emily. Accordingly, to be enforceable it will need to have consideration, which is why B is incorrect. In C, unlike in B, Emily provided consideration to support the sidewalk promise (i.e., she extended the completion date under the contract), and thus C most likely would allow Emily to enforce the sidewalk promise.

Answer to Question 40.

(B) is the correct answer.

There is an offer, an acceptance, and consideration found in the Smith/Jones conversation. Jones made an offer to buy, an acceptance on those terms was agreed to by Smith, and the promises to buy and sell were mutually bargained for [Text §§7.12; 7.3]. The contract will not fail for indefiniteness, for the parties have given themselves until June 1 to cure any indefiniteness as to the subject matter [Text §6.02]. A is incorrect, because both parties are bound to buy and sell, respectively, a car, and C is incorrect, because this was the offer Jones made. Thus, Jones cannot be heard to complain about its "unfairness." D is incorrect, because Smith accepted the offer on its terms and did not propose any additional terms to the bargain [Text §4.0], and thus, his reply cannot be considered a counter-offer [Text §4.411].

Answer to Question 41.

(C) is the correct answer.

Martha made an offer seeking a promissory acceptance, the invited method of which was by return letter. The offer did not specify an exact time, but it was posted by Daisy the morning after it was received, which seems timely enough under the circumstances [Text §4.4122-2]. Because acceptances are effective upon dispatch [Text 4.61] (assuming acceptance by mail is an authorized mode of acceptance and that the letter is properly addressed), a contract was formed as soon as Daisy mailed the letter. Note that Daisy's power of acceptance was still in effect, for Martha became incapacitated only after the acceptance became effective [Text §4.415]. A is incorrect, because while foreseeable reliance on a promise might allow Daisy to collect reliance damages from Martha's estate on a promissory estoppel theory, it would probably not allow Daisy to enforce the contract so as to provide her with the house. [Text §8.4] B is incorrect, for by the time Martha attempted to revoke the offer it had already been accepted, and once an offer has been accepted, the offeree loses his or her right to revoke it [Text §4.1]. D is wrong, because the receipt of Martha's revocation is irrelevant since the offer had already been accepted.

Answer to Question 42.

(B) is the correct answer.

The rule states that upon the death of the offeror, the power of acceptance of the offeree is immediately terminated, regardless whether the offeree knows of the death or not [Text §4.415]. Hence, imagine that an offeree does not know that an offeror had died and is reasonable in not knowing that fact. To a reasonable person in the shoes of the offeree (the objective theory of contracts test) [Text §4.2], it appears that the offer may still be effectively accepted. Because it cannot, the rule seems more consistent with the subjective theory of contracts, i.e. consistent with the idea that there can be no subjective meeting of the minds between the two contracting parties, than with the objective theory.

Answer to Question 43.

(B) is the correct choice.

Because this is a contract for the sale of goods for $500 or more, the transaction will not be enforceable unless the UCC's statute of frauds is satisfied [Text §9.6]. Here, it is Shiela who is the "party to be charged" for it is she who is asserting the defense. [Text §9.62] Accordingly, the Statute cannot be satisfied against her under §2-201 by the check itself, for the check was signed by Bernice, not Shiela; hence Choice III is incorrect. Choice II is correct, because under §2-201(3)(c), performance under a contract satisfies the Statute. While the Code speaks in terms of "performance" and not "part performance" (which was true here), most courts allow part performance to satisfy the statute in a case like this on the grounds that one the cashing of a $15,000 check is sufficient indicia that any oral testimony will rest on a real transaction. [Text §9.6431] Accordingly, when Shiela cashed the check, she lost the statute of frauds defense. Choice I is thus wrong because it is an incorrect statement of the law. Choice IV is incorrect, because the parol evidence rule has nothing to do with whether the statute of frauds is satisfied. [Text §17.5]

Answer to Question 44.

(B) is the correct answer.

The only warranty breached here is an express warranty. The implied warranty of merchantability focuses on the workmanship of the good, i.e., whether it is of average quality, or fit for the ordinary use for which such goods are put [Text §36.22]. Here, Bernice's complaint is not that the car does not run well, but that certain factual representations made about the car, on which she relied in making the purchase, turned out to be false. As such, there has been an actionable breach of express warranty [Text §36.1].

Answer to Question 45.

(C) is the correct answer.

Under UCC §2-508(1), a seller has an absolute right to cure so long as the time for performance under the contract has not yet passed, and so long as the seller gives reasonable notice that he or she is intending to cure [Text §22.241]. Hence Choice I is a correct statement of the law. Under §2-508(2), a seller must establish that it had reason to believe that the goods were acceptable when shipped, that any delay in getting conforming goods to the buyer will not result in commercial hardship to the buyer, and that the buyer is seasonably notified of the seller's intentions, before it has the right to cure [Text §22.2412]. Hence, Choice IV is also a correct statement of the law. Choices II and III are simply incorrect statements of the law.

Answer to Question 46.

(D) is the correct answer.

Under UCC §2-609, a party to a contract who has reasonable grounds to do so is entitled to seek reasonable assurances from the other party as to the other's willingness and ability to perform under the contract [Text §23.32]. An article in a newspaper of general circulation disclosing a buyer's fiscal troubles is generally held to be sufficient for the seller to seek such assurances [Text §23.321]. The failure to give adequate assurances within a reasonable time (not to exceed 30 days) when properly demanded constitutes an anticipatory repudiation [Text §23.32]. The test for whether assurances are adequate is an objective one, i.e., whether a reasonable person in the position of the insecure party would be assured of the other's willingness and ability to perform. Conclusory promises without some detail to back them up are generally not considered sufficient assurances [Text §23.322]. Here, the article gave Sid reasonable grounds to demand assurances, and the response of Buford was insufficient. Hence, D is the correct answer. Note that C is wrong because under the UCC, an anticipatory repudiation may occur either as a result of a definite or unequivocal refusal to perform under §2-610, **or** as a result of the failure to respond to adequate assurances under §2-609. [Text §23.3]

XVI. PRACTICE ESSAY QUESTIONS AND ANSWERS

Question No. 1

Sally owned two adjacent houses on Park Street: 2101 Park Street and 2103 Park Street. Sally lived in the house at 2101 Park Street and rented out the house at 2103 Park Street. At all relevant times the 2101 Park Street house was worth $135,000, and the 2103 Park Street house was worth $100,000.

On June 1, Sally decided to sell 2101 Park Street, so she put a "For Sale" sign in the front yard. Bub was driving through the neighborhood that day, saw the sign, stopped, and rang the doorbell. Sally showed Bub through the house, told him she was asking $150,000 for it, and told him she wanted to deliver the deed on August 1 and receive the $150,000 on the same day. She also said she would have the house painted inside and out before August 1. (The painting would cost Sally $2,000.) In response, Bub asked if she would take $140,000 for the house. Sally said she would have to think about it. Bub told Sally that he would not be able to buy her house unless he could find a buyer for his present house (on Elm Street). Bub said, "If we do make a deal, could we understand that I have to buy your house only if by July 1 I have a contract with a buyer to buy my house on Elm Street?" Sally said that would be "OK" with her.

On June 2, Sally wrote Bub the following letter:

June 2

Dear Bub:

I offer to sell you my home on Park Street for $145,000. If you wish to accept this offer you must let me know before June 10.

If you accept, then you will pay me the $145,000, and I will give you a deed, all on August 1. I will maintain insurance on the house until August 1 and will also take good care of the lawns and plants until that date. My furniture is not included, except for the dining room table (which was specially made to fit the odd shaped dining room), and the six matching chairs. My insurance company has appraised the dining set at $600.

Very truly yours,

/s/ Sally

On June 4 Bub wrote back:

June 4

Dear Sally:

I am happy to accept the offer set forth in your June 2 letter.

Sincerely,

/s/ Bub

On June 10, Bub telephoned Sally and said it did not look like he was going to be able to find a buyer for his Elm Street house, but that he would buy Sally's home anyway. Sally said, "great," and told Bub that she would go ahead and arrange for the house to be painted. Sally immediately called a painter and contracted with her to paint the 2101 Park Street house for $2,000.

On June 12, Bub telephoned Sally and said he had changed his mind; he said he would not buy her home unless he succeeded in finding a buyer for his house. Sally said he was obligated to buy her house anyway.

Bub did not find a buyer for his house. When Sally tendered a deed to him on August 1, Bub refused to pay her the $145,000 or any other amount.

Sally has now sued Bub for damages for breach of contract. Will she prevail? Discuss. Assuming she prevails, what amount of damages will she recover? Discuss.

Question No. 2

Leslie wrote to Tom on December 1, 1988 in an undated letter, saying, "I will lease you my house for a year, while I am away in Europe. You can have the house beginning on January 1, 1989. Write me with your answer within one week." Although Leslie mailed the letter on December 1, it was misplaced for 10 days by the postal service. Thus, it was postmarked December 11 and was delivered to Tom on December 12. The envelope bore no markings on it indicating the misplacement at the post office. But for its misplacement, the letter would have been delivered on December 2. On the morning of December 14, Tom mailed a letter back to Leslie, which stated, "I accept your offer. Please be sure all the locks and built-in appliances are in good working order." The postal service lost Tom's letter, which was properly addressed and stamped. Accordingly, it was never delivered to Leslie.

Meanwhile, on December 10, Leslie leased the house to Xerxes for calendar year 1989. Tom showed up at the house mid-morning on January 1 with a moving van he had rented full of his possessions. Unfortunately for Tom, Xerxes had already moved in. Once Tom assured himself that Xerxes had a lease, he drove straight to his lawyer. The lawyer told Tom that Tom had no claim against Leslie. (Do not necessarily assume the lawyer was competent.) Tom nevertheless sent a demand letter to Leslie, demanding $5,000 in damages to settle his breach of contract claim. Leslie responded with the following letter:

Dear Tom:

I will agree to pay you $600 in full settlement of any claim you may have against me.

/s/ Leslie

Tom immediately mailed a reply, stating, "I agree to your terms."

Leslie never paid Tom anything, so Tom sued Leslie.

Assume the state landlord-tenant law requires landlords to have rented premises in "safe and decent condition" before renting them.

Please discuss the following questions:

(a) Did Tom have a valid contract to lease the house?

(b) If Tom did not have a valid contract to lease the house, can he recover the $600 from Leslie?

(c) Would your answer to (a) be changed if Leslie's December 1, 1988 letter had included the following sentence: "The monthly rent will be as agreed upon between us?"

Please assume that there are no statute of frauds issues.

Question No. 3

Novice Publishing Co. ("Novice") was a new company that was formed to publish law books. Congress was about to pass a bill that would completely rewrite the law of government ethics, so Novice contracted with Priscilla Professor to write a 15-chapter single volume treatise on government ethics law. Both Priscilla and Novice knew that there were already too many treatises in existence on government ethics law for a new one to be profitable unless there was a change in the law, and unless Novice could publish the first book to deal with the new law. Consequently, Novice's president, Newton, orally proposed the following deal to Priscilla:

- Priscilla would write a 15-chapter, one-volume, treatise on government ethics law;

- The first chapter would be "due" in four months, and then one additional chapter would be "due" each month thereafter (Priscilla had truthfully informed Novice that it would be very difficult to complete such a treatise in less than 18 months.);

- Priscilla would be paid $30,000 when the book was completed, but would receive no other payments or royalties from the treatise; and

- Novice could refuse to pay Priscilla if the text was "unsatisfactory to Novice."

Priscilla was concerned that Novice might not have the money to pay her the $30,000, so Newton called Big Bucks into the room. Big Bucks was a wealthy philanthropist with a strong interest in government ethics issues. Indeed, he had suggested that Novice break into the law book market with a government ethics book. Priscilla told Big Bucks of her concern; he said that he personally would ensure that she would be paid. Big Bucks took one of his business cards, wrote on the back of it "$30,000 ensured," and handed it to Priscilla. Priscilla then accepted Novice's proposal.

Priscilla began work on the treatise, but it went more slowly than she expected. It took her four months and eighteen days to complete the first chapter. While that chapter was in the mail to Novice, the U.S. President unexpectedly vetoed the government ethics bill. It was obvious that her veto could not be overridden, and she had 3 1/2 years left in her first term of office. In truth, the government ethics bill was dead as a doornail and so government ethics law would, as a result, remain substantially unchanged for the foreseeable future.

When Priscilla heard of the veto, she called Novice's President Newton to say that she would have to restructure completely her outline of the treatise. Newton said he wasn't sure he could let her have that much time. He truthfully pointed out that publishing costs were rising 1% per month and that the prices at which law books could be sold were not rising at all.

When Newton got Priscilla's first chapter in the mail, he skimmed it quickly and then sent a letter to Priscilla. The letter said that Novice was canceling the contract for "delay and unsatisfactory work."

Discuss the issues raised by these facts.

Question No. 4

Bev owned a business that did a large amount of chrome plating of bumpers and other car parts for Ford and Chrysler. Her contracts with Ford and Chrysler were fixed-price contracts ($20 per bumper, $3 per hood ornament, etc.), so Bev always worried about increases in the price of chromium. The country of Volga was the major chromium producer in the world. Accordingly, Bev had followed the widely reported unrest in Volga ever since 1982. It is now 1988.

In January of 1988, Bev decided to lay in a large stock of chromium, so she pulled out of her desk a brochure she had received the previous week from Sal, a dealer in metals. The brochure discussed various metals, including chromium, that Sal offered for sale, and it included a pre-printed Order Form. Bev filled in the blanks for her name ("Bev"), the type of metal she wanted ("99% pure chromium"), the amount ("five tons"), and the delivery date ("June"). A clause in the middle of the form stated that "Buyer agrees to hold this offer open for 35 days, and Seller may accept at any time within the period." Another clause in the form stated that the price for the chromium under the contract would be the closing price on the New York Commodities Exchange for the day on which the order was accepted. Bev signed on the signature line at the bottom of the form and mailed the order form to Sal on January 10.

On February 7, Sal mailed Bev a typed sheet entitled "Confirmation of Sale." The Confirmation stated that "Seller confirms the sale of five tons of 99% pure chromium to Bev." The Confirmation of Sale also stated that "Seller will not be responsible to deliver metals if availability is materially affected by labor strike, natural disaster, or war (including civil war)." This clause was not in the Order Form. The signature line at the bottom of the confirmation was blank; Sal had forgotten to sign it.

On February 8, before Bev received Sal's Confirmation of Sale, the market price of chromium dropped 10%. Sal anticipated a further drop, so he decided to wait several weeks before buying the chromium he would need to fill Bev's order. Bev also anticipated a further drop. Accordingly, as she had not yet received Sal's Confirmation, she mailed Sal a letter on February 8 saying that she no longer wished to purchase the chromium from him.

On February 9, Bev received Sal's Confirmation of Sale. She knew it was from Sal only because the envelope in which the Confirmation came had his return address on it, and because the Confirmation of Sale referred to five tons of 99% pure chromium, the same amount of the same metal she had ordered from Sal.

On February 10, Sal received Bev's February 8 letter. Sal wrote a note to himself saying "Don't buy chromium for Bev's order."

On February 11, tensions heightened in Volga. The market price of chromium accordingly went up by 15%. Bev immediately mailed a letter to Sal on February 11. In her letter: (1) she thanked Sal for his February 7 Confirmation of Sale; (2) said that he should ignore her February 8 letter; (3) stated that she was "looking forward to delivery of five tons of chromium under our contract;" and (4) signed it "Your loyal customer, Bev."

Sal received Bev's February 11 letter on February 13. He was busy; he glanced at her letter, did not notice it was signed by Bev (although it was), thought it pertained to a deal with a different customer, and threw it away.

On April 15, full scale civil war erupted in Volga. The market price of chromium went up by a factor of ten. On April 25, Bev wrote to Sal stating that she would prefer delivery of the five tons of chromium on June 3. On April 27, immediately after receiving Bev's letter, Sal wrote back, saying, "I believe you cancelled your order and that we do not have a deal. Please advise me immediately if you believe otherwise. Regardless, it does not appear I have any responsibility to deliver chromium. Moreover, I doubt I could get together more than one ton of chromium for you in any case given the civil unrest in Volga." Sal signed the letter, "Best wishes, Sal."

It is now April 30. Bev has come to you for advice. Please advise her: (1) Whether there is an enforceable contract for sale of the chromium? (2) If there is, what should she do? If Bev tells you she believes the price of chromium will rise steadily between now and the end of June, what effect will that have on your advice to her?

Question No. 5

On March 8, Byron went to his tailor, Silvio, and spoke with him about ordering a new suit. However, in the end Byron decided he couldn't afford the suit, but wasn't too clear in telling Silvio that he didn't want the garment. A few days later, Byron received the following letter from Silvio, dated March 10:

Byron,

It was, as usual, a pleasure seeing you again at the shop. I am starting work on the beautiful blue pin stripe suit which you ordered and I guarantee that it will be tailored to your exact measurements. The price, as we discussed, is $650 and it should be ready in two or three weeks. I will call you when it is finished. Thanks again for your order.

/s/ Silvio

Byron never responded to the letter and on April 1, Byron got a call from Silvio, who said, "Your new suit is ready! When will you be by to pick it up?" Byron replied, honestly, "Silvio this is all a misunderstanding. I never meant to order the suit we were talking about when I was in your store last month. I suppose I could see how you might have **thought** I told you to go ahead, but I can't afford it right now and I never wanted you to start making it." In response Silvio said, honestly, "it sure seemed to me like you told me you wanted it. And anyway, what about my letter?"

Byron told Silvio, "I meant to call you about that letter, but I forgot. It's still here sitting on my desk. Anyway, the letter proves nothing and I am not going to pick up the suit because I never ordered it." Byron never took delivery of the suit which was tailored to his measurements.

The suit cost Silvio $400 to make, inclusive both of the time he spent in making it and of the materials.

On his birthday, May 1, Byron treated himself to dinner at his favorite restaurant, Le Cess Poule. He ordered shrimp cocktail to start, sirloin steak with Bernaise sauce, apple pie, and a 1961 Lafite Rothschild as his wine.

As the waiter presented the wine, Byron noticed the waiter had made a mistake and had brought him a 1970 Lafite and not a 1961. Byron had never tasted the 1970 wine, was curious about it, and so said nothing about it. He finished drinking it at the restaurant. Le Cess Poule charges $700 bottle for the 1961, but only $575 for the 1970 Lafite. The retail values of these wines are $250 for the 1961 and $150 for the 1970.

When the waiter came with the appetizer he told Byron that the restaurant had, unfortunately, sold out of the shrimp cocktail but that he had brought Byron crab cocktail in its place as he thought this would be equally acceptable. The waiter additionally explained that while the crab cocktail was more expensive ($18 instead of $12), the restaurant would charge him only $12 due to the inconvenience they were sure Byron had been caused. Byron grumbled but said that it would be OK and ate the crab cocktail.

Byron took a bite of the sirloin when it arrived and exclaimed to the waiter, "this is Hollandaise sauce, not Bernaise!" The waiter promised to bring Bernaise sauce shortly, but never did. Byron took another bite or two of the meat while he was waiting, but finally it got cold and he eventually told the waiter he did not want it any longer and to take it away.

When dessert came, the waiter brought Byron a piece of pecan pie. Byron screamed that he had ordered apple and not pecan. The waiter apologized for his mistake and told Byron he would immediately bring him a slice of apple pie in its place. Byron said "forget it," and walked out of the restaurant without paying.

Discuss liability and damages:

(A) in *Silvio v. Byron*; and

(B) arising out of Byron's dispute with Le Cess Poule.

Question No. 6

Sap Co. ("Sap") was a manufacturer of heavy duty equipment. Bloop Co. ("Bloop") owned a private harbor and needed a large power dredge to keep the channels in the harbor free of silt. (A power dredge is like a small powerful ship but with a scoop attached to its bottom to scoop silt up out of the channels.)

In early March, Bloop discussed its needs with Sap; after extensive discussions, Sap proposed a particular design for the type of dredge Bloop would need and asserted that Sap was capable of making such a custom-made dredge. Sap told Bloop that it would take a few days to figure out the price Sap would have to charge.

Sap thereafter telegraphed Bloop on March 13. The telegram said: (1) the price for the dredge, if the parties agreed to a deal, would be $2.5 million; (2) Sap would have to do one final check of its cost figures before committing to building the dredge; and (3) Bloop would need to pay part of the price several months before delivery.

Bloop then sent Sap the following letter on March 15,:

Dear Sap Co.:

Two and a half million dollars is a lot of money. It is much more than we expected, and frankly we think it is too high. However, we really need a dredge and you seem very qualified to build one. Let us know when we can expect the dredge; any time before December of this year will be OK. We expect to receive full warranties, including a warranty that the dredge will do the job for us. We do not want to be limited to arbitration if there is a dispute, even though we know it is usual to have an arbitration agreement in these sorts of contracts. We are willing to deal with you only on the above terms.

We don't know how we're going to scrape together $2.5 million, so we will **very** much appreciate it if you would reduce your price.

Sincerely,

/s/ President Bloop Co.

P.S. We will pay $100,000 of the total on June 1. We reserve the right to cancel this order at any time up to June 15, by sending you a letter that says we are canceling it. Any payments we make before then will be returned to us if we cancel by June 15.

Sap mailed the following reply to Bloop on March 19:

Dear Bloop Co.:

We will deliver the dredge in October of this year. We will give you a warranty that the dredge will be free from defects in materials and workmanship (for example, that the steel used in it will be good steel and that the parts will be welded together properly), but we will not warrant that the dredge will actually work to dredge the silt in your particular harbor. **There will be NO implied warranty of merchantability or of fitness.** We agree that you will pay $100,000 out of the 2.5 million total on June 1. We will have the same right to cancel by June 15 that you have. Let us know if you agree to these terms; otherwise we will not deliver the dredge.

Sincerely,

/s/ President Sap Co.

No further correspondence was exchanged between Bloop and Sap until June 1, when Bloop paid Sap the $100,000 by check. Sap immediately deposited the check in its account. On June 2, Sap wrote Bloop and said that the price for the dredge would be only $2.3 million. Sap's letter said Bloop need not respond to it and Bloop did not. Bloop received Sap's price reduction letter on June 4.

On June 10, Bloop's president reviewed the file and for the first time noticed all the provisions in Sap's letter of March 19. He wrote Sap on June 10, saying that Bloop objected to the warranty limitations and to the provision allowing Sap to cancel, all of which were in Sap's March 19 letter.

Sap received the letter on June 14 and immediately telegraphed Bloop, stating that Sap would not deliver the dredge.

Bloop comes to you for advice on June 15. Is there a contract? If so, what are its terms? Discuss. Assume there are no statute of frauds issues.

Question No. 7

Joe Freelance was an independent producer of television documentaries and of television news stories. During the past few years, Joe had frequently produced stories for the CBS "60 Minutes" news program. On September 25, Joe had the following conversation with Don Hughclever, who was in charge of producing "60 Minutes."

> Don: We're thinking of running a story on photocopy salespersons. Do they all look like Jack Klugman? What brand of glass cleaner do they use to clean the glass plates on their photocopiers? Inquiring minds want to know!

> Joe: I could do a ten-minute story like that for you, but I'd have to ask at least $25,000.

> Don: We could afford to pay that much for a high quality piece . . .

[Sound of telephone ringing. Don answers it and then turns back to Joe]

> Don: Excuse me, Joe. I have to talk to our nightly news anchorman now. We'll talk again later.

The next day, Don sent the following letter to Joe:

Dear Joe:

CBS is willing to pay $25,000 for a high quality ten-minute piece on photocopier salespersons. We are scheduling it for our December 1, show.

> Very truly yours,

> (Signed) Don Hughclever

Joe did not respond to the letter, but immediately got to work on the story. Accompanied by an associate with a TV camera hidden in a briefcase, Joe went to Maxine's Wonderful World of Photocopiers and posed as a potential buyer. Maxine herself showed Joe several models of photocopiers. Joe said he liked the Z1000 photocopier and asked what he needed to do to get one. Maxine said she could quote him a price of $1,000 for a Z1000, and that he should send in a purchase order.

Joe then returned to his office and, with the television camera focused on his desk, filled out a purchase order. As he did so, Joe said (into the microphone), "We'll send this purchase order to Maxine and see how long it takes her to respond. Television viewers, this is true drama." Joe mailed Maxine the purchase order (which merely stated that he was ordering one Z1000 for $1,000).

Maxine received the purchase order the next day and immediately drove to the post office to mail back an acknowledgment which was sent in an envelope with sufficient postage and addressed correctly. The acknowledgment stated that Maxine would fill Joe's order at the stated price. It also stated, that:

(1) The Z1000 is warranted to work properly for one month or 1,000 copies, whichever comes first;

(2) There is NO IMPLIED WARRANTY OF MERCHANTABILITY OR FITNESS FOR ANY PARTICULAR PURPOSE accompanying the sale of the Z1000;

(3) The $1,000 price for the Z1000 offered by Maxine is a special low price. By ordering a Z1000 at that price, Buyer agrees to buy all photocopy supplies for the Z1000 from Maxine for the next year at Maxine's standard prices; and

(4) The terms of this acknowledgment, and only the terms of this acknowledgment, are the terms of the contract between Buyer and Maxine.

Then Maxine returned from the post office, she found a message from Joe on her telephone answering machine. The message was:

I am doing a story on photocopier salesperson for "60 Minutes." I don't really want a copier. Watch the show on December 1. This is Joe. Good-bye.

Joe never finished the story for "60 Minutes." CBS sued Joe for breach of contract. So did Maxine. Will CBS prevail? Will Maxine prevail? Discuss.

Question No. 8

Sound mixing companies prepare the sound tracks for motion pictures, television shows, and commercials. Johnson worked for a sound mixing company for ten years, learned everything there was to know about sound mixing and about sound mixing equipment, and then decided to start his own sound mixing company. In the fall, he purchased a small house in an area zoned for residential and commercial uses and began to remodel it into a sound mixing studio. He ordered acoustical panelling to put on the walls. On Friday, October 16, the panelling was delivered, and Johnson started to go to the hardware store to buy nails to put up the panelling. As he was about to get in his car, he spotted Neighbor in her front yard and introduced himself. When Johnson said he was going to the hardware store to buy nails, Neighbor said, "I've got a bag of nails I don't need. You can have it for $20. I'm leaving on vacation right now, but if you want the bag, it's in the garage." Neighbor got in her car and drove off. Johnson looked in Neighbor's garage, saw the bag of nails, and saw that it still had a $15 hardware store price tag on it. Johnson took the bag and left a note for Neighbor saying he would pay her only $15 for the nails, since that is what the nails cost her.

On Monday, October 19, Sound Mixing Equipment Sales Co. ("Sales Co.") mailed a letter to Johnson. (Johnson had written Sales Co. asking for its best offer on an Acme X14 Super Sound Mixer.) Sales Co.'s letter stated:

Pursuant to your inquiry, we are happy to quote you an Acme Super Sound Mixer for the low price of $30,000. We do not usually sell X14's for this low a price, but we intend to get lots of business from your new company. You can come by our premises any time before next Thursday, October 29 to give us an answer.

Johnson received Sales Co.'s letter on Thursday, October 22. That same day, October 22, Sales Co., mailed the following letter to Johnson:

After further consideration, we must ask $32,000 for the Acme X14.

On Monday, October 26, Johnson received Sales Co.'s letter of October 22.

On Saturday, October 24, after he had received the 10/19 letter but before he had received the 10/22 one, Johnson mailed the following letter to Sales Co.:

> It's a deal. I insist that if any lawsuit that arises out of this deal, the losing party will pay the prevailing party's attorney's fees.

Sales Co. received Johnson's letter of October 24 on Wednesday, October 28.

Discuss the following questions:

(1) Does Johnson have a contract to pay $20 for the nails?

(2) Does Johnson have a contract to buy an X14?

(3) Assuming he does, regardless of your answer to Part "(b)",

    (a) is the attorney's fee term a part of the contract?

    (b) what price must Johnson pay for the X14?

    (c) is Johnson obligated to buy additional items from Sales Co.?

Question No. 9

Pete, the owner of Pete's Ambulance Service ("Pete's") came into your office today, July 13, and told you the following story:

On June 1, Pete's purchased a new ambulance from Sam's Specialty Chevrolet ("Sam's") for $35,000. Just before the contract was signed, Peter told Sam he needed a reliable vehicle, and related a horror story about what happened a few weeks previously when one of his ambulances got a flat tire on the way to the hospital with a critically ill patient and the driver discovered there was no spare tire. In response, Sam promised personally to see to it that two spares were installed in the new ambulance. Nonetheless, Peter discovered yesterday that no spare tires were ever installed in the vehicle he purchased from Sam's.

The purchase contract was only one page long and paragraph 6 was set out in all capital letters as follows: "SELLER'S RESPONSIBILITIES UNDER THIS AGREEMENT ARE LIMITED SOLELY TO REPAIR OR REPLACEMENT, IN ITS SOLE DISCRETION, OF ANY DEFECTIVE PART OF SUBJECT VEHICLE FOR A PERIOD OF TWELVE MONTHS. IN NO EVENT WILL SELLER BE RESPONSIBLE FOR CONSEQUENTIAL DAMAGES ARISING OUT OF ANY BREACH OF THIS AGREEMENT."

Pete's took delivery on June 1 and drove without incident for two weeks. However, starting June 15 the engine began to stall, and between June 15 and July 7, the ambulance was in Sam's service department being worked on for 10 full days. Each ambulance in Pete's fleet averages two calls a day at $500 per call.

On July 7, Sam told Peter his shop had fixed the stalling problem and indeed the ambulance operated normally until yesterday. At about noon yesterday the ambulance was on its way to the hospital with a heart attack patient when the engine stalled in the middle of an intersection. When the engine stopped, the power steering froze, and the driver crashed into a light pole, injuring herself. The ambulance would not restart, and so another ambulance had to be called to deal with the heart attack victim. The delay in getting another ambulance to the scene caused the patient further injuries.

At about 5:00 p.m. yesterday Peter called Sam to tell him to take his no-good ambulance back, and found out that Sam's was out of business.

Please advise Peter as to all his present options concerning the ambulance arising under **contract law** (do not discuss any tort claims he may have), and what procedures he must follow, if any, to take advantage of each such option. Also discuss any defenses he is likely to face in pursuing each such option, and the damages, if any, available to him under each option.

Suggested Analysis of Essay Questions

Answer to Question No. 1

Will Sally prevail?

Sally will prevail only if there was an enforceable contract that was breached by Bub.

There was a contract.

Sally did not offer to sell the house to Bub for $150,000 on June 1; she merely said she was asking $150,000 for it [Text §3.213]. Anyway, Bub never accepted any offer at $150,000. Similarly, Bub did not offer to buy it for $140,000; he merely asked if she would take $140,000 for it [Text §3.213]. Further, even if Bub somehow made an offer to buy it for $140,000, Sally never accepted any such offer.

Sally's June 2 letter is an offer. It says it is an offer, invites Bub to accept, includes words of commitment ("If you accept, then you will pay... and I will give you a deed..."), and its terms are reasonably definite [Text §3.0]. It was a manifestation of commitment to enter into a bargain so made as to justify Bub in reasonably concluding that his acceptance was invited and would conclude the bargain.

Bub explicitly accepted the offer on June 4, within the time period for acceptance under the offer [Text §4.4] and obviously Bub was a proper offeree, for the offer was plainly directed to him [Text §4.3]. Thus, there was an offer and acceptance.

This is a bilateral contract, and thus, Bub's promise to pay was consideration for Sally's promise to hand over the deed, and **vice versa** [Text §7.2].

 Thus, there was a contract based on the terms of the June 2 and June 4 letters.

The contract may or may not be enforceable under the statute of frauds.

This is a contract for sale of an interest in real property so it is within the statute of frauds [Text §9.21]. Thus, there must be a memorandum of the contract signed by the party to be charged, which identifies the parties, identifies the subject matter of the contract, and **contains all the essential terms** of the contract [Text 9.23]. Otherwise the contract is voidable. [Text §9.02]

Bub is the "party to be charged" under the statute, because he is the one who is resisting enforcement of the contract. The only writing he signed was the letter of June 4. Since that letter expressly refers to the letter of June 2 and expresses his assent to it, all courts will be willing to read the two letters together (integrate them) to see if there is a sufficient memorandum. The two letters together identify the parties (Bub and Sally), more or less identify the subject matter (Sally's home on Park Street), and state a lot of the terms, but not all of them. The letters say nothing about the condition precedent that Bub find a buyer for his house by July 1, nothing about Sally's obligation to paint the house, and do not state which of Sally's houses on Park Street is the subject matter of the agreement.

The issues then are whether the identification of the house is sufficient, and whether the condition precedent and the painting term are essential terms.

You cannot tell from the letters alone what real property is being sold. However, in a sense that is always true. Even if the letters said "2101 Park Street," you still would not know what real property was involved without looking at a parcel map to find Park Street and then looking at the numbers on the houses to find out which one was 2101 and how much surrounding land came with the house. You always have to look at some external facts to apply the contract to the real world. The question should be whether the facts you have to look to are objectively verifiable facts that do not involve a risk of perjury; if so then the description should be considered adequate.

Modern courts will not be bothered by the absence of a specific mention of a particular city and state. There is no indication from these facts that Sally owned a home on any Park Street in any other city. The absence of a street number would not be a problem if Sally owned only one house on Park Street; there, the question of which house on Park Street she owns could be answered by looking to objective facts without any risk of perjury. Here, however, she owns two houses on Park Street, so the question is whether the letters provide us with enough identifying information to decide which house is being sold without there being a risk of perjury. The letters provide two important bits of information: (1) the house that is being sold is Sally's "home;" and (2) the house has an odd shaped dining room. Objective facts can be used to determine which of the two houses was being used as a "home" by Sally, and if only one of the houses has an odd shaped dining room suited for a custom made table and chair set worth $600, then that too is an objective fact that identifies the property that is being sold. A court that took a modern approach to this would almost certainly decide that the property was adequately described. The court might also consider the price in the letters to indicate that 2101 Park Street was intended, since its value is much closer to $145,000 than is the value of 2103 Park Street.

The next question then is whether omission of the painting term and of the condition precedent is fatal to the enforceability of the agreement. We must first ask if these terms were part of the contract. If they were not part of the contract, then it would not matter that they were omitted. To satisfy the statute of frauds, a memorandum must contain all the essential terms of the contract [Text §9.23]. (Below is a discussion as to whether such terms are part of the contract under the parol evidence rule; for now just assume that they were part of it.)

The painting term is relatively minor in value — $2,000 out of $145,000 total — so a court might say it was a mere detail rather than an essential term.

The condition precedent was very important, however. Assuming that there was a real chance Bub might not be able to find a buyer in a month, the condition would make it much less likely that Sally would get the benefit of the contract. Thus, a court could well say the condition was an essential term, and thus hold that the letters were insufficient to satisfy the statute of frauds. On the other hand, conditions precedent like this one can be proved despite the parol evidence rule (as we will see below), even if the writing otherwise is treated as a complete integration. It would seem strange to allow the condition to be proved under one rule which is designed to prevent perjury (the parol evidence rule) but then to throw out the whole contract under another rule that is designed to prevent perjury (the statute of frauds). Accordingly, it is reasonable to suppose that the condition should not be treated as an essential term under the statute of frauds, or that its absence can be excused given that there is no argument that the term was, in fact, part of the contract, and that the contract is thus enforceable under the Statute.

Was the condition precedent part of the contract? Yes.

The condition precedent of Bub obtaining a contract to sell his home by July 1 was a condition that would either have to be fulfilled or excused before either party would owe any enforceable duties to the other under the contract. Thus, evidence of the condition is admissible under the doctrine that the parol evidence rule does not apply to exclude evidence that a condition precedent was not fulfilled [Text §17.23].

Since evidence of the condition is admissible, the only question is whether that evidence will convince the trier of fact that the parties agreed to the condition. Of course, there is no way to predict how a particular jury would view this proof in advance, but there are reasons to think the evidence would be accepted. First, the evidence of the June 1 conversation will establish that both parties agreed that such a condition would be part of any bargain that they ultimately concluded. A reasonable person would therefore think that the condition was part of their ultimate agreement, unless when they formed their contract by correspondence they manifested an intent not to have such a condition. No such intent was manifested. Further, the June 10 telephone conversation indicates that both parties still thought the condition was part of their deal. Why would Bub have said he would buy the house "anyway" if he did not think the condition was part of the original deal? If Sally did not think the condition was part of the original deal, she probably would have protested that there was no such condition at all. She would not have in effect said that since Bub was waiving the condition, she would go ahead and have the painting done without waiting to see if Bub could sell his house.

Thus, evidence of the condition precedent is admissible under the parol evidence rule, and that evidence should be enough to convince the trier of fact that the condition was part of their bargain.

Did Bub waive the condition? Yes.

The condition was waived if Bub led Sally reasonably to believe that he would perform even if the event described in the condition did not occur [Text §20.41]. He told her he would buy her home even if he could not find a buyer for his home, so even though the condition was part of the initial contract, Bub was (as of June 10) obligated to buy the house regardless whether the condition was fulfilled.

Was Bub entitled to reinstate the condition? Perhaps.

At the time of the waiver the condition had not yet failed — it was still possible that Bub might find a buyer by July 1. Thus, his waiver did not become an "election." [Text §20.412] That means the waiver can be retracted (and the condition reinstated) if Bub gave Sally notice of the retraction before she *materially* changed position in reliance on the waiver [Text §20.413].

Bub attempted to retract the waiver on June 12, only two days after making it. However, Sally had already entered into a contract to have the house painted by that time. That is, she had relied on the promise of the waiver of the condition to her legal detriment.

The next issue, however, is whether Sally's reliance was a "material" change of position based on the waiver. A court could say that $2,000 in absolute terms is a lot of money to the average homeowner, so Sally did materially change position if she had the house painted. However, as she apparently only **contracted** to have it painted, she should be able to get out of the painting contract for a lot less than $2,000 — even if the painting contractor is unwilling to negotiate a rescission, Sally could repudiate the contract and probably pay a lot less than $2,000 in damages (although the hassle of defending a lawsuit and the possible injury to Sally's reputation if she repudiates the painting contract might lead the court to consider the whole $2,000 as Sally's reliance). A court might not think that lesser amount would represent a material change in her position.

Further, the court would consider whether Sally was going to have to paint the house anyway to sell it to someone else. If so, her injury from painting it now would be little or nothing. A court might also say that if the house needed painting, and if the painting increased the value of the house, then Sally's reliance did not represent a material change of position.

If the court concludes that Bub was entitled to reinstate the condition because Sally had not "materially" relied on his waiver, then Sally will not prevail in her lawsuit. That is, because the condition (Bub's house selling by July 1) was not fulfilled, Bub had no obligation to buy the home [Text §20.0]. In other words, they were in a valaid contract, but because of the failure of the condition precedent, the duties under the contract were never enforceable. Since the duties were unenforceable, Bub could not have breached by not performing.

If, on the other hand, the court concludes that Bub was not entitled to reinstate the condition, Sally will prevail in her lawsuit. Bub's duty to buy the home would then become unconditional [Text §20.0]. The only condition to Bub's duty to buy the home would be the constructive condition that Sally would have to tender a deed to the home before Bub would be obligated to pay the contract price of $145,000 [Text §21.1]. Sally satisfied that condition by timely tendering the deed. In that case, Bub would be in breach when he failed to tender the purchase price.

Another argument for Sally is that Bub's June 12 telephone conversation acted as an anticipatory repudiation of the purchase contract. That is, the argument is that Bub made a definite and unequivocal expression of his intent not to go forward with the purchase in that conversation. [Text §23.23] His conversation probably is not an anticipatory repudiation, however. Most likely, Bub was merely expressing his view that he could retract his waiver, and not impliedly stating that if he could retract his waiver, he refused to continue with the contract. If Bub's statement **was** an anticipatory repudiation, however, Sally was entitled to treat the contract as breached at that point and sue for total breach damages [Text §23.2].

Was the condition precedent eliminated by an enforceable modification of the parties' agreement? No.

A separate issue is whether the June 10 conversation acted as an oral modification of the contract. In other words, regardless of whether a "waiver" of the condition occured, did the 7/10 conversation eliminate the condition from the deal altogether by means of a modification? [Text §26.0] While Sally would like to argue this is the case, thereby making the contract enforceable, she runs into several problems with that theory. First, a modification of a contract is itself a contract: it is the substitution of a new different contract for the original contract. That means there must be mutual assent (offer and acceptance) **and consideration** for a modification to occur. There probably was an offer and acceptance. Bub certainly manifested assent in the June 10 conversation to an elimination of the condition. There may be some question as to whether Sally manifested assent in return, however. Clearly, Sally did not **expressly** manifest any assent. However, she did say she would go ahead and arrange for the painting. Accordingly, a reasonable person might well interpret that statement as assent to elimination of the condition, so probably mutual assent can be established.

While there is an offer and an acceptance of the modification, there is no apparent consideration for the deal. Bub does not say, "I will agree to eliminate the condition if you will agree to reduce the price by $500" or anything similar. It does not appear that Bub is seeking anything in exchange (i.e., is bargaining) for his action in rescinding the condition [Text §7.63]; he just flatly says that he will buy the house even if the condition is not satisfied. Neither does it appear that Sally is giving him anything **in exchange** for eliminating the condition. She does say she will go ahead and arrange for the painting, but an objective observer would likely not think she is exchanging that promise for his elimination of the condition. Rather, she is most likely reacting to his statement that he will buy the house even if the condition is not satisfied. Thus, because the bargained for exchange requirement is not met, the "modification" is unenforceable because there is no consideration for it. (This is not a UCC Article 2 contract, so consideration or promissory estoppel is needed [Text §§7.633; 26.21]. There are no unanticipated circumstances so Restatment 2d §89(a) does not apply.)

In addition, the statute of frauds bars enforcement of any modification here. The contract as modified is a contract for the conveyance of an interest in land [Text §9.21], so the modification has to be evidenced by a memorandum signed by Bub (the party to be charged, i.e., the party who would be denying that there was a modification which eliminated the condition). [Text §9.23] There is no such memorandum.

Damages, Assuming Sally Prevails

The contract called for Sally to get $145,000 in exchange for a $135,000 house, $2,000 worth of painting, and the $600 dining room set. Thus, if the contract had been performed, she would have gotten $145,000 in cash, but would have given up a total of $137,600 in value. Thus, she would have improved her economic condition by $7,400. [Text §31.3] That is, she would have to receive $7,400 to put her in the same economic position as if the contract had been fully performed. (Her expectation interest is greater than any reliance or restitution interest she may have, so she will seek enforcement of her expectation interest.)

All of this assumes Sally was obligated under the contract to paint the house. If she was not obligated to paint it, and did not paint it, her damages would be increased by $2,000. That is, in such event, the bargain would have been for her to give up only the $135,000 home and the $600 table and chairs in exchange for the $145,000. Accordingly, her expectation damages would be $9,400.

To decide whether she was obligated to paint the house, we must consider the parol evidence rule. Bub's June 4 letter expressed assent to a contract as "set forth in your [Sally's] June 2 letter." That should be enough to constitute adoption by Bub of the June 2 letter as a final statement of the parties' agreement [Text §17.1]. (Of course, Sally adopted it as a proposed final statement of the parties' agreement by signing and sending it.) The June 2 letter does not appear to be tentative and it has some detail in it. Thus, the June 2/June 4 letter agreements, taken together, would at least constitute a partial integration, meaning that neither party could introduce evidence of prior written agreements or prior or contemporaneous oral agreements that "contradict" the terms of the letters. [Text §17.1] Using the "might naturally" test, it would appear the painting requirement is a consistent additional term. That is, if the parties had agreed to it, it is the kind of thing that might naturally have been left out of their contract. [Text §17.14] Thus, Bub can introduce evidence of the term unless the June 2/June 4 letters constitute a complete integration.

Depending on the jurisdiction, a court will apply one of two tests to determine if the June 2/June 4 letter agreement is a complete integration.

Under the "four corners" test, the court will probably conclude that it is a complete integration. [Text §17.131] There is nothing obviously left out, and there is quite a bit of detail in the letter. As such, a court might well conclude the parties' agreement was completely integrated and no additional evidence of its terms will be permitted. However, a court might also say that a $145,000 transaction would probably have additional details, in which case that the letter agreement would be found incompletly integrated.

Under the "reasonably susceptible" test, [Text §17.132] the court considers separately, out of the presence of the jury, all the relevant evidence about the contract. If the court believes the painting term was really a part of the agreement (or at least that there is credible evidence that it was), then the court allows the trier of fact to consider the evidence. Here, there is good evidence that the term was agreed to and that the parties did not intend to eliminate it. Sally's phone response on June 10 is especially persuasive. Accordingly, it is likely that under the reasonably susceptible test the contract will be considered only partially integrated.

Answer to Question No. 2

Part (a) of the question involves 5 issues:

1) whether the letter of 12/1 was an offer;

2) the effect of the delay of the offer in the mail;

3) the effect of the lease to Xerxes ("X");

4) the effect of the loss of the December 14 letter in the mail; and

5) whether the inclusion of the statement "Please be sure all the locks and appliances are in good working order" prevented the December 14 letter from being an effective acceptance.

An offer is a manifestation of willingness (or commitment) to enter into a bargain so made as to justify another in believing that his or her assent is invited and will conclude the bargain [Text §3.0]. The 12/1 letter showed willingness to enter into the bargain and commitment to the proposed bargain. That is, it used words of commitment ("I **will** lease you my house," "You can have the house") and it invited Tom to accept ("Write me with your answer . . ."), thus showing that Leslie was committed to leasing the house to Tom if Tom assented to the proposed deal. Because the letter asked Tom to give an answer, Tom was justified in believing that his assent was invited.

The real issue here was the indefiniteness of the December 1 letter. It did not state the rental price, when rent would be due, how much rent would be paid in advance, how much of a security deposit (if any) would be required, etc. [Text §6.03]. This indefiniteness has two effects: (1) it may make it unreasonable for Tom to believe that Leslie is making a sufficient committment to lease the house to Tom so as to make the letter an offer — a reasonable person would probably want to have these terms settled before being bound to a bargain; and (2) even if Leslie manifested enough commitment, if the bargain is too indefinite it will not be enforced.

As to the first effect, Leslie has used rather clear words of commitment, and she is concerned with nailing down a tenant for her house quickly, because she is about to leave for Europe. Tom could reasonably believe that Leslie was willing to lease the house for a reasonable amount on the usual terms.

As to the second effect, if the parties intended to conclude a bargain (as they apparently did here), courts are hesitant to destroy that bargain for indefiniteness. This is a case of omitted terms [Text §6.021] (not an agreement to agree), so a court could reasonably conclude that the parties intended the rentals to be a reasonable amount on the usual terms; at least the court could conclude that implying such reasonable and usual terms would not unjustly violate the expectations of the parties. This is a lease of property and thus the UCC's gap fillers do not specifically apply, but courts in non-UCC transactions are increasingly willing to imply reasonable and usual terms to save a contract from indefinitness where it does not appear that such implications will defeat the parties' expectations. [Text §6.23]

Fair market rental value can probably be determined sufficiently accurately from the rental price of similar houses in the area, and there probably are fairly standard terms in the area (for example, first and last months' rent in advance plus one month's rent security deposit, with rentals payable monthly on the first of each month). Some courts would imply terms to make the contract enforceable; others would say that more certainty is needed in contracts involving real property than in other contracts and would refuse to imply terms. Assuming a court is willing to imply terms, the contract will be enforceable.

Assuming the December 1 letter was definite enough to be an offer, the next issue is the effect of the delay of the offer in the mail. The rule is that the time to accept an offer which gives a time period for acceptance runs from the time the offer is received, unless the offer states otherwise [Text §4.4123]. However, if the offeree has reason to know that communication of the offer has been delayed, the amount of the delay is subtracted from the period for acceptance [Text §4.4124]. This all, thus, boils down to whether Tom had reason to know that the postal service delayed the offer. If the letter had been dated, perhaps he would have had reason to know. However, since it bore no date, and the envelope gave no indication of the letter's misplacement, he had no reason to know of the delay. Accordingly, the offer was still open and he accepted it in a timely manner, unless it had been effectively revoked.

That takes us to the question of the effect of the lease to X. Did it revoke the offer? The answer is "no." Tom was never told by Leslie that she was revoking the offer, [Text §4.4132] hence her only argument is indirect revocation. However, an indirect revocation is only effective when the offeree obtains reliable information that the offeror has taken action that is inconsistent with an intent to enter into the offered bargain. [Text §4.4133] There is no indication here that Tom obtained **any** information about the lease to X until January 1, long after Tom sent his acceptance. An offeror cannot revoke an offer after it is accepted, of course.

The loss of Tom's acceptance letter in the mail does not matter. Leslie sent the offer via mail, so the mail would normally be a reasonable (and therefore invited) means of sending the acceptance. [Text §4.52] She did not tell him he had to use some other means and she came close to actually telling him to use the mail by asking Tom to write her with his answer. Thus, the mail was an invited means of acceptance. An acceptance sent by an invited means is effective when it is sent, even if it never arrives, so long as it is properly addressed and stamped, which this one was. [Text §4.61]

Finally, there is the question of the statement in the acceptance that Leslie should be sure that the locks and appliances were in good working order. This is not a contract for the sale of goods, so UCC §2-207 does not apply. The old "mirror image" rule applies, so if Tom's letter is *requiring* an added term, it is not an acceptance but rather a counter-offer (which Leslie never accepted). [Text §5.0]

It is possible that Tom is accepting Leslie's offer and merely suggesting or requesting that she make sure the locks and appliances are working. That is, his letter could be interpreted not as adding a term upon which he is **insisting** be included in the deal, but rather as only a letter suggesting or requesting the offeror's consideration of additional terms [Text §§4.4114-2; 4.4114-4]. However, in the letter he asks her to "be sure" about the appliances and such language sounds stronger than a mere request or suggestion, even though he does say "Please." Tom's best argument is that the landlord-tenant law already requires that locks and appliances be in good working order because it requires landlords to have their premises in safe and decent condition. Thus, responsibility for making sure the applicance worked and the locks were fixed would already be understood as part of Leslie's responsibilities without Tom saying anything, and hence he did not add any term that was not already there by operation of law. This is a stronger argument as to locks, and as to those appliances, that either are unsafe if they do not work (such as a gas heater), or which create a less than decent living situation if they do not work (water heater). It is not a very good argument as to appliances such as dishwashers or toasters. This is because such applicances do not directly relate to the "safe and decent" portion of the landlord's duties, so if there are such appliances Tom may be deemed to have added a term. On the other hand, perhaps it is usual in this area for landlords to have all appliances in good working order, and hence Leslie would already have that obligation based on the usual and customary terms of leases in the trade, which is possible because the offer is silent on this point. [Text §18.212] If so, then Tom's letter did not add any term, and his December 14 letter is an effective acceptance.

Part (b)

The question here is whether there is consideration for Leslie's promise to pay the $600. Tom's promise to release a claim that turned out to be invalid can still be consideration. All that is required is that at the time the settlement contract was made Tom had an honest belief of a colorable claim for Leslie's promise to be enforced [Text §2.634]. If Tom believed his attorney, then Tom did **not** honestly believe he had a claim, and there is no consideration. (Tom's quick agreement to accept much less than he demanded may show he did not have much confidence in the validity of his claim, but it will not be conclusive). If Tom did not believe his attorney, then he may have honestly believed his claim might be valid, which would be enough to enforce the promise.

Part (c)

It is much less likely that there will be a contract if the parties agreed to agree. The courts have a harder time implying a reasonable term when the parties have said that they — the parties — are going to determine what the term is [Text §6.023]. Here there is reliance by Tom, which Leslie should have expected. A reasonable rental amount will probably fall close to the amount that the parties would have agreed on if they in fact had gone ahead and agreed on the amount, and it will probably be an objectively determinable and fair amount for the court to force each party to accept. On the other hand, it is a very important term, and the court may refuse to "make an agreement for the parties."

Answer to Question No. 3

Statute of frauds on agreement to write and publish between Priscilla ("P") and Novice ("N").

This contract is not within the one year provision of the statute of frauds because the contract, by its very terms, is not impossible for P to complete in one year [Text §9.31]. Just because all the chapters will not be **due** for 18 months does not mean P must take that long to write them. N is supposed to pay her when she completes the book, so if she completes it in less than a year, N must pay her then. This is a contract for services, rather than goods, so UCC §2-201 does not apply. Thus, this is a contract that, by its terms, can be completed within a year and thus is enforceable even if oral.

Note that N's promise would also likely be enforceable, at least to some degree, on promissory estoppel grounds given the forseeable and actual reliance undertaken by P in putting in 4 months' work on the first chapter. [Text §9.7]

Statute of frauds on guarantee by Big Bucks ("BB").

BB's promise is subject to the suretyship provision of the statute of frauds [Text §9.5]. That is, BB is a "surety" because: (i) N may eventually owe a debt to P; (ii) as between BB and N, N is primarily liable, BB is only secondarily liable for the debt should it become due; and (iii) the promise was made to P, the creditor [Text §§9.51; 9.52]. The "leading object" or the "main purpose" doctrine probably does not apply here, for the economic benefit of the promise was for N, not BB [Text §9.53]. Note, however, that an argument could be made that BB wanted the book written for his own purposes because he was interested in ethics (thereby invoking the "main purpose" doctrine), but as he does not stand to benefit economically, the doctrine likely does not apply.

As the promise is within the Statute, P may or may not be able to enforce it. As the party seeking to enforce the promise, P must establish a sufficient writing, signed by BB. [Text §9.54] Whether BB's business card is a sufficient writing is a close call: BB's printed name on it is probably a sufficient signature since he probably used his card (rather than just any piece of paper) to identify to P the name of the person who was making the promise. In other words, he used it to authenticate his intention to stand behind the guarantee. The writing is probably sufficient to identify the parties to the surety promise, i.e., BB's name is on it and its delivery by him to P should be enough to identify her as the promisee, especially since the identity of the promisee will not likely be disputed. However, it may not have all the essential terms. Perhaps the only essential term is that he is guaranteeing the payment of the $30,000, which the card says, but a court may believe some further description of the debt is needed, e.g., under what circumstance will it be paid, who is the principal, **etc.**

If the card is judged an insufficient writing, however, promissory estoppel may suffice to let P enforce the promise. [Text §9.7]

Effect of 18 day delay in completion of first chapter.

P promised to perform a series of services — completion of 15 chapters. Completion of each chapter on time is not an express condition of N's duty to pay [Text §20.121], but failure to timely perform under a contract is always a breach [Text §20.0]. The question then will be whether P materially breached by submitting the first chapter late [Text §21.22] and, if so, whether she failed to cure that breach within an appropriate time [Text §21.272]. If she did materially breach without curing, N's duties will be discharged and it may cancel the contract. If her delay is only an immaterial breach, N will be obligated to continue performing, but will have a claim against P for partial breach due to the delay.

The relevant factors for determining whether the breach is material or not are listed in Restatement 2d §§241 and 242 [Text §21.242]:

The extent to which the breach will deprive N of the benefit which it reasonably expected (18 day delay seems trivial because it will lead to less than a 1% increase of costs, and because speed is no longer important after the veto, and because P may be able to "make up" the lost time on later chapters);

The extent to which damages can adequately compensate N (if P ends up taking longer than 18 months to finish, N can probably prove the increase in publishing costs caused by the delay, and those expenses will be recoverable for the partial breach);

The extent of forfeiture on P's part if N is permitted to cancel (P's work of more than 4 months will be forfeited;

The likelihood of cure (if P can write the later chapters slightly faster than one per month she can make up the lost time — but perhaps that will be very difficult);

The extent to which P acted in good faith and fairly (she apparently worked very hard to minimize the delay);

The extent to which any delay in allowing N to terminate will prevent N from making substitute arrangements (N does not want to make substitute arrangements for the treatise); and

The extent to which the agreement provides for performance without delay (i.e., there is no agreed upon "time is of the essence clause" here).

As a result, P's breach should only be judged immaterial, and thus the delay does not justify N's cancellation of the contract [Text §21.21].

Effect of President's veto on N's duties.

There are two major issues raised by the President's veto: (1) did the veto frustrate N's purpose in entering into the contract [Text §25.3]; and (2) was existence of the new law an implied-in-fact condition of either party's duties under the contract [Text §21.0]?

Did the veto frustrate N's purpose?

Whether the contract was frustrated depends on how you define N's purposes under it. N will still get a book on government ethics if the contract proceeds, but it will not be the kind of book that will let N break into law publishing in a successful way. Is P's performance essentially worthless to N? Arguably it is, since it will not be financially worthwhile to publish the book. However, it can be used in N's business as part of the range of subjects it covers, even though it will not be profitable. There is a strong presumption against a finding of frustration just because a party will not make as much money from the contract as expected, or even if a party will lose some money [Text §§25.311; 25.312]. Hence, all things considered, it appears that frustration will not provide a successful defense to N because, on these facts, there is insufficient "frustration."

Implied-in-fact condition

The argument here is that since both P and N knew that the market would not support a new book on the old law, the fact of the law's being passed was an implied-in-fact condition of their duties. (It is not a constructive condition for it is not implied by the court as a means of determining the parties' rights and duties.) This is a very close question. The principal argument against it is that if the condition was really that important, it is likely that the parties would have discussed it openly and made it an express condition. However, if it was well understood, even if not overtly expressed, it could be that the passage of the new law is an implied condition precedent, and thus the veto by the President made each party's duties under the contract unenforceable.

Effect of veto on P's duties.

Just as frustration is principally a buyer's remedy, impossibility and impracticability are seller's or supplier's remedies. Here, the veto did not make it impossible for P to finish the book [Text §25.1], but it probably made it impracticable for it to be completed on time [Text §25.2]. That is, the veto was the occurrence of an event, the non-occurrence of which was a basic assumption of both parties on which the contract was made [Text §25.212]. It occurred without P's fault [Text §25.213], and it does not seem that P either explicitly or implicity assumed the risk that the veto would occur, since neither seemed to have considered its possibility. [Text §25.214] This would likely be treated as a case of temporary impracticability, which means that P's delay is excused for a "reasonable period of time," and such delay cannot be considered a breach by N. [Text §25.5] Note that if her delay in performance is "unreasonably" long (e.g., because P stopped working on it for nine months or so), then it would still constitute a material breach, and her failure to satisfy an unexcused constructive condition would justify N's withholding its performance. If the delay continues reasonably, but for a long enough period so that it creates a hardship to N, e.g., where P is working diligently, but it is taking a long time to re-structure her entire book, N would be thereafter justified in canceling the contract, but N would not have an action for breach against P.

The condition of satisfaction.

If the judging of the quality of a manuscript is seen as depending on the tastes of the publisher, then a subjective good faith standard would be applied. [Text §7.622] That is, for N to cancel the contract on the grounds of dissatisfaction, N must **actually** be dissatisfied with the quality of the manuscript, not just with the terms of the deal. If so, application of the good faith promise is a sufficient restriction on N's activities as to cure any illusory promise problems. Since Newton merely skimmed the chapter, it appears he did not in good faith try to see if the chapter was satisfactory but just said it was not in order to be able to cancel the contract. Moreover, it is difficult for Newton to be able to state credibly that the **entire manuscript** would be unsatisfactory by reading just one chapter. The good faith obligations under a contract would seem to require N to at least have told P what was wrong with the chapter so that she could rewrite it and do the other chapters to N's liking. Accordingly there has been a breach of the duty of good faith and fair dealing by N.

Remedies.

If N is able to terminate the contract on grounds of frustration, P should get restitution of any benefits she has conferred on N [Text §25.6]. It is difficult to know if N got any benefit at all. Under the "cost avoided" method of valuation, P would be entitled to the going rate for writing such a chapter for a legal publisher. Under the "net benefit" method, P's recovery would be nothing, for receipt of an unusable chapter has not advanced N's economic interests in the slightest. [Text §32.11]

If N is entitled to cancel the contract as a result of P's breach (i.e., in the unlikely event P's late tender will be judged a material breach), even then P is entitled to restitution [Text §32.3]. However, restitution requires that when a breaching party seeks restitution, the measure of valuation used is the one least favorable to the breacher. [Text §32.111] Hence, on these facts, should P be seeking resitution as the breacher, she would receive little or nothing because her compensation would be determined by the net benefit method.

If N wrongfully canceled, then N repudiated the contract and P can receive damages of $30,000, less whatever amount she can now reasonably earn from comparable employment that she would not have been able to earn if she were still working on the book [Text §31.32].

Answer to Question No. 4

Offer

An offer is a manifestation of willingness to enter into a bargain, so made as to justify another in believing that his assent is invited and will conclude the bargain [Text 3.0]. It must be definite enough to permit a court to determine the existence of a breach and to provide an appropriate remedy. If the manifestation shows that sender does not intend to be bound until he or she manifests further assent, it is not an offer.

Sal did not make an offer by sending the brochure and order form to Bev. Advertising brochures typically aren't offers, for reasons present here [Text §3.214]. The brochure and blank order form do not include any terms of a deal (except price as set by N.Y. Commodities Exchange). When important terms are not stated, that is some indication that only preliminary negotiations are occurring [Text §3.213]. Further, if Bev just wrote in her name and "I accept," and mailed the otherwise blank form to Sal, a court would have no idea how to determine whether a breach occurred or what remedy to give especially since neither quantity nor subject matter appear on the form [Text §6.01]. It is up to the buyer to fill these in and then for Sal to determine if he is willing and able to undertake to fulfill the order. Further, the order from refers to "Buyer" as making an offer and "Seller" as having power to accept, so the brochure must be inviting offers for Sal to consider. It does not show any commitment by Sal to fill orders that buyers send in. For all these reasons, Bev would not be justified in believing her assent would conclude any deal.

Bev made an offer, however, by filling in the order form and mailing it in. All the terms are now definite (except for the June delivery date, which probably would be interpreted as permission to delivery at any time in June, and in any case is not a serious problem given the UCC gap filler on delivery time, §2-309) [Text §6.224]. The order calls itself an offer, and it expressly provides for acceptance by Sal. Sal would be justified in believing his assent would conclude the deal.

Acceptance

Bev's offer is an offer for the purchase of goods. Accordingly, it is governed by the UCC. As the formation and terms of the contract here will be determined through an exchange of writings, the analysis of the issue is governed by §2-207 [Text §5.2].

Sal's 2/7 Confirmation of Sale acts as a valid acceptance under §2-207. Under the common law mirror image rule, it would be a counter-offer since Sal added a "force majeure" clause (the strike, natural disaster, etc. clause); under §2-207(1), however, it is a valid acceptance because it is a seasonable definite expression of acceptance not made conditional on Bev's assent to the force majeure clause. [Text §5.31]

It is **seasonable** because it comes before the offer lapses. By its terms, the offer does not lapse until February 14, 35 days after Bev mailed the offer. The offer is not an **irrevocable** firm offer under §2-205 because **Bev** (the offeror) did not separately sign the 35 day provision on the form which was provided by the offeree Sal, as is required by that section [Text §4.422]. However, that just means Bev *could have* revoked the offer. However, as she did not revoke it (or otherwise terminate Sal's power of acceptance), the offer was accepted when Sal mailed the confirmation of Sal.

The 2/7 Confirmation is a **definite** expression of acceptance because it showed Sal's intent to go ahead with Bev's proposed deal. He confirmed that he would sell her the 5 tons of chromium, and he did not change the major, typically negotiated terms like price, quantity, subject matter, and delivery date. (Changing one of those would make it appear not to be an "acceptance" of the same basic deal proposed by Bev.) [Text §5.311]

The 2/7 Confirmation did not say "No deal unless you assent to force majeure clause," or "Acceptance is conditional on assent to force majeure clause" or anything else that would make the acceptance expressly conditional on Bev's assent to the added term. [Text §5.312]

Thus the requirements of §2-207(1) are met, and the 2/7 Confirmation acted as a valid acceptance.

Attempted Revocation of Offer and Its Effects

Bev's letter of 2/8 was an **attempt to revoke her offer** [Text §4.4]. A revocation is a manifestation by the offeror that he, she, or it no longer wishes to enter into the offered deal. The letter arrived too late for the revocation to be effective, however, because an offer cannot be revoked after it has been accepted. Where use of mail is an invited means of acceptance (as was true here, since the offer was sent by mail), an acceptance is effective upon dispatch [Text §4.61]. Thus, Bev's offer was accepted on 2/7 when Sal mailed the confirmation. One of the consequences of acceptance of an offer is that the offer can no longer be revoked [Text §4.1].

While the 2/8 letter cannot be effective as a revocation of Bev's offer, it might still have effect in one of four other ways:

(1) If an offeree who receives a revocation after accepting the offer **relies** on the revocation, the offeror may be **estopped from enforcing the contract** [Text §4.64]. Here, however, while it is true that Sal wrote a note to himself not to buy chromium for Bev, he had already planned to wait several weeks to buy the chromium anyway. Accordingly, it is not clear that he relied at all on Bev's 2/8 letter. **Perhaps** he would have bought chromium for Bev on 2/11 or 2/12 if he thought she still wanted it. (Any reliance after he received her 2/11 letter on 2/13 would not be reasonably justified.) Prices were rising so his initial thought that he should wait while prices fell might have changed. There are insufficient facts in this fact scenario to tell whether reliance occurred.

(2) The 2/8 letter could have been taken as an **anticipatory repudiation** [Text §23.0]. In some sense the 2/8 letter could be interpreted as an unequivocal statement by Bev that she is unwilling to perform [Text §23.3]. However, when she sent it she did not know there was a contract. Thus, a reasonable person looking solely at the 2/8 letter, would not know whether she would refuse to perform once she found out there **was a** contract. In addition, Sal should have known his acceptance and her revocation crossed in the mail, so probably he would not have been justified in treating this letter as a repudiation.

If the 2/8 letter was a repudiation, however, under §2-611 Bev could retract it until: (1) Sal relied on it, or (2) Sal indicated to her that he was cancelling the deal or that he considered her repudiation final. [Text §23.5] Sal's note to himself was not directed to Bev so (2) does not apply. Under (1), Bev could retract her repudiation unless Sal relied on it. (Whether he relied on it is the same fact question discussed above in relation to estoppel.) Hence, Bev's 2/11 letter would be an effective retraction of the repudiation unless Sal had relied on the repudiation before receiving the retraction on 2/13.

(3) The 2/8 letter could be treated by Sal as an **offer to rescind the contract** [Text §24.4]. However, Sal did not accept that offer and Bev, in effect, revoked the offer of rescission in her 2/11 letter. Sal's note to himself was not communicated to Bev, so it provided no objective manifestation of his acceptance of the offer to rescind.

(4) The 2/8 letter might be considered a **waiver** of Bev's right to insist on delivery of any chromium [Text §§20.41; 26.5]. Again the issue will be whether Sal relied on the 2/8 letter. If he did not, Bev can retract her waiver under §2-209(5) [Text §26.7].

Sal probably did not rely on the 2/8 letter, so Bev can still enforce the contract. (Of course, a court might strain to find reliance since Bev is shifting her position back and forth in response to market shifts, which puts her in a bad light. In fact, she may have acted in bad faith, in which case a court **might** prevent her from introducing her 2/11 letter. However, she was still at risk — if the market had dropped after 2/8, Sal could have held her to the contract. Thus, she should probably be considered as acting in good faith in claiming the benefit of the contract when the market shifted upwards. Moreover, if Sal did not rely on her 2/8 letter, any bad faith on her part did not harm him, anyway.)

Statue of Frauds

Assuming, that the N.Y. Commodities Exchange price for 5 tons of chromium on 2/7 would be at least $500, the contract is within the statute of frauds of Article 2, and thus must satisfy UCC §2-201 to be enforceable. [Text §9.6] Sal will want out of the deal and Bev will want to enforce it, so Sal is the "party to be charged," or, in §2-201's words, the "party against whom enforcement is sought."

There does not seem to be an adequate writing signed by Sal to bind Sal under §2-201(1) [Text §9.62]. The 2/7 Confirmation was unsigned and apparently Sal's signature was nowhere in the Confirmation or on the envelope. There is, of course, an argument that the return address on the envelope would suffice to satisfy the Statute [Text §9.6224], but that argument is not a strong one. Sal probably did not put the address on the envelope to indicate that he was responsible for the contents of the envelope, but rather he put the return address there so that recipients of his letters would know the address to respond to.

However, under §2-201(2), Bev's letter of 2/11 is sufficient against Sal as a merchant's confirmatory memorandum [Text §9.63]. This is, because: (1) it is sufficient against Bev (signed by her, shows a contract for sale was made, indicates quantity); (2) it seems to have been sent within a reasonable time after formation of the contract (only 4 days); (3) it confirms the existence of contract; (4) Sal received it; (5) Sal had reason to know its contents, even though he threw it away; and (6) Sal did not object to its contents until long after the ten days permitted in 2-201(2), the statute is deemed "satisfied" under §2-201(2).

Thus the contract is enforceable against Sal under the statute of frauds.

The Force Majeure Clause

If the force majeure clause in Sal's 2/7 Confirmation is part of the contract, Sal is probably excused from delivering any chromium. This is because the civil war in Volga has presumably "materially affected the availability" of chromium. (Sal says he can only get together one ton.)

Whether the clause becomes a term of the contract depends on UCC §2-207(2) [Text §5.322]. Under §2-207(2), the force majeure clause becomes part of the contract if Bev and Sal are merchants (which is almost certainly the case) unless:

(1) Bev's offer limited Sal to accepting the offer on its terms [§2-207(2)(a)], or

(2) The force majeure clause materially changes the deal [§2-207(2)(b)], or

(3) Bev already objected to the force majeure clause, or objects to it within a reasonable time after getting Sal's Confirmation [UCC §2-207(2)(c)].

There are no facts supporting any reasonable argument that UCC §2-207(2)(a) or §2-207(2)(c) are satisfied. Whether the force majeure clause materially changes the deal depends (according to Comments 4 and 5 of §2-207) on whether it would cause Bev unreasonable surprise or hardship if the provision was included in the deal without her being aware of it. If the doctrine of impracticability would not excuse Sal from performing in the event of a civil war in Volga, then inclusion of the clause would probably unreasonably surprise Bev and cause hardship to her since she would be counting on the contract to protect her against such occurrences. Thus, if the clause would help Sal at all in this case, it probably materially changed the deal.

If Sal cannot establish that the force majeure provision became part of the contract under §2-207(2), Sal might be able to argue that the clause was explicity agreed to by Bev. That is, he may be able to establish that he and Bev entered into a contract modification including the term. Bev's 2/11 letter "thanking" Sal for the Confirmation may be construed as her implied assent to addition of the force majeure term [Text §5.312]. Under §2-207(2), just going ahead with a deal is not an assent. However, Bev's 2/11 letter comes close to endorsing the Confirmation — perhaps a reasonable person would view it as an assent. Under UCC §2-209(1), no consideration is needed for a modification of a contract. So long as Sal is in good faith in proposing this modification, an assent to it by Bev will make it part of the contract. It seems honest and within commercial standards of fair dealing for Sal not to want to take these risks, so he is in good faith. Note, if this argument is successful, there will be no statute of frauds promise associated with the modification for it was done in writing. [Text §26.1]

Impracticability

Assuming the force majeure clause would not become a part of the contract, Sal may still argue that his performance duties are discharged through normal commercial impracticability principles. [Text §25.2] (No frustration of purpose issue is presented since Sal's purpose of getting money is not frustrated, nor is the money he would get from Bev practically worthless.) To establish impracticability, Sal must show that:

(1) Performance by him would be sufficiently impracticable (ten times increase in price may be enough of a cost increase to change the "essential nature of the performance" per §2-615, Comment 4) [Text §25.211];

(2) The impracticability was due to occurrence of an event (the Volga civil war), the non-occurrence of which was a basic assumption of both parties when they entered into the contract. However, the foreseeability of Volga civil war given Volga's recent civil unrest makes it doubtful that the occurrence of civil war was something neither party thought could happen when they entered the deal, especially since the very fact Sal tried to list civil wars in his force majeure clause shows that he was concerned about the occurrence of the event [Text §25.212];

(3) That the party asserting the defense (Sal) did not assume the risk of the civil war's occurence under the contract. Here there was a fixed price contract of a volatile commodity supplied from a country that is in a state of upheaval, and Sal did not include anything in the order form to put this risk on Bev. (If he had, it would have been part of Bev's offer and thus part of the contract. This may show that implicitly Sal assumed the risk.) [Text §25.214];

(4) That the event causing the impracticability was not Sal's fault. Obviously Sal did not cause the civil war, but he did have a chance to buy the chromium on 2/7 or 2/8. Instead, Sal chose to speculate on the price of chromium. Further, if Sal had read his mail carefully, he would have known on 2/13 that Bev was expecting him to buy chromium for her, which would have given him two months to buy it before the war started. Arguably he was also responsible for the impracticability for his performance [Text §25.213].

Accordingly, it appears Sal's performance obligations will not be discharged due to impracticability for he probably cannot establish several of the elements.

What should Bev do?

Bev should immediately demand reasonable assurances of performance under UCC §2-609 [Text §23.32]. Sal's 4/27 letter certainly gives Bev grounds for insecurity, so she should write Sal, include a copy of her letter of 2/11, and insist that he promise to perform and that he give her assurances that he will be able to perform. If he then says he will not perform, or if he fails to assure her within a reasonable time that he will perform, she is entitled to conclude that he has anticipatorily repudiated the contract under UCC §2-610. Accordingly, at that point she is entitled to cancel the contract, buy the chromium elsewhere (cover), and seek damages based the on difference between the cover and contract prices under UCC §2-712 [Text §33.21]. Further, if she chooses not to cover, she is entitled to seek market differential damages based on the difference between the market price for the chromium and the contract price based on the formula given in §2-713 [Text §33.22].

It would not be prudent for Bev to cancel the contract without seeking assurances, however, because it is not clear that Sal's 4/27 letter was a repudiation. It was not unequivocal [Text §23.23]; he said he "believed" there was no deal, and that it did not "appear" he had to deliver chromium, and that he "doubted" he could get together more than one ton. None of those is an unequivocal statement that he is refusing to perform or that he cannot perform, especially in light of his willingness to consider Bev's point of view if she believes there is a contract ("Please advise me. . .").

If Bev cancels the contract now, it is more than likely that **she** would be repudiating the contract under the first material breach doctrine [Text §21.25]. In that case, Sal would be entitled to cancel the agreement.

If Bev believes the price will continue to rise

Bev should immediately buy all the chromium she can if she believes the price will continue to rise. If Sal decides to perform, she can use his low price chromium in her business, or resell it at a big profit. If he does not, she can sue him for the price differential.

Answer to Question No. 5

Silvio v. Byron

The first issue is whether or not a contract was formed between Silvio and Byron. As we are not given the text of the conversation that took place in the tailor shop in the facts, it is impossible to answer definitively whether a contract was formed, or even who was the offeror and who was the offeree. However, typically the buyer will make the offer and the seller will accept it and there are enough facts to analyze the formation issue on that basis.

In the April 1 telephone conversation, Byron admitted that he understood how Silvio "might have thought" Byron told him to go ahead and make the suit. Under the objective theory of contracts, an effective offer is one in which a reasonable person would believe the person making the purported offer was willing to be bound on the terms he presented given those circumstances. [Text §§3.0; 3.2] Accordingly, Byron's admission suggests that he did make an effective offer in the tailor shop.

The next question is whether Silvio properly accepted. He may have accepted orally, promising to make the suit, thereby forming a valid bilateral contract. Once again, by not having the text of their conversation in the facts, it is impossible to say with certainty whether or not formation took place in that manner. However, the facts state that Silvio began performance shortly after Byron left. Under §2-206 acceptance can be made by beginning performance, if such course of action is reasonable. [Text §4.54] Here we have a tailor trying to get a specially made good into the hands of his customer in the shortest possible time, which would certainly pass any commercial reasonableness test. Additionally, Silvio gave prompt notice by the March 10th letter, as required in §2-206(2) [Text §4.5432], making it sound even more like an effective acceptance.

Thus, if no offer was made by Byron, obviously Byron will win since there can be no breach without a valid contract. However, if Byron is judged to have made an offer, as appears to be the case, it was properly accepted by Silvio and a valid contract was formed.

The next issue is whether the contract is enforceable under the statute of frauds. The agreement is subject to the statute of frauds under §2-201(1) as it involved a contract for the sale of goods for of $500 or more [Text §9.6]. The facts reveal no writing signed by Byron evidencing a contract, and thus under §2-201(1) Byron has a valid statute of frauds defense [Text §9.62]. Accordingly, unless one of the exceptions to the statute of frauds listed in §2-201(2) or §2-201(3) comes into play, Byron will prevail as the oral contract will be unenforceable.

Section 2-201(2) states that the recipient of a confirmatory memorandum like Byron, will lose his statute of frauds defense if he does not object properly to the memo within ten days after its receipt. However, the provision explicitly states that it is effective only "between merchants." Obviously Silvio is a merchant as he is in the business of selling suits. The question is, can Byron be called a merchant. As it appears he is merely a consumer, he probably cannot [Text §9.634].

There is no question, however, that the contract is enforceable under 2-201(3)(a). A custom made suit is obviously a specially manufactured good [Text §9.641], and here the suit was made to Byron's "exact measurements." Accordingly, the oral contract between Byron and Silvio is enforceable under §2-201. As Byron refuses to pay for the suit, he is in breach.

The next issue is what damages are collectible by Silvio. Obviously, Silvio would like to sue for the price under §2-709 [Text §33.4]. As Byron has not accepted the suit, Silvio's only chance for the price is under §2-709(1)(b). Under that provision, Silvio may recover for the price of the suit only if he can establish that he cannot obtain a reasonable price for the suit from another despite diligent efforts, or establish that any attempt at resale would be reasonably unavailing [Text §§33.43; 33.44]. As the suit is specially made to fit Byron's measurements, a good argument could be made that attempting a resale of the suit by looking for someone with Byron's exact measurements would be unavailing, thereby entitling Silvio to the full $650. If Silvo cannot find anyone to buy it for a reasonable price, upon satisfaction of a final judgment, Byron would be entitled to possession and title to the suit [Text §33.4].

However, if a court should hold that portions of the material could be reused for scrap, or that the suit could be re-altered to fit someone else with relatively little damage, then Silvio would have to sue under §2-708(2) [Text §33.53]. Under that provision he could recover his profit ($640 - $400, or $250), plus the amount of time and materials expended in making the suit ($400), less the value of the material as scrap or less any proceeds upon resale of the suit to someone else [Text §33.5311].

Byron v. Le Cess Poule

The first issue is whether the transaction in the restaurant is governed by Article 2. Obviously steaks, shrimp, etc., can be identified to the contract and at the time of identification they are movable. Thus, the requirements of Article 2 applicability set forth in §2-105 are met [Text §34.2]. Further, additional support for the premise that the food is covered by Article 2 comes from the language of §2-314(1). Hence, these are clearly Article 2 transactions.

Wine

When Byron noticed the waiter had brought the 1970, as opposed to the 1961, bottle of wine and said nothing about it, he accepted goods under the contract with notice of the defect. Accordingly, under both §2-607(3) and §2-709(1), Byron is liable for the full contract price of the 1961 bottle [Text §§22.311; 33.31]. In other words, it would be wrong to say that under the **contract** he is only liable for the price of the 1970 bottle, despite the fact that he only received the 1970 wine. That is not how §2-709(1) or §2-607 read. If he accepted goods knowing of their non-conformity, he is liable for the full amount of the **contract** price.

However, because he accepted non-conforming goods, he has a breach of express warranty claim against the restaurant. Under §2-714(2), the proper measure of damages for a breach of express warranty is the difference between the value of the goods as promised and the value of the goods received. In this case that is the difference between the 1961 price and the 1970 price i.e., $700 - $575. Thus, he ends up paying only the restaurant's price for the 1970 wine, but that figure is properly arrived at only after holding him liable for the full contract price and offsetting against that damages from his breach of warranty claim. See §2-717 [Text §33.314]. Since he has not paid that price to the restaurant, he is in breach.

Shrimp Cocktail

Le Cess Poule's tender of the crab cocktail instead of the shrimp cocktail is probably best characterized as an accommodation shipment [Text §4.551]. The waiter informed Byron that the restaurant did not have what he asked for, tendered what he thought would be an equally acceptable good, and gave Byron the chance to refuse that selection. In other words, the crab cocktail was a counter-offer, which Byron accepted, and thus he is liable to the restaurant for the special price the waiter quoted him for the crab cocktail, $12. Once again, since he has not paid anything for the crab cocktail, he is in breach.

Steak

The first issue here is whether Byron accepted the steak. As it is difficult to tell by sight whether the sauce was a Hollandaise or Bernaise, taking a bite or two initially would probably be inspection, not acceptance [Text §22.31]. Thus when Byron told the waiter to bring the Bernaise sauce, there was a proper rejection with an assurance of cure by Le Cess Poule [Text §22.24]. However, when Byron took other bites of the steak while waiting for the Bernaise sauce to be brought, there probably was acceptance under §2-606(c). That is, such acts appeared to be inconsistent with Le Cess Poule's ownership of the meat [Text §22.31]. However, Byron still was within his rights at the end of the meal to revoke his acceptance since he only accepted with the assurance that the defect would be cured under §2-608(1)(a) [Text §22.33]. As the defective tender was never cured, Byron's revocation was effective and thus he is not liable for the purchase price of the steak. Although courts have been reluctant to adopt it, Le Cess Poule might have a claim in restitution for any benefits Byron received from eating the steak [Text §22.334].

Pie

When the waiter brought Byron the wrong kind of pie, clearly Byron was within his rights to reject as the pie was a non-conforming good [Text §22.32]. However, the restaurant attempted to cure by replacement under §2-508(2), and possibly §2-508(1) depending on whether the time for performance had passed [Text §22.241]. As there is no evidence that waiting for the apple pie to be brought caused Byron any damage, it is he who is in breach for not allowing cure to be made. Thus, he is liable to the restaurant for the cost of the pie. Perhaps if the waiter intentionally brought him the wrong kind of pie Le Cess Poule would lose its cure rights as it would not have reason to believe that the goods tendered would be acceptable under §2-508(2) [Text §22.2412]. However, there is no evidence of this from the facts and it is highly unlikely that is the case.

Answer to Question No. 6

The 3/13 telegram and the 3/15 letter.

The 3/13 telegram was only a preliminary negotiation, because Sap ("S") expressly stated that S would have to give further assent to the proposed bargain before being committed to building the dredge. That is, there was no commitment to be found [Text §3.213].

The 3/15 letter from Bloop ("B") was an offer [Text §3.0]. B grumbled a lot about the price, but ended up expressing willingness to enter into a bargain at $2.5 million. There is language of commitment ("let us know when we can expect the dredge," "we are willing to deal with you . . .," "we will pay . . .," this "order").

Contract formation under §2-207.

UCC Article 2 applies because this is a contract for the sale of a good, i.e., something that will be movable at the time of the identification to the contract — the dredge [Text §34.1]. S's "acceptance" contains additional and different terms from the offer, and so to resolve whether a contract exists and, if so, what its terms are, §2-207 must be applied [Text §5.2].

Under §2-207(1), to be effective as an acceptance, a purported acceptance containing additional or different terms must be: (i) a **seasonable** expression of acceptance; (ii) a **definite** expression of acceptance; and (iii) not include a term making its effect conditional on the offeror's assent to the additional or different terms found in the document [Text §5.31].

S's 3/19 letter is probably a definite and seasonable expression of acceptance. It is **seasonable** because it was sent only 4 days after the offer was sent and thus probably only a day or two after receipt of the offer. There is no indication that speed is important here, so the reasonable time to accept should extend beyond the minimum that the Restatement 2d gives (midnight of day of receipt) [Text §4.4122-2].

It may be a **definite** expression of acceptance because it assents to the typically negotiated terms in the offer (price, quantity, subject matter, delivery terms), and it shows commitment to going ahead with the bargain ("We will deliver . . ."). However, S's attempt to add a cancellation right for S may change the bargain in such a fundamental way that there is no definite expression of acceptance; in effect S is saying that even if there is a contract S can choose not to perform — that is much more fundamental than warranty or arbitration issues, and may be as fundamental as price and quantity [Text §5.311]. If the letter is not a definite expression of acceptance, it will have to be viewed as a counter-offer, and no contract would be formed by the exchange of writings under 2-207(1).

If the 3/19 letter is a definite expression of acceptance, we still have to ask whether the acceptance is expressly conditional on B's assent to the added or different terms.

S says that unless B agrees to S's terms, S will not deliver the dredge. Thus, S is saying that the deal will not go forward unless B expressly assents to S's terms, and that is the same as saying "no deal unless you agree to my terms." Thus, the acceptance is expressly conditional on B's assent to S's terms, which once again means S's letter is a counter-offer [Text §5.312].

Accordingly, at least due to one, and possibly two, reasons, no contract was formed under §2-207(1).

As a result, if a contract is to be formed at all from this fact situation, it must be formed by §2-207(3) [Text §5.33]. If both parties engage in conduct which would indicate to a reasonable person that a contract exists between them, then there is a contract under §2-207(3). B paid $100,000; S accepted the check and deposited it. Those actions recognize that a contract exists.

Thus, a valid offer and acceptance were exchanged to form a contract by conduct between B and S under §2-207(3).

What are the terms? The §2-207(3) analysis.

If there is no contract formed under §2-207(1), but a contract is formed by conduct under §2-207(3), then the terms are those on which the parties actually expressly agreed, plus any supplementary terms added by the UCC [Text §5.33]. All others are "knocked-out." The parties' letters agreed on price ($2.5 million), quantity (one), subject matter (the dredge), and delivery date (B gave S authority to set the delivery date at any date before December, and S chose October), so these would be enforceable terms. (See below for possible modification of price term.)

Perhaps the parties agreed that there would be no limitation to arbitration; B proposed that term, and S did not object even though S did object to other specific proposals in B's offer. This analysis is borrowed from 2-207(2), under which at least some courts have held that objection to some added terms but not to others is the same as an express assent to the others. It is not clear a court would use this approach under §2-207(3), but it would seem reasonable under these circumstances.

The parties did not agree to exclude any implied warranties, so B will get an implied warranty of merchantability (because such a warranty is implied whenever a sale of goods by a merchant occurs and is not disclaimed, see §2-314) [Text §36.2]; and, perhaps an implied warranty of fitness for B's particular purposes as well [Text §36.3]. That is, B had a specific use for the goods; let S know of their particular use; and let S know it was relying on, and did in fact rely on, S's skill and judgment in selecting, designing, and building the dredge.

The parties did not agree on when the remaining $2.4 million would be paid or where delivery was to take place. However, the UCC gap filler in §2-310(a) states that, in the absence of agreement to the contrary, a buyer must pay for goods at the time and place of delivery [Text §6.225]. Similarly, §2-308(a) provides that, in the absence of agreement in the contract, delivery is to be made at S's place of business [Text §6.223].

The next issue is whether B is bound by the price modification, i.e., whether it becomes part of their contract. S's June 2 letter was a proposal to reduce the price from $2.5 million to $2.3 million. There is no consideration for the reduction but that doesn't matter — no consideration is needed for modification of a contract for the sale of goods under §2-209(1) [Text §26.2]. The modification has to be obtained in good faith, but B is in good faith here; B made no threats and S voluntarily proposed the reduction for S's own reasons. The question then is whether B assented to the proposal — i.e., whether the offer to reduce the price was "accepted" by B so as to say there was an enforceable modification of the contract. S said B did not have to answer the letter, so S is probably assuming B will assent and telling B that silence is an appropriate means of acceptance. B stayed silent apparently with the intention of accepting, so there was an effective acceptance. Acceptance by silence is usually ineffective as a method of acceptance, but when the offeror gives the offeree that power, and where the offeree intends to accept in such a manner, it is effective [Text §4.572].

The consideration problem (the cancellation provision).

Because it was not agreed to by both parties, the cancellation provision does not become part of the contract [Text §5.33]. Probably that is all that needs to be said about the issue, but as a review recall that if one or both parties end up with the right to cancel the contract merely by sending a letter, there is a consideration or a mutuality of obigation issue. Suppose B has the right to cancel. B can then perform by either buying the dredge or by sending the notice of cancellation. Where a party has alternative ways that he can freely choose to perform his promise, his promise is consideration only if both alternatives are sufficient "somethings" and at least one of them was bargained for. The older cases would say there is no consideration here. They would say that sending a letter is not sufficient detriment to B to be a sufficient "detriments," and hence B's promise to buy the dredge or send the notice would not be consideration. The newer cases would say that there is consideration. B had no pre-existing duty to send a letter, and sending such notice is an act, so it is a sufficient "something" to enforce the promise [Text §7.622].

Note, however, that once B makes the $100,000 payment and S cashed the check, the contract should be enforceable by B, even if a court would otherwise have thought the right to cancel meant that there was no consideration for S's promise. That is, even if there as an illusory contract to that point, B's payment and S's receipt of the money constituted mutual agreement that there was a deal, and B's payment would be consideration for S's promise to deliver the dredge.

Answer to Question No. 7

CBS V. JOE

Joe did not finish the piece, so, if he had a contractual obligation to finish it, he breached that obligation, and CBS will prevail in the breach action. Thus, the question is whether Joe had a contractual obligation to finish the piece that he started.

Contracts cannot be formed without assent of both the contracting parties [Text §2.0]. Mutual assent is usually shown by the making of an offer by one party and the acceptance of that offer by the other party [Text §1.2]. Thus, the first question is whether either party here made an offer.

An offer is the manifestation of intent to enter into a bargain so made as to justify another in believing that his or her assent is invited and will conclude the bargain [Text §3.0]. If the putative offeror manifests the intention not to be bound to a bargain until he or she manifests some further assent, then no offer has been made, but rather the party has just engaged in preliminary negotiations [Text §3.213]. Further, a manifestation of assent cannot be an offer unless the proposed bargain is reasonably certain. The traditional view is that all material terms must be reasonably certain; the Restatement 2d view is that a contract is definite enough to be enforced if the parties intended to contract, and if the court can determine who breached and can determine an appropriate remedy [Text §6.2].

Offer

1. *The face-to-face conversation on Sept. 25*

No offers were made in the Sept. 25 conversation between Don and Joe. Even if an offer was made, it was not accepted.

Don's initial statement does not show any commitment to any bargain with Joe and thus is not an offer. Don stated that CBS needed to run a story, but he did not state that he wanted Joe to do the piece, nor did he say that CBS would pay Joe for the piece. In the absence of any manifestation of commitment by Don, Joe would not be justified in believing that Don was inviting his assent or that his assent would conclude a bargain. Further, almost no terms are specified. The subject of the piece is specified, but neither its length, nor the price CBS would pay for it, nor the time when CBS would need it, are stated. This indefiniteness is evidence that CBS is not committed to any bargain; a reasonable person would want the terms specified much more completely before being bound to a bargain.

Further, even if CBS did intend to commit itself to a bargain, the terms of the "bargain" are so indefinite that there would be no valid offer here [Text §6.0]. Under the traditional approach, there are several material terms that are completely uncertain (price, length, time of delivery) [Text §6.1]. Perhaps these could be supplied by usage of trade or course of dealing, but that is unlikely. There is probably not a sufficient usage of trade [Text §6.4]; that is, it is unlikely that independent producers and networks almost always agree to a certain price, length, and time for delivery of such pieces. (If you could show that such news show pieces are almost always eight minutes, that the independent producers almost always get paid $20,000, and that the pieces are almost always considered due within 6 weeks, then you *might* be able to argue that there was a sufficient usage of trade to fill in the omitted terms. That seems very unlikely and is not suggested at all on these facts.) There is also probably not a sufficient course of dealing; that is, it is unlikely that Joe and CBS have repeatedly agreed on the same terms for price, length, and time for delivery in their past dealings. (Even if there were such a usage of trade or course of dealing, there still would be no offer, because CBS has not manifested commitment to the bargain, but at least the indefiniteness problem could be overcome.)

Under the Restatement 2d approach, the indefiniteness in these terms would prevent Don's initial statement from being an offer, because the court could not provide an appropriate remedy [Text §6.01]. Perhaps the court could determine who breached. The court might say that since no time was stated, Joe had a reasonable time to produce the piece [Text §§6.224; 6.23], and if he failed to produce any piece within that time the court might be able to say that Joe breached the contract no matter what length the piece was supposed to be and no matter what the price was supposed to be. However, without knowing how much CBS was supposed to pay, the court would be unable to determine what CBS's expectation interest is. The court could not determine CBS's reliance interest without knowing how long the piece was supposed to be; if at the last minute CBS had to pay a lot extra to get a substitute piece done by another producer as a rush job, it might seem that the court could determine CBS's reliance interest as the extra costs a rush job caused as compared with what CBS normally would have paid for a piece — but those extra costs almost certainly depend on how long the piece was that was done on a rush basis, and we have no way of knowing how long a piece CBS could have relied on Joe providing, since no length was set. (Even if the court could determine what an appropriate remedy would be, so that the court could say that the indefiniteness problem is not insurmountable under the Restatement 2d approach, the court would still hold that there was no offer, because

CBS did not manifest commitment to the bargain. That is, CBS simply did not intend to contract.)

Could Joe's first statement be an offer?

Joe's statement is more definite than CBS's first statement (we now have a length and a minimum price), but there are two reasons why it is not an offer.

First, it does not show commitment by Joe [Text §3.0]. Joe does not say, "I will do a piece," but "I **could** do a piece." He is not committing himself to doing a piece, but rather is saying that it is possible that he could do it. Further, Joe has not said that $25,000 is acceptable to him, but rather that he would need to "ask at least $25,000." The statement of an "asking" price is usually not considered to be a statement that the party is willing to enter into a bargain at that price, but rather is simply preliminary negotiation [Text §3.213]. Joe did not even say that he would have to ask $25,000, but that he would have to ask **at least** $25,000. Thus he is not saying that $25,000 is acceptable to him, but simply that he would not be willing to do it for any less than $25,000. A reasonable person would think that Joe would want to have the price set before being bound to a bargain, so this is additional evidence that Joe has not manifested commitment to a proposed bargain.

Second, Joe's statement may be too indefinite to be an offer even if he intended to contract [Text §6.0]. No time for delivery of the piece is stated, and no firm price is stated.

(Even if somehow this were an offer, the presumption is that CBS's power of acceptance would have lapsed at the end of the face-to-face conversation [Text §4.4122-1]. Joe did not say how long his offer would be open, so contract law presumes that the reasonable time to accept, offers made in face-to-face conversations generally terminates when the conversation ends, unless one of the parties manifests a contrary intent. It is not likely that Don's general "We'll have to talk again later" would be interpreted to mean, "I accept your offer").

Could Don's final statements be an offer?

"We could afford . . ." is not the same as "we will pay;" it does not manifest commitment to any bargain, but just indicates that there is some chance CBS will want to enter into a bargain in the future. Don also manifests an intention not to be bound until he manifests a further assent, when he says, "Excuse me . . . We'll talk again later." Such a manifestation means that Don has merely engaged in preliminary negotiations and has not made an offer [Text §3.213].

2. Don's Letter

Don's letter is probably an offer [Text §3.0]. It manifests commitment to a bargain. In terms of commitment, "willing to pay" is not as strong as "we will pay," but in light of the firm scheduling of the piece for the Dec. 1 show, it does manifest commitment to a bargain. The letter is also definite enough to show commitment [Text §6.0]. It contains price ($25,000), subject matter (ten minute piece on photocopier salespersons), and an implied delivery date (early enough before the Dec. 1 show so that CBS can work it into the show — presumably there is an industry usage on how much time is needed for that) [Text §6.4]. There are no significant terms left open that would make a reasonable person think that CBS would want to have the deal clarified before being willing to be bound to a deal. "High quality" is somewhat indefinite, but it is very likely that Joe and Don know what they mean by a high quality piece because they have worked together numerous times in the past, i.e., there is a course of dealing between them [Text §6.4]. The letter seems to be personally directed to Joe and not to others; thus there is no problem of over-acceptance that could lead a reasonable person to think that CBS would not want to create a power of acceptance that could lead to over-acceptance.

Acceptance

Acceptance is the manifestation of assent to the terms of the offer by a means invited or required by the offer [Text §4.0]. Mike's letter did not specify any particular means of acceptance. Thus, any reasonable means of acceptance under the circumstances is invited [Text §4.52].

This raises three issues. First, whether acceptance by beginning performance was a reasonable means of acceptance under the circumstances. Second, if so, whether Joe's failure to give notice to Don renders the acceptance void. Third, assuming that it does render the acceptance void, what are the rights of CBS in such a situation?

Was acceptance by beginning performance a reasonable means of acceptance?

There may be an argument that Don asked for a promissory acceptance in his letter. At the time of the offer, it was only 2 months until the piece was scheduled to be shown on the air. It is likely that in such a situation Don needed to know and know quickly whether Joe was going to accept; hence the argument that Don was seeking a promissory acceptance. If so, then there was no effective acceptance by Joe when he started performance without promising to complete performance [Text §§4.51; 4.542].

However, whatever benefits Don could receive by a promissory acceptance could just as easily be obtained through Joe's acceptance by beginning performance followed by prompt notice of acceptance. Since the offer is silent as to the method of acceptance, and since the seasonable notice requirement, if fulfilled, would seem to cover Don's concerns, it is likely that acceptance by beginning performance was an acceptable method of performance of the offer [Text §4.543].

Assuming that beginning of performance was an acceptable mode of acceptance, *the next question is what is the effect of Joe's failure to give notice to Don that he had started?*

The general rule under the Restatement 2d is that acceptance by performance must be followed within a reasonable time by notice of acceptance to the offeror [Text §4.5432]. There are only three exceptions to the rule [Text §4.5432-1]:

(1) if the nature of the acceptance is such that the offeror would reasonably know the offer has been accepted. (In the present case, there are no facts that indicate Don would know that Joe accepted so this exception does not apply.)

(2) if the offeror gave the offeree a reason to believe that acceptance by beginning performance without notification was an acceptable mode of acceptance. (Here, again, however, there is nothing in Don's offer to indicate acceptance by silence would be acceptable so this exception does not apply either.)

(3) if due to past dealings between the parties it was reasonable for Joe to believe either that acceptance by beginning performance without notification was a proper means of acceptance. Once again, nothing in the facts indicate that to be the case here.)

Accordingly, on these facts, Joe's beginning performance without giving notice to Don was not an effective acceptance [Text §4.5433].

Note, however, that under the approach of §54 of the Restatement 2d, Joe's beginning of performance acts as an enforceable promise by Joe to CBS that he will finish the piece, even if he does not follow-up those acts with notice. That is, the failure to give notice means that CBS is not bound to pay him upon tender of the finished piece. However, he is obligated to finish the piece for CBS because by beginning of performance he implicitly promised the offeror he would finish. Hence, even though the acceptance was not "effective" from Joe's point of view (in that he cannot enforce it against CBS), it was effective from CBS's view (in that CBS can enforce it against Joe), and thus CBS is entitled to recover from Joe any damages it suffers based on Joe's breach of his implied promise to finish [Text §4.5433].

MAXINE V. JOE

Joe refused to buy the Z1000 photocopy machine. If he had an enforceable contract to buy one, he obviously breached it, and Maxine will prevail. Thus, *the issue of whether there was a contract must be examined.*

Offer

The issue in this transaction turns on whether a contract for the sale of goods, i.e., a photocopier, was formed. As such, it is governed by the UCC [Text §34.1].

Maxine's initial price quotation was probably not an offer. Price quotes are not usually treated as offers but rather as invitations for offers [Text §3.213]. Courts will treat a quote as an offer if the circumstances or the language used shows a commitment to sell at the quoted price and if the terms are definite. Here the quantity seems definite based on Joe's inquiry about "one" photocopier, and the quote can provide the price. If the parties had intended to contract based on this quote, the UCC will fill in the remaining terms with its "gap filler" requirements [Text §6.21] (time of delivery would be a reasonable time, payment is due at time and place of delivery which will be at Maxine's, and the quality required is that the machine be merchantable). However, Maxine did not say she would sell Joe a machine for the $1,000; she merely said she "could" quote him a price of $1,000. That may be even weaker in terms of commitment than the usual "I quote you $1,000." Further, she told him to send in a purchase order; she is probably in effect saying, "Make me an offer by sending in a Purchase Order" ("P.O."). In light of the lack of explicit terms and questionable commitment in Maxine's quote, it seems likely that her statements are no more than an invitation to Joe to make an offer, and not an offer themselves.

As a result, Joe made an offer when he sent in the P.O. We are told little of what the P.O. said, but the reason a person sends a P.O. is to purchase the items listed on the P.O. Thus the recipient of a P.O. is likely to see it as a manifestation of commitment to buy the item [Text §3.0]. Indeed, UCC 2-206(1)(b) implies that an "order" for goods is an offer. Although the P.O. apparently contains only price, quantity, and subject matter, the UCC will fill in the other terms if the parties intend to contract with gap fillers, so there is no serious indefiniteness problem here.

The next issue turns on the objective theory of contracts. That is, Joe obviously was not seriously considering buying a photocopier when he ordered it from Maxine. Indeed, he told Maxine in his phone message that he was not interested in buying a copier; he just wanted to shoot his piece for *60 Minutes*. Thus, it is fair to say there was no *subjective* meeting of the minds to the contract even if Maxine accepted what appeared to be an offer. However, for at least the last century it has been established that the **objective** theory of governs contract formation in American courts. When one party has no reason to doubt that the other party intends to contract, the law does not permit the other party to avoid contractual liability simply because he or she did not actually intend to contract. Thus, because Joe's outward manifestations showed an intent to contract, (i.e., a reasonable person in Maxine's shoes would believe that upon a valid acceptance a contract would be formed), his undisclosed subjective intent does not prevent his P.O. from being an offer that Maxine can accept [Text §3.2].

Acceptance

The next two issues are: (1) Whether Maxine's "acknowledgment" an effective acceptance under UCC §2- 207(1)?; and (2) Whether Joe effectively revoked his offer before Maxine effectively accepted it?

Was Maxine's acknowledgment an effective acceptance under §2-207(1)

Maxine's acknowledgment added terms that as far as we know were not on Joe's P.O. That means the acknowledgment was an attempt to accept the offer and also add terms to the deal. §2-207(1) deals with whether an attempted acceptance that tries to add or change terms is effective as an acceptance. §2-207(1) states that so long as the offeree's writing is a reasonable and definite expression of acceptance, it **will** act as an effective acceptance despite the presence of additional or different terms, so long as there is no "acceptance is expressly made conditioned on offeror's assent" to other terms clause in the offeree's document [Text §5.31].

Accordingly, we must first ask whether the acknowledgment was **seasonable**. The offer had not lapsed; an offer received by mail which does not state how long it will be open ordinarily does not lapse until at least midnight of the day the offer was received [Text §4.4122-2]. Maxine mailed back the acknowledgement the same day she received the offer. Under the mailbox rule, the acceptance (if it was an acceptance) was effective when she posted it, because the mail was an invited means of acceptance and because it was correctly addressed [Text §4.61]. It was an invited means of acceptance because the offer was sent by mail and nothing in the offer or the circumstances indicated that the mail was not a reasonable means of acceptance [Text §4.52]. Thus, Maxine's power to accept the offer had not lapsed before acceptance. However, to be seasonable, an acceptance must become effective while the offer is still open to be accepted, and there is an issue to be discussed below about whether Joe revoked the offer before Maxine could accept it. Assuming he failed to revoke it effectively, the acknowledgment was a seasonable expression of acceptance.

Next we must ask if it was a **definite** expression of acceptance. A definite expression of acceptance is one that indicates commitment to the bargain going forward and which does not try to change one of the basic, typically negotiated terms of the offer, such as price, quantity, subject matter, or perhaps delivery terms. Here the acknowledgment indicated that Maxine would sell Joe a Z1000 for the same price as on the P.O., so it appears to be a definite expression of acceptance. The fact that it attempts to make material changes to the warranty portion of the deal by imposing a short express warranty and eliminating the implied warranty of merchantability does not prevent it from being an effective "acceptance" under §2-207(1) for an acceptance is valid under §2-207(1) even if the offeree's response contains additional or different terms [Text §5.31].

However, the acknowledgment also attempts to add to the subject matter of the contract by requiring Joe to buy his supplies from Maxine. Unless the court sees supplies as being relatively minor compared to the copier itself, the court should decide that this addition makes the acknowledgment **not** a definite expression of acceptance, because one of the typically negotiated terms (quantity and subject matter) is affected, and Maxine's response would be deemed to propose a different deal. In that case, Maxine's letter would really be a counter-offer. That is, ultimately the issue in this case as to whether Maxine and Joe had a contract under §2-207(1) comes down to whether the buyer and seller were buying and selling the same thing. If so, the presence of additional or different terms does not change the effectiveness of the acceptance. If not, then the purported acceptance becomes a counter-offer [Text §5.311].

If the acknowledgment is a definite and seasonable expression of acceptance, the next issue is whether it is expressly made conditional on Joe's (the offeror's) assent to the added terms (thus involving the "unless" clause of Maxine's acknowledgment). If so, once again it is not an effective acceptance but a counter-offer [Text §5.322]. The acknowledgment does say that its terms and only its terms will be the terms of the contract, but it does not say that Joe must **assent** to those terms for there to be a contract. It does not say, e.g., "No deal unless you assent to my terms," or "This acceptance is conditional on your agreeing to my terms," or anything that means that. The acknowledgment did insist on its own terms, but such an insistence is insufficient to turn the offer into a counter-offer. §2-207(1) makes clear that the key is whether the offeror's **assent** is needed before a contract is made. If it says that silence, or inaction, or any other thing short of affirmative agreement on the part of the offeror can lead to the offeror's acceptance of additional different terms, the document is an acceptance and not a counter-offer [Text §5.322].

The revocation/acceptance issue

Joe attempted to revoke his offer by leaving the phone message for Maxine. Joe indicated he did not want the Z1000; his statement is a sufficient manifestation of an intention not to enter into the deal he had offered to Maxine, so it would effectively revoke the offer and terminate Maxine's power of acceptance, **if** the revocation became effective before Maxine accepted the offer. However, once an offer has been accepted, the offeror can no longer revoke [Text §4.1].

As noted above, Maxine's acceptance would be effective under the mailbox rule when posted (dispatched) [Text §4.61]. Maxine did not hear the message until after she mailed the letter, so if she is not deemed to have "received" it until then, the revocation was too late. The facts do not say whether the message was left before she put the acknowledgment in the U.S. mail, and thus there is an issue as to whether the oral revocation even "received" (albeit on an answering machine), before the acceptance's dispatch. While the legal answer to this issue is not that clear, for there are not a lot of cases on point, it is likely that a court would find that Maxine had not "received" the revocation until a reasonable time after she arrived back in the office so that she could check her messages.

Accordingly, as there was a valid offer by Joe in the P.O., a valid acceptance by Maxine, and consideration, an enforceable contract existed [Text §1.2], and if Joe does not pay for the copier, he will be in breach.

Answer to Question No. 8

PART (1)

The first issue is whether Neighbor ("N") made an offer to Johnson ("J"). An offer is a manifestation of willingness to enter into a bargain so made as to justify another in understanding that his assent is invited and will conclude the bargain [Text §3.0]. Central to the concept of offer is that in a valid offer the offeror is committed to the bargain and upon that offeree's acceptance, a contract will be formed. A statement is not an offer if the person to whom it is addressed (the offeree) knows or has reason to know that further communication by the person making the statement is needed to evidence sufficient willingness to enter into a bargain.

N's statement to J is an offer for several reasons. It shows commitment by N to a proposed deal — N says J "can have" the nails for $20 and invites him to take the nails. She would not do that unless she were willing to enter into the bargain of selling the nails to J for $20. She even specifies a means by which J can assent to the deal: by taking the nails in the garage. J will not reasonably believe any further assent by N is needed, since N did not indicate that further assent was needed; also since she is leaving, she will not be around to give any further assent before J takes the nails. The definiteness of the terms also shows N's commitment and that no further assent from N is needed: the price ($20), quantity (one bag), subject matter (nails), and time of delivery (whenever J takes the nails), and place of delivery (the garage) are all stated. Only time of payment is unstated, but since this is a contract for the sale of goods (and thus governed by the UCC), the UCC's time of payment gap filler, i.e., payment is due at the time and place of delivery, can be used to cure any indefiniteness problem [Text §6.225]. Since no important terms are unstated, it makes sense to think N's statement is definite enough to be an offer.

Since N made an offer, the next issue is whether J accepted it. The offer specifies, or at least suggests, a method of acceptance — taking the nails from the garage [Text §4.51]. Since J did that, it looks as though he accepted.

J's only defense is that he left the note specifying he would only pay $15. Under the objective theory of contracts, J would argue that no reasonable person in N's position could believe he was "accepting" N's offer as he specified a price change in the note. At most, J would argue he was making a counter-offer, indicating he was willing to go forward with the deal on different terms [Text §4.411].

The problem with this argument, of course, is that J took the nails. He was not just making a counter-offer. Under Restatement 2d §69(2), when an offeree exercises dominion over offered property ("does any act inconsistent with the offeror's ownership of offered property"), the offeree is bound to the offer's terms unless they are manifestly unreasonable. The rule is the same under the UCC §2-606(1)(c) [Text §4.574]. $20 for a bag of nails that cost $15 at some unspecified time in the past is not manifestly unreasonable, given that J is saved the trouble of a trip to the store. Here the exercise of dominion was wrongful as against the offeror N because J manifested an intention not to accept, so there is an acceptance only if N ratifies J's taking of the nails. Thus, under the last sentences of §69(2) or of UCC §2-606(c), N can choose to hold J to the contract and require him to pay $20. (Note N could also sue J for conversion, but that is a tort remedy, not a contractual one, and thus probably need not be mentioned in any answer to a Contracts problem unless the tort has been discussed by your Contracts Professor.)

This agreement could also, of course, be discussed under UCC §2-207(1). Under §2-207(1), the question would be whether the effect of J's, i.e., the offeree's, note would be to turn his "acceptance" into a counter-offer (thus terminating J's power of acceptance). When an offeree changes a basic, typically negotiated term like price, the offeree has not made the definite expression of acceptance that §2-207(1) requires [Text §5.311]. That is, the buyer and seller simply are not part of the same deal. Accordingly, here J's note means that no contract was formed under §2-207(1).

Once it is concluded that a contract was not formed under §2-207(1), it might be tempting to argue that one was formed under §2-207(3). However, §2-207(3) is designed for the case in which the parties' communications do not show that a contract was formed, but where **both** parties thereafter go ahead and engage in conduct that recognizes the existence of a contract [Text §5.33]. **J** engaged in such conduct (taking and presumably using the nails), but *N* did nothing after making her offer. Thus there is no contract formed under §2-207(1) or (3). However, UCC §1-103 allows general rules of contract law to supplement the Code. That includes the principle of Restatement 2d §69(2). In addition, §2-606(c) also suggests acceptance. Thus, given the above analysis N can sue in contract for $20, or in tort for conversion for the value of the nails. There is a contract if N chooses there to be one.

PART (2)

The first issue is *whether Sales Co.'s 10/19 letter was an offer*.

The 10/19 letter uses the word "quote": the general rule is that "price quotes" are not offers [Text §§4.212; 4.214]. Also the letter does not have any **express** words of commitment that Sales Co. will sell the X14 to J (although the request for J to give an answer comes close to an express commitment). Many cases, especially older cases, look for such express words of commitment and ignore the context of the words. Further, it may be customary in the trade for sales of such complicated, expensive machines to be made pursuant to carefully drafted, written agreements.

However, the modern approach is to realize that: (1) use of the word "quote" does not prevent a communication from being an offer; and (2) commitment can be found in the communication based on its context, even if there are no express words of commitment. Here Sales Co.'s letter is in response to J's request for its "best **offer**;" the letter even states "Pursuant to your inquiry." A reasonable person will thus be inclined to consider a response to be an offer if the facts permit that conclusion. Sales Co. also implies that it is willing to sell the X14 for $30,000 when it says it does not **usually** sell them for the $30,000 price it quoted to J. Commitment to a bargain is also shown by Sales Co.'s invitation to J to give an answer. If Sales Co. is not proposing a bargain, what is Sales Co. asking him to answer? The invitation to give an answer also shows that Sales Co. is inviting J to assent. Nothing in the 10/19 letter indicates that any further assent by Sales Co. is needed before the bargain will be concluded. Indeed, the request for an answer indicates to the contrary. Enough terms are included with enough definiteness — price, quantity ("an" X14), and subject matter — that a reasonable person would have no problem believing that Sales Co. would be willing to be bound without any further clarification of terms [Text §3.0].

The omitted terms — time and place of delivery, payment, quality — etc., are not essential under the UCC, which will fill the gaps with terms from §§2-308, 2-309, 2-310, and 2-314. Thus, likely the letter is definite enough to be an offer.

The next issue is *whether J accepted the offer*.

The first sub-issue is whether a mailed acceptance was an invited manner of acceptance [Text §4.4122-2]. The offer invited J to answer in person, but it did not clearly provide that J could **only** answer in person. Thus answering in person was probably only a suggested means of acceptance. That means that any means of acceptance reasonable under the circumstances is invited [Text §4.51]. Since the offer was mailed, a mailed acceptance seems reasonable.

The only thing in this fact pattern that could be considered an acceptance is J's letter of 10/24. Since, once again, we are dealing with the sale of goods in which the offeree's response attempted to add a term to the deal, §2-207 should be looked to so as to determine if a contract was made. J's 10/24 letter did not merely **suggest** that the attorney's fee provision should be added; it **insisted** that it be added to their deal. At common law, under the mirror image rule, it would *not* be acceptance but rather a counter-offer [Text §5.0]. Under §2-207(1), however, it is effective as an acceptance if:

(1) it is a **definite** expression of acceptance [Text §5.3]. That means the response must **assent** to the **same** basic deal proposed in the offer, without changing any of the typically negotiated terms like price, quantity, or subject matter. "It's a deal" is an assent, and it doesn't change any of those typically negotiated terms. This requirement is satisfied, and thus the 10/24 letter acts as a definite expression of acceptance even though it adds an additional term.

(2) it is **seasonable**. That means that the acceptance had to become effective while the offer was still open to be accepted. The offer said J had until 10/29 to give an answer in person. Probably that means a mailed acceptance would have to be mailed early enough so that is would normally arrive by 10/29. J's mailing of his acceptance on 10/24 was thus seasonable, **unless** Sales Co. effectively revoked its offer, which is discussed below.

(3) it is not expressly conditional on the offeror's assent to the additional or different terms. Here J insisted that his additional attorney's fees term **must** apply, but he did not say that his acceptance would not be effective unless Sales Co. **"assented to"** the attorney's fee term. He did not say "no deal unless you agree to the attorney's fee clause." Just insisting that your terms apply is not enough to prevent your response from being an acceptance under §2-207(1). It is essential that the terms of the offeree's document require the express amount of the offeror to the additional terms before the offeree's response becomes a counter-offer under this provision of §2-207(1) [Text §5.312].

Accordingly, assuming Sales Co. did not effectively revoke its offer, it appears J has a contract to buy an X14.

Hence, *whether the offer was effectively revoked* must be discussed.

The first sub-issue is whether the offer was irrevocable under UCC §2-205, the merchant's firm offer provision [Text §4.422]. Sales Co. is a merchant with respect to X14 machines, so **if** Sales Co. gave assurances that the offer would be held open until 10/29, the offer is irrevocable until then (assuming an authorized Sales Co representative signed the letter). However, the letter does **not** give that assurance, i.e., it does not *promise* that the offer will be held open, but, instead just indicates the time when the offeree's power to accept will lapse. Accordingly, it would be incorrect to conclude that Sales Co.'s offer was irrevocable.

The second sub-issue is the time at which J's acceptance became effective. A mailed acceptance where mailing is an authorized means is effective on dispatch [Text §4.61]. Thus, J's letter was an effective acceptance as of 10/24.

Offers can only be revoked before they are accepted [Text §4.1], so Sales Co.'s revocation was effective only if it occurred before J mailed his letter. Sales Co.'s letter of 10/22 was an attempted revocation of its offer since it manifested Sales Co.'s intent not to enter into the bargain proposed by its 10/19 offer. However, **a revocation is effective only when it is communicated to the offeree**, which in the case of mailed revocations means when the letter is *received*, **not** when it is mailed, or dispatched [Text §4.62]. The revocation was not received by J until 10/26, two days **after** his acceptance became effective, so it was too late. Thus, the offer was not effectively revoked, and J has a contract to buy an X14.

PART (3)

Part (3)(a)

The terms of the contract for a X14 are determined under §2-207(2) [Text §5.32]. The first question is whether the attorney's fee provision will be included. §2-207(2) states that between merchants, an additional term to a contract, such as only if **NONE** of the following are true [Text §5.322]:

(1) The offeror's offer expressly limits acceptance to the terms of the offer, §2- 207(2)(a). Here, there was no express limitation in the 10/19 offer.

(2) The additional term materially alters the contract, §2-207(2)(b). If the addition of an attorney's fee clause would materially alter the contract, then it cannot become part of the contract (unless Sales Co. expressly assents to it, which did not happen here). The tests that may be applied for whether a term materially alters a contract are:

   (a) whether it would cause unreasonable surprise or hardship if it became a part of the contract without Sales Co. actually being aware of it at the time of contracting (UCC §2-207, Com. 4); and

   (b) whether the inclusion of the term would be likely to influence the decision of a reasonable person as to whether or not to enter into the contract.

An attorney's fee clause protects the innocent party in a dispute — it does not change the performance done by either party unless there is a dispute, and it probably is a fairly standard provision in contracts for sale of complicated machines. It therefore does not seem to create unreasonable hardship, nor should it be too surprising to Sales Co. that J might want such a term. On the other hand, attorney's fee clauses can make a party reluctant to litigate even when it believes it has a meritorious position if attorney's fees are likely to be quite large in comparison to the $30,000 cost of the X14.

It probably does not result in unreasonable surprise or hardship, but it *might* be a term that would influence a seller's decision to enter into or not enter into a contract to sell an X14. Hence, whatever the attorney's fee provision materially alters the terms of the contract it is a close question and one on which courts have disagreed. If the term is common in the trade, as it probably is, it probably does not materially alter the contract.

(3) The offeror has already objected to the term, or objects to it within a reasonable time, §2-207(2)(c). The facts show no objection so far, but Sales Co. may still have a few days in which to object. If it does not, then this hurdle is passed.

Part (3)(b):

The offer J accepted was for sale of an X14 for $30,000. (Acceptance under 2-207(1) is an acceptance on the terms of the offer, as supplemented or changed by terms that pass the hurdles of 2-207(2).) Because Sales Co.'s attempted revocation by way of a price increase was not effective until after J's acceptance was effective (see Part (2)), the price increase is contractually ineffective.

Part (3)(c)

The offer J accepted did not require him to promise or commit himself to buy more items. It merely stated Sales Co.'s intent to sell him more ("We intend . . ."). It did not expressly ask J to make such a commitment, nor are there any circumstances that indicate a reasonable person would think he was giving such a commitment by accepting the offer. The indefiniteness of the stated intent ("lots of business") would lead a reasonable offeree to think it could not be asking for a commitment, since a reasonable person would not make such an indefinite commitment.

Answer to Question No. 9

The first issue is **whether Pete's has valid cause of action for breach of express warranty against Sam's as a result of there being no spare tire in the ambulance.**

If Pete, the owner of Pete's Ambulance Service, can surmount the parole evidence rule (see below), he can establish reasonably clearly the elements of a breach of express warranty claim [Text §36.1]. Obviously, Sam made a representation that the tires would be included with the ambulance; the representation was part of the "basis of the bargain" (regardless of whether basis of bargain is defined as reliance or as something taking place before conclusion of the sale [Text §36.12]), and the lack of the tires caused Pete's damages as measured by the difference in fair market value between the ambulance with the tires and the ambulance without.

The issue is whether or not the representation about the tires is admissible at all under the parol evidence rule.

There seems to be no dispute that the contract they both signed contained a final expression of the parties as to at least most of the terms of the sales contract, price, delivery, etc. The question then becomes whether the writing was intended as a complete and exclusive statement of the terms of the agreement under §2-202 [Text §19.11]. While there is no evidence in the facts that the contract contained merger clause, that fact alone is not determinative in deciding whether the contract was intended as a complete and exclusive statement [Text §17.1341]. In this case, both Pete's and Sam's are merchants executing a contract for the sale of a rather expensive good which is important to the running of their businesses. Thus, it would seem likely that the parties' would take care to scrutinize the contract carefully to ensure that written document would contain the final and exclusive statement of all the terms of their agreement. If so, then evidence of the oral promise to install the tire would be inadmissible under §2-202(b) [Text §19.11].

If a court were to construe a contract as not being a complete and exclusive statement of the terms of the agreement, i.e., not completely integrated, then the oral promise to equip the ambulance with new tires could be introduced under §2-202(b) if it passed the "would certainly" test as set forth in Comment 3 to §2-202 [Text §19.1111]. Under that test the court would ask, if the parties had really reached the agreement about the spare tires, can it be said that they would "would certainly" have included such a provision in their contract? It is likely that a judge would find that the evidence would be inadmissible given that test. That is, the installation of two spare tires was obviously quite important to Peter, and thus it is likely a judge would find that had the agreement in fact been made, Peter would have seen to it that the term "would certainly" have been included the final written contract. On the other hand, it is hardly a standard clause for a vehicle sale and a court might decide that it would *possibly*, but not certainly, be in the agreement if the parties in fact reached an accord about the tires and if Peter signed a standard printed automobile sales form contract. Nevertheless, although it is a close question, it seems likely that the evidence would be excluded.

This means that Pete would never be able to establish the first element of an express warranty claim, i.e., that a representation was made, because the parol evidence rule would bar the admissibility of such evidence in the trial.

The next issue is **whether Paragraph 6 of the sales agreement is valid and should be given full effect**.

The resolution of this question is crucial as it is determinative of all remaining issues in the problem. To resolve the issue properly there must be a two step analysis: first, whether the provision is facially valid under the Code must be discussed. If it is determined that the Paragraph is facially valid, then the issue of whether or not Sam's has lived up to its end of the bargain, thus entitling it to the benefits set forth in Paragraph 6, must be analyzed.

Paragraph 6 has two sentences, each of which is properly classified as a limitation of remedy, as opposed to a warranty disclaimer, and thus is governed by the rules of §2-719 and not §2-316 [Text §33.82]. To be facially valid each of the sentences must be conscionable under §2-719 and §2-302. The analysis relating to each of the sentences is somewhat different, and thus they will have to be analyzed independently.

The first sentence ("repair/replacement provision") would likely be judged conscionable under §2-302 [Text §§15.3; 33.81]. It is important to realize that in the repair/replacement provision Pete's has given up all remedies provided by the code, i.e., Pete's cannot reject the ambulance, cannot revoke its acceptance of the ambulance, cannot sue for breach of warranty, cannot sue for cover or market differential damages, etc. Its **sole** remedy under the contract is to have any defective part in the ambulance repaired or replaced. While such a provision would perhaps be held unconscionable in a consumer transaction, it is a different question when dealing between merchants. Here, Peter was buying a piece of machinery with which he was familiar in a type of transaction which he had entered into at least a few times previously. Additionally, it's not as if the provision takes all of Pete's remedies away and leaves it nothing in return. Instead of a lawsuit to recover market differential, warranty, or cover damages (as would be Pete's code-based remedies), Pete's has the right under the contract to have the ambulance fixed whenever a problem comes up. It may be that a court would nevertheless, find sufficient amounts of procedural unconscionability within the ambulance industry to void the provision (especially if the repair/replacement provision was adhesive as to Sam's and standard throughout all ambulance sellers), but if a retailer of ambulances cannot limit the remedies available in a transaction with an established ambulance company, sellers will likely never be able to do so in any transaction. Accordingly, the first sentence is facially valid and survives a conscionability attack [Text §33.81].

The conscionability of the second sentence ("consequential damage provision") is governed by §2-719(3). That provision states that a limitation on consequential damages between merchants is *prima facie* conscionable when the losses excluded by the provision are economic. Accordingly, to the extent the provision is interpreted to limit Pete's ability to recoup lost profits while the ambulance is being fixed, or economic loss suffered by Pete's as a result of the patient not getting to the hospital on time, the clause probably survives a conscionability attack. Of course, §2-719(3) does not state that all economic consequential damage limitations are valid. It merely establishes a presumption of conscionability. However, this is a clause agreed to between two merchants in a transaction of some importance in their businesses. There is no evidence of oppression, unequal bargaining power, confidential relationship, etc., which might suggest unconscionability. Hence, it is unlikely that the presumption of conscionability will be rebutted [Text §33.81].

To the extent Sam's tries to use the consequential damage provision to exclude recovery for non-economic damages, the clause is likely to be found *prima facie* unconscionable under §2-719(3). That provision states that there is a presumption of unconscionability when a party attempts to limit consequential personal injury losses in consumer transactions. It is true that this is a merchant, not a consumer transaction, and there are reasons to treat the two differently. In a consumer transaction, the purchaser has only the seller to look to for personal injury recovery. In a case like this, the availability of corporate health benefits, worker's compensation rights, etc. means that Pete's driver has sources other than the seller from whom he can recover for his injuries. Nonetheless, courts have been understandably reluctant to permit exclusion of damages for personal injuries, and so I believe that to the extent the clause excludes personal injury damage, it is unconscionable.

Under §2-302, a court is empowered to limit application of an unconscionable clause to avoid an unconscionable result [Text §15.2]. As such, the consequential damages provision would likely be interpreted so as to include limitations on economic losses and to exclude limitations for personal injuries suffered by Pete's employees.

Just because the repair/replacement provision and a portion of the consequential damage provision in Paragraph 6 are valid against an attack of unconscionability does not necessarily mean that they are enforceable given this fact situation. The determination as to whether the clauses are enforceable turns on whether §2-719(2) is satisfied. That provision provided that if the conduct of a party asserting the validity of an otherwise valid limitation of remedy provision is so delinquent that the limited remedy fails its essential purpose, the clause will be stricken. The purpose of repair/replacement clause is to ensure that the buyer has a working good, as opposed to having a non-conforming good and the right to reject, sue for breach of warranty, cover, etc. as provided in the Code. In the first five weeks that Pete's owned the ambulance, it was in the shop ten full days, plus it was going to need additional servicing after July 13th. While a day or two for repairs might be within the contemplation of §2-719(2), it is likely that the intrusive interruptions in service that Pete's suffered has deprived it of the benefits of its bargain, i.e., a working ambulance, and thus the repair/replacement provision is unenforceable. In other words, Pete's has been able to realize neither the benefits of its code-based remedies or its contract-based remedies [Text §33.81].

If the repair/replacement provision of Paragraph 6 is unenforceable, Pete's would have available to it any of the remedies set forth in §2-711, with the possible exception of the ability to recover consequential damages, which will be discussed below. One of those remedies is to sue for breach of warranty under §2-714. In such a case Pete's would have to give notice of its intention to sue to General Motors (now that Sam's in no longer in business), would have to keep the ambulance, but would be able to recover the difference between the value of the ambulance as promised and the value of the ambulance actually received, plus any incidental damages and possibly consequential damages as well. As a practical matter, if Pete's decided to keep the ambulance it would probably have the engine repaired by another mechanic so that it did not stall in traffic, and the repair bill would be the bulk of its damages. There should be no problem in recovering these damages against GM as the privity barriers for breach of warranty have long been abolished [Text §36.42].

Pete's also would have the chance to exercise either its rejection or (possibly) revocation rights should it choose not to keep the ambulance [Text §§22.32; 22.33]. The first question that must be answered is whether Pete's has accepted the ambulance under §2-606 [Text §22.31]. The Comments to that section make it clear that neither possession nor payment, by themselves, signify acceptance. The idea behind acceptance is that the purchaser is given a reasonable period of time to test the product to ensure that it is a conforming good under the contract before it will be deemed to have been accepted. Here, Pete's has had the ambulance for approximately 6 weeks, but it has been in the shop often during that time. As automobiles are somewhat sophisticated pieces of machinery, and as courts have given automobile purchasers a fair amount of leeway to test a vehicle before acceptance, it is likely that Pete's will not be deemed to have accepted the car and thus be able to reject. There has been little controversy over a buyer's right to reject against a remote seller, and although that doctrine could be questioned (see below), based on existing precedent there should be no problem in Pete's exercising its rejection rights against GM [Text §22.32].

Should Pete's be deemed to have accepted it under §2-606(b), Pete's may be entitled to revoke its acceptance under §2-608(1)(a) i.e., claiming that its acceptance was based on the reasonable assumption that the nonconformity would be cured [Text §22.32]. Of course, to revoke Pete's would also have to establish that the value of the contract to it has been substantially impaired by the failure of the vehicle to run properly, but this should be no problem since it has obviously lost a good deal of money because of the defect.

While there has been no serious issue raised regarding rejection against remote sellers [Text §32.325], there has been discussion as to whether or not it is proper in revocation situations [Text §32.335]. Those who have argued in favor of revocation against remote sellers have stated that it is likely that the remote seller will have a better means of selling the revoked good in the used markets than will the buyer. This is probably true here as General Motors would seem to have better lines of distribution for used ambulances than Pete's. However, those who argue against a revocation remedy being available a remote seller point out that the remote seller only received wholesale purchase price from its dealer, yet would be forced to refund the full retail purchase price to the revoking buyer (this is also true for rejection against sellers but no one seems to have raised this issue in that context). While each of these arguments needs to be taken into account, the real issue appears to be who should bear the risk of the insolvency of the dealer — the manufacturer who chose to distribute its good though that retailer, or the consumer who chose to purchase from it? The manufacturer would seem to be in a better position to do the background checking so as to ensure the solvency of its dealers, and to get them to post bonds in case they go out of business, etc., rather than imposing on the consumer buyers the obligation to ensure that the dealer has sufficient resources to be in its location for the expected life of the car. Accordingly, it's probably the better rule that the buyer can revoke against a remote seller, at least when the retailer is bankrupt. Again, however, this is a close call.

Upon rejection or revocation there is an issue as to whether or not Pete's has to pay any restitutionary recovery based on the value of any benefit Pete's received from using it during the six weeks. Most courts have held that such recovery is not available, but to the extent Pete's will receive back its full purchase price, plus any cover or market differential damages, it will have been put in a better position than it would have been had the contract been performed. That is, it will have all of its money, plus thirty days or so of using the ambulance for its business without having to pay for that use [Text §22.334]. It would seem that its damages should be offset by its benefits, but it is difficult to find support for such a claim in the case law.

The fact that the repair/replacement position of Paragraph 6 is unenforceable does not necessarily answer the question as to whether or not the limitation on consequential damages for economic loss is unenforceable. The resolution of this question is determined by whether the repair/replacement and consequential damage provisions are considered dependent or independent. If they are deemed dependent, i.e., the only reason Pete's agreed to give up its rights to consequential damages was because it had been promised that a defective part would be promptly repaired or replaced, the consequential damage limitation must also be stricken and such damages would be recoverable. While this approach has been adopted by some courts, others have held that the provisions are independent, and thus the failure of the repair/replacement clause provision has no effect on the consequential damages provision. If so, then the economic loss suffered by Pete's both while the ambulance was being repaired, and by the patient who suffered additional damages while waiting for the substitute ambulance, would still not be recoverable [Text §33.811].

XV. CASE SQUIBS

TABLE OF CASES IN CASE SQUIBS LISTED ALPHABETICALLY

ASSENT

Balfour v. Balfour, 2 K.B. 571 (1919)

In *Balfour*, a husband promised to make certain monthly payments to his wife, with whom he was living amicably at the time of the promise. After the parties separated, the wife sued for payments due under the agreement. The court held that the alleged contract was not enforceable because family members do not normally contemplate legal consequences when they make promises to each other. Such promises are unenforceable after domestic partners separate. Note, however, that there has been some relaxation of the presumption against legal consequences arising from these types of agreements in modern decisions. Thus, where the agreement is made between family members not living together amicably (e.g. where the agreement is entered into by separated marital partners or in a dissolution situation) or where the parties expressly agree to the agreement's enforceability, the contract is likely to be enforced. [Text §2.13]

Varney v. Ditmars, 111 N.E. 822 (N.Y. 1816)

This early case is cited as one of the seminal cases setting forth the indefiniteness doctrine. An architectural draftsman sued his employer over a provision in his employment contract that he would be paid a "fair share of [the employer's] profits" in addition to his regular salary. The court refused to enforce the profit sharing provision, stating that its amount was a matter of "pure conjecture" and "may be any amount from a nominal sum to a material part according to the particular views of the person whose guess is considered. Such an executory contract must rest for performance on the honor and good faith of the parties making it." Accordingly, because the meaning of the term was too indefinite, the promise could not be enforced. [Text §6.022]

OFFER AND ACCEPTANCE

Adams v. Lindsell, 106 Eng. Rep. 250 (1818)

This case is cited as the original decision setting forth the mail box rule. The offeror mailed an offer to sell wool to the offeree. The offeree responded with a letter of acceptance. Subsequent to the offeree's dispatch of the acceptance, but before the offeror received it, the offeror sold the wool to another party and attempted to revoke the offer. The mail box rule says that: (1) properly addressed acceptances are effective upon dispatch, if acceptance by mail is a permissible mode of acceptance under the terms of the offer; and (2) rejections and revocations of offers are effective upon receipt. Thus, in this case, an enforceable contract was formed at the moment of the offeree's dispatch and the attempted revocation was without effect. [Text §§4.6, et seq; 4.63]

Allied Steel & Conveyors v. Ford Motor Co., 277 F.2d 907 (6th Cir. 1960)

This case details effective methods of acceptance where the offer is ambiguous as to whether it is to be accepted by a promise or performance. Ford contracted to buy machinery from Allied. It then sent an amended purchase order to Allied for the purchase of additional machines beyond the quantity agreed to in the original contract. The purchase order stated, "This purchase order agreement is not binding until accepted. Acceptance should be executed on [the] acknowledgment copy which should be returned to buyer." Allied began performance without returning an executed acknowledgment copy. A dispute later arose as to whether a contract had been formed. The key was how a reasonable offeree would construe the terms of the offer. Here, the court held that the offeree reasonably understood the offer not to state that return of the acknowledgment copy was the **exclusive** method of acceptance, but only one of the many permissible ways to accept. Hence, beginning performance was also a permissible method of acceptance, and a contract was formed for the additional machinery when performance was begun. Note that this case is not an exception to the general rule that the offeror is the "master of his offer;" it merely requires the offeror to be unmistakably clear in his or her terms, or risk alternative means of acceptance. [Text §4.52]

Ammons v. Wilson & Co., 170 So. 227 (Miss. 1936)

This case illustrates a scenario where the prior course of dealing between the parties makes it reasonable that the offeree's silence be construed as an acceptance. The seller's salesman took an order from the buyer for prompt shipment "subject to acceptance by seller's authorized agent at point of shipment." The seller did not respond to the order for almost two weeks. During that time period, the market price of the ordered goods rose, and the seller subsequently refused to ship. The court held that a jury question was presented as to whether the seller's silence indicated an implied acceptance. An offer can be accepted by silence when such a pattern has been established by the course of dealing between the buyer and seller. In this case, the seller's salesman had previously taken orders from the buyer, and those orders "had been accepted and shipped not later than one week from the time they were given" without any notice of formal acceptance to the buyer. Therefore, it would have been reasonable for the buyer to assume that if the seller intended to reject the offer that notice would have been forthcoming during the usual time period required for shipping. Since no notice of rejection came, the buyer reasonably assumed that the seller had accepted the offer. [Text §4.5433]

Ayer v. Western Union Telegraph Co., 10 A. 495 (Me. 1887)

This case determined which party bears the risk of an incorrect price quote transmitted through the seller's agent. Ayer contracted with Western Union to transmit a price quote to the buyer as "two ten net cash," but Western Union mistakenly transmitted "two net cash." The buyer accepted Ayer's offer as transmitted, and Ayer supplied the goods at the lower price. The court held that the seller, not the buyer, bears the risk of an error committed by the telegraph company because an offeree must be able to rely on an offer communicated through an agent chosen by the offeror. Because the buyer had no reason to know of the error, and because the seller chose the agent, acceptance by the buyer at the lower price was valid under the objective theory of contracts. However, Western Union was held liable for the difference between the price Ayer quoted and the lower price which Western Union mistakenly telegraphed. [Text §§3.2; 4.2]

Brackenberry v. Hodgkin, 116 Me. 399 (1917)

This case illustrates the irrevocability of offers looking to a unilateral contract once the offeree begins performance. A mother promised to leave her farm to her daughter if the daughter gave up her home to come and care for the mother. The court held that once the daughter began performance by complying with the request, an irrevocable option contract was formed which bound the mother to perform as promised in the offer, provided the daughter completed performance as specified in the offer. Note, however, that the offeree is not bound to complete his or her performance in such a situation, for the offeree may decline to exercise an option offered to him or her. [Text §4.4134-1B]

C. Itoh (America), Inc. v. Jordan Int'l Co., 552 F.2d 1228 (7th Cir. 1977)

This case illustrates UCC §2-207 (3)'s role in determining the enforceability contract by conduct under the UCC, and in regulating what the terms of such a contract will be. The buyer in *Itoh* offered to purchase steel coils from the seller. The seller sent back an acknowlegment which included an additional arbitration clause and provided that "[s]eller's acceptance is . . . expressly conditional on

[b]uyer's assent to the additional or different terms and conditions set forth below and printed on the reverse side." The buyer never notified the seller of his assent to the additional terms. Nonetheless, the seller shipped the steel coils, and the buyer paid for them. The court held that no contract was formed under UCC §2-207 (1), since the seller's acceptance fell within that provision's "expressly conditional" exception to the formation of a contract. However, a contract came into existence under UCC §2-207 (3), since the conduct of the parties recognized the existence of a contract. The terms of the contract were the terms on which the parties' forms agreed plus additional terms automatically provided by the UCC under the "knock out" rule. These terms would not include the arbitration clause. [Text §§5.3123; 5.33]

Caldwell v. Cline, 156 S.E. 55 (W. Va. 1930)

This case determines the allowable time period for acceptance of an offer which provides that the offeree may accept for a specified time period. The offeror in *Caldwell* mailed an offer to the offeree on January 29 which stated that the offeree had eight days to accept or reject the offer. The offeree received the offer on February 2 and telegrammed his acceptance on February 8. This acceptance was received by the offeror on February 9. The court held that the offeree's acceptance was effective because an offer is deemed to be made when received by the offeree, and the period allowed for acceptance is calculated from the date of receipt, **unless otherwise specified in the offer.** [Text §4.4121]

Carlill v. Carbolic Smoke Ball Co., [Text §§4.3313-1, 4.3341; 4.562].

Davis v. Jacoby, 34 P.2d 1026 (Cal. 1934)

If it is unclear whether an offer looks to a unilateral or a bilateral contract, the offer can be accepted either by performance or by a promise to perform. Thus, a letter which promised an inheritance to a woman and her husband if the couple would manage her uncle's affairs and care for his dying wife was an offer which could be accepted either by the couple's arrival, or by their promise to arrive, so long as they undertook preparations to fulfill that promise. The couple had thus accepted by sending a letter promising to perform, and hence the death of the uncle before they actually began did not affect their rights. That is, there is a general presumption in favor of bilateral contracts where the offeror's offer is unclear as to which type of contract was intended. The couple's acceptance of the bilateral contract meant that there was not an offer pending which would have resulted in the termination of the couple's power of acceptance upon the death of the offeror. Instead, they had entered into a contract, the terms of which were enforceable after the death of one party to the agreement (so long as they performed their promise to care for the uncle's wife). Thus, the niece had an enforceable right to an inheritance from her uncle's estate. [Text §4.52]

Dickinson v. Dodds, 2 Ch. D. 463 (Eng. 1876).

This case sets forth the indirect revocation doctrine. The offeree was given "two days" to decide whether to accept an offer to sell some land. During that two day period, the offeree learned from a reliable source that the land had been sold to another. The court held that as soon as the offeree learned of the sale from the reliable source, there was an effective, but indirect, revocation of the offeror's offer. [Text §4.4133-1]

Dorton v. Collins & Aikman Corp., 453 F.2d 1161 (6th Cir. 1972)

This case illustrates the tendency of the courts to strictly construe the "expressly conditional" exception of UCC §2-207(1). The offeree's form in *Dorton* made its acceptance "**subject to** all of the terms and conditions" contained in the form. One of the terms in the form stated that any dispute arising under the parties' contract would be resolved by arbitration. The issue was whether the "subject to" language in the offeree's form made the offeree's acceptance "expressly conditional" on the offeror's assent to the additional terms. If so, the offeree's acknowlegement could not operate as an acceptance; rather, it would operate as a counter-offer. The court held that the "is subject to" language did not have such an effect. The court stated that for the "expressly conditional" exception of UCC §2-207 (1) to become operative, "It is not enough than an acceptance is expressly conditional on additional or different terms; rather, an acceptance must be expressly conditional on the **offeror's assent** to those terms . . . [to make it a counter-offer]." Since the "is subject to" language in the offeree's form did not expressly require the offeror's separate and affirmative assent, the offeree's form operated as a valid acceptance of the offeror's offer. The case was then remanded to determine whether the arbitration clause "materially altered" the agreement under UCC §2-207(2). [Text §5.3123.]

Drennan v. Star Paving Co., [Text §§4.4135-1; 8.342].

Embry v. Hargardine, McKittrick Dry Goods Co., 105 S.W. 777 (Mo. App. 1907)

Embry was one of the first cases to usher in the objective theory of contracts. In that case, an employee threatened to quit if his employment contract was not renewed for another year. The employer replied, "Go ahead, you're all right. Get your men out, and don't let that worry you." Unbeknownst to the employee, however, the employer harbored an undisclosed intent not to renew the contract. Two months later, the employee was terminated, and he sued his employer, alleging that his employment contract had been renewed. The court held that a reasonable employee would have understood the employer's statement to mean that his employment contract was being renewed. Therefore, the employer's subjective intent when the statement was made was irrelevant and the alleged renewal was enforceable. [Text §3.2]

Fairmount Glass Works v. Crunden-Martin Woodenware Co., 51 S.W. 196 (Ky. Ct. App. 1899)

This case demonstrates that in certain cases a "price quote" may amount to an "offer" which empowers the offeree to validly accept the bargain. The buyer in *Fairmount* requested the seller's price for ten car loads of mason jars. The seller wrote back, saying "we quote you" certain jars at specified prices "for immediate acceptance." The buyer accepted and requested delivery of the ten carloads. The seller refused to deliver the jars, claiming its letter did not constitute an offer, but was rather only a quotation of prices, which normally is deemed to be only a solicitation to make an offer. The court held, however, that an offer was created by the seller's correspondence, despite the fact that it never used the term "offer" and used the word "quote." Use of the language "for immediate acceptance" made it clear that the seller was willing to be bound to the terms in the correspondence, and thus the buyer was empowered to accept the seller's offer. [Text §3.212]

Hamer v. Sidway, (Text §4.521 and Case Squibs section on Consideration).

Hawkins v. McGee, 84 N.H. 114 (1929)

Hawkins demonstrates that a patient will be entitled to expectation damages where his or her doctor promises a certain result that does not occur. A young boy's hand was scarred from a severe burn, and the surgeon who was to perform a skin graft operation promised that the boy's hand would be "100% perfect" following the operation. The court held that the doctor made an enforceable promise, under the objective theory of contracts, which was breached when the surgery failed. The plaintiff was entitled to expectation damages equal to the difference between the value of a "100% perfect" hand and the value of his hand in its post-surgery condition. [Text §§2.12, 3.2153.]

Hays Merchandise, Inc. v. Dewey, 474 P.2d 270 (Wash. 1970)

This case illustrates UCC §2-606(1)(c) which holds that a buyer has accepted goods once he or she does an act inconsistent with the seller's ownership of the goods. The retail buyer in *Hays* gave notice of revocation to the seller, but then proceeded to price, display, and sell the goods. These acts are clearly inconsistent with an intent to revoke the goods, and the court held that the buyer had thus accepted the goods. [Text §22.322]

Humble Oil & Refining Co. v. Westside Investment Corp., 428 S.W.2d 92 (Tex. 1968)

This case demonstrates the principle that irrevocable offers are not terminated by the offeree's counter-offer. This is the case with option contracts which are formed when an offeree gives the offeror consideration to keep an offer open. In *Humble*, the seller and buyer agreed to a two-month option on certain real property. The buyer paid seller $50, which made the option irrevocable. During the two-month period, buyer sent a counter-offer stating that it would be willing to exercise its option on different terms. Later, buyer attempted to exercise the option according to its original terms, and seller claimed the option had been terminated by the buyer's counter-offer. The court held that an option contract is an irrevocable offer, and therefore the buyer's power of acceptance was not terminated by his interim counter offer. [Text §4.4211]

International Filter Co. v. Conroe Gin, Ice & Light Co., 277 S.W. 631 (Tex. Comm. App. 1925)

The court in *Conroe* held that bilateral contracts may be effectively accepted without notice to the offeror where the offer expressly allows such an acceptance. The plaintiff sent the defendant a written proposal which stated that the proposal "becomes a contract when accepted by the purchaser and approved by an executive officer" at the plaintiff's office. An officer at the plaintiff's office accepted the proposal by writing "OK . . . P.N. Engel" on the proposal. Subsequently, the defendant attempt to revoke its offer. The court held that the officer's endorsement on the proposal was sufficient to constitute an acceptance of the bilateral contract offer since the proposal expressly authorized acceptance in such a manner. Thus, the express language of the proposal made the officer's acceptance immediately effective without notification to the offeree. [Text §4.572]

Jordan v. Dobbins, 122 Mass. 168 (1877)

This case illustrates the general principle that where either the offeror or offeree of a pending contract dies, the power to accept the contract is terminated. A third party wished to buy goods on credit from a department store. Dobbins executed a standing offer that he would guarantee any of the third party's debts to the department store. Dobbins died, a fact of which the department store was unaware, and the department store sued Dobbins's estate for debts owed by the third party. The court held, however, that the death of Dobbins (the guarantor) operated as a revocation of his guarantee whether or not the department store (the creditor) had notice of the death. Therefore, the debt owed by the third party could not be recovered from Dobbins's estate. [Text §4.414]

Lefkowitz v. Minneapolis Surplus Stores, (see §3.2143).

Livingstone v. Evans, 4. D.L.R. 769 (Alberta 1925)

This case provides an example of a situation where an acceptance which is mailed after the expiration of the offer may be held to be a valid acceptance. In *Livingstone*, the offer stated no specific time period during which the offer would remain open, so the offer remained open for a reasonable time. The offeree failed to accept within a reasonable time, however, and mailed an acceptance at a later date. The late acceptance crossed in the mails with a letter from the offeror indicating that the offer was still open. Thus, the court held that the acceptance, though late according to the original offer's terms, was valid. [Text §4.412]

Lonergan v. Skolnick, 276 P.2d 8 (Cal. Ct. App. 1954)

This case illustrates the general principle that a "quote" does not usually constitute an "offer" to sell. Thus, where the certain piece of property, in response to the plaintiff's inquiry, and with a disclaimer that the letter was a "form letter," the court held that the plaintiff was not reasonable in concluding that the price quote constituted an offer to sell. [Text §3.2121]

Lucy v. Zehmer, 84 S.E.2d 516 (Va. 1954)

This case illustrates the enforceability of a purported agreement under the objective theory of contracts even though one of the parties subjectively had no intention to enter the agreement. The plaintiff offered the defendants $50,000 for their farm. The defendants then drafted a written promise to sell the farm to the plaintiff at that price. The plaintiff took the defendants seriously and later sued them when they refused to convey the farm. The defendants asserted that they were only joking were intoxicated at the time they made the promise, and had no intention of actually selling the farm. The court held that the defendants were bound by the agreement, stating that "[a] person cannot set up that he was merely jesting when his conduct and words would warrant a reasonable person in believing that he intended a real agreement." [Text §3.2152.]

Marchiondo v. Schenk, 432 P.2d 405 (N.M. 1967)

This case holds that when an offer for a unilateral contract requests performance as the appropriate method for acceptance, the offeree's beginning of performance makes the offeror's offer irrevocable. The defendant offered to sell a piece of property to a third party (with a six day time limit on the offer) and also offered the plaintiff (a real estate agent) a commission if the sale was consummated. The offer was made within the six day limit, but the defendant subsequently revoked his offer to sell. The court held that the real estate agent was entitled to his commission because a seller's promise to pay a commission upon the sale of his property becomes irrevocable when the agent begins performance of the unilateral contract by securing a potential buyer. The commission is payable even if the seller later backs out of the sale. [Text §4.4134-1B]

Morrison v. Thoelke, 155 So. 2d 889 (Fla. Ct. App. 1963)

This case illustrates the application of the mailbox rule to offerees. Buyer signed a contract for the purchase of real estate and mailed it to the seller. Seller signed (accepted) the contract and mailed it back to the Buyer. Before the buyer received the accepted contract through the mail, the seller contacted buyer's lawyer and attempted to repudiate his acceptance. The court held that the contract was enforceable at the moment of acceptance by the seller. Thus, an acceptance is effective upon dispatch by the offeree. A rejection dispatched after the acceptance is ineffective, even if received by the offeror before the acceptance. [Text §4.6 *et seq.*]

Petterson v. Pattberg, 161 N.E. 428 (N.Y. 1928)

This case holds that an acceptance of a contract offer unambiguously calling for a unilateral contract is not effective until performance actually starts. Prior to the time performance begins, the offeror can freely revoke his offer. The defendant held a mortgage on the plaintiff's property. The defendant offered plaintiff a partial reduction of principal if plaintiff paid off the mortgage before the end of the month. Before the end of month, plaintiff told defendant he had money to pay off the discounted mortgage, but defendant revoked before the plaintiff could physically tender the payment, stating that he had sold the mortgage to a third party. Plaintiff ended up paying the full principal amount to the third party, so he sued the defendant for the discount. The court held that the plaintiff never effectively accepted the defendant's offer because payment was never actually tendered. The court treated the attempted tender as a mere preparation to perform which was ineffective to accept the defendant's unilateral offer. The defendant was free to revoke his offer until an actual tender of payment was made. [Text §§4.4134; 4.54]

Roto-Lith v. F.P. Bartlett & Co., [Text §5.3122].

Southwest Engineering Co. v. Martin Tractor Co., 473 P.2d 18 (Kan. 1970)

This court held, in accordance with UCC §2-204 (3), that the absence of an important term from an agreement is not necessarily fatal to the formation of the contract. Thus, where plaintiff and defendant failed to agree on a time for payment, the court inserted a "gap filler" payment term provided by UCC §2-310(a) which requires that the goods be paid for upon delivery where the parties' contract fails to specify the payment term. Other indefiniteness problems concerning price and time for shipment or delivery may also be corrected by various gap filler provisions found in the UCC. In addition, it held that printed letterhead, or any other symbol adopted by a party with the present intention to authenticate a writing, is sufficient to meet the "signature" requirement of the statute of frauds. [Text §6.221; 9.6224]

CONSIDERATION/PROMISSORY ESTOPPEL

Allegheny College v. National Chatauqua County Bank, 159 N.E. 173 (N.Y. 1927)

In this case, Justice Cardozo set forth the requirements for valid consideration. A charitable donor promised to donate money to Allegheny College. In return, the College promised to name a scholarship fund after the donor. The court held that an enforceable bilateral contract, supported by valid consideration, had been formed.

Justice Cardozo opined that in order for a promise to be "supported by consideration," three requirements must be met: (1) the promisee must suffer a "legal detriment"; (2) the detriment must induce the promise; and (3) the promise must induce the detriment. Thus, a charitable organization's promise to name a scholarship after a donor is sufficient consideration to make the donor's promise enforceable if it is induced by the promised contribution and the promise to contribute is induced by the promised naming of the scholarship. Although the court held that an enforceable contract had been formed, the case is often noted for Justice Cardozo's statement that "we have adopted the doctrine of promissory estoppel as the equivalent of consideration in connection with our law of charitable subscriptions." Thus, as indicated now under §90 (2) of the Restatement 2d, promissory estoppel may be an alternative basis for enforcing the promise in similar cases. [Text §§7.12; 8.1; 8.22]

Bard v. Kent, 122 P.2d 8 (Cal. 1942)

This case illustrates the revocability of option contracts at common law where there is only a recital, but no actual payment, of consideration i.e., where there is "purported" consideration. The defendant offered the plaintiff a written option to extend his lease of the defendant's property. The option stated that it was granted "for consideration of ten dollars and other valuable consideration." The plaintiff never paid the stated consideration but hired an architect to draw up sketches for improvements to be made to the leased property. Before the plaintiff could exercise the option to renew the lease, the defendant died, and the defendant's estate refused to allow the plaintiff to renew. The court held that an option to renew a lease becomes an irrevocable offer only when consideration is actually paid by the offeree. In the absence of consideration, the option is revoked upon the death of the offeror, even if the offeree incurs expenses in reliance on the option. Thus, the fact that the plaintiff failed to pay the stated consideration prevented him from enforcing the option since it was revoked by the defendant's death.

Note, however, that under §87 of the Restatement 2d of Contracts purported consideration in option contracts is sufficient to bind the party selling the option so long as the option is in writing, the deal is fair, and it is signed by the offeror. [Text §4.4212]

DeCicco v. Schweizer, 117 N.E. 807 (N.Y. 1917)

In *DeCicco*, Justice Cardozo wrote a controversial decision which held that a party's forebearance from exercising his right to rescind an agreement could be sufficient consideration to enforce the other party's promise. The opinion illustrates the general judicial hostility to the consideration requirement inherent in the pre-existing duty rule. In that case, a father promised his daughter's fiance a $2500/year payment if the fiance and his daughter went through with their planned marriage. After making the payments for ten years, the father refused to make any more payments, claiming there was no consideration for his promise because his daughter and her fiance were already engaged to be married when the agreement was entered into. Therefore, the parties were already bound to go through with the wedding (a pre-existing duty), and the fiance's promise to get married could not then be adequate consideration for the promised payment from the father. However, the court found that the father's promise was supported by adequate consideration; it was not merely an unenforceable promise to make a gift. The court reasoned that the couple could have rescinded their engagement, and their forebearance from exercising this right was sufficient consideration for the father's promise. [Text §7.2]

East Providence Credit Union v. Geremia, 239 A.2d 725 (R.I. 1968)

This case illustrates when a promise to procure insurance will be enforceable. The Geremias purchased a car with the help of a loan from the Credit Union. At the outset, the Geremias agreed to obtain insurance on the car. However, Mr. Geremia later became ill and could no longer pay the premiums on the insurance. The Credit Union promised to make the premium payments for the Geremias, and the Geremias agreed to allow the Credit Union to add the amount of these payments to their loan balance. However, the Credit Union failed to make the premium payments. When the car was subsequently destroyed, the Credit Union sued for the balance due on the loan, and the Geremias counterclaimed for the insurance proceeds. The court held for the Geremias on two grounds: (1) the agreement to pay interest on the money borrowed to pay the insurance premium was sufficient consideration to make the Credit Union's promise enforceable; and (2) the promise was enforceable by promissory estoppel, since the Geremias had relied on the Credit Union's promise to make the premium payments which caused the Geremias to forebear maintaining the insurance policy. This last basis for the court's decision is controversial since the facts indicate that the Geremias could not have continued to maintain the insurance policy anyway. Thus, there is a question of whether the Credit Union's promise caused a real forebearance by the Geremias. [Text §7.3; 8.2]

Feinberg v. Pfeiffer Co., 322 S.W.2d 163 (Mo. Ct. App. 1959)

This case upholds by the principle that past consideration is insufficient consideration to make a contract enforcable. However, it also shows that where a contract cannot be enforced due to insufficient consdieration, promissory estoppel can be used to enforce some or all of the promises of that agreement. After the plaintiff had worked for Pfeiffer Co. for 37 years, the company's board of directors passed a resolution entitling the plaintiff to a $200/month pension upon her retirement. Plaintiff continued working for another year and a half and then retired. She was paid her pension for seven years, but the company eventually cut the amount back to $100/month, and the plaintiff brought suit. The court held that the company's promise to pay her pension could not be enforced as a contract, for the company's promise was merely a gift promise based on past consideration. However, the company's promise could be enforced on promissory estoppel grounds, for the plaintiff reasonably, foreseeably, and detrimentally relied on the company's promise in deciding to retire when she did. [Text §§7.51; 8.2]

Fischer v. Union Trust Co., 101 N.W. 852 (Mich. 1904)

This case demonstrates that sham consideration will not suffice to make a gift promise enforceable. In *Fischer*, a daughter paid her father $1.00 at the time he deeded certain property to her in exchange for the father's promise that he would pay off the mortgages on the property when they became due. Following the father's death, the daughter sought to enforce her father's promise against his estate. The court held that the father's promise was an unenforceable gift due to lack of adequate consideration. The facts showed that the father's promise was intended as a gift, and thus the payment of $1.00 was merely sham consideration given the surrounding circumstances. As a result, the father's promise was unenforceable. [Text §7.612]

Foakes v. Beer, 9 App. Cas. 605 (Eng. 1884)

Foakes is the preeminent pre-existing duty rule case. Foakes owed Beer money under a loan and did not have the money to repay the principal when it became due. The loan agreement contemplated this fact and called for him to pay interest on any sum not paid in full when due. Foakes entered into a modification with Beer, whereby they agreed he could repay the principal on fixed schedule, and as long as he stuck to the schedule, he would not have to pay any interest. Foakes stuck to the schedule, but after making the last payment, Beer sued for the interest called for in the original contract. The court held that Foakes had to pay the interest for there was no consideration for Beer's agreement to forego the interest. That is, under the pre-existing duty rule, to be enforceable, a modification must be supported by new consideration. Because Foakes did not promise to do anything he had not already promised, Beer's promise to forego the interest was unenforceable. [Text §§7.6341; 24.33]

Goodman v. Dicker, 169 F.2d 684 (D.C. Cir. 1948)

This case holds that reliance damages are recoverable in an action based on promissory estoppel where the defendant promised the plaintiff a franchise. A higher award of the plaintiff's expectation interest would be inappropriate given that there was no enforceable contract. In *Goodman*, the plaintiff applied to the defendant for a franchise to sell Emerson radios. The defendant led the plaintiff to believe that the franchise had been approved, and the plaintiff spent $1,150 to hire salesmen and advertise before he found out that the franchise had not in fact been approved. The court's holding, which allowed plaintiff his reliance damages, is significant for two reasons: (1) it allowed damages under a reliance measure, whereas the traditional rule would have allowed only a restitutionary recovery; and (2) recovery was permitted even though the franchise was terminable at will. [Text §§8.4; 31.53]

Hamer v. Sidway, 27 N.E. 256 (N.Y. 1891)

This case demonstrates that the forebearance of a legal right is sufficient consideration to support a promise as a contract. An uncle promised to pay his nephew $5,000 if he refrained from smoking, drinking, and gambling until he turned age 21. After turning 21, the nephew sought to enforce this promise. The court held that the nephew's abstention from the specified activities was a sufficient consideration to support the uncle's promise. The fact that the nephew may have actually benefited from this forebearance does not mean that the nephew's performance did not amount to a "detriment." Rather, the nephew's agreement to limit his actions was a sufficient detriment for purposes of consideration. [Text §4.521.]

Harrington v. Taylor, 36 S.E.2d 227 (N.C. 1945)

This case holds that a humanitarian act, voluntarily performed, does not suffice as legal consideration for a subsequent promise. The defendant's wife was assaulting the defendant with an axe when the plaintiff intervened and saved the defendant's life. In the process, the plaintiff's hand was severely injured. The court held that the defendant's oral promise to compensate the plaintiff was unenforceable. That is, where the voluntary act occurs before the defendant's promise is made, the act does not constitute consideration for the promise. [Text §7.52]

Hoffman v. Red Owl Stores, [Text §§8.351; 8.42].

Kirksey v. Kirksey, 8 Ala. 131 (1845)

A gift promise in insufficient consideration to make a promise enforceable. Similarly, the fact that a promisee may have undertaken acts incidental to the receipt of the gift is not a sufficient detriment to make a gift promise enforceable. In *Kirksey*, a man promised his sister-in-law that he would provide a place for her to live at his home after the death of her husband. The sister-in-law thereafter incurred expenses in reliance on the promised place to live by moving her family several hundred miles to the defendant's home. Once she arrived, however, the father-in-law changed his mind and refused to let her stay with him, and the sister-in-law brought suit.

The court held that the father-in-law's promise was only a gift promise, and thus could not be enforced due to a lack of consideration. Further, the sister-in-law's act of moving to Alabama could not be thought of as "substantial reliance" on the offer, which would have made it irrevocable. Rather, moving to Alabama was merely an act incidental to the gift, i.e. it is something the recipient had to do to take advantage of a gift. Since the father-in-law's promise of a place to stay and the sister-in-law's moving to Alabama were in no way bargained for, the promise of a place to stay could not be enforced as an offer. Note, however, that at least the costs of the move would probably be recoverable on a promissory estoppel theory. [Text §§7.5113-2; 8.2]

Kucera v. Kavan, 84 N.W.2d 207 (Neb. 1957)

This case illustrates the principle that reliance in the form of preparation for performance may render a unilateral offer irrevocable under the doctrine of promissory estoppel. The plaintiffs in *Kucera* were looking to purchase a farm. They began to negotiate with the defendant who suggested a joint ownership arrangement whereby the plaintiff and the defendant would become partners in the parcel of land, and the plaintiffs would obtain possession while paying the defendant rent. The defendant agreed that the plaintiffs would have an option to purchase the entire interest in the parcel once the defendant found another parcel to invest her money in. However, plaintiffs never paid consideration for the option. Plaintiffs took possession and began to make several thousand dollars worth of improvements to the property. When the plaintiffs later attempted to excercise the option, however, the defendant refused to honor their right to accept his offer, stating that any such option was unenforceable due to the lack of consideration paid for it. Nevertheless, the court enforced the option agreement on the basis of the plaintiffs' reliance on the unenforceable option. The court quoted the Restatement which provided that "[a] promise which the promisor should reasonably expect to induce action or forbearance of a definite and substantial character on the part of the promisee and which does induce such action or forbearance is binding if injustice can be avoided only be enforcement of the promise." [Text §4.4135-2]

Mattei v. Hopper, 330 P.2d 625 (Cal. 1958)

The court in *Mattei* discussed the situation where one party's duty to perform is dependent on that party's subjective satisfaction with the other party's performance. In this case, one party agreed to purchase a shopping center subject to his satisfaction with leases that were to be secured for the shopping center. The court held that such a contract is supported by adequate consideration. "[T]he promisor's duty to exercise his judgment in good faith is an adequate consideration to support the contract." That is, the personal satisfaction clause did not render the promise illusory, for the determination of any such satisfaction had to be exercised in good faith. The party thus had bound himself to do something he did not have to do before the contract was entered into, i.e., decide in good faith whether he was satisfied with the lease terms, and thus consideration was present and the contract enforceable. [Text §7.622]

Mills v. Wyman, [Text §§7.5211; 7.5222]

Ricketts v. Scothorn, 57 Neb. 51 (1898)

This case illustrates the application of the doctrine of promissory estoppel to enforce gifts that induce detrimental reliance by the donee. A grandfather did not want his grandaughter to have to work outside the home, so he gave her a promissory note as a kind of "nest egg." The daughter quit her job in reliance on the note. Subsequently, the grandfather died, and the daughter sought to enforce the note against his estate. The estate defended on the grounds that there was no consideration for the note, and thus its promise to pay was unenforceable. The court held that while the note could not be enforced as a contract because of the lack of consideration, the grandfather's promise to pay could be enforced on promissory estoppel grounds. That is, it was reasonable to foreseeably expect the daughter to rely on the note, she did in fact rely on the note, and injustice could only be avoided by enforcing the promise. [Text §8.21.]

Webb v. McGowin, [Text §7.5221]

Wheeler v. White, 398 S.W.2d 93 (Tex. 1965)

A party to an otherwise unenforceable agreement may recover reliance damages under the Restatement 2d's view of promissory estoppel where the promise induced his "foreseeable, definite, and substantial reliance." Reliance will put him in the position he would have been in had he not relied on the promise. Plaintiff owned some land which he planned to develop as commercial property. Defendant promised the plaintiff a construction loan, and the parties signed a document which later turned out to be unenforceable as a contract because basic, material terms were omitted from the agreement. Before the loan was to come through, the defendant encouraged the plaintiff to demolish some buildings on the property which had a value around $58,000 so that construction could begin as soon as possible. The promised loan never materialized, and the plaintiff sued the defendant because he was unable to obtain alternative financing. The defendant asserted that plaintiff could have no recovery since the purported loan agreement was unenforceable as a contract. However, the court permitted plaintiff's recovery of his reliance damages in promissory estoppel under the above-stated principle. [Text §8.2; 8.4]

Wood v. Lucy, Lady Duff Gordon, [Text §§7.6222; 7.6241]

STATUTE OF FRAUDS

Azevedo v. Minister, 471 P.2d 661 (1970)

The UCC 2-201 statute of frauds is satisfied by an accounting sent 10 weeks after the formation of an oral agreement, where performance began without objection after the oral agreement was formed. However, the burden of proving the oral agreement remains on the party alleging the contract, despite the other party's receipt of the written memoranda purportedly memorializing the contract. [Text §9.643]

J.J. Brooksbank Co. v. American Motors Corp., 184 N.W.2d 796 (Minn. 1971)

Although the statute of frauds in this case barred the plaintiff's action to enforce the promise of the promisor to answer for the debt of a third party, it did not bar an action against the promisor for breach of an oral agreement to repurchase goods from the plaintiff. The plaintiff operated a Budget Rent-a-Car company. He entered into an oral agreement with American Motors under which plaintiff was to purchase new automobiles for use in his car-rental business, and American guaranteed that the cars would be repurchased by its franchised dealers at a depreciated price approximately one year after plaintiff purchased each car. A dispute arose over three of the cars purchased under the agreement after American's dealer in Minneapolis refused to repurchase its share of the cars. Plaintiff was forced to sell the three cars at an auction and thereafter brought suit for the difference in price between what he would have received if the cars had been sold under the oral repurchase agreement and what he realized at auction.

The trial court barred plaintiff's action, reasoning that American stood in the position of a surety of its dealers' obligations under the oral repurchase agreement. Since the statute of frauds limits the enforceability of oral suretyship promises, the trial court dismissed the plaintiff's suit.

The Minnesota Supreme Court, however, reversed, holding that this case presented an example of the "leading object" or definite interest" exception to the suretyship provisions of the Statute. That is, when the surety makes an oral promise to secure an economic advantage for the surety and not the principal, the transaction is outside the Statute, and thus enforceable even though oral. Here, American made its guarantee to further its own economic interest, and thus, under the "leading object" rule, the Statute did not apply. [Text §9.53]

Crabtree v. Elizabeth Arden Sales Corp., 110 N.E.2d 551 (N.Y. 1953)

This case illustrates the modern view that the statute of frauds may be satisfied by combining the terms in an unsigned document with terms in a separate signed document to form a single memorandum if both documents clearly refer to the same transaction and there is external evidence that both parties assented to the unsigned document. (the "merger" doctrine) In *Crabtree*, an employee sought to enforce an employment agreement against her employer which was evidenced by two payroll cards (signed by the employer) and the employer's memorandum of her oral offer (unsigned by the employer). The court rejected the view held by some jurisdictions that the signed writing must refer to the unsigned writing. It is enough "that a sufficient connection between the papers is established simply by a reference in them to the same subject matter or transaction . . . , and oral testimony is admitted to show the connection between the documents and to establish the acquiescence of the party to be charged, to the contents of the one unsigned." The court was satisfied that the alleged employment contract existed and was set forth in a series of documents some of which were signed by the party to be charged. Thus, the employee was allowed to introduce evidence explaining terms on the documents that were not signed by the employer. [Text §9.231]

MISTAKE

Elsinore Union Elementary School Dist. v. Kastorff, 353 P.2d 713 (Cal. 1960)

The court in *Elsinore* allowed relief for a unilateral mistake where a general contractor made a clerical error in his bid for construction work for a school district. The general contractor submitted a bid which mistakenly omitted a subcontractor's bid for the plumbing on the project. This omission amounted to almost ten percent of the general contractor's total bid, and made his bid of $89,994 more than $11,000 less than the next lowest bid. The school district accepted the general contractor's bid, but before a written contract was sent to him, the general contractor requested to withdraw his bid. The school district was then forced to accept the next lowest bid, and it sued the general contractor for the difference. The court ruled that the general contractor should be released from the contract since the mistake was an honest clerical error. The court noted that the school district intended for the general contractor to furnish plumbing, and therefore the school district must have understood that the general contractor intended for his bid to include the plumbing work. Additionally, the sum omitted, almost ten percent of the general contractor's total bid, was a material amount. Note, however, that the court would be much less willing to grant relief where the mistake was due to an error in business judgment rather than a clerical error. [Text §11.41]

Sherwood v. Walker, [Text §11.321].

Wood v. Boynton, [Text §11.322].

MISUNDERSTANDING

Frigaliment Importing Co. v. B.N.S. Int'l Sales Corp., 190 F. Supp. 116 (S.D.N.Y. 1960)

This case demonstrates that where the parties' contract contains an ambiguous term, the party claiming a breach of the contract has the burden of proving the meaning of the ambiguous term in his or her favor or there is no proven breach. The parties in *Frigaliment* entered into a contract calling for the sale and delivery of "chicken." The seller shipped "stewing chickens," and the buyer rejected them, claiming that the contract was for "broiling chickens," a much higher grade of chicken. The buyer later brought suit for breach. The court assumed that both parties acted in good faith and that they both believed the contract was on their own terms. The court held that the buyer could not sustain its burden of proof that there was a breach. The dictionary and the Department of Agriculture both supported the view that "chickens" meant "stewing chickens." Perhaps more significantly, given the prevailing prices at the time the contract was executed, it should have been clear to the buyer that the seller did not intend to provide broiling chickens. If it had, it would have entered into a losing contract. Thus, if the risk of mistaken views as to the meaning of the term "chicken" was to be allocated to one of the parties, it was properly allocated to the buyer under these facts. Accordingly, the buyer could not sustain its burden of establishing a breach in this case. [Text §11.52]

Raffles v. Wichelhaus, [Text §11.521].

DURESS

Austin Instrument, Inc. v. Loral Corp., 272 N.E.2d 533 (N.Y. 1971)

This case illustrates the principle that a contract modification will be unenforceable where the modification is secured through duress. A general contractor agreed to supply the U.S. Navy with $6,000,000 worth of radar sets. A subcontractor was to supply certain of the components necessary for the general contractor's performance. After the subcontractor began delivery of the components, the Navy granted the general contractor another contract to supply more radar sets. The subcontractor then threatened to stop further deliveries of the components unless it was guaranteed a portion of the work under the second contract and an increased price for the components under the original subcontract. There was no other supplier that could meet the general contractor's supply requirements in a timely manner, so the general contractor relented and agreed to the subcontractor's proposed modification. After full performance under both of the Navy contracts, the general contractor sought restitution of the excess payments made to the subcontractor as a result of the modification. The court held that the contract modification was voidable since the modification was the result of duress caused by the subcontractor. That is, the threat of nondelivery of the goods (which were not readily available from another source) and the requirement that the subcontractor be awarded a second subcontract constituted duress which sufficiently deprived the general contractor of its "free will" to reject the modification. [Text §12.23]

UNDUE INFLUENCE

Methodist Mission Home v. N — A — B —, 451 S.W.2d 539 (Tex. Civ. App. 1970)

This case demonstrates the defense of undue influence to contract actions. A mother had a child out of wedlock, and shortly after the birth, while the mother was experiencing a period of emotional distress, representatives of the maternity home and the mother's counselor encouraged the mother to give up her child for adoption. The court allowed the mother's defense of undue influence to an adoption agreement, taking note of the fact that "an unwed mother who has just given birth is usually emotionally distraught and peculiarly vulnerable to efforts . . . to persuade her to give up her child." Thus, the elements of undue influence, i.e., that there be a "special relationship" between the contracting parties (the Woman and the Home); and that there be "improper persuasion" by the stronger party (the Home) were established. [Text §13.12]

MISREPRESENTATION

Kannavos v. Annino, 247 N.E.2d 708 (Mass. 1969)

Where the misrepresentation by the breaching party to a contract is fraudulent, the innocent party is entitled to avoid the contract even in the absence of proof of justifiable reliance. In *Kannavos*, the plaintiff contracted to purchase a house from the defendant who represented that the house was suitable for multi-family rental use. The plaintiff failed to confirm this representation with the public records, but there was evidence in the case that the defendant knew of the zoning regulation which prohibited multi-family use of the house. Therefore, the plaintiff was able to successfully rescind the contract. [Text §14.42]

Laidlaw v. Organ, 15 U.S. (2 Wheat.) 178 (1817)

This United States Supreme Court case states the general rule (which is subject to several exceptions, none of which are present here) that a party has no duty to disclose beneficial facts during contract negotiations, especially when those facts are equally available to the other contracting party. In *Laidlaw*, a peace treaty was signed which effectively ended the War of 1812 and the British blockade of New Orleans. Organ lawfully learned of the treaty several hours before it became common knowlege. Knowing that with the blockade lifted the price of tobacco for export would rise, Organ purchased a large quantity of tobacco from Laidlaw without disclosing the fact of the peace treaty to Laidlaw. Laidlaw asked him whether he knew of any fact which would increase the value of the tobacco, and Organ simply did not answer. When the price of tobacco subsequently rose, Laidlaw sold the tobacco to another, and Organ sued for breach. However, Chief Justice Marshall stated that Laidlaw "was not bound to communicate" the facts that may be beneficial "where the means of intelligence are equally accessible to both parties" and where it is an arm's length transaction. That is, silence in such cases does not amount to an affirmative misrepresentation. Note the results could well have been different if Organ had affirmitavely misled Laidlaw in answer to his question. [Text §14.4156]

UNCONSCIONABILITY

A & M Produce Co. v. FMC Corp., 186 Cal. Rptr. 114 (App. Ct. 1982)

This court held that a disclaimer of express and implied warranties and a limitation on consequential damage recovery which are in technical compliance with the requirements of the Uniform Commercial Code may still be denied enforceability on unconscionability grounds. A small farming company entered into a contract with a large corporation for the sale of a weight-sizing machine for use by the farming company in harvesting a tomato crop. The farming company had never grown tomatoes before, so it relied on the corporate salesman's judgment regarding the specifications for the particular machine it would need. The salesman recommended a specific machine and assured the farming company that the one selected would work for their needs and that additional equipment would not be necessary.

The parties' written agreement was contained on a preprinted form produced by the corporation. The agreement contained two disclaimers: one disclaimed all warranties, and the other disclaimed consequential damages. Problems arose shortly after delivery of the machine because the machine was unable to properly harvest tomatoes without damaging them. Part of the problem was the need for additional equipment (a cooling unit) which the salesman had said the company would not need. The farming company ended up losing most of its tomato crop, so it wanted to return the weight-sizing machine to the corporation, but the corporation refused and demanded full payment of the balance due on the machine. The farming company subsequently sued for breach of express and implied warranties and for consequential damages, and the corporation defended that the warranties and consequential damage liability had been successfully disclaimed in the parties' written agreement.

The court refused, however, to enforce either the warranty disclaimers or the consequential damage limitation, stating that to do so would lead to an unconscionable result. The court held that the unconscionability doctrine applies to disclaimers of warranty and consequential damage provisions, just as it applies to any other contract provision, and that unconscionability is available to corporations just as it is to consumers. The court also held that that unconscionability has both procedural and substantive elements. The procedural element is met where the parties' agreement involves oppression and surprise for the party of lesser bargaining power. "Oppression . . . arises from an inequality of bargaining power which results . . . in 'an absence of meaningful choice.'" Surprise occurs when the contested terms "are hidden in a prolix printed form drafted by the party seeking to enforce the disputed terms." The substantive element is met where the agreement is "commercially unreasonable," i.e., where a contractual term causes an unjustifiable one-sided result, such as where the term "reallocates the risks of the bargain in an objectively unreasonable or unexpected manner." The procedural and substantive elements work together on a sliding scale, such that the more one of the elements can be shown, the less of the other that must be shown in order for the contested provision to be held unconscionable.

The contested provisions in the *A & M* case were unconscionable because the bargain took place between a large corporation and a small farming company (indicating oppression); both disclaimer provisions appeared on the middle of the back page of the preprinted form contract (indicating surprise); the provisions were never brought to the farming company's attention (indicating suprise); there was no opportunity for individual negotiation during the bargaining process (indicating oppression); the corporation knew the farming company had no expertise with weight-sizing machines and knew the farming company was relying on its expertise in selecting an appropriate machine (indicating oppression and commercial unreasonableness); and the disclaimer provisions resulted in the sale of an expensive piece of machinery with a corporation that guaranteed nothing about its performance (indicating commercial unreasonableness, i.e., a very one-sided bargain). Therefore, having found that the elements for the unconscionability doctrine were met, the court refused to give effect to the disclaimer provisions and upheld the lower court's damage award. [Text §§15.3; 15.4]

Campbell Soup Co. v. Wentz, 172 F.2d 80 (3d Cir. 1948)

This case illustrates the common law application of the unconscionability doctrine. Campbell Soup Company contracted with Wentz, a farmer, for his entire crop of a specific type of carrot at a fair price on the day the contract was signed. Subsequently, a market shortage occurred of the particular strain of carrots used for soup making, so the market price for Wentz's carrots rose sharply. As a consequence, Wentz breached the contract so that he could sell his carrots on the open market. Campbell's sued for specific performance. Normally, courts are amenable to granting specific performance in a shortage situation because the remedy of damages is inadequate where the plaintiff cannot buy a substitute performance in the open market. However, Campell's had imposed a very one-sided bargain upon the plaintiff in that Campbell's could unilaterally cancel the contract with Wentz, while Wentz had to obtain Campbell's approval before he could sell any carrots it had even if Campbell's did not want them. Hence, the court stated that because one part of the contract was unconscionable, Campbell's was not entitled to equitable relief, even though the part of the contract that was unfair had nothing to do with the issue in the present case. Commmon law was very strict about requiring that plaintiffs who sought equity had "to do equity," and thus this case shows that unconscionability was more of a defense to equitable relief at common law than it was a doctrine by which parties sought affirmative relief. [Text §15.21]

Weaver v. American Oil Co., 276 N.E.2d 144 (Ind. 1971)

Although many courts are reluctant to enforce adhesion contracts because of their inherent unfairness, a complaining party usually must show something more than a standardized form agreement to obtain relief from the contract. Courts, such as the court in *Weaver*, often require that the plaintiff additionally show the existence of a gross disparity in bargaining power. In that case, the defendant leased a gas station from the plaintiff, a large oil company. The lease signed by the parties was a standard form agreement which was drafted by the plaintiff's lawyers. The contested provision in the agreement provided that plaintiff could not be held liable for injuries to the defendant occurring on the premises, even if these injuries were caused by the plaintiff's negligence. In addition, the contract also provided that the defendant would be liable for any injuries occurring to the plaintiff, even if caused by the **plaintiff's** own negligence. An employee of the plaintiff spilled gasoline on the defendant and the defendant's employee, and the plaintiff brought a declaratory judgment action seeking a ruling that the plaintiff could not be held liable for the loss. The court held that the clause, which was located in the fine print of the contract, could not be enforced. The gross disparity in the parties' bargaining positions was apparent in that the plaintiff had no opportunity to negotiate any of the lease provisions. Moreover, plaintiff was not well educated, and the defendant never called the plaintiff's attention to the clause. Thus, the court concluded that there was no "real and voluntary meeting of the minds" and refused to enforce the contested provision. [Text §15.3]

Williams v. Walker-Thomas Furniture Co., [Text §15.331].

ILLEGALITY

Bateman Eichler, Hill Richards, Inc. v. Berner, 472 U.S. 299 (1985)

This case illustrates the *in pari delicto* defense in a securities fraud action. A tippee filed a securities fraud action against a tipper for losses incurred on a securities purchase recommended by the tipper. The tipper defended that the tippee should be barred from recovery in the suit because the tippee was *in pari delicto* with the tipper, i.e., the tippee was guilty of wrongdoing since he traded on inside information along with the tipper.

The Court refused to apply the *in pari delicto* defense. The *in pari delicto* defense will only be allowed in a securities fraud case if: (1) as a direct result of his own actions, the plaintiff bears at least substantially equal responsibility for the violations he seeks to redress; and (2) preclusion of the suit would not significantly interfere with effective enforcement of the securities laws and protection on the investing public. The Court held that a tippee is not equally at fault with the tipper, so the *in pari delicto* defense is normally not allowed in these situations. Private enforcement of the securities should be encouraged to protect the public interest; therefore, tippees must be permitted to file suit against tippers. [Text §16.411.]

PAROL EVIDENCE RULE

Danann Realty Corp. v. Harris, 157 N.E.2d 597 (N.Y. 1959)

The parol evidence rule ordinarily does not bar evidence of prior oral agreements which establish fraud in the transaction. However, *Danann* stands for an often criticized minority view that evidence of a misrepresentation is barred if the aggrieved party made a specific disclaimer regarding a particular misrepresentation. In that case, an aggrieved lessee signed a written agreement which contained a specific disclaimer that the lessee had made a "full investigation" and was not "relying upon any statement or representation" not contained in the written agreement. The lessor had made some oral misrepresentations regarding expenses which resulted in the lessee's tort action. Even though an ordinary merger clause does not bar evidence of a fraudulent misrepresentation, when the contract expressly states that the parties are relying only on specific representations mentioned in the contract, they may not later assert their reliance on oral representations not included in the contract. This is true even if the oral representations are fraudulent. [Text §17.25]

Hicks v. Bush, 180 N.E.2d 425 (N.Y. 1962)

The holding in this case determines whether parol evidence is admissible to prove the existence of a condition precedent to the parties' written agreement. The plaintiff and the defendants held significant interests in various corporations. They drew up a written agreement which provided that both parties would tender their stock in the various enterprises in exchange for stock in what was to be a new, consolidated entity. The plaintiff tendered his stock according to the written agreement, but the defendants refused to tender theirs, claiming that there was an oral condition precedent to their duty to do so. This condition provided that the written document would have no effect unless additional capital from other sources could be obtained. The court held that parol testimony was admissible to prove the condition precedent because the condition asserted did not contradict the terms of the written agreement. The court noted that "[i]t is certainly not improbable that parties contracting in these circumstances would make the asserted oral agreement; the condition precedent at hand is the sort of condition which parties would not be inclined to incorporate into a written agreement intended for public consumption." [Text §17.23]

Lee v. Joseph E. Seagram & Sons, Inc., 552 F.2d 447 (2d Cir. 1977)

This court followed the Corbin approach to the admissibility of parol evidence. The parties entered into a written agreement for the sale of plaintiff's liquor distributorship. The parties also had a collateral oral agreement that the defendant would find the plaintiff a liquor distributorship in another city. When the plaintiff sought to prove this oral agreement to the court, the defendant claimed that the parol evidence rule barred evidence of the agreement. The court rejected this contention and adopted the Corbin approach which allows extrinsic facts to be admitted to determine whether the parties intend a written document to be a full integration of their agreement or whether there is an enforceable collateral promise. The court held that the oral agreement in this case was not one which would ordinarily be included in the written agreement because it was based on the parties' personal relationship and would not be expected to appear in the parties' written agreement for the sale of corporate assets. Additionally, there was no merger clause in the written agreement, and the collateral promise did not contradict the terms of the written agreement. [Text §17.132]

Masterson v. Sine, 436 P.2d 561 (Cal. 1968)

This case illustrates the Restatement position on whether parol evidence will be admitted to prove an oral agreement made contemporaneously with the parties' written contract. The plaintiffs conveyed their ranch to relatives. In the written deed, the plaintiffs reserved a ten-year repurchase option over the subject property. Subsequently, the plaintiff filed for bankruptcy, and the trustee in bankruptcy sued the relatives to exercise the repurchase option. The relatives wished to prove a contemporaneous oral agreement to the court that the option was understand to be of a "personal" nature only and was not assignable to persons outside the family. The court held that evidence of the oral agreement was admissible. The court determined that the oral agreement was one which would naturally be made as a separate agreement from the written contract. The deed in this case was a standard deed, and it would not be common for the parties to insert additional provisions regarding the nonassignability of the option. Thus, the court concluded that the deed was not a complete integration of the parties' agreement, and the oral agreement regarding the repurchase option was admissable in the relatives' defense. [Text §17.14]

Mitchell v. Lath, [Text §§17.41, 19.1111-1].

INTERPRETATION

Pacific Gas & Electric Co. v. Thomas Drayage & Rigging Co., 442 P.2d 641 (Cal. 1968)

This case follows the Corbin view and rejects Williston's "plain meaning rule" of contract interpretation. Defendant contracted to repair plaintiff's steam turbine. The parties' agreement stated that defendant promised to indemnify plaintiff "against all damag . . . resulting from injury to property . . . ." The defendant damaged the plaintiff's turbine while attempting to perform the repairs, and plaintiff sued for indemnity under the contract provision. The defendant argued that the parties meant that defendant was to be responsible only for damage to the property of third parties. Under the Williston view, the court would look to the plain meaning of the document and conclude that defendant was responsible for the damage to the turbine. However, the court in *Thomas Drayage* concluded that such a rule ignores the true (and possibly contrary) intention of the parties. Thus, the court held that oral testimony is admissible to ascertain the intent of the parties even if the language of their written document seems clear and unambiguous. However, before looking outside the four corners of the document, the court must preliminarily determine that the document is "fairly susceptible" of the asserted interpretation. [Text §18.221]

EXPRESS CONDITIONS

J.N.A. Realty Corp. v. Cross Bay Chelsea, 366 N.E.2d 1313 (N.Y. 1977)

This case illustrates the "disproportionate forfeiture" exception to the general rule that an express condition must be literally complied with before the other party's obligation under a contract arises. The lessee of a building, through negligence or inadvertence, failed to exercise his option to renew a lease within the time specified in the lease agreement. The lessor brought an action to recover possession of the premises. The lessee, who operated a restaurant on the leased premises, had spent $55,000 on improvements and had built up a substantial amount of customer goodwill during the lease term. Generally, a notice exercising an option is ineffective if not given within the time specified in the lease agreement. However, the court granted equitable relief to prevent forfeiture of the improvements and goodwill. The court stated that if the lessee makes substantial improvements in good faith with an intent to renew the lease, and the lessor would not be prejudiced by the delay in giving notice, then equitable relief may be appropriate. No relief will be granted if the tenant's delay was intentional or undertaken in bad faith. [Text §20.43]

BREACH/CONSTRUCTIVE CONDITIONS

Holiday Inns, Inc. v. Knight, 450 P.2d 42 (Cal. 1969)

The court in this case discussed the potential forfeiture of payments made in the earlier years on a multi-year option contract. The parties' option agreement provided that the yearly option payments were to be made into a designated escrow account by July 1 in each of the five years covered by the agreement. In the fourth year, the plaintiffs mistakenly made payment directly to the seller after the due date for the option payment. Therefore, since the terms of the option agreement were not complied with, the seller returned the payment to the plaintiffs with a notice stating that the option had been cancelled. Thereafter, the plaintiff attempted to exercise the option, but this attempt was rejected. Normally, a breaching party is subject to forfeiture of all preceding payments made on a multi-year option contract if the option is cancelled. However, anti-forfeiture statutes may allow a party to avoid forfeiture and cancellation if the breach is not willful, grossly negligent, or fraudulent and the breaching party makes full compensation to the non-breaching party. This case was decided in California which has an anti-forfeiture statute in its Civil Code. Thus, the court declared that the plaintiffs had successfully exercised their option after the seller had attempted to cancel the option contract. [Text §20.43]

Jacob & Youngs, Inc. v. Kent, [Text §§21.2611, 31.343]

K & G Construction Co. v. Harris, 164 A.2d 451 (Md. Ct. App. 1960)

This case demonstrates the presumption made by courts that promises exchanged in a bilateral contract are mutually dependent. A subcontractor contracted to do some construction work for a general contractor. The general contractor agreed to make progress payments each month, and the subcontractor promised to perform all work in a "workmanlike manner." When the subcontractor's bulldozer damaged the house on the subject property, the general contractor refused to make any more progress payments. Then the subcontractor walked off the job because of the general contractor's failure to make payments. Thus, the general contractor was forced to pay a different contractor more money to complete the job. The court held that the general contractor was not in breach for failing to make the progress payments. The court presumed that the general contractor's promise to make progress payments was conditioned on the subcontractor's workmanlike performance. (Obviously the court assumed that the damage to the house was due to non-workmanlike performance.) Therefore, since the general contractor was not in breach, it was the subcontractor who breached by walking off the job. [Text §24.241]

Kingston v. Preston, 99 Eng. Rep. 437 (K.B. 1773)

This was the first case to hold that, in a bilateral contract, one party's duty to perform is constructively conditioned on the other party's performance. Plaintiff and defendant entered an agreement for the sale of defendant's business. Plaintiff agreed to post a security bond (guaranteeing his payments), and defendant agreed to convey the property. Plaintiff failed to post the bond, so defendant refused to convey the property. Hence, plaintiff sued defendant for breach of contract. The court held that the defendant was excused from his promise to sell his business since the plaintiff breached his promise to post the security bond. The court reasoned that the defendant's performance was conditioned on the plaintiff performing his promise. [Text §21.22]

Kirkland v. Archbold, 113 N.E.2d 496 (Ohio Ct. App. 1953)

If a contract is found to be divisible, i.e., the parties' agreement can be divided into a series of equal units of performance, then for purposes of determining whether a constructive condition has been performed, the contract will be hypothetically divided into a series of separate contracts. However, construction contracts are generally not considered divisible even if the owner is required to make periodic progress payments. This latter view was apparent in *Kirkland*, where the plaintiff agreed to do some construction work on the defendant's house. The contract provided for $1000 progress payments. However, the defendant claimed the plaintiff's work was shoddy and refused to make the first payment in full. Instead, he paid the plaintiff only $800 and ordered the plaintiff off the job. The court held that the plaintiff could only recover the reasonable value of his work for the period and not the entire progress payment due. This is because a construction project is deemed indivisible even if payments are scheduled periodically throughout the project. That is, the individual payments are not intended to equal the value of the work done in the corresponding period. [Text §21.271]

Nolan v. Whitney, 88 N.Y. 648 (1882)

This case demonstrates the minority view in situations where a third party's satisfaction or approval is a condition precedent to another party's duty to perform. This minority view states that where the third party unreasonably withholds approval or unreasonably refuses to express satisfaction, the non-performance of the condition is excused. In *Nolan*, an architect's certificate was required before a mason could request payment from the building's owner for his work. The architect honestly, but unreasonably, expressed his dissatisfaction and refused to issue the certificate. The court held that "[a]n unreasonable refusal on the part of the architect . . . to give the certificate dispenses with its necessity." This minority view is applied only where there is a possibility of forfeiture or unjust enrichment. [See gen. Text §20.4]

Plante v. Jacobs, 103 N.W.2d 296 (Wis. 1960)

This court followed the doctrine of substantial performance. That is, once a contracting party has substantially performed, he or she may sue for his expectation damages if the other party refuses to perform. In other words, the constructive condition stating that one party's performance is constructively conditioned on there being no uncured material breach by the other is satisfied upon substantial performance. Here, when one party asserted that a minor breach on the part of the contractor justified his refusal to pay the contractor, it was **he** who materially breached the contract under the "first" material breach doctrine.

According to the court, a party has substantially performed once his or her performance "meets the essential purpose of the contract." Thus, where a contractor substantially performed a building project on a house, the contractor was entitled to recover the contract price, but was liable for damages resulting from his immaterial breach. Strict compliance with the building plans was not required. In this case, the deviation was the placement of a wall one foot off of the plan specifications, so the essential purpose of the contract had been fulfilled. [Text §§21.5; 21.6]

Second National Bank v. Panamerican Bridge Co., 83 F. 391 (6th Cir. 1910)

This case illustrates the majority view that where a third party's approval of work completed is required as a condition of satisfaction under a construction contract, the unreasonable withholding of that approval will not excuse the performance of the condition unless the refusal is also made in bad faith. Plaintiff agreed to construct a building for the defendant, subject to approval of the plans and construction by the defendant's architect. The architect approved the plaintiff's plans which called for 8-hole rivet connections. However, after the plaintiff had constructed a substantial portion of the building, the architect insisted on 10-hole rivet connections. The defendant refused to pay the plaintiff until these changes were made so that its architect could issue the certificate of approval. The court held that it was not enough for the plaintiff to show that the architect's refusal to approve the project was unreasonable. The plaintiff had to also show that the architect was withholding approval in bad faith. Thus, if the architect was withholding his approval for safety reasons, for example, the plaintiff would not be successful in recovering against the defendant because the architect's approval was an express condition precedent to the defendant's liability for payment and express conditions are strictly enforced. [Text §20.124]

Stewart v. Newbury, 115 N.E. 984 (N.Y. 1917)

This case illustrates the principle that, unless the parties agree otherwise, the duty to pay in a contract for services does not arise until the party to perform the services substantially completes the work. Thus, where plaintiff contracted to do construction work for the defendant, and the parties' agreement did not specify when payment was due from the defendant, plaintiff was not entitled to payment for his first month's work where the work performed was not yet close to completion. [Text §21.12]

ANTICIPATORY REPUDIATION

Hochster v. De La Tour, [Text §23.1].

McCloskey & Co. v. Minweld Steel Co., 220 F.2d 101 (3d Cir. 1955)

This case demonstrates that a promisor's expression of anticipated difficulty in performing is not by enough itself to constitute an anticipatory repudiation. A subcontractor agreed to furnish and erect all of the structural steel on a certain project. The subcontractor experienced some difficulties with his supplier but promised delivery within approximately forty days. The general contractor would have experienced delays under the subcontractor's promised delivery schedule, so it requested delivery within thirty days. The subcontractor responded by explaining the difficulties he was having with his supplier. He also requested the general contractor's help in securing the steel from the supplier and indicated its desire to perform in a timely manner. The general contractor claimed that the subcontractor had anticipatorily breached. The court disagreed, stating that a party has not anticipatorily repudiated a contract absent "an absolute and unequivocal refusal to perform or a distinct and positive statement of an inability to do so." [Text §23.23]

Oloffson v. Coomer, 296 N.E.2d 871 (Ill. Ct. App. 1973)

This case illustrates the majority view of the proper measure of a buyer's recovery upon a seller's anticipatory repudiation. A farmer unequivocally repudiated a contract to sell corn when he stated he would not plant corn that season. The court held that the buyer could recover the difference between the price he contracted for and the price of the corn on the day of the repudiation, whether he replaced the corn immediately or waited until the date when the farmer's performance was due.

UCC §2-713 provides that the "market price" that should be used for purposes of a buyer's market differential damages is the market price pending on the date the buyer learned of the breach. The rationale for that rule, especially in a case like this one, is that it is not "commercially reasonable" to wait to replace a commodity sold in a volatile market when the price might substantially rise in the buyer's favor. [Text §33.521]

Phelps v. Herro, 137 A.2d 159 (Md. 1957)

This case demonstrates that the doctrine of anticipatory repudiation does not apply to situations where one party has fully performed and the only obligation remaining for the other party is the duty to make payment for the performance. Thus, the aggrieved party must await the time for performance and then sue for damages. The plaintiffs agreed to sell certain interests they owned in real property and stock to the defendants for $37,500. The defendants paid a $5,000 down payment and signed a promissory note for the balance. The plaintiffs then fully performed by transferring their property interests to the defendants. However, the defendants notified the plaintiffs that they would not make the required payments on the promissory note, and the plaintiffs instituted an action for breach before even the first payment on the note was due. Plaintiffs claimed the right to sue immediately under the doctrine of anticipatory repudiation. The defendants asserted that plaintiffs' suit was premature since plaintiffs had performed all of their obligations under the contract, and all that remained was for defendants to tender their payment on the due date. The court ruled that with unilateral contracts, or with bilateral contracts that become unilateral by virtue of full performance by one of the parties, where the party still obligated has only a duty to pay money to fulfill his promise of performance, the doctrine of anticipatory repudiation has no application. Thus, plaintiffs' suit was premature, and their only remedy was to await the time for performance and sue for breach at that time. [Text §23.21]

Reliance Cooperage Corp. v. Treat, 195 F.2d 977 (8th Cir. 1952).

The parties entered into an executory contract for the sale of bourbon staves. Treat breached before the time for performance arrived. The court opined that the proper time to measure the non-breaching party's damages in a case involving anticipatory repudiation is at the time set for performance, whether or not the non-breaching party accepts the anticipatory repudiation. That is, a party to an executory contract may refuse to accept an anticipatory repudiation of the contract and may instead insist upon performance. The contract then remains binding on both parties, and no actionable claim arises until the date set for performance. However, if the non-breaching party accepts the anticipatory repudiation, the damages will still be measured as of the time set for performance.

This is very much a minority position. The UCC states that the proper "market price" to be used in the calculation of a buyer's market differential damages under §2-713 is the market price pending on the day the seller learned of the breach, and not the day performance was due. [Text §33.221]

United States v. Seacoast Gas Co., 204 F.2d 709 (5th Cir. 1953)

This case holds that a party may no longer retract his repudiation once the non-breaching party has materially changed his position in reliance on the repudiation or stated that it regards the repudiation as final. Seacoast contracted to supply gas to the United States for a certain period. During the period, Seacoast notified the United States that it would no longer perform under the contract. The United States sought out new suppliers, and when it secured a willing supplier, it notified Seacoast that unless its repudiation was retracted within three days, the United States would accept the new supplier's bid. Seacoast's retraction came after the three days had expired. The court held that Seacoast's retraction was ineffective because the United States materially changed its position when it accepted the new supplier's bid. Also, the United States had notified Seacoast that it intended to treat the repudiation as final after the three day period expired. Thus, the repudiation could no longer be retracted after that point. [Text §23.5]

IMPOSSIBILITY, COMMERCIAL IMPRACTICABILITY, AND FRUSTRATION OF PURPOSE

Albre Marble & Tile Co. v. John Bowen Co., 155 N.E.2d 437 (Mass. 1959)

Albre established a nonbreaching party's right to recover reliance damages for expenditures made in preparation for performance of a contract which is discharged because of impssibility, impracticality, or frustration. A general contractor entered into a contract with the state to build a state hospital. The general contractor hired a subcontractor to complete the marble and tile work on the project. Prior to the actual installation of the marble and tile, the subcontract called for the preparation of samples, shop drawings, tests, and affidavits. After preparation of these items, the hospital contract was cancelled because the general contractor failed to comply with statutory bidding requirements. The subcontractor sought recovery of the expenditures involved in preparing the samples and drawings. The general contractor counter-argued that recovery could only be had for labor and materials actually incorporated into the hospital construction. The court held that the nonbreaching party to a contract which is discharged because of impossibility, impracticality, or frustration may recover his or her reliance damages if the party discharging the contract is "at greater fault" than the nonbreaching party. The fair market value of any expenditures which "would have enured to the benefit" of the breaching party if the contract had been performed are recoverable in such a case. Since the drawings and samples would have enured to the general contractor's benefit had the contract been performed, the subcontractor may recover the fair market value of the expenditures related to that work. However, the court noted that if there is "equal fault" between a plaintiff and defendant, it may not award reliance damages. [See gen, Text §31.5]

Alcoa v. Essex, [Text §25.2144].

American Trading & Production Corp. v. Shell Int'l Marine, Ltd., 453 F.2d 939 (2d Cir. 1972)

The plaintiff in this case unsuccessfully sought to recover additional expenses incurred in shipping oil owned by the defendant by claiming that the agreed route for performance had become commercially impractical. The contract called for the oil to be transported from Texas to India and indicated a per ton charge "for passage through the Suez Canal." However, the Suez Canal was closed due to a state of war, and the shipper was forced to use the longer and more expensive route around the Cape of Good Hope. The court held that the plaintiff could not recover its additional expenses from the defendant because the contract had not become either impossible or impractical. Nothing in the contract provided that delivery **had** to go through the Suez Canal; hence, proceeding around the Cape of Good Hope was an alternative means of performance. The court acknowledged that an extreme increase in cost will excuse the performance of a commercial contract on impracticability grounds where the increase was not foreseeable and the contract did not specifically allocate the risk to the performing party. However, in this case, the increased cost was only a third over the agreed price, and that is an insufficient amount to trigger impracticability. [Text §25.211]

Canadian Indus. Alcohol Co. v. Dunbar Molasses Co., 179 N.E. 383 (N.Y. 1932)

The performance of a contract is not excused on the grounds of impossibility when the seller is unable to obtain an adequate supply from his contemplated source. Here, the buyer and seller (a middleman) entered into a contract calling for the delivery of molasses. The seller contemplated, but did not contract for, receiving a supply of molasses from a particular refinery that it would re-sell to the buyer. The refinery output was not sufficient to meet the needs of the seller, so the seller claimed its delivery obligations under the contract with the buyer should be excused due to impossibility. Justice Cardozo disagreed, stating that where the seller makes an absolute promise to deliver and does not attempt to contract with others to insure an adequate supply of materials necessary to fulfill the obligation, the seller bears the risk that it will not be able to fulfill its promise. The seller may not shift this risk to the buyer after it has promised to deliver. Note, however, that if the seller **had** contracted directly with the refinery to assure an adequate supply, and the refinery had breached the supply contract, the seller would have a much stronger basis to claim impossibility of performance under the contract with the buyer. [Text §25.122]

Iron Trade Products Co. v. Wilkoff Co., 116 A. 150 (Pa. 1922)

This court held that a contracting party who contracts to sell items which are in limited supply bears the risk that the market price on the items will rise and cannot claim impossibility as a result of such a price rise which occurs before the time for delivery arrives. In *Iron Trade*, it was the **buyer's** own purchase on the open market of the items in short supply which caused the seller's cost of performance to drastically rise. Claiming impossibility of performance, the seller refused to deliver the more expensive items at the lower contract price. However, the court concluded that the seller was in breach because there was no evidence that the buyer intended to interfere with the seller's performance. Additionally, the seller's performance, although more difficult to accomplish as a result of the price rise, was not impossible. [Text §§25.211; 25.214]

✦ **Krell v. Henry Coronation Cases,** [Text §25.321].

● **Lloyd v. Murphy,** [Text §25.322].

Mineral Park Land Co. v. Howard, 172 Cal. 289 (1916)

> This case illustrates the modern view that extreme impracticability may be an excuse for performance, whereas the traditional view allowed excuse only where a performance had been rendered impossible. The defendant was building a bridge and contracted for his supply of gravel under a requirements contract with the plaintiff. Under the agreement, the defendant was to excavate the gravel from plaintiff's land and paid a fixed price per yard. Once the defendant began to excavate below the water level on plaintiff's land, however, he refused to continue excavating as required by the contract because the cost to the defendant rose by ten times over the prior costs incurred with excavation above the water level. The court held that the defendant could be excused from excavating below the water level. Where changed or unexpected circumstances lead to a substantial increase in the cost of performance of a commercial contract rendering such performance extremely impracticable, performance may be excused just as though it were impossible. [Text §25.21]

Paradine v. Jane, 82 Eng. Rep. 897 (K.B. 1647)

> This case illustrates the traditional early common law doctrine of frustration of purpose. The court refused to excuse a lessee from paying rent on a contract where the lessee had been ousted from the leased property by a foreigner. The court noted that the ouster did not make the payment obligation impossible to perform. [Text §25.3]

Stees v. Leonard, 20 Minn. 494 (1874)

> This case illustrates that the impossibility defense will not be allowed where a contractor assumes the risk of poor soil conditions on a construction project. Defendant agreed to construct a building for the plaintiff. He began construction twice, and each time the building collapsed because the soil underneath was quick-sand. Although it would have been possible to drain the land and construct a stable building at an increased expense, the defendant refused to make a third attempt at construction. The court held that the defendant could not be discharged from the contract on the basis of impossibility. A building contractor assumes the risk that he will have to drain the soil or reinforce the planned structure because the soil is unforeseeably less stable than expected. The contractor's performance will be excused only if it is absolutely impossible to remedy the condition. [Text §25.114]

✦ **Taylor v. Caldwell,** 122 Eng. Rep. 309 (K.B. 1863)

> This case illustrates that, under the doctrine of impossibility, a contract will be discharged where essential subject matter of the contract is destroyed through no fault of either party. Thus, a singer was excused from her promise to perform in a music hall which was destroyed by fire prior to his scheduled performance. The court noted that the existence of the music hall was the "foundation of the contract," i.e., that it was a mutually shared basic assumption on which the contract was made, and that there was an implied condition that both parties would be excused if the hall no longer existed. [Text §25.112]

United States v. Spearin, 248 U.S. 132 (1918)

> This United States Supreme Court case allows discharge for impossibility of performance where one party requires the other party's performance to comply with its specifications which turn out to be defective. In *Spearin*, a contractor agreed to construct a sewer system for the United States gov-

ernment according to plans provided by the government. The Court held that the contractor could be discharged from the contract on impossibility grounds, and that the United States had breached an implied warranty that the specifications would be adequate. Therefore, the contractor could recover damages against the United States for breach of the implied warranty. [See gen. Text §25.1]

United States v. Wegematic Corp., 360 F.2d 674 (2d Cir. 1966)

This case demonstrates that a vendor who promises a technological breakthrough will not be excused from performance when accomplishing the breakthrough becomes commercially impractical. The United States government advertised for bids on a digital computer system. Wegematic submitted a bid which promised an improved version of a present model on the market for the proposed price of $231,000. However, due to engineering difficulties, Wegematic was unable to deliver the computer by the delivery date in the contract, or even within a reasonable time thereafter. Wegematic requested that it be excused from performance because development of the necessary technology would take its engineers one to two years and would cost between $1,000,000 and $1,500,000 to accomplish. The government sued Wegematic for breach. The court held in favor of the government, stating that a vendor who promises new technology assumes the risk that it will prove impracticable to develop or produce. The court noted that to allow the defense of impracticability would require the bidding purchaser to be bound by contract, while the manufacturer would be "free to express what are only aspirations and gamble on mere probabilities of fulfillment without any risk of liability." In any event, the court noted that while the necessary expenses might seem large in relation to this one sale, economies of a scale would allow the manufacturer to recoup its costs once it sold more of the new systems to additional parties. [Text §25.114; 25.214]

Watkins & Son v. Carrig, 21 A.2d 591 (N.H. 1941)

This case illustrates the general principle that the risk of adverse soil conditions on a building project generally rests with the building contractor. The building contractor usually cannot avoid the contract on the basis of mutual mistake because the builder is generally perceived to have expertise in sub-soil conditions. Hence, the risk is properly allocated to the builder. Thus, in *Watkins*, where a builder made a contract to construct a building and then discovered a large rock in the sub-soil that made his performance much more expensive, the court would not allow the builder to avoid the contract even though both parties adhered to the basic assumption that sub-soil conditions were normal. [Text §25.114]

MODIFICATION

Angel v. Murray, 332 A.2d 630 (R.I. 1974)

This case adopted section 89 of the Restatement 2d of Contracts as the proper rule to govern modifications and rejected the common law pre-existing duty rule requirement that consideration be present to make modifications enforceable. The defendant contracted with the City of Newport, Rhode Island to collect garbage. The contract provided that the defendant was to be compensated at the rate of $137,000 per year over a five year term. During that term, the defendant's costs increased substantially, and the defendant requested an additional $10,000 per year to cover these increased costs. The City of Newport made the additional payments, but a citizen later sued to have the additional payments refunded to the city. The court held that the modification was enforceable despite the lack of additional consideration from the city. A promise modifying a pre-existing legal duty is valid without consideration where the contract has not been fully performed, and the modification is fair and equitable in view of circumstances unanticipated when the contract was formed. [Text §26.21]

Universal Builders, Inc. v. Moon Motor Lodge, Inc., 244 A.2d 10 (Pa. 1968)

This case shows how a "no oral modifications" clause may be waived by a party. A provision in a construction contract required that all changes be in writing. The owner's agent requested a number of changes and promised to pay for them, although written change orders were never issued. This oral modification operated as an effective waiver of the condition that all modifications be in writing because the contractor materially changed his position by carrying out the requested changes in reliance on the agent's oral promise. [Text §26.5]

Wisconsin Knife Works v. National Metal Crafters, [Text §26.55].

THIRD PARTY BENEFICIARY CONTRACTS

Dutton v. Poole, 83 Eng. Rep. 528 (K.B. 1677)

This early English case established the right of a third person to sue as a beneficiary of a contract to which that person was not a party. A father expressed his intention to sell wood to raise a dowry for his daughter. However, his son, who wanted to inherit the wood, promised to pay the father £ 1,000 if the father would promise not to sell the wood. The son never paid the promised sum, so the daughter sued him. The son defended, claiming the daughter had no standing to sue since she was not in privity with the contracting parties. However, the court rejected this argument and allowed the daughter to sue as a third party beneficiary of the contract between the son and the father.

Note that Dutton was overruled in 1861 and the English rule now is that no beneficiary may enforce a contract. However, while a beneficiary is not entitled to enforce a promisor's promise directly in a breach action, the English courts allow an artificial use of trusts in this situation. That is, what the American courts would call a third party beneficiary, is called a beneficiary of an implied trust in the English courts. Thus, while the beneficiary may not sue the promisor on a third party beneficiary theory in the English courts, the beneficiary may sue the trustee of the implied trust (i.e. the promisor) for breach of trust. [Text §27.0; 27.3]

Isbrandtsen Co. v. Local 1291, 204 F.2d 495 (3d Cir. 1953)

This case demonstrates than an "incidental" beneficiary, as opposed to "donee" or "creditor" beneficiaries, of a third party beneficiary contract is not entitled to sue to enforce the promisor's promise. Plaintiff chartered a ship to the Scott Paper Company ("Scott") for the purpose of transporting pulp. Scott agreed to load and unload the ship. Scott subsequently hired Lavino Shipping Company ("Lavino") to do the unloading. However, the employees of Lavino stopped work before the ship was fully unloaded. The work stoppage violated provisions of an agreement the employees' union had with Lavino. The delay in unloading the ship became expensive for the plaintiff, so the plaintiff sued the union for violation of the collective bargaining agreement with Lavino.

The court recognized the ability of donee and creditor beneficiaries to sue as third parties to enforce the obligations of a party under a contract. "If in buying the promise the promisee expresses an intent that some third party shall receive either the security of the executory promise or the benefit of performance as a gift, that party is a donee of . . . the contract right . . . . If, on the other hand, the promisee's expressed intent is that some third party shall receive the performance in satisfaction and discharge of some actual or supposed duty or liability of the promisee, the third party is a creditor beneficiary." All others who may be benefited by a contract's performance are "incidental beneficiaries." The plaintiff could not qualify as either a donee beneficiary or a creditor beneficiary since the plaintiff was completely unknown to the labor union. Therefore, as an incidental beneficiary, plaintiff could not enforce the contract and recover his damages resulting from the work stoppage. [Text §§27.313; 27.322]

Lawrence v. Fox, [Text §§27.3121; 27.3212].

Lucas v. Hamm, 364 P.2d 685 (Cal. 1961)

The intended third party beneficiary of a contract between two parties may sue for a breach of the contract. In *Lucas*, the intended beneficiaries of an invalidated trust sued the attorney who improperly drafted the document for the testator. Because the trust was intended for the beneficiaries' benefit, the court held that the beneficiaries had standing to sue for the attorney's breach. The court reasoned that the beneficiaries were the individuals under the contract to whom the attorney's "performance runs." Nevertheless, the beneficiaries were unable to recover against the attorney because the court determined that the attorney was not negligent and thus did not breach his contract to supply reasonably competent professional services. [Text §27.321]

Martinez v. Socoma Co., 521 P.2d 841 (Cal. 1974)

Members of the public cannot sue as third party beneficiaries to recover for injuries resulting from a private party's failure to perform under a contract with a municipal, state, or federal governmental body, even though such contracts are entered into for the public benefit. Thus, in *Martinez*, where the defendants contracted with the federal government to supply job training and employment opportunities for disadvantaged persons, a class action suit brought by persons who would have qualified for the program which was filed as a result of the defendant's breach was dismissed. An exception arises, however, where the contract expresses the government's intent that individual citizens have the right to sue. [Text §27.331]

Moch Co. v. Rensselaer Water Co., 159 N.E. 896 (1928)

This case illustrates the general presumption that parties intend to contract for their own benefit and not for the benefit of third parties. The defendant promised to supply water for the city's fire hydrants. Plaintiff's building was destroyed in a fire because the defendant failed to supply an adequate amount of water, resulting in a breach of defendant's contract with the city. For policy reasons, i.e., to prevent unlimited liability to all residents of the city, the court held that the plaintiff was not an intended beneficiary of the contract with the city. In general, however, members of the public cannot sue as third party beneficiaries to recover for injuries resulting from a private party's failure to perform under a contract with a municipal, state or federal government, even though such contracts may be viewed as entered into for the public benefit. [Text §27.331]

Rouse v. United States, 215 F.2d 872 (D.C. Cir. 1954)

This case illustrates the application of the defense of fraudulent misrepresentation to a third party beneficiary (or its assignee) of a contract where that defense would be applicable to the original promisee. That is, the assignee merely "steps into the shoes" of the assignor. However, the promisor may not assert defenses the promisee could have asserted against the third party beneficiary (or its assignee) where the promisor expressly assumed liability for the promisee's debt.

As part of the purchase price of a home, Rouse agreed to make payments on a heating system installed by the seller (a contract which benefited the contractor that installed the heating system). Rouse then refused to pay on the contract, alleging that the seller (the promisee) fraudulently misrepresented the quality of the system. The United States sued Rouse as the assignee/guarantor of the contract between the seller and Rouse. Rouse could not assert the seller's defense of defective installation against the third party (the contractor) or its assignee because Rouse expressly assumed payment of the debt owed by the seller to the third party. However, the court held that Rouse could properly assert the defense of fraudulent misrepresentation against the United States (the third party's assignee) because a promisor may assert any defenses against the third party or its assignee that it could have asserted against the seller (the promisee). [Text §27.412]

Seaver v. Ransom, [Text §§27.3111, 27.3211].

ASSIGNMENT AND DELEGATION

Allhusen v. Caristo Construction Corp., 103 N.E.2d 891 (N.Y. 1952)

This case discusses the validity of a contract provision prohibiting the assignment of rights created by the contract. A general contractor contracted with a subcontractor for certain painting work on a project. The contract provided that "the assignment by [the subcontractor] of this contract or any interest therein, or of any money due or to become due . . . shall be void." The subcontractor assigned his right to payment under the contract to a bank, which thereafter assigned its interest to a third party. The assignment by the subcontractor was declared invalid. A freely bargained for "no assignment" clause is valid and will be enforced, so long as the clause is drafted in clear and plain language. However, note that most modern courts view no assignment clauses with hostility and thus construe them narrowly or find that the particular provision at issue was not drafted with the requisite clear and plain language for enforceability. Additionally, Article 9 of the UCC deems no assignment clauses within its purview as ineffective. This would include the assignment of accounts receivable. Thus, the result in *Allhusen* would be different if decided today. [Text §28.323]

Chemical Bank v. Rinden Professional Association, 498 A.2d 706 (1985)

The court in this case found that pursuant to UCC §9-206(1) an obligor had waived its defenses against the assignee of a contract upon assignment of that contract. Chemical Bank was the assignee of a lease-purchase contract for an office phone system. The obligor on the contract was a law firm that refused to make payments once the phone system began to malfunction. The notice of assignment from the obligee contained a "hell or high water clause" which prohibited any defenses the obligor had against the obligee from being asserted against the assignee. However, any claims on the underlying contract could still be asserted against the obligee. This clause was included in the notice as a precondition to Chemical Bank's acceptance of the assignment. An agent of the law firm signed the waiver upon receipt. Chemical Bank brought suit three years later when the law firm refused to make any more payments because of the malfunction of the phone system. The court found that the notice of assignment and waiver were valid under §9-206 (1) because Chemical Bank took the assignment for value, in good faith and without notice of any claim or defense of the obligor against the obligee, i.e., it had holder in due course status. No consideration was required for the waiver to be effective upon assignment under §2-209(1). Thus, the law firm could not assert the defense of malfunction of the phone system against Chemical Bank. [Text §28.52]

Crane Ice Cream Co. v. Terminal Freezing & Heating Co., 128 A. 280 (Md. 1925)

The court in this case exemplified the pre-UCC view that output and requirements contracts cannot be assigned. The owner of an ice cream plant (the buyer) contracted with the seller to purchase his weekly requirements for ice, up to a maximum of 250 tons per week. The buyer agreed under the contract not to purchase ice from other suppliers. The buyer then sold his ice cream plant to a third party who owned several other ice cream plants, and the buyer assigned his rights to the contract with the seller to the third party. The third party sued the seller for breach of contract when the seller refused to make further deliveries. The court held that the contract between the buyer and the seller was not assignable to the third party. The reasoning was that the seller relied on the buyer's credit and the seller's past experience with the buyer in promising to meet the buyer's requirements. The third party might not have the same ability to pay or the same requirements since more ice cream plants were involved. Note, however, that the UCC may permit the assignment of an output or requirements contract if the assignee's output or requirements are not "unreasonably disproportionate" to the assignor's estimated output or requirements [UCC §2-210, Comment 4].

Evening News Ass'n v. Peterson, 477 F. Supp. 77 (D.D.C. 1979)

This case demonstrates the assignability of certain personal service contracts. Peterson was a news anchor of a television station which was sold. As part of the sale, the contracts of all the employees were assigned to the new owners. Peterson claimed his contract was not assignable because it was a personal service contract. The court held such contracts were freely assignable, so long as the assignment did not violate public policy, was not prohibited under the terms of the contract, and would not result in a materially greater burden to the employee (i.e. the "obligor"). While a personal service contract cannot usually be **delegated**, such contracts are freely assignable subject to the limitations stated above. Thus, so long as Peterson would not be required to appear on a greater number of newscasts, for example, his contract would be assignable. All that happened as a result of the assignment was that Peterson received his paycheck from the new owner of the station. Because his obligations under the contract remained the same, and because there was no prohibition against assignments in his contract with the old employer, the assignment was valid. [Text §§28.322; 29.222; 30.223]

Langell v. Betz, 164 N.E. 890 (N.Y. 1928)

This case exhibits an exception to the traditional rule that the assignment of a bilateral executory contract impliedly assigns the assignor's rights and duties under the contract. Seller contracted with purchaser for the sale of land. Purchaser assigned the contract to a third party. On the date set for performance, seller was ready to convey the property, but the third party refused to make payment for the land. The court held that the third party was not obligated to make payment on the assigned contract unless the third party promised he would perform the purchaser's obligations. This exception appears to apply only to contracts for the sale of land. [Text §§28.38; 29.211]

Taylor v. Barton-Child Co., 11 N.E. 43 (Mass. 1917)

This case demonstrates the traditional pre-UCC rule that a right based on a future expectation cannot be assigned. Thus, in *Taylor*, the court refused to recognize the assignment of after-acquired accounts receivable as valid. Today, use of such clauses is a routine business practice, and they are specifically provided for in the UCC. [Text §28.313]

EQUITABLE REMEDIES

Hilmor Sales Co. v. Neushaefer Div. of Surponics Corp., 6 UCC Rep. Serv. 325 (N.Y. 1969)

This case discusses UCC §2-716(1) which allows a buyer the right to specific performance "where the goods are unique or in other proper circumstances." Plaintiff contracted for the purchase of nail polish and lipsticks from the defendant at close-out prices. Defendant refused to perform, and plaintiff requested specific performance alleging that the goods were unique since they could not be replaced at the close out contract price. The court held, however, that the goods were not unique and that plaintiff's legal remedy of money damages would provide an adequate remedy so that the equitable remedy of specific performance was unnecessary. [Text §§30.21; 33.11]

Karpinski v. Ingrasci, 268 N.E.2d 751 (N.Y. 1971)

A covenant not to compete in an employment contract is enforceable if it is reasonable and not unduly broad. In *Karpinski*, plaintiff (an oral surgeon) hired defendant (another oral surgeon) to work for him, and the parties signed an agreement that the defendant would **never** practice oral surgery or general denistry, in competition with the plaintiff, within the same geographic region. The court held that the geographic region specified was not overly broad since it covered the area where plaintiff practiced. The lack of any time limit was also deemed reasonable. However, the court held that the covenant was unduly broad in that it prevented the defendant from practicing general denistry in addition to oral surgery. Therefore, while the defendant was properly enjoined from practicing oral surgery in the same geographical region as his former employer, the provision which attempted to prevent the defendant from practicing general denistry in the same geographical region was held to be unenforcable as unduly broad. [Text §30.2234]

LaClede Gas Co. v. Amoco Oil, [Text §30.2111].

Lumley v. Wagner, [Text §30.12].

Peevyhouse v. Courland Coal & Mining Co. (See Case Squibs, Damages)

DAMAGES

Equitable Lumber Corp. v. IPA Land Development Corp., 344 N.E. 2d 391 (N.Y. 1975)

This decision illustrates the more liberal view of the UCC toward liquidated damage provisions. A construction company contracted with a lumber company for the supply of lumber. The parties' contract specified that if the lumber company had to sue for the purchase price, the construction company would be liable for reasonable attorney's fees, liquidated at thirty percent of the amount recovered. The court held that liquidated damage provisions will be upheld if one of two tests are satisfied: (1) the liquidated damages are reasonable in light of anticipated harm from a breach viewed as of the time was contract was made; or (2) the liquidated damages are reasonable in light of the actual harm caused by the breach. The court remanded the case to determine whether one of these two tests were satisfied. [Text, §§31.7; 33.6.]

Hadley v. Baxendale [Text §31.421].

Hawkins v. McGee, 84 N.H. 114 (1929)

Hawkins demonstrates that a patient will be entitled to expectation damages where his or her doctor promises a certain result that does not occur. A young boy's hand was scarred from a severe burn, and the surgeon who was to perform a skin graft operation promised that the boy's hand would be "100% perfect" following the operation. The court held that the doctor made an enforceable promise, under the objective theory of contracts, which was breached when the surgery failed. The plaintiff was entitled to expectation damages equal to the difference between the value of a "100% perfect" hand and the value of his hand in its post-surgery condition. [Text §§2.11; 3.2153; 31.3]

Jacobs & Youngs Co. v. Kent [Text §§31.343, 21.2611].

Neri v. Retail Marine Corp., 285 N.E.2d 311 (N.Y. 1972)

> This case illustrates the proper measure of recovery against a breaching buyer by a lost volume seller. A boat retailer entered into an agreement with the plaintiff for the sale of a particular boat. Plaintiff provided a $4,250 deposit, and the retailer ordered the boat from the manufacturer. The plaintiff later rescinded the contract, and the retailer retained the entire deposit paid by the plaintiff. The retailer resold the boat to a third party at the same price the plaintiff originally agreed to pay, so the plaintiff sued to recover his deposit, claiming that the retailer had sustained no damages since it was able to secure the subsequent sale. However, the court noted that the retailer was a lost volume seller in that it could have obtained **two** sales had the plaintiff not breached the agreement. Therefore, under UCC §2-708(2) the retailer was entitled to retain the amount of the profit it would have earned on the contract with the plaintiff, plus incidental damages, out of the plaintiff's deposit. Note, however, that this rule is only applicable if the seller has an excess supply of the goods. [Text §§31.3821; 33.53]

Oloffson v. Coomer, 296 N.E.2d 871 (Ill. Ct. App. 1973) (See Case Squibs Section, Anticipatory Repudiation)

Parker v. Twentieth Century-Fox Film Corp., [Text §31.4323].

Peevyhouse v. Garland Coal & Mining Co., 382 P.2d 109 (Okla. 1962)

> This case illustrates the principle of economic waste by holding that the proper measure of expectation damages under a breached agreement to restore the value of property is the resulting diminution in the property value and not the disproportionately greater cost of restoration. The court held that landowners were entitled to expectation damages when a strip mining company breached a promise to restore their land. The proper measure of damages was the $300 difference between the value of the land if restored and the value in its unrestored state. The plaintiffs were not entitled to the $29,000 cost of restoration which was clearly disproportionate to the benefit the owners would have received if the contract had been fully performed. [Text §30.2331]

Rockingham County v. Luten Bridge Co., 35 F.2d 301 (4th Cir. 1929)

> This case applies the concept of avoidability of damages to limit a non-breaching party's recovery. A contractor who completed construction of a bridge could not recover the damages he incurred after a stop work order was issued by the county. The court reasoned that the county could not be held responsible for damages "which need not have been incurred," and could have been avoided without undue risk, burden, or humiliation to the non-breaching party. [Text §31.43]

Seamen's Direct Buying Serv., Inc. v. Standard Oil Co., 686 P.2d 1158 (Cal. 1986)

> The California Supreme Court has long recognized an implied covenant of good faith and fair dealing in every contract. A "bad faith" breach of this covenant by an insurance carrier gives rise to tort damages for breach of contract. The issue in this case was whether a plaintiff can recover tort damages for breach of the implied covenant of good faith and fair dealing in a commercial contract.
>
> Seamen's entered into a lease of city marina property for the purpose of operating a marine fuel dealership and then negotiated with Standard Oil to supply its fuel requirements for a ten year period. Seamen's wished to lease a larger portion of the waterfront area in the city, but the city required evidence of a binding agreement with an oil company before this larger lease could be

secured. In response to Seamen's request for a written, binding agreement, Standard Oil sent Seamen's an offer in which Standard promised to sign a fuel dealership agreement with Seamen's in the future. Seamen's accepted this offer and copies of the signed letter of intent were presented to the city which immediately approved Seamen's request to lease the larger space.

Shortly thereafter, fuel prices rose sharply, and the contemplated fuel dealership agreement was never executed. Then federal regulations went into effect which mandated that oil companies allocate their fuel supplies between **existing** customers, and since Standard Oil had not yet begun to supply Seamen's requirements, Standard Oil claimed it need not go forward with the agreement. However, Standard indicated that the federal regulations were the only reason for its refusal to supply Seamen's, and requested Seamen's help in securing federal approval of their proposed agreement. Seamen's was able to secure this approval, but Standard thereafter changed its position by claiming no binding agreement had ever been reached and refused to go forward with the contract. Standard's refusal to go forward with the contract caused Seamen's to go out of business and lose the city marina project, and Seamen's brought suit seeking punitive damages for a "bad faith" breach.

In remanding the case, the California Supreme Court created a new tort in California, which was the bad faith denial of the existence of a contract. If Standard was found liable for this tort, Seamen's could recover tort damages, including punitive damages, if the requisite standards were met.

In addition, the court held that a breach of contract suit could also give rise to tort damages if the breach is of the covenant of good faith and fair dealing and if the contract is one in which the parties are in a "special relationship" with each other. However, it held that there were no indicia of such a "special relationship" in a commercial contract such as the one at issue in the case, and thus denied Seamen's tort damages for breach of contract in this action. [Text §31.8]

Southwest Engineering Co. v. United States, 341 F.2d 998 (8th Cir. 1965)

This case illustrates the enforcement of a liquidated damages provision where such a provision was a reasonable estimate of the potential loss resulting from a potential breach viewed at the time of contracting. The non-breaching party may collect under the liquidated damages provision even if the later breach results in no actual damages, provided the reasonable estimate requirement is met. In *Southwest Engineering*, the plaintiff contracted to build several projects for the defendant. Each contract between the parties provided for a $50-100 late charge for each day the project's completion was delayed by the plaintiff. Plaintiff was unable to complete some of the projects on time, so the defendant subtracted the late charges from payments made to the plaintiff. The plaintiff sued to recover the late charges because the defendant conceded that no actual loss was suffered by the delays. Nevertheless, the court upheld the defendant's withholding of liquidated damages, noting that liquidated damages provisions are enforceable if at the time of contracting they were a reasonable forecast of estimated losses from a breach of the contract and if actual damages will be difficult to prove with precision. It makes no difference that the defendant sustained no actual damages once the breach actually occurred. [Text §31.7]

Sullivan v. O'Connor, 296 N.E.2d 183 (Mass. 1973)

The court in this case awarded reliance, rather than expectation, damages for a surgeon's breach of a promise to achieve a particular result for his patient, but also allowed the recovery of emotional distress damages as well. A plastic surgeon promised to improve his patient's appearance. The surgeon failed to achieve this result after two operations (in fact, the patient looked worse after the two operations than she did in her pre-surgery state), and a third operation was undertaken to attempt to restore the patient to her pre-surgery condition. The court allowed the patient's recovery of her reliance damages—the difference in value between her appearance before the operation and her appearance after the operation, in addition to the fees she paid and damages for pain and suffering. The court would not allow a recovery of the patient's expectation damages — the difference between the value of the patient's promised appearance and her appearance before the operation—because recovery of such damages would inhibit doctors from performing beneficial surgeries. [Text §31.612; 31.3]

Vitex Mfg. Corp. v. Carbitex Corp., 377 F.2d 795 (3d Cir. 1967)

Generally, a plaintiff's expectation damages are calculated by measuring the benefits plaintiff would have received under the contract and subtracting any benefits plaintiff received from not having to perform. An exception arises, however, in the calculation of plaintiff's overhead costs. Overhead costs are generally considered fixed and not part of the costs saved by a non-breaching party who has not completed performance at the time of the breach. Thus, the non-breaching party's expectation damages will not be reduced by the proportion of overhead expenses allegedly saved because the work was left uncompleted. In *Vitex*, where the parties had a contract for the manufacture of cloth, the court refused to subtract the plaintiff's saved overhead costs as a result of the defendant's breach prior to the time plaintiff completed performance. [Text §31.3]

White v. Benkowski, 155 N.W.2d 74 (1967)

This case holds that punitive damages, i.e., damages beyond that required to compensate a party for his injured expectation interest, are generally not recoverable in contract. Thus, where a homeowner had a contract with his neighbor for the supply of water from the neighbor's well, and the neighbor had shut off the supply for several short periods causing odors to accumulate in the plaintiff's bathroom, the court refused to award punitive damages for the breach of the contract. The court noted that "without exception, punitive damages are not available in breach of contract actions." This is true even if the breach is willful. The court noted that the plaintiff would have to sue in tort if he wanted to recover punitive damages. [Text §31.8]

RESTITUTION

Britton v. Turner, 6 N.H. 481 (1834)

This case allows restitution to be awarded to a party in breach. An employer and employee entered into a one year employment contract which called for $120 in compensation to be paid to the employee. The employee worked for 9 1/2 months and then breached the employment contract without justification. Nonetheless, the court held that the employee could recover $95 for the reasonable value of his services. The employee in this kind of situation is entitled to a restitutionary recovery of the reasonable value of his or her services because he or she has conferred a benefit upon the employer. Note that the jury in this case found the reasonable value of the employee's services to be equal to a *pro rata* amount of the contract price. [Text §32.3]

XVI. TABLE OF RESTATEMENT OF CONTRACTS SECTIONS CITED IN TEXT

References are to section numbers

RESTATEMENT 1ST

90: 8.22, 8.33
133: 27.31
133 (1): 27.311, 27.3111
133 (1)(a): 27.311
133 (1)(b): 27.312, 27.3121, 27.323
133 (1)(c): 27.313

RESTATEMENT 2ND

1: 1.11
12: 10.1
14: 10.1
15: 10.2
16: 10.23
18: 2.0
20: 11.5
20 (1): 11.52
20 (2): 11.52, 11.523
22 (2): 2.2
23: 4.332
24: 1.2, 3.0
25: 4.421
26: 3.213
26 (Com. b): 3.214
26 (Com. d): 3.211
28: 3.5
28 (1)(a): 3.51
28 (1)(b): 3.52
28 (1)(c): 3.53
29: 4.3
29 (Com. b): 4.331
29 (2): 4.52, 4.543
32: 4.52
33: 6.2, 6.23
35: 4.41
36 (Com. c): 4.416
37: 4.4211
38: 4.411
38 (Com. a): 4.4144-3
38 (2)(Com. b): 4.4114-6
38 (2): 4.4114-6
39: 4.411
39 (Com. a): 4.4111

39 (Com. b): 4.4114-2
39 (2)(Com. b): 4.4114-6
39 (2)(Com. c): 4.4114-7
41 (Com. b): 4.4121
41 (1): 4.412
41 (2): 4.4121
41 (3)(Com. e): 4.4122-2
43: 4.4133
43 (Com. d): 4.4133
45: 4.4134-1B, 4.4135, 4.4135-1, 4.4213-1, 4.541
46: 4.4132-1
48: 4.414
48 (Com. a): 4.4141
49: 4.4124
50: 1.2, 4.0
51: 4.332
52: 4.3, 4.32
53: 7.5
54: 4.5433, 4.56
54 (2): 4.5432
58: 4.51
59: 5.5
61: 5.5
63: 4.61, 4.614
67: 4.611, 4.612
68: 4.4132
69 (1): 4.571
69 (1)(b): 4.572
69 (1)(c): 4.573
69 (2): 4.574
71: 1.2, 7.5
71 (1): 7.13
71 (2): 7.13, 7.2
71 (3): 7.2
71 (4): 7.4
73: 7.63
75: 7.3
76 (Com. c): 7.6253-2
78: 7.67
79: 7.61
79 (a): 7.13
82: 7.64
83: 7.64

86: 7.522: 7.5222
87: 7.661
87 (Com. c): 7.661
87 (1)(Com. c): 4.4212
87 (2): 4.4135, 4.4135-1, 4.4213-2, 8.34, 8.342, 31.53
89: 87(2)(Com e) 4.4135-2, 7.633, 26.21, 31.53
90: 1.2, 8.2, 8.22, 8.31, 8.32, 8.331, 9.22, 31.53
90 (2): 8.22, 8.33
95: 8.6
112: 9.5
112 (Com. d): 9.52
116: 9.53, 9.531, 9.532
124: 9.4
125: 9.2
125 (Com. e): 9.213
127: 9.21
129: 9.22
131: 9.23, 9.34, 9.54
139: 8.32, 9.7, 31.53
148: 24.43 24.431
149: 9.8, 26.4
151: 11.1
151 (Com. b): 11.12
152: 11.3, 11.31, 11.313
153: 11.4, 11.41
154: 11.313, 11.321, 11.322, 11.34
159: 14.41
160: 14.415
161 (a): 14.415
161 (b): 14.415
161 (c): 14.415
161 (d): 14.415
161 (Com. e): 14.4154
162 (1): 14.421
162 (2): 14.422
163: 14.3
168 (1): 14.411
168 (2): 14.4111
172: 14.44
174: 12.1
175: 12.2

365: 30.2, 30.23, 30.231
366: 30.2, 30.22, 30.222, 30.223
366 (Com. a): 30.2221, 30.2222
367: 30.2
367 (1): 30.22, 30.223
367 (2): 30.223, 30.2233
367 (Com. b): 30.2232, 30.2233
371: 32.111, 32.23. 32.5
371 (a): 32.11
371 (b): 32.11
371 (Com. b): 32.111, 32.23, 32.4
373: 32.21
373 (Com. a): 32.21, 32.211,
   32.2111
373 (2): 32.21, 32.22, 32.221,
   32.222, 32.232, 32.25
374: 32.3
374 (Com. b): 32.111
375: 32.5
376: 32.5
377: 32.5
384: 32.12, 32.5
384 (1): 32.121
384 (2): 32.12, 32.122

XVII. TABLE OF UCC SECTIONS CITED IN TEXT

References are section numbers

ARTICLE 1

1-106: 30.21, 31.3
1-106 (Com. 1): 31.411
1-107: 7.635, 24.331
1-201 (11): 1.12
1-201 (26): 4.4132, 4.62
1-201 (37): 28.84
1-201 (39): 9.6224
1-203: 7.622, 8.351, 23.1, 31.8, 36.13
1-205: 19.1122
1-205 (2): 19.1123
1-206 (a): 9.61
1-207: 24.3322
1-208: 21.2422-2A, 23.212

ARTICLE 2

2-101: 34.211
2-102: 1.04, 22.0, 34.2, 34.212, 34.222
2-104 (1): 4.422, 36.21
2-105: 34.22, 34.222, 34.4
2-107: 34.4
2-107 (1): 9.212, 34.4
2-107 (2): 9.212, 34.4
2-201: 9.6, 9.61, 9.7, 26.4
2-201 (1): 9.61, 9.62, 9.622, 9.6223, 9.6224, 9.63, 9.631, 9.633, 9.634, 9.635, 9.64
2-201 (2): 9.61, 9.63, 9.631, 9.633, 9.634, 9.635, 17.51
2-201 (3): 9.61, 9.64
2-201 (3)(a): 9.641, 9.644
2-201 (3)(b): 9.642
2-201 (3)(c): 9.643, 9.6431
2-202: 19.0, 19.1, 19.11, 19.1111, 19.112, 19.2, 36.13
2-202 (Com. 3): 19.1111
2-203: 8.6
2-204: 6.2, 6.226
2-204 (2): 2.2
2-205: 4.42, 4.422
2-206: 4.53, 4.55
2-206 (1): 4.551

2-206 (1)(a): 4.52, 4.543
2-206 (1)(b): 4.55, 4.551
2-206 (2): 4.5432, 4.5433
2-207: 5.2, 5.3, 5.3121, 5.3122, 5.33, 5.34, 5.341, 5.4, 5.5
2-207 (Com. 3): 5.323
2-207 (Com. 4): 5.3222
2-207 (Com. 5): 5.3222, 5.3411
2-207 (1): 5.3, 5.31, 5.311, 5.312, 5.3121, 5.3122, 5.3123, 5.32, 5.3222, 5.323, 5.33, 5.34, 5.341, 5.3411, 5.4, 5.41
2-207 (2): 5.3, 5.3123, 5.32, 5.322, 5.323, 5.33, 5.341, 5.3411, 5.4, 5.41, 5.42
2-207 (2)(a): 5.322, 5.3221, 5.3411, 5.41
2-207 (2)(b): 5.322, 5.3222, 5.341, 5.3411, 5.41
2-207 (2)(c): 5.322, 5.3223, 5.341, 5.3411, 5.41
2-207 (3): 5.3, 5.311, 5.3123, 5.33, 5.331, 5.4, 5.41, 5.42
2-208: 19.1121, 19.1124
2-209: 26.0, 26.1, 26.6
2-209 (1): 7.633, 26.1, 26.2, 26.3, 26.4, 26.54
2-209 (2): 26.1, 26.3, 26.5
2-209 (3): 26.1, 26.4, 26.5
2-209 (4): 26.1, 26.5, 26.51, 26.52, 24.53, 26.54, 26.55
2-209 (5): 26.1, 26.6
2-210 (1): 29.222, 29.32
2-210 (2): 28.322, 28.323
2-210 (3): 28.323
2-210 (4): 28.38, 29.211
2-302: 15.1, 15.2, 36.13
2-305: 6.21, 6.221, 19.116
2-305 (Com. 1): 6.212
2-305 (4): 6.211, 19.1111-2
2-306 (1): 7.623, 7.6232
2-306 (2): 7.6222, 7.624
2-307: 6.21, 6.222
2-307 (Com. 3): 6.222
2-308: 6.21, 6.223
2-309: 6.21, 6.224

2-309 (3): 7.6263
2-310: 6.21
2-310 (a): 6.225
2-312: 36.0
2-313: 34.212, 36.0, 36.121
2-313 (Com. 3): 36.122
2-313 (1): 36.11
2-313 (1)(a): 36.11
2-313 (1)(b): 36.11
2-313 (1)(c): 36.11
2-313 (2): 36.11
2-314: 5.331, 5.42, 34.212, 36.0, 36.2, 36.22
2-314 (2): 36.22
2-314 (2)(a): 36.22
2-314 (2)(b): 36.22
2-314 (2)(c): 36.22
2-315: 5.331, 34.212, 36.0, 36.3
2-316: 15.5, 33.82, 36.13
2-316 (1): 36.13
2-316 (2): 36.23, 36.33
2-316 (3)(a): 36.23
2-318: 36.43
2-319: 35.11
2-319 (1)(a): 35.11
2-319 (1)(b): 35.11
2-319 (2): 35.12
2-320: 35.13
2-320 (Com. 1): 35.13
2-320 (1): 35.13
2-320 (3): 35.14
2-328: 3.5
2-328 (2): 3.51
2-328 (3): 3.52, 3.53
2-501: 34.22
2-501 (1)(a): 34.221
2-501 (1)(b): 34.222
2-503: 22.11
2-507: 22.11
2-507 (1): 22.1
2-508: 22.241, 22.2413, 22.2414, 22.2421, 22.333
2-508 (1): 22.2411, 22.2412-1
2-508 (2): 22.2412, 22.2412-1, 22.333
2-509: 35.0

ARTICLE 2A

ARTICLE 3

ARTICLE 8

ARTICLE 9

XVIII. INDEX

Refences are to section numbers

A

"Massachusetts Rule," regarding priority among competing assignments 28.83
Modification by assignee and obligor 28.7 et seq.
    assignments for value 28.71
    gratuitous assignments 28.72
"New York" rule, regarding priority among competing assignments 28.81
"No assignment" clause, effect of 28.323
Notification to assignee 28.33
Notification to obligor 28.34
Obligor
    defined 28.1
    discharge of duties where performance rendered to assignee 28.4
    discharge of duties where performance rendered to assignor 28.4
    duties of 28.4
Option contracts, assignment of rights under 4.323
Oral, effectiveness of 28.39
Partial 28.35
Revocability 28.7 et seq.
Rights to Accept Offers 4.32
Terminology 28.1
Third party beneficiary contracts, relationship to 28.37
Warranties made in assignments for value 28.6
Writing, when required 28.39
AUCTIONS
    See OFFER AND ACCEPTANCE

B

BATTLE OF THE FORMS
    Generally Chap. 5
BENEFICIARIES
    See THIRD PARTY BENEFICIARY CONTRACTS
BEST EFFORTS
    Illusory promises, effect on 7.623; 7.624
    Implied in:
        exclusive dealing contracts 7.624
        output contracts 7.623
        requirements contracts 7.623
BILATERAL CONTRACTS
    Anticipatory Repudiation, Necessity for 23.21
    Consideration for 7.3, 7.122, 7.132
    Constructive conditions of exchange under 21.1; 21.2
    Defined 1.32

Formed upon beginning performance under unilateral offer 4.4134-1C
Material Breach, Necessity for 21.23
Offers to enter into 3.32
BREACH OF CONTRACT
    See also PERFORMANCE
    Generally Chapters 21, 22
    Anticipatory repudiation as 23.1; 23.3
    Consequences of 21.0, 21.22
    Constructive conditions of exchange, relation to 21.1; 21.2; 21.24 et seq.; 22.1; 22.2
    Dependent promises and material breach 21.241
    Determining which party is in breach 21.1; 21.2, 21.25
    Determining whether breach is material or partial 21.24; 22.2 et seq.
    Independent/dependent promises test 21.241
        modern test 21.242
    Determining which party must perform first 21.11; 22.1
    Distinction between material and immaterial breach, when applicable 21.23
    Effect of breach 21.0 21.22
    Excuse of condition by 20.42
    First material breach doctrine 21.25
    Immaterial breach
        constructive conditions of exchange, relationship with 21.21
        defined 21.21
        effect of declaring a breach "immaterial" 21.22
        substantial performance doctrine 21.26
        turning material breach into immaterial breach by
            cure 21.272
            divisibility 21.271
            part performance 21.271
            waiver 21.273
    Independent promises and material breach 21.241
    Material breach
        anticipatory repudiation, relationship with 23.1; 23.4
        constructive conditions of exchange, relationship with 21.2
        defined 21.21
        determining whether breach is material or immaterial 21.24; 22.2 et seq.
        independent/dependent promise test, for determining 21.241

modern test, for determining 21.242
    effect of declaring a breach "material" 21.0 21.22
    immaterial breach followed by repudiation constituting 21.2422
    material breach becoming partial breach 21.27 et seq.
    material breach becoming total breach 21.2421
    suspension of performance as a result of 21.22
    "time is of the essence" clause, effect of 21.2423
    under the perfect tender rule 22.2 et seq
    when important to determine if breach is "material" 21.23
Partial breach
    see Immaterial breach, above
Perfect tender rule
    defined 22.2
    effect 22.2
    generally 22.2 et seq.
    limitations 22.24 et seq.
        course of dealing 22.244
        course of performance 22.244
        cure by seller 22.241
        de minimus non curat lex 22.243
        installment contracts 22.242
        revocation of acceptance 22.245
        usage of trade 22.244
    relationship with material breach 22.2
    statement of rule 22.2
    when it applies 22.2
Restitution available upon material breach 21.28, 32.0, 32.1
    to the breaching party 32.3
    to the non-breaching party 32.2
Substantial performance doctrine 21.26
Tender
    generally 21.1
    defined 21.1
    of delivery 22.11
    of payment 22.12
    of performance 21.1; 22.1
    requirement of 21.1; 22.1
"Time is of the essence" clause, effect of 21.2423
Total breach
    defined 21.2421
    when material breach becomes total breach 21.2421, 21.2422
Under the UCC, generally 22.0
"BROOKLYN BRIDGE" HYPOTHETICAL 4.4134 et seq.
BUILDING CONTRACTS

See CONSTRUCTION CON-
TRACTS

C

CAPACITY
See INCAPACITY
C & F, as mercantile term 35.14
CATALOGUES
Distinguished from offers 3.214
C. I. F., as mercantile term 35.13
COGNITION THEORY 10.2
COMMERCIAL IMPRACTICA-
BILITY
see IMPRACTICABILITY
COMMON LAW DECISION
MAKING 1.01
CONDITIONS
Generally Chapter 20; 21.1; 21.2
Breach
as excuse for enforcing condition
20.42
relationship with constructive
conditions 21.2
Constructive concurrent conditions
generally 21.11
under UCC 22.1
Constructive conditions, generally
defined 20.123
effect 20.125; 21.1 21.2 et seq.;
22.1 et seq.
no strict construction rule 20.125
Constructive conditions of exchange
concurrent conditions 21.11; 22.1
defined 20.1232
immaterial breach, relationship
to 21.21
Material breach, relationship
to 21.21
(one party's performance
constructively conditioned on
there being) no outstanding
uncured material breach of
the other 21.22
use to determine which party must
perform first 21.1 et seq.; 22.1
use to determine material
breach 21.2 et seq.
Disproportionate forfeiture, as
excuse for enforcing condition
20.43
Effect of classifying a condition as
precedent or subsequent 20.114
Excuses for enforcing conditions
breach 20.42
waiver 20.41
generally 20.4
to avoid disproportionate
forfeiture 20.43
Express conditions

Defined 20.121
Effect 20.124
Strict construction rule 20.124
effect of materiality 20.1241
effect of reasonableness 20.1241
Forfeiture, disproportionate as
excuse for enforcing condition
20.43
Implied-in-fact conditions
defined 20.122
effect 20.124
Implied-in-law conditions
see Constructive Conditions
Interpretation, rules of applied to
whether promise is subject to
condition precedent or is
unconditional 20.32 et seq.
Order of performance 21.11
under UCC 22.1
Parol evidence rule, effect of
condition precedent on 17.23
Precedent
Defined 20.111
distinguished from condition
subsequent 20.1 et seq.
effect of construing condition as
precedent rather than
subsequent 20.114
effect of construing promise as
being subject to condition
precedent versus being
unconditional 20.32
Promise/Duty
conditional 20.3
determining if conditional or
unconditional 20.31 et seq.
rules of interpretation 20.32
effect of construction as being
subject to a condition
precedent 20.2
unconditional 20.3 et seq.
Simultaneous performance 21.11
under UCC 22.1
Strict construction rule applied to
express conditions 20.124
Strict construction rule not applied
to constructive conditions
20.125
Subsequent
defined 20.112
distinguished from condition
precedent 20.1
effect of construing condition as
"subsequent" rather than
precedent 20.114
Types
condition precedent 20.111
condition subsequent 20.112
constructive 20.123
express 20.121

implied-in-fact 20.122
implied-in-law 20.123
Waiver
establishing 20.412
as excuse for enforcing condition
20.41
retraction 20.413
election 20.413
CONDUCT
Anticipatory Repudiation by 23.232
Contract by 1.34; 5.33 et seq
Ratification of contract entered into
by mentally infirm by 10.21
Ratification of contract entered into
as minor by 10.122
CONSIDERATION
Generally Chapter 7
Accords 7.634, 24.331
modern view 7.635, 24.3323
Acts incidental to gift promises
insufficient 7.5113
Adequacy of 7.61
Aleatory promises 7.6253-2
Bilateral contracts 7.3, 7.122, 7.132
Defined 7.1 et seq.
bargain theory 7.13
benefit/detriment theory 7.12
criticism of definitions 7.15
will theory 7.11
Exclusive dealing contracts 7.624
Good faith, use with illusory
promises 7.62 et seq.
Gratuitous/gift promises 7.51
acts incidental to gift promises 7.52
Illusory promises
implied promises used to make
enforceable
best efforts 7.624
good faith 7.622
in contracts with
termination-at-will
clauses 7.626
modern view 7.6262
UCC approach 7.6263
in contracts with expressly
conditional promises 7.625
in exclusive dealing contracts 7.624
in output contracts 7.623
in requirements contracts 7.623
Implied best efforts promise 7.624
Implied promise of good faith 7.622
Inadequate consideration 7.61
as evidence of fraud, duress, undue
influence, 7.611
as evidence of sham consideration
7.622
"peppercorn" theory 7.61
Illusory promises 7.62 et seq
modern approach 7.622
traditional approach 7.621

under UCC 33.313
Cost avoided, defined 31.3
Construction contracts
 breach by builder 31.34
 breach by owner 31.35
 special rules for calculating "lost
 value" 31.34
Cover damages, buyer
 defined 33.21
 formula 31.381, 33.211
Cover damages, seller
 defined 33.51
 formula 31.382, 33.511
Direct damages
 defined 31.23
 foreseeability requirement 31.42
 measure for breach of warranty 33.3
 "ordinary course of events" 31.423
"Duty" to mitigate 31.43
Emotional distress damages
 general rule 31.6
 under UCC 33.7
 where breach "particularly likely"
 to result in emotional
 distress 31.62
 where breach results in personal
 injury 31.61
Employment contracts
 breach by employee 31.33
 breach by employer 31.32
Exemplary damages, defined 31.24
 recoverability 31.8
Expectation damages
 avoidability, as limitation 31.43
 certainty, as limitation 31.41
 consequential damages, as
 component 31.3
 construction contracts 31.34; 31.35
 costs avoided, as component 31.3
 employment contracts 31.32; 31.33
 formula, general 31.3
 foreseeability, as limitation 31.42
 Hadley v. Baxendale, rule of 31.421
 incidental damage, as component
 31.3
 land sale contracts 31.36; 31.37
 limitations on recovery 31.4 et seq.
 losing contract situations 31.31
 loss avoided, as component 31.3
 lost value, as component 31.3
Expectation interest defined 31.11
General damages, defined 31.26
Incidental damages
 as consequential damage 31.425
 defined 31.27
 under UCC 33.312
"Interest" analysis 31.0
 expectation interest, defined 31.11
 reliance interest, defined 31.12
 restitution interest, defined 31.13

Land sale contracts
 breach by buyer 31.36
 breach by seller 31.37
 "American Rule" 31.37
 "English Rule" 31.37
Loss avoided, defined 31.3
Lost value, defined 31.3
Lost volume seller 31.3822, 33.531
Liquidated damages
 defined 31.28; 31.7
 distinguished from alternative
 performance clauses 31.72
 standards for enforceable provision,
 31.71
 under UCC 33.6
Limitation of remedy clauses
 see LIMITATION OF REMEDIES
Limitations on recovery
 avoidability 31.41
 certainty 31.43
 foreseeability 31.42
Mitigation
 see Avoidability, above
Nominal damages
 availability upon breach 31.29
 defined 31.29
Out-of-Pocket damages, defined
31.2-10
Pre-judgment interest, recovery
of 31.9
Punitive damages
 bad faith breach 31.81
 commercial contracts 31.81
 defined 31.2-11
 general rule 31.8
 insurance contracts 31.81
 under UCC 33.7
 when breach is also a tort 31.8
Reliance damages
 availability 31.51
 certainty, as limitation 31.521
 defined 31.2-12
 formula for recovering 31.5
 generally 31.5
 limitations on recovery 31.52 et seq.
 losing contract, effect on recovery
 31.522
 loss avoided, as limitation 31.523
Reliance Interest, defined 31.12
Restitution
 see RESTITUTION
Restitution interest, defined 31.13
Seller's damages
 cover 31.382 33.51
 full contract price 33.4
 market differential 33.52
 lost profit 33.53
 lost volume 33.531
Special damages 31.2-13
Stipulated damages, defined 31.2-14

Under UCC
 buyer's breach of warranty
 recovery 31.3812, 33.3
 buyer's cover damages 31.381,
 33.21
 buyer's market differential
 damages 31.381, 33.22
 consequential economic loss 33.313
 consequential personal injury and
 personal property loss 33.313
 emotional distress 33.7
 incidental damages 33.312
 lost volume seller 31.3822, 33.531
 liquidated damages 33.6
 punitive damages 33.7
 seller's cover damages 31.382,
 33.51
 seller's lost profit recovery 31.3822,
 33.53
 seller's market differential
 damages 31.382, 33.52
 warranty damages 33.3
DEATH
 Of the party performing a specialized task in a personal services
 contract 25.121
 Of offeree
  effect on irrevocable offer 4.4211
  effect on revocable offer 4.415
 Of offeror
  effect on irrevocable offer 4.4211
  effect on revocable offer 4.414
 Of thing essential to performance of
 contract other than offeree or offeror 4.416
DELEGATION OF DUTIES
 See also ASSIGNMENT OF
 RIGHTS
 Generally Chapter 29
 Anti-assignment clauses, effect of
 29.223
 "Assignment of contract" clause
 29.211
 Assumption of duty by delegate
 29.34; 29.4
 Delegate, defined 29.1
 Delegating party, defined 29.1
 Delegator, defined 29.1
 Distinguished from novation 29.4
 Duties of delegate upon valid dele-
 gation 29.3
 Duties of delegating party after
 valid delegation 29.3; 29.32
 Discharge of delegating party's
 duties upon performance of
 delegate 29.33
 Elements of effective delegation
 29.2
 Limitations on right to delegate
 public policy 29.221

See DAMAGES
RESTATEMENT OF
CONTRACTS
 Described 1.03
RESTITUTION
 See also DAMAGES; EQUITA-
 BLE REMEDIES
  Generally Chapter 32
 Award based on value of benefits
  actually received by benefited
  party 32.0
 Breach, availability as remedy for
  generally 32.2
  limitations on recovery by
  non-breaching party:
   breach must be total breach 32.211
   must be mutual 32.12
   possible notice requirement 32.2
   presumption of recovery using
   value calculation method
   yielding the greatest amount
   32.111; 32.23
    where aggrieved party has
    performed and benefited party
    only has to pay money 32.22
 Cost Avoided method of value
  calculation 32.11
 Distinguished from reliance
  damages recovery 32.0
 Doctrine explained 31.13;
  32.0 et seq.
 Duress, recovery upon 12.3; 31.5
 Frustration of purpose, recovery
  upon 25.6; 32.5
 Illegality, when recovery permitted
  16.3; 16.4; 32.5
 Impossibility, recovery upon 25.6;
  32.5
 Impracticability, recovery upon
  25.6; 32.5
 Incapacity, when recovery permitted 10.12; 10.13; 32.5
 Losing contract situations, use in
  31.31 31.522, 32.231
 Measure of recovery
  cost avoided method 32.11
  net benefit method 32.11
 Mutual restitution, requirement of
  32.12
 Net benefit method of value calculation 32.11
 Presumption of proper valuation
  method:
  recovery by breaching party
   32.111; 32.32
  recovery by non-breaching party
   32.111; 32.23
  recovery in quasi-contract
   situations 32.4
 Quasi-contract, recovery in 32.4

Recovery by breaching party
 damages of non-breaching party
  must be subtracted from 32.32
 presumption of recovery using
  value calculation method
  yielding the least amount
  32.111; 32.32
Unjust enrichment, goal to avoid
 32.0
Use where value of services
 exceeds contract price 32.232
REVOCATION OF ACCEP-
 TANCE UNDER UCC
 See also REJECTION OF GOODS
 Generally 22.3
 Against Remote Sellers 22.335
 Cure, relationship with 22.333
 Damages available upon rightful
  and effective revocation 31.381,
  33.2 et seq
 Effect 22.33 et seq.
 Elements necessary to establish
  22.331
 Restitution upon revocation 22.334
REVOCATION OF OFFERS
 See OFFER AND ACCEPTANCE
RISK OF LOSS
 Generally 35.0
 In absence of breach
  destination contracts 35.012
  shipment contracts 35.011
 When breach has occurred
  buyer's breach 35.023
  seller's breach followed by revoca-
  tion of acceptance 35.022
  seller's breach that gives buyer right
  to reject 35.021

S

SEAL, CONTRACTS UNDER 8.6
SHIPMENT CONTRACT 35.011
SILENCE
 Acceptance by 4.57
 Ratification by 10.123; 10.21
SPECIFIC PERFORMANCE
 See EQUITABLE REMEDIES
STATEMENT OF FUTURE IN-
 TENTION
 As distinguished from factual
  statement in misrepresentation
  14.412
STATUTE OF FRAUDS
 Generally Chapter 9
 Failure to satisfy, effect of 9.02, 9.9
 Marriage contracts 9.4
  pre-nuptial agreements 9.41
 "Merger" Doctrine 9.231
 Modifications of contracts 9.8;
  26.1, 26.2, 26.4

One year provision 9.3
 contracts with early termination
  clauses 9.32
 full performance by one party,
  effect of 9.33
 part performance 9.331
 satisfaction of one year provision
  9.34
Origins of 9.0
Parol evidence rule, relation to 17.5
Purpose 9.01
Rationale 9.01
Reliance, effect of 9.22, 9.7
Restitution, when required 9.93
Sale of goods 9.6 et seq
 divisible contracts 9.6221
 limit enforcement to less than
  $500 9.6222
 quantity term 9.6223
 satisfaction by:
  admission 9.642
  complete performance 9.643
  merchant's confirmatory
  memorandum 9.63
   failure to object, effect of 9.632
   objecting, effect of 9.633
   party not a merchant 9.634
  part performance 9.6431
  performance 9.643
  specially manufactured goods 9.641
 "signed by" requirement 9.6224
Surety contracts 9.5
 definition of "surety" 9.51
 leading object rule 9.53
 main purpose rule 9.53
Terminology 9.11
Transfer of an interest in land 9.2
 satisfying land portion of statute
  9.23
  application to sale of goods
  attached to land 9.212
Waiver, relationship with 26.5
STATUTE OF LIMITATIONS
 Enforceability of promises to pay
  debt otherwise unenforceable by
  its running 7.64
 Under UCC 34.212
SUB-CONTRACTORS
 Bids to general contractors tempo-
  rarily irrevocable 4.4135;
  8.34 et seq
 Low bid to general contractor as
  unilateral mistake 11.411
SUBSEQUENT AGREEMENTS
 See ACCORDS; NOVATION; MU-
 TUAL RESCISSION; RE-
 LEASES SUBSTITUTED
 CONTRACTS; SUBSTI-
 TUTED PERFORMANCE
SUBSEQUENT CONDITIONS

of the implied warranty of
merchantability 36.23
Express warranty
disclaimer 36.13
elements 36.1
Horizontal privity 36.43
Implied warranty of fitness for a
particular purpose
disclaimer 36.33
elements 36.3
Implied warranty of merchantability
disclaimer 36.23
elements 36.2
Limitation of remedy clause 33.81;
33.82
Notice by buyer of breach, require-
ment of 36.41
Parol evidence rule, effect on ex-
press warranty disclaimer 36.13
Puffing 14.414; 36.11
Remote manufacturer, right to re-
cover against 36.42
Sample of model, basis for express
warranty 36.11
Vertical privity 36.42
Warranty of title 36.0
"WOULD CERTAINLY" TEST
UNDER PAROL EVIDENCE
RULE 19.1111

XIX. CAPSULE OUTLINE

I.   INTRODUCTION TO OUTLINE

II. 10-5-2 HOUR STUDY GUIDE FOR CONTRACTS

III. INTRODUCTION TO CONTRACTS

CHAPTER ONE: A CONTRACTS OVERVIEW

    A. **SOURCES OF CONTRACT LAW. [§1.0]** There are four principal sources from which we get contract law: (1) common law judicial decision making; (2) treatises; (3) the Restatement of Contracts; and (4) The Uniform Commercial Code.

    B. **DEFINITION OF CONTRACT. [§1.1]** There are at least two different definitions of "contract":

        1. **RESTATEMENT DEFINITION. [§1.11]** The Restatement 2d defines a contract as "a promise or set of promises for the breach of which the law gives a remedy, or the performance of which the law in some way recognizes as a duty."

        2. **UCC DEFINITION. [§1.12]** The UCC defines a contract as "the total legal obligation which results from the parties' agreement."

        3. **SIGNIFICANCE OF DISTINCTION BETWEEN RESTATEMENT AND UCC DEFINITIONS. [§1.13]** The Restatement 2d definition does not cover transactions resulting in the simultaneous exchange of cash for products, services, or land. That is, unless there is at least one **promise** remaining to be performed after contract formation, that agreement is not a "contract" under the Restatement 2d's definition.

    C. **ELEMENTS OF A CONTRACT. [§1.2]** A contract consists of: (1) an offer; (2) an acceptance; and (3) consideration. Sometimes individual promises in a contract rendered unenforceable because of a lack of consideration can be enforced due to promissory estoppel.

    D. **TYPES OF CONTRACTS. [§1.3]**

        1. **UNILATERAL CONTRACTS. [§1.31]** Unilateral contracts are contracts in which the only effective mode of acceptance is the performance of an act by the offeree.

        2. **BILATERAL CONTRACTS. [§1.32]** Bilateral contracts are contracts formed by the exchange of mutual promises.

        3. **EXPRESS CONTRACTS. [§1.33]** Express Contracts are contracts resulting from words.

        4. **IMPLIED-IN-FACT-CONTRACTS. [§1.34]** Implied-in-fact contracts are contracts whose offer, acceptance, or both, are implied from conduct rather than evident from words.

        5. **"IMPLIED-IN-LAW" CONTRACTS OR "QUASI-CONTRACTS". [§1.35]** Quasi-Contracts are not contracts at all. Rather, the term

describes situations in which one party enriches another and it is unjust for the benefited party to have accepted those benefits without paying for them.

IV.   OFFER AND ACCEPTANCE

CHAPTER TWO: MUTUAL ASSENT

A. **MUTUAL ASSENT. [§2.0]** To have an enforceable contract, the parties must be mutually bound to the same transaction; however, mutual assent does not require agreement on **all** terms, only on essential ones. The presence of mutual assent is judged by objective factors, and there is a presumption against mutual assent in domestic or social situations.

CHAPTER THREE: OFFERS

A. **OFFER. [§3.0]** An offer is the manifestation by one party of the willingness to enter into a bargain with another. It creates in the offeree a power of acceptance, and the determination of whether an "offer" has been extended is made under an objective theory.

1. **DISTINGUISHING OFFERS FROM OTHER TYPES OF COMMUNICATION. [§3.21]** In analyzing fact patterns, an offer must be distinguished from:

    (1) a statement of future intention;

    (2) a request for a price quotation;

    (3) preliminary negotiations or invitations to make an offer; and

    (4) advertisements and catalogue descriptions that specify neither a quantity term nor a permissible mode of acceptance.

    (5) A statement made in jest, in anger, in a grumbling manner, or while intoxicated, however, **can** be a valid offer under the objective theory of contracts.

B. **TYPES OF OFFERS. [§3.3]** There are 3 types of offers:

1. **UNILATERAL CONTRACT OFFER. [§3.3]** Where the offeror is seeking actual performance by the offeree.

2. **BILATERAL CONTRACT OFFER. [§3.32]** Where the offeror is seeking a promissory acceptance from the offeree.

3. **GENERAL CONTRACT OFFER. [§3.33]** Where the offer can be accepted potentially by a large number of persons.

CHAPTER FOUR: ACCEPTANCE

A. **ACCEPTANCE. [§4.0]** An acceptance is the manifestation by the offeree that he or she assents to the terms of the offer and is willing to be bound to those terms. Assuming the existence of consideration, timely acceptance of a valid offer by one who has the power to accept that offer creates an enforceable contract. Whether acceptance has taken place will be judged under an objective theory.

B. **WHO IS ENTITLED TO ACCEPT THE OFFER. [§4.3]** A valid offer may only be accepted by the person or persons in whom it is reasonably apparent that the offeror intended to create the power of acceptance when the offer was made, as judged under the objective theory of contracts.

1. **POWER TO ACCEPT IS NOT GENERALLY TRANSFERABLE. [§4.32]** A power to accept an offer is generally not transferable to another. However, the power to accept an offer granted under an option contract is assignable as any other contract right.

2. **SPECIAL PROBLEMS CONCERNING WHO CAN ACCEPT "GENERAL" OFFERS. [§4.33]** A general offer is an offer that creates a power of acceptance in potentially unlimited numbers of people, such as a reward offer. Usually it is construed as capable of being accepted only by the **first** person to meet all the conditions of the offer.

C. **DURATION OF THE POWER OF ACCEPTANCE IN A REVOCABLE OFFER. [§4.4]** A revocable offer remains open, and thus the offeree has a power of acceptance under it, unless:

(1) the offeree has made a rejection and/or counter-offer;

(2) the offer has expired by its terms, or has expired after a reasonable time if no specific limit is set in the offer;

(3) the offer has been revoked by the offeror;

(4) the the offeror has died or become incapacitated before acceptance;

(5) offeree has died or become incapacitated before acceptance;

(6) any person or thing essential for performance of the contract has either died, been destroyed, or become incapacitated before acceptance;

(7) the acts called for in the offer have become illegal; or

(8) any condition of acceptance specified in the exchange has not yet occurred. If an offeree attempts to accept an offer in one of these situations, the purported acceptance is really a counter-offer.

D. **DURATION OF THE POWER OF ACCEPTANCE IN AN IRREVOCABLE OFFER. [§4.42].** There are two types of irrevocable offers: (1) merchant's firm offers under the UCC (§4.4222) and option contracts. An option contract is a contract, the subject matter of which is the option to accept another offer. It must be supported by its own consideration to be enforceable. The most important diference between a revocable and an irrevocable offer is that an offeree has only a *power* to accept under the former, but both a power *and a right* to accept under the latter. This means that under an "irrevocable" offer, the offeree's power and right of acceptance can only be terminated by: (1) lapse of time; (2) death or destruction of a thing essential for performance under the agreement; (3) supervening illegality; or (4) the non-occurrence of a necessary condition. Most importantly, such an offer is **not** automatically revoked upon a rejection or counter-offer by the offeror, or upon an attempted revocation by the offeree.

E. MODES OF ACCEPTANCE. [§4.5] There are only four ways to accept an offer: (1) by promise (bilateral contract); (2) by performance (unilateral contract); (3) by beginning performance; and (4) by silence.

1. **GENERAL RULE REGARDING ACCEPTANCE OF AN OFFER WHICH SPECIFIES METHOD OF ACCEPTANCE. [§4.51]** If the offer sets forth how it is to be accepted, a buyer must accept it precisely in that way to have a valid acceptance.

2. **BEGINNING PERFORMANCE AS ACCEPTANCE IN RESPONSE TO AN UNAMBIGUOUS UNILATERAL CONTRACT. [§4.541;4.4134].** There are three theories as to the effect of a party's beginning of performance in response to an unambiguous offer to enter into a unilateral contract: (1) that such an act is not an acceptance, and thus the offeror may revoke it at any time up until the point of formal acceptance by full performance; (2) that the beginning performance establishes a unilateral option contract under §45 of the Restatement 2d whereby the offeror's offer is irrevocable for a reasonable period of time, but the offeree is not bound to complete performance; and (3) that the beginning of performance by the offeree turns the contract into a bilateral one, wherein both parties are thereafter promissorily bound and are obligated to complete performance. Note these rules only apply when the offer is unambiguous, i.e. one for a unilateral contract

3. **GENERAL RULES REGARDING ACCEPTANCE OF AN OFFER WHICH DOES NOT SPECIFY METHOD OF ACCEPTANCE [§4.52]** The general rule regarding offers which do not specify their mode of acceptance, or which do so ambiguously, is that the offeree may accept in any manner and by any medium reasonable under the circumstances.

    a. **When Beginning Performance is Intended to Act As An Acceptance. [§4.54]** When an offeree's beginning performance is, under the circumstances, a reasonable mode of acceptance of an ambiguous offer, the act of commencing performance generally acts as an effective promissory acceptance subject to a condition subsequent. That is, by beginning performance in such cases, the offeree has validly accepted the offer **and** has implicitly promised that he, she, or it will complete performance, or be in breach for failing to do so. However, the agreement will become unenforceable if the seller does not satisfy the implied condition subsequent by notifying the offeror of such acceptance within a reasonable time after beginning performance.

    b. **The "Unilateral Contract Trick" Under The UCC. [§4.55]** If shipment of goods is a reasonable mode of acceptance in a contract governed by the UCC, shipment of non-conforming goods acts as a simultaneous acceptance and breach. If a seller sends an accommodation a letter along with the non-conforming goods, however, shipment of non-conforming goods is only a counter-offer.

4. **ACCEPTANCE BY SILENCE. [§4.57]** Generally acceptance by silence is an ineffective mode of acceptance. It is only effective when: (1) there has been a silent acceptance of services under circumstances in

which a reasonable person would realize an implied-in-fact contract has been formed; (2) previous conduct between the parties has made silence a permissible mode of acceptance; and (3) where a contract can be implied from the silent use of another's property.

F. **THE MAILBOX RULE. [§4.6]** Properly addressed acceptances are effective on dispatch, so long as acceptance by mail is a permissible mode of acceptance. Offers, revocations, and rejections are effective on receipt. However, with option contracts, acceptances are valid only on receipt.

CHAPTER FIVE: WHEN THE "ACCEPTANCE" VARIES FROM THE OFFER: THE MIRROR IMAGE RULE AND UCC §2-207

A. **COMMON LAW MIRROR IMAGE RULE. [§5.0]** At common law, the offer and acceptance had to match exactly, i.e., be mirror images of each other, before a contract was formed. Due to the unfairness of this rule in certain cases, the mirror image rule has been replaced by UCC §2-207.

B. **EXAM APPROACH TO ANALYSIS OF §2-207 PROBLEMS. [§5.3]** Proper analysis of a §2-207 problem is in three steps:

1. **FIRST, IT MUST BE DETERMINED WHETHER THE PARTIES HAVE A CONTRACT BASED ON THEIR WRITINGS UNDER §2-207(1) [§5.31].** That is, does the offeree's document act as a "definite and seasonable expression of acceptance?" If so, it is an "acceptance" even if it contains terms additional to or different from the terms of the offer. Or, does the offeree's document expressly make acceptance "conditional on [the offeror's] assent to additional or different terms?" If so, the document is a counter-offer.

2. **SECOND, IF IT IS DETERMINED THAT THE PARTIES HAVE A CONTRACT BASED ON THEIR EXCHANGED WRITINGS UNDER §2-207(1) (SEE ABOVE), THEN §2-207(2) GOVERNS WHAT TERMS MAKE UP THE CONTRACT [§5.32].** If either party is a non-merchant, the additional terms in the offeree's document are only proposals to contract. If both parties are merchants, the offeree's additional terms become part of the contract unless: (1) the offer expressly limited acceptance only to the terms of the offer; (2) the additional terms materially alter the contract; or (3) notification of rejection to the offeree's additional terms has already been made, or is made within a reasonable time, by the offeror. There are two views as to the proper treatment of "different" terms under §2-207(2). This is an issue because the words "different terms" are included in §2-207(1), but not in §2-207(2).

3. **THIRD, IF NO CONTRACT IS FORMED UNDER 2-207(1) BASED ON THE EXCHANGED WRITINGS, AN IMPLIED-IN-FACT CONTRACT MAY BE FORMED BY THE PARTIES' CONDUCT UNDER §2-207(3). [§5.33]** If so, then the contract is made up of all the terms on which the parties agree plus any UCC gap fillers, under §2-207(3)'s "knock-out" rule.

   a. **When the Additional or Different Terms Are Found in a Confirmation Instead Of An Acceptance. [§5.34]** If the additional or different terms are found in a confirmation as opposed to a acceptance, the contract should be treated as the offer, and the confirmation as the acceptance.

CHAPTER SIX: THE INDEFINITENESS DOCTRINE

A. THE INDEFINITENESS DOCTRINE. [§6.0] The indefiniteness doctrine states that a contract will not be enforced if a court cannot determine its essential terms with reasonable certainty. Indefiniteness problems are of three types: (1) where parties to a contract have not agreed to a term; (2) where parties have agreed to a term, but the term is so indefinite that its impossible to ascertain its meaning; and (3) where the parties have agreed to agree to a term after contract formation, but fail to do so.

B. COMMON LAW RULE ON INDEFINITENESS. [§6.1] Common law was relatively strict in applying the indefiniteness rule, and required the parties to reach agreement on several material terms or their "contract" would not be enforceable.

C. MODERN RULE ON INDEFINITENESS. [§6.2] Modern contract law has relaxed the indefiniteness rule in two ways. First, courts now have broader interpretive powers to decide what ambiguous contract terms should mean. Second, the UCC has supplied "gap filler" terms that should be used if the contract, as written, is so indefinite that it would be unenforceable.

    1. THERE ARE SIX GAP FILLERS UNDER THE UCC. [§ 6.22] (1) the price (reasonable price); (2) the mode of delivery (delivery in a single lot); (3) the place of delivery (seller's place of business); (4) the time of delivery (reasonable time); and (5) the time and (6) place for payment (at time and place for delivery).

V. CONSIDERATION AND ITS "SUBSTITUTES"

CHAPTER SEVEN: CONSIDERATION

A. THE CONSIDERATION DOCTRINE. [§7.0] Consideration is the doctrine by which the legal system separates those promises that will be enforced by a court from those that will not. Without consideration, no agreement can be enforceable as a contract, although various promises in such an agreement may be enforceable by promissory estoppel.

B. DEFINITIONS OF CONSIDERATION. [§7.1] The two most common theories used to define consideration are: (1) the benefit/detriment theory; and (2) the bargain theory.

    1. THE BENEFIT/DETRIMENT THEORY. [§7.12] The benefit/detriment theory holds that consideration exists when the promisee acts or promises to act **in exchange** for the promisor's promise and such act or promised act is either a legal detriment to the promisee or a legal benefit to the promisor.

    2. THE BARGAIN THEORY. [§7.13] The bargain theory of the Restatement 2d states that consideration exists when the promisee's return promise or act is both **sought by**, i.e., *bargained for* the promisor **in exchange for his or her promise, and is given in exchange** for that promise.

C. TYPES OF CONSIDERATION IN UNILATERAL CONTRACTS. [§7.2] There are three types of bargained for consideration that can support the enforceability of the offeror's promise to enter into a unilateral contract:

(1) an act; (2) a forbearance; or (3) the creation, modification, or destruction of a legal relationship.

D. TYPES OF CONSIDERATION IN BILATERAL CONTRACTS. [§7.3] In a bilateral contract, each party's promise serves as consideration for the return promise of the other, so long as the promises were bargained for, and so long as the promised performance by each party would be valid consideration if it would be performed.

E. THE RETURN PROMISES OR PERFORMANCES BY THE PROMISEE CAN BE VALID CONSIDERATION EVEN IF GIVEN TO A THIRD PARTY. [§7.4] So long as it is bargained for and given in exchange, consideration is valid even if the benefit of the promisee's promise or act goes to a third party.

F. TRANSACTIONS WITHOUT CONSIDERATION BECAUSE THEY LACK A BARGAINED FOR EXCHANGE. [§7.5] A number of kinds of transactions have been identified over the years as being unenforceable due to a lack of consideration. These include: (1) gift promises; (2) transactions based on past or moral consideration; and (3) unsolicited actions. Note, however, that the Restatement 2d has taken the position that sometimes moral or past consideration **can** serve as valid consideration. This is true: (a) any time a promisor's promise is made in recognition of a benefit previously received by the promisor, unless the promisee intended the benefit received by the promisor as a gift, or unless the value of the promisor's promise is clearly disproportionate to the benefit received by the promisor; or (b) when it's a promise to pay a valid debt that is currently unenforceable (see 7.64).

G. SPECIFIC TYPES OF TRANSACTIONS RAISING CONSIDERATION ISSUES. [§7.6]

1. TRANSACTIONS IN WHICH THE CONSIDERATION OF ONE PARTY IS WORTH SUBSTANTIALLY LESS THAN THE OTHER. [§7.61] Courts will not generally inquire into the adequacy of consideration, but too great disparity in the bargain may be evidence of fraud, duress, undue influence, unconscionability, or sham consideration.

2. ILLUSORY PROMISES. [§7.62] Promises that lack a definite commitment were held to be without consideration in early common law. However, modern courts hold that the implied covenant of good faith and fair dealing is usually a sufficient restraint on the exercise of a party's unfettered discretion to make such contracts enforceable. Contracts that raise illusory promise issues include personal satisfaction contracts, requirements contracts, and output contracts. The obligation of good faith is also used to support contracts in which performance is conditioned on the occurrence of **an event somewhat within the promisor's control.** Moreover, an implied "best efforts" covenant also makes an exclusive dealing agreement enforceable, as does the implied notice of termination requirement in at-will employment agreements.

3. TRANSACTIONS RAISING ISSUES UNDER THE PRE-EXISTING DUTY RULE. [§7.63] The pre-existing duty rule is in two parts: (1) contracts may not be enforceably modified without the payment of new consideration; and (2) a contract is not enforceable if it requires a party to pay additional consideration just to get the same contract rights he or she is already owed. The first part of the rule has been largely overruled by modern contract modification rules. The second part of the rule, however, remains valid.

4. **PROMISES TO PAY DEBTS MADE UNENFORCEABLE UNDER THE STATUTE OF LIMITATIONS OR BY BANKRUPTCY.** [§7.64] The Restatement 2d provides that if a debtor promises to pay a debt that is unenforceable due to the running of the statute of limitations, the promise can be enforced. Similarly, a promise to pay a debt that has been discharged in bankruptcy, or is currently the subject of bankruptcy proceedings, is also enforceable under the Restatement 2d.

CHAPTER EIGHT: PROMISSORY ESTOPPEL AND THE SEAL

A. **THE PROMISSORY ESTOPPEL DOCTRINE.** [§8.0] If a promise is unenforceable due to a lack of consideration, it may be enforceable by promissory estoppel. Promissory estoppel is a morally-based doctrine that makes enforceable promises that a shared sense of justice mandates should be enforced. It is not an absolute "substitute" for consideration [§8.1]

B. **ELEMENTS OF PROMISSORY ESTOPPEL UNDER THE SECOND RESTATEMENT.** [§8.2] The elements a party seeking to enforce a promise based on promissory estoppel must establish are: (1) that the promisor should reasonably have expected his or her promise to induce action or forbearance on the part of the promisee; (2) that the promisee did in fact induce foreseeable action or forbearance by the promisee; and (3) that injustice can only be avoided by enforcement of the promise.

C. **TYPES OF PROMISES ENFORCEABLE UNDER PROMISSORY ESTOPPEL.** [§8.3] The types of promises that are most often enforced by means of promissory estoppel, because they lack bargained for consideration, include: (1) gift promises; (2) oral promises to convey land; and (3) charitable subscriptions, whereby a charity can enforce a promised donation even without reliance under Restatement 2d §90(2).

D. **OFFERS THAT INDUCE FORESEEABLE RELIANCE OF A SUBSTANTIAL NATURE BECOME IRREVOCABLE.** [§8.34] Promissory estoppel can also be used to make certain offers irrevocable. An offer which the offeror should reasonably have foreseen would induce an offeree to undertake substantial action in reliance thereon, and which does in fact induce such reliance, is irrevocable. The most common application of this rule is between sub-contractors and contractors, where a sub-contractor's bid becomes irrevocable until a reasonable time after the developer awards the job to a contractor.

E. **ACTIONS TAKEN IN RELIANCE ON PROMISES MADE IN PRELIMINARY NEGOTIATIONS.** [§8.35] Promissory estoppel can be used to make enforceable certain promises made in preliminary negotiations. A party who does not make a contractual offer, but who does make a promise during preliminary negotiations that he or she reasonably should have expected would induce the offeree's substantial reliance, and which does induce such reliance, may be liable at least for out-of-pocket expenditures of the other if the party making the promise fails to perform it.

F. **REMEDIES WHEN A PROMISE IS ENFORCED UNDER PROMISSORY ESTOPPEL.** [§8.4] Promissory estoppel is not a complete "substitute" for consideration. Instead, it says that promises should only be enforced, if they are to be enforced at all, to the extent justice allows. Many times this means a party will only be awarded his or her reliance expenditures, and not the full amount of his or expectation damages.

G. EXAM APPROACH TO PROMISSORY ESTOPPEL PROBLEMS. [§8.5] In approaching a contracts problem, promissory estoppel should only be used to support a promise after it is determined that the promise cannot be supported by consideration.

H. THE COMMON LAW SEAL. [§8.6] At common law the seal was a complete substitute for consideration. The seal is no longer in use.

VI. VOIDABLE AND VOID AGREEMENTS

CHAPTER NINE: THE STATUTE OF FRAUDS

A. THE STATUTE OF FRAUDS DOCTRINE. [§9.0] The Statute of Frauds evidences the legal system's general preference for a written contract over an oral one by holding that certain oral contracts will not be enforceable.

B. MAJOR TYPES OF CASES COVERED BY THE STATUTE. [§9.1] There are five major types of cases that are governed by some part of the Statute:

(1) Contracts for the transfer of an interest in land that is anything other than a license.

(2) Contracts which, by their very terms, cannot be performed within a year of their making.

(3) Contracts made in consideration of marriage;

(4) Contracts where one party acts as a surety for another; and

(5) Contracts for the sale of goods for $500 or more under UCC §2-201.

C. SATISFYING THE STATUTE. [§9.62-9.7] The Statute can be satisfied for all of these contracts by a written agreement, clearly indicating the essential terms of the contemplated transaction, and signed at least by the party against whom the contract is trying to be enforced. In addition, some jurisdictions allow any part of the Statute to be satisfied by reliance, and all courts allow an oral promise to transfer an interest in land to be enforced if the seller of the property foreseeably induces the buyer to rely on the transfer of the property. Lastly, the statute under the UCC can be satisfied by either the sending of a merchant's confirmatory memorandum and the failure to respond to it within 10 days, or by one of the three exceptions of §2-201(3), i.e., specially manufactured goods, admission of the elements of a contract under oath, or performance [§9.64].

D. CONSEQUENCES OF NOT SATISFYING THE STATUTE OF FRAUDS. [§9.02; 9.9] If a contract is within the Statute, and it is not satisfied, then the contract cannot be enforced against the party who has not signed a writing or otherwise satisfied it. However, if a party who has the power to cease performance wishes instead to continue performance under the contract, he or she is permitted to do so, for failing to satisfy the Statute only makes a contract voidable, not void. That is, it provides a defense to a party who does not perform, but it does not require the party who holds the defense to cease performance.

1. **RESTITUTION PERMITTED UPON DISAFFIRMANCE. [§9.93]**
The party who avoids the contract under the Statute is entitled to restitution from the other.

CHAPTER TEN: INCAPACITY

A. **THE INCAPACITY DOCTRINE. [§10.0]** The idea behind the incapacity doctrine is that to have a valid contract, the contracting parties must have sufficient judgment to decide voluntarily to enter into a legally binding document. There are two circumstances in which the law expresses a belief that a person does not have that judgment: (1) when the party is a minor; or (2) when the party is mentally incapacitated.

B. **INCAPACITY DUE TO INFANCY/MINORITY. [§10.1]** The general rule is that any contract entered into by a minor is voidable at the option of the minor until he or she reaches majority. At that point, the minor has a reasonable period of time either to disaffirm the contract, or to ratify it. If he or she does nothing, it will be considered implicitly ratified.

   1. If the contract is disaffirmed either before or within a reasonable time after the minor turns 18, the minor need only return whatever is left of the goods or services purchased on credit, and he or she is entitled to the return of all monies he or she has paid for the goods, land, or service. That is, there is no obligation on the minor to account for the restitutionary value of the goods while in his or her possession, except for those jurisdictions adopting the "New Hampshire" rule.

   2. The non-minor is entitled to restitution for the economic benefits of goods of services provided a minor under a contract the minor later validly disclaims if the transaction: (1) is for cash and not on credit; (2) is for "necessities"; or (3) is one in which the minor misrepresents his or her age. In fact, e.g., in some states a minor who misrepresents his or her age loses the power to disaffirm the contract at all and thus is potentially liable in contract for the full contract price, not just restitution.

C. **INCAPACITY DUE TO MENTAL INFIRMITY: THE COGNITION THEORY. [§10.2]** The general rule is that if, at the time of the making of the contract, a party lacked the ability to understand the nature and consequences of the agreement, the contract is voidable at the option of the mentally infirm party or by his or her guardian. A party who recovers from mental incapacity has a reasonable time to decide whether to ratify or disaffirm the contract. If he or she does nothing, the contract will be deemed implicitly ratified upon a reasonable time after a recovery. Upon disaffirmance, most jurisdictions permit the non-incapacitated party to recover in restitution, unless the incapacity was obvious. However, all jurisdictions allow the non-infirm party to recover in restitution for the supply of necessities to a mentally incompetent individual.

   1. **INTOXICATION AND OTHER DRUG USE. [§10.23]** Most states provide that a party temporally incapacitated due to alcohol or other drug use is entitled to disaffirm any contract made during this period, regardless of whether such intoxication was voluntary or involuntary (cognition test). The Restatement 2d, however, takes the view that such a contract should be voidable only if the incapacitated party fails the cognition test and the non-incapacitated party had reason to know of the incapacity of the other.

CHAPTER ELEVEN: MISTAKE AND MISUNDERSTANDING

A. **THE MISTAKE DOCTRINE. [§11.0]** A "mistake" in contract law is a belief that is not in accord with the true facts. A "mistake" is **not** an improvident act, entering into a losing contract nor is it a erroneous belief as to future events. If a party can establish that a sufficient mistake was present at the time of contract formation, the contract is voidable by that party.

   1. **MUTUAL MISTAKE. [§11.3]** Mutual mistake occurs when both parties to a contract are under substantially the same erroneous belief as to the true facts present at the time of contract formation. A party seeking to establish mutual mistake must prove: (1) the mistake was as to a basic assumption on which the contract was made; (2) the mistake has a material effect on the agreed transaction; and (3) the party seeking to avoid the contract must not have borne the risk of making the mistake [§11.313]. The party seeking to avoid the contract must do so within a reasonable time after he or she should have discovered the mistake, and if the contract is avoided, a restitution action is permitted.

   2. **UNILATERAL MISTAKE. [§11.4]** A unilateral mistake occurs when only one party to a contract has an erroneous belief as to the true facts present at an exchange. To establish unilateral mistake, the party seeking to avoid the contract must prove all the elements necessary for avoiding the contract under mutual mistake, **plus** either: (1) that the effect of the mistake is such that enforcement against the mistaken party would be unconscionable; or (2) that the non-mistaken party had reason to know of the mistake. The party seeking to avoid the contract must do so within a reasonable time after he or she should have discovered the mistake, and he or she loses the right to disaffirm the contract if the non-mistaken party relies on the contract to his or her detriment. Once again, if the contract is avoided, a restitution action is permitted.

B. **THE "MISUNDERSTANDING" DOCTRINE. [§11.5]** Misunderstanding occurs when the parties agree to a term in their contract, but each has a different meaning of that term. The rules in misunderstanding cases are:

   1. If neither party knows or has reason to know of the meaning of a material term attached by the other, no contract is formed.

   2. If the parties have different meanings as to a material term, but one party knows of this misunderstanding and the other does not, a contract is formed and the meaning of the disputed term is construed to be the meaning ascribed by the party who was unaware of the misunderstanding.

CHAPTER TWELVE: DURESS

A. **THE PROBLEM OF DURESS. [§12.0]** The duress doctrine gives an aggrieved party a right to avoid a contract if it was not entered into voluntarily, but rather as a result of either physical compulsion or improper threat. If a contract is avoided on the grounds of duress, a restitution action is permitted [§12.3].

B. **DURESS BY PHYSICAL COMPULSION. [§12.1]** Any contract entered into by a party solely as a result of physical force is void. However, this doctrine only applies when imminent actual physical force, and not merely the threat of physical force, is used to secure agreement.

C. DURESS BY IMPROPER THREAT. [§12.2] A contract entered into by a party as a result of an improper threat is voidable by that party. What threats are sufficiently "improper" to trigger this doctrine depends on whether the terms of the exchange appear fair.

  1. IMPROPER THREAT WHEN TERMS OF THE EXCHANGE APPEAR FAIR. [§12.22] Where the terms for the exchange appear fair, a threat made to induce a party to enter into the contract is "improper" for purposes of duress if: (1) what is threatened (or the threat itself) is a crime or tort; (2) what is threatened is criminal prosecution; (3) what is threatened is the bad faith use of the civil process; or (4) the threat is a breach of the duty of good faith and fair dealing.

  2. IMPROPER THREAT WHERE TERMS OF THE EXCHANGE APPEAR UNFAIR. [§12.23] Where the terms of the exchange appear unfair, a threat made to induce a party to enter into a contract is improper if: (i) the threatened act would harm the recipient and not benefit the party making the threat; (ii) prior dealings of the parties increase the effectiveness of the threat; or (iii) the threatened action is a use of power for illegitimate ends.

CHAPTER THIRTEEN: UNDUE INFLUENCE

  A. UNDUE INFLUENCE. [§13.0] The undue influence doctrine allows a party who suffers from some sort of mental weakness (short of incapacity), and is subject to improper persuasion (short of duress), by someone who is in a "special relationship" with the party, to avoid a contract entered into on that basis. If a contract is avoided, a restitution action is permitted [§13.2].

  B. ELEMENTS OF UNDUE INFLUENCE. [§13.1] To avoid a contract on undue influence grounds, a party must establish: (1) a "special relationship" with the other party to the contract; and (2) there has been improper influence of the victim by the stronger party in obtaining the aggrieved party's consent to enter a contract.

CHAPTER FOURTEEN: MISREPRESENTATION

  A. THE MISREPRESENTATION DOCTRINE. [§14.0] In certain cases, contract law allows a party to avoid a contract based on the misrepresentations made to him or her during the bargaining process. A misrepresentation claim must be brought within a reasonable time after discovering the misrepresentation, and when a contract is avoided on misrepresentation grounds, a restitution action is permitted. Actionable misrepresentation is of two types:

  1. FRAUD IN THE *FACTUM* [§14.3] Fraud in the *factum* occurs when there has been a misrepresentation as to the very nature of the document presented to the innocent party. In such cases, the contract is **void**, not just voidable.

  2. FRAUD IN THE INDUCEMENT. [§14.4] The most common type of misrepresentation case occurs when a seller misrepresents the attributes of the good, land, etc., he or she is selling as an inducement for the innocent party to enter a contract. To establish an actionable misrepresentation claim for fraud in the inducement, the innocent party must prove: (1) there was a misrepresentation of fact made to him or her; (2) the misrepresentation was **either** fraudulent or material; (3) the misrepresentation induced actual reliance; and (4) such reliance was reasonable.

CHAPTER FIFTEEN: UNCONSCIONABILITY

A. **THE UNCONSCIONABILITY DOCTRINE. [§15.0]** The unconscionability doctrine allows a court to "step in" and correct a situation in which one contracting party makes too good a deal for himself or herself, even in the absence of duress, undue influence, misrepresentation, etc. If a court finds that a contract, or a portion of a contract, is unconscionable, it is entitled to: (1) refuse enforcement of the entire contract; (2) enforce the contract without the unconscionable clause or clauses; or (3) modify or limit the application of any clause to avoid an unjust result. While modern unconscionability largely grew out of §2-302 of the UCC, the doctrine applies to both UCC and non-UCC contracts.

B. **ELEMENTS OF UNCONSCIONABILITY. [§15.3]** There are two types of unconscionability: (1) procedural, meaning that one party has no meaningful choice to deal elsewhere and/or that the objectionable terms are hidden in the prolix of the agreement; and (2) substantive, meaning that the terms are unreasonably favorable to one party. To establish that a contract, or part of a contract, is unconscionable, a party must show the presence of both procedural and substantive unconscionability. While there is no necessary quantum of proof that must be met for each of these factors before unconscionability is established, the more substantive unconscionability present, the less procedural unconscionability need be proven, and *vice-versa*.

CHAPTER SIXTEEN: ILLEGALITY

A. **ILLEGALITY. [§16.0]** A contract is illegal if either its formation or its performance is criminal or otherwise against public policy. Illegal contracts need not call for criminal acts to be "illegal" in the contracts sense. Rather, an illegal contract is one in which the societal interest in its enforcement is clearly outweighed by public policy concerns [§16.1].

B. **COMMON TYPES OF ILLEGAL CONTRACTS. [§16.2]** The most common forms of illegal contracts are:

   (1) agreements for the performance of criminal acts such as prostitution, murder, etc.;

   (2) gambling contracts in most states;

   (3) contracts associated with bribery;

   (4) contracts in which one party attempts to release another from tort liability;

   (5) agreements with parties who should be, but are not, licensed; and

   (6) agreements in which the seller is aware that the goods or services he or she is providing will be used by the buyer for an illegal purpose.

C. **EFFECT OF FINDING A CONTRACT ILLEGAL. [§16.3]** If a contract is found to be illegal and performance under it is wholly executory, the general rule is that the agreement is "void" and neither party may enforce it. If at the time of the making of the contract one party was justifiably ignorant as to the facts which made the contract illegal, he or she may treat it as voidable, however. Further, if a statute that makes a contract illegal is designed to protect a particular class of persons, an individual in that class has the option of avoiding or affirming the contract.

1. If a contract is found to be illegal and performance under it has been partially or wholly executed, the general rule is that the agreement is "void" and neither party may either enforce it or seek restitution under it [§16.4]. However, a party who is at lesser fault regarding the illegality is entitled to seek restitution under the *in pari delicto* doctrine [§16.41]. Similarly, a party is also entitled to restitution if he or she repudiates an illegal contract before its illegal purpose has been either attempted or obtained, so long as the illegality is minor, under the *locus poenitentiae* doctrine [§16.42].

VII. THE PAROL EVIDENCE RULE AND INTERPRETATION

CHAPTER SEVENTEEN: THE PAROL EVIDENCE RULE

A. **THE PAROL EVIDENCE RULE. [§17.0]** The parol evidence rule both states contract law's preference for enforcing only the final agreement of the parties, and sets forth the rules to follow when the parties disagree as to what their final agreement actually was. Parol evidence describes terms one party says should have been included in the final written agreement of the parties (because they were part of the parties' final deal), but which are not present in that writing. While parol evidence can be written or oral, a parol evidence issue always arises in the same way, i.e., when one party seeks to introduce parol evidence of some term he or she says was agreed to during contract negotiations, but which do not appear in the parties' signed contract.

B. **STATEMENT OF THE PAROL EVIDENCE RULE. [§17.1]** The parol evidence rule is in two parts: (1) if the writing is partially integrated, no evidence of an allegedly agreed-upon term made either contemporaneous with, or prior to, the written agreement can be introduced into evidence if such term will contradict (as measured by the "might naturally" test) a term of the written contract; and (2) if the writing is totally integrated, no evidence of prior or contemporaneous agreements, can be admitted at all.

1. The rules governing when a contract is partially or totally integrated are discussed in §17.13.

2. When a parol term "passes" the parol evidence test, it does not automatically become part of the contract. Rather, a party is thereafter entitled to offer evidence at trial that the particular term was mutually agreed upon during negotiations. The trier of fact can either accept or reject that evidence [§17.4].

C. **SITUATIONS IN WHICH THE PAROL EVIDENCE RULE DOES NOT APPLY. [§17.2]** There are six situations in which the parol evidence rule does not apply: (1) when a party wants to introduce evidence of a modification to an existing contract; (2) where a party wishes to introduce evidence to show that no valid agreement ever existed between the parties; (3) where a party seeks to introduce evidence of an unfulfilled condition precedent; (4) where a party introduces evidence to establish the failure of the other to tender consideration; (5) where evidence is offered to show a contract was voidable; and (6) where "parol" evidence is contained in a side agreement made contemporaneous with the written contract.

CHAPTER EIGHTEEN: INTERPRETATION

A. **INTERPRETATION. [§18.0]** Interpretation is the general doctrine governing what meaning courts are to give words. The interpretation doctrine is in two parts: (1) rules of construction, which apply to every contract; and (2) rules of interpretation, which govern how a court is to discern the meaning of a term under a particular contract.

B. **RULES OF CONSTRUCTION. [§18.1]** There are six generally recognized rules of construction:

1. An interpretation that gives meaning to all terms is preferable to an interpretation making a part of the agreement surplusage;

2. If two clauses are in conflict, the more specific acts as an exception to the more general;

3. Separately negotiated terms are given greater weight than standardized terms;

4. Handwritten terms generally control over typed or printed ones; typewritten terms generally control over printed ones;

5. If a term is ambiguous, it should be resolved against the party who drafted it; and

6. The expression of one thing is the exclusion of others.

C. **RULES OF INTERPRETATION. [§18.2]** The general rules governing interpretation are:

1. Language is to be given its generally prevailing societal meaning; and

2. Terms are to be interpreted in light of their meaning within the usage of trade, course of dealing, or course of performance.

   a. **Hierarchy of Express Terms, Usage of Trade, Course of Dealing, and Course of Performance. [§18.2121]** If the same word is interpreted differently in different contexts, then: (1) the meaning of the express terms of the contract controls over any meaning given the term through a course of performance, course of dealing or usage of trade; (2) the meaning ascribed to a term by course of dealing controls over the meaning given that term through a course of performance or usage of trade; and (3) the meaning given a term by course of performance controls over the meaning given that term through usage of trade.

D. **ADMISSIBILITY OF EXTRINSIC EVIDENCE TO PROVE THE PARTIES HAD THEIR OWN SPECIAL MEANING FOR A TERM. [§18.22]** The decision as to whether one party will be entitled to introduce evidence that the parties had agreed to use their own special meaning for a contract term, different from the ordinary meaning of that term, depends on whether the jurisdiction has adopted the strict "plain meaning" rule, or the more liberal "reasonably susceptible" rule.

CHAPTER NINETEEN: UCC §2-202

A. **UCC §2-202. [§19.0]** In UCC §2-202, the drafters have attempted to combine both the parol evidence rule and the interpretation rules in one section. As stated in §2-202, that provision governs how terms in a written document may be both "supplemented" and "explained."

B. **APPROACH TO A §2-202 PROBLEM. [§19.1]** Assuming the UCC applies to the transaction, the first step in a §2-202 problem is to determine whether the contract is partially or totally integrated. If it is partially integrated, then no evidence of any supplementary term which contradicts (as measured by the "would certainly" test) any term in the writing will be admitted. However, course of performance, course of dealing, and usage of trade are freely admissible to explain (but not supplement) any terms in the writing. If the writing is totally integrated, no evidence as to supplementary terms is allowed, but again course of performance, course of dealing, and usage of trade is freely admissible to explain any terms of the writing.

  1. **HIERARCHY OF INTERPRETATION. [§19.124]** The UCC hierarchy of interpretation when the same word has a different meaning based on the express language of the contract, the course of performance, the course of dealing or the usage of trade, is the same as the hierarchy used in common law interpretation. (18.2121)

C. **SITUATIONS WHERE §2-202 DOES NOT APPLY. [§19.2]** The parol evidence function of §2-202 does not apply to exclude evidence in the same six situations in which the common law parol evidence rule does not apply to exclude evidence.

VIII. CONDITIONS

CHAPTER TWENTY: CONDITIONS

A. **CONDITIONS GENERALLY. [§20.0]** Conditions are devices that allow parties to a contract to be bound by a valid agreement, but to have the duties under that agreement be (or become) unenforceable.

B. **DISTINGUISHING AMONG DIFFERENT KINDS OF CONDITIONS. [§20.1]**

  1. **CONDITION PRECEDENT. [§20.111]** A condition precedent is an event, not certain to occur, but which must occur before performance under a contract is enforceable, unless the non-occurrence of the event is excused.

  2. **CONDITION SUBSEQUENT. [§20.112]** A condition subsequent is an event, the occurrence of which is not the result of a breach of the obligor's duty of good faith which, if it occurs, terminates a party's duty to perform, unless its occurrence is excused.

   a. **Effect of Classifying a Condition as "Precedent" or "Subsequent" [§20.114]** A party who presently claims to be owed an enforceable duty bears the burden of proof to establish that a condition precedent was satisfied. The party who at one time owed an enforceable duty of performance to the other bears the burden of proof to establish that a condition subsequent has occurred.

3. **EXPRESS CONDITIONS. [§20.121]** An express condition is a condition expressly agreed upon by the parties as evidenced by their words. Express conditions are strictly enforced.

4. **IMPLIED-IN-FACT CONDITIONS. [§20.122]** An implied-in-fact condition is a condition agreed upon by the parties as evidenced by their actions. Such conditions are treated like express conditions.

5. **CONSTRUCTIVE CONDITIONS. [§20.123]** A constructive condition is a condition not expressly agreed to by the parties, but rather implied by a court to determine the parties' rights and duties under a contract. Constructive conditions are not subject to the strict enforcement rule [§20.125].

C. **EFFECTS OF CONSTRUING A PROMISE AS BEING SUBJECT TO CONDITION PRECEDENT AS OPPOSED TO BEING UNCONDITIONAL. [§20.2]** The principal effect of construing a promise as being subject to a condition precedent rather than being unconditional is that the risk of the non-fulfillment of the condition is shifted from one party to the other. Thus, if the condition is never fulfilled, the party whose duty is conditional on its occurrence will not be in breach.

1. **WAYS TO INTERPRET PARTY'S OBLIGATIONS. [§20.31]** An obligation of a party under a contract can be construed: (1) as a conditional promise; (2) as an unconditional duty; and (3) as both a conditional promise and a unconditional duty. There are outcome-determinitive consequences to the innocent party depending on which construction is adopted.

   a. **General Rules of Interpretation for Determining Whether an Obligation Is a Conditional Promise, an Unconditional Duty, or Both. [§20.32]** There are two general presumptions regarding whether a party's contractual obligation should be construed as a conditional promise, an unconditional duty, or both: (1) an interpretation that a promise is an unconditional duty rather than a conditional obligation is favored when the event necessary to fulfill the condition is within the obligee's control; and (2) the interpretation that reduces a promisor's risk of forfeiture is preferred.

D. **EXCUSE OF CONDITIONS. [§20.4]** A condition can be excused in three ways: (1) by waiver; (2) by material breach; and (3) where enforcement of the condition would cause a disproportionate forfeiture.

IX.   PERFORMANCE, NON-PERFORMANCE, AND MODIFICATION OF DUTIES

CHAPTER TWENTY-ONE: PERFORMANCE AND BREACH IN CONTRACTS NOT GOVERNED BY THE UCC

A. **DETERMINING BREACH: CONSTRUCTIVE CONDITIONS OF EXCHANGE, TENDER, AND THE ISSUE OF WHICH PARTY MUST PERFORM FIRST. [§21.1]** When it is unclear who must perform first under a contract, constructive conditions of exchange are used to determine the order of performance. These constructive conditions state that: (1) if performance of each party can be rendered simultaneously, tender of each party's performance is due simultaneously; and (2) if the performance of one party requires a period of time to complete, and the other does not, performance of the time-consuming duty must be rendered first.

B. MATERIAL AND IMMATERIAL (OR PARTIAL) BREACH. [§21.2] A material breach occurs when a party fails to perform a duty due under a contract which results in the unexcused non-occurrence of a constructive condition of exchange. An immaterial breach occurs when a party fails to perform a duty under a contract that results in the excused non-occurrence of a constructive condition of exchange.

1. **CONSEQUENCES OF DECIDING THAT A BREACH IS MATERIAL OR IMMATERIAL. [§21.22]** The principal difference between the consequences of declaring a breach material as opposed to immaterial is that the non-breaching party is entitled to cease performance upon the other party's material breach, but must continue performance if the breach is immaterial. In other words, the performance of a party under a contract is constructively conditioned on there being no outstanding unexcused material breach by the other.

2. **THE ONLY SITUATION IN WHICH THE DOCTRINE OF MATERIAL BREACH APPLIES: BILATERAL CONTRACTS IN WHICH THERE ARE EXECUTORY DUTIES REMAINING ON BOTH SIDES AT THE TIME OF THE BREACH. [§21.23]** The only time it matters whether a breach is "material" or not is when the contract involved is bilateral and there are executory duties remaining by both parties at the time of breach.

3. **HOW TO DETERMINE WHETHER A BREACH IS MATERIAL OR IMMATERIAL. [§21.24]** In deciding whether a particular breach is "material," i.e., whether it results in the unexcused failure in the occurrence of a constructive condition, a court is directed to examine the following factors: (1) the extent to which the non-breaching party will be deprived of a reasonably expected benefit of the bargain; (2) whether the non-breaching party can be fully compensated for the breach; (3) the extent to which the breaching party will suffer forfeiture if the breach is declared material; (iv) the likelihood of cure by the breacher; and (v) the good or bad faith of the breaching party [§12.242].

4. **THE TEST FOR WHEN A MATERIAL BREACH BECOMES A TOTAL BREACH: WHEN THE BREACH IS NEITHER CURED NOR EXCUSED AFTER A REASONABLE TIME. [§21.2421]** A material breach becomes a total breach when it is neither cured nor excused after a reasonable time, or when a partial breach is accompanied or followed by a repudiation, unless the partial breach followed by a repudiation concerns a breach of the payment of money in installments.

5. **THE SUBSTANTIAL PERFORMANCE DOCTRINE. [§21.26]** The substantial performance doctrine states that so long as a party has substantially performed a duty under a contract, any discrepancy between actual and promised performance is only an immaterial breach. The substantial performance doctrine typically applies to construction contracts, and the principal determinant as to whether there has been "substantial performance" in such cases is whether the owner has (or will have) received the essential part of his or her bargain under the contract if the breach is treated as an immaterial one.

6. **DOCTRINES THAT TRANSFORM MATERIAL BREACHES INTO IMMATERIAL BREACHES. [§21.27]** A material breach can be transformed into an immaterial one upon: (1) application of divisibility principles and part performance; (2) cure of the material breach by the breaching party; or (3) the non-breaching party's waiver of the material breach.

CHAPTER TWENTY-TWO: PERFORMANCE AND BREACH UNDER THE UCC

A. **TENDER AND CONCURRENT CONDITIONS OF EXCHANGE UNDER THE CODE. [§22.1]** Tender of performance by one party is a constructive condition to the performance of the other under the UCC, just as in non-UCC agreements [see §§21.11 and 21.12 respectively for the definition of seller's and buyer's tender obligations under the UCC].

B. **THE PERFECT TENDER RULE UNDER THE UCC. [§22.2]** The so-called "perfect tender rule" of the UCC states that in single lot delivery contracts governed by the Code, if either the goods, or the manner of their tender, fails in any respect to conform to the contract, such non-conformity constitutes a material breach.

    1. **LIMITATIONS ON THE PERFECT TENDER RULE. [§22.23]** There are five potential limitations on the application of the perfect tender rule:

        a. In many cases a seller has the right to cure his or her performance, transforming a material breach into an immaterial one;

        b. In installment contracts, the perfect tender rule is replaced by the "substantial impairment" test. This test holds that no material breach occurs until there has been a "substantial impairment" of the innocent party's bargain. Otherwise, any breach is only an immaterial breach;

        c. Most courts hold that if the non-conformity is minimal, no material breach will be found;

        d. Usage of trade, course of dealing and course of performance can transform a material breach into an immaterial one; and

        e. The perfect tender rule ceases to apply after a buyer has accepted the goods. That is, if the buyer attempts to revoke his or her acceptance, there is no material breach unless, *inter alia*, the nonconformity of the good "substantially impairs" the value of the good to the buyer.

C. **PERFORMANCE UNDER THE UCC: ACCEPTANCE, REJECTION, AND REVOCATION. [§22.3]** Once goods are tendered to a buyer, the UCC gives the buyer three options: (1) the buyer may accept the goods; (2) the buyer can reject the goods; or (3) the buyer may initially accept them, but later revoke that acceptance.

    1. **ACCEPTANCE OF GOODS UNDER THE UCC. [§22.31]** A good becomes accepted either: (1) when the buyer informs the seller of acceptance; (2) upon the expiration of a reasonable time, or (3) when the buyer uses the goods inconsistently with the seller's ownership rights.

a. **Effect of Acceptance. [§22.311]** Once a buyer "accepts" a good: (1) the buyer is obligated to pay the full contract price for the good; (2) the buyer can no longer reject it; (3) the burden of proof to establish the good's non-conformity switches to the buyer; and (4) the buyer must give notice to the seller of any non-conformity or be barred from recovery.

2. **REJECTION. [§22.32]** For a rejection to be effective, a buyer must: (1) reject the good within a reasonable time after delivery; (2) seasonably notify the seller of the decision to reject; (3) hold and store the goods with reasonable care; (4) follow the seller's reasonable instructions, especially if the buyer is a merchant; and (5) attempt to re-sell goods if they are perishable.

   a. A buyer may not exercise any indicia of ownership of the goods after rejection or else the rejection will not be effective.

      (1) **Grounds for Rejection. [§22.324]** A buyer whose contract is governed by the perfect tender rule is entitled to reject a good for any non-conformity with the contract. A buyer under an installment contract is entitled to reject a particular installment only when its non-conformity causes a substantial impairment to the buyer's bargain under contract. A buyer under an installment contract is entitled to cancel the contract only if the breach by the seller substantially impairs the value of that entire contract the buyer.

3. **REVOCATION OF ACCEPTANCE. [§22.33]** To establish an effective revocation of acceptance, a buyer must prove: (1) receipt of non-conforming goods (or a non-conforming tender of the goods) whose problems substantially impair the value of the contract to him or her; (2) the revocation occurred within a reasonable time after the non-conformity should have been, or was, discovered; (3) the revocation occurred before any substantial change in the condition of the goods not caused by their non-conformity; and (4) **either**: (a) that the buyer had reasonable grounds to expect that the non-conformity would be cured by the seller if the goods were accepted by the buyer with knowledge of this non-conformity, or (b) that the buyer accepted the goods without knowledge of their non-conformity because the non-conformity was difficult to discover.

CHAPTER TWENTY-THREE: ANTICIPATORY REPUDIATION

A. **ANTICIPATORY REPUDIATION. [§23.0]** The rule today is that upon receipt of an actionable anticipatory repudiation, the aggrieved party is no longer under a duty to perform under the contract, and may immediately bring suit for breach of the contract.

B. **ELEMENTS TO ESTABLISH A CLAIM FOR ANTICIPATORY REPUDIATION IN NON-UCC TRANSACTIONS. [§23.2]** To establish that an anticipatory repudiation has taken place in a contract governed by common law contracts principles, the aggrieved party must demonstrate: (1) there has been a repudiation of a bilateral contract with duties owing under that agreement by both parties; (2) the repudiated duty results in a material breach; and (3) the repudiation was definite and unequivocal. An effective repudiation may be communicated by words or by conduct, and may be directed to only a part of a contract.

C. **ELEMENTS FOR ANTICIPATORY REPUDIATION UNDER THE UCC. [§23.3]** There are two ways to anticipatoraly repudiate a contract under the UCC: (1) under general anticipatory repudiation rules found in §2-610; and (2) by failing to provide reasonable assurances of performance under §2-609:

   1. **ANTICIPATORY REPUDIATION UNDER UCC §2-610. [§23.31]** To establish an effective repudiation under UCC §2-610, the aggrieved party must show: (1) the existence of a bilateral contract with executory duties on both sides; (2) that the repudiation, whether by words or by conduct, definitely and unequivocally illustrated the repudiator's unwillingness or inability to perform his or her promised duties; and (3) that the failure to perform such duties would substantially impair the value of the performance to the aggrieved party.

   2. **ANTICIPATORY REPUDIATION BY FAILING TO PROVIDE REASONABLE ASSURANCES UNDER UCC §2-609. [§23.32]** When a party has reasonable grounds to be insecure about the willingness or ability of the other to perform under their contract, he or she may demand reasonable assurances of performance. If the other party does not provide such assurances within a reasonable time (not to exceed 30 days) after they are justifiably demanded, the party seeking the assurances is entitled to treat the contract as anticipatoraly repudiated.

D. **THE REPUDIATING PARTY'S RIGHT TO RETRACT THE REPUDIATION. [§23.5]** A party who anticipatoraly repudiates a contract is free to retract that repudiation up until the time of performance (although if the timing of such retraction causes a hardship to the innocent party, that party will get an extension of time in which to perform). The innocent party can make the repudiation irrevocable, however: (1) if the innocent party gives notice to the repudiator that he or she considers the repudiation final and the contract terminated; or (2) if the innocent party materially relies on the repudiation.

CHAPTER TWENTY-FOUR: DISCHARGE OF DUTIES BY SUBSEQUENT AGREEMENT — SUBSTITUTED PERFORMANCE, SUBSTITUTED CONTRACTS, ACCORDS, MUTUAL RESCISSION, AND RELEASES

A. **SUBSTITUTED PERFORMANCE. [§24.1]** Substituted performance is an agreement in which a party owed a duty under a contract discharges that duty by agreeing to accept a different performance than that called for in the original contract.

B. **SUBSTITUTED CONTRACTS AND NOVATIONS. [§24.2]** A substituted contract is a transaction in which a party owed a duty under a contract discharges it by agreeing to accept the promise of a different performance than that originally called for under the contract. When the new promise comes from a third party, it is a special type of substituted contract called a novation. If the new promise is not performed, the promisee is only entitled to enforce the **new** promise made in the substituted contract because the old duty was discharged.

C. **ACCORDS. [§24.3]** An accord is a transaction in which a party owed a duty under a contract agrees to enter into what would otherwise be a substituted contract, except that the original duty owed under the first contract is discharged only after actual performance of the duties promised under the accord, i.e., when the accord is "satisfied." Hence, upon the breach of an accord, there is an option of suing to enforce either the original duty promised under the first contract, or suing to enforce the new duty promised in the accord.

D. **MUTUAL RESCISSION. [§24.4]** Mutual rescission is an agreement whereby each party to a bilateral contract agrees to discharge all remaining unexecuted duties of the other.

E. **RELEASES. [§24.5]** A release is an enforceable promise by a party that he or she is discharging a duty owed him or her either immediately, or upon the occurrence of a condition, such as a payment of money.

CHAPTER TWENTY-FIVE: DISCHARGE OF DUTIES BY IMPOSSIBILITY, IMPRACTICABILITY, OR FRUSTRATION OF PURPOSE

A. **IMPOSSIBILITY. [§25.1]** Impossibility of performance is a defense to a breach of contract suit whereby the party asserting the defense seeks a declaration that his or her duties under the contract have been discharged due to the occurrence of an unexpected event or series of events. It is principally used by sellers or suppliers.

1. **Elements [§25.11]** To establish the defense, a party must prove: (1) the occurrence of an event which makes performance of a contractual duty impossible; (2) that the non-occurrence of the event was a basic assumption of both parties when they entered into their contract; (3) that the event occurred without the fault of the party asserting the defense; and (4) that the party asserting the defense had not assumed the risk of the event's occurrence.

B. **COMMERCIAL IMPRACTICABILITY. [§25.2]** Commercial impracticability is also a defense to a breach of contract action whereby the party asserting the defense seeks a declaration that his or her duties under the contract have been discharged due to the occurrence of an unexpected event or series of events. It is also principally used by sellers or suppliers.

1. **Elements [§25.21]** To establish the defense, the party asserting it must prove: (1) the occurrence of an event which makes performance commercially impractical; (2) that the non-occurrence of such event was a basic assumption of both parties when they entered into their contract; (3) that such event occurred without the fault of the party asserting the defense; and (4) that the party asserting the defense had not assumed the risk of the event's occurrence.

C. **FRUSTRATION OF PURPOSE. [§25.3]** Frustration of purpose is a defense to a breach of contract suit whereby the party asserting the defense seeks a declaration that his or her duties under a contract have been discharged due to the occurrence of an unexpected event or series of events. It is principally used by buyers.

1. **Elements [§25.31]** To establish the defense, a party must prove: (1) the occurrence of an event that frustrates the party's principal purpose for entering into the contract; (2) that the non-occurrence of the event was a basic assumption of both parties when they entered into the contract; (3) that such event occurred without the fault of the party

asserting the defense; and (4) that the party asserting the defense had not assumed the risk of the event's occurrence.

CHAPTER TWENTY-SIX: MODIFICATION AND WAIVER UNDER UCC §2-209

A. **MODIFICATION. [§26.0]** The rules governing modifications of agreements under the UCC are set forth in UCC §2-209:

1. **A MODIFICATION NEED NOT BE SUPPORTED BY CONSIDERATION TO BE ENFORCEABLE UNDER UCC §2-209(1). [§26.2]** Unlike the common law rule, a modification of a UCC agreement is enforceable in the absence of new consideration to support the modification.

2. **AN ORAL MODIFICATION IS UNENFORCEABLE IF THE PARTIES HAVE AGREED TO A "NO MODIFICATION EXCEPT IN WRITING" CLAUSE UNDER UCC §2-209(2). [§26.3]** No modifications except in writing clauses are specifically held enforceable in §2-209(2). Hence, if such a clause is validly a part of a contract, any modification to that agreement must be in writing to be enforceable.

3. **IF THE CONTRACT, AS MODIFIED, IS WITHIN THE STATUTE OF FRAUDS, IT MUST SATISFY THE STATUTE OR IT WILL BE UNENFORCEABLE UNDER UCC §2-209(3). [§26.4]** The most generally accepted interpretation of §2-209(3) is that if the agreement, as assertedly modified, is subject to the statute of frauds, the modified agreement as a whole must satisfy the Statute. If it does not, the modification will be unenforceable, and the terms of the original contract will control.

4. **A MODIFICATION THAT IS UNENFORCEABLE BECAUSE IT IS NOT IN WRITING MAY STILL OPERATE AS AN ENFORCEABLE WAIVER UNDER UCC §2-209(4). [§26.5]** A modification that cannot be enforced because it is not in writing may still be operable as a waiver under §2-209(4). There are four theories as to how the "waiver" provision should be interpreted: (1) the writing requirement may be waived by the parties, but only in writing; (2) all attempted oral modifications act as implied waivers of any writing requirements; (3) evidence that a party's unilateral decision not to enforce a promise can be freely admitted into evidence, but the terms of the bilateral modification are not admissible; and (4) evidence of the modification is admissible upon a showing of reliance.

5. **A WAIVER OF A TERM MAY BE UNILATERALLY RETRACTED IN SOME CASES. [§26.6]** A modified agreement may not be unilaterally retracted. However, a party's waiver of his or her rights is freely retractable unless the other party has foreseeably and materially relied on the waiver.

X. RIGHTS AND OBLIGATIONS IN CONTRACTS INVOLVING MORE THAN TWO PARTIES

CHAPTER TWENTY-SEVEN: THIRD PARTY BENEFICIARY CONTRACTS

A. **THIRD PARTY BENEFICIARY CONTRACTS. [§27.0]** A third party beneficiary contract is one between a promisor and a promisee, wherein performance of the duties promised by the promisor under that agreement will benefit a third party, i.e., the beneficiary.

B. **THE RIGHTS OF THE BENEFICIARY TO SUE THE PROMISOR FOR BREACH. [§27.3]** Under modern contract law, "intended" beneficiaries are entitled to sue the promisor for breach, whereas "incidental" beneficiaries are not [§27.32]. A beneficiary of a promise is an "intended" beneficiary if recognition of a right to performance is appropriate to carry out the intentions of the promisor and promisee, **and** where either; (1) performance of the promise will satisfy an obligation of the promisee to pay money to the beneficiary; or (2) where the circumstances indicate that the promisee intended to make a gift to the beneficiary. All other beneficiaries of contract promises are "incidental" beneficiaries.

   1. An intended beneficiary is entitled to enforce the promisor's promise even if: (1) performance of the promisor's promise was not made directly to the beneficiary; (2) the precise identity of the beneficiary was not known at the time the promisor and promisee entered into their contract; and (3) the beneficiary did not know that he or she was an intended beneficiary at the time promisor/promisee contract was made [§§27.324-27.3244].

C. **RIGHTS OF THE PROMISOR IN A SUIT BROUGHT BY THE BENEFICIARY. [§27.4]** When an intended beneficiary sues a promisor for breach, the following doctrines provide the promisor with a partial or total defense: (1) the beneficiary is subject to any defense the promisor could assert in a suit brought by the promisee, i.e., the beneficiary "steps into the shoes" of the promisee; (2) the beneficiary's rights are subject to any limiting terms of the promisor/promisee contract; and (3) the beneficiary's recovery is subject to offset for any damages the promisor suffers due to an immaterial breach by the promisee.

D. **RIGHTS OF AN INTENDED BENEFICIARY TO SUE THE PROMISEE. [§27.5]** An intended beneficiary retains whatever rights he or she had to bring suit against the promisee before the promisor/promisee agreement was made.

E. **RIGHTS OF THE PROMISEE AGAINST THE PROMISOR. [§27.6]** If a promisor breaches a third party beneficiary contract, the promisor is liable to both the promisee and the intended third party beneficiaries of that contract.

F. **RIGHTS OF THE PROMISEE AND PROMISOR TO MODIFY THEIR CONTRACT TO THE DISADVANTAGE OF AN INTENDED BENEFICIARY. [§27.7]** There are three views as to when the rights of an intended beneficiary under a third party beneficiary contract vest, thereby depriving the promisor and promisee of the power to modify their agreement to the disadvantage of the beneficiary: (1) the majority view, adopted by the Restatement 2d, holds that a beneficiary's rights vest upon the beneficiary's reliance on the promisor's promise; (2) one minority view holds that the beneficiary's rights vest as soon as the beneficiary learns that he or she is an intended beneficiary; and (3) the other minority view holds that the beneficiary's rights vest as soon as the promisor/promisee agreement is made.

CHAPTER TWENTY-EIGHT: ASSIGNMENTS

A. **ASSIGNMENTS. [§28.1]** An assignment is the transfer of contractual rights. In an assignment, the assignor transfers to the assignee his or her rights under a contract with the obligor. Assignments can be "gratuitous," where the assignor intends to make a gift of the transfer of rights to the assignee, or can be "for value," where the assignor receives consideration for his or her transfer of the rights to the assignee [§28.2].

B. **ELEMENTS NECESSARY TO MAKE AN EFFECTIVE ASSIGNMENT. [§28.3]** An effective assignment has three elements:

1. First, the assignor must manifest a present intention to transfer an existing right, rather than merely make a promise to assign a right in the future.

2. Second, there must be no legal prohibition against assignment of that particular right. That is: (1) it must be the kind of assignment that does not violate public policy; (2) the assignment must not materially and adversely affect the obligor's rights, duties, and justified expectations of return performance; and (3) the assignment must not violate a valid "no assignment" clause, although such clauses are typically read narrowly.

3. Third, the assignee must agree to the assignment before it becomes effective, unless a third party other than the assignee has given the assignor consideration for the assignment, or unless the assignment is irrevocable because of the delivery of a writing or other token chose to the beneficiary.

4. An assignment can be partial and/or conditional, and still be effective. Notification to the obligor of the assignment is not necessary. Lastly, oral assignments are usually valid unless the subject matter of the assignment is itself within the statute of frauds.

C. **DUTIES OF AN OBLIGOR AFTER VALID ASSIGNMENT. [§28.4]** After a valid assignment, the obligor owes the assignee his or her performance obligations under the contract the obligor initially made with the assignor. Thus, the duties under that contract may only be discharged by performance if the performance is made to the assignee. If the obligor does not know of the assignment, however, rendering performance to the assignor will discharge the obligor's duties.

D. **CLAIMS AND DEFENSES THAT CAN BE ASSERTED BY THE OBLIGOR AGAINST THE ASSIGNEE AFTER A VALID ASSIGNMENT. [§28.5]** After a valid assignment, the assignee "stands in the shoes" of the assignor. Thus, an obligor can assert any defenses in a suit brought by the assignee after an assignment that the obligor could have asserted in a suit brought by the assignor had no assignment taken place.

The one exception to this rule is where the assignee is a "holder in due course" of a negotiable instrument. Such a "holder" is only subject to the defenses of which he, she, or it was aware upon the assignment, and to the so-called "personal" defenses in a breach action brought against the obligor. The holder in due course doctrine does not apply in consumer contracts [§28.52].

E. **RIGHTS OF THE ASSIGNEE TO SUE THE ASSIGNOR: THE IMPLIED WARRANTIES INHERENT IN ASSIGNMENTS FOR VALUE. [§28.6]** Upon an assignment for value, the assignor impliedly warrants to the assignee that: (1) he or she will do nothing to impair the value of the assignment; and (2) that the assigned right exists and is subject to no reasonably unforeseeable defenses.

F. **ATTEMPTED MODIFICATION OF AN ASSIGNMENT BY THE ASSIGNOR AND THE OBLIGOR. [§28.7]** The assignor and obligor do not have the contractual right to modify effectively the terms of an assignment for value. However, gratuitous assignments are freely revocable and modifiable by the assignor and obligor unless: (1) the assignment is by means of a writing signed by the assignor; (2) the assignment is accompanied by a token chose; (3) the assignee has relied on the assignment; or (4) the assignee has already received performance by the obligor.

G. **RIGHTS OF THE ASSIGNEE AMONG COMPETING CLAIMS OF OWNERSHIP. [§28.8]** There are four views regarding which assignee has priority if the assignor assigns the same rights to more than one party at the same time: (1) the "New York" rule states that the first assignee always has priority; (2) the "English" rule states that the first assignee to notify the obligor of the assignment has priority; (3) the "Massachusetts/Restatement 2d" rule states that generally the first assignee prevails, subject to four exceptions; and (4) the rules of Article 9 of the UCC provide that the first to file and perfect a financing statement has priority.

CHAPTER TWENTY-NINE: DELEGATION

A. **DELEGATION. [§29.0]** A delegation is the transfer of an obligation to perform a duty under a contract. That is, the delegating party transfers to the delegate the obligation to perform a duty that the delegating party owes the obligee.

B. **MECHANICS OF AN EFFECTIVE DELEGATION. [§29.2]** An effective delegation has two elements:

1. the delegating party must manifest an intention to delegate a duty; and

2. there must be no prohibition against the delegation of that particular duty. That is, the delegation must not: (1) violate public policy; (2) be of a duty that the obligee has a "substantial interest" in having the delegating party personally perform; or (3) violate a valid "no delegation" clause.

3. The obligee need not assent to the delegation in order for it to be effective.

C. **PRINCIPAL CONSEQUENCES OF AN EFFECTIVE DELEGATION. [§29.3]** An effective delegation has five consequences:

(1) the delegate thereby becomes entitled to perform the delegated duty;

(2) the duty of the delegating party to render performance is not automatically discharged upon the delegation;

(3) full and complete performance of the duty by the delegate **will** discharge the delegating party's duty to render that same performance;

(4) a delegate acquires an enforceable **obligation** (as opposed to an entitlement) to perform the duty only when he or she *specifically assumes such a duty*; and

(5) the delegating party and the delegate have enforceable rights against each other as promisor and promisee under a third party beneficiary contract.

XI.   REMEDIES

CHAPTER THIRTY: EQUITABLE REMEDIES

A. **EQUITABLE RELIEF.** [§30.0] The most common types of equitable relief granted for breach of contract are specific performance and injunctions.

B. **REQUIREMENTS FOR OBTAINING EQUITABLE RELIEF FOR BREACH OF CONTRACT.** [§30.2] There are three requirements for obtaining equitable relief for breach of contract:

1.   A showing that an award of money damages would be inadequate to put the non-breaching party in the position he or she would have been in had the contract been performed. The factors that go into this determination are: (1) the difficulty in proving damages with reasonable certainty; (2) the difficulty of procuring suitable substitute performance upon an award of monetary damages; and (3) the likelihood that an award of damages could be collected.

2.   No undue practical burdens that would follow if a court granted such relief. The factors that go into this determination are: (1) whether the terms of the contract are too uncertain to be specifically enforced; (2) whether the supervisory burden on the court is too great; and (3) whether the contract is one for "personal services".

3.   Certain equitable principles cannot be violated upon an order for such relief. The factors are: (1) whether an equitable award will itself be inequitable (violate public policy); (2) whether the breaching party's assent to the contract was induced by unfair business practices; (3) whether such an order would cause unreasonable hardship on the breaching party; and (4) whether it appears the non-breaching party will perform if equitable relief is granted.

CHAPTER THIRTY-ONE: MONEY DAMAGES

A. **THE "INTEREST" ANALYSIS OF CONTRACT LAW AND THE CONCEPT OF ECONOMIC BREACH.** [§31.0] The most common remedy for breach of contract is an award of money damages. Such award is calculated by the extent to which the non-breaching party failed to receive the economic benefits of full performance promised by the breaching party.

B. THE DIFFERENT ECONOMIC INTERESTS RESULTING FROM CONTRACT FORMATION. [§31.1] There are three ways to measure the protected economic interest one party receives in the other's performance. That is, upon a breach the non-breaching party may sue to recover damages based on the interference with his or her: (1) expectation interest; (2) reliance interest; or (3) restitutionary interest:

1. **THE EXPECTATION INTEREST. [§31.11]** An award of expectation damages is designed to give the non-breaching party a sum of money that would put him or her in the position he or she would have been in had the contract been performed.

2. **THE RELIANCE INTEREST. [§31.12]** An award of reliance damages is designed to give the party a sum of damages equal to the expenses (including labor) reasonably incurred by that party up to the time of the breach.

3. **THE RESTITUTIONARY INTEREST. [§31.13]** A restitutionary award is designed to give the aggrieved party a sum of money equal to the amount of benefits the benefitted party has actually received from the aggrieved party.

C. CALCULATION OF EXPECTATION DAMAGES. [§31.3] Expectation damages are the most common type of monetary damages. The general formula for calculating them is:

> **Expectation Damages = Lost Value Due to the Breach + Incidental Damages + Consequential Damages - Costs Avoided/Saved as a Result of the Breach - Loss Avoided Due to the Breach.**

D. THREE LIMITATIONS ON THE RECOVERABILITY OF EXPECTATION DAMAGES: CERTAINTY, FORESEEABILITY, AND AVOIDABILITY. [§31.4] There are three limitations on the recoverability of damages in general, but which have their greatest effect on limiting the recovery of expectation damages:

1. **CERTAINTY [§31.41].** The non-breaching party must be able to prove his or her damage with reasonable certainty This rule has its greatest application in limiting the buyer's recovery of lost profits in collateral transactions.

2. **FORSEEABILITY [§31.42]** The kind of loss suffered by the non-breaching party must have been reasonably foreseeable to the breaching party at the time the contract was entered into as per *Hadley v. Baxendale* and the modern construction of that holding. That is, with regard to direct damages, foreseeability is established as a matter of law, i.e., direct damages are damages that follow in the ordinary course of events after a breach. With regard to consequential damages, the non-breaching party must make a special showing of foreseeability to establish that the breaching party was made aware that such consequential losses would follow from a breach of this particular contract.

3. **AVOIDABILITY OR MITIGATION [§31.43]** A contract loss is not recoverable if the non-breaching party could have avoided it without undue risk, burden, or humiliation.

E. RELIANCE DAMAGES. [§31.5] Reliance damages are always available to the non-breaching party as an alternative to expectation damages. They are equal to the amount of expenses reasonably incurred by the non-breaching party up to the time of the breach.

1. **LIMITATIONS ON RELIANCE DAMAGES RECOVERY. [§31.52]** Recovery of reliance damages is subject to four limitations: (1) the damage must be proven with reasonable certainty to be recoverable; (2) any amount of provable loss the non-breaching party would have suffered upon full performance must be subtracted from the amount the non-breaching party spent in reliance up to the point of the breach; and (3) the value of any salvageable materials in the possession of the non-breaching party must be subtracted from that party's reliance damage recovery as a loss avoided; and (4) any damages claimed must not have been available by the non-breaching party without undue burden, risk, or humiliation.

F. **EMOTIONAL DISTRESS DAMAGES ARE GENERALLY NOT AVAILABLE. [§31.6]** Damages for emotional distress in breach of contract suits are recoverable **only** when the breach results in tangible personal injury [§31.61], or when the breach is "particularly likely" to bring about such distress [§31.62].

G. **LIQUIDATED DAMAGES. [§31.7]** Liquidated damages are damages, the amount of which parties have stipulated in advance will be due upon a breach of their contract. Liquidated damage provisions will be upheld only if the precise amount of the actual damage suffered by a party will be difficult to prove with certainty, and the liquidated amount is nevertheless a reasonable estimate of those damages in light of the anticipated or actual loss that the non-breaching party will suffer upon a breach.

H. **PUNITIVE DAMAGES IN BREACH OF CONTRACT SUITS. [§31.8]** Punitive damages are not generally recoverable for breach of contract. However, most states allow for their recovery for the bad faith breach of an insurance contract.

I. **THE INJURED PARTY'S RECOVERY OF PRE-JUDGMENT INTEREST. [§31.9]** If the amount of a non-breaching party's breach of contract damages is a sum certain, the non-breaching party is entitled to pre-judgment interest on the award. If the amount in controversy is not a sum certain, recovery of such interest is within the court's discretion.

CHAPTER THIRTY-TWO: RESTITUTION

A. **RESTITUTION. [§32.0]** Restitution provides that a person who has been unjustly enriched by another must account for that enrichment by restoring the value of the benefits actually received through a payment of money. The amount of the restitutionary interest due a party is valued under either the "net benefit" or the "cost avoided" method [§32.11]

B. **RULES REGULATING ALL RESTITUTION ACTIONS. [§32.1]** The following rules govern restitution:

1. Restitutionary recovery is based on the **value** of the enrichment **actually received** by the benefited party, and neither on the value of the promised performance of the other, nor on the value of the expenditures made by the other that were not actually received by the enriched party.

2. Restitution is available as a remedy: (1) to a party who has breached a contract; (2) to the non-breaching party under a contract; (3) to a party who has either avoided a contract or who otherwise cannot enforce a contract; and (4) or to a person seeking quasi-contractual recovery. A party seeking restitution must make restitution, i.e., to be effective restitution must be mutual.

C. **VALUING THE BENEFITS RECEIVED. [§32.11]** A non-breaching party is presumptively entitled to restitutionary recovery based on whichever of the cost avoided or net benefit method of valuing benefits yields the largest result. A breaching party is presumptively entitled to restitutionary recovery based on whichever of the cost avoided or net benefit methods yields the least generous result, and from that figure any losses suffered by the non-breaching party must be substracted to calculate the appropriate amount of the breacher's restitutionary award. An aggrieved party seeking restitution in quasi-contract must base his or her recovery on the cost avoided method of valuing benefits. In all other cases, a court is free to base a restitutionary award on whichever method is the most "just" for that situation.

D. **RESTITUTIONARY RECOVERY FOR BREACH OF CONTRACT.** **[§32.2]** There are two limitations on the aggrieved party's entitlement to seek restitution for breach of contract: (1) restitution is only available if the injured party would be able to sue the breacher for total, and not just partial, breach; and (2) restitution is not available to a non-breaching party where he or she has performed all the duties required under the contract, and the only remaining performance owing by the breacher is the payment of a definite sum of money.

CHAPTER THIRTY-THREE: REMEDIES FOR BREACH UNDER THE UCC

A. **A BUYER'S RIGHT TO EQUITABLE REMEDIES UNDER THE UCC. [§33.1]** There are two equitable remedies available to a buyer under the Code: (1) specific performance, which is ordered when the buyer can establish that securing replacement goods is unreasonably burdensome; and (2) replevin, a pre-judgment attachment order.

B. **A BUYER'S RIGHT TO SUE FOR DAMAGES IN CASES WHERE HE OR SHE DOES NOT HAVE THE GOODS. [§33.2]** If a buyer chooses not to keep non-conforming goods, or if the buyer never was tendered goods in the first place, he or she is entitled to: (1) purchase replacement goods ("cover") and sue for the price differential, along with related damages; or (2) sue for the price differential between the market and contract price for the goods without replacing them, along with other related damages:

1. **UCC §2-712: COVER DAMAGES. [§33.21]** A non-breaching buyer is given some flexibility to purchase replacement goods under the Code so long as he or she does not act in bad faith or without unreasonable delay. If so, the buyer is entitled to recover:

   [(Cost of Cover) - (Contract Price)] + Incidental Damages + Consequential Damages - Costs Avoided as a Consequence of the Breach.

2. **UCC §2-713: MARKET DIFFERENTIAL DAMAGES. [§33.22]** A non-breaching buyer does not have to purchase replacements in order

to get relief under the Code. In such a case, he or she is entitled to recover:

$$[(Market\ Price) - (Contract\ Price)] + Incidental\ Damages +$$
$$Consequential\ Damages - Costs\ Avoided\ Due\ to\ the\ Breach.$$

The proper "market price" to be used in the formula is the one pending on the day the buyer learned of the breach, either in the market of tender (if the seller never sends the goods), or in the market of delivery (if the seller sends the goods but they are rightfully and effectively rejected, or the buyer's acceptance of them is properly revoked).

C. **BUYER'S RIGHT TO WARRANTY DAMAGES. [§33.3]** If a buyer keeps non-conforming goods, or goods which were tendered improperly, he or she is entitled to sue for breach of warranty. In such cases, a buyer is entitled to recover:

$$[(Value\ of\ the\ Good\ as\ Warranted) - (Value\ of\ the\ Good\ as\ Received)]$$
$$+ Incidental\ Damages + Consequential\ Damages.$$

Incidental damages have the same meaning under the Code as in non-Code cases, i.e., expenses incurred after the breach in an attempt to avoid losses for the breacher. However, the UCC separates consequential loss into two types: (1) consequential **economic** loss, whose recoverability is governed by normal contract foreseeability rules; and (2) consequential **personal injury** and **personal property** loss, whose recoverability is governed by tort proximate cause foreseeability rules.

D. **SELLER'S RIGHT TO SUE FOR THE FULL CONTRACT PRICE UPON BUYER'S BREACH. [§33.4]** A seller is entitled to bring an action against the breaching seller for the full contract price whenever: (1) the buyer has accepted the goods; (2) the goods are lost or destroyed during transit after the risk of loss has passed to the buyer, and (3) when the seller cannot obtain a reasonable re-sale price for wrongfully rejected or revoked goods, either because no one will offer such a price, or efforts to re-sell the particular good would be unavailing.

E. **SELLER'S RIGHTS TO SUE FOR DAMAGES OTHER THAN THE FULL CONTRACT PRICE UPON A BUYER'S BREACH. [§33.5]** When a seller is not entitled to maintain an action for price, the non-breaching seller has three options: (1) the seller is entitled to actually re-sell wrongfully rejected or revoked goods and recover the difference between their re-sale and contract price, along with other associated damages; (2) the seller can sue for market differential damages, along with other associated damages while holding onto the goods; or (3) if the seller is a lost volume seller, the seller is entitled to recover for lost profits, along with other associated damages.

1. **RECOVERY UNDER §2-706: SELLER'S "COVER" DAMAGES. [§33.51]** So long as he or she does so in a good faith and in a commercially reasonable manner, a seller is entitled to re-sell wrongfully rejected or revoked goods and recover for:

$$[(Contract\ Price) - (Re\text{-}sale\ Price)] + Incidental\ Damages.$$

2. **RECOVERY UNDER §2-708(1): SELLER'S MARKET DIFFERENTIAL DAMAGES. [§33.52]** A seller is entitled to keep wrongfully rejected or revoked goods, and recover for:

[(Contract Price) - (Market Price)] + Incidental Damages.

The "market price" to be used in the formula is the one pending at the time and place for tender.

3. **RECOVERY UNDER §2-708(2): SELLER'S LOST PROFIT RECOVERY. [§33.53]** A "lost volume" seller is one who has an excess supply of a fungible good. If a buyer breaches a contract with a lost volume seller, the seller is entitled to recover for:

Profit on the Contract that was Breached + Incidental Damages + Costs Reasonably Incurred in Performance.

The formula of §2-708(2) also requires deduction for payments or proceeds of any re-sale, but that portion is ignored by courts in recovery by lost volume sellers.

F. **LIMITATION ON, OR MODIFICATION OF, CONTRACT REMEDIES. [§33.8]** Parties of roughly equal bargaining power are free to limit, modify, or even eliminate Article 2 remedies, except in two instances: (1) where the parties try to replace the Article 2 remedies with liquidated damages, in which case the Code's liquidated damage rules control; and (2) any limitation on the recoverability of consequential personal injury or personal property loss is *per se* unconscionable

If a limited warranty "fails of its essential purpose" the buyer is generally thereafter entitled to recover under any UCC remedy [§33.81].

XXII. MISCELLANEOUS UCC PROVISIONS

CHAPTER THIRTY-FOUR: APPLICABILITY OF ARTICLE TWO OF THE UCC

A. **APPLICABILITY OF ARTICLE TWO. [§34.0-34.1]** Article 2 applies to "transactions in goods". Today, probably the only type of transaction subject to Article 2 is a "sale", although in those jurisdictions that have not yet adopted Article 2A, leases may also qualify. A "good" is personal property, i.e., something movable at the time it is identified to the contract. Article 2 is not limited to merchants.

B. **ARTICLE TWO APPLICABILITY TO SALES/SERVICES "HYBRID" TRANSACTIONS. [§34.3]** When the same transaction involves both the sale of a good and the sale of a service, the courts have developed two tests to determine whether the buyer's rights should be governed by the UCC or by torts principles: (1) the predominant purpose test (asking which aspect of the transaction predominates); and (2) the graveman test (asking what is the gravaman of the planitiff's cause of action).

C. **ARTICLE TWO APPLICABILITY WHEN THERE IS A SALE OF SOMETHING ATTACHED TO REALTY. [§34.4]** When a transaction involves the sale of a good attached to real estate, the UCC applicability rules are: (1) if it is a sale of minerals or of a structure, it is only an Article 2 transaction if the seller severs the goods from the property; (2) if it is a sale apart from the land of crops, timber, or anything else that can be severed from the property without material harm, it is an Article 2 transaction regardless of who severs the goods.

CHAPTER THIRTY-FIVE: RISK OF LOSS AND MERCANTILE TERMS

A. **RISK OF LOSS. [§35.0]** Risk of loss rules determine which contract party still has the obligation to perform when goods are lost, damaged, or destroyed during transit. Whether the buyer or seller has the risk of loss depends on whether or not there has been a breach:

1. **RISK OF LOSS IN THE ABSENCE OF BREACH. [§35.01]** If the contract is a shipment contract, then in the absence of breach the risk of loss shifts to the buyer when the goods are first transferred to the buyer or the buyer's agent, usually at the seller's place of business. In a destination contract, the risk of loss remains with the seller until the goods are delivered to a particular point, usually the buyer's home or place of business.

2. **EFFECT OF BREACH ON RISK OF LOSS. [§35.02]** When the seller breaches in such a way as to give the buyer a right of rejection, the risk of loss stays with the seller until the seller cures any problem and/or the buyer accepts the goods. When the seller breaches and the buyer revokes his or her acceptance, the buyer is entitled to treat the loss as having rested on the seller from the beginning, to the extent of any deficiency in his or her effective insurance coverage. If the buyer wrongfully repudiates or breaches before the risk of loss has shifted, the seller may treat the risk as having rested on the buyer for a commercially reasonable time, to the extent of any deficiency in his or her effective insurance coverage.

B. **MERCANTILE TERMS. [§35.1]** Mercantile terms are abbreviations used in commercial law to denote a lengthy series of terms. Among the most common are: (1) F.O.B.; (2) F.A.S.; (3) C.I.F.; and (4) C & F.

CHAPTER THIRTY-SIX: WARRANTIES

A. **EXPRESS WARRANTIES UNDER THE UCC. [§36.1]** To establish that an actionable express warranty was made to him or her in a sales contract, the buyer must establish that: (1) the seller made a sufficiently factual promise relating to the qualities or attributes of the goods by means of an affirmation, promise, description, or sample; and (2) that such factual warranty was part of the basis of the bargain of the transaction. Basis of the bargain has been interpreted either: (1) as being a synonym for reliance; or (2) as meaning only that the warranty was made by the seller sometime before the sale.

1. **DISCLAIMING AN EXPRESS WARRANTY. [§36.13]** Express warranties can be disclaimed. If the words of the disclaimer and of the warranty cannot be read consistently, the words of the disclaimer are inoperative if, **but only if**, the words creating the express warranty can be introduced into evidence under the parol evidence rule.

B. **IMPLIED WARRANTY OF MERCHANTABILITY. [§36.2]** To establish that a seller has breached the implied warranty of merchantability, a buyer must establish that: (1) the seller was a merchant; and (2) the goods sold were unmerchantable, e.g., they were not fit for the ordinary purposes for which such goods were used.

1. **DISCLAIMER OF IMPLIED WARRANTY OF MERCHANTABILITY. [§36.23]** To effectively disclaim only the implied warranty of merchantability a seller may orally or in writing make it clear to the buyer that the merchantability warranty has been disclaimed, and must use the word "merchantability" in doing so. To effectively disclaim the implied warranty of merchantability as part of a general disclaimer of **all** implied warranties, the seller must conspicuously use words like "with all faults" or "as is" for the disclaimer to be effective.

C. **THE IMPLIED WARRANTY OF FITNESS FOR A PARTICULAR PURPOSE. [§36.3]** To establish an actionable implied warranty of fitness for a particular purpose, the buyer must prove that: (1) he or she had a particular purpose in mind for the goods; (2) the seller had reason to know of this particular purpose; (3) the seller had reason to know the buyer was relying on the seller's skill or judgment to select furnish goods to meet the buyer's needs; and (4) the buyer actually relied on the seller's skill and judgment.

1. **DISCLAIMING THE IMPLIED WARRANTY OF FITNESS FOR A PARTICULAR PURPOSE. [§36.33]** To effectively disclaim only the implied warranty of fitness for a particular purpose, the seller must do so in writing. No special words need be used, but it must be clear that the seller is disclaiming the warranty. To effectively disclaim the implied warranty of fitness as part of a **general** implied warranty disclaimer, the rules discussed above apply.

D. **DOCTRINES APPLICABLE TO ALL WARRANTY CLAIMS. [§36.4]** The following doctrines are applicable to all breach of warranty claims:

1. **THE NOTICE REQUIREMENT UNDER UCC §2-607(3). [§36.41]** A buyer who does not give notice of a breach to the seller within a reasonable time after which he or she actually discovers, or should have discovered, the breach, is barred from remedy.

2. **VERTICAL PRIVITY IN WARRANTY. [§36.42]** Today virtually all vertical privity requirements to bring a warranty claim have been eliminated.

3. **HORIZONTAL PRIVITY IN WARRANTY. [§36.43]** There are four views as to how far horizontal privity should extend to allow by-standers and other third parties to bring suit for breach based on a warranty not given them, but given the buyer: (1) only members and guests of the buyer's household can recover; (2) all reasonably affected persons can recover, but only for personal injuries and personal property loss; (3) all reasonably affected persons can recover for any kind of loss; and (4) whatever rules regulate third party claims in tort law also govern them in warranty.

4. **WARRANTY DEFENSES. [§36.5]** There are two warranty defenses: (1) voluntary assumption of the risk; and (2) unforeseeable misuse of the product.